THE EVOLUTION OF LABOUR LAW
(1992-2003)
VOLUME 2: NATIONAL REPORTS

Employment & social affairs

Industrial relations and industrial change

European Commission

Directorate-General for Employment, Social Affairs and Equal Opportunities
Unit D.2

Manuscript completed in June 2005

This report was financed by and prepared for the use of the European Commission, Directorate-General for Employment, Social Affairs and Equal Opportunities. It does not necessarily represent the Commission's official position.

If you are interested in receiving the electronic newsletter "ESmail" from the European Commission's Directorate-General for Employment, Social Affairs and Equal Opportunities, please send an e-mail to empl-esmail@cec.eu.int. The newsletter is published on a regular basis in English, French and German.

**Europe Direct is a service to help you find answers
to your questions about the European Union**

Freephone number:
00 800 6 7 8 9 10 11

A great deal of additional information on the European Union is available on the Internet.
It can be accessed through the Europa server (http://europa.eu.int).

Cataloguing data can be found at the end of this publication.

Luxembourg: Office for Official Publications of the European Communities, 2005

ISBN 92-894-9894-3

Printed in Belgium

PRINTED ON WHITE CHLORINE-FREE PAPER

General table of contents

THE EVOLUTION OF LABOUR LAW IN BELGIUM

1992-2002

Final report 4 June 2003

Chris Engels
Lawyer-Partner Claeys & Engels
Prof. K.U. Leuven

Table of contents

Chapter I:
Introductory section

1. Trade unionisation

While worldwide trade unionisation levels may have been declining, the same cannot be said for Belgium. Trade unions and employer federations remain extremely important. In fact, the degree of unionisation remains high and is even reported to be on the rise, be it only slightly.

Belgium has three major trade unions. Each of these unions corresponds ideologically to one of the major political parties:

1. ACV/CSC is related to the Christian democrat party
2. ABVV/FGTB is related to the socialist party and
3. ACLCB/CGSLB is related to the liberal party.

In terms of membership, the first two unions are by far the most important. While the socialist trade union used to be the biggest in the French-speaking part of the country, over the last couple of years the Christian trade union has become the biggest in both Flanders and Wallonia.

With regard to membership figures, no official figures are available. The trade unions themselves report – in an unverified way – on the number of their affiliates. Instead of decreasing numbers, the Belgian trade unions have reported a slight increase over the last couple of years. The Christian trade union reported an increase of 30 000 members over the last three years.

Trade Union Membership in absolute figures

ACV/CSC	1 600 000
ABVV/FGTB	1 200 000
ACLVB/CGSLB	280 000

All three trade unions are represented in both linguistic parts of the country. The trade unions are organised on an industry basis rather than an occupational one, with the exception of white-collar workers.

The overall unionisation level is more than 50%. Unionisation is higher among blue-collar workers (manual labour) than among white-collar (intellectual) workers. Both kinds of workers are represented through different organisations within the three trade unions.

2. Collective bargaining

2.1. Introduction

Collective bargaining in Belgium is entirely regulated by the Act of 5 December 1968 on Collective Bargaining Agreements (C.B.A.s) and Joint Committees.[1] This Parliamentary Act foresees the possibility for engaging in collective bargaining at the various levels of industrial relations.

The 1968 Act sets out the rules that govern collective bargaining in Belgium. It determines the scope of collective bargaining with respect to the people covered by it, as well as with respect to the issues that can be addressed in a collective bargaining agreement. It defines what a collective bargaining agreement is, which rules it has to obey, who can negotiate it, what its binding force will be, whether it can be extended to cover the entire workforce, etc. The 1968 Act also regulates the scope of the various kinds of collective bargaining agreements and other sources of labour and employment law.

The 1968 Act defines a collective bargaining agreement as an agreement concluded between one or more employee organisations (read: trade unions) on the one hand and one or more employers' associations or one or more employers on the other. In addition, the Act states that a collective bargaining agreement regulates individual and collective relations between employers and employees at the level of the company or the level of the industry and defines the rights and obligations of the contracting parties.[2]

---

1   Act of 5 December 1968, Official Gazette, 15 January 1969, often amended thereafter.
2   Act of 5 December 1968, Official Gazette, 15 January 1969, often amended thereafter, Article 5.

2.2. Personal coverage of collective bargaining agreements

The Act of 5 December 1968 is applicable to workers executing an employment contract and to employers. In Article 2, paragraph 3, it excludes from its scope the personnel of the State, the provinces, the communities and public sector workers. A few exceptions are explicitly foreseen in the Act.[3] In principle, public sector employees are therefore not covered by collective bargaining agreements.

In Article 19, the Act of 5 December 1968 further specifies that a collective bargaining agreement is binding on:

1. 'The organisations that concluded it and the employers that are members of such organisations or that have concluded the agreement, from the date that it comes into force;

2. The organisations and employers subsequently acceding to the agreement and the employers who are members of such organisations, from the date of their accession;

3. Employees who became affiliated to an organisation bound by the agreement, from the date of their affiliation; and

4. All workers in the service of an employer are bound by the agreement.'[4]

Even if some of the workers do not agree with the provisions, this will not affect the binding nature of the collective bargaining agreement on them.[5]

The above does not mean that the parties to the collective bargaining agreement cannot determine the personal scope of application of their own collective bargaining agreements. When concluding the collective bargaining agreement they can determine the conditions that need to be satisfied in order to be able to benefit from the application of the agreement, unless the choice of the worker to whom the agreement would be applicable is discriminatory and in violation of the law.

For a collective bargaining agreement to be in force, it does not matter if an employee is unionised or not. For a compa-

ny-level agreement, the rule is that it is applicable to who ever is employed by the employer, regardless of whether he or she is considered a free-rider. Trade union membership is thus not required in order to be able to be covered by a collective bargaining agreement.

Membership of an organisation that concluded a collective bargaining agreement may be important for an employer when dealing with sector collective bargaining agreements that are not rendered generally binding by the King. In that case, an employer will only be bound by the sector-level agreements if he is himself a member of the employers' association that concluded the agreement.

2.3. Types of collective bargaining agreements

With respect to the types of collective bargaining agreements, a two-fold distinction will be made. On the one hand, there is a distinction regarding the duration of the collective bargaining agreements (fixed-term or not), and on the other hand there is a distinction based on the level of the industrial relations system at which the collective bargaining agreements have been concluded.

Article 15 of the Act of 5 December 1968 explicitly foresees three kinds of collective bargaining agreements in this respect:

1. Collective bargaining agreements for a fixed term, indicating the duration of their validity;[6]

2. Collective bargaining agreements for an indefinite period of time; and

3. Collective bargaining agreements for a fixed term with a renewal clause.

Collective bargaining agreements can be concluded at the national inter-industry level in the National Labour Council, thereby covering the various levels of industrial relations in Belgium. The National Labour Council is composed of employer and employee representatives and is presided by a civil servant that is not a party to the collective bargaining agreements as such. Collective bargaining agreements concluded within the National Labour Council are almost

---

3   Article 2, paragraph 3, Act of 5 December 1968, Official Gazette, 15 January 1969, often amended thereafter.
4   Article 19, Act of 5 December 1968.
5   Supreme Court, 1 February 1993, *Rechtskundig Weekblad*, 1993-94, 47; Labour Court, Liège, 26 May 1998 and 24 November 1998, *Sociaalrechtelijke Kronieken*, 1999, 237.
6   See also: Article 16, 5°, Act of 5 December 1968, Official Gazette, 15 January 1969, often amended thereafter.

always rendered binding by Royal Decree and then become applicable to all employers and employees in the private sector.

Situated directly below the industrial relations level of the National Labour Council is the level of the various industries or sectors of business. Sector-level collective bargaining takes place in the joint committees of industry set up by sector of industry. Distinct joint committees are generally set up for blue- and white-collar workers, so that bargaining for the two kinds of workers often takes place separately. There are over one hundred of these joint committees in Belgium, where several hundreds of collective bargaining agreements are concluded each year. It is fair to say that the majority of the wages and working conditions for a large number of employees are set at the level of the joint committee of industry.

One level below is the level of the individual enterprise. It should be taken into account that lower-level collective bargaining agreements cannot go against the content of higher-level collective bargaining agreements. They may not foresee conditions and benefits that are less advantageous to the employee. However, they can foresee conditions that are more advantageous. Various parliamentary acts foresee that certain topics (such as night work and weekend work, under certain conditions) need to be regulated by an enterprise collective bargaining agreement. It is therefore not surprising that over the last couple of years more and more emphasis has been placed on enterprise level bargaining, especially if one looks at the number of collective bargaining agreements that are concluded per year.

2.4. Content of the collective bargaining agreements

Collective bargaining agreements in Belgium deal with wages and working conditions in the broadest sense. The 1968 Act states that they determine individual and collective relationships between the parties to it.[7]

A collective bargaining agreement is often referred to as a double-yolked egg.[8] This means that it has a double content: on the one hand, it regulates labour and employment conditions for employers and employees, both at a collective and at an individual level. This regulation has a normative nature, imposing norms on employers and employees and regulating their specific conditions. On the other hand, the collective

bargaining agreement also stipulates the rights and obligations of the parties who conclude the agreement. This constitutes what is referred to as the obligatory part of the collective bargaining agreement.

With respect to the normative part of the collective bargaining agreement, a further distinction needs to be made between the individual and the collective normative parts. Individual normative stipulations are the rules concerning the wages and working conditions of the individual employees. This includes stipulations about wages and benefits, cost of living clauses (indexing of wages in line with the increase of the cost of living), job classifications, working time issues, holidays, vacations, etc. Collective normative stipulations govern the collective relationship between the social partners at the level the collective bargaining agreement is concluded. This could be the enterprise level or any higher level of collective bargaining. Examples of such collective normative stipulations are the establishments, the conditions for establishment and the function of the trade union delegation in the company, procedures for the settlement of industrial disputes, etc.

2.5. Binding force of collective bargaining agreements

2.5.1. Agreements not rendered generally binding

A distinction has to be made between the normative and obligatory provisions of the collective bargaining agreement, as discussed above.

With respect to the normative provisions, it must be stressed that these provisions bind the employer that concluded the agreement or that acceded to it, or the employer that is a member of the employers' association that concluded the agreement or of one that acceded to it. In any of these cases, the provisions of the collective bargaining agreement have a more binding effect than the individual employment contracts. For other employers, the individual normative provisions have an effect beyond the contract parties or their members. The 1968 Act foresees a supplementary binding effect of the normative individual provisions of a collective bargaining agreement on employers who are not members of a signatory party, but who fall within the scope of a joint committee in which the agreement is concluded. The binding force is supplementary only inasmuch as individual written employment contracts make deviations from the provisions possible.[9]

---

7   Article 5, Act of 5 December 1968, Official Gazette, 15 January 1969, often amended thereafter.
8   See: R. Blanpain and C. Engels, Belgium, in *International Encyclopaedia for Labour Law and Industrial Relations*, R. Blanpain (ed.), The Hague London Boston, Kluwer Law International, s.d.; Nos 571, 275.
9   Article 26, Act of 5 December 1968, Official Gazette, 15 January 1969, often amended thereafter.

When a collective bargaining agreement (which is higher in the hierarchy of sources than an individual employment contract) that implicitly modified the provisions of an individual employment contract ceases to be applicable, the employment contract will remain modified, unless the collective bargaining agreement contains a stipulation that foresees the contrary.[10] This means that the modified individual contract will remain in force even after the notification and the lapse of the notice period. Given the fact that one is then dealing with an individual employment contract, it is clear that the parties may bargain on an individual basis in order to change the said contract. Incorporation of the provisions of a collective bargaining agreement can occur only with respect to individual normative provisions and not with respect to the collective normative ones.[11]

2.5.2. Agreements rendered generally binding

Only agreements concluded in a joint body can be rendered generally binding by Royal Decree. This would give the collective bargaining agreement a greater binding force since it would move up in the hierarchy of sources (see supra). The violation of collective bargaining agreements that are rendered generally binding by Royal Decree is subject to criminal sanctions.

If a collective bargaining agreement that contains collective normative provisions is rendered generally binding, the collective normative provisions will then become applicable also to the employers that belong to an employers' association that did not sign the agreement.

Extension is only possible if the parties to the agreement ask for it. Of course, the extension ends when the agreement is terminated. The government continues to play a secondary role, even when it puts the governmental power at the disposal of the social partners as in the case of extension.[12]

2.5.3. Hierarchy of sources

Article 51 of the 1968 Act sets out a hierarchical list of the legal sources that regulate employment relations. From the highest to the lowest level these are:

1. The mandatory provisions of the law

2. Collective bargaining agreements that are rendered generally binding, in the following order:

   a. Agreements concluded in the National Labour Council
   b. Agreements concluded in a joint committee of industry
   c. Agreements concluded in a joint sub-committee

3. Collective bargaining agreements that are not rendered generally binding, where the employer is a signatory thereto or is affiliated to an organisation that is a signatory party to the agreement, in the following order:

   a. Agreements concluded in the National Labour Council
   b. Agreements concluded in a joint committee of industry
   c. Agreements concluded in a joint sub-committee
   d. Agreements concluded outside a joint body

4. An individual agreement in writing

5. A collective bargaining agreement in a joint body but not declared generally binding where the employer, although not a signatory thereto or not affiliated to an organisation that is a signatory thereto, is within the jurisdiction of the joint body in which the agreement was concluded

6. Company work rules

7. The supplementary provisions of the law

8. A verbal individual contract of employment

9. Customs.[13]

The hierarchy that is established by Article 51 of the Act of 5 December 1968 does not prevent individual bargaining between an employer and an employee, nor does it prevent collective bargaining at a lower level of industrial relations such as the company level. It is foreseen, however, that the results of the lower level bargaining (whether individual or collective) cannot go against the provisions of the higher-level collective bargaining agreement.[14] In case the lower-level agreement foresees better terms and conditions than the higher level agreement, this is not considered to be contrary to higher level provisions. Unless explicitly foreseen

10   Article 23, Act of 5 December 1968, Official Gazette, 15 January 1969, often amended thereafter.
11   See: Labour Court Brussels, 18 June 2001, *Journal des Tribunaux de Travail*, 2001, 481.
12   See: R. Blanpain and C. Engels, Belgium, in *International Encyclopaedia for Labour Law and Industrial Relations*, R. Blanpain (ed.), The Hague London Boston, Kluwer Law International, s.d.. No 588, 281.
13   Article 51, Act of 5 December 1968, Official Gazette, 15 January 1969, often amended thereafter.
14   Article 9, Act of 5 December 1968, Official Gazette, 15 January 1969, often amended thereafter.

differently, Belgian law always allows deviation from the higher norm to the benefit of the workers concerned.[15] A collective bargaining agreement can never go against the provisions of a mandatory provision of the law.[16]

3. Regional or Community-wide extension of collective bargaining agreements

Recently there has been a discussion about whether regional collective bargaining agreements would be possible. The question arose as to the validity of a regional government rendering collective bargaining agreements dealing with regional or community matters generally binding. The Act of 5 December 1968 only foresees that the King (read the Minister of Labour) can render a collective bargaining agreement generally binding.

In a recent recommendation (24 January and 28 March 2002) the Council of State stated that when dealing with community or regional matters, the Federal Government would not be able to render collective bargaining agreements that deal with either regional or community matters generally binding. This means that only the regional or community government should be able to do so and that the regional or community legislator should therefore pass legislation in order for its governments to be able to do so.[17]

The entity of the state that will be able to render collective bargaining agreements generally binding will thus depend on the corresponding competence of either the federal state or the region or community, in line with the constitutional division of competencies. It is clear that the legislative framework will now have to be amended accordingly.

A decree of the Flemish Community of 29 November 2002 (Official Gazette, 17 December 2002) foresees that the Flemish Government will be competent to render collective bargaining agreements generally binding in the area in which the Flemish Community is competent. This means that when issues such as training and mobility are dealt with in a collective bargaining agreement between the social partners, this agreement will now have to be rendered generally binding by the Flemish Government and no longer by the Federal Government.

The Prime Minister introduced a procedure for the annulment of the Flemish Decree to the Court of Arbitration on 30 April 2003 (case No 2000696).

4. Collective action and dispute resolution

4.1. Collective disputes

There are almost no legal rules that govern strike action in Belgium, except for some rules with respect to guaranteeing essential services. The determination of what could be considered as essential services is left up to the social partners at sector level. They also determine the procedures that need to be followed in order to guarantee these services. The Act of 19 August 1948 that regulates this matter provides for government intervention if the social partners cannot come to an agreement.

The right to strike is considered to be an individual right of the employees. This was confirmed by a decision of the Supreme Court in 1981 and in the European Social Charter that Belgium ratified in 1991. This implies that mere participation in a strike cannot, as such, justify dismissal. It also implies that workers can go on strike with or without the approval of the trade unions and without respecting the provisions of collective bargaining agreements intended to set up procedures to be respected in case of a strike. There is no sanction mechanism for not respecting the peace obligation that a trade union took on in a collective bargaining agreement.

Both the company trade union delegation and the joint committees play an important role in the settlement of industrial disputes. Trade union delegations have a right to be heard by the employer when an industrial conflict arises or is about to arise. These delegations are often assisted by the regional secretaries of the trade unions.

If no solution can be found at company level, the (potential) conflict can be referred to the conciliation committee that is established within the joint committee of the industry. On the basis of the Act of 5 December 1968 (which also deals with collective bargaining agreements), the joint committees have the task of preventing and settling disputes. In case of a potential conflict, either of the parties can contact the chair-

---

15   See: C. Engels, 'Deregulation and Labour Law: The Belgian case', in *Deregulation and Labour Law in search of a Labour Law Concept for the 21st Century*, The Japan Institute of Labour, 1999, 63.

16   Supreme Court, 10 January 2000, *Rechtskundig Weekblad*, 2000-2001, 692; Supreme Court, 27 January 1994, *Sociaalrechtelijke Kronieken*, 1994, 75.

17   See: P. Populier, Vlaamse C.A.O.'s [Flemish Collective Bargaining Agreements], *Rechtskundig Weekblad*, 2002-2003, 154.

man of the joint committee who is a neutral civil servant of the Ministry of Labour. Unless foreseen differently, the chairman is supposed to call together the parties within a period of seven days.

Other government officials, such as social conciliators, can also play a role in the settlement of industrial disputes. Generally, the chairperson of the joint committees is appointed as a social conciliator.

It should finally be noted that none of these settlement procedures can 'force' a decision on the social partners with respect to the outcome of the industrial conflict, even though the purpose of the procedure is to bring the parties together. If the process fails, the parties remain free to engage in action. There is no real binding arbitration in collective disputes.

A more recent phenomenon deals with court interventions in case of strikes and the use of injunctions against striking workers who clearly exceed their right to strike. Injunctions are obtained from the presidents of civil courts in cases where the trade unions or the employees on strike clearly engage in actions that surpass their right to strike. This may include, for example, situations in which the striking workers, most often aided by external union representatives and workers not belonging to the company on strike, try to block access to the buildings both for management and for employees who are not willing to go on strike. Sometimes the company premises are not only blocked for the employees but also for third parties such as companies delivering services and clients of the company. In some cases the strikers even try to occupy the premises of the company, forcing themselves in. Blockades of public roads, etc. Also form part of the arsenal of the strikers.

Any such action clearly falls outside the scope of the right to strike, which means the right to peacefully refrain from working. Besides not working, Belgian law also allows strikers to form picket lines by which they try to convince those workers who are not on strike to also refrain from working.

The procedures in court are unilateral since the employer, when requesting the injunction from the judge, does not know the identity of those who want to or are already blocking the entrance. Furthermore, trade unions often work with 'flying picket lines', replacing the individuals once they have been identified.

Trade unions have vehemently complained against these procedures and have stated time and time again that these kinds of injunctions were an attack against their right to strike. Clearly, they are wrong. While the right to strike must be fully guaranteed, the rights of others must equally be respected. The actions they have been engaging in are a clear infringement of the rights

of others, such as the right to work and the right of the employer (property rights), rights which are equally protected under Belgian law.

In response, the Minister of Employment has introduced a proposal for a new legislative act that would regulate the injunctions and the procedures to obtain them. Labour courts, instead of the ordinary civil courts, would become competent to deal with these matters.

Neither the trade unions nor the employers' associations were in favour of this kind of legislative intervention. They instead came to a compromise aimed at giving the social dialogue its rightful place (again) within the Belgian system of industrial relations. They stressed the importance of a normal social dialogue, as well as the necessity to seek conciliation as foreseen in the Belgian system. The employers' associations have declared that they will advise their members not to use civil court injunctions unless all means of conciliation have been exhausted. The trade unions have declared that they will make an effort to avoid physical and material violence and preserve company property. The solemn declaration was made on 15 February 2002. However, it has not significantly affected the actions of either social partner. Trade unions still go on strike before the means of conciliation have been exhausted and employers still react by requesting courts for an injunction when illegal activity accompanying strikes occurs.

4.2. Individual disputes

Individual disputes over rights can always be brought before the labour courts. Labour courts are generally composed of a professional judge and two lay judges, one of whom represents the employees' side and is chosen by the representative trade unions and the other one chosen by the representative employers' associations. Decisions are always made on the basis of consensus. There are no dissenting opinions to the court's judgment.

Trade union representatives can assist the employee when going to court.

The trade union delegation of the company can always assist employees when they have an individual conflict with the employer. The trade union delegation generally has the right to be heard by the employer.

Arbitration does not really play a role in employment law conflicts. In general, the Act of 3 July 1978 on employment contracts declares arbitration clauses null and void if concluded before the conflict arises. Such clauses would only be valid for the highest level of white-collar workers in charge of the day-to-day management of the company.

Chapter II:
From job security to employability

1. Individual employment security

1.1. Blue- and white-collar workers

A significant distinction still exists with respect to the employment security of blue- and white-collar workers (for a qualitative comparison, see below). The terms of notice or the indemnities to be paid to white-collar workers in lieu of notice are substantially higher than those paid to blue-collar workers. The Act on Employment Contracts (1978) has cemented these differences. While several attempts have been made to have this distinction declared unconstitutional, none of these attempts was successful. The social partners have finally agreed to reduce/eliminate the differences over time through collective bargaining. However, not much has happened yet. The structure of the trade unions themselves is likely to act as an impediment to any fundamental changes in the very near future.

The term of notice or notice period an employer needs to respect when terminating a blue-collar worker's contract only takes into account the years of seniority the worker has built up with the same employer. The law is straightforward and determines that the term of notice is 28 calendar days for workers who have up to 20 years of seniority, regardless of any other circumstances, such as the age of the worker or his income.[18] In case the employee has more than 20 years of seniority the term of notice to be respected by the employer doubles to 56 days.[19]

This period differs greatly with the term of notice an employer needs to respect when terminating white-collar workers' contracts. A white-collar worker who has concluded an employment contract for an indefinite period of time, not containing a trial clause, is immediately more protected than the blue-collar worker who has 30 years of seniority. The Act on Employment Contracts indeed contains a provision setting the minimum term of notice at three months per five-year period of employment with the same employer.

In order to determine the exact term of notice, one must also make a distinction between various sub-categories of white-collar workers. The distinguishing criterion is the annual income the employee earns (including the value of the benefits in kind the individual is receiving). This means that the legislator does not only take into account the years of seniority with the same employer, but also the annual income earned. The annual income is adjusted to a cost of living index once per year. For 2003 the amount was set at EUR 25 921.

If the white-collar worker earns less than the threshold amount mentioned, the Act on Employment Contracts explicitly determines the term of notice that has to be

Seniority	Term of notice	
	White-collar minimum	Blue-collar
0-less 5 years	3 months/90 days	28 days
From 5 years to less than 10	6 months/180 days	28 days
From 10 years to less than 15	9 months/270 days	28 days
From 15 years to less than 20	12 months/360 days	28 days
From 20 years to less than 25	15 months/450 days	56 days
...	[+3months/+90 days]	56 days

18   Article 59, paragraph 3, Act on Employment Contracts.
19   See footnote 18.

respected: three months of notice per five-year period of seniority with the same employer.[20] This is the minimum legal notice period for white-collar workers. This period is already substantially more beneficial for the worker than the period of notice the blue-collar worker would obtain after 30 years of work for the same employer.

White-collar workers earning more than the threshold amount mentioned above can count on receiving terms of notice that are extremely advantageous compared to those of blue-collar workers. The Act on Employment Contracts states that the above-mentioned periods are the legal minimum below which a judge can never set the judgment when asked to determine the notice period the worker concerned would be entitled to.[21]

For employees earning above EUR 25 921 annually (amount valid during 2003) the Act on Employment Contracts only mentions the minimum period of notice to be respected. The actual terms of notice (either the length of the notice period or the indemnity in lieu of notice in case the period is not respected) have to be set by the parties or by the court in case the parties can not come to an agreement. Courts will take into account all circumstances proper to the individual case, but aim to reward seniority on the one hand and look at the ability of the worker concerned to find a comparable job, on the other hand.

Prior to 1994, the parties could not come to an agreement on the term of notice before the employer had actually notified its intention to terminate the contract of employment. Any earlier agreement, even when more beneficial to the employee concerned, was considered to be null and void. In the absence of a clear standard in the Act itself, several doctrinal formulae have been developed, all aimed at predicting the level of the notice period or indemnity in lieu that would be granted in an individual case.

Since 1994, parties are granted the ability to contractually determine the period of notice to be respected. Several conditions would have to be satisfied simultaneously:

- The annual remuneration of the white-collar worker needs to surpass an annually adjusted income level, set at EUR 51 842 for the year 2003;

- Parties need to come to an agreement on the notice period once the employee starts performing the contract (at the latest); and

- The term of notice that is contractually stipulated needs to respect the minimum legal notice the Act on Employment Contracts foresees for the white-collar worker earning less than EUR 25 921 per year (three months of notice per period of seniority of five years).

With respect to white-collar workers there is thus a distinction between three categories of workers, based on their annual salary. For the category earning the least, the Act explicitly determines what the term of notice is. For the categories earning the most, contractual freedom reigns, at least inasmuch as the minimum legal rules applicable to the lowest level of white-collar workers are respected. For the intermediary category (including those who earn above threshold level, but who did not enter into a (valid) agreement), the term of notice needs to be set taking all factors of the case into account, and looking primarily at the seniority of the employee, age and annual income as factors that could give an indication of the ease with which the worker concerned will be able to obtain comparable employment. These white-collar workers almost always obtain substantially higher terms of notice than the minimum stipulated in the law. As illustrated below, the social partners, both at the national inter-industry level and at the level of the sector of industry, have increased the terms of notice to be respected in case of dismissal of blue-collar workers. However, equality of treatment has certainly not been reached yet.

Further distinctions between blue- and white-collar workers with respect to employment security relate to the length of trial clauses and the requirement to justify the dismissal of blue-collar workers when they claim their dismissal was unjustified (abusive dismissal). The trial clause of a blue-collar worker cannot surpass 14 days (with a minimum duration of seven days),[22] while the minimum trial clause for a white-collar worker is one month and can run up to six months or even one year depending on the annual income of the white collar worker.[23]

The Act on Employment Contracts includes a provision on the abuse of the dismissal right by an employer, but does so

---

20   Article 82, paragraph 2, Act on Employment Contracts.
21   Article 82, paragraph 3, Act on Employment Contracts.
22   Article 48, paragraph 2, Act on Employment Contracts.
23   Article 67, paragraph 2, Act on Employment Contracts.

only with respect to blue-collar workers.[24] There is no similar provision for white-collar workers. However, case law has developed an abuse of rights theory, although it does not go as far as the explicit legal provision dealing with blue-collar workers. In case an employer is not able to rebut the presumption of abusive dismissal invoked by the blue-collar worker, the latter receives an indemnity equal to six months of pay. This indemnity is clearly substantially higher than the indemnity in lieu of notice the same blue-collar worker would be able to claim on the basis of the Act on Employment Contracts.

1.2. Employee representatives

A very elaborate form of job security is guaranteed to employee representatives in works councils and health and safety committees by a Parliamentary Act of 19 March 1991 (Official Gazette, 29 March 1991). Employee representatives can be dismissed for only two reasons:

1. Economic or technical reasons and

2. Just cause reasons allowing an immediate termination of the employment contract, without any termination indemnity being paid.

Very strict procedures need to be respected by the employer invoking either of the two categories of dismissal. In case of an intended dismissal for economic or technical reasons, a procedure needs to be followed by the joint committee of the industry to which the company belongs. The employer cannot dismiss the worker concerned during the procedure. Depending on the outcome of the procedure, the employer may have to follow a procedure before a court of law before actually terminating the employment relationship concerned. In case of an intended dismissal for just cause, court intervention is required from the beginning.

If the above procedures are not followed, this may lead to the application of severe sanctions. The employee concerned can then claim termination indemnities equal to several years of pay, with an absolute maximum of eight years of pay. The indemnity is composed of two parts. A first part (either two, three or four years of pay) depends on the number of years of service the worker concerned has (less than 10, 10-20, and more than 20). The second part of the indemnity is equal to the employee's salary for the remainder of his or her position as an employee representative to the works council or the health and safety committee (maximum four years).

At the level of the different sectors of industry, trade union representatives also enjoy some protection against dismissal. This protection is less far-reaching than that foreseen for works council members or members of the health and safety committee and is entirely regulated by sector-level and company-level collective bargaining agreements, unless the trade union delegation has taken up the duties of the works council in which the works council legislation – including the Act of 19 March 1991 – become entirely applicable.

1.3. Special forms of protection

Several specific forms of protection have been introduced in Belgium over the years:

- Protection against abusive dismissal for blue-collar workers (see infra) (Article 63, Act of 3 July 1978 on Employment Contracts).

- Protection against dismissal of a pregnant worker for reasons related to her pregnancy (Article 40, Act of 16 March 1971, Official Gazette, 30 March 1971, often amended subsequently). According to the amended text (1995), the protection is enforced from the moment the employee notifies the employer of the pregnancy.

- Protection of the employee who is breastfeeding. This protection was introduced by an inter-industry-wide C.B.A. of 27 November 2001 that was rendered generally binding by Royal Decree of 21 January 2002 (Official Gazette, 12 February 2002).

- Protection of an employee on parental leave when maternity leave is converted into paternity leave (Royal Decree, 17 October 1994, Official Gazette, 9 November 1994). Under certain conditions, maternity leave can be converted into paternity leave. This is the case when the mother has died or when she has been hospitalised.

24   Article 63, Act on Employment Contracts.

- Protection of workers on parental leave (C.B.A. No 64, 29 October 1977, Official Gazette, 7 November 1997).

- Protection for equal treatment on the basis of sex (Act 7 May 1999, Official Gazette, 19 June 1999).

- Protection for workers that benefit from the credit or all kinds of interruption of their professional career. (C.B.A. No 88bis, 9 December 2001, modified by C.B.A. No 77 ter, 10 July 2002).

- Protection against violence, harassment and sexual harassment at work (Act of 11 June 2002). The Act installs protection for employers filing a complaint or an action in court, as well as for the witnesses.

- Protection for workers who exercise a political mandate (Act of 13 July 1976, Official Gazette, 24 August 1976).

- Protection of employees filing remarks with respect to the draft text (or modifications) of the company work rules (Article 12, Act of 8 April 1965, Official Gazette, 5 May 1965).

- Protection of employees who entered into a night work regime after 7 April 1998 and who exercise their right to return to a day time regime within their trial period (Article 9, paragraph 3, Act of 17 February 1997, with respect to night work, Official Gazette, 8 April 1997).

The various acts that establish these forms of protection foresee a shift in the burden of proof. The employer has to prove that any dismissal that occurred was unrelated to the reasons for which the protection was granted. If the employer is not able to carry the burden of proof, an indemnity equal to six months of pay needs to be paid by the employer.

The implementation of the Framework Directive on discrimination follows the same principle (see infra).

2. Inclusion of risk group

2.1. Introduction

The social partners that concluded the inter-professional agreement for 1989 and 1990 decided to make special efforts for persons they considered to be 'groups at risk' among the unemployed as a whole.

Generally, groups at risk are understood as long-time unemployed, young people and persons with lower levels of education. Over the last decade the notion 'groups at risk' has also come to include older employees.

Since 1998, a 'National Action Plan for Employment' (NAP) is drafted every year. The measures to enhance the employment of groups at risk generally make up for a large part of these NAPs.

2.2. Employment fund

The employment fund destined to finance measures to increase the employment of risk groups already existed before 1992. However, since 1993[25] the social partners determine, by way of a collective bargaining agreement, what they view as groups at risk within the sector in which they are operating. Each such collective bargaining agreement is concluded within the competent joint committee or at company level.

2.3. Young people

2.3.1. First job contract ('starbaanovereenkomst') or 'Rosetta-plan'

The 24 December 1999 Act to enhance employment introduced the system of first job contracts and abandoned the system of internships for young people that had been in existence since 1983. The 30 March 2000 Royal Decree carried out some of the provisions of the 1999 Act.

The system applies to employers from both the private and public sectors. Employers from the private sector with at least 50 employees have to engage a number of young workers equal to at least 3% of their personnel (calculated in full-time equivalents). Collectively, all the employers from the private sector, including the ones that employ less than 50 employees, have to engage a number of young workers equal to at least 1% of the personnel of all companies employing at least 50 employees (calculated in full-time equivalents). Employers that engage such young workers will benefit from reductions on their social security contributions.

The goal of the first job contract system is to give young people the opportunity to obtain a position on the labour market within six months of leaving school. The main category of young people concerned by this system are persons no longer subject to compulsory education (thus older than

---

25   Act on the implementation of some elements of the 9 December 1992 inter-professional agreement of 10 June 1993.

18), who are not yet 25 years old and who left school less than six months ago. If the number of such workers is insufficient, the first job contract system will apply to workers less than 25 years old who are looking for a job. Finally, if there are not enough of the latter the system will apply to persons less than 30 years old who are looking for a job. Since the 5 September 2001 Act, the system can also apply to unemployed persons over 45 years of age, in case there is a lack of young people in the other three categories. The 24 December 2002 Act stipulates that the first category will be abandoned as of 1 January 2004.

Three different kinds of contracts can be offered: a normal employment contract, an employment contract combined with schooling and an indenture. In the first instance, the maximum duration of the first job contract will be 12 months. Even if the contract that has been concluded lasts for more than 12 months, only those first 12 months will be considered a first job contract. For the other two types of contracts a maximum of 24 months applies (36 months as of 1 January 2004).

2.3.2. Mobilisation course (*inschakelingsparcours*)

During the last decade, several cooperation agreements were concluded between the federal state, the regions and the communities. These cooperation agreements aimed at increasing the chances of job seekers on the job market and the support of their efforts in view of concluding a first job contract. Each one of these cooperation agreements was concluded for a limited duration and each abrogated the previous one. However, the latest cooperation agreement, of 31 August 2001 was concluded for an unlimited duration.

This cooperation agreement concerns persons not older than 25, that have left school less than three months ago, that at the very maximum) enter their third month as job seeker and that do not possess a degree of higher education.

Before the end of their third month as a job seeker, the person concerned will receive an invitation from the competent regional placement service. Before the end of the fourth month, interviews will be conducted in order to develop a personalised mobilisation course for the job seeker. This course deals with the different steps and elements that are necessary in order to find a job, such as adaptation of the person's determination to find a job, additional training, etc. In addition, a special mobilisation contract will be concluded between the job seeker and the regional placement service. Young persons that agree to follow additional schooling within the framework of a mobilisation course will receive allowances. Persons that refuse to cooperate will face sanctions.

2.4. Long-time unemployed persons/older unemployed persons

2.4.1. Local employment agencies

The system for local employment agencies already existed, but was seriously reformed by the **30 March 1994** Act. The creation of local employment agencies in municipalities has a twofold objective. On the one hand, it aims to find a solution for activities that cannot be found in the normal labour circuit. On the other hand, it gives work to long-time unemployed persons.

The following unemployed persons are concerned: 1) persons that have been unemployed for at least two years and that have been receiving allowances; 2) persons older than 45 who have been unemployed for at least six months; 3) unemployed persons that in the 36 months preceding their registration at the local employment agency have received allowances for at least 24 months.

The unemployed persons that are registered at a local employment agency are allowed to perform services at the request of private persons, educational institutions, etc. They are allowed to work a maximum of 45 hours a month. Their services are paid for in 'local employment agency cheques'.

2.4.2. Activa Plan

Measures such as the 'service jobs', job-plans and the insertion of temporary workers have been replaced as of 12 January 2002 by the Activa Plan, developed in the 19 December 2001 Royal Decree. With this plan, the government hopes to increase the employment rate of long-time unemployed persons and older unemployed persons. The government seeks to obtain this by a combination of two measures. Firstly, employers will receive a reduction on the employer's social security contribution. Secondly, there is a 'reactivated unemployment allowance' that the employer can deduct from the net remuneration he or she has to pay.

2.4.3. Employers' social security reductions

Belgian legislation provided for numerous reductions on employers' social security contributions when hiring long-time unemployed persons, old or young employees. Since these measures could be found in various acts and royal decrees, a harmonisation was necessary. This harmonisation was carried out by the 24 December 2002 Act. Since many of its provisions will enter into force on 1 January 2004, transition measures apply in the meantime.

The 24 December 2002 Act stipulates that employers that engage long-time job seekers will enjoy reductions of the employer's social security contributions. A Royal Decree will determine who should be considered a long-time job seeker.

2.5. Older employees

2.5.1. Bridge pension

Much political attention has been given to increasing the participation of older workers in the labour market. However, the system of pre-pension rights that grants workers that terminate their active life a security of income, sometimes from an age as early as 50, certainly works against this policy. It has often been stated that the system should be abolished, however, no government has had the courage to do so. The system of the pre-pensions is often used to restructure companies in a less painful manner.

2.5.2. Prohibition of discrimination

The 13 February 1998 Act on provisions concerning the improvement of employment includes a prohibition on discrimination with regard to age in employment relationships. When organising the recruitment of a new employee, an employer is not allowed to fix a maximum age for a candidate for a certain job. Similarly, an employer is not allowed to fix a maximum age for applicants for a certain position.

2.5.3. Employers' social security reduction and subsidy

The 15 September 15 2001 Act stipulated that the reduction on employers' social security contributions, which already existed for certain employees, could be increased by Royal Decree if those employees reach the age of 58. This measure was confirmed in the 24 December 2002 Act.

Furthermore, the employer can obtain subsidies from the government for undertaking actions that would improve the quality of the working conditions for older workers. A Royal Decree of 30 January 2003 spells out the details.[26]

A collective bargaining agreement at sector or company level is a prerequisite. The actions or studies undertaken by the employer must relate to job safety, the health of the worker, ergonomics or the psycho-social pressure of the employee's work. Actions need to be aimed at employees who are 55 years or older. Priority is given to actions that prevent risks, that are innovative and that can also be applied in other companies (examples of best practices). The level of subventions depends on the size of the employer.

2.5.4. Outplacement

Recently,[27] the National Labour Council added another termination entitlement to the list of the dismissed employees of 45 years or older; outplacement. To benefit from outplacement at the expense of the (former) employer, the employee must meet the following conditions:

- Be 45 years or older at the time of the dismissal

- Have at least 1 year seniority

- Not be dismissed for serious cause

- Be registered for employment (and thus not benefit from the pre-pension regime).

The employee must apply for such outplacement.

The entitlement to outplacement is valid for a period of 12 months. It is split up in three phases, of 20 hours each. The first phase takes place the first two months of unemployment. If the employee has not found a new job by then, phases two and three take place respectively during the following four and the last six months.

The entitlement to outplacement naturally comes to an end if the employee finds a new job. If he or she loses this new employment within three months, the outplacement can be revived upon his or her request. However, the original 12-month period cannot be exceeded.

Some sectors of industry have bargained over the issue and have come to sectoral arrangements with respect to the outplacement to be offered by the employer.

For example, within J.C. No 218 (which gathers a large amount of white-collar workers) the outplacement services are organised by CEVORA, which is the training institute of the Joint

---

26   Royal Decree, 30 January 2003, determining the criteria, the conditions and rules for granting subventions in support of actions that relate to the improvement of the quality of the working conditions of older workers and the amount of the subventions, Official Gazette, 7 February 2003.

27   C.B.A. No 82 concluded in the National Labour Council on 10 July 2002 and rendered generally binding by Royal Decree of 20 September 2002.

Committee of Industry No 218. Hence, the employee must apply for outplacement with CEVORA within two months of their dismissal. There is no extra cost for the employer.

2.6. Lifelong learning

2.6.1. Educational leave within the framework of lifelong learning

The **September 15 2001 Act** simplified the system of paid educational leave. According to this Act, employees will receive extra leave hours for training attended during their free time or they will be granted leave in case the training takes place during the normal working hours. The employee will receive normal remuneration for the hours during which he or she is absent. The employer can claim a reimbursement for this expense from the Ministry of Employment and Labour.

2.6.2. Training cheques (*opleidingscheques*)

Both the Flemish and Walloon regions have organised a system of 'training cheques'. The basic system was established in the Flemish region by the 14 December 2001 Decree and in the Walloon region by the 23 July 1998 Decree.

Employers can buy training cheques from the regional government. With these cheques they pay for the training of their employees in a recognised training institution. The region bears part of the cost of the training.

2.6.3. Also see the following section on *Immigrants*

2.7. Immigrants

Subsidies can be requested from the Flemish Government for projects that involve training[28] for low-skilled workers, workers over the age of 45 (with the exception of managers) and for immigrants (referred to as 'allochtonen' and defined as people coming from outside the EU).

Projects need to be discussed at company level with the employee representative bodies. Among other things, projects in the ICT area and Dutch language classes are foreseen.

Subsidies can run up to EUR 1 million (including those received from the ESF).

Recently, the Flemish Parliament adopted another Decree (not yet published) setting up a framework for the 'inclusion' policies of the Flemish Government as concerns immigrants. They can receive additional training and guidance in order to ensure their position on the labour market.[29] This framework aims at better integrating immigrants in society at large.

3. Company restructuring

The legislation dealing with collective dismissals primarily dates back to the 1970s. However, a very significant piece of legislation was passed in 1998. Articles 62-70 of the Act of 13 February 1998 are generally referred to as the Renault Act, since this legislation was passed after the French car manufacturer Renault decided to close its plant in Vilvoorde, Belgium, in absolute violation of all of the existing rules on information and consultation of the workforce and their representatives. The Renault Act did not abolish any existing legislation in the area. However, it was said to render the existing obligations more explicit and to foresee additional sanctions.

Before any collective dismissals are announced or effected, the employer must consult the workers' representatives within the works council in relation to the proposals and their consequences. In the absence of a works council, the employer should consult the union representatives and in the absence of union representatives, the employer should consult the employees.

Prior to the consultation, the employer must provide oral and written information about the intended collective dismissal to the appropriate representatives. Written information must include:

1. The reasons for the proposed dismissals

2. The number and categories of workers to be dismissed (but not their identities)

3. The number and categories of workers normally employed

---

28   Flemish Decree, 27 September 2002 with respect to the conditions and rules for subsidies for continuing training for workers and companies, part on 'herfboomkrediet-opleidingen', Official Gazette, 11 December 2002.

29   Draft text No 1545 (2002-2003), 1. Session 29 January 2003. The text was adopted by the Flemish Parliament.

4. The period in which the proposed dismissals are to be carried out

5. The proposed criteria for selecting workers to be made redundant and

6. The method for calculating any redundancy payments other than those arising from legislation or collective bargaining agreements.

A copy of this information must also be sent to the head of the Regional Bureau of the National Employment Agency.

The employer must hold several meetings with the workers' representatives to consult on general employment issues arising from the proposed dismissals. In particular, they should discuss how to avoid the dismissals, or at least reduce their scope and mitigate their consequences. This will involve consideration of measures to redeploy or retain redundant workers. The employer must allow the workers' representatives to ask questions and to make proposals. The employer must respond to all their questions, arguments and proposals.

After the consultation with the workers' representatives has been completed, the employer must notify the head of the regional unemployment office of the proposed collective dismissals. No dismissals can be made within one month of this notification. This period may be extended by a further month.

It is common practice for the employer and the trade unions to produce a social plan containing measures and mandatory compensation designed to alleviate the consequences of the collective dismissals. Such a social plan is, however, not mandatory.

If the employer fails to comply with the relevant procedure, the workers' representatives in the work council have up to 30 days following the notification of the dismissals to contest the procedure (this is known as a collective challenge). If they fail to do so, the procedure is deemed to have been carried out correctly. Employees can also challenge whether the employer has complied with the procedure up to 30 days after the dismissal.

If the employee contests the procedure, the notice period will be suspended for a period of 60 days following receipt by the regional unemployment office of a new notification that does comply with the legal requirements. During this period, the employer must provide work to the employee and pay his or her salary. If the employee has been dismissed without notice, the employee can claim reinstatement. If it appears that the information and consultation procedure was not followed, the employer must reinstate the employee and pay backdated salary from the date of dismissal.

If the dismissed worker cannot be reinstated, the employer must pay the worker's salary for up to 60 days after the notification of the head of the regional unemployment office.

Proposals are on the table to make the Renault Act stricter, since its five-year application has shown that alternatives to the intended collective dismissals are not often found. The objective is to foresee a reimbursement of any reduction in taxes and/or social security contributions over a five-year period of time for those companies that do not fully comply with the provisions of the Renault Act.

Chapter III:
Labour law and adaptability

1. Employed or self-employed persons

The classic question of the distinction between self-employed workers on the one hand and subordinate employees on the other hand, remains of critical importance in Belgian labour and employment law. However, over the last couple of years there has been an increasing tendency to include self-employed workers in the scope of some protective legislation, such as health and safety legislation. The Act on the well-being of workers, passed in 1996, now explicitly foresees that a number of provisions have to be included in the agreement between the self-employed worker and the company for whom the self-employed person is performing services at the premises of this company. The area of health and safety is most likely to be the least controversial for applying some protective legislation. It is clear that all workers whether they are self-employed or subordinate employees, should be protected from the dangers inherent in the workplace. A certain degree of coordination between the company and the self-employed worker is put forward by the 1996 Act on the well-being of workers. In a separate section, namely chapter IV of the Act of 4 August 1996, a number of provisions are put forward with respect to the coordination of work being performed within a company, either by a self-employed worker or by another worker coming in to do the work with his or her own personnel. Information needs to be exchanged between both parties involved with respect to the inherent risks of the work to be performed and the place where it is to take place. (Article 8 e.s. Act of 4 August 1996, on the well-being of workers in the performance of their work, Official Gazette, 18 September 1996, often amended subsequently). The Act also foresees that one party can take precautionary measures with respect to safety at the expense of the other party in case the latter does not respect its obligations.

With respect to non-discrimination principles, it should be noted that the implementation of the Framework Directive has led the Belgian legislator to act both with respect to subordinate workers and with respect to self-employed contractors (see *infra*).

1.1. Subordination or authority as a crucial concept

A distinguishing feature of an employment contract is the existence of a continued and personal relationship of subordination of the employee or worker towards the employer. It is indeed the latter characteristic which distinguishes the self-employed worker from the employee and which will be important in determining whether parties are bound by an employment contract or not.

The Supreme Court has defined a relationship of subordination as:

The legal authority of the employer, who has the right to give orders to employees concerning the organisation and the performance of the work agreed on.

The labour courts look at a number of objective factors to determine whether there is a link of subordination.

1.1.1. Factors indicating a link of subordination

- The obligation to regularly draft reports and attend meetings where instructions are given and, generally, the right to give instructions and the correlated obligation to respect them

- The reimbursement of expenses, including travel expenses

- The obligation to respond to a defined working time schedule and to justify the use of his or her time; the obligation to respond to a working time schedule applicable to other (subordinate) workers within the same company/group

- The obligation to justify his/her absences (namely illnesses)

- The obligation to ask prior approval in order to take vacation

- A guaranteed income

- A vacation allowance

- The use of a company car

- The existence of an exclusive commitment

- Supervision of the employee's performances

- The obligation to complete a trial period

- The fact that the worker is listed in the employer's personnel register

- The fact that the worker is listed on the same telephone list as other (subordinate) workers within the same company/group

- The fact that the company concluded an insurance policy for work accidents for the worker, etc.

Please note that the existence of a single factor is not sufficient in order to establish a relationship of subordination.

1.1.2. Factors not indicative of a relationship of subordination

The Labour courts have held that certain factors do not imply a relationship of subordination. In general, the following factual criteria are not considered as indicia for subordination:

- General instructions given in the context of a corporate strategy

- The obligation to dedicate time to the activity

- The fact that the worker performing the activity in the principal's offices, if the worker pays part of the costs

- A fixed fee

- A standard competition clause

- A standard confidentiality clause

- A mutually agreed schedule, if the worker decides himself/herself to use a replacement.

1.1.3. Factors indicating the independence of the worker

The courts have also held that the following factors are likely to exclude the existence of an employment contract or should at least, together with other factors, be looked upon as a sign of independence:

- The worker may be replaced (and can himself/herself decide on the replacement) or hire his/her own staff, remunerated by himself/herself

- The work is non-exclusive – the worker may also work for third parties

- The worker may freely organise his/her time, decide when to be absent from work or and when he or she is incapable of working without any external control being possible

- There is no minimum guaranteed remuneration.

As a general rule, employment contracts require the worker to be a physical person. While the Employment Contracts Act of 3 July 1978 does not mention this condition explicitly, it is generally considered to reflect the spirit of the act. Therefore, in case of a Personal Service Company (PSC) established by one of the lawyers, the fact that one is dealing with a legal entity rather than a physical person prevents the agreement between these entities to be considered an employment contract under Belgian law. The mere existence of a corporate entity through which the performances are delivered is not a guarantee, however, that the contract for the performance of the services will not be considered an employment contract as far as the actual performer of the services is concerned. Indeed, the fact that the formal agreement is concluded between two legal entities (and thus not with a worker, as a physical person) does not mean that there cannot also be an agreement between the worker as a physical person on the one hand, and the 'employer' on the other hand. Several court of appeal cases over the last decade explicitly confirmed this point of view.

1.2. The 'Unizo-test' – an expression of economic dependence

Unizo (an organisation representing small and medium-sized employers) developed a formula, allegedly based on the criteria used by the labour courts, which makes it possible to verify mathematically whether a person is an employee or a self-employed worker. Unizo has selected 12 factual criteria and each criterion is given a number of points. The total amount of points determines whether or not the person is a self-employed worker or an employee: if the result of the formula is below 40, the person is not considered to be self-employed. If the result exceeds 60, the person is considered to be a self-employed person. If the result is between 40 and 60, a ruling commission should decide whether or not the worker is self-employed. The formula reads as follows:

	Criterion	Points
1.	Substantial participation in the profit	13
2.	Important professional investments	13
3.	Responsibility and power to decide in order to keep the company profitable with capital equipment	13
4.	Variable income without a minimum income guarantee	9
5.	Possibility to work for several clients	9
6.	Manifest himself towards a third party as a company	9
7.	Have his own infrastructure and equipment	4
8.	Not subject to control/sanctions	4
9.	Purchase freedom or free price-fixing	4
10.	Organise his own working time	9
11.	Real possibility of recruiting own staff	9
12.	Possibility to engage himself as a self-employed person	4
Total		**100**

This mathematical approach can be criticised, as each case should be decided upon its own merits, taking into account all its individual circumstances and peculiarities. The presence of certain criteria must be evaluated on a case-to-case basis and in conjunction with other criteria.

A draft text of a modification to the Act on Employment Contracts, as well as a draft Royal Decree, are presently under discussion. The 12 criteria mentioned above are enumerated. If a worker (working for remuneration of some

kind) satisfies more than half of the criteria mentioned, he or she would be presumed to be a subordinate employee. The presumption would remain rebuttable. It cannot be rebutted, however, by using criteria related to the formal labelling of the contract, as the draft text states.

1.3. Recent Supreme Court case law: moving away from economic dependence

In a few very recent cases, the Supreme Court clearly goes against the suggested legislative approach. The Supreme Court held on 23 December 2002 (Supreme Court, 23 December 2002, case No S010169F) that the following facts were not incompatible with the status of an independent contractor:

1. One contract party was working eight or nine hours a day for another party and was therefore not able to have his or her own clientele;

2. Prices were set by one party;

3. The person performing the services had no stake in the commercial property and no real freedom of economic administration;

4. The rooms in which the performances had to be delivered, as well as the materials and equipment with which the work was to be performed, were not held by the one performing the services;

5. The one performing the services was not carrying the economic and financial risk.

6. More recently, the Supreme Court once again clearly confirmed its position (Supreme Court, 24 April 2003, case No S01.0184.F).

It is clear that the discussion on this basic concept of labour and employment law in Belgium is far from over. The National Labour Council that was asked to deliver an opinion on the draft text of the Royal Decree is not expected to render a unanimous recommendation on the draft text. The draft (pre-) text of the recommendation confirms that there is no unanimous acceptance by the trade unions and employers' associations with respect to the draft legislative texts.

2. Fixed-term contracts

2.1. Formal requirements

Belgian employment law considers an employment contract for an indefinite period of time the ultimate and most desirable form of protection for employees. Fixed-term employment contracts must therefore respect various formal conditions in order to be considered valid. Such an employment contract needs to be formalised in a written document signed by the parties before the employee begins performing the job. If the contract is already being executed, the Supreme Court clearly holds that the contract for a fixed period of time cannot be concluded any longer (Supreme Court, 7 December 1992, *Rechtskundig Weekblad*, 1992-93, 1375 – Supreme Court, 20 September 1993, *Sociaalrechtelijke Kronieken*, 1994, 30). This condition does not apply to indefinite employment contracts. Such contracts do not even need to be concluded in writing.

Furthermore, a fixed-term employment contract must clearly indicate the period of time during which it needs to be executed. If it does not, it is presumed to be an indefinite employment contract (Article 9, Act of 3 July 1978 on Employment Contracts.

The Act foresees that for certain sectors of industry and certain categories of workers no written document is required. The social partners at sector level should conclude a collective bargaining agreement to this extent. For example, one could refer to the sector-level agreement concluded in the sector of horticulture that stipulated that no written contracts are required (Collective Bargaining Agreement, 18 April 1995, rendered generally binding by Royal Decree, 10 June 1996, Official Gazette, 23 August 1996).

2.2. Successive contracts

Since the legislator considered the indefinite employment contract more desirable than fixed-term employment contracts, it established a presumption that successive employment contracts for a fixed period of time are presumed to be an employment contract for an indefinite period of time.

The difference primarily relates to the provisions that govern the termination of the contract. When a fixed-term contract comes to an end, no termination indemnities have to be paid. When indefinite employment contracts are terminated the employer has to pay (depending on the particular circumstances of each case) relatively large termination indemnities or has to respect long terms of notice.

Prior to 1994, it was possible to conclude successive employment contracts but a specific justification was needed. The employer was allowed to prove that successive contracts were required because of the nature of the work or other justified reasons (Article 10, Act of 3 July 1978 concerning employment contracts). In 1989 a provision was added that stated, by Royal Decree, that the situations in which the employer would not be allowed to come up with such evidence would be defined. During the period discussed in the present report, the government did not issue a Royal Decree that would prevent an employer from proving that the successive employment contracts were justified because of the nature of the work or other justified reasons. Given the fact that successive employment contracts for a fixed term are to be considered the exception to the rule, the exceptions have to be narrowly construed.

In 1994 the rules on successive employment contracts for a fixed period of time were relaxed by the legislator, who realised that such contracts could be beneficial to the economy and to the potential inclusion of job seekers in the labour market. A new article 10bis was therefore introduced in the Act of 3 July 1978 concerning employment contracts. It now allows successive employment contracts to be concluded without being considered to be an indefinite employment contract if certain conditions are satisfied.

Two distinct situations are now foreseen in the 1978 Act. The first situation leads to successive employment contracts being concluded for a maximum period of two years and the second envisages a three-year period of time.

The total duration of the successive employment contracts can increase to two years if:

1. Each separate employment contract has a duration of at least three months

2. The maximum number of contracts that concluded is four and

3. The total duration does not surpass two years.

If these conditions are all cumulatively satisfied, no justification has to be given for the conclusion of the successive employment contracts.

The Supreme Court ruled that the presumption is installed for the benefit of the worker and can be invoked by the worker only. Once invoked by the worker, the employer can rebut the presumption. However, the employer cannot make the presumption if the worker has not done so (Supreme Court, 2 December 2002, RARG, 2003, p. 5).

The total duration of the successive employment contracts can go up to three years if:

1. Each separate employment contract has a duration of not less than six months

2. The maximum number of contracts concluded is six

3. The total duration does not surpass three years

4. In addition, the prior permission of a civil servant is required. The employer can, according to a Royal Decree of 17 June 1994 (Official Gazette, 25 June 1994) ask the permission of the Inspector, who is head of the district of the inspection of labour legislation of the place where the company is located, by fax or by registered mail. The request should mention the reasons why successive contracts would be justified.

This possibility of concluding successive contracts for a fixed period of time was introduced in the Act of Employment Contracts, by an Act of 30 March 1994. It was meant to cover the period of time between 1 April 1994 and 31 December 1997. According to the Act of 13 February 1998, which contains measures to promote employment, the measure was made permanent without changing anything with respect to the content of the measures and the conditions to be satisfied.

Employers are, especially in the first instance, free to conclude successive employment contracts for a fixed period of time, without having to justify or specify the reasons why they do not want to conclude an indefinite employment contract.

3. Equal treatment principles

See infra.

4. Triangular employment relationships

4.1. Temporary work

4.1.1. Applicable legal sources

In Belgium, the issue of temporary work is regulated by various legal documents. The first is the 24 July 1987 Act on temporary work and putting workers at the disposal of a user (hereafter referred to as '1987 Act'). This 1987 Act is mainly concerned with defining the formal aspects of temporary work (such as the existence of two contracts), labour conditions, termination of the contract, the relationship between the temporary employment agency and the user and the relationship between the temporary worker and the user.

During the last decade, various new legal documents have been added. A very important one is the collective bargaining agreement concluded within the National Labour Council on 7 **July 1994** (hereafter referred to as '1994 C.B.A. No 58'). The 19 February 1997 Royal Decree regulates the measures that need to be taken in order to ensure the health and security of temporary workers. Moreover, in 1993 the Joint Committee No 322 for temporary work was created. Within this Joint Committee, numerous collective bargaining agreements have been concluded since then, regulating the working conditions of temporary workers.

4.1.2. Definition

Temporary work necessarily implies the involvement of three parties: the temporary worker, the temporary employment agency and the user. Although the temporary employment agency is the temporary worker's employer, the employer's authority over the temporary worker is exercised by the user. While the temporary worker works for the user, the user is responsible for the application of the rules regarding the regulation and protection of labour and the rules concerning safety and protection in the workplace.

Two contracts are needed. Firstly, an employment contract needs to be concluded between the temporary worker and the temporary employment agency. The law determines a number of mandatory provisions to be included in the employment contract. The second contract is concluded when the temporary worker is put at the disposal of a user and is concluded between the temporary employment agency and the user.

4.1.3. Permissible use

Temporary work can only be used in a limited number of clearly defined circumstances.

4.1.3.1. Excluded situations

Collective labour conflicts, such as a strike or a lock-out

Temporary employment agencies are not allowed to put temporary workers at work with an employer in case of a collective labour conflict. Temporary workers that are working for an employer when a collective labour conflict breaks out need to be called back. (Article 8, C.B.A. No 58, 7 July 1994 replacing the C.B.A. No 47 of 18 December 1990 concerning the procedure to be followed and the duration of temporary work, rendered generally binding by Royal Decree 23 September 1994, Official Gazette, 18 October 1994, often amended thereafter).

Prohibitions to make use of temporary workers in certain branches of industry

This prohibition is limited to blue-collar workers, to remaining companies, to companies involved in the storage of furniture and to construction companies.

4.1.3.2. Permissible use

Temporary workers are to be used exclusively for the execution of permitted temporary work in the private sector.

Replacement of a regular employee

'Replacement of a regular employee' refers to the following situations (Article 1, paragraph 2, 1987 Act):

- Temporary replacement of an employee whose employment contract has been suspended

- Temporary replacement of an employee whose employment contract has been terminated.

The 1994 C.B.A. No 58 stipulates the procedure that needs to be applied in case of the temporary replacement of an employee whose employment contract has been terminated with a notice or for a serious cause, and the prolongation of this replacement. It involves the trade union delegation of the user company. This procedure does not need to be applied in case of the temporary replacement of an employee whose employment contract has been terminated for other reasons. However, this procedure also needs to be followed when prolonging the replacement of such an employee.

With regard to this procedure, a distinction needs to be made between companies that have a trade union delegation and companies that do not have one.

- Companies with a trade union delegation (Article 6, paragraph 2, 1994 C.B.A. No 58)

    The trade union delegation needs to give its preliminary permission. Within three working days of the reception of the permission, the employer needs to inform the competent inspector of the Administration for Labour Relations and Labour Rules. If the trade union delegation grants its permission, the employer can proceed with the replacement. Once again, the employer needs to inform the competent inspector.

- Companies without a trade union delegation (Article 6, paragraph 3, 1994 C.B.A. No 58)

    If a company does not have a trade union delegation, the temporary employment agency needs to give the name, address and number of the applicable joint committee to the Social Fund for Temporary Workers before the 20th day of the month in which the temporary worker started working. A notification also needs to be made to the employee representatives in the Fund. A second notification needs to be sent when the duration of the replacement reaches five months and will go beyond six months. The employee representative – the Fund – can approve such prolongation. The user then needs to stop working with the temporary worker within a period of seven days following such a notification.

If the employment contract of the employee that is being replaced was terminated with a period of notice, if the employment contract was terminated for serious cause, or if the employment contract was terminated for other reasons the replacement is limited to six months, although a prolongation of six more months is possible (Article 5, 1994 C.B.A. No 58).

Increase of work

- Companies with a trade union delegation (Article 7, paragraph 1, 1994 C.B.A. No 58)

    If the company has a trade union delegation, the company needs to request the trade union delegation's permission. This request is renewable.

- Companies without a trade union delegation (Article 7, paragraph 2, 1994 C.B.A. No 58)

  If the company has a trade union delegation, the maximum duration is six months. However, a prolongation of another six months is possible. The above-mentioned procedure concerning the replacement of a regular employee applies. If another prolongation is sought after 12 months, the temporary agency needs to apply for the permission of the Commission of Good Services. If a prolongation is sought after 18 months, yet another procedure applies.

Exceptional work

In principle, temporary workers are allowed to perform this kind of work for a maximum of three months. However, a prolongation of up to 12 months is possible if a new function is created or while awaiting new recruits, on the condition that a special procedure is followed (Article 2, C.B.A. No 36, concluded within the National Labour Council on 27 November 1981).

4.1.3.3. Potential sanctions

- Presumption of an indefinite employment contract with the user. No rebuttal of this presumption is possible. (Article 31, paragraph 3, al. 1 1987 Act; Article 9, 1994 C.B.A. No 58)

- Potential termination of the indefinite employment contract by the employee and without a term of notice. (Article 31, paragraph 3, al. 2 1987 Act)

- Joint liability between the (original) employer and the user, including liability for termination indemnities and social security contributions (Article 31, paragraph 4, 1987 Act)

- Criminal sanctions could apply as well.

4.1.3.4. Health and safety of temporary workers

The 19 February 1997 Royal Decree enacts measures to enhance the health and safety of temporary workers. This Royal Decree determines the obligations concerning the health and safety of the temporary workers that are to be fulfilled by the user and the temporary employment agency respectively.

Before a temporary worker is employed, the user is obliged to describe in an accurate way the position that is open and the qualifications needed (Article 2, 3 §1, 5 §2 and §3, 19 February 1997 Royal Decree).

The temporary employment agency is responsible for the medical supervision of the temporary workers. If the user requires a medical examination before employing anyone, the temporary employment agency will also be responsible for this (Article 3, paragraphs 2-4, 6-8, 19 February 1997 Royal Decree).

The temporary employment agency is also responsible for the application of the protection concerning motherhood (Article 4, 19 February 1997 Royal Decree).

The user has to ensure that the temporary workers enjoy the same level of protection as the regular employees with regard to safety and hygiene on the work floor (Article 5, paragraph 1, 19 February 1997 Royal Decree).

The user also has to maintain a list of all temporary workers it employs, including the positions they hold (Article 5, paragraph 4, 19 February 1997 Royal Decree).

Temporary workers are not allowed to perform certain tasks, such as the handling of poisonous waste (Article 11, 19 February 1997 Royal Decree).

4.1.3.5. Some important C.B.A.'s concluded within Joint Committee No 322, regulating the working conditions of temporary work

The Act of 24 July 1987 explicitly determines in its Article 10 that the remuneration of the temporary worker should not be less than the remuneration that the worker would have received if he or she had been hired as a permanent worker of the user.

A deviation is possible through a collective bargaining agreement. However, such a deviation is only allowed if equivalent benefits are granted.

- **Labour Regulations:** The 20 March 1995 C.B.A. (R.D. 10 June 1997) enacts a model of labour regulations that could apply between the temporary worker and the temporary employment agency.

- **Racial discrimination:** The 7 May 1996 C.B.A. (R.D. 9 September 1996) establishes a code of conduct in order to prevent racial discrimination.

- **Year-end premium:** The 10 December 2001 C.B.A. (R.D. 12 June 2002) affirms the right of the temporary worker to a year-end premium. This C.B.A. replaces C.B.A. No 36 concluded in 1986. The year-end premium is paid by the Temporary Workers Social Fund.

- **Reception of temporary workers by the temporary employment agency and by the user:** The 10 December 2001 C.B.A. (R.D. 22 August 2002) determines the way in which temporary workers have to be received by both the temporary employment agency and the user.

- **Incapacity to work:** The 10 December 2001 C.B.A. (R.D. 12 June 2002) entitles the temporary worker to additional allowances if his or her incapacity to work starts after the employment contract for temporary work has ended and at the latest on the first working day following the end of this employment contract. This allowance is not due when the incapacity begins during the employment contract for temporary work.

- **Guaranteed income:** The 18 December 1990 C.B.A. (R.D. 15 September 1994) establishes a right to a guaranteed income in case the employment contract comes to an end during the seven-day period mentioned in Article 52, paragraph 1 and Article 71 of the 3 July 1978 Act on Employment Contracts, or during the 30-day period mentioned in Article 70 of the 3 July 1978 Act on Employment Contracts or during the 23-day period mentioned in Article 3 of the 26 February 1979 C.B.A. No 12bis or in Article 3 of the 26 February 1979 C.B.A. No 13bis.

4.2. Putting workers at the disposal of a user company

4.2.1. Introduction

Putting regular workers at the disposal of a user company was very strictly regulated by an Act of 1987 (Act of 24 July 1987 regulating fixed-term work, temporary work and the putting of workers and the disposal of users, Official Gazette, 20 August 1987, often amended thereafter). The conditions this Act imposed were so stringent that they were almost never fully respected when an employer tried to make his or her employees available to a third party user. Nevertheless, this kind of activity was often undertaken by employers working, for instance, in the software business and developing programmes for users at the user's premises.

The 1987 Act was recently modified. In the framework of service-level agreements between companies (the employer's company and the user company) it should now be possible to perform work for third parties (user companies) without violating the provisions of the (modified) 1987 Act as explained below. While the Act seems, in principle, to uphold the prohibition of lending out employees to third party users, its wording allows for this prohibition to be easily by-passed.

4.2.2. Principled prohibition remains intact

The Parliamentary Act of 24 July 1987 on fixed-term work, work through temporary employment agencies and putting workers at the disposal of users, regulates this matter in a very stringent way.[30]

Article 31 of the Parliamentary Act of 24 July 1987 deals with the issue of putting workers at the disposal of users outside of the context of fixed-term work and work through temporary employment agencies.

In principle, the Act severely limits the activity of a physical person or legal entity that puts employees at the disposal of third parties and that would exercise any of the employer's normal authority over them.[31]

The prohibition is restricted in its scope to subordinate workers. This means that a company can contract an independent consultant/specialist, in order for the latter to perform certain jobs at the premises of a third party or user (the client).

The 1987 Act only prohibits putting subordinate workers at the disposal of users when such leasing of personnel is accompanied by a delegation of some part of the employer's authority. It should be noted that only a small part of the employer's authority needs to be delegated before the Act becomes applicable.

However, a modification of the Act in the year 2000 severely reduced the scope of the prohibition. In practice, the modified Act now leaves some room for putting employees at the disposal of another employer.

Severe sanctions are applied in case of a violation of the provisions of the Act. A limited number of exceptions are foreseen within the scope of the Act itself.

The Act only foresees a limited number of situations in which to the delegation of authority from one employer to another would be allowed. Even in these circumstances, additional limitations come into play.

---

30   Act on Temporary Employment. See: C. Engels, *Overdracht van Onderneming en outsourcing*, Larcier, Brussels, 2000, 127-154.
31   Article 31, paragraph 1, Act of 24 July, 1987.

4.2.3. Exceptions to the prohibition

4.2.3.1. Without delegation of authority

Situation prior to the law of 12 August 2000[32] – still applicable

In order to fall within the scope of the prohibition it is not required that the original employer transfer his or her authority entirely. It would suffice that only part of this authority is transferred to the user.

To prevent the restrictions from being applied, the user must refrain from exercising any authority over the workers. In order to determine whether the user is exercising any form of authority over the workers, the same indicia are taken into account as those used to determine whether an employment relationship exists.

In this context it is important to stress that Belgian labour courts are quite liberal in their interpretation of whether or not an employment contract exists. This means that the courts are willing to accept the existence of an employment relationship in circumstances where the alleged employer's actual or potential exercise of authority over the alleged employee is not so apparent. Quite often the employer's authority is derived from secondary, rather than primary, indicia of subordination. Primary indications would be the fact that the (alleged) employer gives the worker mandatory instructions in respect of what, where, and when to perform the work. The same is true when the employer effectively controls the way the worker performs the services.[33]

Situation since the Act of 12 August 2000 – extending the possibilities outside the scope of the Act

The Act of 12 August 2000 does not remove the prohibition of putting employees at the disposal of another employer in Belgian law.

However, by adding a paragraph to Article 31 of the Act of 24 July 1987, it renders the principled prohibition meaningless, at least when dealing with employers that formalise their relationship with partners where the employer's employees are going to perform services.

The new paragraph introduced into the Act of 24 July 1987 reads as follows:

The observation by the third party [read: user] of the obligations that rest on him with respect to the well-being at work, as well as the instructions the third party gives in furtherance of the agreement reached with the employer, both with regard to working time and rest time, as well as with regard to the execution of the agreed work, will not be considered as an exercise of authority in the sense of this Article.

When a third party user instructs the employees of another employer regarding health and safety matters, it is clear that this should not be seen as an exercise of authority over the worker concerned.[34] Furthermore, the Act on well-being at work foresees that certain health and safety measures, precautions and obligations need to be respected beyond the context of an employer/employee relationship.[35]

Equally, giving instructions with respect to working time and time off is not an indication of the employer's authority being exercised in this context. It can be explained by the practical necessity of coordinating the work of one's own employees with that of external workers to deliver services in the company.

More surprising is the reference to 'instructions with respect to the work to be performed'. It is surprising that the Act now states that such instructions are not to be seen as an expression of the employer's authority over the workers concerned. This exception seems to be very broad and would allow workers to be placed at the disposal of another employer if the employer and the user enter into a decent service agreement in which they describe the work to be performed.

All instructions that the user wants to give with respect to the work to be performed by the employees of the contracted party will thus not be seen as an expression of the employer's authority, in application of the Act of 24 July 1987.

If the courts were to broadly interpret the reference to 'instructions with respect to the work to be performed', the prohibition of putting workers at the disposal of a user will become an empty shell, at least in comparison to the situation prior to the year 2000 when the modification of the Act took place.

---

32   Article 181, Act of 12 August 2000, Official Gazette, 31 August 2000.

33   See: C. Engels, 'De Juridische duiding van de overeenkomst tussen ziekenhuis en ziekenhuis geneesheer, Arbeidsovereenkomst of overeenkomst tot zelfstandige samenwerking', in *Arbeidsrecht, een confrontatie tussen theorie en praktijk*, O. Vanachter (ed), Antwerpen – Apeldoorn, Maklu Uitgevers, 1993, 31, 56-63.

34   C. Engels: *Het ondergeschikt verband naar Belgisch Arbeidsrecht*, Brugge, Die Keure, 1989, 75.

35   Article 8, e.s., Act of 4 August 1996 with respect to the Well-Being of Workers in the Execution of their Work, Official Gazette, 18 September 1996 modified thereafter.

This raises a question as to the instructions a user could give the workers of a third party without violating the prohibition contained in the Act of 24 July 1987.

This might include instructions regarding disciplinary sanctions, decisions on wage increases, evaluations and promotions.[36]

What becomes evident is that the service agreement between the employer and the user must clearly define the work that needs to be performed for the user. Any subsequent instructions the user gives to the third party employees performing the work will therefore not lead to a violation of the Act of 24 July 1987.

4.2.3.2. With delegation of authority to the user

Exceptionally, an employer can put some of its regular workers at the disposal of another employer and hereby delegate some of its normal authority over the workers concerned. However, as a general rule, a government authorisation is required. In order to obtain this authorisation, the consent of the trade union delegation within the user company is also required.

However, neither the trade union delegation's consent, nor the government's authorisation is required if a worker-whose original contract of employment is preserved – is exceptionally put at the disposal of a third company under the following exceptional circumstances:

1.   Within the framework of collaboration between employers of the same economic and financial entity

2.   In light of the short-term performance of specialised tasks that require special professional qualifications.

No authorisation or consent is needed in these circumstances. However, the government needs to be notified 24 hours before the worker is put at the disposal of the user.

A written document needs to be drafted and signed by the three parties involved: the (normal) employer, the user and the worker concerned. It needs to be signed before the employee is put at the disposal of the user.

The employment contract between the original employer and the worker remains in existence. However, the original employer and the user become jointly liable for the payment of all wages, indemnities, benefits and social security contributions.

The 1987 Act further states that the worker that is put at the disposal of the user should not be treated in a less favourable manner than the user's normal workers that perform the same kind of jobs. This means that the employment conditions (including wages and all kinds of benefits) of the worker should not be inferior to the wages of the user's employees with the same job description.[37] Clearly, this provision does not apply to forms of subcontracting that fall outside the scope of the Act of 24 July 1987. If the Act is not applicable and a third party comes to do work at the user's premises, there is no obligation for the third party to pay its workers the same level of remuneration and benefits as the user's workers that are doing the same or similar work.

A few of the provisions of the 1987 Act that deal with temporary employment agencies are also applicable to the situation of workers put at the disposal of a user.[38]

In 2000, a modification of the Act of 24 July 1987 granted the National Labour Council the authority to define the concepts of 'short-term performance' and 'the requirement of special professional qualification'. To date no such collective bargaining agreement has been concluded. It is clear that it will be very hard, if not impossible, to come up with acceptable definitions at national level, across the various industries.

Prior to its modification on 13 February 1998, the Act stated that putting a worker at the disposal of another employer had to remain exceptional. While it was not exactly clear what the term 'exceptional' really meant in this context, it seemed, however, to exclude the idea of permanently putting workers of one company at the disposal of the other.

Since the modification of the Act of 24 July 1987 on 13 February 1998, it has become clear that the circumstances in which employers are allowed to put normal workers at the disposal of users need to be not only restricted in time. The amended version of the 1987 Act now states that the employer, contrary to the general prohibition (stated in Article 31 of the same Act) is allowed to put its permanent

---

36   See: C. Engels, *Overdracht van onderneming en outsourcing*, Brussels, Larcier, 2000, 133.
37   Article 32, paragraph 4, Act on Temporary Employment.
38   Act 19, paragraph 1, Act on Temporary Employment.

employees at the disposal of a user if a number of conditions are cumulatively satisfied:

- The workers can be put at the disposal of the user for only a limited period of time and

- The employer may put workers at the disposal of a third company only when this does not form part of the employer's ordinary or normal activities.

The parliamentary discussion highlighted that putting workers at the disposal of a user should not form part of the employer's normal activities.

The modification of the Act in 2000 further states that a collective bargaining agreement concluded with the National Labour Council can define the concept of a 'limited period of time'.

Furthermore, the Act now expressly states that it is possible to put permanent workers at the disposal of a user for only a limited period of time (beperkte duur/durée limitée).

5. Outsourcing

It is clear that in a number of circumstances it is very hard, if not impossible, to predict whether the Directive[39] and its implementing legislation (in the case of Belgium, an inter-industry collective bargaining agreement, No 32bis concluded within the National Labour Council) apply to a business transaction that is primarily aimed at taking over the economic activity that is the core of the business that is targeted. In order to safeguard the rights of the employees, a few sectors of industry have concluded a sector-level collective bargaining agreement determining the rights of the employees in case of a take-over of an economic activity. Such is the case in the security industry or in the cleaning business, for example. The sector-level collective bargaining agreement determines that, in the case of loss of a contract, the new contractor must take over a percentage of the old workforce, or at least offer them a contract depending on the sector of industry. It is clear that such sector-level collective bargaining agreements grant employees additional rights they would not have otherwise, since the collective bargaining agreement that implemented the Directive on the Transfer of Undertakings may in these cases not apply.

Inasmuch as the Directive and its implementing legislation would already be applicable, it is clearly not possible to restrict the scope of the Directive and its implementing legislation. However, inasmuch as the Directive would not be applicable (if the transaction were not considered a transfer of a business) the sector-level collective bargaining agreements extend the scope of the collective bargaining agreement implementing the Directive on the Transfer of Undertakings in Belgian law. Recently, at the time of the bankruptcy of the Belgian national airline, a discussion took place on the taking over of some parts of the bankrupt airline. It is clear that some of the activities in an airport depend on being granted a license to operate. A loss of the license would mean that the employer would be out of business at that particular airport. A potential employer at the airport proposed to extend the principles of the Directive on the Transfer of Undertakings to a situation where an employer would be faced with the loss of a license. The trade unions embraced the idea. However, nothing has come out of the discussion yet, even though it has now been taking place for a couple of months. Some have even argued that such collective bargaining agreements are in conflict with the principle of freedom of movement of services and all the anti-competition and anti-monopoly provisions. It is clear that the implication of the airline industry and surrounding businesses in such collective bargaining agreements has raised a number of European law issues. At the national level, judges have not yet formulated any clear answers. The issue of the validity of the collective bargaining agreements in the other sectors has not resulted in any significant discussion.

5.1. As a transfer of a business

The first question to be asked should therefore be about the applicability of the European Directive dealing with the transfer of businesses or parts thereof. The scope of the Belgian legislative measures implementing the Directive is to be determined in the same way.[40]

Outsourcing of company activities can fall within the scope of the Directive on the Transfer of Undertakings and its implementing Belgian legislation, but this is not necessarily so.

If the outsourcing does not involve more than the transfer of a mere economic activity, it will not be considered as a

---

39   Directive 2001/23/EG, 12 March 2001.

40   Inter-industry wide Collective Bargaining Agreement, No 32bis, concerning the rights of workers in case of change in employer, in case of a contractual transfer of a business and concerning the rights of workers taken over in case of transfer of assets upon bankruptcy or judicial agreement with conditions in return for relinquishing assets, 7 June 1985, rendered generally binding by Royal Decree of 25 July 1985, Official Gazette, 9 August 1985, amended thereafter.

transfer of a business. If it involves more than the transfer of an economic activity, it may be, depending on 'how much more' is being transferred.[41]

In order to determine whether the outsourcing activity is to be treated as the transfer of a business, one must take – as already indicated – the relevant case law of the European Court of Justice as a reference.

Belgian courts remain very faithful to the Directive and the case law of the European Court of Justice.

The employee protected by the Directive and the implementing Belgian Collective Bargaining Agreement No 32bis has the right to continue performing his or her employment contract or employment relationship under the same conditions as before the transfer. The Directive requires that they remain in service under the same conditions. One is dealing here with a right, rather than a duty, to transfer under European law. This Directive can therefore not be interpreted as containing an obligation for the employees concerned to transfer to the new employer. Such an obligation would jeopardise the fundamental rights of the employee, who must be free to choose his employer and cannot be obliged to work for an employer whom he has not freely chosen. The Court considers that the worker that refuses the transfer does not need the protection of the Directive.

In these circumstances (refusal of the transfer by the employee concerned), the Directive leaves all options open for the Member States. It is up to national law to decide the fate of the employment contract of the employee who has refused the transfer.

Even though case law is scant, Belgian courts seem to require employees to transfer with the business. Under Belgian law it might be stated that the employee has a duty

to transfer together with the business or the part of the business the employee has been performing in.

The employee that refuses to transfer with the business or the part of the business he or she was performing in should resign or should be considered as resigning. The latter seems to be the case since the employee under these circumstances refuses to execute one of his or her essential duties under the employment contract, meaning the performance of his or her contractual duty.[42]

The question of whether and to what extent collective bargaining agreements remain in force for the employees who are (automatically) transferred with the part of the business in which they work, is of utmost importance in Belgium, given the fact that working conditions are largely determined by collective bargaining agreements.

There are significant differences in treatment between the collective bargaining agreements of different sectors of industry.

The difference in one of the very few cases that came before a court of law (and that was published) dealt with the protection of employees in case of termination of their contract of employment in the insurance industry.[43] This sector has particular collective bargaining agreements that foresee certain procedures in case of termination. If the procedure is *not* properly followed and the worker concerned is terminated in violation of it, the worker is entitled to receive an additional termination indemnity equal to six months of pay. If the worker has five years of seniority or more, the indemnity increases to nine months of pay.

The case referred to concerned a worker whose contract was terminated. The company worked for belonged to the insurance sector. Even though the person concerned

---

41 See: C. Engels and L. Salas, 'Cause and Consequence, What's the Difference in respect of the EC Transfer Directive', in *Labour Law and Industrial Relations at the Turn of the Century, Liber amicorum in Honour of Prof. Dr. Roger Blanpain*, Kluwer Law International, 1998, 275, 282-286; C. Engels and M. Weiss (eds); Engels, *Overdracht van onderneming en outsourcing, Arbeidsrechtelijke aspecten* [Transfer of a Business An Outsourcing, Labour Law Aspects], Brussels, Larcier, 2000, 252 pp, 5-33; C. Engels, 'Outsourcing: enjeu et conséquences au regard de la Convention Collective No 32bis relative au transfert d'entreprise et de la loi du 24 juillet 1987 relative au détachement et au prêt de personnel', [Outsourcing: stake and consequences with respect to collective bargaining agreement No 32bis relating to the transfer of businesses and the Act of 24 July 1987 relating to putting workers at the disposal and binding them out] in *Le contrat de travail et la nouvelle économie* [The Contract of Employment in the New Economy], Editions du Jeune Barreau de Bruxelles, 2001, 69-124.

42 See: C. Engels, *Overdracht van onderneming en outsourcing, Arbeidsrechtelijke aspecten* [Transfer of a Business An Outsourcing, Labour Law Aspects], Brussels, Larcier, 2000, 43-44.

43 Labour Court Antwerpen, 17 May 1999, *Journal des Tribunaux du Travail 2000*, 24, note. C. Engels, *Wijziging van paritair comité bij overgang van onderneming en het lot van de collectieve arbeidsovereenkomst* [Changes of joint committee in case of transfer of a business and the fate of the collective bargaining agreements]. See also: C. Engels and R. Blanpain, 'Continued applicability of sectoral collective agreement in case of transfer of a business accompanied by change of sector', case note under Labour Court Antwerp, 17 May 1999, *International Labour Law Reports*, Vol. 19, Martinus Nyhoff Publishers, The Hague/Boston/London 2001, 473-481.

worked in an insurance brokerage office and not in the insurance activity as such, he was covered by the sector-level collective bargaining agreements of the insurance sector. This is because the Belgian system of industrial relations upholds the principle that a company necessarily belongs to one sector of industry only, namely the sector determined by its principal activities. If the worker concerned had worked for an insurance brokerage company (from the beginning) that was not involved in the insurance activity, the worker would have been covered by the collective bargaining agreements of this first sector of industry only and not by these of the insurance industry.

The insurance company underwent some form of restructuring/outsourcing, thereby putting non-core activities in separate legal entities and thus separate companies. Since the primary activity of the company, as a legal entity, determines to which joint committee of industry the company belongs, outsourcing of the non-core activities resulted in the new legal entities being engaged in an activity other than the insurance activity. In the sector of the insurance brokers, different collective bargaining agreements were applicable. In the latter sector no specific procedures in case of dismissal were applicable.

The company that employed the worker at the time of the termination did not belong to the sector of industry of the insurance companies and would thus, as such, not be bound by the collective bargaining agreements of the latter sector, including the one dealing with special protection in case of dismissal. The company terminated the employment relationship of an employee without respecting the termination procedures that would apply in insurance companies. The worker stated that the company should have respected the collective bargaining agreements from the insurance sector since, as a worker, he transferred with part of the insurance company (non-core activity of insurance brokerage) to a new legal entity. For this reason, the worker argued, the employer should have respected the collective bargaining agreements from the insurance sector that were certainly applicable at the time of the transfer of the part of the business. The worker further argued that the change of

the sector of industry did not influence the applicability of the collective bargaining agreements from the former sector of industry, given that the transfer of part of the business had taken place.

The Belgian legislative measure (*sensu latu*) through which the Directive is implemented does not address the issue of the continued validity or binding nature of collective bargaining agreements in the case of a transfer of a business or part of a business.

An existing piece of legislation dealing with collective bargaining agreements and joint committees of industry, which dates back to 5 December 1968, was presumed to sufficiently implement the relevant provision of the Directive as far as Belgian law was concerned.[44]

Where the Directive leaves the Member States the option of restricting the continued binding nature of the collective bargaining agreement in the case of a transfer of a business to one year, Belgian law did not implement this option. The 1968 Act does not foresee anything at all in this respect.

The 1968 Act addresses a number of hypotheses with regard to the continued binding nature of collective bargaining agreements. In this respect, the Belgian Act seems to go even further than the Directive itself. The Directive only requires that the *terms and conditions* set by the collective bargaining agreements be respected. The 1968 Act deals with the continued *binding nature of the collective bargaining agreement itself*, and thus not only with the working conditions resulting from it.[45]

Two provisions of the 1968 Act are particularly relevant to the issue of the continued validity of collective bargaining agreements in case of transfer of a business.

Article 20 of the 1968 Act states:

In case a company is wholly or partially transferred, the new employer has to respect the agreement that was binding on the previous employer until it ceases to have binding force.

---

44   Act of 5 December 1968, concerning collective bargaining agreements and joint committees, Official Gazette, 15 January 1969, often amended thereafter.

45   See: C. Engels, 'Wijziging van paritair comité bij overgang van onderneming en het lot van de collectieve arbeidsovereenkomst' [Changes of joint committee in case of a transfer of a business and the fate of collective bargaining agreements], case note under Labour court Antwerp, 17 May 1999, *Journal des Tribunaux du Travail*, 2000, 28; C. Engels, 'Outsourcing, de individuele en collectieve rechten van de werknemers bij overgang van onderneming' [Outsourcing, the individual and collective rights of workers in case of a transfer of a business], *Journal des Tribunaux du Travail*, 2000, 129-144.

Article 23 of the same Act states:

The individual contract of employment that is implicitly modified by a collective bargaining agreement remains in existence as it is, when the collective bargaining agreement ceases to have binding force, unless differently stipulated in the agreement itself.

Article 20 of the 1968 Act addresses the direct binding force of collective bargaining agreements, while Article 23 can be said to address the indirect binding force.

Article 23 of the 1968 Act, quoted above, deals with the incorporation of provisions of the collective bargaining agreement into the individual employment contract. It addresses the fact that certain provisions of a collective bargaining agreement will actually remain in force through their incorporation in the individual employment contract, even though the collective bargaining agreement itself ceases to have binding force and expires.

The provisions of the collective bargaining agreement that modified the provisions of the individual contract of employment either by granting additional new rights to employees or by granting the workers a more beneficial treatment than that foreseen in the individual agreement, modify the individual contract permanently, unless the collective bargaining agreement stipulates the contrary.[46]

The new employer is held to the provisions of the enterprise-level collective bargaining agreement, the same way the previous employer was.

This means that the agreement will automatically come to an end at the date foreseen in it, when it is a collective bargaining agreement for a fixed duration. If the agreement is not for a fixed period of time, the possibility to give notice has to be foreseen. This means that the new employer must have the right to give notice to end the binding force of the agreement.

Given the fact that under Belgian law the sector of industry to which a company belongs is determined by the main activity of the legal entity concerned, outsourcing may often lead to a change in the sector of industry concerned. When one considers that most cases of outsourcing actually include a return of the company to its core activities and the sourcing out of supporting services to separate units, it is clear that such forms of outsourcing will often lead to a change in the sector of industry to which the companies performing the outsourced activities belong.

If the outsourced part of the business remains engaged in the same or in a similar activity, the Directive and its implementing legislation generally remain fully applicable.[47]

Up until very recently, Belgian case law showed only one case that directly addressed the issue of the continued applicability of sector-level collective bargaining agreements in case of a transfer of a business (or part of a business) accompanied by a change of joint committee of industry. In a 1984 case, the Labour Court of Brussels decided that the collective bargaining agreements of the previous joint committee remained applicable as such.[48] The court did not explain why it defended this position. Indeed, the doctrine has generally rehashed the 1984 decision of the Labour Court of Brussels without questioning its validity and correctness.

An interpretation of the Belgian legislation in light of the Directive does not seem to require that the collective bargaining agreements of the previous sector should, as collective bargaining agreements, remain fully applicable in a case of change of the sector of industry to which a company belongs.[49] The argument for the continued applicability is unconvincing, since the Directive does not require the collective bargaining agreements to remain applicable. It merely foresees the continued application of employment terms and conditions resulting from the collective bargaining agreements. The incorporation of the terms and conditions foreseen in the sector-level collective bargaining agreements have implicitly modified the individual employment contracts. They keep their 'modified state' after the collective bargaining agreements of the previous sector cease to have effect. This form of

---

46   See: Labour court Brussels, 14 March 1989, *Sociaal Rechtelijke Kronieken*, 1989, 347; Labour Court Brussels, 17 January 1990, *Sociaal Rechtelijke Kronieken*, 1990, 190.

47   See: C. Engels & L. Salas, 'Cause and consequence, what's the difference in respect of the EC Transfer Directive', in *Labour Law and Industrial Relations at the Turn of the Century, Liber amicorum in Honour of Prof. D. Roger Blanpain*, C. Engels & M. Weiss (eds), Kluwer Law International, The Hague London Boston, 1998, 275 es.

48   See: Labour court of Brussels, 2 October 1984, *Journal des Tribunaux du Travail*, 1985, 116.

49   See however: C. Wantiez, *Transferts conventionnels d'entreprise et droit du travail* [Contractual Transfer of a Business and Labour Law], E.D.S., s.p.r.l., Bousval, 1996, 126, No 99.

incorporation could therefore be seen as a sufficient implementation of the relevant principle of this Directive in Belgium.

Furthermore, the Directive states that the terms and conditions of the collective bargaining agreements need to remain applicable until the moment the collective bargaining agreements expire, or until the entry into force or application of another agreement. A change of sector of industry most often implies the applicability of a different set of sector-level collective bargaining agreements. Even though the protection that is actually granted by the sector-level collective bargaining agreements may differ, most often there are some collective bargaining agreements that come into play.

Finally, it could also be argued that the collective bargaining agreements of a given sector should no longer be applied to a company that has changed sectors since one of the conditions of applicability for the sector-level collective bargaining agreements is no longer satisfied. In order for a sector-level collective bargaining agreement to be applicable, the company needs to belong to the scope of the joint committee of industry within which the collective bargaining agreements is concluded. In the case of a change of sector, this condition is no longer satisfied.

This position was confirmed in a 1999 decision of the Labour Court of Appeals in Antwerp.

5.2. Not as a transfer of a business

In the absence of the applicability of the Directive on the Transfer of Undertakings and the Collective Bargaining Agreement No 32bis, there will be no automatic transfer of employment contracts for workers engaged in the performance of the activity that was outsourced. Their right to transfer is not guaranteed by the Directive and the implementing Belgian legislation.

In the absence of a transfer of a business in the sense of the Directive, employment contracts do not transfer automatically. This means that workers need to be re-hired by the company that took over the activities. From a purely legal point of view, the company that takes on the outsourced activity has a free choice of who takes over and the employment conditions to be implemented. While the new company has no duty to take over the employees that were engaged in the outsourced activity by the outsourcing com-

pany, the employees concerned have no duty to transfer with the business either.

6. Telework

6.1. Introduction

A 1996 Parliamentary Act defines and regulates telework. The 1996 Act inserted a new chapter dealing with telework in the Act on Employment Contracts.

Previously, there was discussion as to what kind of contract the teleworker had under Belgian law. The Supreme Court had recognised that employer authority (which is required as an essential element of an employment contract) could be exercised over a teleworker. However, it has held that the employment contract for telework was not regulated by the Act of 3 July 1978 concerning employment contracts. In a case dealing with terms of notice for teleworkers under an employment contract, the labour court of appeal judged that the terms of notice foreseen in the Act of 3 July 1978 on employment contracts were not applicable to the teleworker.

In a decision of 30 November 1992 (*Rechtskundig Weekblad*, 1992-1993, 851) the Supreme Court accepted the idea that one was dealing with an employment contract. However, this employment contract seemed to be an unregulated one that was not covered by the Act on Employment Contracts. This meant that the employment contracts of teleworkers were regulated by the ordinary principles of our civil code on contracts, and thus also by the contract stipulations as agreed between the employer and the employee.

The 1992 Supreme Court case resulted in some legislative action being taken. As indicated above, a new chapter (chapter IV) was introduced in the Act of 3 July 1978 concerning employment contracts. The Act addresses the specificity of telework, as compared to 'normal employment relationships'.

6.2. The employment contract

The employment contract for telework is a contract by which an employee, the teleworker, undertakes to perform services in exchange for remuneration and under the authority of the employer, at his or her home or another location that he or she has chosen, without being under the supervision or direct control of the employer.

The employment contract must be in writing. The agreement must be entered into with every single teleworker individually and prior to the actual start of the work.

The employment contract must contain information on a number of issues (the identity of the parties (name, surname, main residence, registered office, etc.), the wages or the way and criteria for calculation of the wages, the arrangement for the reimbursement of (extra) costs related to the telework (e.g. electricity, heating, telephone, etc.), the place(s) chosen by the teleworker to perform the work, the job description, the agreed working time, working schedules or the minimum level of performance and the joint committee to which the employer belongs).

In the absence of the mandatory stipulations, the employee may terminate his or her employment contract at any time without notice and without severance pay.

In the absence of a stipulation with regard to the reimbursement of costs related to the telework, a lump sum indemnity equal to 10% of the gross wages is due as reimbursement of the (extra) costs related to working at home. The employee may, however, prove that the costs of the telework were actually higher than 10% of the gross wages. The amount of 10%, as the reimbursement of costs, is added to the normal wages and is generally considered to be free of social security contributions and taxes.

6.3. Working conditions

The regulations concerning working time and Sunday rest (*i.e. The* maximum working time per week and per day, the minimum working time of three hours per day, overtime, overtime pay, compensatory rest, etc.) are not applicable to teleworkers.

The legislation on the prevention and protection of employees at work (Act of 6 August 1996 and the General Regulation on Labour Protection) applies to teleworkers. The Crown may, however, determine special 'safety' measures for teleworkers.

If the employee works on a computer, the provisions of the Royal Decree of 27 Augustus with regard to picture screen hardware must also be complied with. This Royal Decree

provides special rules for the organisation and the furnishing of the workplace.

7. Working and family life balance

Over the last decade, various new pieces of legislation have been enacted in order to reach a more acceptable balance between working life and family life. Generally speaking, one can divide this new legislation into two categories: 1) various forms of career interruption, including the so-called time-credit and 2) general and collective reductions of working time.

7.1. Career interruption

7.1.1. Systems currently in force

Career interruption is not a new phenomenon; it appeared on the Belgian social landscape in 1985. However, during the last decade some important developments with regard to this matter have taken place.

There are currently three different systems of career interruption in Belgium: 1) the 'classic' career interruption, 2) thematic leave, and 3) time-credit.

7.1.2. Classic career interruption

7.1.2.1. Application ratione personae

The classic system of career interruption applies to persons working in the public sector and to employees in the private sector that entered into a system of career interruption before 1 January 2002.[50] For the private sector, the system has been changed for the future.

7.1.2.2. Development[51]

Complete suspension of the employment contract

Classic career interruption was already established by the 22 January 1985 Act. However, the system was further developed over the last decade.

Since 1 March 1996,[52] the duration of the period during which the employment contract can be completely sus-

---

50   Various transition systems regulate the situation of these employees. These transition systems will not be discussed in this report.

51   In the classic system of career interruption applied in the private sector, an employee needed the employer's permission before he could enter into a system of career interruption. Between 1985 and December 2001, Royal Decrees and collective bargaining agreements changed this and established a right to career interruption (e.g. 10 August 1998 Royal Decree). However, since private sector employees have to use the time-credit system as of 1 January 2002, this report does not address this issue.

52   2 January 1991 R.D.

pended, is a minimum of three months and a maximum of twelve. It is possible to extend the original period of suspension whereby the minimum of three months no longer applies.

A person can apply for several periods of complete suspension of their employment contract during their professional career. However, in 1991 a Royal Decree stated that the total of all periods of suspension could not exceed 60 months. It must be noted that, since 1 October 1998, certain periods of suspension no longer count towards the maximum of 60 months, including periods of leave due to palliative care or care for a seriously ill person and parental leave.

During the suspension of the employment contract the employer is not liable to pay any remuneration. The employee will receive 'interruption allowances', which are paid by the government. Originally the employee could only receive these allowances if his employer replaced him during the period of the suspension. Since 1 January 2002,[53] the employee can receive the allowances irrespective of his employer replacing him or not.

Partial suspension of the employment contract

Since 1 May 1996,[54] employees have the opportunity to partially suspend their employment contract. It is thus possible to individually reduce the working time by one fifth, one fourth or one third.

The minimum period for this type of reduction is three months. The maximum duration varies in accordance with the age of the employee. If the employee is not yet 50 years old, the maximum duration is 60 months. When he or she reaches 50 there is no longer a maximum duration.

7.1.3. Thematic leave

7.1.3.1. Leave due to palliative care

The 21 December 1994 Act gives employees the right to career interruption in the form of a leave due to palliative care. Contrary to the classic system of career interruption, neither the permission of the employer is needed, nor a collective bargaining agreement establishing a right to this type of leave.

Palliative care is defined as 'every form of assistance at the medical, social, administrative and psychological level, as well as the care that is given to a person suffering from an incurable disease and going through the terminal phase'.

The full-time employee can either completely suspend his employment contract or reduce his or her working time by one fifth or one half. A part-time employee can only completely suspend his or her employment contract.

The maximum duration of the leave is one month per person, although an extension of one more month is possible. The employee receives interruption allowances.

7.1.3.2. Leave due to care for a seriously ill family member

The 6 February 1997 Royal Decree established the right to leave in order to take care of a seriously ill family member. However, this Royal Decree was set to expire on 31 December 1998. The 10 August 1998 Royal Decree removed this time limit.

'Seriously ill' is understood as any illness or medical operation that the treating M.D. considers as such and where the physician thinks that any form of social, familial or emotional assistance or care is necessary for the recovery.

The full-time employee can choose between a complete suspension of his employment contract or a reduction by one fifth or one half.[55] The part-time employee cannot obtain the complete suspension of his employment contract.

In case of complete suspension of the employment contract, the total duration of the leave is of 12 months. In case of a reduction, the total duration of the leave is of 24 months, both for a reduction of one fifth or one half.

The employee receives interruption allowances. Since 1 January 2002[56] the employer is no longer obliged to replace the employee.

7.1.3.3. Parental leave

The right to parental leave has been established by the 29 **April 1997** C.B.A. No 64 and the 29 **October 1997** Royal Decree. Both systems are mutually exclusive.

---

53   Act concerning the reconciliation of job opportunities and the quality of life of 10 August 2001.
54   See footnote 52.
55   Before 1 January 2002 reductions of one fourth or one third were also permissible.
56   Article 19, 3°, Act concerning the reconciliation of job opportunities and the quality of life of 10 August 2001.

The Royal Decree establishes a right to parental leave either at the occasion of the child's birth (until the child is four years old) or at the occasion of the adoption of a child (until the child is eight years old). The employee can enjoy this right if he or she has been employed by the employer for at least 12 months. The employee can opt for a complete suspension of the employment contract with a maximum duration of three months. Since 1 October 1998,[57] the employee can also reduce the working time by one half, with a maximum duration of six months. Since 1 **February 2002**,[58] the employee can also reduce his working time by one fifth for a maximum period of 15 months. During the parental leave the employee receives interruption allowances. Since 1 January 2002 the employer is no longer obliged to replace the employee.[59]

The Collective Bargaining Agreement does not apply to persons that are not bound to an employer by way of an employment contract. The occasions on which parental leave can be obtained are the same as the ones in the Royal Decree. Of the 15 months before the request of parental leave, the employee has to be bound to the employer by way of an employment contract for at least 12 months. The employee can either opt for a complete suspension of his employment contract for a maximum of three months or reduce the working time. With regard to the reduction, the parties are free to set the percentage and the corresponding period. The employee is not entitled to interruption allowances.

7.1.4. Time-credit

One of the goals of the 2001-2002 Inter-professional Agreement concluded at national inter-industry level was to reconcile private and working life. In order to achieve this, the social partners developed the system of 'time-credit' in C.B.A. No 77, concluded within the National Labour Council on 14 February 2001. In a recommendation to the Belgian Federal Government, the National Labour Council requested that the existing legislation be adapted so that the time-credit system could enter into force on 1 January 2002. The Federal Government did so in Chapter 4 of the 10 **August 2001** Act concerning the reconciliation of job opportunities and the quality of life.

There are three different types of time-credit:

1. A complete career interruption or a career reduction by one half for all employees, with a maximum duration of one year, unless a collective bargaining agreement extends this period to five years.

2. A career reduction by one fifth for all employees, with a maximum duration of five years.

3. A career reduction of one fifth or one half until the age of retirement. However, this only applies to employees that are at least 50 years old.

It is important to notice that a reduction by one third or one fourth is no longer allowed.

The employees that have suspended their employment contract or reduced their working time under the time-credit system receive allowances from the government. The amount of these allowances and the conditions on which it will be granted, have been determined in the 12 December 2001 Royal Decree.

The employer is not obliged to replace the employee that suspended the employment contract or reduced their working time under the time-credit system.

7.2. General and collective reduction of working time

7.2.1. Obligatory 38-hour working week

As of 1 January 1999, the weekly working time was reduced to 39 hours. The 10 August 2001 Act concerning the reconciliation of job opportunities and the quality of life stated that as of 1 January 2003 the weekly working time had to be further reduced to 38 hours. This reduction could be achieved by effectively reducing the weekly working time, by granting resting time or by a combination of both. A collective bargaining agreement states the way in which the reduction to 38-hours a week will be reached.

---

57   Article 2, 29 October 1997 R.D.
58   See footnote 57.
59   See footnote 56.

In order to entice the employers to establish the 38-hour working week before 1 January 2003, the 10 August 2001 Act provided for several reductions of the employer's social security contributions in case the reduction was carried out before 1 January 2003.

7.2.2. Voluntary collective reduction

The 10 August 2001 Act also aimed to encourage companies to reduce the weekly working time even further. It therefore foresaw two possibilities: either a conventional collective working time reduction or the introduction of a working week of four days.

7.2.2.1. Conventional collective reduction

The employer can reduce the weekly working time below 38 hours either by a collective bargaining agreement (at sector level or company level) or in the labour rules that apply within the company.

If the employer does so, he or she will receive two different reductions to their social security contributions. Firstly, they will receive a once-only reduction of EUR 800 per employee concerned, per hour reduction. Secondly, they will benefit from an additional reduction determined by the total weekly working time that is reached: a reduction of EUR 62.50 if the weekly working time is 37 hours, EUR 100 if the weekly working time is 36 hours and EUR 150 if the weekly working time is 35 hours or less. The second reduction is only granted in the fourth quarter, following the quarter in which the once-only reduction was granted. It is granted for a period of ten years.

7.2.2.2. Working week consisting of four days

Employers that introduce a working week of four days will receive a once-only reduction of their social security contributions of EUR 400 per employee concerned.

7.2.2.3. The future?

It should be noted that the 24 December 2002 Act has changed the system of reductions that are granted in case of voluntary collective reduction. The draft Royal Decree foresees the following: 1) in case of a reduction of the weekly working time below 38 hours, a reduction of EUR 400 will be granted for a period of 8, 12 or 16 trimesters; 2) in case the introduction of a working week of four days, the reduction will be of EUR 400, granted for a period of four trimesters.

A combination of a reduction with the introduction of a four-day working week is also foreseen, and entitles the employer to higher social security reductions.

7.3. Flexible working time

The 'flexibilisation' or making flexible of working time came at the request of employers. Concerns over the ability to harmonise working time and family life were not taken into account.

7.3.1. Annual working time – annualisation

The Social Recovery Act of 22 January 1985 introduced the concept of the annualisation of working time. The normal daily and weekly limits of work (eight hours and 40 hours respectively) can be exceeded on the condition that a legally binding collective bargaining agreement exists that contains provisions on the following:

- The average weekly working time, as well as the total number of hours over a period of 12 consecutive months

- The number of hours during which work can be performed, below or above the daily limit, without exceeding two hours a day and without exceeding a daily working time of nine hours

- The number of hours during which the work can be performed, below or above the weekly limit, without exceeding, five hours a day or 45 hours a week.

Specific rules apply to determine what hours can be considered working hours with regard to public holidays, hours lost to mechanical breakdowns, etc.

Overtime regulations may differ according to the applicable working time schedule. The social partners have continually expressed a willingness to reduce overtime in an effort to redistribute available labour (see *supra*).

7.3.2. New and flexible working patterns

An agreement reached in the National Labour Council on 23 March 1986 called for Parliament to vote on an act institutionalising prior working time experiments (Hansenne-experiments, named after the then Minister of Employment). The Parliamentary Act of 17 March 1987 and the national inter-industry wide collective bargaining agreement No 42 of 2 June 1987, allow 12-hour working days for economic reasons, Sunday work, and night work for economic reasons for men. The Parliamentary Act determined that the working time schemes so introduced should have a positive impact on employment.

7.3.3. Shift work with night work

This national inter-industry-wide agreement is applicable to employers employing workers that perform in systems of continuous, semi-continuous and fixed night work (enterprises working 24 hours a day) between 11 p.m. And 6 a.m. In principle, only employees with an individual employment contract for an indefinite period of time may perform under these kinds of working time systems. Participation is voluntary. The above-mentioned working time systems must be the result of a collective bargaining agreement with the trade union delegations represented in the enterprise.

Collective Bargaining Agreement No 46 also deals with transportation, remuneration, weekly working time, compensatory rest, rights of trade union delegations, training, hygiene, occupational safety and medicine, and social infrastructure.

Many provisions allow collectively bargained alterations at the level of the sector and/or the enterprise.

8. Data protection issues

8.1. Introduction

Employers monitoring employees visiting Internet sites or using electronic mail must comply with the C.B.A. No 81 of 26 April 2002 of the National Labour Council *regarding the protection of the privacy of employees vis-à-vis the control of electronic online communication data*.

This C.B.A. provides for restrictive means of control, specific rules regarding monitoring activities, an information procedure for the works council, safety committee or trade union delegation and of the individual employees and specific rules regarding the identification of individual employees.

This agreement did not abolish some of the general legal provisions that considerably limited the employer's ability to exercise control, such as the secrecy of communications (Article 314bis Criminal Code and Article 109ter D Belgacom Act) and the Data Protection Act of 8 December 1992 (implementing the EU Directive). These provisions still apply, together with the Collective Bargaining Agreement No 81.

8.2. C.B.A. No 81 of 26 April 2002

8.2.1. Purposes of the control

An employer can only control the use of the e-mail and Internet infrastructure for one or more of the following purposes:

1. Preventing unlawful or defamatory acts, acts that contravene common decency or acts that can harm the dignity of another person

2. Protecting the economic, commercial and financial interests of the company which are confidential and the prevention of practices that contravene these interests

3. Protecting the safety and/or the technical integrity of the IT-network systems of the company, including cost-controlling, and the physical protection of the installations of the company

4. Ensuring compliance with the company's principles and rules for the use of online technologies in good faith.

The employer must clearly and explicitly describe the purposes of the control.

8.2.2. Information

8.2.2.1. To the employee representatives

An employer that plans to install a monitoring system must inform the works council of all aspects thereof. This means that the works council has to be informed before the installation of the monitoring system. In the absence of a works council, the information has to be given to the safety committee; in the absence thereof, to the trade union delegation, and if there is no trade union delegation, to the employees directly.

The information has to relate to the following aspects of the control system:

- The policy on monitoring and the prerogatives of the employer and the supervising personnel

- The purpose(s)

- Whether or not the personal data are stored, the place and the duration of the storage

- Whether or not the monitoring is permanent.

8.2.2.2. To the individual employees

At the moment a monitoring system is installed, the employer must inform the employees of all aspects of the monitoring.

This information should relate to the aforementioned aspects of collective information, and to the following additional aspects:

- The use of the instruments that are put at the employee's disposal for the execution of the work, including the limitations regarding the use as part of the function;

- The rights, duties and obligations of the employees and the prohibitions regarding the use of the electronic online communication means of the company;

- The sanctions provided for by the work rules in case of non-compliance.

The employer can choose the means of informing employees: general guidelines (circulars, posting, etc.), work rules, employment contract, instructions at the start up of the computer or of the programme. However, some information must be mentioned in the work rules.[60]

8.2.3. Evaluation

The installed monitoring systems must be evaluated on a regular basis, in order to propose possible adaptations resulting from technological developments. This evaluation takes place in the work council.[61] The report preceding C.B.A. No 81 specifies that the possibilities of better achieving non- or minimal intrusion of the privacy of the employees should be investigated).

8.2.4. Monitoring

In principle, the monitoring of electronic online communication data may not interfere with the privacy of the employees. If, however, the monitoring does lead to interference in this privacy, this interference must be restricted to a minimum (proportionality principle).

The commentary regarding Article 6 of C.B.A. No 81 (containing the proportionality principle) clarifies that only the data that is necessary for the monitoring may be processed and collected. This implies that only the data that interferes the least with the privacy of the employees, taking into account the purpose of the monitoring, can be used. At this stage, only global data can be collected and the identification of individual

employees is not allowed. A distinction is made between monitoring of surfing and monitoring of the use of e-mail:

- **Internet:** the employer can collect data regarding the duration of the connection per PC, but cannot individualise the visited web sites

- **e-mail:** the employer can collect data regarding the number and volume of sent e-mails per PC, but cannot identify the employee that has sent those e-mails.

C.B.A. No 81 does not clarify how global monitoring without identification of employees should or can be carried out. According to a possible interpretation, a distinction should be made between the data on the PC (server) on the one hand and the way this data is processed and reproduced on the other. To ensure conformity with C.B.A. No 81, it should be impossible to deduct the identity or responsibility of individual employees from the output of the monitoring programme. For example, the number of sent and/or received e-mails per PC could be indicated, without specifying to which individual employee the PC concerned belongs.

In this interpretation, it basically comes down to drawing up lists with global data in such a way that is not possible to identify, on the basis of those lists, individual employees who are responsible for sending e-mails, visiting web sites, etc. If, on the basis of this global data, the employer presumes that irregularities have occurred, he can proceed to the identification of the individual employees, on the basis of the other data collected and located on the PC (server) (see further: individualisation procedure). This seems to be the only useful and feasible interpretation of the said provisions, but case law will have to clarify this position in the future.

8.2.5. Individualisation of electronic online communication data

C.B.A. No 81 contains specific rules regarding individualisation, which is defined as 'the processing of electronic online communication data that was collected by the employer, in order to attribute them to an identified or identifiable person'.

The individualisation must be carried out in good faith and according to the given purposes.

Only the electronic online communication data that is necessary for the given purpose(s) of the monitoring may be individualised. It must be adequate, relevant and not excessive in relation to the purposes.

---

60   Although the C.B.A. No 81 only refers to the clause regarding 'sanctions', it is generally admitted that the 'rights and obligations of the supervising personnel' and the facts which can justify a 'dismissal for urgent cause' must also be mentioned in the work rules.

61   This should take place in the safety committee if there is no work council or in the trade union delegation if there is no safety committee.

According to the purpose of the employer, a direct or indirect procedure must be followed.

8.2.5.1. Direct procedure

Direct individualisation is allowed if the employer pursues one or more of the purposes mentioned under point 8.2.1, No 1-3.

An employer that finds an irregularity when pursuing one of those purposes may directly individualise the electronic online communication data, in light of the global data at his or her disposal. For example, irregularities can be discovered by controlling the global data (e.g. statistical data), or by means of any other source of information.

8.2.5.2. Indirect procedure

When pursuing the purpose mentioned under point 8.2.1, No 4, the employer must follow a specific procedure to be allowed to individualise the data.

Firstly, the employer must inform the employees of the fact that an irregularity has been detected and that the electronic online communication data will be individualised if such irregularity is detected again. The employer must also further specify or remind employees of the applicable principles and rules in order to prevent a new irregularity from occurring.

Subsequently, when an individual employee is found responsible for a (new) irregularity, he or she must be invited by the employer for a personal discussion. This conversation must take place before any decision or evaluation regarding the employee is made. The discussion is supposed to give the employee the opportunity to justify his or her use of the electronic online communication means and to explain his or her objections to the intended decision or evaluation.

8.2.6. Reading of the employees' e-mail

It is not clear whether C.B.A. No 81 allows the employer to read e-mails sent or received by his employees.

C.B.A. No 81 states that only the data that is adequate, relevant and not excessive in relation to the purposes of the control can be individualised. The report preceding this

agreement clarified that *the content may not be individualised, unless the parties and certainly the employee have given their consent according to the Belgacom Act and the Data Protection Act.* Indeed, general provisions such as the secrecy of communications still apply. These provisions considerably limit the ability of the employer to read his employees' e-mails (see further).

Article 11 of the C.B.A. explicitly states that the rules regarding individualisation do not apply *to the subject and the content of the electronic online communication data of which the professional character is not contested by the employee.*[62] It is unclear how an employer, in order to know if the individualisation procedure has to be complied with, can determine whether the data has a private or a professional character before the individualisation itself has taken place.

The report preceding C.B.A. No 81 clarifies that:

• If the subject *and the content* of the electronic online communication data has a professional character that is not contested by the employee, the employer can take cognisance of this data without having to follow a procedure

• If the private character of the content of the data is put forward, *namely by a reference in the subject*, the employer has to follow the individualisation procedure, but cannot take cognisance of the content.

One of the possible interpretations of these provisions is that the employer can oblige the employees to put the mention 'private' in the subject of private e-mails, combined with certain rules regarding the use of e-mail for private purposes (e.g. Time, number, prohibition to add attachments, etc.) By doing so, it would be sufficient to verify whether the applicable rules are respected by establishing a statistical list mentioning the number of e-mails having the mention 'private' in the subject and for example the time of sending, the presence of an attachment, etc. On the other hand, it would then be possible to take cognisance of the content of e-mails that do not have the mention 'private' in the subject (and taking into account what will be discussed below). It is clear that in the future case law will have to clarify whether such a method of control complies with C.B.A. No 81 or not.

---

62   All electronic online communication data cannot be qualified as professional or as private, as this would render the guarantees provided by C.B.A. No 81 ineffective.

8.3. Secrecy of communications

8.3.1. Article 314bis Criminal Code

The Criminal Code (Article 314bis) prohibits intercepting, reading or recording private (tele)communications during transmission. Professional communications, such as e-mail, that are not intended to be heard or read by other persons than the correspondents, are protected by this provision. As a consequence, employers reading the content of e-mails sent or received by their employees could be criminally sanctioned.

However, according to some legal experts this provision does not prohibit an employer from checking the mailbox of an employee, as this control method is not carried out 'during the transmission' of the communication. Moreover, it can be argued that Internet monitoring through the registration of website addresses is not envisaged by this provision.

8.3.2. Article 109ter D of the Belgacom Act

Under the Belgacom Act of 21 March 1991 (Article 109ter D), it is prohibited monitor *data concerning telecommunications related to another person*. According to most legal experts, this provision applies to employers monitoring their employees' use of e-mail and the Internet. Others argue that this is not the case.

Belgian labour courts are also divided on this issue, but in the majority of decisions it is stated that the Belgacom Act applies.

As C.B.A. No 81 explicitly refers to Article 109ter D and states that this Article applies in case of monitoring of e-mail and Internet usage, it has become very difficult to hold the contrary.

8.3.3. Exceptions

There are two relevant exceptions to Article 314bis of the Criminal Code and Article 109ter D of the Belgacom Act:

1.   Permission by law

At present, no specific law expressly allows employers to register and monitor their employees' e-mail and Internet activities. According to some legal experts, the employers' authority (laid down in Articles 2, 3 and 17 of the Employment Contracts Act) constitutes a 'permission by law'. Others state that a more specific rule is required.

In a Decision of 22 June 2000, the Labour Court of Brussels decided that the employer can invoke Article 16 of the Employment Contracts Act (protection of common decency – case of dismissal for serious cause of an employee sending a pornographic picture by e-mail to a female colleague).

2.   The consent of all persons involved in the (tele)communication

There is no breach of Article 314bis of the Criminal Code or Article 109ter D of the Belgacom Act if the employer obtains the consent from all persons involved in the (tele)communication.

As far as Internet use is concerned, the consent of the employees suffices. However, legal experts are divided on the extent to which an employee can give his or her consent. For some legal experts, a general provision in the work rules or in the employment contract is sufficient. For others, the employee should specifically agree every time he or she uses the Internet (for example, by clicking on an 'I agree' button when starting up the Internet browser).

With regard to the control of the use of electronic mail, consent may constitute a practical problem, since all parties involved must give their consent. Obviously, it is difficult to obtain the consent of participants to the communication that are not part of the personnel of the company. It can be argued, however, that implicit consent suffices. Such consent could be obtained by using a specific standard clause in every e-mail, stating that the e-mail can be read by the employer.

8.4. Article 8 of the European Convention on Human Rights

Article 8 of the European Convention on Human Rights (ECHR) prohibits interference with a person's private life. This prohibition also applies to the employer – employee relationship. The right to privacy is not absolute, however.

A breach of privacy is permitted if the following conditions are met:

- The interference is in accordance with an existing, clear and accessible norm (*legality principle*)

- The employer must have a legitimate purpose, notably the necessity to protect a fundamental right (*finality principle*)

- The interference has to be 'proportional' (*proportionality principle*): a breach of privacy is only permitted if it is not excessive in relation to the purposes for which it is intended.

As these principles are also laid down in C.B.A. No 81, one can argue that an employer complying with the C.B.A. Is not violating Article 8 of the ECHR.

8.5. Data Processing Act of 8 December 1992

The Data Processing Act of 8 December 1992 defines 'personal data' as 'any information relating to an identified or identifiable natural person'. Information on an employee's use of e-mail and Internet falls within the scope of this definition, as the login name, the e-mail address or the PC number can be linked to an employee.

Processing personal information is only permitted in certain cases, notably among others if the data subject explicitly agrees, if access is necessary to perform an agreement with that person or to enforce a legitimate interest (provided that the data subject's interests and fundamental rights do not take precedence).

Processing abilities are limited. Personal data must be:

- Processed fairly and lawfully

- Collected for specified, explicit and legitimate purposes and not further processed in a way that is incompatible with those purposes

- Adequate, relevant and not excessive in relation to the purposes for which it is collected or further processed (according to the Commission for the protection of privacy in its recommendation of 3 April 2000, it is disproportionate for an employer to read the e-mails sent or received by his employees)[63]

- Accurate and, if necessary, kept up to date; inaccurate or incomplete data must be erased or rectified

- Kept in a form that allows identification of data subjects for no longer than necessary for the purposes for which the data is collected or for which it is further processed.[64]

Under the Data Processing Act, employers processing personal data have to comply with several obligations. Non-compliance with most of these obligations is criminally sanctioned.

An employer processing personal data must:

- Inform the employees thereof

- Fulfil certain obligations concerning the confidentiality and security of the processed data

- Notify the Commission for the protection of privacy of the processing (the notification should take place before carrying out the processing).

The risks of non-compliance with the provisions discussed above are double:

- Employers violating most of the above-mentioned provisions can be criminally sanctioned (*e.g. As a result of a complaint made by an employee*)

- If a control is illegitimate because it violates one of the provisions discussed above, evidence produced by such a check will be considered as irregularly acquired and a Labour Court will most likely not take it into account (*e.g. In case of dismissal for serious cause*).

8.6. Medical Testing Data

The employee's privacy protection is further enhanced by a new Act of 28 January 2003 (Act with respect to medical examination in the framework of employment relations (Official Gazette, 9 April 2003).

The Act clearly prohibits biological tests, medical examinations or oral information gathering with respect to an employee's or applicant's health or family history unless they are related to their present ability to perform the job and the specific requirements of the job.

HIV/AIDS tests and predictive genetic research are absolutely prohibited. The prohibited examinations will, as an exception, be allowed only in cases set by Ministerial Decree.

---

63 Although the recommendation of the Commission only has a moral value, it is likely to be used as a guideline by Belgian Labour Courts in order to evaluate if a specific control method complies with the Data Protection Act.

64 According to the EU Data Protection Working Party (Directive 95/46/EU), data regarding the use of e-mail and Internet should be stored no longer than three months.

A specific information procedure towards the individual must be followed prior to the examination. The employer needs to notify the employee of the data that is being researched, which examination will be performed and why it will be done.

The employer must also notify employees or potential candidates of the illnesses that can be aggravated by the work to be carried out.

Chapter IV:
Promoting equal opportunities

1. Blue- and white-collar workers

1.1. Difficulties in making the distinction

The 3 July 1978 version of the Belgian Act on Employment Contracts (often modified thereafter) makes a clear distinction between white- and blue-collar workers. Both kinds of workers are dealt with in separate chapters of the Act.

White-collar workers are defined as those primarily engaged in intellectual labour,[65] while blue-collar workers primarily perform manual duties.[66] The criteria the Act sets out for making the distinction is unclear and unspecified, relying on the judges and courts to make it more concrete and fit for application.

This distinction creates problems both from *qualitative* and from *quantitative* points of view for courts confronted with making the distinction.[67] The courts will first determine whether a given kind of performance, as well as the different tasks the workers concerned are involved in, are of an intellectual nature or of a manual nature. Next the courts will then have to decide whether the intellectual or manual performances are predominant. Furthermore, the dominant character of one kind of performances is not necessarily or entirely determined by the number of hours spent on each of the different kind of tasks.

The combination of both manual and intellectual activities makes decision-making more difficult for judges. In addition, it is not always easy to determine what is to be considered intellectual or manual. It will not come as a surprise that contradictory decisions with respect to the same or very similar jobs are manifold.[68]

Over recent decades, the difficulty in making such a distinction has led courts to take into account various other criteria than the nature of the performances delivered.[69]

Since the 1950s, it has been argued that the difference between blue- and white-collar workers is no longer warranted. It has caused difficulties in application for decades. Technological developments made it possible to cut out a large section of the hard and dirty manual labour.[70] Furthermore, the manual operations required to make certain equipment function required a certain degree of intellectual application. This holds for almost any kind of manual labour – a certain degree of reflection and intellectual knowledge is required. On the other hand, it is clear that a number of jobs that were traditionally seen as white-collar have become more and more repetitive and less stimulating, resulting in a recognition that the distinction between white- and blue-collar workers may no longer be valid. Some courts have explicitly stated that they consider the distinction an artificial one.[71]

The artificial nature of this distinction has forced employers who had to prove that a worker was a blue-collar worker to basically argue in court that the workers concerned were ignorant.[72]

---

65   Article 3, Act on Employment Contracts of 3 July 1978, Official Gazette, 22 August 1978, often amended afterwards [hereafter Act on Employment Contracts].

66   Article 2, Act on Employment Contracts.

67   See C. Engels, 'Het onderscheid werkman/bediende, een ongrondwettige discriminatie in strijd met de artikelen 6 en 6bis van de Belgische grondwet' [The distinction between manual/intellectual workers, an unconstitutional discrimination in violation of the Article 6 and 6bis of the Constitution], *Rechtskundig Weekblad*, 1991-92, 729, 737 [hereafter Het Onderscheid].

68   See: C. Engels, 'Het Onderscheid', 739; D. Cuypers, 'Het onderscheid tussen werklieden en bedienden' [The distinction between blue -and white-collar workers], *Oriëntatie* 1991, 57, 60.

69   See: C. Engels, 'De statuten van werkman and bediende : een juridische benadering' [The status of blue- and white-collar workers: a legal approach], in *Statuut werkman – bediende , Arbeidsrechtelijke en sociologische kanttekeningen* [The status of blue- and white-collar workers, A labour law and sociological approach], *Belgische Vereniging voor Arbeidsverhoudingen* (ed.), Brugge, Die Keure, 1990;7, 13 [hereafter C. Engels, Belgische Vereniging voor Arbeidsverhoudingen].

70   See: Labour Court Liège 10 March 1976, *Jurisprudence de Liège*, 1975-76, 234.

71   See: Labour Tribunal Brussels, 3 March 1988, *Rechtspraak van de Arbeidsgerechten te Brussel*, 1988, 158.

72   See: R. Blanpain, *Sire, zijn er domme werknemers in ons land?* [Your Majesty, are there any ignorant workers in our country?], Brugge, Die Keure, 2001, 25

1.2. The importance of the difference

The difference in treatment between blue- and white-collar workers is important not only from a labour law perspective, but also with respect to social security contributions. Social security contributions for blue-collar workers are much higher than for white-collar workers. Furthermore, holiday pay is regulated differently for the two kinds of workers.[73]

Within the trade union organisations, white-collar workers are organised across the different sectors of industry, in a single white-collar worker trade union. Most blue-collar workers are organised on an industry basis.

The form of trade union organisation goes hand in hand with the organisation of collective bargaining in Belgium. The Belgian Act on Collective Bargaining did not require the organisation of separate joint committees of industry in which the bargaining at sector level takes place for white- and blue-collar workers.[74] However, in most sectors of industry, different bargaining structures for blue- and white-collar workers exist.[75] These facts clearly result in substantial differences in the outcome of collective bargaining at sector level.

The Act on Employment Contracts contains a number of important differences in treatment between blue- and white-collar workers as has been explained above (see Chapter II, section 1.1).

1.3. Reducing the gap contractually

1.3.1. The inability to contractually abolish the distinction

Employers and workers have come to reduce the difference through negotiations. Employers can grant workers the benefit of the white-collar worker status in the individual employment contracts that they conclude. They may label the agreement as an agreement for a white-collar employee, even though the work to be done is primarily and predominantly of a manual nature. They may explicitly foresee that the worker concerned will receive all the benefits he or she

would be able to derive from the status granted. It is clear, however, that the worker concerned will, even under these circumstances, still be considered a manual worker if not predominantly involved in work of an intellectual nature.

The distinction between white- and blue-collar workers is of a mandatory nature, which means that the parties cannot contractually modify it. However, the worker concerned could nevertheless be granted the advantages that are attached to another status than the one he or she is granted by law. The Act on Employment Contracts explicitly foresees that all contract provisions that are contrary to the provisions of the Act and its implementing Decrees will be considered null and void if they reduce the rights the worker is granted under the Act or impose more (including more far-reaching) duties on the worker concerned.[76] Practically speaking, this means that the blue-collar worker will be able to benefit from the white-collar status that has been granted to him or her contractually and will at the same time be able to rely on his (mandatory) legal rights as a blue-collar worker under the law if and when these rights are more beneficial to him or her than the white-collar provisions that have been contractually extended to him or her. One such example would be the application of the legal provision of the Act on Employment Contracts that deals with abusive termination of employment contracts and is only applicable to blue-collar workers. The contractual granting of white-collar worker status does not take this protection away. While benefiting from the advantages of white-collar status, he or she will be able to combine these with the advantages of the other status.

1.3.2. Collective bargaining efforts to reduce the gap

Collective bargaining efforts at the various levels of our system of industrial relations have addressed the (unjustified) distinction between white- and blue-collar workers. Some companies have made the decision to treat all of their workers alike, regardless of the nature of the performances they deliver. As indicated above, such collective bargaining agreements, entered into between the trade unions and an employer, will not be able to eradicate the distinction between the two kinds of workers.

---

73 See: R. Blanpain, *Sire, zijn er domme werknemers in ons land?* [Your Majesty, are there any ignorant workers in our country?], Brugge, Die Keure, 2001, 25.
74 Act concerning collective bargaining agreements and joint committees of industry of 5 December 1968, Official Gazette, 15 January 1969, often amended afterwards.
75 See: C. Engels, *Belgische Vereniging voor Arbeidsverhoudingen*, 28.
76 Article 6, Act on Employment Contracts.

At sector-level, various initiatives have been undertaken to try to reduce the gap between white- and blue-collar workers. With respect to the difference in treatment as far as security of employment, and more precisely to the terms of notice, various sector-level collective bargaining agreements have addressed the issue. The Act on Employment Contracts even contains an explicit provision through which the legally determined terms of notice can be modified.[77]

The provision of the Act on Employment Contracts states that a Royal Decree, on the basis of a proposal by the joint committees of industry (social partners at the level of the sector of industry) can modify the terms of notice foreseen in the Act itself in the interest of specific categories of workers or for terminations on the basis of social or economic reasons. The Royal Decrees that result from such initiatives can both prolong the terms of notice or reduce them. In many sectors of industry, such deviating terms of notice have been set but this does not benefit the workers concerned in all sectors. Some sectors of industry, such as the building industry, now have even shorter periods of notice than those foreseen in the Act. In most sectors of industry the terms of notice have, however, been prolonged. But in most of these sectors the actual terms of notice for blue-collar workers still fall far below the minimum terms applicable to white-collar workers.

Under the pressure of public opinion, some action was also undertaken at the national inter-industry level of Belgian industrial relations. The social partners concluded a collective bargaining agreement on 20 December 1999 extending the terms of notice of blue-collar workers (under certain conditions).[78]

This Collective Bargaining Agreement sets the terms of notice as shown in the table below.

While the terms of notice of the national collective bargaining agreement are substantially better than those in the Act on Employment Contracts, there is still a very ample difference between white- and blue-collar workers. The table below clearly shows that the minimum terms for white-collar workers are at least three to four times as favorable as the enhanced terms of notice for blue-collar workers.

More importantly, however, the national collective bargaining agreement restricts its own scope very substantially. It states that the extended terms of notice will not be applicable if, at the level of the sector of industry, there is either:

• A Royal Decree or a collective bargaining agreement that contains terms of notice that are different from the ones contained in the Act on Employment Contracts

or

• An applicable collective bargaining agreement that foresees an extended system of employment or income security through supplementary income guarantee or equivalent rules.[79]

Seniority	Term of notice	
	White-collar Legal term Act	Blue-collar C.B.A.
0-6 months	3 months/180days	28 days – 28 days
6 months-less than 5 years	3 months/90 days	28 days – 35 days
5 years to less than 10	6 months/180 days	28 days – 42 days
10 years to less than 15	9 months/270days	28 days – 56 days
15 years to less than 20	12 months/360 days	28 days – 84 days
20 years to less than 25	15 months/450 days	56 days – 112 days
...	[3 months/90 days]	56 days – 112 days

77 Article 61, Act on Employment Contracts.
78 Article 2, Collective Bargaining Agreement No 75, 20 December 1999, concerning terms of notice for blue- collar workers; rendered generally binding by Royal Decree, 10 February 2000, Official Gazette, 26 February 2000.
79 Article 3, Collective Bargaining Agreement No 75, 20 December 1999, concerning terms of notice for blue-collar workers; rendered generally binding by Royal Decree, 10 February 2000, Official Gazette, 26 February 2000.

The deviating terms of notice the collective bargaining agreement refers to do not have to be beneficial to the worker concerned. Furthermore, even a limited improvement to a small category of workers would suffice to render the national collective bargaining agreement not applicable. If a system of employment security were to introduce an additional procedure to be followed in case of dismissal, the collective bargaining agreement would not be applicable either. The same would hold if sector-level pre-pension arrangements were in place or if a system has been set up to provide the workers with some supplements to unemployment benefits in case of dismissal, even if this is only for a (very) limited period of time.

It is clear that the national inter-industry level collective bargaining agreement will not be applicable in very many instances. One may wonder whether it is a mere form of window dressing.

1.4. A case of unacceptable unequal treatment?

The Belgian Constitution explicitly stipulates that there is equality among its citizens: all Belgians are equal before the law.[80] Article 11 of the Constitution further stipulates that all citizens must be able to equally enjoy all rights and privileges. It has been suggested that this constitutional provision could be used to challenge the inequality of treatment of white- and blue-collar workers under Belgian labour and employment law.[81]

The Belgian Court of Arbitration, which is a quasi-constitutional court, is competent to deal with the issue of the alleged unconstitutionality of legal provisions.

The Court has held that the above-mentioned constitutional prohibition on discrimination prohibits any form of discrimination, whatever its origin.[82] The provisions of the Act on Employment Contracts will have to be scrutinised for any such form of unconstitutional discrimination. This does not mean that any form of distinction or differentiation is no

longer allowed. The Court of Arbitration recognised this in stating that the principles of non-discrimination and equal treatment do not exclude distinctions being made between different categories of persons, inasmuch as the distinguishing criterion is reasonable and objectively justified. Such a justification, the court stated, needs to take into account the purpose, the consequences and the nature of the provisions under discussion. The principle of equality is violated in the absence of a reasonable relationship of proportionality between the means that are used and the purpose to be achieved. The distinguishing criteria used must be pertinent and adequate.[83]

It is doubtful that the foreseen distinction between blue- and white- collar workers in the Act on Contracts of Employment is sufficiently justified.[84] It is impossible to find a decent justification for the differences in treatment at present. Furthermore, the criteria used to make the distinction leads to a great number of problems both from a qualitative as well as a quantitative point of view (see above) when applied.

The Court of Arbitration had to examine the distinction between white- and blue-collar workers more closely in a case that focused on the difference in terms of notice or indemnities in lieu, on 8 July 1993.[85] Even though the Court recognised that the distinctions that are made between blue- and white-collar workers are no longer justified, it lacked the courage to actually make the 'right decision'.

The Court stated that a distinction based on the manual versus intellectual nature of the performances could hardly be called objective and reasonable at the present time. However, this does not imply that the legislator had violated the provisions on equal treatment by not abolishing the distinction when it implemented the Act on Employment Contracts. The Court further emphasised that the distinction existed well before the introduction of the Act on Employment Contracts. Equally important was the fact that improvements in the protection of blue-collar workers had already been introduced and opportunities for improvement were provided for in the Act.

---

80   Article 10, Belgian Constitution.
81   See: C. Engels, 'Het onderscheid', 729-742; C. Engels, 'De toenadering tussen de statuten van werkman en bediende en de ongrondwettelijkheid van het nog bestaande onderscheid' [Closing the gap between white- and blue-collar workers and the unconstitutionality of the remaining distinction], *Oriëntatie* 1992, 13-24; D. Cuypers, 'Het onderscheid tussen werklieden en bedienden' [The distinction between white- and blue-collarworkers], *Oriëntatie* 1991, 57, 65.
82   Cour d'Arbitrage, 13 October 1989, No. 23/89 Official Gazette, 8 November 1989, B.1.2.
83   Cour d'Arbitrage, 31 October 1991, no. 30/91, Official Gazette, 15 November 1991, B.2. *See also* the case law cited in C. Engels, 'Het onderscheid', 735.
84   See: C. Engels, 'Het onderscheid', 735,f.
85   Cour d'Arbitrage, 8 July 1993, No. 56/93, Official Gazette, 27 August 1993.

The Court emphasised that the distinction has had pervasive effects far beyond the mere terms of notice. The Court stressed that an immediate eradication would not be feasible, but that this should happen over time.

The Court also stressed that it needed to restrict itself to the limits of the case that had been presented to it (discrimination with respect to terms of notice only) while the differences in treatment go far beyond that, extending into labour and employment law in general and even into social security law.

The Court lacked the courage to declare the distinction between white- and blue-collar workers unconstitutional.[86] Even though it is true that the Court could have passed judgement only with respect to the issue of the terms of notice that are different, it is clear that the said decision would have practically forced the legislator and the social partners to engage in a full overhaul of the system in order to avoid unjustified distinctions and discriminations.

Since its landmark judgement on 8 July 1993, the same Court of Arbitration has rendered a number of judgements in which it seems to go further in the fight against discrimination. In three of its 1996 decisions (in other areas of law than mere employment and labour law) the Court addressed the matter of the unconstitutionality of the absence of action by the legislator.[87] One of the cases dealt with the issue of granting civil servants a limitation of liability for actions undertaken in the performance of the employment relationship, similar to the limitation of liability granted to employees through the Act on Employment Contracts. As no act was in force for civil servants, the general rules on liability were applicable. The Court held that the mere fact of not passing a legislative measure that would grant a group of workers a similar right to the that granted to other similarly situated workers was in itself unconstitutional, thereby forcing the legislator to act.[88]

While these decisions were viewed as a new step in the case law of the Court of Arbitration, it could be argued that these cases should also be the starting point for taking another and even braver step. While the failure to provide any specific rules (without justification) can be regarded as unconstitutional, the Court should take one more additional step.

If not taking any measure with respect to a particular group of similarly situated people can be regarded as unconstitutional, refusing to abolish discriminatory rules, even when they were justified at their inception, should also be deemed unconstitutional.

Even though the social partners and the legislator have time and again declared that they are willing to address the issue of the abolition of the discrimination between white- and blue-collar workers, it is hard to avoid the conclusion that not much has been done yet. Perhaps the Court of Arbitration can help all involved to take a definitive and decisive step towards full equality by holding that the absence of a decision to abolish a discrimination that is no longer justified could be seen as unconstitutional, in the same way a mere absence of legislative action has been seen as such.

However, in a recent 2001 case dealing with the difference in legal treatment between blue- and white-collar workers in the area of abusive dismissal law, the Court of Arbitration merely reiterated the reasoning it had developed in its 1993 case with respect to terms of notice.[89] It thereby still declined to show the required courage to bring about a much-needed change in the law.

Recently, two separate political initiatives have been taken to abolish the distinction (Proposal for a Law introducing a unitary status for subordinate workers, Chamber of Representatives, Session 2001-2002, 21 June 2002, Document 50, 1881/001; Proposal for a Law with respect to the status of subordinate workers and suppressing the distinction between blue- and white-collar workers, Senat, Session 2001-2002, 30 September 2002, Document 2, 1278/1).

2. Public and private sector

The existing difference between public and private sector employment does not facilitate the transfer from one system to the other. Legislative action has been proposed to remove the differences in treatment.

Public sector employment is regulated by administrative law rather than employment law. The systems are very different, in terms of both employment security and pension rights.

---

86   See: C. Engels, Note under Cour d'Arbitrage, 8 July 1993, No. 56/93, *Fundamentele Rechtspraak*, 6 September 1993, 16-17; R. Blanpain, *Labour Law in Belgium*, The Hague, London, Boston, Brussels, Kluwer/Bruylant, 1996, no. 24.

87   See: A. Alen, 'Ongrondwettige lacunes in de wetgeving volgens de rechtspraak van het Arbitragehof' [Unconstitutional absence of lawmaking in the case law of the Cour d'Arbitrage] in *Liber Amicorum Prof. Dr. Roger Blanpain*.

88   Cour d'Arbitrage, 18 December 1996, No. 77/96, Official Gazette, 8 February 1997.

89   Cour d'Arbitrage, 21 June 2001, No. 84/2001.

Clearly, mobility between the public and private sector is very much reduced, as the transfer from one sector to the other will lead to loss of rights.

However, the public sector employs more and more workers that do not have the status of civil servants and whose employment status is regulated by employment law. The fact that these so-called contractual workers fall within the scope of employment law (as opposed to administrative law) in general, unfortunately does not grant them the full protection of employment law. Quite a number of legislative acts refer to the Act of 6 December 1968 concerning collective bargaining agreement and joint committees (see introduction) for their scope. The latter Act is clearly not applicable to the public sector.

Recently some legislative action has been taken in this respect (See Act, 22 April 2003, modifying the Articles 38bis, 51bis and 59 of the Act of 3 July 1978 concerning Contracts of Employment, Official Gazette, 13 May 2003).

Collective bargaining agreements, in the context of the Act of 6 December 1968, are not applicable to the public sector or to the contractual workers of this sector.

This means that the national inter-industry wide collective bargaining agreement that increased the term of notice for blue-collar workers is not applicable to blue-collar workers in the public sector. The above-mentioned Parliamentary Act of 22 April 2003 explicitly foresees the same terms of notice as those foreseen in the collective bargaining agreement for any notice given after 13 May 2003.

3. Fixed-term and part-time workers

Council Directive 97/81/EC of 15 December 1997 concerning the Framework Agreement on part-time work concluded by UNICE, CEEP and the ETUC was implemented both by an inter-industry wide collective bargaining agreement of 27 February 1981 (modified by agreement on February 9, 2000) and by an Act of 5 March 2002 concerning the non-discrimination of part-time workers (Official Gazette, 13 March 2002).

The Belgian Act defines part-time work as any work that is performed for less than the working time of a comparable worker in a comparable situation. The comparable worker is defined by reference to the same kind of employment contract and the same kind of function. Comparisons should be made within the same establishment or, in the absence of a comparable full-time worker, in the same establishment in the same undertaking or, in the absence of the latter point of reference, in the same sector of industry.

Differences in treatment based on objective reasons can justify distinctions being made. Where appropriate, rights can be rewarded *pro rata temporis*. In case objective reasons justify it, the access to certain working and employment conditions can be made dependent on a certain level of seniority, working time or remuneration. The original collective bargaining agreement already established a priority for part-time workers with respect to vacancies at the company concerned.

Based on the general principles contained in the Act of 3 July 1978, a full-time worker cannot be forced to accept part-time work against his or her own will. A reduction of working time (and the accompanying reduction in remuneration) would be considered tantamount to a constructive discharge, thereby entitling the worker to a termination indemnity.

Under Belgian law, working time is strictly regulated for part-time workers. Their working time schedules need to be properly announced and any deviations from the normal working time schedule need to be well-documented. If this is not the case, the worker could claim full-time wages. This presumption was established in 1989 and resulted in quite a lot of case law during the 1990s on the question of whether or not the presumption was refutable. Since the text of the law was changed in 1996, it seems that the presumption is now refutable, even though the discussion is most likely not over yet.

A Parliamentary Act of 5 June 2002 implements Council Directive 1999/70/EC of 28 June 1999 concerning the Framework Agreement on fixed-term work concluded by ETUC, UNICE and CEEP (Act of 5 June 2002 concerning the non-discrimination of workers with a fixed-term contract, Official Gazette, 26 June 2002).

Belgian legislation foresaw elaborate protection against the 'misuse' of successive fixed-term employment contracts and generally foresees that they are to be considered as an indefinite employment contract unless the succession of such contracts can be justified (see *supra*).

Similar definitions are to be found in the legislation on non-discrimination of part-time workers with respect to comparable workers and the potential to still make justified distinctions between workers with a fixed-term contract and those under a contract for an indefinite period of time.

The Act explicitly states that it is not applicable to temporary workers (Article 3, paragraph 2).

The Act places a positive obligation on the employer to inform those workers with a fixed-term contract of any vacancies for an indefinite period of time.

On-call contracts as such are unknown under Belgian employment law. In doctrine, such contracts are defined as contracts that stipulate that the employee is not aware of the days and hours that he or she will perform tasks for the employer. The employee must wait to be called in by the employer and will work for as long as the employer needs him or her. (See: Labour Tribunal Dendermonde, 18 December 1996, Tijdschrift voor Gentse Rechtspraak 1997, 93).

No specific legislative act or collective bargaining agreement regulates this kind of employment. If the worker must be at the disposal of the employer at all times, the contract is considered to be null and void, without limiting the worker's rights to pay for the performances (Labour Tribunal Brussels, 11 June 1992, Sociaal Rechtelijke Kronieken 199, 40). The Supreme Court seems to have indicated that the worker would not be entitled to full-time wages (Supreme Court, 16 March 1992, Rechtskundig Weekblad 1992-93, 401).

4. Sex and race discrimination and the Framework Directive

4.1. Legal provisions

Please note that many of the EU Directives dealing with discrimination have also been implemented through adaptations of scattered pre-existing legal provisions, such as:

- The Act of 4 August 1978 regarding economic re-orientation, State Gazette, 17 August 1978

- The Act of 30 July 1981 regarding the punishment of certain acts inspired by racism and xenophobia, State Gazette, 8 August 1981, as amended last time by the Act of 7 May 1999, State Gazette, 25 June 1999

- The Act of 7 May 1999 on the equal treatment of men and women with regard to working conditions, access to employment and promotion, access to an independ-

ent activity and additional social security schemes, State Gazette, 19 June 1999, Ed. 1

- The Act of 5 March 2002 on the principle of non-discrimination with respect to part-time workers, State Gazette, 13 March 2002

- The Act of 5 June 2002 on the principle of non-discrimination with respect to fixed-term work.

4.2. The extent of the prohibition on sex and race discrimination

4.2.1. Recruitment situation

When hiring employees, employers cannot discriminate (directly or indirectly) on the basis of sex. The same principle of non-discrimination on grounds of sex is to be respected with regard to access to independent activities (Act of 7 May 1999).

Discrimination on the basis of race, skin colour, descent or nationality is forbidden during employment finding, job offering and recruitment (Act of 30 July 1981).

However, the Act of 7 May 1999 does not obstruct measures aimed at the promotion of equal opportunities for men and women, such as the removal of factual inequalities that negatively influence women's chances on the labour market.

The Act of 7 May 1999 has implemented Directive 97/80 on the burden of proof in cases of sex discrimination. Any person can bring an action to court in order to enforce the provisions of the Act of 7 May 1999. If this person establishes facts that demonstrate that there has been direct or indirect discrimination, the burden to prove that there has been no infringement of the principle of equal treatment shifts to the defendant (i.e. The employer).

Provisions contrary to the principle of equal treatment as defined in the Act of 7 May 1999 are null and void. In addition, such infringements also constitute criminal offences subject to imprisonment and/or penalty payments.

4.2.2. During the employment relationship

Employers cannot discriminate on the basis of sex (be it directly or indirectly) with respect to promotion opportunities, working conditions and supplementary social security schemes (Act of 7 May 1999). For the application of the Act of 7 May 1999, sexual harassment at the workplace is assumed to constitute an instance of discrimination on the grounds of sex.

The Act of 7 May 1999 does not obstruct measures aimed at the promotion of equal opportunities for men and women, in particular those that seek to remove factual inequalities that negatively influence women's chances in the labour market.

Sanctions

Provisions contrary to the principle of equal treatment as defined in the Act of 7 May 1999 are null and void. In addition, such infringements also constitute criminal offences subject to imprisonment and/or penalty payments.

4.2.3. The dismissal stage

The Act of 7 May 1999 provides that an employer cannot terminate the employment contract or unilaterally change the working conditions of an employee who filed a complaint, went to court or for whom someone else went to court in order to have the provisions of this Act respected, unless such termination or unilateral change is not related to the complaint or court action.

The Act of 30 July 1981 provides that dismissal because of someone's race, skin colour, descent or nationality is forbidden.

If an employer terminates an employment agreement or unilaterally changes the working conditions contrary to the provisions of the Act of 7 May 1999, the employee concerned or his employee organisation may request, by registered mail and within 30 days of the termination or the announcement thereof, or within 30 days of the unilateral change of working conditions, that he or she be allowed to take up his or her function within the company under the same conditions as before. The employer should react within 30 days of the notification of the registered letter.

If the employer accepts that the employee work again in his or her former function, the employer must pay to the employee the income missed because of the termination or the change in working conditions. In addition, the employer must pay the employee and employer's social security contributions on the missed income.

If the employer does not want the employee to work in his former function and if it has been judged that the dismissal or the unilateral change of working conditions is contrary to

the Act, the employer must pay the employee a compensation which is, at the employee's discretion, either equal to a lump sum corresponding to six months' gross wages, or equal to the damages actually suffered. In the latter case the employee is to prove the extent of the damages suffered.

The employer is obliged to pay the compensation mentioned in the above paragraph, without the employee having to request the permission to take up his function again, if:

• The employee terminates the employment contract because the employer's behavior is contrary to the provisions of the Act, which is for the employee a reason to terminate the employment contract without notice or before the contract has ended

• The employer has terminated the employee for serious cause, on the condition that the competent judicial body does not declares the dismissal an infringement of the Act.

4.3. Framework Anti-Discrimination Act

A new anti-discrimination Act was passed on 25 February 2003 (Official Gazette, March 17, 2003). It is the implementation of the EU Framework Directive. The new Act has considerable labour law implications and will therefore deeply influence the daily human resource practices of companies.

4.3.1. New definition of discrimination

The Act distinguishes between direct and indirect discrimination. Direct discrimination occurs when a person is treated differently without this treatment being reasonably and objectively justified and if this treatment is directly based on sex, assumed race, colour, ascendance, national or ethnic origin, sexual orientation, civil status, birth, fortune, age, religious or philosophical conviction, actual or future health, disability or physical feature. The list of prohibited criteria is considerable longer than that of the Framework Directive.

Indirect discrimination is said to occur when a regulation, criterion or practice, held to be neutral, has harmful repercussions on persons to whom one of the quoted discrimination grounds applies, unless the regulation, criterion or practice is objectively and reasonably justified.

Furthermore, the Act addresses the lack of reasonable adjustments for disabled persons. A reasonable adjustment is defined in the Act as one that does not cause disproportionate burden, or for which the burden is sufficiently compensated by existing measures.

The Act also considers harassment as discrimination if there is undesirable behaviour that is linked with the above quoted discrimination grounds and that aims or causes the slurring of a person's dignity or the creation of a threatening, hostile, insulting, humiliating or harmful environment.

It should be noted, however, that the Act allows positive discrimination, although it is not clear what exactly is seen as positive discrimination and what sort of positive discrimination measures would be acceptable.

It is obvious that this new Act contains a large number of grounds for discrimination that were mostly unknown in Belgian legislation. The principle of equal treatment between male and female workers has already been embedded in our legislation for several years. However, grounds for discrimination such as civil status, fortune, health, or future health and physical features have not. Many of these new discrimination grounds are vague and not clearly defined. Inevitably they will cause interpretation difficulties that the judges will need to solve.

4.3.2. The range of application

The Act clearly stipulates that any form of direct or indirect discrimination is forbidden regarding:

• The conditions of access (selection and appointment criteria included) to salaried and unpaid employment or to a self-employed relationship, in any activity or branch and on each level of professional hierarchy, promotion opportunities included

• The terms of employment, dismissal and salary, both in the private as well as in the public sector.

More particularly, the new Act will apply to employment offers, application procedures, promotion opportunities, salary policy (level of basic salary; bonuses, granting of a company car and other extra-legal benefits), terms and stipulations/modalities and conditions of supplementary pension schemes applicable in the company, dismissal and dismissal procedures.

It is important to stress that the new Act not only applies to individual employment relations (employer-employee), but also to collective employment relations and negotiations between employers and unions. In other words, stipulations of a Collective Employment Agreement should be in accordance with the new Act's stipulations. It must be stressed that the Act also applies to contractual relations with and between self-employed persons.

4.3.3. When is unequal treatment justified?

In general, the Act stipulates that discrimination has not occurred if a difference in treatment can be objectively and reasonably justified. In consequence, it is possible to make certain distinctions, provided an objective and reasonable justification can be given. In this aspect, the legislator found it necessary, regarding employment relations, to demand a more severe criterion to justify unequal treatments. Specifically, the Act lays down that in employment relations, different treatment is objectively and reasonably justified, if such a characteristic (i.e. Age, fortune, civil status, physical features,) constitutes an essential and determining professional requirement because of the nature of the professional activity and of the context in which it is performed, if the goal is legitimate and the requirement is proportional to that goal. The criterion of the essential and determining professional requirement seems to be, at first sight, extremely severe. One may consider, for example, sex or a specific physical feature for a role in a movie or the visual abilities of an aircraft pilot. On the basis of the Act's preparatory work in Parliament, however, it is not clear if this requirement shall be applied with full rigour. Reference to the preparatory works and the observations made by the competent minister allow argument to be made in both directions.

4.3.4. Nullity of conflicting clauses

The Act expressly states that the clauses of an agreement that conflict with the Act's stipulations are null. In particular, this might imply that social plans, fixed in collective bargaining agreements and for instance supplementary pension schemes that contain clauses conflicting with the anti-discrimination Act, will be ignored. Evidently, this nullity may cause considerable problems, not only regarding human resources, but also from an economic point of view.

4.3.5. Claim to cease and desist

The Act provides that persons that consider themselves victims of discrimination can bring the case before the competent court and submit a claim for a cease and desist order. This means that, through a shortened procedure, an alleged discriminatory action, decision or policy can be terminated. The concerned employee and the representative employee organisations (unions), institutions or associations with a statutory goal to defend human rights or to combat discrimination can file a request for such an injunction.

It is important to note that within the scope of this procedure, the burden of proof in certain circumstances does not rest with the plaintiff. If the concerned employee or the group that defends the employee's interests is able to prove, for example, by statistics or practical tests that a presumption of discrimination exists, the burden of proof lies with the employer. According to the Act, the practical test can be executed with the help of a bailiff. The bailiff could, for instance, record how many people of a certain ethnic origin or a certain age work in a company. More detailed regulations on these practical tests must be set by Royal Decree.

The Act provides the possibility for judges to order that their decision be posted or even published in the newspapers. Finally, it is stated that the court's order to cease the discrimination can be sanctioned by a penalty.

4.3.6. Employment protection

A final item that deserves special attention is the employment protection for an employee that has submitted a complaint of an alleged discrimination. This employment protection prevails regardless of whether the complaint is submitted at company-level, at Employment Law Inspection Services level or before the court.

A twelve-month protection period starts from the moment a complaint is submitted. In the case of court claim, the protection period lasts for three months after a final judgement. In cases where a complaint is submitted on Employment Law Inspection Services level, employment protection is created even if the employer is not yet informed. The question arises if, in this case, the employer should be informed of the identity of the plaintiff.

The employment protection, as it is stipulated in the anti-discrimination Act, implies that the concerned employee cannot be fired, except for reasons unrelated to the complaint or to the claim.

An employee that is fired without the employer respecting the employment protection may ask for reintegration into the company. In some cases, this obligation does not exist (for instance, when the court considers the discrimination facts proven or when the employee terminates the employment agreement for serious cause committed by the employer). If the employer refuses the reintegration, he or she must pay the employee a lump sum of six months salary as damage compensation or any other compensation for the actual damages suffered (here the employee must be able to prove the scale of the damages suffered).

A specific Act dealing with the prevention of and protection against harassment and sexual harassment at work dates from 11 June 2002 (Official Gazette, 22 June 2002). It targets physical or psychological violence, repeated harassment and sexual harassment at work. The legislator paid close attention to the prevention of any such forms of harassment occurring. The employer must draft a prevention plan in order to reduce and prevent harassment. A specific prevention advisor specialised in the psychological aspects of violence at work must be appointed. The prevention advisor is protected in a similar manner as the worker representatives in the work council.

If harassment occurs, the worker can file a complaint:

• At company level with the prevention advisor who will try to reconcile those involved

• With the inspector of the medical inspection, or

• With the public prosecutor acting in labour law matters.

The victim may also start a civil action to obtain an injunction, as foreseen in the Act of 9 May 1999 (see *supra*).

A reversal of the burden of proof is foreseen in case the employee comes up with facts that may presume there was some violence, harassment or sexual harassment. The Minister declared that the three levels of potential conciliation have to be used before the presumption and reversal of the burden of proof come into play.

Specific protection against dismissal is foreseen, as well as the indemnity that needs to be paid on top of the normal termination indemnities, in case the employer terminates the employee because he or she filed a complaint or acted as a witness that testified in any of the complaint procedures. The level of additional indemnity is set at six months of pay.

Chapter V:
Concluding remarks

Belgian labour and employment law has undergone a number of changes. The number of legislative acts (in the broadest sense) that have been passed has not been reduced. On the contrary, it seems that the number of Parliamentary Acts and Royal Decrees regulating various aspects of individual and collective labour relations has increased.

This does not mean, however, that other sources of obligations in the labour and employment field have disappeared. Actual working conditions are often – as they have always been – determined not by the legislation, but by the social partners themselves. Collective bargaining takes place at the various levels of industrial relations in Belgium.

The national inter-industry-wide level bargaining takes place in the National Labour Council, also referred to as the Social Parliament of Belgium. The collective bargaining agreements concluded at that level are most often rendered generally binding by Royal Decree, which means that these collective bargaining agreements are applicable to all employees in the private sector. Given the 1968 legislation that governs collective bargaining agreements, public sector employees are excluded from the scope of the national inter-industry-wide collective bargaining agreements.

As a consequence, the implementation of European directives through national inter-industry-wide collective bargaining agreements has an inherent shortcoming. The directives that have been implemented in this way do not cover the public sector as defined by Belgian law. However, it is certainly true that some enterprises fall within the definition of public sector as operated in Belgium, but are at the same time engaged in economic activities as interpreted by the European Court of Justice. These kinds of enterprises are not excluded from the scope of the European directives and the implementing legislation should therefore cover them. This means that the national inter-industry-wide collective bargaining agreements need to be supplemented by additional legislative acts, which is not always the case.

For certain issues, the collaboration between the National Labour Council and the Belgian legislator runs very smoothly.

If the provisions of a Belgian Parliamentary Act need to be modified (e.g. With respect to the competence of the Belgian labour courts for employment-related matters), a national collective bargaining agreement will be passed to implement a European directive and the legislator will take simultaneous action. A good example of this is the implementation of the EU Directive dealing with European works councils. In order to make Belgian courts competent to deal with issues involving European works councils, the Code of Civil Procedure needed to be modified. The same was also true for legislation dealing with confidential information and legislation dealing with the protection of employee representatives. Legislative Acts were passed in this respect, albeit a bit late. A national inter-industry-wide collective bargaining agreement was passed in order to implement the body of the European Works Council Directive. The extension to the public sector (as far it was engaged in economic activities), however, did not take place.

Belgium has a long tradition of implementing legislation through inter-industry-wide collective bargaining agreements, even before this was explicitly foreseen at the European level. There are no indications of any shift in this practice.

Furthermore, the National Labour Council is always asked for advice before labour legislation is passed, so that the Minister and the Parliament are always informed of the Council's opinion. Clearly, the Parliament and the Minister are not bound by the recommendations of the Council, but these carry considerable weight in parliamentary discussions.

The involvement of the National Labour Council in legislative work (both by granting advice and by passing collective bargaining agreements) has proven effective over the years. Given the fact that the social partners in the National Labour Council represent a large section of employees in Belgium, their active involvement has brought and continues to bring added-value to the discussion.

The issue of rendering collective bargaining agreements that deal with employment issues and with professional training and education generally binding by Decree of the Flemish Community has stirred up a new debate. It remains to be seen how the Council of State will deal with the issue. It seems possible that they will reject the claim for the annulment introduced by the Prime Minister.

In addition to the 'legislation' that is produced by the National Labour Council (and rendered generally binding through a formal government intervention), the number of legislative acts (Parliamentary Acts) and government acts (Royal or Ministerial Decrees) has increased over the years. Legislative intervention remains high on the agenda, except in the area of collective industrial conflicts. This area remains highly unregulated. Even though collective bargaining agreements contain provisions that deal with the peace obligations of the parties and with the procedures to be respected in case of collective conflict, these provisions are not always applied in practice. Most often the parties invoke a reason (changed circumstances) not to live up to these obligations. The interpretation by the trade unions of their right to strike is very extensive and includes actions which clearly violate other parties' rights, such as the constitutional right of workers to prefer working over a strike and the property rights of employers to their premises, machinery and goods. In the absence of enforceable legal procedures guaranteeing them these rights, there has been an increase in litigation before civil courts that are not competent to deal with individual labour and employment law conflicts; as these belong to the sole competence of the labour courts.

Such civil courts and their presidents are not entirely familiar with labour and employment law, but are willing to enforce the rights of the non-striking workers and of the companies involved. Their intervention is, from a legal point of view, entirely justified, however upsetting it may be to the social partners. When rights are granted, such as the right to strike, it is clear that they can be abused and that these abuses must be sanctioned. Furthermore, the injunctions obtained from the presidents of the labour courts do not prohibit strikes at all. They only indicate that goods cannot be obstructed or that employees who want to work should not be prevented from entering their workplace by the striking workers. While one may question why the police does not just intervene in these situations (there seems to be some form of instruction from the Ministry not to intervene), it is certain that the injunctions do nothing more than confirm the existing rights of the third parties that do not participate in the strike. In order to make the injunctions more effective, the judge declares that a violation will be punished with a monetary sanction or fine.

The Belgian industrial relations landscape has seen an increasing number of such injunctions over the years, especially since the beginning of the 1990s. These injunctions are not likely to disappear unless a Parliamentary Act prohibits unilateral actions with the civil courts. An alternative would be the regulation of strikes. However, given the involvement of the social partners in the National Labour Council and their close ties with the different political parties this is not likely to happen. The trade unions would certainly consider any regulation of strikes an infringement of their rights and would thus lobby against it.

It has already been stated that there is an increasing number of acts regulating labour and employment matters, making it extremely difficult for employers to know all of their obligations. Throughout the 1990s, a large amount of legislation (sensu latu) was directly inspired or required by the obligation to implement European directives. Most directives are implemented very faithfully and often the European texts are reproduced at the national level. References to the European directives that are implemented by the national legislation are now included in the text of the legislative acts.

With respect to the content of the legislative action and the changes that occurred in the 1990s, it must be stressed that the concept of 'subordination' that is the cornerstone for the application of Belgian labour and employment law remains a focal point of discussion. However, this is not entirely new. Over the decades, the concept has led to an overwhelming number of cases appearing before the Belgian labour courts. It is indicative that courts increasingly look at the external circumstances in which performances are delivered as opposed to the key message of subordination, namely that one receives instructions from the employer and works under his or her supervision and control. Lower-level courts tend to take into account factual indicia that refer to the economic dependence of the worker towards the company he or she is performing for, rather than the effective or potential authority of the employer. In the battle against the 'fake' self-employed, the organisation that represents small businesses came up with a mathematical formula that reflects a tendency to take into account criteria that refer to the economic dependence of the workers. The formula is, however, in conflict with the case law of the Belgian Supreme Court, which has always held that economic dependence is not a sign of subordinate employment status. It is most likely in reaction to the publication of the formula and its use by some lower-level labour courts that the Supreme Court delivered some very important and clear decisions. These decisions implicitly rejected the formula by indicating that a large number of the factors taken into account should not be seen as indicia for a subordinate employment status.

While the discussion on the criteria to distinguish subordinate employees from self-employed workers is not new, and has been going on for decades (even before the 1990s), the debate has clearly intensified. The attempts by both workers and employees to avoid paying the high social security contributions levied on subordinate employment are certainly factors that have contributed to the intensification of the debate. While there has been much talk about reducing the cost of labour in Belgium, no real action has been taken.

The Minister of Labour (before the last elections in May 2003) came up with a legislative proposal that would basically convert the formula that was developed into law. Once a majority of the factual indicia (that conflict with the case law of the Supreme Court) are satisfied, it is presumed that an employment contract exists. If the text becomes a law, it will be very hard to rebut the presumption in practice. The legislative proposal starts from the erroneous idea that all workers should be subordinate employees, completely covered by all protective provisions of Belgian labour and employment law, including all collective bargaining agreements. It seems to be inspired by an underlying assumption that people cannot make their own decisions about their potential self-employed worker status and that they need to be protected against themselves, either by legislative acts or by collective bargaining agreements that are concluded above their heads. The freedom of contract has largely disappeared.

An area in which more leeway was created for companies over the last ten years deals with triangular employment relationships. Temporary work through temporary employment agencies has been a fact of life in Belgium even before the beginning of the 1990s. It is reported that quite a few workers actually make a deliberate choice to work as temporary workers and are thus not 'forced' into this system. At least 8% of all temporary workers consider temporary work an additional source of income. Furthermore, temporary work has also been an important tool to obtain more permanent employment within a company. Figures report that at least 10% of workers are recruited via temporary work and 26% of all workers once worked (at least one day) as a temporary worker. The latter number is increasing, given the constant growth of the temporary sector in Belgium over the last decade. Apart from a recruitment tool, temporary work grants the employers a flexible way of coping with an increased workload. The legislative framework, combined with the collective bargaining agreements specifically for the sector of temporary work, provide sufficient breathing room for the temporary employment agencies and companies and a sufficient degree of protection for the temporary workers. The system has been in place for a long time, but was completed and improved over the years.

One remaining issue is the idea that temporary employment agencies cannot conclude employment contracts for an indefinite period of time with the temporary workers, even though some of the agencies are willing to do so, even providing the pay of the workers concerned for the period in which they are not employed by a user company.

In this respect, temporary work would conceptually come very close to putting workers at the disposal of a user company. While the applicable legislative act that emerged in 1987 foresaw a number of articles dealing with the issue, the conditions that were imposed were so stringent that it was almost impossible to put a worker at the disposal of a user company in practice. A modification of the Act in the late 1990s made it even more difficult. A very recent modification of the Act, however small the amendments to the legislative act actually were, only left the system intact in principle. The current Act now allows for the leasing out of personnel if decent service agreements are concluded between the actual employer of the worker involved and the 'user' company. The legislative Act still contains a general prohibition of this kind of activity in principle. It would have been much clearer and better to actually bring the Act in to line with company practices, whereby workers are put at the disposal of other companies to work in the framework of service agreements between the companies. However, any further modification of the 1987 Act in this direction is unlikely, as it would be too politically sensitive. Temporary work and the leasing of employees in the framework of service agreements grants employers the ability to flexibly react to changes in the market conditions. Fixed-term employment contracts can serve a similar purpose. Belgian legislation still considers that the employee should be primarily employed with an employment contract for an indefinite duration, since this presumably grants the worker a higher degree of employment security. The basic 1978 Act on Employment Contracts therefore installed a presumption that successive employment contracts are to be considered an indefinite employment contract unless the employer had valid reasons to conclude successive contracts. The rebuttal of the presumption is not easy to carry. In the early 1990s, a temporary exception was introduced allowing basically successive employment contracts for a fixed-term (of up to two or three years in total). The temporary exception was later made permanent.

The distrust of fixed-term employment contracts comes from the idea that the fixed-term contracts do not grant the employees concerned a sufficient degree of employment security compared to permanent employment contracts. This may be true for white-collar workers that enjoy a large degree of employment security based on legislation. In particular, white-collar workers that earn an annual income of around EUR 26,000 benefit from extremely favourable terms of notice that represent a very high cost to an employer that would like to downsize or terminate an employment relationship because the employee is incompetent. Courts have been granting the high indemnities and there is no real indication that they reduced their awards in the 1990s. Since 1994, the Act on Employment Contracts foresees a limited possibility for white-collar workers earning around EUR 52,000 annually to come to an agreement concerning the term of notice to be respected by the employer in case of termination. The contractual freedom of the individual is recognised again, be it still within the limits of a mandatory framework set by the law.

In this respect, attention must also be drawn to the fact that there is an enormous distinction between blue- and white-collar workers with respect to terms of notice and employment security. While there has been much discussion on the fact that the distinction is no longer warranted in the course of the last ten years, not much has been done in practice. The social partners stated they would tackle the problems, but little has been done since this promise was made.

With the encouragement of the EU and as a reaction to a specific Supreme Court case, a new employment contract was created, namely the employment contract for the teleworker, which could cover any form of teleworking and paid attention to the specifics of working at home. This kind of contract may not be used that much yet, but certainly has a lease on the future.

In the same manner as the employment contract for home work was established because of the need to accommodate home and teleworking practices and recognise its specificities, the issue of data protection was also regulated. Besides the general law on data protection that was implemented and amended to correspond fully to the EU Directive, the social partners also tackled the issue of Internet and e-mail use. A national inter-industry-wide collective bargaining agreement was concluded to provide the employer with some possibilities for controlling Internet and e-mail if these facilities are granted to the employees of the company. The employee representative bodies at company-level have an important role to play in this. The interests of all involved are balanced. Furthermore, a legislative act was passed to regulate the new phenomenon of genetic testing of employees, restricting the employer's ability to ask for medical tests unless these are job-related. Belgian legislation *sensu latu* has thus reacted swiftly and in a balanced way to a number of issues posed by recent developments.

Another recent development is the issue of outsourcing. In this field, the EU Directive on the Transfer of Undertakings has been faithfully implemented and applied in Belgium. There is no indication whatsoever that Belgian courts would be more restrictive in their interpretation than the European Court of Justice. The issue of the application of the Directive is time and again a hot issue for debate when dealing with the practical aspects of mergers and acquisitions. The stringent nature of the principles contained in the Directive often make actual integration of the various companies or parts of companies involved quite difficult. However, Belgian law is at least as strict as the Directive. Practical problems with outsourcing also occur in the area of putting workers at the disposal of other companies. This, however, is a very common practice in outsourcing deals. The modifications that have been brought to the legislation (see supra, re-leasing of personnel) have made this practice legal in line with real business needs. Collective bargaining agreements have also tried to cope with the problems that emerged in outsourcing deals where the Directive would not apply by trying to extend the scope of the Directive partially or completely. These agreements have tried to foresee similar rules as those put forward by the Directive.

Other forms of company restructuring, such as collective dismissal and company closures, have drawn increased attention during a number of highly publicised individual company reorganisations. The legislation of company closures and collective dismissal was modified and sanctions in case of violation of the information and consultation duties were stiffened. The aim was to give the workers and their representatives the possibility to influence decision-making by suggesting alternatives to the intended measures. It is clear that the modification had the effect of making employers much more aware of their obligations and much more careful in the ways they communicate with their personnel and the outside world. This is an advantage in itself. However, it is doubtful that the impact on the actual decision-making process has been as high as expected. Hence the continuing frustration of the employee representatives with these processes. Even though European initiatives have been taken to strengthen the pro-active forms of consultation of employee representatives, the question should be asked as to whether this is truly a realistic way of approaching company restructuring.

The harmonisation of working life and family life has been high on the agenda, especially since the second half of the 1990s. The numerous forms of career leave that were introduced caused the system to become very complicated. A new and more transparent system has since been set up which allows for all kinds of justified and unjustified leave. While previously there were obligations on the employer to replace the employee on leave, this is no longer true. This means that an additional burden on the employer has been removed. On the other hand, the various leaves quite often pose an organisational problem for the employer. Flexible working time regimes were primarily introduced to grant employers the ability to make more optimal use of the available working time and cope with peaks and troughs in production. The rights of the employees are granted through the mandatory participation of employee representatives to install flexible working time regimes.

In the same line of thought with respect to the harmonisation of working life and family life, the government has tried to reduce working time even below the levels that are set in sector-level collective bargaining agreements. It therefore gives incentives in the form of a reduction in social security contributions that can vary according to the number of hours of working time reduction below 38 hours a week. Furthermore, the introduction of a four-day working week can lead to a reduction in social security contributions. The legal acts do not oblige the employer to hire additional personnel, although this was certainly one of the aims of the legislative acts.

Employees that are on career leave or that have filed a request to go on leave are protected against dismissal. This is just one additional protection against dismissal granted by Belgian employment law. It is part of a long list of specific protections that have been established over the last couple of years and in which the government uses the technique of the reversal of the burden of proof. If an employee is dismissed during the protected period, the employer must reverse the presumption and prove that the particular dismissal has occurred for reasons other than the ones for which the protection was granted . In practice, this burden of proof is quite heavy. However, it is a technique that is increasingly used by the government and the legislator, forcing employers into finally putting all appraisals and everything that happens with respect to an employee down on paper or to send registered letters warning employees in order to show the court his or her good faith.

The same techniques are also to be found in the various acts that deal with employment discrimination through which the Belgian legislator implemented the European Directives. The reversal of the burden of proof comes into play if the employee comes forward with facts that prove that discrimination may be involved in decision-making. The legislator has indicated that statistical evidence and trial cases can be used in order to prove discrimination. A Royal Decree is still required in order to make this operative.

The text of the general 2003 Discrimination Act is a full implementation of the Directive. However, the Act goes a lot further than the Framework Directive does, since it not only directs itself at the forms of discrimination prohibited by the Directive but includes a long list of additional criteria that can no longer be part of the employment decision-making process. While the legislative Act may be based on great principles with respect to non-discrimination and equal treatment, the inclusion of many of the factors the Act mentions will lead to impossible situations. Some of the grounds that are mentioned leave even employment specialists clueless. In an employment relationship, what does it mean to discriminate on the basis of birth, fortune, or ascendance? It is clear that this Act is not well thought through and has not at all taken into consideration the situation of employers who have to put the Act in practice. Furthermore, the Minister of Employment disregarded the advice of the National Labour Council in order to explicitly foresee the exceptions to the principle of non-discrimination the EU Framework Directive allowed Member States to legislate on. The Act indicates that only bona fide occupational qualifications can justify alleged discrimination, both direct and indirect. If judges decide to apply the Act according to its strict wording, no human resources policy would be acceptable any longer. The Minister has indicated that exceptions to the Directive could still be invoked in Belgium. However, the text of the Act seems to indicate the contrary.

Since the second half of the 1990s, the legislator has introduced various instances in which an employer is confronted with a reversal of the burden of proof. Furthermore, the concept of cease and desist orders was also introduced. Cease and desist orders were previously primarily known in commercial law and were requested, for example, in files in which there was a violation by one party of commercial trade secrets. This technique is now generally introduced in the area of employment discrimination. While practical experience does not exist, it is presumed that this legislation will introduce more procedural burdens on employers. It is clear from all of this that the employment relationship is certainly not moving away from deregulation; instead it is going in the direction of increased government intervention and formalism.

Belgium has proven faithful to European legislative acts (although their implementation has not always been timely). It has also followed up on European calls for initiatives to include risk groups by taking measures to reduce the costs of employing workers that belong to the group of those at risk from exclusion. Furthermore, various actions of a more qualitative nature have been undertaken in order to better prepare those looking for employment. Incentives to engage in training and lifelong learning have been established. It is not clear to what extent these kinds of government intervention have led to a reduction of unemployment. It seems that the government was, at least over the past years, riding on the wave of the economic boom. When economic times become more difficult again, it may be harder to provide actual evidence that the government measures have led to any increase in jobs.

In this respect, it is important to bear in mind that government – except for the public service – does not actually create any jobs. The whole mechanism of European coordination of employment policies and reactivation of the unemployed may be a fantastic effort to make people aware of the issues we are currently facing. However, a direct creation of jobs will not be the result. Only companies create jobs and they need the appropriate environment to do so. This means an environment free from over-regulation and intervention. It should be clear from the above that we are not yet there.

In his declaration to form a new government on 3 June 2003, the Prime Minister declared his intention to intensify the policies of activation of the unemployed. By reducing contributions and costs for employment by EUR 1 500 million, the government hopes to create 210 000 jobs for low-skilled workers (including youngsters), part-timers, older workers, workers in the care sector and knowledge workers. Social security contributions for highly-skilled and creative workers may be capped.

The Prime Minister also declared that the equal treatment of blue- and white-collar workers would be introduced by legislation and within a short time frame to be discussed with the social partners. The new government also seems to want to modify the system of career interruptions to allow workers to step into systems of 'time-saving' that would permit a worker to convert part of his wages into days off or save days from unused holidays in order to use this saved time for a career interruption. This would then allow a more flexible career in which periods of more intense work could be combined with time off. It is presently unclear how the existing system of career interruption would be combined with the new proposal. The unemployed would get a better system of follow-up in their search for employment, laws on opening hours for shops would be further liberalised, etc.

The question of whether these principles can be actually introduced should also be asked, given the fact that quite a number of these issues have been debated over the last decade without the desired results having been obtained.

THE EVOLUTION OF LABOUR LAW
IN DENMARK, FINLAND
AND SWEDEN

1992-2003

Niklas Bruun & Jonas Malmberg

Table of contents

Table of contents

Executive summary

I. Denmark

The industrial relations regime in Denmark is commonly referred to as 'the Danish model'. A distinctive feature of this model is that there is a high trust tripartite cooperation between trade unions, employers' organisations and the government. There has been a long-standing consensus that the state shall not interfere in regulation as regards wages and other employment conditions, without a joint request from the social partners. And the social partners have generally preferred regulation through collective agreements. Thus, legislation has traditionally played a minor role in the field of labour law. Another feature of the Danish model is that the social partners play a predominant role in dispute settlement through industrial bodies, such as the Labour Court and industrial arbitration tribunals.

The predominant issue in the evolution of labour law in Denmark since 1992 has been how to integrate EC labour law into the Danish model. As for implementing EC directives, the procedure used in practice is to transpose the directive into national law. After that the legislator will adopt the statutes necessary to guarantee that every employee is ensured the rights of the directives. The opinion that it is possible to implement an EC directive only through traditional collective agreements seems to have been abandoned. Several different techniques have been used when drafting the statutes. The act transposing the directive is usually semi-mandatory, i.e. The statutes apply only in workplaces not covered by collective agreements. This kind of legislation has, for instance, been used in relation to the Working Time Directive and the Fixed-Term Work Directive. While implementing the Part-Time Directive, the major Danish collective agreements on its implementation were given an *erga omnes* effect through legislation. Here too, the individual contract was given preference to the clauses in the collective agreements. This change occurred after the shift in political power from the Social Democrats to the Conservative/Liberal coalition in 2001. The legislation issued by the new government led to a complaint to the International Labour Organisation (ILO). The ILO held it not to be consistent with the basic conventions on free collective bargaining.

On the whole, however, the procedure used in transposing EC directives shows that tripartite cooperation in the field of labour law still is a reality in Denmark. The state still accepts the idea that regulation of employment conditions is mainly an issue for the social partners. From this aspect the Danish model has survived.

On the other hand, it must be stressed that the number of labour law statutes has increased dramatically during the last decade. Although there are some examples of purely national legislation adopted during the last decade, the bulk of new legislation has been introduced in order to transpose EC directives. Furthermore, individual human rights have become more important. In 1997, the European Convention on Human Rights was incorporated into Danish law. The Convention has had a significant impact on the labour law debate (e.g. The questions on negative freedom of association and *locus standi* for individual employees).

New forms of employment (such as agency work and fixed-term work) have not been a major issue in Denmark.

II. Finland

The Finnish development of labour law since the early 1990s can be characterised by consensus and tripartism. The national income policy that coordinates collective bargaining and Finnish membership of the European Union are factors that have particularly marked the evolution of labour law. Although EC law set the agenda for labour law to a large extent, an extensive modernisation of national labour law has taken place in parallel.

During the last ten years a remarkable renewal of Finnish labour law legislation has occurred. The process has been driven especially by the central employers' organisations TT and the central trade union SAK. The Employment Contracts Act, the Act on Working Time, legislation on health and safety, protection of young employees, personal integrity in the working place and legislation on so-called alteration leave are only some examples of an impressive list of legislative achievements during this period. The content of this legislation can be described in a few catchwords: simplification, modernisation and continuity.

From the perspective of substance, the main trends of the evolution can be summarised in four points:

• Individual constitutional and human rights have clearly gained importance in Finnish labour law.

• Also on a more general level individual labour law and the rights and duties of the individual worker have gained importance.

• The effort to combine flexibility for employers with security for workers has been strongly felt in the development of different legal instruments. The high level of unemployment has been an important factor that has been taken into account in the legislative process.

• The collective bargaining system is still an important and central regulator of the terms and conditions on the Finnish labour market. The bargaining system has to a large extent, however, been decentralised from within.

III. Sweden

The development of labour law in Sweden has since the 1990s evolved around three different – but partly interrelated – themes: the discussion on flexibility, the Europeanisation of labour law and importance of equal treatment and other individual human rights.

The starting point in the debate on the evolution of labour law has usually been the economic crises of the early 1990s. The argument has been that the labour law must provide more room for flexibility in order to promote economic growth and rise in employment. The discussion has often focused on the Employment Protection Act. The private employers' confederation, with support of among others the Conservative Party, has argued for a far-reaching deregulation, while the trade unions, mostly backed by the Labour Party, have defended the existing legal regulation. The debate has been rather hostile and the social parties have not been able to influence the legislator. The debate has resulted in some changes of the regulations of the Employment Protection Act regarding redundancies and fixed-term work. Most of the changes were later repealed and the law

was restored to its former condition. The changes that have survived concern minor issues. Despite the extensive debate the legislative changes that have actually taken place have been rather few. On the other hand the substance of collective agreements concluded during the same period have undergone a dramatic decentralisation, in moving from detailed regulation to framework agreements, leaving generous leeway for negotiations at company level.

Sweden became a member of the EU in 1995. This event is certainly the most important factor in explaining the development of Swedish labour law during the last decade. A series of new acts have been adopted in order to transpose EC directives. It is no exaggeration to say that most of the legislation adopted during the period is a response to the demands of the Community legal acts.

The discrimination legislation constitutes an area where the changes that have taken place are most significant. A new Equal Treatment Act was adopted in 1991 and this Act has been strengthened several times. In 1999 Acts concerning discrimination on the grounds of ethnical origin, sexual orientation and disability were adopted. This development is partly due to the membership of the Community, partly a response to domestic political demands.

Alongside the equal treatment issues, individual human rights issues have gained importance. In 1994 the European Convention on Human Rights was incorporated into Swedish law. The Convention has had a significant impact on the labour law debate (e.g. The questions on negative freedom of association and privacy for employees).

Chapter I:
Denmark

1. Introduction

1.1. The Danish model

The Danish labour market, more so than the labour markets of other EU Member States, is regulated by collective agreements between the social partners. By international standards, employment legislation is relatively restricted. Apart from the Annual Holidays Act (*Ferieloven*) and the White-Collar Workers Act (*Funktionærloven*), the majority of statutes governing the relationship between employers and employees are a consequence of Danish membership of the EU.

In Denmark, trade unions, employers' associations and the government cooperate closely on labour market issues. One aspect of this tripartite relationship is the shared understanding that the government should only intervene with legislation at the joint request of the social partners. The fact that there are current exceptions to this rule does not alter the overall picture.

The social partners share a preference for regulating relations between employers and employees by collective agreement rather than legislation. One advantage of agreements is that they can be adjusted better and more quickly to the specific needs of different sectors and companies. Another is that the social partners are more likely to accept and abide by rules which they themselves have taken part in drawing up. However, the social partners have not always shared this preference for collective agreements. During the late 1980s and early 1990s, the trade union movement proposed more extensive legislation, particularly in the area of individual employment rights.

The tripartite approach is an integral part of labour market policy. The social partners take part in the drafting of regulations even on issues which are not subject to collective agreements, but which instead are regulated by law, such as the work environment, job placement services or unemployment insurance schemes. The social partners are regularly consulted on draft labour market legislation.

1.2. The social partners

By international standards, trade union membership is remarkably high in Denmark. More than 85% of workers indicate professional affiliation. The majority of trade unions are members of one of the three central organisations: the Danish Confederation of Trade Unions (*Landsorganisationen i Danmark* – LO), the Salaried Employees' and Civil Servants' Confederation *Funktionærenes og Tjenestemændenes Fællesråd* – FTF) and the Danish Confederation of Professional Associations (*Akademikernes Centralorganisation* – AC). LO is the dominant central organisation, representing not only workers, but also some groups which in other countries would belong to organisations representing white-collar workers. Approximately 70% of all trade union members belong to unions that are affiliated to LO (1995). FTF represents white-collar workers and civil servants and AC represents graduate professionals.

Traditionally, trade unions in Denmark have been organised along occupational lines to a greater extent than in the other Nordic countries. During the last decade, however, a shift has taken place and employees are increasingly organised according to sector or industry. Only a few trade unions are not members of the large central organisations. Trade unions are not differentiated by religious or political beliefs. It is relatively uncommon for trade unions to be competing for the same members.

The main central organisation on the employers' side is the Danish Employers' Confederation (*Dansk Arbejdgiverforening* – DA). DA covers employers in the private sector from industry, crafts, trade and services. In addition to DA, there are separate employers' organisations in specific sectors, such as in agriculture (SALA) or the financial sector.

1.3. Decentralised regulation through collective agreements

It is estimated that almost 80% of workers are covered by collective agreements. However, coverage varies between sectors. All public sector workers are covered by collective agreements.

The last decades have witnessed a significant decentralisation of collective bargaining. From the 1950s to the late 1970s, LO and DA played a key role in wage setting. Since the 1980s, by contrast, the main wage agreements have been concluded at sectoral level. For a long time, however, wage agreements at sectoral level were closely coordinated, with wage agreements in certain sectors, most notably the metal industry, setting the trend. This development is best described as a decentralisation rather than the outcome of the process. At the same time, the content of sectoral agreements has changed. Collective agreements based on the standard-wage system (*normalløn*), whereby the wage levels for different occupations are set at federal level without the possibility of local adjustment, have increasingly been replaced with a wage system in which actual wages are set at local level, and often for each employee individually.

1.4. The private law nature of labour law and labour law in the public sector

In Denmark, with the exception of work environment law, labour law is considered private rather than public law.

With regard to the public sector, in Denmark a distinction is made between 'crown servants' (*tjenestemandsanstatte*) and other public employees (*offentligt ansatte* or *overenskomstansatte*). 'Crown servants' is a separate category of employees governed by separate legislation (mainly the Crown Servants Act – *tjenestemandsloven*). Crown servants may not, for example, engage in strike actions. All other public employees are, in principle, subject to the general employment and work environment legislation. However, public employers are expected generally to observe the principles of administrative law in relation to their employees.

1.5. Dispute resolution in legal disputes

Danish rules on the handling of legal disputes in the field of employment law are complex. Employment law disputes may be handled by a variety of bodies. Disputes relating to collective agreements are handled within the so-called 'industrial system' (*fagretlige system*), that is, either by the Labour Court or by special industrial arbitration tribunals (*faglig voldgift*). Decisions by the Labour Court and decisions by the arbitration tribunals are final and may not be appealed. By contrast, the ordinary courts handle disputes relating to legislation or individual contracts of employment. Other bodies exist for the purpose of deciding specific issues.

The industrial system acquired its general structure as far back as the first decades of the twentieth century, and in several respects its rules of procedure differ from those applicable before the ordinary courts. The social partner organisations play a central role in the industrial system. First, the signatory parties to a collective agreement have the right of interpretation. If the parties agree on an interpretation, that interpretation subsequently applies. The members of the social partner organisations, as well as employers who are party to a local collective agreement, become bound by the interpretation. Only the parties to a collective agreement may decide to bring disputes before the Labour Court or the industrial arbitration tribunals. An organisation may enter pleas both on its own behalf and on behalf of its members. However, individual employers (which are bound by a collective agreement by virtue of their membership of an employers' association) and individual employees do not have the right to plead within the industrial system.

For a long time it remained unclear whether a member of a trade union could pursue a claim on the basis of a collective agreement. A 1997 change in the law made it clear that individual trade union members may pursue a claim if the trade union refrains from getting involved in the dispute. In that case, the claim will be pursued before the normal courts. The change in the law was claimed to be necessary in order to comply with Article 6 of the European Convention on Human Rights. Already in 1994, a judgement from the Danish Supreme Court, referring to the European Convention, had established that such a subsidiary right existed.

1.6. Economic and demographic changes

Danish industry has long been characterised by a relatively large number of small and medium-sized enterprises. In the 1990s, a significant structural change took place, increasing the proportion of large firms.

Ever since the 1973 oil shock, Denmark has had varying levels of unemployment. Unemployment rose significantly during the 1990s, but has since fallen. In 2002, unemployment was at its lowest level in 25 years. In the EU, Denmark has one of the lowest unemployment rates and one of the highest rates of labour force participation. Nevertheless, significant groups of people of working age remain outside the labour market. In the years to come, demographic evolutions will lead to a reduction of the labour force. According to estimates from the Ministry of Finance, provided that the rate of labour market participation remains unchanged, the labour force will decrease by a total of 66 000 persons in the period 2000-2010. It is therefore one of the Danish government's top political priorities to increase the number of people in work.

1.7. Migration

It is estimated that the number of immigrants and their descendants aged 16-66 is approximately 265 000 in Denmark. Of these, roughly one-third originate from the EU, the Nordic countries and North America, while two-thirds originate from other countries. At an estimated 13%, unemployment is higher among immigrants.

One way of increasing labour market participation among immigrants has been specifically to try to increase the recruitment of immigrants to the public sector. Since 1998, the proportion of immigrants in public employment has risen from 1.6% to 2.0% (year 2000).

In 2000, the government launched a programme aimed at integrating immigrants through more intense and effective use of three tools: more traineeships for immigrants, support to enter the labour market, and the teaching of Danish within companies. The government's programme has been controversial.

The social partners have also actively taken part in various local and regional integration initiatives, including the framework of the joint LO and DA multi-annual initiative for improving integration in the future. Separate agreements have also been concluded, such as that between LO and SALA.

1.8. Mediation and resolution of interest disputes

The industrial arbitration tribunal was established for the purpose of preventing unnecessary labour market disputes.[1] The institution is to contribute to resolving disputes between employers and employees. The institution is not empowered to rule on the substance of collective agreements through, for example, binding arbitration. However, the institution can suspend an announced strike action for two weeks.

In Denmark, it is not unusual for the parliament (*Folketinget*) to intervene with legislation to settle an ongoing labour dispute. This would typically take the form of an act of parliament providing that a collective agreement with certain content shall apply between the parties. Such interventions by the parliament were commonplace in the 1970s and 1980s. During the 1990s, the parliament seemed more hesitant to intervene in ongoing disputes. Such interventions did, however, take place, *inter alia* during two strikes by nurses (1995 and 1999) and during the major industrial dispute between

LO and DA in 1998. The ILO's Committee on Freedom of Association has regarded some of these interventions as a breach of ILO Conventions No 87 on freedom of association and No 98 on the right to collective bargaining.

1.9. Constitutional reforms

The Danish constitution has traditionally had a remarkably small impact on labour law. It is highly unusual for labour market legislation to be challenged as unconstitutional or for the constitution to be invoked for the purpose of interpreting labour market legislation.

No constitutional reforms of relevance to labour law have been carried out during the period under consideration.

However, the European Convention on Human Rights has been incorporated into Danish law.[2] The Convention has had a significant impact on the labour law debate (e.g. The question of the negative right of association).

1.10. Government

In 1992, a coalition government composed of the Social Democratic Party (*Socialdemokratiet*) and the Social-Liberal Party (*Det Radikale Venstre*) came to power. It was replaced in November 2001 by a coalition of the Liberal Party (*Venstre*) and the Conservative Party (*Det Konservative Folkeparti*).

2. From employment protection to employability

2.1. Employment protection

Denmark has no general legislation on employment protection. The traditional view was that the parties were able to terminate the employment relationship subject only to a duty to observe a certain period of notice. Over time, however, a considerable number of restrictions on the employer's ability to terminate employment have been introduced. Rules on termination of employment are contained in laws governing specific groups of employees (e.g. private employees, crown servants) or specific grounds for termination (e.g. right of association), as well as in collective agreements and individual contracts of employment.

---

1   The institution is governed by the Arbitration Act.

2   Act No 183 of 12 March 1997 incorporating the European Convention on Human Rights.

2.1.1. Collective redundancies

In 1992, a directive amending the Collective Redundancies Directive was adopted.[3] For the purpose of implementing this Directive, a specific law on collective redundancies was introduced in Denmark: Act No 441 of 1 June 1994 on notification, etc. In connection with large-scale redundancies.[4] On the same occasion, previous provisions on collective redundancies contained in the Unemployment Insurance Act were repealed.

2.1.2. Information on employment conditions

In 1993, the Proof of Employment Act (*Ansættelsesbevisloven*) was introduced.[5] The Act is based on the Written Statement Directive[6] and aims to provide employees with improved protection against possible infringements of their rights and to create greater transparency on the labour market. Following the judgement of the European Court of Justice in *Lange*,[7] the law was amended in 2002 so as to make it clear that the employer's duty to inform extends to all essential elements of the employment relationship and is not restricted to those specifically mentioned in the law.

2.1.3. Transfers of undertakings

In 2001, following the amendment of the Transfers of Undertakings Directive[8] a number of minor adjustments were made to the Danish Transfers of Undertakings Act.[9] This included specifying that the law applies to public bodies exercising an economic activity. An administrative reorganisation of public administrative bodies or a transfer of administrative functions between such bodies is not to be considered a transfer. It was further specified at what moment the rights and obligations of employees affected by the transfer would come into play.

2.1.4. Information related to employees' health

In 1996, a law was adopted on employers' handling of information related to employees' health.[10] The law covers the use of health-related information in the labour market and aims to ensure that such information is not used to restrict the employee's ability to obtain or keep a job. As a general rule, in connection with or as part of recruitment, an employer may request information related to the employee's health for the sole purpose of establishing whether the employee suffers from or has suffered from an illness which may significantly affect his ability to perform the work in question. In principle, the law prohibits the employer from gathering or using health-related information concerning the risk of the employee developing an illness. In connection with the recruitment or at the request of the employer, the employee must indicate whether he suffers from or has the symptoms of an illness which may significantly affect his ability to perform the work in question. Prior to any medical examination, the person carrying out the examination must ensure that the employee has been informed, both in writing and verbally, of *inter alia* the purpose, nature and method of the examination.

2.2. Improving employability

2.2.1. Employment policy

Employment policy is an area subject to rapid and often recurrent amendments to existing legislation. During the period under consideration, a series of reforms have been implemented in this area. A recurring theme in these reforms has been the tightening of the conditions for entitlement to unemployment benefits and a reinforcement of the requirement to be active, for example in vocational training.

When the Social Democratic government came to power in 1992, the official unemployment rate in Denmark exceeded 10%. In 1993, a new law was adopted in the area, the so-called Activation Act (Act on an Active Employment Policy – *aktiveringsloven – lov om aktiv arbejdsmarkedspolitik*). The main objective of the law was to reinforce the activity requirement in employment policy. The law makes it possible to arrange different kinds of rehabilitation, vocational training

3   Council Directive 92/56/EEC of 24 June 1992 amending Directive 75/129/EEC on the approximation of the laws of the Member States relating to collective redundancies. Now Directive 98/59/EC.

4   Lov nr 441 af 1.6.1994 om varsling m.v. I forbindelse med afskedigelser i større omfang.

5   Act No 392 of 22 June 1993 on the employer's obligation to inform employees of the conditions applicable to the employment relationship (*Lov nr 392 af 22. Juni 1993 om arbejdsgiverens pligt til at underrette lønmodtageren om vilkårene for ansættelsesforholdet*).

6   Council Directive 91/533/EEC on an employer's obligation to inform employees of the conditions applicable to the contract or employment relationship.

7   Case C-350/99 *Wolfgang Lange*, ECR 2001 p. I-1061.

8   Council Directive 98/50/EC of 29 June 1998 amending Directive 77/187/EEC on the approximation of the laws of the Member States relating to the safeguarding of employees' rights in the event of transfers of undertakings, businesses or parts of businesses. Now Directive 2001/23/EC.

9   Act No 11 of 21 March 1979 on the safeguarding of employees' rights in the event of transfers of undertakings (*Lov nr 11 af 21.3.79 om lønmodtagernes retsstilling ved virksomhedsoverdragelse*).

10   Act No 256 of 24 April 1996 on the use of health-related information, etc. In the labour market (*Lov nr 256 af 24.4.1996 om brug af helbredsoplysninger m.v. på arbejdsmarkedet*).

and traineeships. This requirement is linked to the rules of the unemployment insurance scheme insofar that unemployed persons who fail to satisfy the activity requirement may be denied benefits. The activity requirement for benefits under the unemployment insurance scheme has been reinforced through successive reforms in 1994, 1996 and 1998. The reinforcement of the activity requirement represents a radical reorientation of Danish employment policy. The purpose of this policy was to reduce unemployment, in particular long-term unemployment, and to prevent new groups of unemployed persons becoming permanently excluded from the labour market. The current centre-liberal government is in the process of reorganising employment measures by integrating activation of unemployed.

In addition, in 1994 so-called social chapters were introduced in collective agreements. Common to these are, *inter alia*, that employees with reduced capacity for work are to be kept in the labour market by virtue of employers creating new jobs adapted to the special needs of the employees. The idea was that these jobs would not replace already existing job openings.

2.2.2. Employers' responsibility for professional training

The question of employers' responsibility for improving the knowledge, skills and qualifications of those in employment gained prominence during the 1990s. This should be seen against the background of a general tendency in the labour market towards flexibility and company restructuring. In the private as well as in the public sector, collective agreements have been concluded containing so-called skills packages. In these agreements, employees agree to contribute to restructuring through continued training while employers undertake to provide for such training. The agreements also provide the employers with an opportunity to place new demands on the employees. The substance of these agreements has developed gradually. By now, they often contain, for example, a requirement for the development of written training plans.

2.2.3. Covenants in restraint of competition

Another issue which affects the worker's employability in practice, is the permissibility of covenants in restraint of competition, i.e. contractual provisions which prohibit the employee from engaging in certain types of business or to take up employment in such types of business. In 1999, the rules in the White-Collar Workers Act (*Funktionærloven*) relating to competition clauses (Section 18) were amended. Such clauses may only be used where the employee holds a position of trust or has agreed with his employers on the rights to exploit an invention made by the employee. It is a further requirement that the crown servant is compensated for the duration of the obligation and that the right to compensation is enshrined in a written contract. The compensation shall be at least 50% of the salary at the time when the employment ceased. The purpose of the amendment was to ensure that competition clauses are formulated in such a way that the employee retains his employment prospects and is able to exploit his training and qualifications.

2.3. Integration of vulnerable groups

2.3.1. Employment policy

It has been a persistent theme in the last ten years' employment policy – under both the Social Democratic government (1992-2001) and the current Conservative/Liberal government – to stress the activation of the unemployed and vulnerable groups, such as the long-term unemployed. This has been pursued partly through financial incentives (e.g. shortening of the period of entitlement to benefit), and partly through increased training and the creation of real jobs.

As indicated above, the current Conservative/Liberal government has stressed the importance of integrating immigrants and refugees by boosting the incentive for these groups to seek work actively. This has, *inter alia*, been done by lowering the benefit levels. In addition, the government is trying to change the prevailing view regarding knowledge of the Danish language. Previously, it was thought that learning the Danish language was a prerequisite for finding work. However, the government is arguing that knowledge of the language is best acquired in a working environment and that Danish should be taught in the workplace and in parallel with normal work.

Efforts are also being made to prevent excessive early departure from the labour market. In this context, the early retirement (so-called *efterløn*) system has been tightened. The early retirement system used to enable those aged 60-66 with long-term membership of an unemployment insurance fund to retire early on relatively favourable terms. The system has now been changed, making it far less advantageous for those aged 60-61 to use the system. This is expected to lead to an increase in the labour force of 10-20 000 people between now and the year 2010.

2.3.2. The requirement for employers to take active measures

Danish legislation in the area of discrimination does not, unlike for example in Sweden, contain any requirements for the employer to promote equality between men and women or to promote equal rights and opportunities regardless of ethnic background. In fact, the legislation rests solely on the prohibition of discrimination. It is thus voluntary for employers to, for example, draw up equality plans.

There are, however, collective agreements within both the private and the public sectors which require the employer to work actively for equality between women and men.

3. Labour law and companies' adaptability

3.1. Fixed-term employment

In contrast to the situation in Finland and Sweden, the proportion of fixed-term employees did not rise significantly during the 1990s. In 1999, the proportion of fixed-term employees was about 10%.

Given the absence of any general legislation on employment protection, there is also no general regulation on fixed-term employment in Denmark. Traditionally, the following has applied. Collective agreements tend to be based on the assumption that the employment contract is of an indefinite duration. This does not prevent the employee and the employer from concluding an employment contract for a fixed period or a specific job (fixed-term employment). Collective agreements have not, traditionally, contained any real restrictions on the employer's ability to recruit for a fixed period or a specific job. The White-Collar Workers Act also assumes that, as a general rule, the contract of employment is of indefinite duration. That law also does not prevent employers and employees from concluding fixed-term contracts. Employment contracts concluded for a fixed period or a specific job come to an end when their term is complete, without any requirement of prior notice. There is thus no requirement to provide any form of justification. However, according to established case law, an employee whose employment is based on successive fixed-term contracts may legitimately expect that, in fact, his employment is permanent and therefore covered by the rules on termination applicable to permanent employees.

In 2003, the Act on Fixed-Term Employment,[11] implemented the Fixed-term Work Directive[12] in Denmark. Prior to that, many sections of the labour market had already reached collective agreements implementing the Directive. In the private sector, an agreement was concluded between LO and DA in August 2002.

The Act was adopted with a view to ensuring that the Fixed-term Work Directive would apply even to employees not covered by the collective agreements implementing the Directive. The law provides that the employment conditions of fixed-term workers may not be less favourable than those of comparable permanent workers except where this can be justified on objective grounds. The renewal of a fixed-term contract must also be justified on objective grounds. Special rules apply to the public research and teaching sector, where fixed-term contracts may be renewed up to two times. The law only applies to employees who are not covered by a collective agreement; thus guaranteeing that the employee, at a minimum, enjoys the rights laid down in the Directive.

At the same time, the White-Collar Workers Act was clarified and amended in several respects. It was made clear that the law applies to fixed-term employees and a provision was added explicitly providing that fixed-term contracts may only be renewed where this is justified on objective grounds.

3.2. Part-time work

For the implementation of the Part-time Work Directive[13] in Denmark, a new combination of legislation and collective agreements was used, which had partially been used for the implementation of the Fixed-term Work Directive. First, collective agreements on the implementation of the Part-time Work Directive were concluded in various sections of the labour market. Such an agreement was concluded between LO and DA. Similar agreements were also concluded in the public sector. Subsequently, the Part-Time Act (*Deltidsloven*) was adopted in 2001.[14] The law extended the main collective agreements on the implementation of the Part-time Work Directive to employees not covered by the agreements. This applies only where the employees in question are not covered by collective agreements offering protection for employees that is at least equivalent to that offered by the Directive. The agreement between LO and DA was extend-

---

11   Lov nr 370 af 28.5 2003 om tidsbegrænset ansættelse.
12   Council Directive 99/70/EC of 28 June 1999 concerning the framework agreement on fixed-term work concluded by ETUC, UNICE and CEEP.
13   Council Directive 97/81/EC concerning the Framework Agreement on part-time work concluded by UNICE, CEEP and ETUC.
14   Act No 443 of 7 June 2001.

ed to employees in the private sector. In the public sector, the most representative collective agreements were extended to the state or local sectors.

Originally, the Part-Time Act contained no rules on the employer's ability to recruit part-time employees or the employee's right to request part-time work. In workplaces covered by collective agreements, the question of the employer's ability to recruit part-time employees was dependent on the substance of the agreement. Approximately 6% of employees were covered by collective agreements which did not allow part-time work.

A change in the law in 2002 enabled employers and employees to agree on part-time work, also where this would go against an applicable collective agreement. The provision was implemented by the Conservative/Liberal government as part of its 'freedom package for the labour market'. The new legislation has been criticised heavily, especially by the trade union movement, given that this is an issue which, according to established Danish practice, is addressed through collective bargaining. The legislation issued by the new government led to a complaint to the ILO. The ILO held it to be inconsistent with the basic conventions on free collective bargaining.

Until 2001, the White-Collar Workers Act would only apply to employees working at least 15 hours per week. The implementation of the Part-time Work Directive raised concerns that this requirement might be contrary to the Directive and, possibly, Article 141 of the Treaty (indirect sex discrimination). The minimum working time requirement was therefore reduced to eight hours per week and thus came to reflect the rule contained in the 1993 Proof of Employment Act.

3.3. Agency work

In 1990, the state monopoly on employment services was abolished (except for nurses). As a result, previous restrictions on employment agencies (vikarbureauer) were also removed. There is no legislation on employment agencies in Denmark. Thus, there is, for example, no explicit ban on charging jobseekers. However, such a ban is included in the code of conduct established by the Danish Association of Employment Agencies.

During recent years, the use of agency workers (vikarer) has increased steadily. In 1992, there were 73 registered employment agencies employing a total of 3 000 people. In 1999, the corresponding figures were 346 agencies employing a total of 35 000 people. Agency work is common within the

health sector. Other large user groups include production, warehouse work and driving, as well as office work.

3.4. Economically dependent employees

There is no uniform definition of the term 'employee' in Denmark. Its meaning varies from law to law. In order to determine whether a person should be considered an employee ('lønmodtagar'), it is therefore necessary to consider the relevant law. The term is, on the whole, imperative. An overall assessment taking into account a wide range of factors is normally used for determining whether a person is an employee. This includes consideration of whether the person performing the work is working under the employer's supervision and instruction and whether he is paid for his work in the form of a wage. Other factors include the form of payment, as well as whether the person performing the work is under a duty to work, the duration of the work, etc. The courts also consider whether the person performing the work is comparable to normal employees in social and financial terms. Additional considerations may apply in respect of individual laws.

A working group under the Ministry of Labour was charged with defining and analysing the expansion of the 'third group', i.e. persons who are neither employees nor typical self-employed persons, but something in between, and who are covered by, or should be covered by, some form of protection under the law with regard to employment and/or social security. The working group concluded that it was difficult to form a clear picture of the expansion and presence of the third group in different sectors given the lack of surveys and analyses. However, the working group did conclude that the category is more prevalent in the service and IT sectors, where it encompasses a significant proportion of employees. The group also exists in the health sector (e.g. specialist doctors performing certain operations in private hospitals), in teaching, in the media (where, traditionally, many people work on a freelance basis), in the insurance industry and in a number of other professions, such as chiropractors, physiotherapists, architects, engineers and artists.

3.5. Teleworking

During the 1990s, teleworking increased sharply in Denmark. Approximately 18% of employees telework. According to a survey carried out by Eurobarometer, the employees largely determine the terms and conditions for telework in Denmark. In other countries, such as the United Kingdom and

Germany, the employer most often determines the terms and conditions for telework.

There is no legislation governing teleworking. Instead, the issue is often regulated by collective agreements. In 2000, for example, a collective agreement on telework for employees in shops and offices was concluded. According to the agreement, telework (*telearbejde*) involves an employee working at home on previously agreed days and, where possible, with computer equipment paid for by the employer. The agreement also contains rules on the organisation of working time. The agreement came in response to a call on the social partners from the then Social Democratic Minister of Labour to reach a collective agreement on teleworking.

In Denmark, the framework agreement on telework between UNICE, CEEP and ETUC will be implemented through collective agreement.

3.6. Working time

Standard weekly working time in Denmark is, by collective agreement, 37 hours. Traditionally, Denmark has had no general working time legislation. Instead, questions relating to the duration and organisation of working time have been regulated by collective agreement. Against this background, a central question in connection with the implementation of the 1993 Working Time Directive was the extent to which it could be implemented in Denmark by collective agreement.

In 1993, the Danish parliament urged the Danish government to work actively for the development of the EU's social dimension. At the same time, the parliament underlined its desire for Denmark to retain its model in the employment field and for EC directives to be implemented first and foremost by collective agreement. In 1996, DA and LO concluded a basic agreement on the procedure for implementing EU directives. The agreement urges the Ministry of Labour to ask the social partners, whenever a new directive has been adopted, whether they want to implement the directive by collective agreement. If the social partners decide to conclude a collective agreement in the area, it will be for the government, in cooperation with the social partners, subsequently to determine whether further measures are required in the form of legislation.

This procedure for implementing EU directives was first used for the implementation of the Working Time Directive. Some provisions were deemed to fall within occupational

health and safety law and were implemented by occupational health and safety legislation. Other parts of the Directive were left to the social partners, including the rule on maximum weekly working time. These parts of the Directive were also incorporated into the main part of the collective agreement in the public as well as the private sector. In agreement with the social partners, the government and the parliament subsequently opted not to legislate in this area. The decision not to legislate has been described as political rather than legal and has been said to have been intended to signal the importance of collective agreements in the Danish labour market model.

In 2001, the European Commission sent Denmark a reasoned opinion claiming that the Working Time Directive had not been implemented correctly and threatening to take Denmark to the European Court of Justice. The reason was the fact that a significant proportion of the labour force (approximately 30%) was not covered by collective agreements. This prompted the government and the social partners to agree to table draft legislation implementing the Working Time Directive. The draft legislation was adopted in 2002.[15] The law may be described as semi-binding, albeit subject to restrictions under EU law. It applies only to employees who are not covered by a collective agreement that guarantees employees at least the same rights as those laid down in the Working Time Directive. The collective agreement may continue to apply in its normal field of application, but the law also allows the parties to an individual employment relationship to agree to apply a given collective agreement which meets the requirements, in which case the material provisions of the law do not apply.

3.7. Unemployment legislation

As part of the fight against unemployment, several laws were introduced in the early 1990s allowing employees to take (unpaid) leave from work.

The Equal Treatment Act contains rules on the right to leave during pregnancy and following the birth of a child. Either the mother or the father may, within certain limits, take leave following the birth of a child. The law does not contain any rules obliging the employer to pay any form of compensation during the period of leave. Such an obligation follows from the White-Collar Workers Act and collective agreements. The Daily Allowances Act (*Dagpengeloven*) grants workers the right to daily allowances during the period of leave. The local authority pays the daily allowances. In 2002,

---

15   Act No 248 of 8 May 2002 on the implementation of the Working Time Directive (*Lov nr. 248 af 8.5.2002 om gennemførelse af dele af arbejdstidsdirektivet*).

the rules on parental leave (*barselsorlov*) were amended. In simple terms, the legislative amendment involved extending the period of entitlement to full daily allowances from 32 weeks to 52 weeks.

Another measure used in Danish employment policy is 'job rotation'. This involves a company hiring an unemployed person as a substitute for an employee taking study leave. Financial support may be granted to both the employee for his education/training and the employer for hiring the substitute.

4. Discrimination and equal treatment

4.1. Equal treatment of women and men

The key laws on equal treatment of men and women are the Equal Pay Act (*Ligelønsloven*) and the Equal Treatment Act (*Ligebehandlingsloven*).[16] These laws date from the 1970s and were adopted with a view to implementing EC directives in the area. During the 1990s, several amendments were made to these laws, albeit of limited significance. The Equal Treatment Act has, *inter alia*, been amended with a view to implementing the Burden of Proof Directive[17] and the so-called Motherhood Directive.[18]

In 2001, the Social Democratic government tabled a proposal for a significant new element in the Equal Pay Act. The proposal required employers with more than ten employees to draw up pay statistics by gender and other relevant criteria at the request of the employees, the trade union or the Equality Board (*Ligestillingsnævnet*). The proposal was adopted by the Danish parliament in June 2001. When the Conservative/Liberal government came to power, the provision was amended so that the changes would only take effect on the decision of the Minister for Employment. The purpose of postponing the entry into force was to offer the social partners an opportunity to come up with alternative ways of ensuring respect for the principle of equal pay. The law has yet to enter into force (February 2004).

In 1999, the White Collar Workers Act was amended to entitle pregnant workers to full pay during periods of absence

due to illness. The amendment resulted from a judgement by the European Court of Justice and removed the distinction between pregnancy-related absences and other absences.

Equality legislation is generally subsidiary to collective agreements, provided the latter provide the same level of protection as the law (or the directive behind the law).

Collective agreements are assumed to rest on the principle of equal pay. Furthermore, the cooperation agreement between LO and DA contains an additional agreement on equal treatment of men and women concluded in May 1999. The agreement covers all aspects which promote equal treatment of men and women. In the public sector a circular exists with a similar content.

4.2. Discrimination on the grounds of ethnic origin, disability and sexual orientation

In 1996, the Discrimination Act (*Diskriminationsloven*)[19] was adopted. The law was adopted in response to the concern that Denmark was failing to live up to its international obligations, in particular ILO Convention No 111 on discrimination in employment and occupation, which Denmark has ratified. The law prohibits direct and indirect discrimination on grounds of race, skin colour, religion, political opinions, sexual orientation and national, social or ethnic origin. The law covers neither disability nor age (dealt with in Article 13 of the EC Treaty). The law is essentially structured like the Equal Treatment Act.

In January 2003, a draft amendment of the Discrimination Act was tabled with a view to implementing the two new discrimination directives adopted in 2000: the Race Equality Directive[20] and the general Employment Equality Directive.[21] The proposal introduced a new discriminatory ground in the form of protection against discrimination on the grounds of belief. The proposal also specified that harassment constitutes a kind of difference of treatment, which is covered by the prohibition of discrimination. The prohibition of discrimination was further extended to also encompass different treatment by employers' associations and trade unions in

---

16   In addition, there is the Act on Equal Treatment of Men and Women in Occupational Social Security Schemes, principally pensions.

17   Council Directive 97/80/EC on the burden of proof in cases of discrimination based on sex.

18   Council Directive 92/85/EC on the introduction of measures to encourage improvements in the safety and health at work of pregnant workers and workers who have recently given birth or are breastfeeding.

19   Act No 459 of 12 June 1996 prohibiting discrimination in the labour market, etc. (*Lov nr 459 af 12.6.1996 om forbud mod forskelsbehandling på arbejdsmarkedet m.v.*).

20   Council Directive 2000/43/EC implementing the principle of equal treatment between persons irrespective of racial or ethnic origin.

21   Council Directive 2000/778/EC establishing a general framework for equal treatment in employment and occupation.

their acceptance and treatment of members. The proposal was not adopted by the parliament.

5.   Personal integrity

In Denmark there is no special legislation protecting the personal integrity of employees but, as previously mentioned, employees' health-related information is protected.

Denmark has implemented the Directive on the protection of personal data through a Personal Data Act (*Persondataloven*).[22] The law affects working life in various ways, including in terms of how personal data is handled and with regard to the protection of sensitive personal information.

The basic agreement between DA and LO contains provisions on the procedures for establishing principles on the handling, collection and storage of personal data.

6.   Concluding remarks

A central and recurring theme in the Danish labour law debate has been how to incorporate EC labour law into the Danish model. As regards directives concerning employment conditions, a process has been developed whereby the social partners initially conclude the collective agreements necessary for implementing the directive within their respective sectors. This form of regulation by collective agreement is then supplemented by legislation aimed at guaranteeing the application of the directive to employees not covered by collective agreements. The idea that EC Directives might be implemented by collective agreement without supplementary legislation would now appear to have been abandoned. Various models have been developed for this type of supplementary legislation. In several cases so-called semi-binding legislation has been adopted, i.e. laws from which it is possible to deviate through collective agreement. In such cases, the collective agreement must satisfy the requirements of the directive. Such legislation was for example used for the implementation of the Working Time and Temporary Work Directives. Another approach was used for implementing the Part-Time Work Directive, whereby a specific law was adopted for the purpose of giving *erga omnes* effect to the main collective agreements.

The manner in which EC labour law directives have been implemented in Denmark shows that tripartism in labour market matters generally works well and that the legislator in general accepts the principle that matters affecting employers and employees in should be dealt with in the first instance by the social partners. In this respect, the Danish model is still strong. The intervention of the current Conservative/Liberal government to allow part-time work (see section 3.2) independently of any collective agreements does, however, provide an example of legislation adopted against the wishes of the social partners. It remains to be seen if this example marks a new trend.

At the same time, it should be stressed that labour market legislation has increased significantly in scope. It will suffice to recall the Working Time Act, the Part-Time Act, the Act on Temporary Employment and the Discrimination Act. This new legislation has mainly been prompted by EU directives or other international obligations. The Act on the use of health-related information in the labour market, as well as the restrictions on the use of covenants in restraint of competition are, however, purely domestic legislative products.

Another feature of the Danish model is that the social partners within the framework of the so-called 'industrial system' handle interpretation and dispute resolution in the labour market to a large extent. However, it can be argued that the control exercised by the social partners over interpretation and dispute resolution has decreased in the last decade. One reason for this development is the possibility of challenging national law through preliminary rulings by the European Court of Justice. The growth in legislation has also increased the importance of the ordinary courts. The granting to trade union members of a subsidiary right to be heard by the ordinary courts on matters primarily falling within the remit of the industrial system marks a step in the same direction.

Unlike in Sweden, there has been no political debate in Denmark on a more flexible approach to labour law. This can be partly explained by the fact that Denmark escaped the worst of the economic recession of the beginning of the 1990s and by the absence of detailed employment protection regulation such as that contained in the Swedish Employment Protection Act (LAS – *Lagen* (1982:80) *om anställningsskydd*). Another and probably more important explanation is the well-functioning tripartite system involving the social partners and the government. The collective bargaining system also seems to have allowed considerable scope for 'flexibility' (see section 3).

The evolution of Danish labour law over the last 10 years can thus be summed up as follows:

1.   Individual labour law has become more important and more prominent. This is a result partly of the influence

22   Act No 429 of 31.5.2001.

of the EU, and partly of developments in national law. Ten years ago, only crown servants (White-Collar Workers Act) were subject to detailed individual labour law. Today, such regulation is widespread.

2. Noticeable attempts have been made in Denmark to combine flexibility and security and to boost wage earners' employability. Employment policy and its regulation must be described as successful during the ten-year period under consideration.

3. Danish collective labour law finds itself in a regulatory crisis. The fact that different and technically rather complicated models were chosen for the implementation of key directives indicates that an appropriate tool for handling the relationship between individual and collective labour law has yet to be found. In addition, there has been a breakthrough for the revolutionary idea that the individual parties to an employment relationship might be empowered by law to depart from what has been agreed in a binding collective agreement. However, this rule is so new that it would be premature to assess its practical impact.

Chapter II:
Finland

I. Introduction

1.1. Historical background

Modern Finnish labour law has its roots both in continental Europe (Germany, Austria, etc.) and in the other Nordic countries (Sweden and, to some extent, Denmark), as well as in the International Labour Organisation (ILO) system in which Finland has taken an active part since the 1920s. The German influence in the Finnish legal system was strong during the first decades of the 20th century. Since the Second World War, however, the Scandinavian influence has become considerably stronger.

The prevailing legal tradition in Finland marks labour law, in the sense that legislation is extensive and detailed. Work is thus to a large degree *governed by legislation and extensively regulated*, although collective bargaining has also played a key role in the development of the labour market and labour law during the second half of the 20th century.

As early as 1922, the project of creating an extensive Employment Contracts Act governing individual working conditions was realised. This legislation, in an amended form, remains central to individual labour law.

The legal regulation of collective agreements was, somewhat paradoxically, introduced in 1924, at a time when collective bargaining was very rare. The legislation was, to a large extent, based on a German draft law, which was never adopted in Germany. A law on Mediation in Labour Conflicts was adopted in 1925. This regulation and collective bargaining practice have evolved and have been influenced by the other Nordic countries.

Following Finland's accession to the European Union in 1995, EU regulation has been the main international legal influence on Finnish labour law. Within the framework of its so-called *social dimension*, the EU has carried out extensive harmonisation of the legislation of the Member States with regard to free movement of workers, employment protection, working time, gender equality, worker involvement and collective redundancy protection. The body of European legislation is constantly expanding. Today, the vast majority of Finnish labour market legislation is adopted within a framework decided at EU level.

In general terms, developments in the last ten years are best described as cooperative tripartism and political stability. Whereas, at the onset of the period under consideration, the Finnish economy was in deep recession with unemployment running high (approximately 20%), by the end of the 1990s it was benefiting from the so-called 'IT boom' and from successful Finnish actors in the global market, with Nokia as the prime example.

1.2. The social partners

Membership levels in the Finnish labour market organisations are high both for employers' organisations and trade unions. The rate of trade union membership is regularly said to be approximately 90%. However, if pensioners and other special groups are discounted, the membership rate falls to approximately 72%.

The largest trade union, the Central Organisation of Finnish Trade Unions (*Suomen Ammattiliittojen Keskusjärjestö, SAK*) has about 1 million members organised along industrial federation lines. The industrial federation principle basically means that all employees within a given branch of industry belong to the same trade union. This implies that the metal workers' federation, for example, counts not only metal workers, but also joiners and cleaners who work in the metal industry, among its members. The Finnish trade union movement also caters for public and private sector salaried employees. Almost half of SAK's members belong to federations of industrial workers. The other federations are the public sector federation, the private service sector federation and the transport sector federation.

The second-largest trade union is the Finnish Confederation of Salaried Employees (*Toimihenkilökeskusjärjestö, STTK*), with about 650 000 members. These include health care personnel (excluding doctors) and clerical and technical staff within industry, services and the public sector. STTK is Finland's largest central organisation for salaried employees.

The third central organisation, the Confederation of Unions for Academic Professionals (AKAVA), has approximately 432 000 members, the majority of whom are graduates. The confederation describes itself as a trade union for those with higher-level education. Like the other two central organisations, AKAVA draws its membership from both the private and the public sector.

There are four major organisations representing employers at national level. The main central employers' organisation is the Confederation of Finnish Industry and Employers (*Teollisuuden ja Työnantajain keskusliitto, TT*). TT has over 5 600 member companies employing 530 000 people. The central organisation is composed of 30 branch federations. As the name suggests, industrial companies dominate the organisation, but other sectors such as transport and services are also represented. The member companies account for over 75% of both the industry's added value and its export earnings.

The service sector has its own central organisation for employers, the Employers' Federation of Service Industries (*Palvelutyönantajat, PT*). It has approximately 9 000 member companies from the commerce, hotel, restaurant, banking, insurance and other branches of the private service sector, employing over 363 000 people.

Within the public sector, there are two major social partner organisations on the employers' side. The Department of Public Personnel Management (*Valtion työmarkkinalaitos, VT*) looks after the interests of the State as employer, while the Commission for Local Authority Employers (*Kunnallinen työmarkkinalaitos, KT*) represents the local authorities. The Evangelical-Lutheran Church also has its own negotiating delegation.

The public sector is a large employer. The State employs over 120 000 people, of which 100 000 are civil servants and about 20 000 are blue-collar workers. The local authorities employ 422 000 people, divided into even amounts of civil servants and blue-collar workers.

1.3. Income policy

Since the 1960s, a state incomes policy has been used in Finland to regulate wages and other employment conditions. This incomes policy has involved the social partners and the government negotiating an overall agreement. This overall agreement provides the framework for wage, tax and social policy for a given period. Since 1968, only a few negotiating rounds have failed to produce a central agreement. These central incomes policy agreements are not, legally speaking, collective agreements. Collective agreements are negotiated

separately at branch or federation level within the framework established by the central agreement, and only rarely do the social partners derogate from that framework.

The incomes policy has both required and promoted the emergence of a neocorporatist governmental political system. It is remarkably top-down insofar as the framework is negotiated by the central employers' organisations and trade unions in cooperation with the government. The government's involvement in the negotiations has varied considerably over the years. Another aspect of the neocorporatist decision-making pattern is the presence of the central social partner organisations on a variety of government bodies. The incomes policy has contributed to a growing centralisation of the social partner organisations.

A certain decentralisation has, however, taken place during the 1990s. Indeed, since the conclusion in 1997 of the centralised wage agreement for 1998-1999, the room for manoeuvre for the federations and for individual workplaces has increased as a result of the relative flexibility of that agreement. The latest central agreements cover the years 2001-2002 and 2003-2004. Finland's membership of the single currency, in particular, has encouraged a continuation of the incomes policy tradition in order to keep national wage developments under control, and at central level an agreement was even reached on the establishment of buffer funds for countering the feared negative consequences of the single currency.

1.4. Decentralised legislation and collective bargaining: new forms of regulation

It has been argued that collective bargaining in Finland is extremely centralised. The main regulation does, however, take place at trade union level through collective bargaining. Collective bargaining has become increasingly decentralised to the local level. This development is also evident in the working time legislation and the new Employment Contracts Act, which establish the legal framework for local bargaining.

The Finnish labour law tradition is characterised by a unique national mixture of legislation and collective agreements. Within this mixture, legislation plays a key role in the establishment of frameworks, rules and rights. This legislation may be mandatory, semi-mandatory or optional. In addition, the provisions of the Employment Contracts Act regarding *erga omnes* collective agreements may extend the legally binding status of a given collective agreement. An employer who, pursuant to the Collective Agreements Act, is not bound by a given collective agreement (e.g. An employer who is not a member of an employers' organisation) may nevertheless be compelled to observe a collective agreement. A binding effect may result from the Employment Contracts Act's provisions on *erga omnes* collective agreements. The employer may often be unable to make use of the possibility provided for in the collective agreement for derogating from its provisions.

To some extent, so-called soft law has also entered Finnish law. In some cases, the social partners have adopted joint recommendations on, for example, sexual harassment in the workplace. Certain important government programmes deserve mention in this respect. During the 1998-2002 period there was a national programme to raise awareness of the problems experienced by older workers (see below). Previously, there was a similar national programme for the promotion of gender equality.

1.5. The private law nature of labour law, sources and labour law in the public sector

The Finnish labour market system covers the public as well as the private sector. Over time, the public sector has grown, gradually leading to a regulation of employment conditions similar to that within the private sector.

The main sources of Finnish labour law are legislation, collective agreements and individual employment contracts. Employment contracts are regulated by the 2001 *Employment Contracts Act*.[23] The equivalent basic regulation within the public sector is the 1994 *Civil Servants' Act*.[24] The new *Local Officials Act* from 2003 regulates the working conditions of approximately 50% of all local officials.[25] Over 200 000 employees working for the municipalities are contractually employed and their working conditions are governed by the Employment Contracts Act. As a result, the state and local government sector in Finland has *two main groups of employees*. There are a significant number of public sector workers with private law employment relationships. They are covered by the same labour law regulation that applies in the private sector.

Collective agreements, which play a significant role in practice, are governed by the 1946 *Collective Agreements Act*.[26] The central and local *civil servants´ collective agreements* are each governed by a separate Act (1970).[27] The 1978 *Cooperation Within Undertakings Act* grants employees the right to influence such issues as may affect their work and workplace.[28] The 1988 *Cooperation (State Employees) Act* likewise applies to state employees.[29] Within the local government sector, co-determination is based on an agreed arrangement. On the basis of the cooperation legislation, a *cooperation agreement* may be concluded, which has the same effect as a collective agreement. Also on the basis of the Cooperation within Undertakings Act, *workplace rules* may be drawn up.

In the private as well as in the public sector, central agreements are concluded. In the private sector, these are referred to as general labour market agreements, which have been simplified and standardised in recent years. In the public sector, the agreements are referred to as basic agreements. These agreements are designed to remain in force for a lengthy period of time.

In Finland, labour market legislation, individual as well as collective, is first and foremost considered private law. On the other hand, the economic legislative nature of labour law, halfway between public and private law, has often been stressed. Occupational health and safety legislation, the regulation of employment services and the public social security system have all been categorised as subject to public law. In addition, the regulation of employment in central and local government has traditionally been considered subject to public law.

The other categories of public sector employees are the state and the local government civil servants. In comparison with other workers, civil servants have traditionally enjoyed a separate status and they have been subject to separate legislation. This group has often been described as a category of employees who typically exercises public power. In 1970, a collective bargaining system for civil servants was introduced, which in key parts is based on the Collective Agreements Act. However, the system is more centralised, and the freedom to conclude agreements and the right to strike are more restricted than in the private sector. The regulation of individual employment relationships has also become increasingly standardised, although separate rules apply to senior civil servants. Today, the prevailing view is that labour law also covers civil servants in the public sector, despite the fact that the Employment Contracts Act and several other key labour laws do not apply to them.

---

23   Arbetsavtalslag 26.1.2001/55.
24   Statstjänstemannalag 19.8.1994/750.
25   Lag om kommunala tjänsteinnehavare 16.4.2003/304.
26   Lag om kollektivavtal 7.6.1946/436.
27   See lag om statens tjänstekollektivavtal Act 6.11.1970/664 and lag om kommunala tjänstekollektivavtal 6.11.1970/669.
28   Lag om samarbete inom företag 22.9.1978/725.
29   Lag om samarbete inom statens ämbetsverk och inrättningar 1.7.1988/651.

The specific rules which apply to these groups have increasingly come to resemble those which apply to private employees.

In recent years, the distinction between private and public employees has been brought into sharp focus, mainly as public activities have been opened up to competition or have been privatised. This has led to groups of employees being transferred from public law employment relationships to private law employment relationships, which at times has involved a loss of rights. This has given rise to a series of court cases and judgements, but also to a growing convergence between public civil servants and private employees.

1.6. Dispute resolution in the labour market

In the Finnish labour market, trade unions and shop stewards appointed by them play a key role in monitoring the application of the law and collective agreements. The vast majority of disputes are handled and resolved through this labour market system.

A special *Labour Court*[30] has been established to deal with disputes concerning the 'validity, duration, substance and scope' of collective agreements. The Labour Court is also empowered to decide whether a practice is in breach of the Collective Agreements Act, the Civil Servants Collective Agreements Acts or the provisions of collective agreements. The Court has also ruled on breaches of the peace obligation. It also decides on the sanctions to be applied to breaches of the collective agreements legislation.

The composition of the Labour Court is different to that of other courts. It is composed of representatives of the three parties, so-called *interest representation*. The President of the Labour Court is appointed for a renewable three-year term.

The plaintiffs and the defendants before the Labour Court are generally organisations which are parties to the agreement. The Court deals with approximately 100 cases per year. The Court's judgements are final and there is no leave to appeal against a judgement which the Labour Court has handed down. As a general rule, it is a precondition for seeking a review by the Court that the parties have tried to negotiate a resolution of their dispute.

The Labour Court does not have jurisdiction over disputes concerning individual labour law. In Finland, the general courts deal with such disputes.

1.7. Demographic changes, migration and statistics

Women have played a significant role in the Finnish labour market for many years. Women entered the labour market *en masse* immediately after the Second World War, when there was a shortage of labour. As early as 1950, 41% of the working population were women, most of them in full-time employment. By 1993, the proportion had risen to 51%. Statistics for 2000 indicate that 17% of female wage earners work part-time. The corresponding figure for male wage earners is 8%. Among women, 21% are in fixed-term employment, compared to 15% of men. However, the Finnish labour market is relatively segregated and women tend to work in lower-paid jobs.

The Finnish labour force is clearly ageing. From 2010, the proportion of the population of working age will start to fall significantly as the big post-Second World War generations retire. This will have a dramatic impact on the supply of labour. Today, the proportion of foreigners in Finland is about 3%, or 130 000 people, but a marked increase in foreign labour is expected. Finnish immigration policy has been rather restrictive, given the high level of unemployment. In this respect, a change of policy is likely and can already be gleaned from various policy documents.

The entire post-Second World War period has thus been characterised by unemployment and recession, resulting *inter alia* in significant emigration to Sweden during the 1960s and 1970s. However, between 1950 and 1990, unemployment never exceeded 7%. By contrast, during the 1992-94 recession, unemployment rose explosively to over 20%. Since 1995, the trend has been towards falling unemployment, albeit only slowly. In 2002, the number of unemployed people was 237 000, an equivalent rate of 9.1%. The number of long-term unemployed (people who have been unemployed for more than a year) was over 76 000, compared to 100 000 in 1999. The overall unemployment rate is currently below 10%, but unemployment remains above 20% in several areas of northern Finland, despite improvements brought about by active labour market initiatives targeted specifically at these areas.

---

30   Lag om arbetsdomstolen 31.7.1974/646.

1.8. Mediation and resolution of interest disputes

The Finnish conciliation service plays a key part in mediating interest disputes, in particular during negotiations on collective agreements. It is compulsory to take part in conciliation and the mediator is empowered under certain defined circumstances to postpone announced strike action. However, there is no obligation to accept the mediator's conciliation proposals and the parties cannot have an agreement imposed on them which some of them refuse to recognise.

In practice, the mediator has become a key part of the incomes policy mechanism. The mediator is widely seen as the guarantor of the general nationally agreed wage level. Both the social partner organisations and the mass media are highly critical of organisations that seek to achieve additional advantages through strike action.

1.9. Constitutional reform

In Finland, a constitutional reform was implemented in 1995 which added a new chapter on fundamental rights to the Constitution. An overall review of the Constitution followed in 2000.[31] The new 1995 rules were integrated in the new Constitution. The incorporation of the European Convention on Human Rights into Finnish law in 1990 also helped focus attention on fundamental rights in the Finnish legal system.

The Finnish constitutional reform enshrined a series of key fundamental rights in the Constitution. The right to privacy, the right to freedom of assembly and association, the right to equality, the right to work and social security are all guaranteed by the Finnish Constitution. The right to work includes a prohibition of unlawful dismissal.

This reform has had several important implications for labour law. First, the fundamental rights argument has taken on greater significance, also outside the public sector. The starting point is that fundamental rights may also be relevant to relationships between individual legal entities, although a degree of uncertainty remains over exactly what should apply. In addition, the fact that a right is recognised as a fundamental right means that, generally speaking, that right may only be set aside or restricted by a law adopted by the parliament. Moreover, fundamental rights have a significant impact as a factor of interpretation in situations where values protected by the Constitution are at stake.

In practice, the new Constitution has had an impact on labour market regulation in various ways. First, the employment protection of certain groups which previously had no legally regulated protection is now subject to regulation. The main group to whom this applies are local government salaried employees. Secondly, fundamental rights have been given greater prominence in the Collective Agreements Act and a separate Act on Personal Integrity in Working Life has been adopted. *Protection of privacy, personal integrity* and protection of personal data are enshrined in the Constitution and have the same human rights status as the right to protection against discrimination. The basic idea underpinning the protection of privacy is that the employee, despite his subordinate position, has a right to human dignity. The employee's private life must not be subjected to further restrictions than necessary in a given situation. It has also been worded in such a way that the individual enjoys protection not only *vis-à-vis* the State. An employee does not renounce all his fundamental freedoms and rights when he concludes an employment contract and starts working for an employer.

The protection of personal integrity can be summed up in a few principles or interests. The employee has an interest in having *access* to his personal data collected or used in his working life. He has a right to control and influence which of his personal data are used, *an interest in discretion*. There is a quality requirement regarding the data which are collected and used, *an interest in exhaustiveness*. It is clear that these principles cannot fully guide legislation in this area. When legislating, these interests must be weighed against other principles involving the interests of employers or society as a whole in management, control and security.

The principle of *protection from discrimination* and arbitrary treatment is expressed differently in Finnish legislation. The Constitution provides that all persons are equal before the law and that without good reason, nobody should be treated differently because of gender, age, origin, language, religion, belief, opinion, health or disability or any other personal characteristic. The Constitution explicitly provides that gender equality must be promoted in social activities and in working life, particularly as far as pay and other working conditions are concerned. The principle of non-discrimination is further regulated in the Equality between the Sexes Act, the Employment Contracts Act and the Act on Equality that came into force on 1 February 2004.

---

31   Finlands grundlag 11.6.1999/731 (the law entered into force on 1 March 2000).

2. From employment protection to employability

2.1. Introduction

The principle of *employment promotion* has, particularly during the 1990s, affected labour law in various ways. According to the Constitution, the government must promote employment and work to ensure for every person the right to work. Unlawful dismissal is also prohibited. Employment promotion has also been expressed in legislation aimed at distributing work more evenly among different groups. An example is the Alternate Leave Act (*Lagen om alterneringsledighet*).[32] The Act entitles an employee to take leave from his work for a certain period (between three months and one year) on the condition that an unemployed person is taken on as a substitute for the same period of time. Rules considered to present obstacles to new recruitment were also reviewed or made more flexible during the 1990s.

Work on reforming the body of labour market legislation has taken place within a tripartite framework in which the largest organisations (FFC and TT) have played a leading role. The organisation representing small businesses has been sceptical about some of the results of the consensus policy, as has the organisation representing graduates (AKAVA). The reform efforts have been guided by the idea of reconciling flexibility and security, so-called flexicurity. This legislative strategy has been combined with active investment in education/training, IT and support for small businesses. The policy has been successful in the growth areas of southern Finland, whereas workers laid off in the countryside and in the cities of sparsely populated areas have often drifted into long-term unemployment.

2.2. Employment protection

The Finnish rules on employment protection in the Employment Contracts Act aim to create security for employees without preventing effective management and a smooth adjustment of the workforce to the labour supply. The basic instruments of employment protection are *individual and collective redundancy protection*, *termination of the employment relationship* and *dismissal*. These instruments were recently revised in Finnish law in conjunction with the adoption of the new Employment Contracts Act 2001, and their main provisions are outlined below.

Termination on personal grounds (grounds for termination linked to the person of the employee) requires objective and *weighty reasons* since the employer is terminating without the consent of the employee.

Objective and weighty reasons for termination on personal grounds flow from an overall assessment. All the relevant facts of the case need to be taken into account when assessing whether the measure is reasonable. Previously, reasons for termination on personal grounds were defined only negatively. Acceptable reasons were not indicated, only unacceptable reasons. The new Employment Contracts Act builds on a slightly different regulatory approach. The Employment Contracts Act (7:2) specifies in general terms reasons for termination which may be viewed as objective and weighty and thus provide legal grounds for the employer to terminate the contract of employment. In addition, in accordance with previous practice, the Act specifies reasons for termination which are not acceptable.

There are two types of objective and weighty reasons for termination on personal grounds:

1. A serious breach of the employee's obligations towards the employer. This concerns obligations which follow from the employment contract or from the law, and these obligations must be of significance to the employment relationship.

2. A significant change in the employee's personal circumstances which cause him to no longer be able to carry out his work duties. The draft legislation reveals that this provision was not intended for situations where the employee's capacity for work is reduced as a result of illness or disability.

An employee who has failed to observe his obligations may not, as a general rule, be terminated if the employer has failed to give him a *warning*.

The objective and weighty grounds for termination are also delimited by negative definitions. The Employment Contracts Act lists individual reasons which are not considered acceptable grounds for dismissal. Some of them are categorical, while others are of a more relative nature.

An employee may not be dismissed on grounds of illness, disability or accident. This does not, however, apply in all situations. Reduced capacity for work for the aforementioned rea-

---

32   Lag om försök med alterneringsledighet 22.12.1995/1663. The Act was renewed at the beginning of 2003 (2002/1305).

sons may, in certain circumstances, constitute a valid ground for dismissal. In such cases, the capacity for work would have to be so *significantly* and *enduringly* reduced that it would be unreasonable to expect the employer to continue the employment relationship. The determining factor is the employee's ability to carry out his or her work. It also has to be considered whether the employer could reasonably have transferred the employee to other tasks which he was able to carry out.

The law also explicitly bans the employer from terminating the employment contract on the grounds that the employee took part in a strike action.

It follows from the *freedoms of conviction and religion* that an individual employee's political, religious or other convictions do not constitute valid grounds for dismissal. The employee's participation in social or association activities does not constitute grounds for dismissal. This prohibition flows from the general prohibition of discrimination in labour law.

Prior to carrying out a dismissal, the employer shall hear the employee in order to ascertain whether the dismissal might be avoided by transferring the employee to another job (7:2.4). If the grounds for dismissal constitute such a serious breach that it would be unreasonable to expect the employer to continue the employment relationship, the employer need neither warn the employee nor consider the possibility of a transfer (7:5).

During *pregnancy or parental leave* the employee enjoys strong protection from dismissal. An employer may not terminate a female employee on the grounds of her pregnancy (7:9). The fact that an employee is exercising his/her right to parental leave also constitutes a prohibited ground for dismissal. At the request of the employer, the employee shall provide proof of her pregnancy.

Employee representatives (förtroendeman) and employee delegates (förtroendeombud) have been given a special place in the regulation of employment protection. The task of an employee representative is to represent the employees and look after their interests in their dealings with the employer. The employee representative plays a particularly important role in ensuring that the employees' rights, as laid down in the law, employment contracts or collective agreements, are realised. Many provisions are also drawn from local agreements with the employee representative. These tasks may place the employee representative in a delicate position.

An employer is entitled to terminate the employment contract of an employee representative on personal grounds (7:2) only if the majority of the employees that he represents give their assent. The assent requirement thus supplements the personal grounds for dismissal. Health and safety representatives enjoy the same form of protection. The special provision on the protection of employee representatives has been supplemented by a similar provision on *employee delegates*. 'Employee delegate' is the term used to describe an 'employee representative' whose position has not been established by the provisions of a collective agreement.

Employment protection in the context of collective redundancies. Collective employment protection is substantial and procedure-based.

Grounds for collective redundancies. According to the Employment Contracts Act, the employer may terminate a contract of employment if the amount of work available has significantly and enduringly decreased for economic or production-related reasons or for reasons related to the reorganisation of the employer's business. The provisions on collective redundancies are aimed at arbitrary measures by the employer. However, they also restrict the employer's right to recruit and to terminate the employment relationship, as well as his right to manage and to supervise the work. An employer may not replace an employee merely because he finds another employee more qualified. As an additional requirement, the employee may not be transferred to or retrained for other duties.

The decrease in the amount of work may be due to a fall in demand and thus be caused by the reactions of the market and, possibly, indirectly by the actions of the employer. But the decrease may also be a direct result of the employer's actions. An employer may decide to close a production unit regardless of whether it is profitable. The closure will cause a decrease in the amount of work available as provided for in the Employment Contracts Act (7:3.1). The decrease in work may also be the result of rationalisation, whereby automation reduces the need for labour. The company may be reducing the administrative workload connected with human resource management by buying in services from outside. This may also create grounds for redundancies.

It is a requirement that the decrease in the amount of work available be significant and enduring. This requirement may be described as a kind of *general clause* on the substantial grounds for collective redundancies. No guidelines on the amount and duration of the reduction in work may be gleaned from existing case law. It is therefore important that the provisions have been supplemented by a list of events in which the employer is considered not to have valid grounds for collective redundancies (7:3.2). These so-called *point bans* have two objectives. First, they describe situations in which collective grounds are not sufficiently weighty and, secondly, they aim to make it difficult to circumvent individual grounds for dismissal. The notion of circumvention implies that actual individual grounds for dismissal are camouflaged by economic and production-related reasons.

The employer's obligation to transfer implies that he must consider whether the employee could be transferred to other duties. The transfer obligation also applies where a transfer is possible subject to such training as the employer can reasonably be expected to provide.

In the first instance, the employer must offer the employee work equivalent to that agreed in the employment contract. Where the employer is unable to offer such work, he must, *in the second instance*, as far as possible, offer work which corresponds to the employment contract, i.e. Work which presents sufficient similarities to the work described in the employment contract.

Where the employer is unable to offer other work as described above, he must, *in the final instance*, offer the employee work commensurate with his education/training, skills or experience (7:4.1). In the present context, 'commensurate with' should be understood as tasks which the employee, due to his qualifications, is expected to be able to perform.

The employer's obligation to transfer, immediately or subject to special training, is often said to apply within his sphere of competence. The employer's obligation to offer work is not geographically restricted in the Employment Contracts Act. Where an employer has businesses in several different places, he is under an obligation to offer work on the aforementioned conditions in any of his places of business where such work is available. However, under the terms of the Employment Contracts Act, the national organisations representing employers and employees may limit the geographical extent of the obligation to transfer by collective agreement.

In labour law (and other fields of law), the problem arises of how to deal with conglomerates and other groupings of companies. Is the concept of employer to be understood in its formal sense or can a parent company in its capacity as employer be held liable for the actions of its subsidiary? The literature contains differing opinions on the subject. In case HD 1998:77, the Supreme Court held that a parent company exercising a significant degree of influence over its subsidiary should have considered the possibility of transferring to the subsidiary company an employee who had been made collectively redundant.

In the light of this decision and of certain specific labour law provisions, the new Employment Contracts Act expands the obligation to transfer. An employer who, in practice, exercises a dominant influence over personnel issues in another company or another grouping than the company in which redundancies are threatened, must identify and offer work or training in other companies under his dominant influence.

The fact that a company with powers of decision in another or other companies reduces its staff does not create an obligation to transfer. An additional requirement is that the companies share a sufficient number of common denominators. The case law has focused on joint management of personnel issues, similarities in the companies' areas of business as well as the companies' joint business activities. These criteria drawn from previous case law are important in the interpretation of the new legislative provisions on work which might be offered to the employee.

Ordinarily, a fixed-term employee may not be laid off and may not himself terminate his contract of employment, except where the parties have agreed on a separate termination clause. A fixed-term employee who, as a result of a business transfer, is moved from the transferred company to the receiving company is entitled to terminate his employment contract on the same conditions as *permanent employees*. The employee may terminate the contract with effect from the day of the transfer. This presupposes that the employer or the new business owner has notified the employee of the transfer at the latest one month before the transfer. Where the employee has been notified later than that, he is entitled to terminate the contract with effect from the day of the transfer or later, albeit at the latest within a month of being notified.

The redundancy procedure. The notice periods are the same for individual and collective redundancies. Like lay-offs and transfers to part-time work on grounds of collective redundancy, dismissals are *subject to consultations within the meaning of the Cooperation Within Undertakings Act* (Section 6(3)(b) and (a)). According to the Cooperation Within Undertakings Act, the employer is under special information and consultation obligations and may only make a decision once the legally required consultations have been completed.

The purpose of the consultation procedure is to ensure adequate provision of information to enable for example workforce-related questions to be considered from a variety of angles. The procedure is intended to give the employees a genuine opportunity to influence the decision. The consultation procedure does not restrict the employer's freedom of action in the matter, as he is not bound by the views and opinions of the employees.

However, the Cooperation Within Undertakings Act does not apply to companies with less than 30 employees. In cases of collective redundancies not covered by the Cooperation Within Undertakings Act's provisions on information and consultation, the employer is subject to a separate obligation to inform (9:3). The information which the employer must provide includes the reasons for the redundancy and the alternatives. Where redundancy concerns more than one employee, the information may be given to the employee representative (or, in the absence of a representative, to all the employees concerned). The employer must provide the information prior to announcing any redundancies and in as good time as possible.

The provisions are intended to make up for the limited scope of the Cooperation Within Undertakings Act. In that respect, it is an unsatisfactory solution, given that the Act aims to ensure a two-way communication whereas the separate obligation to inform foresees no exchange between the parties. The Cooperation Within Undertakings Act provides that the procedure must be carried out prior to any decision. According to the wording of Section 9(3), the obligation to inform must be fulfilled before any redundancies are affected. The decision may therefore already have been taken. The duty to inform may also come into play with respect to redundancies resulting from restructuring, the employer's bankruptcy or the employer's death.

Priority order in the context of collective redundancies. A company that reduces its workforce on business grounds may have to decide which employment contracts to terminate. The reduction in the work available may affect only parts of the company. In such situations, the employer will be forced to choose. Finnish legislation contains no explicit general rules on priority ordering. The ban on discriminatory treatment in the Employment Contracts Act and the Equality Between the Sexes Act does, however, impose certain restrictions on the employer's choice. The employment protection enjoyed by the employee representative and the employee delegate also affects the priority order. Workers on parental leave also enjoy stronger employment protection and may only have their employment contract terminated if the company ceases altogether (7:9).

Local collective agreements often contain a *provision on priority ordering.* Seniority will play a key part in priority ordering. This at once clear and schematic principle is softened somewhat by significant exceptions. These are dictated by both business and social policy considerations. The employer is, *inter alia,*

entitled to give priority to employees who, because of their skills, are particularly important to the company. Persons who have lost part of their capacity for work in the service of the employer would, in principle, be in an equally strong position.

Consequences of unfair dismissal. The provisions on compensation for unlawful dismissal in the new Employment Contracts Act are the same for individual and collective dismissals. On this point, the rules have been made simpler and clearer. An employer who has terminated an employee's employment contract on grounds other than those provided for in the Employment Contracts Act must pay *compensation* (korvaus) to the employee of between three and 24 months' pay. However, for the unlawful dismissal of an employee representative or delegate, this may rise up to 30 months' pay. The criteria for awarding compensation laid down in 12:2 differ from those for awarding damages. Apart from the fact that damages are intended to compensate for an injury suffered, they also have a penal purpose. An unfairly dismissed employee who has not suffered a material injury is nevertheless entitled to minimum compensation.

It is clear from the provisions on compensation that the intention was to make the employer pay the employee affected for the breach of the law alone. A motivation behind this solution may have been the absence of a legal instrument for preventing an unlawful dismissal or compelling an employer to re-instate unlawfully dismissed employees. Where a dismissal has been carried out unlawfully, a court may award compensation, but the employee still lost his job. Whether the employer will make good his error and reinstate the employee in his job is a different matter. The same applies to all other ways of terminating an employment relationship.

These provisions on compensation also apply to collective redundancies (7:3) and redundancies connected with restructuring (7:7). They further apply where the employer has prolonged the probation period unlawfully or on unacceptable grounds (8:1).

An employee is entitled to financial compensation for unlawful termination of the employment contract on collective grounds on the basis of the same provisions that apply to termination on individual grounds. A distinction should, however, be made. In the context of collective redundancies (and of transfers of undertakings) there is no fixed minimum amount of compensation.

The Employment Contracts Act lays down rules on how the employee's right to daily unemployment allowances affects the payment of compensation. The starting point is that any daily unemployment allowances already paid shall be deducted from the compensation awarded to the employee as a result of his unlawful dismissal. The employer is to pay an equivalent amount into the so-called unemployment insurance fund.

Redundant workers' financial position and voluntary redundancy payment. During the last 10-15 years, medium-sized and large businesses have been more involved in take-overs than at any time previously. In that context (but without any link), a number of companies have encouraged employees to give notice of termination. In some cases, older employees have been offered early retirement. Regardless of age, however, severance pay in the order of 3-6 months' pay has often been offered in addition to the salary during the notice period. The employer has also helped with additional training aimed at improving the position of the employee in the labour market.

In case of unemployment, the worker is entitled to *income protection*. The size of the financial benefits will depend on whether the unemployed person is a member of an unemployment insurance scheme. The entitlement to benefits also depends on the unemployed person's willingness to undergo training and preparedness to accept any work offered.

Lay-offs are common in Finland. A lay-off involves the temporary suspension of the employment relationship, so that the employer does not have to pay wages and the employee does not have to work. The idea is that a lay-off is a softer measure than redundancy and that it may be used in response to a temporary work shortage. A lay-off may take different forms, ranging from complete cessation of the work to a reduction in the working week.

A lay-off decision may be taken either by agreement between the employer and the employee or by the employer alone. The employer may lay off an employee regardless of the latter's opinion on two grounds. First, the employer has a right to lay off an employee on the ground of *a shortage of work which would represent grounds for collective redundancies.* Secondly, he has a right to lay off an employee if his ability to offer work has *diminished temporarily* and if he *cannot, within reason, find other appropriate work* for the employee or training which fits his needs. A reduction in the available work or the ability to offer work will be considered temporary if it is not expected to exceed 90 days. If the cessation is longer, the lay-off is considered a redundancy.

The employer and the employee may also *agree on a lay-off* during the employment relationship. The agreement must be for a fixed term and acceptable grounds include needs resulting from the employer's business or financial situation.

In the private sector, the employee's redundancy protection is illusory insofar as the employment relationship ceases at the expiry of the period of notice. A decision by the employee to contest the grounds for the termination or to take legal action in the courts would essentially have no effect on this. Equally, there is no legal means for restoring an unlawfully terminated employment relationship without the consent of both parties. In the public sector, by contrast, as a general rule the employment relationship continues during any legal action challenging the decision. If the employer loses the case, the employee may continue in his job.

During the recession of the 1990s, redundancies and lay-offs numbered hundreds of thousands. From an EU perspective, the redundancies were relatively quick and cost-free for the employer. It is difficult to make detailed international comparisons of employment protection. In an EU context, there are no grounds for claiming that employment protection is greater in Finland than in other Member States. Indeed, the opposite is the case.

Transfer of an employee to part-time work. When a shortage of work constitutes grounds for collective redundancies (7:3) the employer is entitled to unilaterally change the employment relationship from full-time to part-time. The employer must observe a period of notice and the change will only come into effect at the expiry of the employee's notice period.

Hence, during shortages of work, a transfer to part-time work may represent an alternative to redundancy or lay-off. The idea is that lay-offs are used as a solution to a temporary problem. Lay-off may take the form of a reduction of the working day or the working week or both.

The change of the employment relationship to part-time work can be interpreted as a mutually agreed change to the employment contract. The transfer provision is important insofar as it defines the instances in which the employer may implement the change without the consent of the employee.

2.3. Improvement of employability

It has long been clear that the needs of employees for security cannot primarily be ensured through employment protection, but must involve giving employees the abilities and possibilities, through education and training and lifelong learning, to remain attractive to employers in a changing labour market.

In the field of education policy, a number of initiatives have been taken to better adapt education to the labour needs of the business world. The system of training agreements has been developed and the number of places has increased significantly. The system, which is equivalent to a form of traineeship combining training and work, remains relatively limited in volume in Finland.

As far as other educational initiatives are concerned, measures have to a greater extent been tailored to the needs of different groups. New legislation on labour market support requires an action programme to be drawn up for each individual employee, and various forms of training are a key element of these action programmes. The demand for educational initiatives has also increased in line with improvements in the level of education of the workforce.

The various possibilities of getting leave for, inter alia, education and skills development may also lead to the individual increasingly being able to look after his own employability.

However, the general idea in Finnish legislation remains that the employer alone is responsible for the kind of practical training which the employee is required to have in order to carry out his tasks. Education is generally considered a matter for society as a whole.

In encouraging companies to keep so-called personnel accounts it was the intention to draw attention to the importance of the skills and, indirectly through those, the employability of the employees.

Since 2000, development projects have been carried out in 831 workplaces within the framework of the governmental Finnish Workplace Development Programme. The projects have been aimed at improving well-being at work, developing teamwork, personnel management, the substance of the work and the skills and ability to handle the work. In all, more than 75 000 people have taken part in these projects.

2.4.   Integration of vulnerable groups

In Finland, there has been a strong focus on trying to reduce long-term unemployment. Those affected have been offered special training and service, but those who have failed to meet the expectations of the authorities have also had their benefits reduced.

During 1998-2002, a comprehensive national age-awareness programme was implemented, which highlighted the need for special measures targeted at older employees and warned that early retirement was too widespread in Finland.

Various equality measures and the activities of the equality ombudsman have aimed at promoting equality in the labour market. Segregation remains significant, with many branches dominated by women who are relatively low-paid.

The immigrant population is relatively small in Finland. Detailed legislation on discrimination on grounds other than gender is currently in preparation on the basis of the relevant EU directives.[33] This legislation came into force on 1 February 2004. A separate authority, the minority ombudsman, was earlier established to better monitor and improve the position and rights of foreigners and ethnic minorities.[34] The new Act on equality covers almost all the grounds for discrimination mentioned in the Constitution as ethnicity or race, nationality, age, language, religion, belief, opinion, health, disability, sexual orientation or any other similar reason. The scope of application and the sanctions in the new Act vary however largely depending on which ground for discrimination is in question. The general sanction is compensation (usually not more than 15 000 euros).

2.5.   Occupational health and safety and medical care

Legislation on occupational health and safety was comprehensively reviewed at the beginning of the 21st century.[35] The legislation was first and foremost brought up to date, but also developed in a direction which focused the attention on preventive health and worker protection, risk assessment and good practice with regard to occupational health. Increased attention was also focused on the psychological working environment, harassment problems, etc. All in all, however, the legislation was developed on a tripartite basis and thus strongly inspired by previous traditions. It also aims to enable Finland to fully meet its EU obligations in the field of occupational health and safety. The strong emphasis in the legislation on preventive measures should also be seen as part of the effort to avoid situations in which a person's employability suffers as a result of burn-out, stress, etc.

---

33   Council Directives 2000/43/EC and 2000/78/EC.

34   Lag om minoritetsombudsmannen 660/2001.

35   Ses lagen om företagshälsovård (1383/2001) and lagen om skydd i arbete (738/2002).

3. Labour law and flexibility

3.1. General

There are grounds for claiming that the Finnish labour law system has become smoother and easier to adjust to the needs of individual companies than before. This increased flexibility has, however, been allowed to develop subject to tight control and regulation. The main trend in the evolution of labour law is better described as modernisation and simplification than actual deregulation. At a general level, the Finnish legal system appears relatively flexible, but it is still subject to criticism from small companies, not least because of the lack of any relaxation of the generally applicable collective agreements as described below.

The scope of labour law is often described as relatively broad. With respect to working time regulation, in particular, Finnish law has been applied rather more narrowly than EU law. This has led to some tension. In connection with the application of the Employment Contracts Act, the application of the law to various previously problematic groups (different leisure pursuits, sports, etc.) was clarified, but the rules essentially remained unchanged. Ongoing discussions on telework and different types of 'teamwork' have yet to leave their mark on the legislation.

3.2. Fixed-term employment

Fixed-term employment is a controversial issue in Finnish employment policy. Fixed-term employment contracts are relatively common and they affect women in the public sector disproportionately. Whereas approximately 18.2% of all wage earners in Finland are on fixed-term contracts, as indicated above, women account for 21% and men for 15%. The rules of the new Employment Contracts Act are not radically different from what applied before, although the liberalisation introduced in the mid-1990s, by which the conditions under which fixed-term contracts might be concluded were relaxed, has disappeared.

Open-ended or permanent employment contracts remain the rule. Subject to certain limitations, the contract may also be concluded for a *fixed term*. A fixed-term contract may be concluded for a specific date, a specific time period, the completion of a particular task or the occurrence of a specific event (e.g. for a substitute until the return to work of the employee).

The scope for concluding fixed-term employment contracts has been restricted with a view to preventing the undermining of employees' redundancy protection. The Employment Contracts Act provides that there must be valid grounds for concluding a fixed-term contract, but it does not list any such grounds. A fixed-term contract is binding upon both parties for the period agreed. A contract that has been concluded without valid grounds or that is allowed to continue after the expiry of the agreed period is regarded as open-ended.

The new Employment Contracts Act contains two important innovations with regard to fixed-term employment. First, where several fixed-term employment contracts have been concluded successively between the employer and the employee without periods of interruption or with only brief interruptions, the employment relationship will be considered continuous for the purpose of calculating benefits.

In addition, the Employment Contracts Act provides that part-time or fixed-term employment relationships may not, by virtue of their duration or the length of the working time, offer less favourable employment conditions than other forms of employment relationship unless there are objective grounds for doing so. The provision has been included in order to meet the requirements of the EU directives on part-time work and fixed-term work.[36] The provision has led to a number of cases being brought before the Finnish Labour Court concerning the proportional rights of part-time employees.

3.3. Part-time work

An employee may be transferred to part-time work on the ground of redundancy. On the other hand, part-time work may also be a first step onto the labour market and, with that in mind, the Employment Contracts Act introduced an obligation on the employer to offer extra work to part-time employees. If the employer needs labour for extra work, he must first offer it to his part-time employees before recruiting new employees (2:5). The employer may also be responsible for providing the training necessary to enable the employee to accept such work. In addition, according to established practice, the employer must provide information within the company or place of work on any posts which become vacant. The idea is to enable part-time and fixed-term employees to apply for these posts on the same basis as ordinary employees or permanent employees. As previously mentioned, discrimination against part-time employ-

---

36   See Council Directive 97/81/EC (part-time work) and Council Directive 99/70/EC (temporary work).

ees is prohibited. Part-time work has also been promoted through better possibilities for part-time pensions.

3.4. Agency work

A company *supplying labour* to another company is considered the employer and a party to the employment contract's provisions on pay and other obligations. This has been clarified considerably in the new Employment Contracts Act. The company in which the work is performed (the user company) is responsible for the actual management and any measures decided in that respect in relationship to the employee. The user company must also ensure adequate health and safety protection, although the supplier company shares the responsibility in accordance with EU rules.[37] Concerning the relationship between collective bargaining and agency work, see the next section.

3.5. Flexibility within the collective agreement system

As a result of the rules obliging employers to abide by the provisions of generally applicable collective agreements, the Finnish collective agreement system is often criticised for being too rigid and unfair to small businesses. The revision of the Employment Contracts Act has increased the transparency of the system and clearly improved the legal protection of employers. Previously, generally applicable agreements would apply immediately, whereas now a separate decision by the authorities is required. The decision can be appealed and the collective agreement must be published.

The difficult question of the relationship between agency work and generally applicable collective agreements has been resolved so that the employment agency (the employer) must pay the minimum wage as defined in the collective agreement that applies to the user company, unless a separate collective agreement is concluded for the agency sector.

At a general level, however, it should be noted that the trend in wage bargaining has been towards greater decentralisation and that an increasing proportion of pay is in the form of different performance-related bonuses. Similarly, the regulation of working time through collective bargaining enables local agreements, a trend which is also supported by the new Working Time Act.

3.6. Leave-related legislation

Leave-related legislation is the key to reconciliation of working and family life and to equal parental responsibility. The new Employment Contracts Act contains detailed provisions on different kinds of parental leave. An employee is entitled to parental leave or partial parental leave during the first three years of the child's life.

An important kind of leave which offers an opportunity both for unemployed persons to enter the labour market and for those who wish to educate themselves further to take career breaks or sabbaticals is the so-called alternate leave. Alternate leave may be of between three months and one year. For an employee to be able to take advantage of this right he must have worked for a total of 10 years and have been with his current employer for at least 12 months. Persons on alternate leave are entitled to a benefit of up to 70% of income support for unemployed persons (80% in some exceptional cases). The purpose of alternate leave is to improve the employee's health and motivation through a brief absence from work and to create better employment opportunities for unemployed workers. The law is temporary and in force only until the end of 2007.

4. Discrimination, equal treatment and integrity

4.1. Discrimination and equal treatment

In 1995, following Finland's accession to the EU, the Finnish Equality Between the Sexes Act was amended accordingly.[38] This Act contains a series of *so-called soft law* rules aimed at promoting equality in various areas, in particular working life. The general incomes policy agreements have also aimed to promote equality through so-called equality pools, although these take the form of low-wage increases. This means that wage increases have been concentrated on the low-wage, mainly female dominated, groups, but the actual wage increase has been paid to both women and men at that particular wage level.

Mainly, Finnish sex equality legislation fulfils the requirements of EU legislation. A specific feature of Finnish equality legislation is that it applies to all areas of society, not just working life. A proposal for an amendment of the sex equality rules has been drafted, aimed at implementing the revised EU Equal Treatment Directive.[39] A formal government proposal is

---

37   See Directive 91/383/EEC.
38   Lag om jämställdhet mellan kvinnor och män, 8.8.1986/609, as amended 17.2.1995/206.
39   See Council Directive 76/207/EEC as amended by Directive 2002/73/EC

expected in autumn 2004 and the draft legislation would reinforce the duty of employers to reveal wage differentials within the company.

In addition, in compliance with the Constitution, Finnish legislation contains a general prohibition of discrimination on all internationally recognised grounds. To this day, discrimination on grounds other than gender has not been the subject of special rules in Finnish law and the case law is limited. With the implementation of the EU Anti-Discrimination Directive, this has changed radically with the new general Act on Equality (see above).

4.2. Protection of personal integrity in working life

The manner in which the position of the employee is viewed and the legal regulation of that position have gradually changed in Finland, and these changes are evident in legislation which has been adopted in the last 10 years. As far as fundamental freedoms and rights are concerned, previously the relationship between the individual and the State was the main consideration. Provisions on protection such as those contained in anti-discrimination legislation, equality legislation and integrity legislation are based on the idea that an individual may require protection from other individuals, including his employer. This has also been expressed in the sense that an employee does not renounce all his fundamental freedoms and rights simply by entering into an employment relationship. It is seen as the responsibility of the State to protect the individual's human dignity from both the State itself and other individuals.

A separate law on the protection of personal integrity in working life entered into force in 2001.[40] The Act on the Protection of Personal Integrity in Working Life has priority over general law on integrity. Questions not covered by the Working Life Personal Integrity Act must be resolved by reference to other legislation, such as the Personal Data Act (1999), the Act on the Protection of Personal Integrity in Telecommunication and Data Protection within Telebusiness (1999), the Occupational Health Act (2001:1383) and other health and safety legislation, and the Cooperation Act.

The protection of personal integrity is largely concerned with questions relating to *handling of personal data*. An employer requires data on an employee for a variety of reasons. These may be business-related, be connected with management functions or with employer duties under the

law or a collective agreement (e.g., the duty to pay wages). The data is often collected by the employer in connection with decisions that concern the employee, e.g. The decision to recruit a jobseeker or on selection for education/training or for promotion, as well as decisions to dismiss an employee on grounds of negligence. In terms of fairness, it is vital that the data are correct and adequate for the purpose.

Like the EU Personal Data Directive, Finnish personal data legislation assumes that personal data have a kind of life-cycle.[41] The concept of *handling of personal data* refers to all phases of this life-cycle, including gathering, processing, storage, use and transfer. The handling of personal data is regulated through both comprehensive general provisions and specific provisions adapted to various situations. The provisions governing the employer's right to process health-related information on an employee falls into the latter category.

It is one of the general comprehensive requirements that an employer may only process personal data of *direct relevance* to the employee's employment situation. The data must be connected with the handling of the rights and obligations of the parties to the employment relationship or with the benefits offered to the employee by the employer or with the specific nature of the tasks. Exemptions from this relevance requirement are subject to the consent of the employee.

When processing personal data, an employer must take care and observe good data handling. These requirements mean that the processing must observe the constitutionally based right to privacy. Processing is also bound by the *end-purpose requirement*. Personal data may only be processed for the end-purpose for which they were originally gathered. The employer must ensure that incorrect, incomplete or out-of-date personal data are not processed (absence of error requirement, Section 9(2)).

The general personal data legislation also *prohibits the processing of sensitive data*. Sensitive data are defined in the law and include data referring to or intended to refer to racial or ethnic origin, a person's social or political opinions or religious beliefs, membership of a trade union, health, illness, disability or treatment, a person's sexual orientation or behaviour (Section 11). There is a long series of exemptions from this prohibition, in all 13 points. Despite the prohibition, such processing may take place as the person concerned has given his explicit consent for this. The requirements of such explicit consent are relatively high and correspond, *inter alia*, to the notion of 'informed consent'.

---

40   Lagen om integritetsskydd i arbetslivet (477/2001).
41   Council Directive 95/46/EC, Personal Data Act 22.4.1999/523.

Gathering of the employee's personal data. Where an employer gathers personal data on an employee he must, in first instance, do so from the employee himself. As a general rule, the consent of the employee (or jobseeker) is required for the employer to be allowed to gather personal data from another source. Personal credit data or extracts from the criminal records aimed at establishing the trustworthiness of the employee are exempt.

Personality and aptitude tests. During the 1990s, it became common place to carry out personality and aptitude tests. They are used for both recruitment and selection for training or promotion. Companies often purchase the services or test methods from specialised companies. A person cannot be legally required to be submitted to such a test. In practice, however, a refusal might jeopardise a person's chances of being recruited or promoted within the company. A test may only be carried out with the consent of the employee (Section 5(1)).

The questions raised by requests to submit to these tests are, in practice, difficult to resolve. As in questions relating to the gathering of personal data, issues of legal certainty are the key. The individual must be able to assume that any data gathered on him and subsequently used as a basis for a decision are reliable. Tests and companies specialising in testing are not subject to certification (unlike, for example, health and safety personnel). The law provides an initial solution to this problem by making the employer *responsible for the quality* of any tests used. The employer must ensure that reliable test methods are used and that competent persons carry out the tests. The employer's responsibility extends to ensuring that any data obtained is correct. The law provides that the data must be correct 'considering the nature and quality of the test method' (Section 5(1)).

The quality requirement is combined with a provision on *access.* The employer or a person carrying out the test on behalf of the employer must, at the request of the employer, grant the employee access to the written assessment free of charge. Where the assessment was verbal, the employee is entitled to a description of the content of the assessment.

Health monitoring and test. Health is an area in which the protection of personal integrity, in the form of confidentiality rules applicable to medical files, etc., goes back a long time. Monitoring and tests of the employee's health carried out on behalf of the employer may only be carried out by qualified members of the health and nursing professions, persons with adequate laboratory training. The same applies to sampling. Health and nursing services must be used in accordance with the provisions of the relevant legislation. The legislation on workplace health and safety specifically imposes an obligation on employees to take part in monitoring of the health situation.

Alcohol and drugs tests. The provisions relating to health and nursing services in the Act on the Protection of Personal Integrity in Working Life also cover alcohol and drug tests (Section 6). For work-related drug tests, the same basic rules apply as in the case of medical examinations and tests. This concerns both consent and the requirements with regard to the personnel carrying out the test or processing it.

Genetic examination. The employer may not demand that an employee submits himself to a genetic examination. This applies during both the recruitment process and the employment relationship. The employer is also not entitled to information about whether the employee has undergone a genetic examination (Section 7).

Data relating to the employee's health. The general rule is that an employer is *entitled to process* data relating to an employee's health where the data have been gathered from a specified source and are used for a specific purpose. It is a requirement that the data be gathered from the employee or from another source with the employee's written consent. Persons who process health-related data are bound by *professional secrecy.* They may not disclose the data to persons outside the employment relationship, even after the cessation of the employment relationship.

Technical monitoring and computer networks. Modern information technology has given new meaning to traditional questions relating to monitoring. Two overlapping questions, in particular, have been raised. The first concerns the employer's right to monitor the employee's behaviour with the help of technical devices (e.g. Video cameras). The other concerns monitoring the employee's use of IT equipment (e.g. The Internet, e-mail). The new law covers these questions, but it fails to provide actual answers.

The purpose, use and methods of electronic surveillance of employees were made the *subject of consultations* in the Protection of Personal Integrity Act. The same applies to use of electronic mail and computer networks. Separate rules on employees' right to be heard apply to companies which, by virtue of their low number of employees, fall outside the scope of the Cooperation Act.

Electronic mail. The employer's right to monitor his employees' use of electronic mail at work is a topical issue for which Finnish law provides no answer.

When the Finnish parliament adopted the Protection of Personal Integrity in Working Life Act, it was on the understanding that the government would draft supplementary legislation on technical monitoring at work, monitoring of computer networks and e-mail, as well as more detailed provisions relating to drug tests. A government proposal 162/2003 is currently being debated in the Finnish Parliament and it seems likely that new legislation will come into force during the second half of 2004.

5. Conclusion

5.1. Pragmatic tripartism

The development of Finnish labour law in the last decade has been characterised by consensus and tripartism. During this period, the main elements of Finnish individual labour law and occupational health and safety law, including legislation on young employees,[42] has been amended within the framework of agreements and compromises between the main social partners. The pension system has also been reformed through partial agreements, aimed at increasing flexibility and keeping pension costs under control when the large generations born in the second half of the 1940s retire.

Finland's membership of the EU would appear to have boosted the national sense of mutual understanding between the social partners, particularly at the level of the central organisations. Without embarking on an analysis of the various social and economic preconditions for this cooperation, which undoubtedly improved with the high growth in Finland in the second half of the 1990s, a number of factors can be mentioned here.

For a small country like Finland, EU membership has been seen as a big challenge, and the social partners – on both sides of industry – have systematically stressed the many common interests in EU membership.

The role of the central organisations has increased as a result of their participation in the EU social dialogue process, including negotiations on new directives in accordance with the procedure laid down in Article 139 of the Treaty.

There has also been cooperation at national level aimed at implementing EU legislation. In this regard, a pragmatic approach has prevailed, whereby, on the understanding that Finland must fulfil its national obligations correctly, the two

sides have agreed that employers should not seek to exploit the possibility sometimes offered by EU legislation to water down existing legislation, in return for which the trade unions would generally refrain from demanding rules which go beyond what the directives require.

The Finnish system of generally applicable collective agreements and relatively detailed legislation means that the kind of problems with regard to the national regulatory tradition (i.e. exclusively on the basis of collective agreements) which has arisen in Denmark has not been an issue in Finland.

There are plenty of practical examples of this. One such example is the Supreme Court's judgement in Case 2001:72, in which it held that voluntary pension schemes were not covered by transfer of undertakings, given that this was not a requirement of the relevant directive. Traditionally, no such exception had been made in Finland for voluntary pension schemes, and the social partners, who had taken part in the implementation of the directive, indicated that the intention had not been for the position of employees to be weakened as a result of the implementation of the directive. The government subsequently tabled a legislative amendment aimed at safeguarding what was perceived as the previous legal situation. The amendment was implemented with the support of the social partners.[43]

5.2. Assessment of the substance of legislative developments

Large areas of labour law have been modernised in the last decade. A modernisation of the Holiday Act and the Cooperation Within Undertakings Act remains a part of the reform programme drawn up by the parties. The Collective Agreements Act is relatively old, but it is still considered to provide an adequate framework for collective bargaining. In addition the implementation of many EU legislative instruments has taken place within the framework of a flexible tripartite system.

Legislation has mainly been adopted through consensus and compromise, often resulting from lengthy negotiations. A policy of mutual understanding such as this, obviously restricts the scope for radical changes to the form and substance of the law. Instead, a modernisation and partial simplification of the laws demonstrate that reform has taken place. Within this social dialogue, the employee's side has displayed a certain traditional scepticism towards so-called

---

42   Lag om unga arbetstagare 19.11.1993/998 (amended in 1996 and 1998), implementing Directive 94/33/EEC.

43   Lag om ändring av arbetsavtalslagen(943/2002).

soft law, partly explaining why Finnish legislation has not really developed in that direction. On the other hand, the law has only to a limited extent been adjusted to new challenges such as public procurement, competition rules or new company structures. This is explained by the employer side's systematic pursuit of as much freedom as possible for business.

On the basis of the above, the evolution of the substance of Finnish labour law in the last decade may be summed up in three main points:

1. Greater emphasis on fundamental individual rights. This is evident not least in the areas of personal integrity and discrimination.

2. Greater emphasis on individual labour law and the role and opportunities of the individual. This is clear from the fact that the role of the individual is taken into account not only in terms of rights, but also in terms of procedural rules. In addition, the individual's needs for flexibility is taken into consideration in the various types of parental leave and alternate leave.

3. An effort to reconcile business flexibility and employee security. Investments in training, development of the substance of the work and skills development are the watchwords of official labour market policy. The legislative solutions regarding agency work and working time are other examples of the effort to reconcile flexibility and security.

In all three areas, the EU can be said to have contributed to and accelerated the evolution of the law. By contrast, it is hard to find a single instance of national development being at odds with the general direction of the EU. However, within the Finnish labour market system, EU regulation is often criticised for being too complicated and technically detailed to enable implementation in a simple and transparent manner.

The evolution described above has taken place within a labour market system characterised by a concentration of issues related to legislation, policy and the EU in the central labour market organisations. At the same time, the evolution was characterised by a decentralisation of collective bargaining, in particular on wages and working time, to the local level. The collective bargaining system has retained its strong role in regulating employment conditions in most branches.

The evolution of labour law has not, however, been able to prevent a certain polarisation within Finnish labour between a group of more or less permanently unemployed persons lacking the qualifications sought by employers and a group of well-paid employees specialising in the new tasks of the information society. Another problem is the apparent growth of the informal economy. Such developments are particularly evident in branches employing labour from the various countries of the Baltic region, including construction, transport or catering work. Tripartite discussions are currently under way on how to improve the national monitoring systems with a view to countering this development.

Chapter III:
Sweden

1. Introduction

1.1. Brief history

By the late 1930s, the view had developed in Sweden that regulation of the labour market was a matter for the social partners and that the legislator (the government and the parliament) should refrain from intervening with legislation. Over the subsequent decades, both the legislator and the social partners accepted this distribution of the roles. The legislation adopted was limited and aimed mainly at evening out differences between various groups of employees with regard to, for example, holidays and working time. By contrast, many issues became the subject of collective agreements, including the influence of works councils and a degree of employment protection. The legislator's reluctance to intervene in matters of labour law came to an end in the early 1970s with the adoption of a number of new laws. Prominent among these were the Employment Protection Act (1974) and the Co-Decision Act (1976). The implementation of these new laws led to a considerable deterioration in the social partners' prospects for cooperation and joint responsibility. The legislation adopted in the 1970s remains controversial. Thus, the Employment Protection Act has since been the subject of no less than five government reviews. In spite of this the labour laws adopted in the 1970s remain essentially unchanged.

Since Sweden became a member of the European Union in 1995 there has been 'a second wave' of legislation. A series of new acts have been adopted in order to transpose EC directives.

1.2. The social partners

By international standards, trade union membership is remarkably high in Sweden. Almost 80% of employees indicate professional affiliation. There are three union confederations representing the employees. The Swedish Trade Union Confederation (*Landsorganisationen – LO*) organises blue-collar workers and represents approximately half of all employees in Sweden. The Swedish Confederation of Professional Employees (*Tjänstemännens Centralorganisation – TCO*) caters for salaried

employees and represents approximately one third of all employees. The Swedish Confederation of Professional Associations (*Sveriges Akademikers Centralorganisation – SACO*) represents about 12% of the labour force. The Confederation of Swedish Enterprise (*Svenskt Näringsliv*, previously SAF) is the central organisation representing private employers. The Confederation of Swedish Enterprise represents about 57 000 companies, together employing approximately 75% of all employees in the private sector. In its capacity as employer, the State is represented by a separate authority, the Swedish Agency for Government Employers (*Arbetsgivarverket*). At council and county council level, the Swedish Association of Local Authorities (*Svenska Kommunförbundet*) and the Swedish Federation of County Councils (*Landstingsförbundet*) respectively serve as employers' organisations.

Only a small number of employers' organisations and trade unions are not affiliated to the large central organisations. Trade unions are not structured along religious or political lines. It is relatively rare for trade unions to be competing for the same group of employees.

Swedish industrial relations can be seen as both highly decentralised and highly centralised. Trade unions are strongly represented in most workplaces except in very small workplaces. Local trade union representation monitors compliance with the law and with collective agreements and is responsible for co-determination. However, decisions with policy implications and difficult legal questions are preserved for the national-level federations.

In Sweden, employee representation is channelled exclusively through the trade unions. In principle, works councils do not exist (with the exception of European works councils).

1.3. Decentralised regulation through collective bargaining

Despite the recent growth in labour market legislation, collective agreements remain the most important instrument for regulating wages and other employment conditions. Swedish collective agreements cover virtually every aspect of an employment relationship and it is estimated that 90% of employees are covered by a collective agreement. In the public sector, all employees – blue-collar workers as well as salaried employees – are covered by collective agreements. In the private sector, the coverage is somewhat lower and varies between different sectors.

Collective agreements are generally concluded at three levels: national cross-sectoral agreements, national sectoral agreements and local or company-level agreements.

At the *national cross-sectoral level*, agreements are concluded between central organisations or negotiating cartels. At this level, basic agreements are concluded, laying down the rules for subsequent collective bargaining. The basic agreements often contain provisions on industrial disputes and negotiating arrangements. Specific agreements are also concluded at this level, on issues such as co-determination, insurance and pensions. The national cross-sectoral level has traditionally played a key role in wage bargaining. Between the mid-1950s and 1981, the level of wage increases was agreed between the central organisations in the private sector, i.e. LO and SAF (the Confederation of Swedish Enterprise). These agreements were seen as setting the trend for other labour market sectors, i.e. for the public sector and for the white-collar workers in the private sector. Since 1981, wage agreements are no longer concluded between LO and SAF.

The most important collective agreements are concluded at *sectoral level*. Sectoral or federation-level agreements lay down a detailed regulation of employment conditions and contain provisions on most aspects of the employment relationship, such as wages, working time, holidays, periods of notice, travel allowances, etc. Increasingly, these agreements have become framework agreements, leaving broad scope for local adjustments and derogations. Sectoral agreements tend to leave it to the local parties to agree both on the size of any wage increase as well as on its distribution between individuals. However, agreements often contain 'fall back' provisions which must be applied if the local parties fail to agree. These rules usually indicate the level of the overall wage increase within the company and a minimum increase for each employee. The sectoral agreement also leaves the local parties free to agree on the length and organisation of working time.

In recent decades, the evolution has generally been towards more decentralised collective bargaining. This decentralisation is evident through two developments. Firstly, bargaining between the central organisations at national level has become less significant. Secondly, the nature of national sectoral agreements has changed from detailed regulation to framework or process agreements leaving greater scope for regulation at company level. At this level, regulation may be agreed either between the employer and the local trade union representatives or, directly, between the employer and the employees concerned. In the latter scenario the employees would possibly also be assisted by trade union representatives. Wages and working time are among the issues increasingly dealt with at company level. This trend is strongest for salaried employees. Company-level bargaining is generally subject to a peace obligation.

1.4. The private-law nature of labour law and labour law in the public sector

Swedish labour law tends to be viewed as private law. Legislation creates rights and obligations for individuals which may be relied upon in a court. The remedies, which may be imposed, are mainly derived from private law, such as annulment and damages. Public law mainly applies in the area of occupational health and safety.

Successive legislative amendments (1965, 1976 and 1994) have 'privatised' the public employment relationship, in the sense that, broadly speaking, the same rules apply to the private and the public sectors. Everyone employed in the public sector, whether blue- or white-collar, is an employee. The current employment protection of public-sector employees is governed by the Employment Protection Act,[44] which applies to both private- and public sector employees.[45] This Act contains only a limited number of specific rules for public-sector employees. Judges with tenure do, however, enjoy stronger employment protection.[46] In addition, public employees enjoy virtually the same rights as private employees with regard to strike action. The idea that private and public employees should be governed by the same rules is prevalent in Swedish law. Thus, when implementing the Transfers of Undertakings Directive,[47] Sweden chose to make the rules fully applicable to the public sector, regardless of whether or not the employer is engaged in an economic activity.

In recent decades, the public sector has been opened up to significant competition. This is mainly because publicly funded activities which were previously managed by the public

---

44   Lagen (1994:260) om offentlig anställning.
45   Lagen (1982: 80) om anställningsskydd.
46   Lagen (1994:261) om fullmaktsanställning.
47   Directive 2001/23/EC on the approximation of the laws of the Member States relating to the safeguarding of employees' rights in the event of transfers of undertakings, businesses or parts of undertakings or businesses.

sector itself are now, to a large extent, handled by private contractors. This raises questions concerning, *inter alia*, the protection of employment and employment conditions when contractors change. Given that the law makes virtually no distinction between private and public employment, the legal effects of the privatisation of public activities have probably been less dramatic in Sweden than in many other countries.

1.5. Dispute resolution in legal disputes

Both the general courts of first instance (the district courts – *tingsrätterna*) and the Labour Court have jurisdiction over labour disputes. The Labour Court is the highest instance in labour law disputes and it covers the entire country. It is composed of both legally trained judges and representatives of employers' organisations and trade unions. Some types of disputes are brought directly before the Labour Court. This is primarily the case when the case is brought by an employers' organisation or a trade union and concerns employment relationships regulated by collective agreement. In other types of disputes, the case must be brought before the district court. This concerns, *inter alia*, cases brought by non-union employees or trade union members who are bringing their case before the court without the support of their union. The decision of the district court may be appealed to the Labour Court. The decision of the Labour Court may not be appealed. The Labour Court decides between 100 and 200 cases per year.

Trade unions play a key role in monitoring the application of the law and of collective agreements. Both labour law and the bargaining arrangements laid down in collective agreements provide that negotiations must take place with a view to resolving the dispute before a case is brought before the Labour Court. Ordinarily, negotiations are first conducted at local (company) level. Where no solution is found, the parties may request central negotiations, i.e. negotiations between the sectoral employers' organisation and the trade union. It is estimated that only a very small proportion of disputes which have been the subject of central negotiations are brought before the Labour Court.

1.6. Economic and demographic changes

Up until the beginning of the 1990s, Sweden had a significantly higher rate of employment and lower rate of unemployment than most EU countries. At the beginning of the 1990s, however, Sweden was hit by a deep economic recession, which caused an exceptionally fast rise in unemployment. The initial wave of redundancies within manufacturing industry caused a contraction of the tax base at a time when the

costs of unemployment were rising fast. A second wave of mass redundancies then hit the public sector as many activities, particularly health, education and care, were restructured or rationalised. The economy recovered during the mid-1990s, although unemployment remained high. Only by the end of the decade did unemployment start to fall. The rate of unemployment currently stands at around 4%.

During the 1990s, the population of working age increased. Despite this increase, labour force participation was lower than in 1990. This was partly due to the increase in the proportion of older people (the 45-54 and 55-59 age groups). The proportion of people aged 25-34 remained unchanged, while the proportion of other age groups fell. It should also be noted that the proportion of older people is expected to rise further during the first decades of the 21st century.

Sick leave, particularly long-term leave, has increased dramatically in Sweden in recent years. The number of sick leaves exceeding 365 days rose from 75 000 to 120 000 between 1997 and 2001. During this four-year period, the number of people taking early retirement or receiving a disability pension also increased.

In 2001, the total number of days lost in sick leave, including qualifying periods, paid sick leave and sickness benefit days was equivalent to 400 000 man-years. Absences due to early retirement or disability pension were also equivalent to 400 000 man-years. This means that absences from working life on the grounds of ill health totalled 800 000 man-years in 2001 or, put differently, 14% of the working population.

1.7. Migration

The Swedish population has changed considerably in the last few decades and Sweden is now a country of many different cultures, languages, religions and traditions. More than 10% of the population was born abroad. The immigrant population may be divided into three groups of roughly equal size: one third was born in other Nordic countries, one third was born in other European countries, and one third was born outside Europe. The immigrant population is a disparate group of people in terms of the duration of their stay in Sweden, their country of origin, etc. Their economic backgrounds vary at least as much as for people who are Swedish by birth. Of all residence permits granted in 2000, 23% were issued on grounds of refugee-status, need for protection or humanitarian grounds and 51% were issued on family grounds. The remaining 26% were granted for study visits, work, adoption or other EEA-related grounds.

In 1997, the Swedish parliament (*Riksdagen*) adopted new guidelines for integration policy. The guidelines provide that general policy must take into account the ethnic and cultural diversity of society and that special solutions for immigrants should generally be limited to the period immediately following their arrival in Sweden. The general aim of integration policy must be to help individuals look after themselves and be part of society, protect fundamental democratic values, promote equal rights and opportunities for women and men and prevent and combat ethnic discrimination, xenophobia and racism.

1.8. Mediation and resolution of interest disputes

Questions relating to wage formation and industrial disputes have generally been considered the responsibility of the social partners. Nominal wage increases have been higher in Sweden than in the rest of the world, leading to higher inflation and undermining real wages. Despite total wage increases in the order of 150%, real wages did not increase at all between 1980 and 1995. In order to safeguard jobs, Sweden was forced into successive currency devaluations, in turn driving up the rate of inflation. In 2000, new rules on mediation were introduced in an attempt to improve the prospects of combining moderate real-wage increases with low unemployment and stable prices. The new rules may also be seen as a measure preparing for a possible membership of the economic and monetary union. The amended legislation established a new National Mediation Office (*Medlingsinstitutet*). The Office is not only charged with the task of mediating between the social partners, but also of 'contributing to a well-functioning labour market'. In comparison with its predecessors, the Office has been given more extensive powers. The Office may, without the consent of the social partners, appoint a mediator in threatened disputes and may, in certain circumstances, postpone announced strike action.[48] The social partners may avoid the intervention of the Mediation Office by agreeing certain procedures for cooperation during collective bargaining. Such agreements now cover large parts of the labour market.

1.9. Constitutional reform

The Swedish Constitution has traditionally had a surprisingly limited impact on labour law. It is highly unusual for labour law to be challenged on constitutional grounds or for the Constitution to be invoked in the interpretation of labour law.

No constitutional reforms with implications for labour law have taken place during the period under consideration.

In Sweden, the positive right of association is guaranteed in the Constitution. In a legislative context, the question of whether the negative right of association should be included in this constitutional guarantee has occasionally arisen. Proposals to that effect have not led to any legislation.

In 1994 the European Convention for the Protection of Human Rights and Fundamental Freedoms (ECHR) was incorporated into Swedish law through an Act of Parliament. The Act has no formal constitutional status. However, it follows from the Swedish constitution (*Regeringsformen*) that the courts or administrative agencies shall refuse to apply statutes or regulations, which *manifestly* conflict with the ECHR. Since the incorporation, the Convention has been invoked several times in the case law of the Labour Court in cases regarding negative freedom of association and privacy of the employees.

1.10. Government

From 1991 until 1994, Sweden was governed by a centre-right coalition of the Moderate Party, the Christian Democrats, the Liberal Party and the Centre Party. The September 1994 general election brought a Social Democratic minority government to power, supported by the Green Party and the Left Party. The Social Democratic government was re-elected in 1998 and 2002.

2. From employment protection to employability

2.1. Employment protection

The current Employment Protection Act was adopted in 1982,[49] but is essentially based on a law from 1974. The Employment Protection Act has been the subject of several government reviews during the period under consideration. Two questions, in particular, have generated debate: the rules relating to redundancies and the permissibility of fixed-term work. The latter is dealt with in section 3.1.

The Employment Protection Act applies to both private and public employees. Small businesses are not exempt. The Act makes a distinction between dismissal on personal grounds and redundancies. Redundancies are defined as dismissals on

---

48   46–53 §§ lagen (1976:580) om medbestämmande i arbetslivet.
49   Lagen (1982:80) om anställningsskydd.

grounds that are not related to the person of the employee concerned. The Act does not require that a certain number of employees be laid off.

In principle, the Labour Court does not review an employer's grounds for resorting to dismissal, nor does the law contain any rules on severance pay, etc. (apart from the rules on notice periods). The protection of employees in the event of redundancies is mainly ensured through the employer's obligation to respect certain rules regarding priority ordering. As a general rule, a priority order must be established for every workplace. In addition, separate lists are drawn up for blue-collar workers and salaried employees. Within the scope of the priority order, employees with greater seniority (i.e. length of service) have priority to remain in their jobs. Factors such as ability and dependants must not be taken into account. However, if an employee may only be kept on, subject to a transfer, he must be adequately qualified for the new job.

The rules on priority ordering are semi-mandatory, i.e. They may be derogated from by collective agreement. Following a change in the law in 1997, such agreements may be concluded at central as well as at local level. This option contributes to strengthening the influence of trade unions during company closures. Any employer who wishes to derogate from the relatively strict rules on priority ordering must seek the agreement of the trade unions concerned.

Employers, among others, have claimed that the rules on priority ordering are too rigid and fail to take into account a company's need to continue to operate. Others have criticised proposals to change the rules as undermining employment protection.

The strict seniority principle means that the selection category (i.e. The group of employees who are compared against each other when the selection is done) takes on central significance. The wider the selection category, the greater the significance becomes of the seniority principle, and vice versa. Discussions have focused on the possibility of exclusions from the priority order. In 1993, the then centre-right government introduced the possibility of excluding two employees from the scope of the priority order, but the incoming Social Democratic government in 1994 removed this possibility. The possibility of exclusions from the scope of the priority order was re-introduced in 2001. The amendment was pushed through by the centre-right parties and the Green Party, against the wishes of the Social Democratic government. The amendment allows employers with maximum ten employees to exclude two employees from the priority order.

2.2. Improving employability

During the 1990s, the fight against unemployment was a key government objective. When it came to power in 1994, the Social Democratic government declared its intention to reduce official unemployment by half, to 4%. This objective was reached in 2000.

2.2.1. Education policy

The general education policy has been viewed as an important element in the government's work to increase employment. Investment in public education has been considered the basis for life-long learning and thus for increased employment and improved growth. During the 1990s, the education system was expanded in several respects. In 1997, the so-called 'adult education initiative' (Kunskapslyftet) was launched, a five-year adult education programme covering over 100 000 people every year. The aim of the knowledge drive was to give those with less education an opportunity to combine work with further education. The primary target group were unemployed adults, completely or partially lacking three-year upper secondary education. The universities were also comprehensively expanded during the 1990s. The expansion covered the entire country, but was concentrated on the newer and smaller universities. The purpose was to develop strong universities in every county.

In 2002, the Swedish parliament approved guidelines for a new system for stimulating individual skills development. The idea was to enable the individual to make tax-deductible deposits on a 'skills savings account' (kompetenssparkonto). Incentives for the employer to pay into an employee's skills savings account will also be introduced. The interest rate on the skills savings account will be taxed in the same way as ordinary capital income. Initially, a public authority will manage the skills savings accounts. Withdrawals from the skills savings account will be taxed as employment income. An incentive is that when withdrawals are made for the purpose of skills development, a skills premium will be given in the form of a tax reduction. The size of the reduction will be determined by the duration of the skills development. The type of skills development sought with the system shall be broadly defined. The Prime Minister's Office is currently working on the rules required for the individual skills development system. No proposal has yet been submitted to the parliament.

2.2.2. Employment policy

The responsibility for improving the employability of unemployed persons and persons threatened by unemployment rests mainly on public employment policy. Swedish employment policy has traditionally followed the 'work line', i.e. The principle that jobseekers should first and foremost be offered work or inclusion in employment policy measures as opposed to cash benefits. In recent years, the work line has evolved into a 'work and skills line'. This means that where no work can be found, unemployed persons should be offered appropriate training or traineeships which may lead to a job, instead of passively receiving cash benefits.

An employment policy measure aimed at improving the employability of unemployed persons is the offer of labour market training, that is, professionally adapted training aimed at enabling the individual to find or keep a job and at preventing skills shortages in the labour market.[50] In 2002, an activity guarantee was introduced with the aim of breaking the vicious circle of unemployment and employment policy programmes for the long-term unemployed. The activity guarantee is aimed at providing extra support to enter the regular labour market in the form of measures tailored to the individual.

2.2.3. Employers' responsibility for skills development

Skills development and life-long learning for employees is primarily a matter for employers. The employer's investment in skills development can to a large extent be seen as an investment in the future, which employers like to influence.

Collective agreements at various levels lay down certain rules on employers' obligations with regard to skills development. Such agreements have existed for a long time, but they seem to have become more widespread. Large parts of the labour market are also covered by so-called *redundancy programme agreements* which aim to facilitate the employee's conversion to other work or training in the event of redundancies. This is done through active conversion work, starting at the time of redundancy or earlier and implemented in cooperation with the redundant employees by the security committees established by the parties to the conversion agreement. These activities are financed by the participating companies paying a fee calculated as a percentage of the wage bill.

Collective agreements on skills development are often of a general nature, offering considerable scope for local cooperation on specific issues relating to skills development. Arrangements concerning the funding of skills development vary with each collective agreement. In some cases, the employer alone

bears the costs. In other cases, employers and employees share the costs. In still other cases, skills development is paid for via separate skills development accounts.

To some extent, labour law may also be said to include an obligation for the employer to support the employee's skills development. The requirement in the Employment Protection Act, that the employer must provide objective grounds for dismissal, implies that employers may not dismiss an employee on the grounds of inadequate skills if the employer could reasonably have been expected to take measures to correct this situation, including through training. Employers must also grant leave for various types of skills development.[51] An employee who has been on leave is explicitly entitled to return to the same or an equivalent position with regard to employment conditions as if no leave had been taken, which may affect any right to skills development which may have been lost during the leave.[52]

When offering the employees skills development the employer is normally considered to be engaged in work or company management. As a result, the granting of skills development on discriminatory grounds may therefore be challenged on the basis of, *inter alia*, anti-discrimination law, in the same way as any other management decision.

2.3. Integration of vulnerable groups

2.3.1. Employment policy

One of the main aims of employment policy is to support those least able to find work and to prevent the marginalisation of groups with little or no foothold in the labour market. Employment policy thus contains a series of measures and programmes aimed at vulnerable labour market groups.

Persons born outside Sweden were hit particularly hard by the increased unemployment in the first half of the 1990s. Immigrants who had just arrived were especially vulnerable. Despite the fall in unemployment among immigrants towards the end of the decade, significant differences remain between immigrants and persons born in Sweden in terms of both unemployment and labour force participation. Employment policy should, in principle, be universal. This implies that, basically, immigrants' labour market needs should be resolved within the framework of universal measures. Nevertheless, the body of labour market legislation contains a number of special rules aimed directly at meeting the particular needs which immi-

---

50   Förordning (2000:634) om arbetsmarknadspolitiska program.

51   See, for example, lagen (1974:981) om arbetstagares rätt till ledighet för utbildning och lagen (1986:613) om rätt till ledighet för svenskundervisning för invandrare.

52   Provisions on the right to return can, for example, be found in Section 9 of the Study Leave Act, Section 17 of the Parental Leave Act and Section 4 of the Employee Representation Act.

grants may have. For example, immigrants are offered Swedish language training partly as labour market training. The same applies to some extent to regular primary and secondary school education. Special rules for immigrants also apply to in-work training and business support (start-up grants).

Unemployment among *persons with a reduced capacity for work* has fallen significantly since the end of the 1990s. Sweden has the highest rate of labour force participation by disabled persons among the OECD countries. Various employment policy programmes are aimed specifically at persons with a reduced capacity for work, for example in the form of help with auxiliary means of assistance in the workplace, a personal assistant or the possibility of wage contributions.[53]

Older employees constitute another vulnerable labour market group. By international standards, labour force participation by older people is high in Sweden. In 2001, the average rate of employment among those aged 55-64 was 67%. A number of employment policy programmes and measures are aimed at helping older employees. Thus, employers who employ a person who has reached the age of 57 and who is long-term unemployed may be entitled to an employment grant.

A number of employment policy measures also aim to help the *long-term unemployed* to return to the regular labour market. The so-called activity guarantee was mentioned above. Another measure entitles employers who employ a long-term unemployed person to some financial support (employment support).[54]

2.3.2. Active measures under the Equal Opportunities Act and the Act on Ethnic Discrimination

Under the *Equal Opportunities Act*,[55] employers must take measures specifically targeted at actively promoting equality in working life. This is to be done in cooperation with employees and trade unions. The requirement to take active measures implies that employers must adapt the working environment to suit both women and men, help both female and male employees reconcile work and family life and take measures to prevent and protect employees from sexual harassment. The employer must also work to ensure that both women and men apply for vacant posts and generally promote equal representation of women and men in various kinds of work. Employers with ten or more employees must draw up an annual equality plan.

Under the 1999 *Act on Ethnic Discrimination*,[56] the employer is also under an obligation to adopt measures to promote equal rights and opportunities regardless of ethnic origin in matters relating to work, employment conditions and other aspects of work as well as opportunities to develop on the job. This must be done in a planned manner. The active measures shall be drawn up and implemented in cooperation with the employees and the trade union representatives. The requirement to take active measures implies that the employer must enable persons with different ethnic backgrounds to apply for vacant posts and take measures to prevent and protect employees from harassment on ethnic grounds. The employer must also, within reason, ensure that the working environment is suited to all employees regardless of ethnic origin.

The employer's obligations under these Acts with regard to active measures may not be the subject of legal claims by individuals. The rules are ultimately enforced by the possibility of a fine being imposed by the Equality Commission or the Anti-Discrimination Commission in response to a complaint from the Equality Ombudsman, the Ombudsman for Ethnic Discrimination or a concerned central trade union.

The laws against discrimination on the grounds of sexual orientation or disability do not impose any obligation with regard to active measures.

3. Labour law and company adaptability

3.1. Fixed-term work

The number of fixed-term workers increased considerably during the 1990s. These workers now represent at least half a million employees or over one-sixth of the total labour force. Fixed-term work is widespread within the nursing and care sectors, various business services, commerce and education and research. There is a clear trend in the labour market towards increasingly organising work on a project basis. Fixed-term work is common among younger employees and women. People of non-Swedish origin are also clearly over-represented within certain sectors. The impact on the individual varies, but generally speaking, by comparison with permanent employees, fixed-term workers have limited access to skills development, have less control over how their tasks are

---

53   Förordning (2000:630) om särskilda insatser för personer med arbetshandikapp.
54   Förordning (1997:1275) om anställningsstöd.
55   Jämställdhetslagen (1991:433).
56   Lagen (1999:130) om åtgärder mot diskriminering i arbetslivet på grund av etnisk tillhörighet, religion eller annan trosuppfattning.

carried out, suffer worse health risks and experience greater financial uncertainty. This less secure form of employment also has more overarching social effects, such as problems establishing a family or having children and problems of integration. It also creates costs associated with ill health for both the individual and society. Many fixed-term workers do eventually secure permanent employment, but it is a tough journey. During the 1990s, over half of those in fixed-term work still found themselves in such employment or in no employment at all after two years. These developments are explained by a variety of connected factors, inter alia the economic crisis and structural changes. This involves new forms of work organisation characterised by slimmed-down core businesses and outsourcing, a shift towards services and service-based production, altered patterns of consumption and increased internationalisation, but also political decisions to curb spending, widespread opportunities to take leave, etc.

Rules on fixed-term work can be found mainly in the Employment Protection Act. The protection of employment under the Act refers to permanent employment. Provisions on protection for fixed-term workers apply only to a few, limited circumstances, including the right of fixed-term workers to be considered first for permanent employment after a certain period of time (normally 12 months' employment). The 1974 Act included a very restricted list of circumstances in which fixed-term work was allowed. The provisions of the Act could be set aside by collective agreements. The law has since evolved in a more liberal direction on the question of fixed-term work. The 1982 Employment Protection Act thus increased the number of permissible forms of fixed-term work. The penalties for illegal fixed-term work were also relaxed. Previous possibilities for the authorities to intervene in clear situations of abuse were also abolished. In 1993, the then centre-right government extended the maximum periods of probation and of work during surges of work from six to nine months. These changes were 'reset' by the new Social democratic government in 1994. In 1997, the Social Democratic government implemented further amendments to the Employment Protection Act aimed at creating 'labour law for increased growth'.[57] These amendments included the introduction of yet another form of employment relationships – collectively agreed fixed-term employment relationships – concluded for a fixed term of between 12 months and three years and covering a maximum of five employees at any given time. Simultaneously the law introduced the possibility of allowing fixed-term work in other circumstances than those laid down in the law provided that the terms were agreed by parties that

were covered by central collective agreements or that the local agreement was approved by a central organisation. On the other hand, a maximum period of substitute employment (three years) was introduced, at the expiry of which the employment relationship would automatically become permanent. As a consequence of the Fixed-Term Work Directive[58] in 2002 a law was introduced prohibiting discrimination against fixed-term employees in terms of employment conditions.[59]

In 2002, a government review resulted in a proposal for entirely new rules on fixed-term work. Under this proposal, fixed-term work contracts would be allowed for a duration of up to 18 months (within a period of five years) except in specifically indicated circumstances. Another feature was a strengthening of the right to priority re-employment for fixed-term workers. Under the proposal, anyone employed on a fixed-term basis and who has not found permanent work at the end of the employment contract must have priority for re-employment. This right applies after six months' employment within a two-year period. The right to priority re-employment applies from the moment notice is given that the employment relationship will cease until nine months after the employment relationship ceased. In addition, a new penalty is proposed. Employers who breach the rules on the maximum period of fixed-term work or the right to priority re-employment must pay compensation amounting to one third of a monthly wage for each completed month of employment, or a maximum of three months' wages. The proposal aims to facilitate job creation (for example during periods of economic growth), prevent lengthy and/or repeated fixed-term work contracts and 'channel' fixed-term workers towards permanent employment. The proposal is currently under consideration by the government.

3.2. Part-time work

3.2.1. Evolution of the labour market

The need to stimulate part-time work is a central issue in the discussion of part-time work at international level. Thus, it is a stated aim of the Part-Time Work Directive[60] to facilitate the development of part-time work on a voluntary basis and to contribute to a flexible organisation of working time in a manner which takes into account the needs of both employers and employees.

The situation in Sweden is different. Part-time work has long been an integrated part of the Swedish labour market. Part-

---

57   See the governmental bill Proposition 1996/97:16.

58   Directive 99/70 EC on the framework agreement on fixed-term work concluded by ETUC, UNICE and CEEP.

59   Lagen (2002:293) om förbud mot diskriminering av deltidsarbetande och arbetstagare med tidsbegränsad anställning.

60   Directive 97/81/EC on the framework agreement on part-time work concluded by UNICE, CEEP and the ETUC.

time work mainly increased before 1980. Between 1965 and 1980, the number of part-time workers doubled from half a million to one million. Since the early 1980s, the proportion of part-time workers has been 23-25%. Over 80% of all part-time workers are women. Against this background, it is often considered strange to speak of part-time jobs as atypical jobs.

Instead, the problem with regard to part-time work in the Swedish labour market is the fact that many part-time workers are *under-employed*, i.e. They work less than they would like. Approximately 21% of the part-time workers are under-employed. A majority of these are women (77%). The majority of those who work part-time cite the nature of the labour market as the reason for not working more.

3.2.2. Measures to prevent involuntary part-time work

The Parental Leave Act[61] contains rules which entitle parents of young children to reduced working time. Both the father and the mother are entitled to a reduction of their normal working time by a quarter to care for a child who is not yet eight years old or who is older but has not yet completed his first year at school. There are no rules on the right to work part-time.

Against the background of the high number of under-employed persons, the government has declared that full-time work must be striven for and that part-time work should only be used to meet the needs of the business or the wishes of the employee. In order to facilitate part-time workers' transfer to full-time work, a rule was introduced in 1996 giving priority to a higher degree of employment.[62] According to this provision, a part-time employee who has indicated to his employer that he would like a higher degree of employment, although full-time at most, has priority for such employment. The provision implies that, in case of an increase in the need for labour, the employer must try to accommodate this wish by offering a part-time employee the higher degree of employment for which he has indicated an interest. The need for additional labour may, for example, be generated by additional work, but it may also result from an employee retiring or reducing his working time, etc. Generally speaking, rather than recruiting a new employee, the employer must then transfer the new tasks to an existing employee. However, for a part-time worker to enjoy the right to priority it should be considered that his transfer to full-time work must enable the employer to meet his labour needs and his qualifications must be adequate for the new tasks.

A separate problem is the status of unemployed part-time workers with regard to *unemployment benefits*. This has been the subject of repeated legislative amendments. Persons in part-time employment who have previously worked full-time are considered to be 'part-time unemployed' and should be entitled to unemployment benefits supplementing the part-time work income. If such so-called top-up benefits become permanent they may contribute to make part-time work and part-time unemployment permanent, since employees have few economic incentives to work more. If, on the other hand, top-up benefits are limited in time, a recipient may be forced to quit his part-time job in order to become full-time unemployed. During the 1990s, the rules were amended several times. At present, the right to top-up benefits will be tested every six months and entitlement to benefits will only continue on certain conditions, e.g. The person has passed his 55th birthday or has been offered, but not yet started, a full-time job.

In order to reduce part-time unemployment and increase the degree of employment among part-time employees, the Swedish Labour Market Board (*Arbetsmarknadsstyrelsen*) has in recent years adopted a practice whereby part-time workers in the health and care sectors are requested to provide a certificate from their employer showing that requested working time cannot be offered.

3.2.3. Discrimination against part-time workers

In principle, Swedish labour law applies to all employees, regardless of their degree of employment. There is no minimum working time required to give a person employee status. The law can be said to rest on the assumption that the part-time workers should be treated in the same way as other employees, and the starting point is that labour law is fully applicable to part-time employees. In the Swedish labour market it is however not unusual for collective agreements to provide different employment conditions for full-time and part-time workers. A more detailed analysis of existing agreements will not be provided here. Suffice it to say that in many areas, collective agreements contain so-called thresholds for exempting part-time employees from all or part of the agreement. The limit is often set at 16 hours per week or 40% of normal working time.

In order to implement the Part-Time Work and Fixed-term Work Directives, a new law came into force in 2002 prohibiting discrimination against part-time and fixed-term workers.[63]

---

61   Föräldraledighetslagen (1995:584).
62   Section 25(a) of the Employment Protection Act (1982:80).
63   Lagen (2002:293) om förbud mot diskriminering av deltidsarbetande arbetstagare och arbetstagare med tidsbegränsad anställning.

The law aims to prevent discrimination against such employees with regard to wages and other employment conditions. The law prohibits both direct and indirect discrimination. As a consequence of the law, the social partners have started reviewing their collective agreements to ensure that they comply with the principle of non-discrimination.

3.3. Agency work

Employment agencies and private employment services were, until the 1990s, in principle prohibited by law. The prohibition was relaxed in 1991. Employment agencies and private employment services are now governed by the Act on Private Employment Services and the Employment Agencies.[64] The provision of agency workers is defined in the law as a legal relationship between a user and an employer which involves the employer providing workers to the user against payment and for the purpose of carrying out work within the business of the purchaser. The law defines employment services as an activity aimed at finding work for jobseekers or labour for employers and which does not involve the provision of agency workers. No permission is required to provide agency workers or offer private employment services. However, employment services for sailors may not be offered against payment. The law also abolished the supervisory tasks previously carried out by the Labour Market Board.

Under the law, anyone offering employment services or agency work shall not request, agree or accept payment from jobseekers or employees in return for offering or finding them work. Agency workers may not, with reference for example to provisions of collective agreements, be prevented from accepting employment with the user company for which they perform or have performed work. Nor may an employee who has left his employment and has taken up employment with an employment agency be hired out to his previous employer within the first six months of leaving that employer.

Following deregulation, the market for agency work has expanded considerably. Nevertheless, at present it still only covers less than 1% of employed persons.

The agency work sector seems to be on the way to becoming fully integrated into the normal labour market. The association of temporary work agencies has concluded collective agreements with organisations representing both blue-collar workers and salaried employees. The collective agreements for blue-collar workers and salaried employees respectively are based on two partly different principles. The collective agreement for blue-collar workers assumes that the agency worker's wages are set in relation to the wages of the employees of the user company, whereas for salaried employees, the agency work sector is viewed as a separate sector with its own wage levels.

3.4. Economically dependent employees

3.4.1. The concept of employee in civil law

In civil law, persons who perform work for others against payment are divided into two categories: employees (*arbetstagare*) and self-employed persons (*uppdragstagare*). Labour law covers employees whereas self-employed persons are covered mainly by general civil law. The concept of employee is not defined in labour market legislation. The concept is assumed to be known. When determining whether a person is an employee, the courts carry out an overall assessment of the relevant circumstances in each individual case. With reference to case law, schemes and factors have been listed that suggest the existence of a work or employment relationship. Examples of circumstances which normally suggest that the person performing the work is to be considered an employee are: the fact that the person must perform such work as the principal assigns to him; the fact that the work is performed under the direction and supervision of the principal; and the fact that the party performing the work is a part of the principal's organisation. It is clear that the courts, to a considerable extent, work through and 'tick off' such lists of characteristics during the review. These lists are not exhaustive and other factors may be taken into account. It is also impossible to say anything precise about how the different factors are weighted by the courts. The concept of employee is mandatory in the sense that, in principle, the parties are not free to decide whether or not the party performing the work is to be considered an employee.

In 1993, a government review called for the inclusion of an explicit definition of the concept of employee in the Employment Protection Act. In principle, the concept would still be mandatory, but any understanding shared by the parties should be respected unless powerful reasons were to suggest otherwise. In addition, it was proposed that if the party performing the work was registered with the tax authorities as a businessman (so-called 'F' self-assessment form, see below) he should be considered self-employed. The proposals resulting from the review were not translated into legislation. In 2000, another review was charged with examining the employee concept. According to its 2002 report, the review did not find sufficient grounds for intervening legislatively, but instead suggested that the definition of employee, as before, should be developed through case law.

---

64   Lagen (1993:440) om privat arbetsförmedling och uthyrning av arbetskraft.

3.4.2. Tax and social security law

As far as the employee concept concerns civil law there were no legislative amendments adopted during the 1990s. By contrast, the areas of tax and social security were subjected to wide-ranging changes. Previously, the concept of the employee was of great significance in these areas, but in recent years another concept has come to play a far greater role.

The Tax Payment Act[65] contains provisions on accounting and payment of tax on account and final tax, as well as social charges. The law provides a definition of an expanded concept of employer. According to that definition, anyone who provides a certain minimum amount of payment for work is an employer and anyone who receives the payment is an employee, regardless of the existence of an employment relationship. The concept thus covers significantly more than the term 'employers' does in its common labour law meaning. A new Social Charges Act[66] has been in force since 2001. When this law was introduced, the concepts of employer and employee were discussed with regard to liability for social charges. At that time, it was pointed out that a wide employer concept is applied in the context of tax law, whereas it is used in a far more restricted sense within other fields of law. In common parlance the concept also has a much narrower meaning. Since in tax law the concept may be replaced by 'the person providing a payment', the employer concept should not be used differently in the context of social charges. Nor, therefore, should the employee concept be used differently in the Social Charges Act.[67] As a result, the employer and employee concepts have been abolished in the context of liability for social charges and they are not included in the new Social Charges Act.

Since 1993, in practice the question of liability for social charges is governed by the tax authority's decision about the procedure for completing the tax return. Prior to this, the parties themselves were responsible for determining the existence of an employment relationship. If that were indeed the case, the employer was to withhold and pay the employee's taxes and pay employer charges. On the other hand, if the party performing the work was running a business, he was responsible for paying his own taxes. The tax authority could hold the principal retroactively responsible for employer charges if he had misjudged the existence of an employment relationship. Nowadays, the following applies. There are two kinds of tax on account: F-tax and A-tax.[68] The particular kind of tax to which a person is subject determines how he is to pay tax on account and social charges on any payment received for his work. If the party performing the work has a so-called F-tax return, the principal is not liable for employer charges. The F-tax return is equally important for establishing a liability for withholding tax on a payment. It is up to the party performing the work to pay tax on account and social charges. The F-tax return is issued to taxable persons who run their own business, whereas the A-tax return is issued to employees and self-employed persons who do not run their own business. With the introduction of the F-tax reform, the tax authority took over responsibility for determining who is liable for tax on account and social charges and the taxable person can now rely on the tax return which has been issued. In order to safeguard against the payer (the principal) taking part in circumventing the rules, the principal is obliged to declare work to the tax authority regardless of the existence of an F-form, when it is clear that the work is actually performed on an employee basis. If no such declaration is made, the principal will be held jointly and severally liable for the tax on account.

3.5. Telework

In Sweden, there is no generally accepted definition of telework, nor are there any reliable statistics on the number of teleworkers. Depending on how the group is defined, estimates vary between 30 000 and one million teleworkers.

In 1997, the government launched a review aimed at finding out more about the existence of various forms of telework and the consequences of such work for employment conditions, and to assess future trends. In addition, the review was charged with mapping and identifying legislation that is relevant to telework, as well as any collective agreements that might have been reached on the issue.

In order to prevent teleworkers from ending up worse off than their colleagues at the main place of work with regard to redundancies, the review proposed a slight adjustment to the Employment Protection Act. Under the proposal, the law would make it clear that the mere fact that an employee had his place of work transferred to his home did not make him part of a separate priority order. The proposal was implemented in 2000. Otherwise the review did not consider it necessary to amend existing labour law.

---

65   Skattebetalningslagen (1997:483).
66   Socialavgiftslag (2000:980).
67   Governmental bill Proposition 2000/01:8 p. 74.
68   Chapter 4, Section 6 of the Tax Payment Act.

3.6. Working time

3.6.1. Reduction of working time and influence on the organisation of working time

During the 1990s, the regulation of working time was a politically controversial subject. A significant minority in parliament was pushing for a reduction in working time and increased influence for employees on the organisation of working time. Against this background, the legislation on working time has been reviewed several times in the last 15 years. However, proposals emanating from these reviews have only led to limited legislative amendments. One reason for this is the different views held across society, at the political level and among the social partners, regarding the issue of working time and the best way to handle it. The issue of working time is multifaceted and concerns the length and organisation of working time, flexibility in measuring working time with reference to a 24-hour period, a week, a year or even the economic cycle, and the question of influence on the organisation of working time. The differences of opinion concern not only substantial issues, but also the question of whether changes should be introduced by law or be handled exclusively by the social partners.

In 2002, a review proposed a law on flexible leave which would entitle employees to take leave of an equivalent of up to to five working days per year. According to the proposal, each employee would have a time account with the employer. Leave would be calculated in hours and could be deposited in either hours or entire days. The leave would be organised according to the wishes of the employee, e.g. so as to reduce daily or weekly working time over a period. The leave would thus give every employee the ability to influence his working time arrangements. It is questionable whether the proposal will become law.

No reduction in working time has been prescribed by law. However, since 1998, in large parts of the labour market collective agreements have introduced possibilities of reducing working time through deposits on working time accounts or similar arrangements. Under these agreements, the individual employee may choose to be compensated for the hours which he has accumulated either in the form of leave or in cash.

3.6.2. The EU Working Time Directive[69]

The Working time Directive should have been implemented by 1996. In connection with the implementation of the Directive in Sweden, in 1995 a working time committee carried out a comprehensive overview of the Working Time Act. Pending the publication of its final report, the committee made a proposal for the provisional implementation of the Working Time Directive. In its interim report, the committee assumed that the Swedish working time regulation provided employees with protection of at least the same degree as the Directive, despite various differences. The committee proposed a legislative amendment which was subsequently implemented. The amendment means that collective agreements or approved exemptions regarding derogations from the Working Time Act may not result in the application of less advantageous rules than those contained in the Directive. In its final report, which contained a proposal for a new Working Time Act, the committee proposed further changes to the rules with reference to the Directive. This proposal was never implemented. This was however, mainly because of political disagreement on issues unrelated to the implementation of the Working Time Directive. The legislative amendment which was said to be provisional in 1996 has thus become permanent.

In March 2002, the European Commission sent a so-called letter of formal notice to the government. The Commission claims that the Directive's provisions on daily rest periods, maximum weekly working time, annual leave and night work have not been implemented correctly in Sweden. A review conducted in the autumn of 2002 has tabled a proposal for changes to the Working Time Act which would address the Commission's criticism. The government has yet to table a proposal on the subject.

3.7. Leave-related legislation

In Sweden, the possibility of facilitating employee's access to further education/training, with a possible view to change jobs, is primarily covered by the 1974 Act on Educational Leave.[70]

In 1997, a separate act was adopted which grants employees the right to take leave from their job to engage in an economic activity.[71] The law aims to encourage the establishment of new businesses, not least by women, by helping employees establish and run their own business. The period of leave may last a maximum of six months. The employee's business may not, however, be in competition with that of the employer.

---

69   Council Directive 93/104/EC of 23 November 1993 concerning certain aspects of the organization of working time.
70   Lagen (1974:981) om arbetstagares rätt till ledighet för utbildning.
71   Lagen (1997:1293) om rätt till ledighet för att bedriva näringsverksamhet.

It should also be mentioned that some local communities are running pilot projects on so-called sabbaticals.[72] During a sabbatical, the employee is granted leave from his job for a period of up to one year for personal development or skills development while a jobseeker registered with the public employment service is taken on by the employer. The employee on leave is entitled to some compensation from the County Employment Board.

A person who is unemployed or threatened by unemployment and who is seeking work through the public employment service may, subject to certain conditions, receive a business start-up grant.[73]

4. Discrimination and equal treatment

Discrimination is the area in which changes to the law have undoubtedly been most significant during the period under consideration. This is partly a consequence of an adjustment to EU legislation and partly a response to political demands for tighter regulation.

4.1. Equal treatment of women and men

The first Equal Opportunities Act was adopted in 1979. At the same time, the equality ombudsman (JämO) was established. In 1991, a new Equal Opportunities Act replaced the 1979 Act.[74] The new Act aimed, *inter alia*, to adapt Swedish legislation to EU law. The law explicitly provided that the prohibition of gender discrimination covered both direct and indirect discrimination. It also made it possible to challenge an appointment from two applicants with equal merits if the employer had behaved in a discriminatory manner. With regard to pay discrimination, the law relaxed the previous rule that two jobs should only be considered as being of equal value if this followed from a collective agreement or established practice within a given sector or from an agreed job valuation. Sexual harassment was also explicitly prohibited. The rules requiring employers to take active measures to promote equality were expanded. The law has since been amended on several occasions.

One of the most high-profile issues has been wage discrimination. In 1994, an obligation was imposed on employers with 10 or more employees to establish a clear picture of wage differentials between women and men in the workplace and to include this picture in the equality plan which the employer

must draw up annually. In addition, the rules requiring employers to take active measures to promote equality and to draw up an equality plan were amended to oblige the employer to observe the provisions of the law even where a collective agreement applies. Finally, it was made clear that the assessment of what work should be viewed as of equal value should be independent of any values laid down in collective agreements.

Wage discrimination was subject to a series of high-profile court cases during the late 1990s. Mostly, the issue was the occurrence of wage discrimination between different professional groups employed by the same employer, e.g. midwives and hospital technicians. Thus, in the case of AD 1996 No 41, the Labour Court established that the fact that wages were set in a collective agreement did not exclude application of the prohibition of wage discrimination where an independent job-valuation differed from the valuation of the social partners. In the specific case, however, the independent valuation invoked failed to meet the relatively strict standards of legal certainty drawn up by the Court. In a subsequent case (AD 2001 No 71), a female intensive care nurse and a male medical-technical engineer were considered to be performing work of equal value within the meaning of the Equal Opportunities Act. However, after considering the respective market positions of the two employees, the Court concluded that the wage differential between them was not gender-based (see also AD 2001 nr 13).

In 2000, the Equal Opportunities Act was comprehensively revised. As part of this revision, the prohibition of discrimination was given a wording more closely reflecting that used in Community law. Furthermore, a definition of work of equal value was introduced and the employer's duty to take active measures to promote equal opportunities for men and women with regard to wage developments was strengthened. Employers must, on an annual basis, provide a clear picture and detailed analysis of, on the one hand, the provisions and the established practice with regard to wages and other employment conditions which they apply and, on the other hand, any wage differentials between women and men who perform equal work or work of equal value. The purpose of this picture and analysis of the wage structure is to identify, address and prevent unjustified differences in wages and other employment conditions between women and men. An employer with 10 or more employees must, annually and on the basis of this mapping and analysis work, draw up an action plan on equal pay.

In 1998, certain amendments were made to the law on sexual harassment. The amendments were aimed at clarifying

---

72   Förordning (2001:1300) om friåret.
73   Förordning (2000:634) om arbetsmarknadspolitiska program.
74   Jämställdhetslagen (1991:433).

the employer's duty to take active measures to prevent any employees being subjected to sexual harassment in the workplace.

4.2. Discrimination on the grounds of ethnic origin, disability or sexual orientation

The 1986 Act on Ethnic Discrimination in Working Life established an ombudsman for ethnic discrimination (DO) charged with the task of countering this type of discrimination. However, the prohibition of discrimination laid down in the Act was not accompanied by any remedies. Such penalties were only introduced in the 1994 Act Prohibiting Ethnic Discrimination. The definition of discrimination provided in the Act differed from the definition of gender discrimination in Community law. In 1999, a new Act Prohibiting Ethnic Discrimination was introduced.[75] In this Act, the prohibition of discrimination more closely reflected the EU's prohibition of discrimination in the field of equality (mainly the so-called Burden of Proof Directive).[76] The Ethnic Discrimination Act also contains provisions on so-called active measures, i.e. The employer's duty to carry out work specifically aimed at promoting ethnic diversity in working life. The requirement to take action is not, however, as wide-ranging as that contained in the Equal Opportunities Act.

In parallel with the 1999 Ethnic Discrimination Act, laws prohibiting discrimination on the grounds of sexual orientation[77] and discrimination against persons with disabilities[78] were enacted. Compliance with these laws is monitored by the ombudsman for discrimination on the grounds of sexual orientation (HomO) and the disability ombudsman (HO) respectively. The wording of the prohibitions of discrimination in these laws reflects the Ethnic Discrimination Act. By contrast, the laws contain no rules on active measures.

It should be pointed out that the Swedish legislation preceded the two anti-discrimination directives adopted by the EU in 2000.[79] These two directives were implemented in 2003.[80]

5. Concluding remarks

The changes of Swedish labour law during the 1990s can be said to have evolved around three different, but interconnected themes.

5.1. The debate on greater flexibility

The debate on the evolution of labour law was, to a large extent, motivated by the recession which hit Sweden in the first half of the 1990s. The debate has been focused on how labour market regulation might be changed to provide greater flexibility and thereby create conditions for growth and reduced unemployment. In particular, the debate has focused on the Employment Protection Act (see section 3.1). Long-standing demands for de-regulation have been met with a strong defence for the existing order. In this respect, the debate has been characterised by disputes and the inability of the social partners to exercise joint influence on the legislative process. Changes to the Employment Protection Act have taken the form of 'repairs' and adjustments of individual issues on the basis of a short-term outlook. Despite wide-ranging discussions and reviews, significant legislative reforms have been few and limited. However, as described in section 1.3, the substance of collective agreements has changed considerably, providing greater scope for regulation at the level of the company and the individual.

5.2. The Europeanisation of labour law

In addition to the debate on greater flexibility, the evolution of Swedish labour law during the 1990s was mainly influenced by the Swedish *membership of the European Union*, which was preceded by the EEA Agreement. It would be no exaggeration to claim that EU-based legislation dominated the legislative agenda in Sweden during this period. A number of specific labour market laws were adopted to implement EU directives, including the Act on European Works Councils,[81] the Act on the Right to Leave on Urgent Family Grounds,[82] the Act on

---

75   Lagen (1999:130) om åtgärder mot diskriminering i arbetslivet på grund av etnisk tillhörighet, religion eller annan trosuppfattning.

76   Council Directive 97/80 on the burden of proof in cases of discrimination based on sex.

77   Lagen (1999:133) om förbud mot diskriminering i arbetslivet på grund av sexuell läggning.

78   Lagen (1999:132) om förbud mot diskriminering i arbetslivet på grund av funktionshinder.

79   Council Directive 2000/43/EC implementing the principle of equal treatment between persons irrespective of racial or ethnic origin and Council Directive 2000/78/EC establishing a general framework for equal treatment in employment and occupation.

80   Lagen (2003:307) om förbud mot diskriminering.

81   Lagen (1996:359) om europeiska företagsråd.

82   Lagen (1998:209) om rätt till ledighet av trängande familjeskäl.

the Posting of Workers,[83] and the Act (2002:293) Prohibiting Discrimination against Part-Time and Fixed-term Workers.[84] In addition, efforts to revise a number of key laws have, to a large extent, been set in an EU context. Examples include the Equal Opportunities Act, as well as legislation on working time and occupational health and safety. A number of amendments to the Employment Protection Act were also brought about by the EU directives on transfer of undertakings and on the employer's duty to inform the employee of the terms and conditions of the employment relationship. In addition, the relationship between labour law and economic legislation (public procurement, free movement of goods and competition rules) has come under review in connection with new regulation and important judgements of the European Court of Justice. Thus, for Sweden, EU membership has generated a significant increase in legislative activity.

5.3. Anti-discrimination legislation

Discrimination is the area in which Swedish labour law has undergone most changes. Since 1991, the anti-discrimination legislation has been gradually tightened and extended to a growing number of issues. This development, which was touched upon above, has partly been driven by Sweden's membership of the EU. As previously indicated, Swedish equality law has undergone successive amendments in order to comply better with the requirements of Community law. Nevertheless, Swedish legislation has in many cases gone beyond those requirements. Thus, the duty to take active measures under the Equal Opportunities Act and the Ethnic Discrimination Act has no equivalence in Community law. Moreover, laws prohibiting discrimination on grounds of ethnic origin, disability or sexual orientation were adopted in Sweden prior to the corresponding EU directive. In some cases, the Swedish legislator's efforts to achieve gender equality have even been questioned as being contrary to Community law.[85]

---

83   Lagen 1999:678 om utstationering av arbetstagare.

84   Lagen (2002:293) om förbud mot diskriminering av deltidsarbetande arbetstagar och arbetstagare med tidsbegränsad anställning.

85   C-407/98 Abrahamsson, [2000] ECR I-5539 (concerning positive discrimination in the appointment of university professors).

Selected bibliography (in English)

Aarvaag Stokke, T. (2002) 'Mediation in Collective Interest Disputes', *Stability and Change in Nordic Labour Law, Scandinavian Studies in Law*, Vol. 43, pp. 135-158.

Bruun N., Flodgren B., Halvorsen M., Hydén H. & Nielsen R. (1992) *The Nordic Labour Relations Model*, Aldershot: Dartmouth.

Bruun, N. (2000) 'The Challenges of Europeanisation and Globalisation in the Field of Labour Law: The Nordic Case', in J. Shaw, *Social Law and Policy in an Evolving European Union*, Oxford: Hart Publishing.

Bruun, N. (2002) 'Labour Law and Non-Discrimination Law', in J. Pöyhönen (ed), *An Introduction to Finnish Law*. Kauppakaari, Finnish Lawyers' Publishing, Helsinki 2002, pp. 169-210.

Bruun, N. (2002) 'The Future of Nordic Labour Law', *Stability and Change in Nordic Labour Law, Scandinavian Studies in Law*, Vol. 43, pp. 375-385.

Edström, Ö. (2002) 'Co-Determination in Private Enterprises in Four Nordic Countries', *Stability and Change in Nordic Labour Law, Scandinavian Studies in Law*, Vol. 43, pp. 159-188.

Eklund, R. (1998-1999) 'Deregulation of Labour Law – the Swedish case', *Juridisk Tidskrift*, pp. 531-551.

Eklund, R. (2002) 'Temporary Employment Agencies in the Nordic Countries', *Stability and Change in Nordic Labour Law, Scandinavian Studies in Law*, Vol. 43, pp. 311-333.

Elvander, N. (1997) *The Swedish Bargaining System in the Melting Pot,* Solna: Arbetslivsinstitutet.

Fahlbeck, R. & Sigeman, T. (2001) *European employment and industrial relations glossary: Sweden*, Sweet & Maxwell: Luxembourg.

Fahlbeck, R. (1993) 'Strikes, Lockouts and other Industrial Actions', in R. Eklund et al (eds.), *Studier i arbetsrätt tillägnade Tore Sigeman*, Uppsala: Iustus.

Fahlbeck, R. (1995) 'Past, Present and Future Role of the Employment Contract in Labour Relations in Sweden', in L. Betten (ed), *The Employment Contract in Transforming Labour Relations*, The Hague: Kluwer.

Fahlbeck, R. (1997) *Labour and Employment Law in Sweden*, Lund: Juristförlaget.

Fahlbeck, R. (1999) 'Employee Loyalty in Sweden', *Comparative Labor Law and Policy Journal*, Vol. 20, pp. 297-319.

Fahlbeck, R. (1999) *Nothing succeeds like success: trade unionism in Sweden*, Lund: Juristförlaget.

Fahlbeck, R. (2002) 'Industrial Relations and Collective Labour Law: Characteristics, Principles and Basic Features', *Stability and Change in Nordic Labour Law, Scandinavian Studies in Law*, Vol. 43, pp. 87-133.

Fahlbeck, R. (2003) 'Lex Laboris – Quo Vadis? The Swedish experience', in Blanpain et al (eds), *Changing Industrial Relations and Modernisation of Labour law*, Kluwer: The Hague, pp. 127-138.

Fransson, S. (2000) 'Freedom of Contract, Parity and Collective Regulation: Collective Labour Law in Sweden', in M. Van der Linden & R. Price, *The Rise and Development of Collective Labour Law*, Bern: Peter Lang.

Hasselbalch, O. & Jacobsen, P. (1999) *Labour Law and Industrial Relations in Denmark,* The Hague: Kluwer.

Hasselbalch, O. (1998) *European employment and industrial relations glossary: Denmark*, Sweet & Maxwell: Luxembourg.

Hasselbalch, O. (2002) 'The Roots – the History of Nordic Labour Law', *Stability and Change in Nordic Labour Law, Scandinavian Studies in Law*, Vol. 43, pp. 11-35.

Knudsen, H. & Bruun, N. (1998) 'European Works Councils in the Nordic Countries: An Opportunity and a Challenge for Trade Unionism', *European Journal of Industrial Relations,* Vol. 4, No 2, pp. 131-155.

Källström, K. (1999) 'Employment and Contract Work', *Comparative Labor Law and Policy Journal*, Vol. 21, pp. 157-158.

Källström, K. (2002) 'Employment Agreements and Contract Work in the Nordic Countries', *Stability and Change in Nordic Labour Law, Scandinavian Studies in Law*, Vol. 43, pp. 77-86.

Lija, K. (1998) 'Finland: Continuity and Modest Moves Towards Company Level Corporativism', in A. Ferner & R. Hyman, *Changing Industrial Relations in Europe*, Oxford: Blackwell.

Malmberg, J. (2002) 'The Collective Agreement as an Instrument for Regulation of Wages and Employment Conditions', *Stability and Change in Nordic Labour Law, Scandinavian Studies in Law*, Vol. 43, pp. 189-213.

Nielsen, R. (1995) *Equality in law between men and women in the European Community, Denmark*, Dordrecht: Nijhoff.

Nielsen, R. (1996) *Employers' prerogatives – in a European and Nordic perspective*, Copenhagen: Handelshøjskolens Forlag.

Nielsen, R. (2002) 'The Europeazation of Nordic Labour Law', *Stability and Change in Nordic Labour Law, Scandinavian Studies in Law*, Vol. 43, pp. 37-75.

Numhauser-Henning, A. (2001) 'Flexible Qualification – a Key to Labour Law', *The International Journal of Comparative Labour Law and Industrial Relations*, Vol. 17/1, pp. 101-115.

Numhauser-Henning, A. (2002) 'Fixed-term Work in Nordic Labour Law', *Stability and Change in Nordic Labour Law, Scandinavian Studies in Law*, Vol. 43, pp. 277-310.

Numhauser-Henning. A. ed. (2001) *Legal Perspectives on Equal Treatment and Non-Discrimination*, The Hague: Kluwer.

Nycander, S. (2003) 'Misunderstanding the Swedish Model', in R. Blanpain (ed), *Collective bargaining, discrimination, social security and European integration*, The Hague: Kluwer.

Nyström, B. (2003) 'The legal Regulation of Employment Agencies and Employment Leasing Companies in Sweden', *Comparative Labour Law and Policy Journal*, Vol. 23, pp. 173-210.

Roseberry, L. (2002) 'Equal Rights and Discrimination Law in Scandinavia', *Stability and Change in Nordic Labour Law, Scandinavian Studies in Law*, Vol. 43, pp. 215-256.

Rönnmar, M. (2001) 'Redundant Because of Lack of Competence? Swedish Employees in the Knowledge Society', *The International Journal of Comparative Labour Law and Industrial Relations*, Vol. 17/1, pp. 117-138.

Scheuer, S. (1998) 'Denmark: A less Regulated Model', in A. Ferner & R. Hyman, *Changing Industrial Relations in Europe*, Oxford: Blackwell.

Sigeman, T. (2002) 'Employment Protection in Scandinavian Law', *Stability and Change in Nordic Labour Law, Scandinavian Studies in Law*, Vol. 43, pp. 257-275.

Sigeman, T. (2002–03) 'Nordic Labour Law – A brief presentation from a comparative perspective', *Juridisk Tidskrift* 2002–03, pp. 497-503.

Suviranta. A. (2000) *Labour Law in Finland*, Helsinki: Kauppakaari.

von Koskull, A. (2002) 'Employment Privacy Protection – Nordic Comparative Perspectives', *Stability and Change in Nordic Labour Law, Scandinavian Studies in Law*, Vol. 43, pp. 335-356.

THE EVOLUTION OF LABOUR LAW
IN GERMANY AND AUSTRIA
1992-2002

by Prof. Dr. Ulrich Zachert
HWP – Hamburger Universität für Wirtschaft und Politik
with Dr Thomas Radner
Tyrol Chamber of Labour
March/April 2003

Table of contents

Abbreviations used in the text

German abbreviation	Full wording in German	English translation
AFG	Arbeitsförderungsgesetz	Employment Promotion Act
AFRG	Arbeitsförderungsreformgesetz	Employment Promotion Reform Act
AGBG	Gesetz zur Regelung des Rechts der Allgemeinen Geschäftsbedingungen	General Contract Terms and Conditions Regulation Act
AKG	Arbeiterkammergesetz	Chambers of Labour Act (Austria)
AltTZG	Altersteilzeitgesetz	Age-related Part-time Working Act
AlVG	Arbeitslosenversicherungsgesetz	Unemployment Insurance Act (Austria)
AMPFG	Arbeitsmarktpolitikfinanzierungsgesetz	Labour Market Policy Funding Act (Austria)
AngG	Angestelltengesetz	Employees Act (Austria)
ARÄG	Arbeitsrechtsänderungsgesetz	Labour Law Amendment Act (Austria)
ArbSchG	Arbeitsschutzgesetz	Industrial Safety Act
ArbVG	ArbeitsverfassungsGesetz	Works Constitution Act (Austria)
ArbZG	Arbeitszeitgesetz	Working Time Act
ASRÄG	Arbeits- und Sozialrechtsänderungsgesetz	Labour and Social Law Modification Act (Austria)
ASVG	Allgemeines Sozialversicherungsgesetz	General Social Security Act (Austria)
AüG	Arbeitnehmerüberlassungsgesetz	Temporary Employment Act
AVRAG	Arbeitsvertragsrechts-Anpassungsgesetz	Employment Contract Law Modification Act (Austria)
AZO	Arbeitszeitordnung	Working Time Order
BAG	Bundesarbeitsgericht	Federal Labour Court
BAG	Berufsausbildungsgesetz	Vocational Training Act (Austria)
BDA	Bundesvereinigung der Deutschen Arbeitgeberverbände	Federal Union of German Employer Associations
BDI	Bundesverband der Deutschen Industrie	Federal Association of German Industry
BErzGG	Bundeserziehungsgeldgesetz	Child Allowance Act
BeschFG	Beschäftigungsförderungsgesetz	Employment Promotion Act
BetrVG	Betriebsverfassungsgesetz	Works Council Constitution Act
BGB	Buergerliches Gesetzbuch	Civil Code
BMVG	Betriebliches Mitarbeitervorsorgegesetz	Corporate Employee Provision Act (Austria)
BPGG	Bundespflegegeldgesetz	Federal Care Allowance Act (Austria)
BVG	Bundesverfassungsgericht	Federal Constitutional Court
CDU	Christliche Demokratische Union	Christian Democratic Union
DAG	Deutsche Angestelltengewerkschaft	German employees' union
DGB	Deutscher Gewerkschaftsbund	German trade union confederation
DPG	Deutsche Postgewerkschaft	German post office workers' union
EBRG	Europäische Betriebsrätegesetz	European Works Council Act

Abbreviations used in the text

German abbreviation	Full wording in German	English translation
EFZG	*Entgeltfortzahlungsgesetz*	Sick Pay Act
EFZG	*Entgeltfortzahlungsgesetz*	Continuation of Payment Act (Austria)
EZG	*Elternzeitgesetz*	Parental Leave Act
FDP	*Freie Demokratische Partei*	Free Democratic Party
FPÖ	*Freiheitliche Partei Österreichs*	Freedom Party of Austria
GBG	*Gleichberechtigungsgesetz*	Equal Treatment Act
	Gesetz zur Änderung des Bürgerlichen Gesetzbuchs und des Arbeitsgerichtsgesetzes	Civil Code and Labour Court Act Amendment Act
GFS	*Gesetz zur Förderung der Selbstständigkeit*	Self-employment Promotion Act
GMDA	*Gesetz für Moderne Dienstleistungen am Arbeitsmarkt*	Modern Services in the Labour Market Act
GSVG	*Gewerbliches Sozialversicherungsgesetz*	Social Security Act for freelance workers in the industrial sector (Austria)
HAG	*Heimarbeitsgesetz*	Home Working Act
HBV	*Handel, Banken und Versicherungen*	Commerce, banks and insurance union
JASG	*Jugendausbildungs-Sicherungsgesetz*	Youth Training Guarantee Act (Austria)
Job-AQTIV	*(Activate, Qualify, Train, Invest, Place ['vermitteln'])*	Activate, Qualify, Train, Invest, Place
KSchG	*Kündigungsschutzgesetz*	Protection Against Dismissal Act
MSchG	*Mutterschutzgesetz*	Protection of Mothers Act (Austria)
NachwG	*Nachweisgesetz*	Employment Conditions Information Act
ÖGB	*Österreichischer Gewerkschaftsbund*	Austrian trades union confederation (Austria)
ÖTV	*Öffentliche Dienste, Transport und Verkehr*	Public services, transport and traffic union
ÖVP	*Österreichische Volkspartei*	Austrian People's Party
SchwBAG	*Gesetz zur Bekämpfung der Arbeitslosigkeit Schwerbehinderter*	Combating Unemployment among Severely Disabled Persons Act
SchwbG	*Schwerbehindertengesetz*	Severely Disabled Persons Act
SMG	*Schuldrechtsmodernisierungsgesetz*	Law of Obligations Modernisation Act
SPD	*Sozialdemokratische Partei Deutschlands*	Social Democratic Party
SPÖ	*Sozialdemokratische Partei Österreichs*	Social Democratic Party of Austria
	Sozialrechts-Änderungsgesetz	Social Law Amendment Act (Austria)
StGG	*Staatsgrundgesetz*	Basic Law on the General Rights of Citizens (Austria)
TVG	*Tarifvertragsgesetz*	Collective Agreement Act
TzBfG	*Teilzeit- und Befristungsgesetz*	Part-time Work and Fixed-term Employment Contracts Act
UrlG	*Urlaubsgesetz*	Leave Act (Austria)
ver.di	*Vereinigte Dienstleistungs-gewerkschaft*	Union of service trade unions
VKG	*Väter-Karenzgesetz*	Paternal Leave Act (Austria)

Executive summary [(*)]

A description of labour law in Germany and Austria over the last ten years could present developments in this area chronologically. However, this method seems hardly suitable for drawing legal and political conclusions at European level from a comparison with the legal landscape in other countries. Another method should therefore be chosen in order to better identify similarities and differences in labour law in the other EU Member States. The description will not be chronological but will take a problem-oriented approach like the reports 'Transformation of labour and future of labour law in Europe' and 'Report of the High Level Group on Industrial Relations and Change in the European Union'.[1] An overview of the **characteristic basic structures of labour law** in the two countries is comprised in Chapter I. This is followed by the main developments, categorised in three main **content-based groups** in Chapter II.

The chapters 'From making employment more secure to employability' (German report, Chapter II, section 1), 'Labour law and adaptability' (Chapter II, section 2) and 'Promoting equality of opportunity' (Chapter II, section 3) look at how particular trends and initiatives have changed German and Austrian labour law. The aim is to fit in with indicators in the Council's annual employment policy guidelines provided for in Article 128 of the EC Treaty.[2] We will be looking at the **overall changes** not only at state level but also at the level of autonomous collective law, collective agreements and legal precedence (of the Supreme Court). As far as content goes, neither government policy nor that of the parties to collective agreements follows a scientific scheme. It follows that any attempt to take stock of the situation in this field is the result of an attempt to subsequently categorise individual initiatives on a scientific basis. As the categories cannot be precisely separated from each other, they must therefore be of a general nature and will consequently often cover several facets of changes at state and collective agreement level at the same time. The innovations in question are therefore cat-egorised under the **most relevant heading**. This does not however, exclude the possibility that they may be explained under other headings as well.

The final chapter (Chapter III) starts with a systematic overview of the changes that have arisen at the most important **regulatory and implementation levels**, i.e. state law, institutional co-determination (works constitutions), collective agreements and the law governing industrial disputes (autonomous conflict resolution). A link is again made to Chapter I. These chapters are followed by a summary of the main results and an outlook for the future.

Where possible, the objective is to present not only the law as seen in the statute book but also **its practical operation**. This means that, in addition to looking at the legislative level, we will also be examining the results of the changes in practice.

[(*)] The overall concept was drawn up by Ulrich Zachert, who also wrote the executive summary and Part 1 for Germany. Part 2, on Austria, was written by Thomas Radner.

[1] Supiot et al., *Transformation of labour and future of Labour law in Europe*, 1998; High Level Group, *On Industrial Relations and Change in the European Union*, 2002; the High Level Group agreed on these principles at its meeting on 19 February 2003 in Brussels.

[2] Hemmann, *Bundesarbeitsblatt 2002*, p. 18 ff. with references.

Part 1: Germany

Chapter I:
The structure of labour law relations and how they have changed

1. Labour law structures: an overview

1.1. State law

1.1.1. Employee rights in the Constitution

The **Constitution** of 23 May 1949, the supreme source of law in Germany, contains relatively few explicit employee rights compared to the constitutions of other European countries such as Spain and Italy[3] or the European Charter of Fundamental Rights of December 2000.[4] The most important is the freedom of association guaranteed in Article 9(3). However, over the post-war history of the Federal Republic of Germany, the ***Bundesverfassungsgericht*** (Federal Constitutional Court) has derived many individual guarantees for employees from Articles 1-20 of the Constitution, which justifies talking about an overall 'mosaic of employee basic rights'.[5]

1.1.2. State employee protection law

Below the Constitution, there are many employee protection laws on various matters. The Civil Code (BGB) of 1 January 1990 still contains, in §§611-630, some relevant labour law provisions, e.g. on employment contracts, gender equality, and some marginal references to employment protection, periods of notice and certificates of employment. Following an amendment to the Civil Code on 1 January 2002, form-based employment contracts are now, in principle, subject to an examination of their contents, in accordance with §310(4) of the Civil Code and §305 ff. of the Civil Code (for-

merly the *Gesetz zur Regelung des Rechts der Allgemeinen Geschäftsbedingungen* (General Contract Terms and Conditions Regulation Act)). Somewhat surprisingly, the legislator amended the Industrial Code with some provisions relating to general labour law (structure of contracts, the authority to give directions, arrangements for the payment of wages, references, competition prohibitions) in June 2002, and extended it to all – i.e. not just industrial and commercial – workers.[6]

This legal basis is too fragmentary to be considered a general part of state labour law. We also have to refer to individual acts regulating areas such as working time, paid leave, sick pay, protection against dismissal and particularly vulnerable groups such as young people, the severely disabled, etc. In contrast to, say, Spain and France, Germany has no uniform labour code. The last attempt, for the time being at least, to create a labour code was undertaken on the occasion of the German Lawyers' Congress in 1992 and was a failure.[7] In contrast to many other EU Member States, no general minimum wage law has been passed yet. The 1952 *Gesetz über Mindestlohnbedingungen* (Minimum Wage Conditions Act) has so far not been applied. The social partners are (still) strong enough to regulate this central issue independently through collective agreements. One exception is the construction industry, for which a minimum wage has applied since 1996 under the *Arbeitnehmerentsendegesetz* (Employee Posting Act).

---

3   Overview: Iliopoulous-Strangas, ed. *La protection des droits fondamentaux* (The protection of fundamental rights), 2000.
4   Zachert, NZA 2000, p. 621 ff. = more comprehensive in *Lavoro e Diritto* (Labour and Law) 2000, p. 507 ff.; idem, NZA 2001, p. 1041 ff.; Philippi, *Die Charta der Grundrechte der Europäischen Union* (The EU Charter of Fundamental Rights), 2002; Däubler, *AuR 2001*, p. 280 ff.; Weiss, *AuR 2001*, p. 374 ff.
5   See Gamillscheg, *Die Grundrechte im Arbeitsrecht* (Basic rights in labour law) 1998; Kühling, *AuR 1994*, p. 126 ff.; Söllner, *NZA 1992*, p. 221 ff.; Zachert, *BB 1998*, p. 1310 ff.
6   See Chapter III, section 2.3 of the German report.
7   Working group on German legal unity in labour law, report D on the 59th German Lawyers' Congress 1992; critical: Weiss, *Theses*, 2nd part, p. 9 ff. and Däubler, *AuR 1992*, p. 192 ff.; comparative: Zachert, *AuR 1993*, p. 193 ff.

1.2. Autonomous collective law

1.2.1. Bases

An overview of German labour law would be incomplete if it looked only at state labour law. In contrast to many European countries, e.g. France and Spain, working conditions in Germany are regulated less by statute than by collective agreements.

The German constitution enshrines the legal basis of free collective bargaining, i.e. the right to structure economic and employment conditions through the conclusion of collective agreements. Article 9(3) guarantees the right to form associations to safeguard and improve working and economic conditions (freedom of association). It is true that Article 9(3) does not explicitly mention collective agreements. However legal precedent and the prevailing opinion in legal studies rightly assume that freedom of association includes the power to autonomously conclude collective agreements.[8] Moreover, this provision of the Constitution also protects trade union activity and the right to strike.[9]

1.2.2. Players in autonomous collective labour relations

The main players in collective labour relations are the coalitions: on one side, the **trade unions** and, on the other side, the **employer associations** (or individual employers).

Trade unions are structured on the basis of the organisational principles of the **non-partisan trade union** and the **sectoral trade union**. The umbrella organisation, the *Deutscher Gewerkschaftsbund* (DGB – German trade union confederation), currently comprises eight single-industry unions (sectoral unions). The DGB has existed since 1949. The organisation of workers in non-partisan unions, regardless of political or religious opinion, is primarily the result of the lessons learnt from the disastrous political split in the workers' movement at the time of the Nazi dictatorship. The merging of unions over the years had led to a steady drop in the number of sectoral unions. In the spring of 2001, the following unions merged: *Öffentliche Dienste, Transport und Verkehr* (ÖTV – public services, transport and traffic), *Deutsche Postgewerkschaft* (DPG – German post office workers' union), *Handel, Banken und Versicherungen* (HBV – commerce, banks and

insurance), *IG Medien* (IG media) and the *Deutsche Angestelltengewerkschaft* (DAG – German employees' union). They formed the new service union known as *ver.di* (*Vereinigte Dienstleistungsgewerkschaft* – union of service trade unions).

The DAG, as the employees' union, now belongs to the DGB, and *ver.di* has become another large sectoral union, alongside *IG Metall*. About two thirds of the 8-9 million members of unions affiliated under the DGB are now in the new service union *ver.di* or *IG Metall*. Altogether, the level of unionisation among employed workers is between 30% and 35%.

The **employer associations** are organised in parallel with the trade unions. The *Bundesvereinigung der Deutschen Arbeitgeberverbände* (BDA – Federal Union of German Employer Associations) is the responsible umbrella organisation for the area of labour and social policy, including collective agreements.[10] More than 40 industry-specific associations belong to it, such as *Gesamtmetall* for the metalworking industry, the *Arbeitgeberverband des privaten Bankgewerbes* (Federation of employers in the private banking sector), and so on. The organisation rate of employers is between about 40 and 45% of all companies.

It is very important, in practical terms, that the unions and employer associations at industry level are responsible for **collective bargaining policy**, and that this responsibility does not lie with the respective umbrella organisations (the DGB and the BDA).

1.2.3. Collective agreements

The legal principles of collective agreements are laid down in the 1949 *Tarifvertragsgesetz* (TVG – Collective Agreement Act). Collective agreements are concluded with legislative effect (§4 of the TVG), and typically as general collective agreements at regional level. The number of new and amended collective agreements each year is steady at around 8 000. There are currently more than 50 000 general collective agreements and some 6 000 single-company collective agreements in force.[11] Although, according to §3(1) of the TVG, collective agreements are in principle only valid if **both** parties are bound to them, they apply to almost 80% of all employees. There is a possibility to declare collective

---

8   E.g. Federal Constitutional Court 26.6.1991, *BVerfGE 84*, 212, 229; Federal Constitutional Court 2.3.1993, *BVerfGE 88*, 103, 114; Federal Constitutional Court 24.4.1996, *BVerfGE 94*, 268, 284 f.

9   E.g. Federal Constitutional Court 26.6.1991, *BVerfGE 84*, 212; new overview: Zachert, AR-Blattei SD 1650.1 'Vereinigungsfreiheit/Koalitionsfreiheit' (Freedom of association/freedom of coalition), 2001, notes 1 ff.

10   In fact, over recent years, the President of the powerful Bundesverband der Deutschen Industrie (BDI – Federal Association of German Industry), Olaf Henkel, has had considerable influence on collective bargaining policy. A firm opponent of the growing importance of federation and collective bargaining policy, he retired on age grounds at the end of 2000; e.g. Henkel, *Jetzt oder nie* (Now or never) 1998, p. 148 ff.

11   Annual statistics of the German Federal Ministry of Labour, Clasen, *Bundesarbeitsblatt 7/8 2002*, p. 41 ff.; Bispinck/WSI-Tarifarchiv, *WSI-Mitt. 2002*, p. 371 ff.

agreements universally applicable, under §5 of the TVG. In addition to this, individual contracts of employment usually refer to the relevant collective agreements, thus making them part of the content of individual labour relationships.

Contrary to the legal situation in many other European countries, it is generally accepted in Germany that collective agreements oblige their parties not to take industrial action. This means that, during the period of the collective agreement, the parties must not take any form of industrial action and must dissuade their members from doing so or from deteriorating working conditions.[12] In addition to 'traditional issues', such as pay and working time, issues such as job protection and training have also played a role in collective agreements recently. This will be investigated in more detail below, as will the relationship between state and collective bargaining law. In general, the relationship is the following: a minimum level of working conditions is laid down by law and improved upon by collective agreements in many areas.

The provisions of group collective agreements, which are often necessarily quite vague, are typically implemented by works councils in the context of co-determination under the 1972 *Betriebsverfassungsgesetz* (BetrVG – Works Council Constitution Act) as amended in July 2001. The results achieved are then established in individual **company agreements**. The negotiating partners here are not the unions and the employer associations or individual employers, but rather the works council elected by **all the employees** of a particular company and the **management** of that company. Similar provisions under specific laws apply in the public sector. This is the second level of the collective agreement structure, contributing decisively to a **decentralised implementation** of general collective agreements in accordance with the specific situation in each individual company.

Whilst it is a typical feature of German law for works councils to play an important role in implementing and, increasingly making, collective agreements more concrete, the order of precedence between collective agreements and individual company agreements is clearly established by law. In particular, §§77(3) and 87(1) of the Betriebsverfassungsgesetz (BetrVG) provide that collective agreements have precedence over individual company agreements. This order of precedence reflects the **dual principle of the representation of interests** in Germany ('double channel'). Put very simply, the unions are responsible for the sector and

the region, and the works council for the company in question. This precedence of collective agreements over individual company agreements is based not only on §§77(3) and 87(1) of the BetrVG, but also on Article 9(3) of the Constitution.

In practice, there is a multilayered **interplay between collective agreements and company co-determination**. Recent developments have seen clear shifts in powers from the level of collective agreements to that of company agreements. The **increasing importance of the corporate level** may provide greater flexibility for companies and, at the same time, take better account of employees' wishes for greater flexibility, for example in the area of the organisation of working time. However, this shift in powers is problematic. This is not only because it reverses the traditional precedence of collective agreements over individual company agreements, but also because works councils (in contrast to unions) do not have the right to initiate industrial action in the event of disputes, according to §74(2) of the BetrVG.

Further developments will depend on whether the parties to collective agreements manage to structure and limit these decentralisation/flexibilisation processes, primarily through provisions in collective agreements themselves.[13] This will be discussed further below.[14]

1.3. Institutional (corporate) co-determination

Unlike most other European countries, Germany has a long tradition of **corporate co-determination**. Works councils, voted for by all the staff members of companies with at least five employees, have more than just information and advisory rights, unlike the systems set up, for example, in Spain and France and under the *Europäisches Betriebsrätegesetz* (European Works Council Act) of October 1996, based on Directive 94/45/EC. German works councils can intervene – often on an equal footing – in central labour law issues such as wages and working time (under the 1972 *Betriebsverfassungsgesetz*, as amended by the *Betriebsverfassungs-Reformgesetz* (Works Council Reform Act) of 23 July 2001, works councils). In cases of doubt, a **company conciliation board** with representation on the principle of parity and a neutral chairman decides according to §76 of the BetrVG.

12 For example, BAG 21.12.1982, AP No 76 on Article 9 of the German Constitution, industrial disputes.
13 The following documents are essential reading: monographic, with empirical references, e.g. Oppolzer/Zachert, *Krise und Zukunft des Flächentarifvertrages* (Crisis and future of the general collective agreement), 2000; Höland/Reim/Brecht, *Flächentarifvertrag und Günstigkeitsprinzip* (General collective agreements and the favourability principle), 2000.
14 See Chapter III, section 4 of the German report.

This does not rule out conflict between the workforce/works council and the employer. However, the logic of this form of conflict resolution lies in the general attempt to solve industrial disputes as early as possible through **dialogue and discussion** (§§2(1) and 74(1) of the BetrVG).

Agreements between employers and works councils with longer-term effects are generally laid down in **company agreements**. These are also collective agreements which operate in a very similar way, according to §77 of the BetrVG. They focus on social matters, where works councils have enforceable co-determination rights (§87 of the BetrVG). As already emphasised, collective agreements have precedence over individual company agreements (§§77(3) and 87(1) of the BetrVG).

Germany has some 40 000 companies, in which around 220 000 works councils and staff councils (in the public service) have been elected.[15] After the last works council elections in spring 2002, some 77% of works council members belonged to a union that was part of the *Deutscher Gewerkschaftsbund*. However, the number of non-unionised works council members is slowly rising.[16] The amendment to the *Betriebsverfassungsgesetz* of July 2001 is designed to address the problem of the lack of representation in small companies by making the voting procedure easier in companies with up to 50 employees.[17]

1.4. Legal precedence/case law

Gaps in the legislation, caused by the fact that there are often only very general legal framework provisions to go on for the settlement of disputes, are typically filled in German labour law by **case law**. There are specific labour courts in Germany, comprising three instances, the highest of which is the ***Bundesarbeitsgericht*** in Erfurt, Thuringia. The first two instances comprise a professional judge and two honorary judges, in practice proposed by the trade unions and the employer associations. The ***Bundesarbeitsgericht*** has ten divisions, each of which has three professional judges and two honorary judges.[18]

In practice, the labour courts play an extremely important role. In quantitative terms, for example, they dealt with some 570 000 new employment cases in 2001. Most of the cases concerned individual disputes, but there were also collective disputes for which the labour courts are also competent.[19]

As the saying goes, the courts are the real masters of labour law.[20] Even if pronouncements of this kind are to be taken with a pinch of salt, it is true that, in practice, the courts often have almost legislative power, mainly because of the many statutory general clauses.[21] In this context there are clear parallels with English (respectively Anglo-American) case law.[22] Court rulings in Germany have led to a fine network of case law principles that operate as legal norms and have their own focuses compared to amendments to state labour law. This will be discussed further below.

2. Reasons for changes in labour law structures

2.1. Political changes

Looking at ten specific years in the development of labour law (1992-2002) is by necessity an arbitrary exercise.[23] Developments in labour law in EU Member States over the last decade will be different if only because, over this period, some Member States had elections leading to changes of government. Other social factors have also had varying impacts on labour law over this period.

In 1992, Germany was roughly in the middle of a sixteen-year period of conservative/liberal government. German Reunification took place in 1989/90. It followed that the core of the Federal Republic's (i.e. the old *Bundesländers'*) labour law was applied also in the former East Germany (the new *Bundesländer*).[24] In fact, differences could be seen for a long time after the official legal unification and have still not been overcome completely − in particular against the background of above average unemployment in the new *Bundesländer*.

15   Data from, for example, Kittner, *Arbeits- und Sozialordnung*, 27th edition 2002, p. 448.

16   In the metalworking industry, the unionisation rate of IG-Metall works councils has fallen from almost 78% to almost 74%: direct, published DGB, 3/2003, p. 2.

17   Rudolph/Wassermann, *Die Mitbestimmung 2002*, p. 62 ff.

18   For more on conciliation procedures, see Chapter III, section 4.5 of the German report.

19   The number of cases was broadly the same as in the previous years; for the statistics and a breakdown, see Grotmann-Höfling, *AuR 2002*, p. 449 ff.

20   Gamillscheg, *AcP 164* (1964), p. 385, 388.

21   On the question of whether case law is a legal source or merely a legal finding, see Zachert, *FS 100 Jahre Deutscher Arbeitsgerichts-verband* (100 years of the German labour court association), 1994, p. 573, 579 f. with references.

22   Reinhardt, *Konsistente Jurisdiktion* (consistent jurisdiction), 1997.

23   For the period 1986-1996, see Zachert, *Relaciones Laborales* (Labour relations) 1996, p. 193 ff.

24   From many contributions: Dieterich, *NZA 1995*, p. 553 ff.; also Budde, *AuR 1996*, p. 1 ff.

In October 1998, following its election victory, the new government published the coalition agreement between the SPD and Bündnis 90/the Greens.[25] This document undertook to repeal certain initiatives of the previous conservative/liberal administration, in particular the limitations on protection against dismissal and the 20% cut in sick pay. New focus was promised on areas such as economically dependent work, part-time work and the extension of co-determination.[26]

Labour market policy was the focus of the Red/Green coalition's labour law reforms in the second legislative period, which started in September 2002,[27] as proposed by the Ministry of Labour and Economic Affairs.[28] The policy was based on a set of proposals made by the Hartz Commission to reintegrate the unemployed more quickly and efficiently in the labour market.[29] The German government was under pressure from the stagnating economic situation, caused, in addition to domestic factors, by instability abroad (Iraq conflict), entrenched, slowly rising unemployment and stronger conservative/liberal opposition in the regional elections in early 2003. In this situation the German government made some surprising concessions (on economically dependent work and small-scale part-time work) to policy proposals made by the current (conservative) opposition. The controversy, in the specialist press and at general political level, about the dismantling of protection against dismissal and modifying the primacy of collective agreements compared to company agreements, shows that German labour law is currently in a period of uncertainty, making it difficult to make predictions about the future. More about this will follow below.

2.2. Changes in society

Over the period in question, labour law was affected not just by political factors, such as the change of government – a series of social factors also played a role. Only a few of these, of particular significance for labour law, can be highlighted here. It must be emphasised that the issue of the importance of these individual developments for labour law has certainly not yet been clarified. However, it should be agreed that a direct causal link between developments in labour law and developments on the labour market cannot be proved.

In January 2003, **unemployment** in Germany was running at 8.6%, according to (consolidated) data from the Statistical Office of the European Communities (Eurostat). This corresponds to the EU average. In Germany, the worst affected regions are in the new *Bundesländer* in the East, as well as economically weaker parts of the West (e.g. the unemployment rate in Saxony-Anhalt and Mecklenburg-Vorpommern is around 20%). There are also so-called 'problem groups' on the labour market, such as young people, senior citizens, women, foreigners and the severely disabled. These people have even more difficulties if they are unskilled.[30]

At the end of 2000, just under 7.3 million foreigners lived in Germany, i.e. around 9% of the total population. The proportion of foreigners in the unemployment figures is about 17%.[31] However, it is expected that the number of people **migrating** to Germany to look for work following the accession of the EU candidate countries (in eastern Europe) will be low.[32] Attempts to use modern migration law to manage immigration to meet specific needs in the labour market (e.g. to make up for the ageing domestic population, or the need for skilled workers in certain sectors) have so far not led to any results because of disagreements between government and opposition.

With regard to the **structure of the economy**, over 25% of all workers are still employed in industry, and studies confirm the continuing importance of this sector, including the supply industry.[33] This is the case despite the growth in the services sector. Almost 5 million people work in the public sector – around 15% of the entire employed population of almost 33 million. In addition to workers and employees, to whom the general labour law regulations apply, this figure includes around 1.7 million civil servants.[34] These are subject to their own regime (e.g. pay laid down by law, not by collective agreement, freedom of association but not to strike,

25   Labour law part, e.g. *AuR 1998*, p. 476 f.

26   Assessment, e.g. Zachert, Int. J. Comp. L. L. I. R., 1999, p. 21 ff., revised version: *Il diritto del Mercado del Lavoro* (Labour market law) 2000, p. 89 ff.; Weiss/Schmidt, Marlene, Int. J. Comp. L. L. I. R., 2000, p. 145 ff.

27   This may lead (in the medium term) to a weakening of the unions' influence: Leisner, *ZRP 2002*, p. 501 ff.

28   Employment law part, e.g. *AuR 2002*, p. 456 f.

29   Commission 'Moderne Dienstleistungen am Arbeitsmarkt' (Modern services in the labour market), 8/2002, p. 12.

30   *Statistisches Bundesamt, data report 2002*, p. 101 ff.; comprehensive: Eichhorst/Profit/Thode, *Benchmarking Deutschland 2001*, p. 65 ff.; latest figures: 'Entlassungswelle ebbt nur langsam ab' (Wave of redundancies receding only slowly), Handelsblatt 5.3.2003, p. 6.

31   *Statistisches Bundesamt, data report 2002*, p. 45 ff., 105 updated.

32   Less than 2 million over ten years: Werding, *NZA 2003*, p. 207 ff.

33   Institut der deutschen Wirtschaft, *Die Industrie, Drehscheibe der globalen Dienstleistungsgesellschaft* (Industry, hub of the global service society) 1998, p. 10.

34   *Statistisches Bundesamt, data report 2002*, p. 235 ff.

etc.). Large areas of the public service have been privatised, e.g. the railways, the postal service and local corporations.[35] In many cases, the impact on those workers involved has been managed in a socially responsible way through collective agreements.[36]

It is not possible here to describe individually all the aspects associated with '**changing values**' and '**individualisation**' and their impact on labour law which were discussed during the reporting period.[37] To summarise, it must be said that the actual situation provides a contradictory picture. Consequently labour law has had to deal with **various different realities** over this period. The old and the new continue to coexist and overlap; Taylorist and modern production concepts; old hierarchies and open forms of management; the traditional employment relationship ('standard employment relationship'), which applies to almost 74% of employees; and new (flexible) forms of contracts. The weakening of the social players in Germany and also in many other European countries was, *cum grano salis*, limited – the examples could go on and on.

However, it is noticeable that the identifiable trends, certainly on the labour market, seem to be evolving at a faster pace than in previous decades. Labour market theoretical studies talk of '**high-speed labour markets**' and '**transitional labour markets**'. One feature is the need to quickly change jobs. This poses new challenges for labour law, too. Its role is to make new institutional arrangements available for interrupted occupational pathways, including bridges between paid work and other productive activities. This includes the entitlement to plan and negotiate these pathways through collective agreements, company agreements and statutes, and the combination of low pay or uncertain income with transfers and the funding of work rather than unemployment.[38]

This differentiated and contradictory situation is a problem for labour law and is likely to remain so for some time.[39] It may continue to have an impact on important subjects such as balances of power, the opportunities for discursive processes and the relationship between individual and col-

lective freedoms. These issues will be dealt with under their respective headings.

3. Result: relative stability of German labour law

Even the legislative element of German labour law has a complicated structure. However, to really understand the changes of the last ten years, it is important to look not only at statute law but also at the **overall structures**. On the one hand, this confirms the ability of labour law to change and adapt against a background of political and economic change. On the other hand, different legal bases have often complemented each other or balanced each other out, as in a system of communicating pipes.

There are examples where, for instance, the dismantling of statutory employment protection in periods of conservative government was absorbed or cancelled out by collective standards. Case law, which is in many aspects independent, and the practice of corporate co-determination, have led to several (conservative) government initiatives being amended or modified.

These are just some of the reasons why the labour law environment in Germany has remained relatively stable over the past decade, despite all the changes to the small print and some innovative initiatives.

---

35   Sterzel in: Blanke/Trümner, ed. *Handbuch der Privatisierung* (Handbook of privatisation), 1998, notes 146 ff.

36   For the complex labour law questions, see, for example, Blanke in Blanke/Trümner, *Handbuch der Privatisierung*, note 793 ff.; for European issues, see Sterzel, ibid., note 238 ff.

37   Zachert, FS Dieterich, 1999, p. 699 ff.; abundant material also in the reports on the 63rd German Juristentag (Lawyers' Conference) 2000 by Kleinhenz und Hanau, and the papers by Däubler and Heinze, each with references.

38   Rogowski/Schmid, *WSI Mitt.* 1997, p. 568, 576 ff.; many other ideas in Schmid, G., ed. *Labor Market Institutions in Europe*, 1994; also: ibid., Transfer 2001, p. 227 ff.; bringing into context with regard to empirical data: Bosch, *GMH 2002*, p. 688 ff.

39   A more post-modern approach is taken by Supiot, *Transformation of Labour and future of Labour law in Europe*.

Chapter II:
The development of central labour law themes over the last ten years

1. From making employment more secure to employability

1.1. Individual protection against dismissal/redundancy

1.1.1. Principles and controversies

One of the most controversial subjects of the last decade was, and still is, (individual) protection against dismissal/redundancy. As in most EU Member States[40] (for reasons of social justice) dismissals and redundancies in Germany are subject to certain conditions which must be presented and, if necessary, proved by the employer. The *Kündigungsschutzgesetz* (KSchG – Protection Against Dismissal Act) (§1(2)) makes a distinction between grounds based on the person and behaviour of the employee (dismissals) and urgent, company-related (commercial) grounds (redundancies). In the case of redundancies for commercial reasons, employers must also take social considerations into account when selecting the employees to be made redundant (§1(3) of the KSchG). Furthermore, the workers' representation body must be informed before any redundancies are made – it has limited monitoring and objection rights (§102 of the BetrVG). Under the *Kündigungsschutzgesetz*, protection against dismissal can be invoked if the employee in question has worked for the same business or company for more than six months (§1(1) of the KSchG). Moreover, under current law, the business must have at least six employees (§23 of the KSchG). The courts have developed a comprehensive case law to decide whether redundancies/dismissals are 'socially justified'.

The controversy in labour law circles about protection against dismissal and redundancy reflects positions that have

been put forward for years in the economic and labour market policy debate. In the economic discussion in particular, the **neoclassical idea** has a considerable weight. According to this idea companies' competitiveness can be strengthened by lowering dismissal/redundancy protection standards and by cutting efficiency-dampening transaction costs. Even the labour market situation can be improved at the same time.[41] This is contradicted by comprehensive **institutional (labour market) theories**. These theories claim that employment stability, which is the aim of such protection, has motivational, trust-building and thus productivity-raising value.[42] These positions also refer to empirical investigations, according to which the German labour market is characterised by a high turnover rate.[43] Furthermore, international comparative analyses show no clear relationship between the level of national regulation on protection against dismissal/redundancy and the labour market situation.[44]

1.1.2. Diverse legislative initiatives and their assessment

With the *Beschäftigungsförderungsgesetz* (Employment Promotion Act) of 25 September 1996, which reduced or restricted some aspects of protection against dismissal, the conservative/liberal legislature followed the neoclassical approach to a certain extent.

A number of changes followed. Raising the threshold for the applicability of the Protection against Dismissal Act is one example. The law was made applicable to companies with eleven or more employees (previously, with six or more). Part-time workers were counted pro-rata.[45]

Moreover, the amendment weakened the principle used in the case law in the event of redundancies for commercial reasons. This prinicple consists of an examination on a case-

---

40   For an overview, see, for example, European Commission, *Termination of Employment Relationships*, 1997.
41   Most recently: Reuter, *FS Wiedemann*, 2002, p. 449 ff.
42   From the comprehensive discussion only: Dörsam, *ZWS 1997*, p. 55 ff.; Kleinhenz, report part B on the 63rd German Juristentag, 2000, p. 52 ff.; the comparison of the situation in Germany and the USA is informative: Finkin, *RdA 2002*, p. 333 ff.
43   Kleinhenz, ibid., p. 26 f.
44   OECD, *Employment Outlook*, 1999; Kleinhenz, ibid., p. 66 f. Similar, but with reference to diversionary tactics to circumvent employment restrictions in Germany: Eichhorst/Profit/Thode, *Benchmarking Deutschland*, 2001, p. 169 ff.
45   The old rules led to orders of reference to the European Court of Justice: ECJ 30.11.1993, DB 1994, 50 = AiB 1994 with note by Däubler.

by-case basis of criteria such as length of service, age and dependants. At the same time, those employees whom the employer considered to be assets to the company were not included in the 'social selection'. The legislator expressly recognised the importance of a 'balanced personnel structure', which weakened the relative importance of length of service and age.

Finally, the amendment limited the protection of workers made redundant against an unfair social selection. This limited protection took place in cases where guidelines to this end had already been agreed with the works council or – in the absence of a works council – as long as the employer made this decision with the approval of two-thirds of the workforce.

Following the change of government in the autumn of 1998, the new government (SPD/Greens) repealed most of these amendments with the *Gesetz zu Korrekturen der Sozialversicherung und zur Sicherung von Arbeitnehmerrechten* (Social Security Correction and Employee Rights Reinforcement Act) of 19 December 1998. Consequently the old legal situation was re-established. In addition (also in its first legislative period) the new governing coalition introduced the obligation to use the written form for ending employment relationships through dismissal/redundancy and for annulment agreements and the setting of time limits in the *Arbeitsrechtsbereinigungsgesetz* (Labour law Reorganisation Act) of 30 March 2000.

With regard to the applicability of the *Kündigungsschutzgesetz* in small companies, studies in the handicrafts sector showed that raising the threshold in 1996 (whereby 80% of (small) companies, representing almost 20% of employees, were removed from the field of application) did not have a (significant) impact on employment.[46]

The controversy about the value of protection against dismissal/redundancy to solve labour market problems remains. Various proposals have been and are still being made in the legal debate to weaken the limited protection offered by the current law in favour of compensation arrangements.[47] Conservative-liberal circles want to completely do away with protection against dismissal for certain groups (older people, the long-term unemployed), in favour of compensation.[48]

Since the beginning of 2003, the debate has become even more intense. The consolidation of conservative tendencies in the winter of 2002/03 led the Red/Green coalition to make proposals to limit protection against dismissal and redundancy, to be implemented in mid 2003. Broadly speaking, the proposals concern; an extension of the maximum period for temporary employment (four, rather than two, years, without confirmation from the courts) for small companies with five employees or fewer; the alternative of compensation to solve dismissal disputes; and certain openings in social selection in the case of redundancy for economic reasons. This has led to controversy in academic circles.[49] The latest empirical studies confirm that German labour law, with a turnover of 3.5-4.5 million employment relationships per annum (out of almost 33 million employed workers), is very flexible, that the turnover in small companies is even higher than in large companies and that redundancy settlements are paid only to a very small number of those affected (around 10%).[50]

1.1.3. Minimum protection against dismissal and redundancy necessary under the Constitution

The academic discussion and developments in the case law, triggered by the conservative/liberal government's initiatives to limit protection against dismissal and redundancy in 1996, could be of interest not just for German labour law but also for the European debate. The exclusion of many employees by the 1996 *Beschäftigungsförderungsgesetz* (Employment Promotion Act) raised the question of whether any protection against dismissal within certain limits even existed outside the *Kündigungsschutzgesetz*. Jurisprudence answered this question with a resounding 'yes', pointing to general civil law principles such as actions *contra bonos mores* (§138 of the Civil Code) or contravening good faith (§242 of the Civil Code), as well as new constitutional law developments. For example, the constitutional guarantee of minimum protection against dismissal [51] is derived from Article 12 of the German Constitution.[52] The case law of the *Bundesverfassungsgericht* and the specialised labour courts has confirmed a view, according to which no-one may be dismissed on arbitrary or irrelevant grounds. It also stipulates that in the case of social selection, a certain degree of social consideration is called for, with account taken of employees' expectations that long service will be rewarded. In procedural terms, the

---

46   Information from Hanau, report on the 63rd German Juristentag 2000, part C, p. 27.
47   Bauer, *NZA 2002*, p. 529 ff.; Buchner, *NZA 2002*, p. 533 ff.; Hromadka, *NZA 2002*, p. 783 ff.; Schiefer. *NZA 2002*, p. 770 ff.; representing the other side of the argument: Däubler, *NJW 2002*, p. 2292 f.; idem, *AiB 2002*, p. 457 ff.; for a comparative overview: Rebhahn, *RdA 2002*, p. 272 ff.
48   Overview of the parties' proposals for the Bundestag election in September 2002, e.g. *AuR 2002*, p. 337 ff.
49   On one side, Däubler, *Die Mitbestimmung* (Co-determination) 2003, p. 37 ff.; on the other side Stein, Peter, *Die Mitbestimmung 2003*, p. 20 ff.; see also Preis, Ulrich, *NZA 2003*, p. 252 ff.
50   Bielinski/Hartmann/Pfarr/Seifert, H., *AuR 2003*, p. 81 ff.
51   Preis, *NZA 1997*, 1256 ff.; Oetker, *AuR 1997*, p. 41 ff.; Bepler, *AuR 1997*, p. 54 ff.
52   Federal Constitutional Court 24.4.1991, *BVerfGE 84*, 133, 'Holding pattern ruling'.

principle of a graduated burden of proof applies.[53] The definition of a business in §23 of the KSchG, which is decisive for establishing the number of employees and thus the applicability of the *Kündigungsschutzgesetz*, is interpreted restrictively in order to protect small businesses. The small business clause applies, in principle, only where personal cooperation and a specific relationship of trust exist and, typically, where the company is small.[54]

These principles could provide reference points for minimum standards for European protection against dismissal, which is recognised, in principle, in Article 30 of the European Charter of Fundamental Rights (December 2000).[55]

1.2. Active labour market policy: the interface between labour law and social law

1.2.1. The relationship between labour law and social law in Germany

It should be emphasised first of all that, in the German system, the distinction between labour law and social law is much clearer than in many other EU Member States. However, there have always been areas where they touch or overlap. The overlaps have increased over recent years, to the extent that social law, to which employment promotion law belongs, is promoting a more structural and prevention-based approach, rather than financial compensation in the case of claims.[56]

It would therefore appear sensible and necessary to pay more attention to social law than in the past, also from a labour law perspective, and to include legal initiatives at the interface between labour and social law in this paper.

1.2.2. Important legal initiatives and their legal policy background

Although it would be impossible here to treat the complex area of employment promotion law anywhere near exhaustively, the following should be stated at the outset.[57] Employment promotion law used to be governed by the 1969 *Arbeitsförderungsgesetz* (AFG – Employment Promotion Act). On 1 January 1998, it was incorporated as Volume III in the

Social Code by the *Arbeitsförderungsreformgesetz* (AFRG – Employment Promotion Reform Act).

The *Bundesanstalt für Arbeit* is responsible for employment promotion. It is self-governing body, with a tripartite representation from employers, employees and public corporations.

Unemployment insurance is funded by **contributions** from employers and employees and a federal contribution from tax revenue. The employee and employer currently contribute 3.25% each of the employee earnings.

Workers who are temporarily unemployed and fulfil the eligibility criterion of 12 months' employment are eligible for **unemployment benefit.** The length of entitlement to unemployment benefit is between 6 and 32 months. Unemployment benefit for unemployed people with at least one child is at least 67% of the last average net pay, whilst all other employees receive 60%. Those unemployed people with no entitlement to unemployment benefit receive unemployment assistance. For unemployed people with at least one child, this is equivalent to 57% of average net pay – the figure for all other unemployed people is 53%. Reform considerations associated with the autumn 2002 Hartz Commission[58] anticipate far-reaching changes. Above all an amalgamation with social security benefits and shortening the period when unemployment benefit can be drawn.

Moreover, the *Bundesanstalt für Arbeit* is responsible for many measures to actively influence the labour market: career advice, placement of employees, promoting occupational training and continuing education, job-creation measures and training measures to improve employability, etc.

1.2.3. The legal policy background of the main legislative initiatives

The incorporation of the *Arbeitsförderungsgesetz* (in the third part of the Social Code (Social Code III) by the conservative/liberal government on 1.1.1998) brought to an end a development whereby the 1969 *Arbeitsförderungsgesetz* was gradually adapted to a worsening employment situation on the labour market and the associated problems of funding unemployment insurance. The SPD/Green government, with

53   Federal Constitutional Court 27.1.1998, *BVerfGE 97*, 169, 179; BAG 12.11.1998, *DB 1999*, 965; BAG 21.2.2001, *RdA 2002*, 99 with note Otto AiB 21002 with note Bachmeister; BAG 25.4.2001, *DB 2001*, 2504.

54   See Federal Constitutional Court 27.1.1998, *BVerfGE 97*, 169, 179; BAG 15.3.2001, *NZA 2001*, 831; Hamburg Labour Court 10.3.1997, *DB 1997*, 2439 = AiB 1998, 120 with note Bösche.

55   Zachert, *NZA 2001*, p. 1041, 1045.

56   On this debate, see, *inter alia*, Schmidt, Ingrid, *AuR 1997*, p. 461 ff.; ibid., *NZA 1999*, p. 124 ff.; Hanau/Peters-Lange, *NZA 1998*, p. 785 ff.; crit. Heinze, *SGb 2000*, p. 241 ff.

57   Short summary in Kittner, *Arbeits- und Sozialrecht*, 27th edition 2002, Chapter 30 (Social Code III); description under 'employability' in English: Weiss/Schmidt, *Marlene in Job creation and Labour law*, ed. Biagi, 2000, p. 145 ff.

58   See Chapter II, section 1.2.10 of the German report.

its Job-AQTIV (Activate, Qualify, Train, Invest, Place [*vermitteln*]) Act of 10 December 2001 (in force since 1 January 2002), brought in a set of innovations whose individual impact is difficult to estimate but which, in their overall design, signify a shift in labour market policy. This reform is the expression of an active labour market policy (explicitly §5 of Social Code III), aiming at a supply and demand equilibrium on the labour market and using various measures and instruments to achieve this. The idea of improving employability, mainly through training, plays a central role, as expressed by the acronym AQTIV, which stands for Activate, Qualify, Train, Invest, Place [*vermitteln*]. From a European perspective, it is interesting to note that experiences in neighbouring countries have served as examples for several aspects of the reform. The main elements of this reform and the prospects for their further development are described below.[59]

1.2.4. Job rotation

The Job-AQTIV Act introduced **job rotation**, which has already been successful in other countries, particularly Denmark,[60] into German labour law. If an employer takes on a jobseeker in order to allow another worker to undertake vocational training, this person's pay can be subsidised by the employment office at a rate of between 50% and 100% (§§229 ff. of Social Code III). The maximum subsidy period is 12 months. Providing a substitute for the employee who is temporarily absent is a relevant ground for a temporary contract of employment. In practice, however, this possibility has not yet been taken up to the expected extent. In November 2002 there were fewer than 400 recorded cases of job rotation in Germany. This may be because employment office staff are not (yet) familiar with the relatively laborious implementation of measures of this kind.

1.2.5. Placement by (private) agencies

The Job-AQTIV Act also regulates the option of using **third party agencies** to find positions for jobseekers. The employment office approves these agencies. Pursuant to §§37 f. of Social Code III, the employment office has to examine whether calling in third-party agencies would increase the placement rate.

The details of the Act were relatively complicated and were simplified on 1.4.2002. Further openings in favour of private agencies have been anticipated in the current debate on further, far-reaching reform of labour market policy, presented by the commission on Modern Services in the Labour Market, the so-called **Hartz Commission**, on 21 August 2002.[61] The model for these and future arrangements were and still are the parastatal 'START' agencies in the Netherlands. Similar agencies based on this model were founded in North Rhine-Westphalia in 1995.[62]

1.2.6. Integration agreements

Integration agreements are similar to the 'New Deal' scheme in the United Kingdom, i.e. the attempt to find employment for people in the primary labour market through individual counselling and compulsion.[63] The amendment of December 2001 describes in §35 of Social Code III the respective obligations of the unemployment office and the jobseeker and associated benefits.[64] The Hartz Commission proposals (autumn 2002) are for these bilateral obligations to be deepened and, if necessary, enforced by stricter penalties.[65]

1.2.7. Transfer social plans

The bridge between employment promotion and corporate co-determination is formed by **transfer social plans.**[66] Social plans are negotiated between the works council and the employer in order to balance out or mitigate the economic disadvantages that hit employees in the event of a company crisis. The works council has co-determination rights here, pursuant to §112 of the BetrVG. Under §254 of Social Code III, provisions of social plans that serve to integrate employees in the labour market may be subsidised by the employment offices. This option was also available under the old law. However, since the reform of works constitutions in July 2001, there is an explicit provision in the *Betriebsverfassungsgesetz* (§112(5)(2) of the BetrVG), creating a link between public promotion and corporate co-determination.

The background to these changes is that, for decades, the practice was, and usually still is, to accept that some jobs will

---

59 On Social Code III and amendments to it, above all in the Job-AQTIV Act, a great deal of literature exists, including: latest, monographic: Kruse/Zamponi, *Das neue Recht der Arbeitsförderung* (New Employment Promotion Law), 2002; also, in English: Weiss/Schmidt, *Marlene in Job creation and Labour Law*, Biagi, ed. 2000, p. 145 ff.

60 Overview: Eichhorst/Profit/Thode, ed. *Benchmarking Deutschland 2001*, p. 225 ff., 308 f. with references.

61 More under Chapter II, section 1.2.10 of the German report.

62 Eichhorst/Profit/Thode, ed. *Benchmarking Deutschland 2001*, p. 228 f. with empirical references regarding the results.

63 Eichhorst/Profit/Thode, ed. *Benchmarking Deutschland*, p. 227 f.

64 Muted assessment of this practice with empirical references by Stindt, *FS Weinspach*, p. 147, 163.

65 More in Chapter II, section 1.2.10 of the German report.

66 An informative description of this problem area with references to the comprehensive discussion from Däubler in Däubler/Kittner/Klebe, *BetrVG*, 8th edition 2002, § 112, 112 a, note 155 ff.; more normative: Fitting/Kaiser/Heither/Engels/Schmidt, *BetrVG*, 21st edition 2002, §112, note 141 ff.

be lost following a company transfer,[67] and to mitigate their impact mainly through the payment of compensation. This practice does not take sufficient account of §2 of Social Code III which, since the reform of the Job-AQTIV Act, has expressly obliged employers to take steps to avoid redundancies or to organise transfers to other employment relationships (§2(3) No 5 of Social Code III).

In practice, it is becoming clear that the agreements and compensation payments provided for in the social plans are not enough in times of mass unemployment. The prospect of finding a suitable job, at least within a certain period, is more important. This is where **employment plans** (transfer social plans) come in. They provide for training for those affected, oblige companies to develop new products and open up new markets, regulate the introduction of new technology, or make money available for creating employment and training companies and/or for their application.

In this context, Social Code III now provides a whole range of possibilities to facilitate these objectives.[68] They include; subsidies for integration measures, primarily through retraining; further training and preparation for starting one's own business (§255 of Social Code III); and so-called *Strukturarbeitergeld*, which is now available to small businesses too, thanks to the Job-AQTIV Act (§175 of the Social Code III), and the funding of structural adjustments (§272 ff. of Social Code III); and infrastructure measures (§279a ff. of Social Code III).[69] The co-funding options offered by the employment authorities are very complex, and initial empirical studies suggest that they are being taken up rather hesitantly. However, they seem to be gradually gaining favour in practice.[70]

1.2.8. Special measures to promote training

The objective of Social Code III to **permanently improve training** against the background of changing demands in the world of work (e.g. §2(2) No 1 of Social Code III) is given concrete form in various provisions of the amendment to the Job-AQTIV Act.[71] For example, the new §235 c of Social Code III promotes further vocational training for workers without

a vocational qualification via **subsidies to employers**. The new §417 of Social Code III provides the opportunity of taking on further training costs for workers in ongoing jobs, as long as the further conditions for this provision are met.

Here too, the link with the tasks of the parties in the context of corporate co-determination should be mentioned.[72] The reform of the *Betriebsverfassungsgesetz* in July 2001 rearranged and gave greater emphasis to employers' responsibility to properly train their employees. The aim is to avoid unemployment as far as possible. According to §97(2) of the BetrVG, employers and works councils (§2(2) No 1 of Social Code III) are responsible for providing training for employees, where the employer is planning or has carried out measures which lead to the nature of the job changing, with the consequence that employees' vocational knowledge and skills are no longer sufficient. Works councils have a right of initiative and co-determination here, i.e. they can say whether and how such a measure will be implemented, with the aid of the company conciliation board.

1.2.9. Targeted assistance for (problem) groups on the labour market: young people, older workers

Compared to other countries, **youth unemployment** in Germany over the past decade (and even before then) has been relatively low. An important reason for this is the dual system of vocational training in a public technical school and at the workplace. One problem – especially since the accession of the new *Bundesländer* in 1990 – is a lack of on-the-job training places.[73] This problem worsened in 2002 against the backdrop of the sustained economic and labour market crisis.[74]

Over the reporting period, wage subsidies were paid to employers via state measures (the 1997 *Arbeitsförderungs-Reformgesetz* – Employment Promotion Reform Act) to promote young people's transition to work. These measures have been extended and differentiated under the new government. Moreover, an immediate aid programme for young people found training opportunities for around 500 000 youngsters

---

67   With regard to the notification obligations pursuant to the Collective Redundancies Directive 98/59/EC and their implementation in German law: Wank, in Hanau/Steinmeyer/Wank, *Handbuch des europäischen Arbeits- und Sozialrechts* (Handbook of European Labour and Social Law) 2002, notes 190 ff., 205 ff. with references.

68   Most recently Weiland, *BB 2002*, p. 570 ff.; Wendeling-Schröder/Welkoborsky, *NZA 2003*, p. 1370; also Däubler, in Däubler/Kittner/Klebe, *BetrVG*, § 112, 112 a, note 159 ff. Lieb, ed. *Der Transfer-Sozialplan* (the transfer social plan), 2000.

69   On positive experiences with integration subsidies in Ireland: Eichhorst/Profit/Thode, *Benchmarking in Deutschland*, p. 229.

70   Empirical data in Kleinhenz, 63rd *German Juristentag*, Report, Part B, p. 30; Stindt, *FS Weinspach*, p. 147, 157.

71   On the further training possibilities offered under Social Code III: Mayer, *Udo AiB 2002*, p. 714 ff.

72   Thannheiser, *AiB 2002*, p. 720 ff.

73   Overview in Weiss/Schmidt, *Marlene, Job creation and Labour law*, Biagi, ed. p. 145, 147; in detail Zachert, country report in: *La transizione dei giovani verso la vita attiva* (Young people's transition to working life), Ministero del Lavoro e della Previdenza Sociale (Labour and Social Security Ministry), volume III, 1997, p. 77, 78 ff.

74   Sehrbrock, *Gewerkschaftliche Bildungspolitik* (Trade union training policy), 2003, p. 10 ff. with statistical information.

between early 1999 and 2001. Some of the provisions of this immediate aid programme (integration subsidies, allowances for measures to prepare people for work, placement premiums, etc.) are reflected in the Job-AQTIV Act.

The **social partners** have long supported this policy with standard clauses about maintaining or increasing training places and, above all, the recruitment of young people once they have finished their training. 52 economic sectors/collective agreement areas, representing some 10.5 million employees, have rules on taking on trainees once they have finished their traineeship.[75]

With regard to **older workers**, the measures implemented so far have concentrated more on facilitating early retirement[76] rather than re-integration. Entry-into-work rates show that job prospects for the over 55s are much worse than for young people (e.g. 15.6% compared to 50.1% of the under 55s).[77]

1.2.10. Interim results and outlook

1.2.10.1. New conceptual focuses

An assessment of government activities to promote employability on the labour market shows up three particularly interesting aspects.

Firstly, the greater emphasis on an **active labour market policy**, as laid down in §5 of Social Code III, amended by the Job-AQTIV Act: unemployment should be avoided, not just temporarily, and the development of long-term unemployment should be prevented.

Secondly, and associated with the first aspect, the focus on **best practice in other European countries** (especially Denmark, the Netherlands, the Republic of Ireland and the UK).

Thirdly, more than ever before, **links** are being forged between the opportunities for exploiting the options in Social Code III **and workers' representation bodies**. This reflects the observation that the starting point for an efficient labour market policy must be companies themselves. The collaboration and co-determination rights of works councils (e.g. §§92a, 97(2) of the BetrVG), which were considerably extended in July 2001, demonstrate this and provide a specific basis.

1.2.10.2. The Hartz Commission (overview)

All of these schemes, initiatives and measures have to be accepted in practice. Their impact will be limited if the overall economic situation is weak.[78] For this reason, the Red/Green coalition, re-elected in September 2002, created a commission on modern services in the labour market, known as the **Hartz Commission**, at the end of the previous legislative period. Although it is not possible here to describe individually all the many proposals made by this commission (which came into force with the *Gesetz für Moderne Dienstleistungen am Arbeitsmarkt* (Modern Services in the Labour Market Act) of 1 January 2003) the underlying philosophy was to build on the Job-AQTIV Act whilst setting some new focuses. One of the main innovations was the Personnel Service Agency (PSA). The idea is that each employment office should set up its own or an outsourced Personnel Service Agency.[79] In principle, jobseekers should be employed there and receive net pay at the level of their unemployment benefit, in order to be hired-out as soon as possible to a third party company. Conditions set out in collective agreements should apply to this work. Before the jobseekers are posted, they should receive training. If, after three to six months, a jobseeker refuses to work for the Personnel Service Agency, his or her unemployment benefit is cut.

The employment offices should become more effective (job centres with greater powers), and help for specific groups (e.g. young people) should become more targeted.

The Commission's report foresees a change in focus, from active to activating labour market policy, in line with the European Union's employment policy guidelines.[80]

The Hartz Commission's proposals raised controversy about their implementation as soon as they were published. In addition to organisational issues (private, mixed or public sector organisation, or publicly-owned operation), the question of the employment conditions for the seconded workers is also controversial. The Hartz Commission assumed that the Per-

---

75   Bispinck/Dorsch-Schweizer/Kirsch, *WSI Mitt. 2002*, p. 213 ff.; overview in Zachert, country report in: *La transizione dei giovani verso la vita attiva*, p. 77, 80 f.

76   See Chapter II, section 3.6 of the German report.

77   Kleinhenz, report on the 63rd *German Juristentag*, 2000, part B, p. 24 and 34.

78   For a discussion of the various factors relevant to a successful labour market policy, comparing Germany and the USA: Finkin, *RdA 2002*, p. 333 ff.

79   On the organisational implementation: Bertelsmann-Stiftung/Bundesanstalt für Arbeit/McKinsey and Company, ed. *The Personnel Service Agency*, 2002, p. 34 ff.

80   Commission, '*Moderne Dienstleistungen am Arbeitsmarkt*' (Modern services in the labour market), 8/2002, www.bma.bund.de/hartz-kommission. Summary: *Bundesarbeitsblatt 9/2002*, p. 21 ff.

sonnel Service Agencies would be exempt from the protection provisions of the *Arbeitnehmerüberlassungsgesetz* (Temporary Employment Act) if **collective agreements** were concluded with them. The aim is to make sure that temporary workers are not discriminated against. Temporary workers will not be placed on an equal footing by law until 2004. Employers and trade unions should use the one-year deferment to conclude collective agreements on temporary work with the agencies. If they are unable to do this by the end of 2003, the remuneration and employment terms and conditions for regular workers, established by collective agreement, will also apply to temporary workers by law from 2004. Payments in excess of the collective agreement will not be taken into account in the equal treatment arrangements.[81]

These objectives are essentially in line with the proposals at European level in the Proposal for a Directive of the European Parliament and the Council on working conditions for temporary workers (COM 2002 149). The starting point of this European initiative is that, during the period of their employment, temporary workers must have at least the same rights as comparable regular workers in the company engaging them (Article 5(1)). However, the Proposal for a Directive does allow certain exceptions.[82] With regard to the Personnel Service Agencies, it is doubtful, notwithstanding the setting of a deadline with the threat of penalties, that the parties to the collective agreement will be able to generate enough negotiating power and pressure to enforce the ban on discrimination sufficiently.[83]

The first collective agreements were concluded in February 2003. It remains to be seen how the situation will develop.[84]

1.3. Working time policy

1.3.1. Working time policy's contribution to job security

The **shortening of the working week** was pushed forward step-by-step by the German trade unions (they were the pioneers in Europe, since the major collective agreement

disputes of 1984). The trade unions pursued a number of objectives with various elements right from the start, including health and safety at work, more free time for own activities and the principle of sharing the available work among as many workers as possible. The aim was to contribute to improving the situation on the labour market.[85]

The issue of whether shortening working time in this way really does promote employment is still controversial. However, a positive effect on employment is generally found. Many empirical studies assume that between around a half and two thirds of the working time reduction led to the creation of new jobs or the reinforcement of existing ones.[86]

Since then, other European countries have also implemented their own working time reduction policies, in particular France, which introduced a mixed package of state and collective initiatives under the Jospin government up until 2002, and the Netherlands, which significantly extended part-time work.[87] In Germany, this development appears to have come to an end, at least for the time being. At the same time we can see new trends relating to working time policy and job security.

1.3.2. Government working time policy

The gap between statutory working time and that agreed upon in collective agreements is striking. As a response to Directive 93/104/EC concerning certain aspects of the organisation of working time, the conservative/liberal government adopted the *Arbeitszeitgesetz* (ArbZG – Working Time Act) on 6 June 1994,[88] thus repealing, after many legislative attempts, the 1938 *Arbeitszeitordnung* (AZO – Working Time Order), which continued to apply as Federal law after the end of the Second World War and the creation of the Federal Republic. The *Arbeitszeitgesetz* keeps the upper limit of 8 hours per day and 48 hours per week (§2 of the ArbZG), but grants companies (not bound by collective agreements) the freedom, under certain conditions, to operate working weeks of up to 60 hours (§7 of the ArbZG). Contrary to the provisions of the AZO, statutory overtime

---

81 For the latest, see Baur, *Bundesarbeitsblatt 1/2003*, p. 4 ff.

82 Wank, *NZA 2003*, p. 14 ff.; Thüsing, *DB 2002*, p. 2218 ff.

83 With regard to the situation for the temporary agency 'Start': collective agreement between START Zeitarbeit NRW GmbH and the ÖTV union of 1.7.2000 (equal rights for temporary workers); agreement between START Zeitarbeit NRW GmbH temporary work-ers/assistants and the *ver.di* union of 28.12.2001 (lower pay than other workers employed by the engaging company); on the alternatives: Kempen/Zachert, *TVG*, 3rd edition, 1997, §1, note 204.

84 More detailed information on this under B.II.1.7.3 of the country report; critical evaluation of these instruments by Däubler, *AiB 2002*, p. 729 ff.

85 In detail, Zachert, *ZTR 1995*, p. 435 ff.

86 On the various positions: Eichhorst/Profit/Thode, *Benchmarking Deutschland*, p. 302 ff. with references from the wide debate; also Bach, *IAB short report* No 3, 2001.

87 A brief overview in Eichhorst/Profit/Thode, *Benchmarking Deutschland*, p. 303 f.

88 On the far-reaching impact of the European Court of Justice case law in this area, see the consequences of the SIMAP ruling: ECJ, 3.10.2000, European Court Reports 2000, I 07963-SIMAP, also BAG 18.2.2003, *AuR 2003*, 119: 'Bereitschaftsdienst als Arbeitszeit' (On-call time as working time).

supplements are no longer provided for. Moreover, the *Arbeitszeitgesetz* contains various provisions to protect the health and safety of workers, e.g. relating to breaks (§§4, 5) and night and shift work (§6).

1.3.3. Negotiated shorter working hours policy

Rather than the statutory weekly working time framework, the unions pursued the reduction of working time by negotiating agreements to that effect. Following widespread warning strikes in the spring of 1990, the parties to the collective agreement in the metalworking industry agreed on the phased shortening of the working week to 35 hours by October 1995. Other sectors followed. At the same time, the parties maintained and extended the exceptions for longer working hours (flexibilisation), also agreed in 1984. Overall, negotiated working time was only slightly reduced over the reporting period, from 38.7 hours in 1991 to 37.4 hours in 2001 (Eastern Germany: 39.2 hours). In terms of actual working time, Germany, with 41.1 hours per week on average, was clearly above the EU average of 39.3 hours.[89] One reason for this could be the gradual move over the last decade from the prevailing model of regular 'normal working hours' divided into equal-length shifts to working time systems based on working time accounts. In these systems, regular daily working hours are less important than annual working time as a calculation basis.[90]

1.3.4. Employment security through a (temporary) far-reaching reduction of working time

A collective agreement which came into force on 1 January 1994, constituted a new approach to using a reduction in working hours – together with a number of other measures – to safeguard jobs in times of economic recession. The agreement in question was concluded between IG Metall and the VW Group at the end of 1993. The preamble to this agreement expresses its objectives: 'The parties agree that the far-reaching economic and structural problems and societal trends call for new approaches, also from the parties to the collective agreement, to safeguard employment.'

This agreement provides for an immediate cut in working time of 7.2 hours a week, from 36 to 28.8 hours. In order to justify economically such a drastic cut in working time (20%), the principle operated was that working time was purchased in the context of 'concession bargaining', in order

to safeguard employment. Although the monthly level of pay remained almost the same, employees gave up, in particular, their bonus payments of around 16% gross in return for the company's assurance that there would be no redundancies for commercial reasons for two years. This avoided some 30 000 redundancies, and the public purse was spared around DM 367 million in unemployment assistance payments. The benefit to the company was a saving of around 16% in working costs and redundancy payments.[91]

The VW collective agreement broke new ground, not only for the metalworking industry, but also for other sectors. As early as 1995, collective agreements were concluded for some 10 million workers which provided for the possibility of reducing working time to less than 30 hours per week, with a corresponding cut in wages, in order to safeguard jobs for a specific period (usually between 2 and 4 years). Legally, this happens using **saving clauses** in collective agreements. These clauses grant decision-making flexibility and structuring options in the standard elements of collective agreements for the parties to the agreement, the works council and the employer.[92]

This form of conditional job safeguarding in times of temporary crisis has evidently been so successful that the parties have not only been continuing to use it but have extended it in various ways. A study from 1999/2000 on *Betriebliche Bündnisse für Arbeit* (company alliances for labour) shows that savings clauses in collective agreements provide the parties with significant room to manoeuvre in order to make operational adjustments in times of crisis. Fixed-term employment guarantees are included in a good three quarters of all such agreements. The companies undertake either not to make any redundancies for commercial reasons or to maintain the existing level of employment. The bulk (50%) of the guarantees are for periods of two years or more. Some 16% of works councils say that these agreements are unlimited until such time as notice is given. In terms of content, the range of undertakings made by employers goes beyond employment guarantees and promises not to make redundancies for commercial reasons. They include provisions relating to the structuring of working time, usually via the reduction of overtime (21%), undertakings to invest in the location (37%) or to keep existing production lines at the location (20%).[93]

---

89 Eichhorst/Profit/Thode, *Benchmarking Deutschland*, p. 289 f. with references. Bach, *IAB short report No 3*, 2001, p. 5 f.

90 Seifert, Hartmut, *WSI Mitt. 1998*, p. 579, 585; ibid., *WSI Mitt. 2001*, p. 84 ff.; for example the key messages of the IG Metall collective bargaining conference of 24/25 October 2002 on working hours policy: IG Metall Presse und Funknachrichten No 126 of 30.10.2002.

91 For more information, see Peters, *Modellwechsel (Change of paradigm)*, 1994.

92 Overview: Zachert, *ZTR 1995*, p. 435, 437 with references; ibid., *Relaciones Laborales 1998*, p. 84, 87 f.

93 Seifert Hartmut, *WSI Mitt. 2000*, p. 437, 440; Maurer/Seifert, Hartmut, *WSI Mitt. 2001*, p. 490 ff.

1.3.5. Age-related part-time work

In its first legislative period (1999-2002), the Red/Green government in particular tried to improve opportunities for older people on the labour market with a number of measures. This led to a drop in the unemployment rate for the over-55s of 36% between April 1998 and April 2002.[94]

One contributory factor was **age-related part-time work**, an example of a hybrid state and social partner initiative. Pursuant to the 1996 *Altersteilzeitgesetz* (Age-related Part-time Work Act), amended in 1999 and 2000, an employer and an employee aged at least 55 years can agree that, until the employee retires, he or she will work part-time, and the employer will make an additional payment to top up the lower wages, and to increase pension contributions. The condition for this arrangement is the conclusion of a **collective agreement.** If the employer then fills the jobs that have become free by recruiting jobseekers or people who have concluded their training, he can claim back the payments made to the part-time worker from the *Bundesanstalt für Arbeit*.

As a rule, the collective agreements used by around 100 000 employees are more generous than the *Altersteilzeitgesetz*. Whilst this Act provides for 70% of the corresponding full-time net wage, and 90% of the pension contributions for half-time workers, most of the collective agreements provide for net wages of 85% or more and, in some cases, full pension contributions. In practice, however, age-related part-time work is a rarity. In most cases, the 'block model' is used, in which employees work full-time during the first phase of the block and then do not work at all during the second phase. In this sense, rather than reducing working time, this is more a case of lowering the pension age.[95]

1.3.6. Collective provisions on training and lifelong learning

Over recent years, training and further training have also been much-discussed policy issues. The general consensus on the importance of lifelong learning, in order to successfully cope with the rapid pace of structural and technological change, led the members of the *Bündnis für Arbeit* – a social dialogue under the auspices of the State[96] – to agree on a training campaign, including vocational training activities by the parties to collective agreements, in 2001. Under this agreement, the parties to collective agreements undertook

to agree framework conditions for further training in the sense of lifelong learning. Investing time in training was defined as a new task of working time policy. In this context, the parties want to use long-term time accounts and other working time tools to make sure that time credits for further training are also investments in working time.[97]

A collective agreement concluded in the metalworking and electronics industries in Baden-Württemberg in July 2000 is particularly interesting. Its innovative feature is that employees are involved in ascertaining their training needs and the associated individual training agreements. In this way, modern need establishment methods are laid down in collective agreements with the participation of those involved. The decision is thus no longer a pure managerial decision. Under certain conditions, employees are individually entitled to sabbatical leave for training purposes. These can last up to three years and include the right to return to a job of at least the same status as their old one. The sabbatical must however be for the purposes of training that is both relevant to the job and needed by the company.[98]

2. Labour law and adaptability

2.1. Adaptability of employees

2.1.1. Standard employment relationship and exceptions

The subject of 'flexible contract structuring' is based on the idea of the 'standard employment relationship', a controversial theme of the legal and social science debates of the 1980s. The debate in Germany was prompted by the *Beschäftigungsförderungsgesetz* (Employment Promotion Act) of 1 May 1985. This was the core of the conservative/liberal government's labour law deregulation policy following the change of government in 1982. Under the motto of greater flexibility, the aim was to allow companies to create a need-related employment policy. The main instrument was to make it easier to hire workers on fixed-term contracts, with the aim to help create more jobs.

In general, a standard employment relationship is considered to be a full-time job with an open-ended contract, characterised by a certain level of protection against

---

94   Bieber/Prahs/Klebula, *Bundesarbeitsblatt 9/2002*, p. 27, 29.

95   For the most recent overview: Bispinck/WSI-Tarifarchiv, *Elemente qualitativer Tarifpolitik No 49*, 2002, p. 10 ff.

96   More on the Bündnis für Arbeit under Chapter III, section 4.5 of the German report.

97   On the practical implementation possibilities: Dobischat/Seifert, H., *WSI Mitt. 2001*, p. 92 ff. Bahnmüller, *WSI Mitt. 2002*, p. 38 ff.

98   Huber, Berthold/Hofman, Jörg, *WSI Mitt. 2001*, p. 464 ff.

dismissal/redundancy.[99] However, certain conceptual grey areas exist, leading to different assessments of the extent of 'non-standard' forms of employment. Nevertheless, and in spite of the definitional differences, it can be empirically demonstrated that the standard employment relationship is still by far the most common, although the proportion of workers in temporary employment relationships, part-time work with various specific features, economically dependent work, etc. has risen.[100]

The Red/Green government repealed the 1985 *Beschäftigungs-förderungsgesetz* (which had been extended in 1996 until 31.12.2000) and replaced it with the *Gesetz über Teilzeitarbeit und befristete Arbeitsverträge* (Part-time Work and Fixed-term Employment Contracts Act) of 31.12.2000 (*Teilzeit- und Befristungsgesetz*, TzBfG). This Act transposes into German law Directives 97/81/EC (Part-time work) and 99/70/EC (Fixed-term work), concluded on the basis of social dialogue (Article 139 of the EC Treaty). In fact, this Act goes further than the Directives, making the protection standards even stronger in some aspects and facilitating bridges between full-time and part-time work, without representing a radical break with the fundamentals of previous provisions in the *Beschäftigungsförderungsgesetz*. Various aspects of the *Teilzeit- und Befristungsgesetz*[101] are considered below.

2.1.2. Standard part-time working and small-scale part-time working: empirical data

According to the legal definition in §2(1) of the TzBfG, part-time work exists when an employee's regular weekly working time is less than that of a comparable full-time employee.

The micro-census found that some 6.8 million people in Germany, almost 21% of all employed workers, were employed part-time in May 2002. This represents a rise of 3.7 million since 1991.

The term 'part-time work' hides many different forms of employment, from public officials, such as judges or teachers, working half-time to cleaners working less than 15 hours

per week.[102] In Germany, which is in the middle of the field when compared internationally, part-time work is characterised by a low number of hours.[103] In Germany part-time employees work an average of 8.6 hours per week, compared to an EU average of 21 hours.[104] Of the 6.8 million part-time workers in Germany in 2002, some 4 million were employed less than 15 hours per week, earning no more than EUR 325 per month (§8 of Social Code IV).[105]

2.1.3. Part-time work as the interface between paid and non-paid work

Part-time work is an essential element of the bridge between non-paid and paid work and can fit in with the different life plans of men and women. As the working week becomes ever shorter, the boundaries between full-time and part-time work are becoming more blurred. Nevertheless, there are still differences between part-time work and the so-called standard full-time employment relationship. These differences are not just in terms of protection standards, for instance equal treatment, but above all, in the gender make-up of these forms of work. The vast majority of part-time work in Germany – around 85% – is done by women. This reflects the increase in the number of working women, in particular among married women (60% of women aged 30-50 years in Germany work, and this figure is set to rise to 75-85% by 2010). Women's increasing need to find fulfilment in paid work has eroded the traditional model of the male bread-winner.[106] The reason most frequently given by women for working part-time is to have more time to look after children or other personal interests, followed by labour market-related part-time working and the desire to have more time for further training.[107]

2.1.4. Traditional arrangements and new focuses on part-time work in the Teilzeit- und Befristungsgesetz (TzBfG)

The *Teilzeit- und Befristungsgesetz* acts as a kind of bridge between full-time and part-time work. In addition to the objective of combating discrimination and promoting part-time work (as set out explicitly in §1) the statement of

---

99 Däubler, *AuR 1988*, p. 302 ff.; Zachert, *Die Sicherung und Gestaltung des Normalarbeitsverhältnisses durch Tarifvertrag* (Securing and structuring the standard employment relationship by collective agreement), 1989, p. 14 ff.

100 Hoffmann/Walwei, *Mitteilungen aus der Arbeitsmarkt und Berufsforschung 3/1998*, p. 409 ff.; also under Chapter I, section 2.2. of the German report.

101 In the comprehensive literature on the TzBfG, just two descriptions with different assessments: on the one hand, Däubler, *ZIP 2001*, p. 217; on the other hand, Richardi/Annuß, *BB 2000*, p. 2001 ff.

102 For more on the structure of part-time working: Heilmann/Martin Troyano, in: Martin/Nienhüser, ed. *Neue Formen der Beschäftigung* (New forms of employment), 2002, p. 153, 158 ff.

103 According to the OECD Employment Outlook 2001, in Eichhorst/Profit/Thode, *Benchmarking Deutschland*, p. 294 f.

104 OECD and Eurostat studies, in Eichhorst/Profit/Thode, *Benchmarking Deutschland*, p. 90 f.

105 For the latest statistics, which contradict each other in some respects: Rudolph, *Die Mitbestimmung* (Co-determination) 2002, p. 29 f.; Heilmann/Martin Troyano in: Martin/Nienhüser, ed. *Neue Formen der Beschäftigung* (New forms of employment), p. 153, 155 ff. and Becker/Jörges-Süß in: Martin/Nienhüser, ed. *Neue Formen der Beschäftigung*, p. 119, 123 f. on small-scale part-time working.

106 Zachert, *WSI Mitt. 2000*, S. 283, 286 with references.

107 Data from Viethen/Scheddler, *Bundesarbeitsblatt 11/2002*, p. 5, 6; also Schiek, *KJ 2002*, p. 23 with references.

grounds cites, first of all, the promotion of flexible forms of work, followed by a reference to the employment policy importance of part-time work.[108]

To realise these objectives, the fundamental protection provision for part-time workers is the **ban on discrimination** in §4 of the TzBfG. According to this, part-time workers must not be treated worse than comparable full-time workers. This applies in particular to pay. Part-time workers must be paid at least the same proportion of the full-time wage as the proportion of the full-time hours they work.[109]

One new feature is the **right to work part-time** under §8 of the TzBfG under certain conditions laid down by law (size of company: 16 employees or more, length of employment: longer than six months). This has been heavily criticised by employers and in some academic circles. Employers must discuss employees' requests with them and approve them if there are no commercial grounds for refusing. Grounds for a refusal may include significant harm to the organisation, work processes or safety of the company. If an employer refuses to allow an employee to work part-time and the latter wishes to appeal, the employer must then call on the labour court to rule on the justification of the application. If part-time workers wish to (re-) increase their working time, employers must consider them, under §9 of the TzBfG, when filling any corresponding vacancies, unless this is not practical for operating reasons or in the interests of other employees deserving greater social protection.

So far, the empirical data and rulings in the first instance do not confirm the fear of a wave of litigation to force employers to comply. A survey in the autumn of 2001 found that some 85 000 employees, of whom 66 000 were women, had applied to reduce their working hours. Nearly all (around 95%) of these applications were approved.[110] The courts expect employers to provide rational, comprehensible grounds of significant importance to justify a refusal to grant part-time work.[111]

2.1.5. Special forms of part-time work: on-call work and job-sharing

Compared to its predecessor, the *Beschäftigungs-förderungsgesetz*, the *Teilzeit- und Befristungsgesetz* does not provide any new focus on special forms of part-time working such as **on-call work**, whereby employees have to

remain on-call in case they are needed, and the rare institution of **job-sharing**. Fundamentally, the existing minimum statutory requirements remain in force. In the case of on-call work, these are a minimum of 10 hours per week and 3 hours per day, and a minimum 4-day period of notice for work (§12 TzBfG). In the case of job-sharing, the substitution obligation is limited, and a certain level of protection against redundancy is guaranteed (§13 of the TzBfG).

2.1.6. Small-scale part-time working

2.1.6.1. Legislative developments

One of the most controversial labour policy proposals of the first Red/Green government involved reforming **small-scale part-time work** and making changes to the conditions for economically dependent work. The 1st April 1999 (1999: 630 DM) small-scale part-time work got defined as less than 15 hours per week and wages of up to EUR 325 per month. Neither reform relates (directly) to labour law, but rather redefines certain provisions of the Social Code (§8 of Social Code (SGB) IV: small-scale part-time working; §7(4) of Social Code IV: (apparent) self employment).

The core of the original law on small-scale part-time employment was that the associated income was free of social security contributions, but that the employer would deduct a flat rate of 22% income tax. In the 1990s, it became increasingly obvious that, despite the imprecision of the statistics, this way of structuring small-scale part-time employment relationships (which, like part-time work in general, concern mainly women) was inadequate in many respects. There was evidence that in some sectors such as retail, full-time jobs were being split up into several part-time ones. It also appeared that many jobs on which social security contributions were payable were being converted into jobs exempt from such contributions. The social security funds were experiencing estimated losses of contributions of between 5 and 6 billion DM per year because of this type of contract.[112]

Comparative studies showed that this misuse could most effectively be combated by abolishing or at least significantly lowering the social security thresholds, with corresponding exceptions for certain groups of persons or activities and sectors.[113] With the new legislation of April 1999 (§8 of Social Code IV in conjunction with §§168(1) No 1b and 249b of Social Code IV), the legislator did not choose this

---

108 BT-Drucksache 14/4374, p. 1, 11.

109 For more on the ban on discrimination, see Chapter II, section 3 of the German report.

110 IAB representative survey in Magvas/Spitznagel, *Bundesarbeitsblatt* 11/2002, p. 10 ff., 11; and *AuR 2002,* p. 413, 416.

111 Recent overview: Reiserer/Penner, *BB 2002*, p. 1694 ff.

112 Sitte, *WSI Mitt. 1997,* p. 780, 787; Information from 'Aus der Gesetzgebung' (From the legislation), *AuR 1999,* p. 55, 57.

113 Bieback, *Die mittelbare Diskriminierung wegen des Geschlechts* (Indirect sexual discrimination), 1997, p. 145 ff.

route, although it did take the first steps towards protecting part-time workers (mainly women) by making pension and health insurance contributions obligatory for them. The employer pays the contributions, and the flat-rate tax is no longer applicable.[114] Several small-scale part-time jobs are added together so that, if the small-scale threshold is passed, a full obligation to pay social security contributions arises. The problem of transfers (from part-time to full-time) remained, as the threshold for full tax liability was 630 DM (now EUR 325).

2.1.6.2. Controversy about the new provisions and outlook

The new provisions raised controversy, particular with regard to the issue of whether the reform had led to a drop in small-scale part-time work. The statistics are contradictory. The German government, citing a number of studies, has found an increase in this type of employment, which, for the first time, can be statistically recorded with a certain level of accuracy by the social security authorities.[115] Other surveys have assumed a decrease in small-scale part-time jobs (in certain sectors, e.g. trade, hospitality).[116] However, it is certain that the new provisions have not led to a collapse of this sector through a mass exodus into illegal work – as predicted by some critics.[117] Overall, the number of small-scale part-time **secondary jobs** has declined, whilst the number of **small-scale part-time only jobs** has increased.[118]

With regard to transfers on the other side of the EUR 325 income threshold, the debate concerns a subsidised low-income bracket (combi-wage).[119] Under the so-called Mainz Model, tested throughout Germany since 1 March 2002, workers earning between EUR 325 and 897 receive an allowance for their social security contributions and/or extra child benefit.[120] The Hartz Commission recommends that, for the domestic services sector, the income threshold be raised from EUR 325 to 500 per month, subject to a social security contribution rate of 10%.[121]

2.1.6.3. Prospects: Turnaround?

The latest legal policy developments (December 2002) are bringing some surprising results. The following agreement was reached between the governing coalition (SPD/Greens) and the opposition (CDU/FDP), on whose agreement the government had to rely for certain aspects of the Hartz plan, because of the political composition of the *Bundesrat* (Upper House). From 1.4.2003, the following applies:

- The 15-hour threshold is scrapped.

- For **small-scale domestic part-time jobs** yielding up to EUR 400, the employer (alone) has to pay a flat-rate charge of 12 % (5% for health, 5% for pension insurance, and 2% tax). These expenses are partially tax-deductible.

- For **other small-scale jobs**, the employer (alone) has to pay a flat-rate charge of 25% (12% for health insurance, 11% for pension insurance and 2 % tax). The principle of counting several secondary jobs together, so that a full social security obligation may arise, is maintained. However, one secondary job may be performed at a preferential social security rate, in addition to a main job where social security contributions are compulsory. The opposite solution was a core element of the 1999 reform, with the aim of stopping the splitting up of full-time jobs into several part-time ones.

- Above EUR 400 to 800 there is now a **sliding zone**, where employers pay 21% social contributions. Employees' contributions rise step-by-step from 4% to 21%.

The overall aim is to simplify the procedure.

It is estimated that the reforms will lead to a loss of around EUR 1 billion per annum for the social security funds. This should however be balanced out by an increase in employment.

114　For further details, see e.g. Feldhoff, *AuR 1999*, p. 249 ff.

115　E.g. data in *AuR 2000*, p. 134.

116　E.g. data in *AuR 1999*, p. 344.

117　Recently, with differentiated empirical data: Rudolph, *Die Mitbestimmung* (Co-determination), 2002, p. 29, 30.

118　Becker/Jörges-Süß in: Martin/Nienhüser, *Neue Formen der Beschäftigung* (New forms of employment), p. 119, 124.

119　From the debate, for example, Streek and Bieback in: Otto-Brenner-Stiftung, ed. *Niedriglohnsektor und Lohnsubventionen im Spiegel des Arbeits- und Sozialrechts* (Low pay sector and wage subsidies reflected in employment and social law), 2000.

120　Jülicher, *Bundesarbeitsblatt 8/2002*, p. 18 ff.; according to the Bundesanstalt für Arbeit, around 10 000 workers had taken up this option by March 2003.

121　E.g. *Bundesarbeitsblatt 9/2002*, p. 21, 25.

This system is so new that any assessment can only be provisional.[122] The simplification of the administrative procedures and the attempt to mitigate the impact of the threshold for full social security charges (EUR 325) by using transitional arrangements are to be welcomed. It remains to be seen whether the (new) preferential flat-rate charge for small-scale **secondary jobs** will again lead to abuses (e.g. the splitting up of full-time jobs into several part-time ones). Broadly speaking, developments suggest that the part-time sector is in a state of flux. It is not yet possible to clearly discern the impact of these provisions.

2.1.7. Short-term contracts and temporary work via agencies

2.1.7.1. Legal and de facto developments and assessment of these contracts

The figures show that the proportion of all employees on temporary contracts was around 9% (approximately 3.3 million) in 2000. With this temporary employment rate, Germany is in the mid range by European standards, as it is for part-time work.[123] New recruits are particularly likely to be on fixed-term contacts.[124] Around half of all fixed-term contracts[125] eventually lead to a permanent contract, as do between 18% and 30% of temporary postings via agencies, according to (unsubstantiated) estimates.[126]

With regard to **fixed-term contracts**, these have been approved for a long time in Germany, as they have in other countries (§620 of the Civil Code). However, they are monitored by the courts, since a whole host of protection rights (in particular, against dismissal/redundancy) do not apply to those on fixed-term contracts. Because of these dangers, the **labour courts** examine whether **objective reasons** exist for fixed-term contracts, in terms of their content and duration. Legal practice has developed an elaborate case law – as happened with redundancies – and broadly accepted fixed-term contracts. The classic fixed-term contract cases are

cover for sick leave or holiday leave, casual work, seasonal work, maternity cover, etc. In all these cases, the courts accept that a fixed-term contract is justified on relevant grounds. The condition is that fixed-term contracts must not be concluded abusively. For example, employers may not shift economic risks onto their employees. Following an intense and controversial debate, the situation changed somewhat with the conservative-liberal government's *Beschäftigungs-förderungsgesetz* (BeschFG – Employment Promotion Act) of 1 May 1985. Since then, fixed-term contracts can be concluded for up to 1½ years (and up to 2 years since the 1996 amendment) with no specific justification, if the employer is recruiting the worker for a new job (§1 of the BeschFG).

If we accept the Supreme Court's jurisprudence[127] that the 'standard' form of employment is one with a (certain) level of protection, then fixed-term contracts – and thus also temporary agency work as a specific type of temporary work – cannot be seen as fundamentally equivalent alternatives to the 'standard' form of employment in the same way as part-time work. Accordingly, the entry into force of the *Beschäftigungsförderungsgesetz* in 1985 was heavily criticised in academic circles.[128] However, subsequent developments showed that the labour market situation did not improve. Neither did the fear that the traditional standard of protection against redundancy would be further eroded materialise. The number of fixed-term employment relationships rose slightly, but not significantly, as a response to the many extensions of the *Beschäftigungsförderungsgesetz*.[129]

The number of temporary **agency workers** in Germany rose disproportionately in the 1990s – in keeping with developments in other EU (and OECD) Member States. However, as it accounts for less than 1% of all employees (around 340 000), this kind of work is still not a mass phenomenon.[130]

In spite of continuing criticism of temporary agency work there has recently been an increase in opportunities for transferring from temporary agency work to full-time per-

---

122 For the latest developments: Rolfs, *ZIP 2003*, p. 141 ff.; idem, *NZA 2003*, p. 65 ff.; critical: Mayer, Udo, *AiB 2003*, p. 69 ff.

123 Schiek, *KJ 2002*, p. 18, 23 with references.

124 Sample surveys suggest that 2/3 of all new recruits in the metal working sector are hired on fixed-term contracts: Gerntke, *Soziale Sicherheit 2000*, p. 385 ff.

125 Bielinski, *WSI Mitt. 1997*, p. 532, 535.

126 Kittner, *Arbeits- und Sozialordnung*, p. 99 with references.

127 BAG GS 27.2.1985, AP No 14 on §611 of the Civil Code, employment obligation in the case of an equivalent request; Federal Constitutional Court 24.4.1991, *BVerfGE 84*, 133 ff. Warteschleifen ruling; Federal Constitutional Court 27.1.1998, *BVerfGE 97*, 169, 179 = *AuR 1998*, 207 with note by Buschmann: Kleinbetriebsklausel (SME clause).

128 Herschel, *AuR 1985*, p. 265: 'Gefährdung der Rechtskultur' (Endangering the legal culture).

129 Bielinski, *WSI Mitt. 1997*, p. 532 ff. Sitte, *WSI Mitt. 1997*, p. 780 ff.

130 For the latest, e.g. Krasnieka/Werwatz, *Bundesarbeitsblatt 2/2003*, p. 2 ff; and Nienhüser/Baumhus in Martin/Nienhüser, ed. *Neue Formen der Beschäftigung* (New forms of employment), p. 61, 70; Walwei, *EuroAS 2002*, p. 149 11; however, some of the statistics are contradictory: the *Bundesverband Zeitarbeitpersonal-Dienstleistungen* (Federal Association of Temporary Workers – Services) gives a figure of 782 000 temporary workers in 2001: Globus-Infografik, 18.11.2002, IG Metall Presse- und Funk-Nachrichten, 22.11.2002.

manent work. The precondition for greater acceptance is that certain minimum conditions are met, in order to protect employees from abusive employment practices.[131]

2.1.7.2. Fixed-term work in the Teilzeit- und Befristungsgesetz (Part-time Work and Fixed-term Employment Act)

Accordingly, the provisions on fixed-term contracts in the *Teilzeit- und Befristungsgesetz* of 31 December 2000 do not break with the tradition of previous employment promotion laws. They do however try to codify a list of examples (§14(1) of the TzBfG) and outlaw or otherwise restrict certain particularly blatant abusive practices.

The most important and, in employment policy terms, most controversial change is the outlawing of 'chain employment contracts' with the same employer under §14(2) of the TzBfG.[132]

§14(3) of the TzBfG, which allows fixed-term contracts without objective grounds for employees over 58 years old, will have to be tested against the ban on age-related discrimination in Article 2 of Directive 2000/78/EC and the Fixed-term Work Directive (1999/70/EC). The same is the case for the latest proposals from the Hartz Commission,[133] to lower the threshold to 52 years.[134]

2.1.7.3. Amendments relating to temporary agency work in the Arbeitnehmerüberlassungsgesetz (Temporary Employment Act) and the ideas of the Hartz Commission

The 1972 *Arbeitnehmerüberlassungsgesetz* (AüG) – the main legal basis for temporary work in Germany – was not significantly amended over the reporting period. Its main characteristics are:

- the delineation of employee transfers (permitted) from employee placement (not allowed) and the formulation of conditions under which the commercial placement of employees is allowed

- the formulation of minimum standards for the legal status of temporary agency workers and

- safeguards for temporary agency workers in cases of banned placement of employees remain in force.[135]

The most important changes were made gradually, in particular in conjunction with the reform of employment promotion law, including the Job-Aqtiv Act.[136] They relate to the maximum time limit for employee placement (three months when the Act came into force in 1972, repeatedly extended and, since 1 January 2002, 24 months: §3 No 6 of the AüG). The new provisions in §10(5) of the AüG should be noted, whereby the agency must grant temporary agency workers the same working conditions as are enjoyed by employees of the client company from the 13th month of the assignment onwards. This is broadly in line with the European Commission's proposal for a directive establishing that temporary agency workers should, in principle, receive the same pay and the same benefits as regular workers performing a comparable job after just six weeks of activity in a company.[137]

It can be assumed that temporary agency work will grow considerably as a result of the reforms proposed by the **Hartz Commission**, implemented in September 2002 by the re-elected Red/Green government through the *Gesetz für moderne Dienstleistungen am Arbeitsmarkt* (Modern Services in the Labour Market Act) of 1 January 2003. Following the Dutch model and the initial experiences in North Rhine-Westphalia (START agencies), Personnel Service Agencies (PSAs) are to be set up to place jobseekers with third parties for payment. Collective agreements between the unions and the PSAs should ensure that the usual collective conditions apply to these workers as well, so that, by the beginning of 2004, the statutory restrictions in the AüG can be repealed.[138] In this context, the unions are demanding that, when jobseekers are placed with companies, the latter's collective and standard industry terms and conditions apply.[139] This demand will encounter difficulties and opposition, as shown by the example of the *START Zeitarbeit GmbH*

---

131 E.g. the discussion between Klös and Seifert, Hartmut in: *Die Mitbestimmung 2000*, p. 38 ff.

132 Criticism from the employer side: *BdA-pro-job.de 2002*, p. 29 ff.; from the industry associations: Girndt, *Die Mitbestimmung 2001*, p. 41; clearly in favour, e.g. Blanke, T., *AiB 2000*, p. 729, 734.

133 Commission *Moderne Dienstleistungen am Arbeitsmarkt* (Modern services in the labour market), 2002, p. 117.

134 E.g. Schiek, *KJ 2002*, p. 18, 30 ff. with references.

135 For the latest labour law overview: Wank, *EuroAS 2002*, p. 167 ff.; for a social law overview: Vor, *EuroAS 2002*, p. 175, ff.

136 E.g. Düwell, *BB 1997*, p. 46 ff.; idem, *BB 2002*, p. 98 ff. also relating to the implementation problems; Ulber, *AuR 2001*, p. 451 ff.; different assessment by Boemke/Lembke, *DB 2002* p. 893 ff.

137 Documentation: *AuR 2002*, p. 173; Wank, *NZA 2003*, p. 14 ff.; Thüsing, *DB 2002*, p. 2218 ff.

138 Commission *Moderne Dienstleistungen am Arbeitsmarkt* (Modern services in the labour market), p. 153, 156, 157; also under Chapter II, section 2.10.2 of the German report.

139 *DGB-Bundesvorstand* (German Trade Union Confederation Executive Committee) Social Security 2002, p. 261, 262; for the latest: Ulber, *AuR 2003*, p. 7 ff.; Reim, *AiB 2003*, p. 73 ff.; Wank, *RdA 2003*, p. 1 ff.; Thüsing, *DB 2003*, p. 446 ff.

in North Rhine-Westphalia.[140] The first collective agreements between unions affiliated to the German Trade Union Confederation and the *Bundesverband Zeitarbeit* (Federal Association of Temporary Work Businesses) which are generally in line with these principles but allow lower pay for hard-to-place groups, were concluded on 20 February 2003.

Several unions, led by IG Metall, already concluded collective agreements for these workers at EXPO 2000 (in Hanover, Lower Saxony).[141] This can be seen as a change in the thinking of the trade unions which, for a long time, demanded that temporary agency work be restricted or even banned, because of the risks to those involved. The unions are now, in principle, ready to help structure this kind of work under certain circumstances, above all through collective agreements.

2.1.8. (Apparent) self-employment and economically dependent work

2.1.8.1. Employees, quasi-employees, teleworking

German labour law contains no legal definition of an 'employee'. Rather, the **courts** have developed a very flexible list of criteria in order to clarify the concept of an employee from that of a self-employed worker.[142] The key concept in Germany – as in many other countries – is that of **personal dependence** or **personal subordination**. The courts look at whether a person is obliged to follow someone else's orders in relation to working time, and the location and content of the work. In addition to this primary criterion for delineating employment from self-employment, the courts look at whether the person in question is part of a **third-party work organisation**.

In contrast to many other European countries, the delineation between employees, who are protected fully under labour law, and the self-employed, who are excluded from this protection, has never been accepted as a satisfactory solution in German labour law.[143] For this reason, a **third category** was developed early on in case law, to define people who, although they are self-employed, have an economic situation which is closer to that of an employee. The deter-

mining factor for this group is **economic dependency**, not 'personal subordination'. These people are described as **quasi-employees**. Since 1951, special statutory rules have applied to such people who are active as **home workers**. The *Heimarbeitsgesetz* (Home Working Act) provides certain employment protection rules for them. Since 1974, quasi-employees have been defined in the *Tarifvertragsgesetz* (Collective Agreement Act). An amendment provides that collective agreements can be concluded for people who are economically dependent and, like employees, require social protection (§12a TVG). For these people, diluted employment protection rights apply.

The issue of whether **teleworkers**, the number of whom rose annually by 34% between 1994 and 1999, constitute home workers or employees depends on the chosen form of organisation. Domestic teleworking *may* do so if the person concerned is not connected on-line with the company. It will usually be considered as outsourced dependent employment. The first collective agreements for teleworking have already been concluded.[144]

2.1.8.2. Changes in the de facto situation

According to the *Statistisches Bundesamt*, of Germany's approximately 38.5 million workers, some 4 million are self-employed. This corresponds to about 11% of the total working population. The number of self-employed people in Germany has never been as high as in other European countries. Nor has it grown as fast over recent years as in some of our neighbouring countries, in particular Italy and the Netherlands.[145] Nevertheless an increase in self-employment in certain sectors was seen in the 1990s. For example in; the services sector, in particular restaurants and shops; freelancers in the mass media; and small companies in the new technologies, such as software and Internet businesses; training and consultancy firms, particularly in the public sector; and finally in the transport sector.

Empirical surveys also show significant abuses in this area. Surveys were carried out by the *Institut für Arbeitsmarkt- und Berufsforschung* (IAB – Institute for Labour Market and Voca-

---

140   The collective agreement between the ÖTV union and the START Zeitarbeit NRW GmbH of 1.7.2000 provides for equal entitlements; the collective agreement between the Ver.di union and the same company, entitled 'Leiharbeitnehmer/Helfer' (Temporary workers/assistants), of 28.12.2001 establishes lower remuneration for low-skilled workers.

141   In *RdA 2000*, p. 183 ff.; also Schwitzer, *AiB 2000*, p. 241 f.

142   From the broad discussion, see Hilger, *RdA 1989*, p. 1 ff.; Griebeling, *NZA 1998*, p. 1137 ff.; in English: Weiss, *Festschrift für Hamani*, 2000, p. 242 ff.

143   For the latest: Appel/Frantzioch, *Sozialer Schutz in der Selbstständigkeit* (Social protection for the self-employed), *AuR 1998*, p. 93 ff.; Frantzioch, Abhängige Selbstständigkeit im Arbeitsrecht (Dependent self-employment in labour law), 2000.

144   See Chapter II, section 1.8.5 of the German report.

145   Statistical data: Eichhorst/Profit/Thode, *Benchmarking Deutschland 2001*, p. 353 ff.

tional Research) at the *Bundesanstalt für Arbeit*,[146] commissioned in the mid 1990s by the conservative/liberal government which was at that time still in power. The abuse relates to employees whose official status is self-employed but who, in fact, worked as **dependent self-employed** people with no economic freedom or flexibility.

The IAB study provided, for the first time, representative figures showing that, depending on the definition, between about 200 000 and 1 million people are working in the grey area where it is unclear whether they are self-employed or employed. The social security funds are estimated to lose between EUR 3 and 3.5 billion annually because of this.

2.1.8.3. Response of the legal system to actual changes

Academic circles have suggested that personal subordination should no longer be the decisive feature for determining employee status. This proposal should be understood against the background of the changes in personnel policy and business organisation. The latest view is that employees are people who are **economically** – not necessarily personally – **dependent** on somebody else. The question to ask is about economic risk. This must be balanced by appropriate opportunities to make a profit on the market. The criteria for being an employee are that the work must be long-term and for just one client, performed by oneself rather than by one's staff, and in principle without own capital or organisation.[147]

Individual **regional labour courts** have followed this approach.[148] However, the case law of the *Bundesarbeitsgericht* tends to stick to the traditional criteria of personal dependence.

This preliminary work in academia prompted the Red/Green government to make an amendment to **social law** in line with the criteria of **economic** dependency. Under §7(4) of Social Code IV, the obligation to contribute to health, pension and unemployment insurance will apply to anyone who is economically dependent on another person. Personal subordination will no longer be necessary.[149]

The formal legal-technical details of this provision are (were) relatively complex. The legislator is working with assumed situations leading to a reversal of the burden of proof. The

amendment was introduced on 1.1.1999, shortly after the change of government, revamped following intense discussion at the end of 1999 and amended with retrospective effect by the *Gesetz zur Förderung der Selbstständigkeit* (Self-employment Promotion Act) of 20 December 1999.[150] The general objectives of the new legislation are (were), on the one hand, to improve the recording of abuses and, on the other hand, to ensure that people who want and are able to become self-employed – some people are talking about a new 'culture of self-employment' – can do so without being hindered by too much red tape. The stricter presumption rules can be avoided by an inquiry procedure, in accordance with §7a of Social Code IV, by the responsible social security board (the *Bundesversicherungsanstalt für Angestellte* – Federal Insurance Board for Employees). The general rules then apply (§7(1) of Social Code IV). This is also attractive to those concerned because, in this case (inquiry procedure), any insurance obligation on the employee may be established **ad hoc**, i.e. not, as in the normal case, with retrospective effect (§7(6) of Social Code IV). Moreover, the presumption provision for economic dependency under §7(4) of Social Code IV, etc. applies only if the work is performed for a client in the **long term**. Self-employed people should not count as employees just because, in the initial phase – in practice three years – they work for just one client.[151]

2.1.8.4. Prospects: Another turnaround?

Together with the amendment relating to small-scale part-time workers ('EUR 352 workers'), this amendment was and still is one of the most controversial labour law reforms introduced by the SPD/Green coalition. However, we are not yet certain of its impact in practice and whether it had, or has, any perceptible consequences. The issue of whether the presumption provision in social law, with its criterion of economic rather than personal dependency, will have an impact on the **labour law definition** of an employee, is also still open for debate.

In December 2002, the Red/Green government scrapped the presumption provisions without prior discussion, claiming that they were too bureaucratic and complicated. This happened in the context of negotiations about the Hartz plan with the conservative opposition.

The inquiry procedure in §7a of Social Code IV has been retained, and preferential treatment is given to those people

146 Dietrich, BMA volume 262, *Empirische Befunde zur Scheinselbstständigkeit* (Empirical findings on apparent self-employment), 1996; Wank, *Empirische Befunde zur Scheinselbstständigkeit*, legal part, 1997.

147 Wank, *Arbeitnehmer und Selbstständige* (Employees and the self-employed), 1988, p. 128 f.; idem, *DB 1992*, p. 90, 91.

148 E.g. LAG Köln 30.6.1995, *AuR 1996*, 413.

149 Bieback, *SGb 2000*, p. 189 ff.; Wank, *AuR 2001*, p. 291 ff. and 327 ff.

150 On the basis of the report from the Dieterich commission. Dieterich is the former President of the Federal Labour Court; see documentation in *RdA 1999*, p. 5 ff.

151 Wank, *AuR 2001*, p. 291 ff. and 327 ff. Bieback, *SGb 2000*, p. 189 ff.; Reiserer/Freckmann, *NJW 2003*, p. 180 ff.

who cooperate with the social security board responsible for the assessment (the *Bundesversicherungsanstalt für Angestellte*). It remains to be seen whether this incentive is enough to combat abuses in the grey area between self-employment and dependent employment.[152]

2.1.8.5. Union initiatives

Not only academic and legislative circles but also the **unions** have spoken out about new forms of employment in the grey area between dependent employment and self-employment. However, the practical results of the unions' endeavours in this area have not been very successful so far. (Public) television and broadcasting companies have long had collective agreements for freelance staff, based on the reform of the *Tarifvertragsgesetz* of 1974, in accordance with §12a of the TVG.[153] Moreover, during the reporting period, company collective agreements to protect and structure teleworking were occasionally concluded, regulating the contractual terms and conditions of the teleworkers themselves, as well as union information rights and the relations between the teleworker and the company. These tended to reflect the spirit of the framework agreement on teleworking that resulted from the social dialogue of July 2002.[154]

2.1.9. Greater organisational flexibility through collective systems

Over the reporting period, industry's desire for greater flexibility has been met above all by **flexible working time systems** at the level of collective agreements, rather than at statutory level. These new, open, flexible forms comprise variable working time structures, in terms of duration, location and distribution. Their common feature is to fix a number of regular hours which on average have to be worked over a particular period.[155] The main forms in collective agreements are working time accounts and working time corridors.

In principle, **working time accounts** function by letting the collective agreement provide the option of different arrangements by company agreement. For example, the collectively

agreed weekly working time for employees can be extended. The difference is then credited to individuals' personal working time accounts. The time credit must then be taken within a particular time frame. Information about the spread of working time account systems varies. They are more common in large than in small companies.[156] However, every study shows a rapid development of account systems over the last decade.

Working time corridor and fluctuation range models allow deviations from the regular working time within certain limits. These must then be compensated for within specific deadlines: generally 6 or 12 months in the metalworking and electronics industries, or 24 months in exceptional cases.[157] In 1999, almost a third of companies in the metalworking industry had working time corridor models, covering around 16% of the industry's employees, mainly in production.[158]

These examples show that working time policy in Germany has moved on significantly over the last decade. Companies and workers are given considerable flexibility within a framework established (roughly) by the collective bargaining and corporate parties. Recently, and going even further along this road, the issue of working time on trust, which represents a major move towards a results-based approach, has been discussed, against the backdrop of the first practical experiences of this system, in which performance and pay are dependent on tasks being completed by a particular deadline.[159]

2.2. Adaptability of businesses

2.2.1. Adaptability of employees among companies: a necessary interaction

The adaptability of employees and that of companies can be differentiated from each other analytically. But in practice they each depend on the other and affect each other directly. This should be borne in mind when modernisation steps taken by companies are discussed below. These steps are characterised

---

152   For the latest: Rolfs, *NZA 2003*, p. 65 ff.; critical: Mayer, Udo, *AiB 2003*, p. 69 ff.

153   Kempen/Zachert, *TVG*, 3rd edition, 1997, §12a, note 5 ff.

154   E.g. Tarifvertrag über Telearbeit bei der Deutschen Telekom AG, der T-Mobil (Collective agreement on teleworking at Deutsche Telekom AG, T-Mobil), in *RdA 1999*, p. 208 ff.; latest overview on teleworking: Ridder/Jensen in: Martin/Nienhüser, ed. *Neue Formen der Beschäftigung* (New forms of employment), p. 207 ff., on the European framework agreement on teleworking: Prinz, *NZA 2002*, p. 1268 f.; the framework agreement of the European social partners is printed in *RdA 2003*, p. 55 f.

155   Promberger et al., *Chancen, Risiken und Grenzen zeitlicher Flexibilität* (The opportunities, risks and limits of time flexibility), 2001, p. 55.

156   Latest information in Munz/Bauer/Groß, *WSI Mitt. 2002*, p. 334, 335 with references: in companies with 20 employees or more, 78%; in all companies around 35%.

157   Ohl et al., *Handbuch Manteltarifverträge* (Handbook of umbrella collective agreements), 2000, p. 161 ff.

158   Herrmann et al, *Forcierte Arbeitszeitflexibilisierung* (Forced working time flexiblisation), 1999, p. 144 ff.

159   Critical, from a legal position: Trittin, *NZA 2001*, p. 1003 ff., also Zachert, *AuR 2002*, p. 41, 46; from the social science debate: Germanis, *WSI Mitt. 2002*, p. 347 ff.

not by the individual and collective structuring of work, in particular with regard to working time, but rather by the aspects of work organisation and management strategies. The respective initiatives of the legislator and the social partners are just parts of the complex and, in some respects, contradictory processes of change and are, moreover, of varying significance.

2.2.2. Working conditions and industrial safety

Significant changes were made to industrial safety law during the reporting period. Initiatives at European level played a decisive role. Industrial safety is one of the core elements of EU law, with its central legal bases in points (a) and (b) of Article 137, paragraph 1, of the EC Treaty (ex Article 118a). The terms 'working environment' and 'working conditions' used in the EC Treaty are characterised above all by the Scandinavian model of a holistic, preventive and dynamic understanding of industrial safety.[160] The Framework Directive 89/391/EEC 'to encourage improvements in the safety and health of workers at work', based on Article 118a (now Article 137) of the EC Treaty was implemented by the conservative/liberal government in the *Arbeitsschutzgesetz* (ArbSchG – Industrial Safety Act) of 7 August 1996.[161] This not only introduced for the first time a uniform general industrial safety law in Germany, but also reflected the fundamental ideas behind and models of modern industrial safety, as expressed in European law.

For example, the prevention philosophy is expressed explicitly in §4 of the ArbSchG, where the general principles for planning, structuring and organising industrial safety are set out. As a basis for this, §5 of the ArbSchG obliges employers to carry out a risk assessment. The results of this assessment and the resulting conclusions are to be recorded: §6 of the ArbSchG. The exemption in §6(1) point 3 of the ArbSchG, which releases employers with ten or fewer employees from this recording obligation, was ruled to be contradictory to Directive 89/391/EEC by the European Court of Justice.[162] §17 of the ArbSchG sets additional accents for German law. Under §17(1), employees must be free to make suggestions to their employer at any time about any aspect of health and safety. If the employer does not respond to these initiatives or complaints, the employees concerned can, according to §17(2) of the ArbSchG, turn to the competent authorities.[163]

The most controversial question was whether the works council has co-determination rights in the implementation of the *Arbeitsschutzgesetz*, in particular the risk assessment in §5 of the ArbSchG. This is answered in the affirmative in the majority of the case law and in academic papers.[164]

2.2.3. Health protection/sick pay

The *Entgeltfortzahlungsgesetz* (EFZG – Sick Pay Act) of 26 May 1994, introduced by the conservative/liberal government, pursued two main goals. Firstly, it consolidated the rules on sick pay and, for the first time, standardised them for workers and employees.[165] Secondly, it cut the amount of sick pay, the six-week duration of which remained unchanged, to 80% of normal wages, and allowed one day's leave to be given up in exchange for full pay. The aim here was to reduce the level of absenteeism.

However, this change did not extend to sick pay laid down by collective agreement, which provided for full pay (100%) for around 80% of employees. Numerous legal disputes therefore arose concerning the issue of whether the collective agreements in question merely repeated the content of the legislation for form's sake, or whether they constituted an independent (more favourable) basis for claims. Above all, the new legislation incurred protests and resistance from employees and trade unions, and intensified the academic debate about sustainable, efficient health protection in companies. It is broadly acknowledged that this cannot be achieved (primarily) by enforcing penalties. Rather, measures to improve job satisfaction are called for, such as giving employees scope to structure their activities and occupational development opportunities. Moreover, physical and mental stress should be reduced or removed as far as possible.[166]

Despite the criticism, the conservative/liberal government stuck to its guns. However, the relevant provisions were repealed by the Red/Green coalition in its *Gesetz zu Korrekturen der Sozialversicherung*, with effect from 1 January 1999. The rate of absenteeism has not risen since then. Since 1998, the annual average has been around 4%. Studies show that the sickness rate is influenced fundamentally by the situation on the labour market.[167]

---

160 E.g. Kittner/Pieper, *ArbSchR*, 2nd edition 2002, introduction, note 9 ff., 12 ff. with references.

161 On the many individual directives for different areas and technical industry safety, see Wank in Hanau/Steinmeyer/Wank, *Handbuch des europäischen Arbeits- und Sozialrechts*, §18, note 430 ff., 432 ff.; Schaub, *Arbeitsrechts-Handbuch*, §152, note 10 ff.

162 European Court of Justice 7.02.2002, *EuZW 2002*, p. 372 ff.

163 On the issue of the right to bring a complaint to third parties in German labour law, see: Le Friant, *Die straf- und verwaltungsrechtliche Verantwortung des Arbeitgebers* (Employers' criminal and administrative liability), 1987, p. 62 ff.

164 E.g. Fitting/Kaiser/Heither/Engels/Schmidt, *BetrVG*, §87, note 292 ff.; Klebe in Däubler/Kittner/Klebe, *BetrVG*, §87, note 188a with references.

165 Exception: Pay-as-you-go systems for small businesses with 'workers' pursuant to the Lohnfortzahlungsgesetz remain.

166 From the broad debate, e.g. Oppolzer, *Die Angestellten-Versicherung* (Employee insurance), 1999, p. 226 ff.; Oppolzer/Zachert, *BB 1993*, p. 1353 ff. with references.

167 E.g. Zoike, *Soziale Sicherheit 2000*, p. 49 ff.; Jaufmann, *Die Mitbestimmung 2001*, p. 32 ff. with country comparisons.

2.2.4. Group work

During the reporting period, changes were also made to **group work**, which, despite all its ambivalence,[168] can be a way of giving individuals more freedom, variety and training opportunities. As part of the reform of works constitutions in July 2001, the works council was granted a co-determination right for semi-autonomous group work (§87(1) No 13 of the BetrVG). The aim was to reduce the risk of internal pressures within the group leading to the exploitation of its members and the exclusion of less effective workers.[169] Under §28a of the BetrVG, the works council can, under certain circumstances, delegate tasks to working groups. It remains to be seen whether and how these changes will work out in practice. However, this is the first time that the German legislator has created the opportunity to link forms of more autonomous working with the demand for flexible production and organisational methods.

2.2.5. Holistic approaches

At collective agreement level, reference should be made to a company collective agreement concluded in August 2001 between Volkswagen AG and IG Metall, in which the company undertook to create 5 000 jobs. This agreement was the cause of great controversy beforehand. It still gives rise to differing assessments because, with regard to wages and working time, it deviates from the standards of VW's own collective agreement in some areas. However, notwithstanding the assessments of some of its parts, this agreement is noteworthy because it is based on a holistic approach. Firstly it creates a project collective agreement concerned with; working time, including an individual flexi-time account, pay; general terms and conditions, including work in a project team and personal and performance measurement, i.e. basic pay plus profit-sharing. Next a training collective agreement sets out the training principles, i.e. three hours of in-service training. Finally, a co-determination collective agreement regulates co-determination, including the size and parity composition of the supervisory board, and qualified majorities on this board, beyond the standard level.[170]

This is similar to the method collective agreements concluded in France at the end of the 1980s at national and sectoral level, which were also based on a comprehensive modernising approach. However, these were not a lasting success in practice.[171]

2.2.6. Bridges and change-overs

The importance of labour law standards serving to guarantee or facilitate change-overs between different life stages has already been addressed several times. These include instruments and approaches such as job rotation, transfer social plans, age-related part-time working[172] and part-time working as a bridge between paid and non-paid employment,[173] as well as parental time/leave.[174]

This approach is taken into account in the section on transfers of undertakings in §613a of the Civil Code. The aim is to safeguard the rights of employees at times of changes to company structures. Based on Directive 77/187/EEC, it gave rise to an intensive debate during the reporting period. This was spurred on by rulings of the European Court of Justice and amendments to the Directive itself.

The question of what exactly constitutes a transfer of an undertaking has led to different emphases and assessments in the case law of the European Court of Justice[175] and the *Bundesarbeitsgericht.*[176] The positions have now converged, and it can be stated that even a transfer of services can constitute the transfer of an undertaking, if the new owner performs the same or a similar activity, and the transferred unit therefore retains its economic identity. This corresponds fundamentally to the wording of the amending Directive 98/50/EC, which, otherwise, did not bring about any real changes to German law.[177]

168　Kleinschmidt/Pekruhl, *Kooperative Arbeitsstrukturen und Gruppenarbeit in Deutschland* (Cooperative working structures and group work in Germany) 1994; European comparison: Benders/Huijgen/Pekruhl, *WSI Mitt. 2000,* p. 365 ff.

169　E.g. Klebe in Däubler/Kittner/Klebe, *BetrVG,* §87, note 301 ff.

170　Assessments by Schwitzer, *AuR 2001,* p. 441 ff.; Bispinck/WSI-Tarifarchiv, *WSI-Mitt. 2002,* p. 67, 71 ff.; Hildebrandt, *GMH 2002,* p. 335 ff.

171　Le Friant in Zachert, ed. *Die Wirkung des Tarifvertrages in der Krise* (The impact of collective agreements in times of crisis), 1991, p. 103, 151 f.

172　See Chapter II, section 1.2 of the German report.

173　See Chapter II, section 2.1.3 of the German report.

174　See Chapter II, section 3.3 of the German report.

175　Especially ECJ 14.4.1994, *European Court reports 1992,* 5755-Christel Schmidt; ECJ 11.3.1997, *European Court reports 1997,* 1259-Ayse Süzen.

176　A more recent overview of the discussion can be found in Wank in the *Handbuch des europäischen Arbeits- und Sozialrechts,* Hanau/Steinmeyer/Wank, §18, note 36 ff.; from a comparative perspective: Davis/Laulom/Dal-Ré/Lo Faro in: *Labour law in the Courts,* ed. Sciarra, p. 131ff.; Ojeda Avilés/Rodrígues Ramos/Gorelli Hernández, in: *La transmisión de empresas en Europa* (The transfer of companies in Europe), Univ. di Bari/Socrates 1999, p. 265 ff.

177　Wank, *Handbuch des europäischen Arbeits- und Sozialrechts,* Hanau/Steinmeyer/Wank, §18, note 153 ff.; also Zachert/Kocher, *Euro-AS 1999,* p. 213 ff.

The implementation of the latest update to the Transfer of Undertakings Directive (Directive 2001/23/EC) has been criticised, however, mainly with regard to the reinforcement of the information obligation towards employees affected by a transfer.[178] According to the new §613a of the Civil Code, paragraphs 5 and 6, the old employer and the new owner must, before the transfer, inform the employees affected in writing of the date or planned date of the transfer, the reason for it, the legal, economic and social impact on employees and the measures taken to protect them. The employees are entitled to lodge an objection in writing within one month of receiving this information.

3. Promoting equal opportunities

3.1. The equality principle as an all-encompassing legal principle

The following section looks at various issues whose common denominator is the principle of equality. This fundamental legal principle is reflected not only in Article 3 of the German Constitution, but also in European Community law.[179] It is expressed in Articles 3(2), 14 and 141 of the EC Treaty and in the Preamble and Articles 20-26 of the European Charter of Fundamental Rights of 7 December 2000.

3.2. Equality between men and women

With regard to the relationship between men and women, the equality principle has now been clearly defined and permanently influenced labour law in Germany and other Member States,[180] in various directives based on Article 141 (ex-Article 119) of the EC Treaty, in particular Directives 75/117/EEC, 76/207/EEC (now: 2002/73/EC)[181] and the case law of the European Court of Justice. The subjects covered range from equal pay, a ban on indirect discrimination (part-time workers), discriminatory hiring practices and other personnel decisions, to issues of promoting women and quotas. In the case of **Tanja Kreil**, the European Court of Justice even ruled that a constitutional rule, in this case the ban on women bearing arms in Article 12a of the German Constitution, violated the principle of equal treatment and free choice of occupation under European law.[182] Overall, the case law of the European Court of Justice and the *Bundesarbeitsgericht*, which transposed the European standards very carefully into national law during the reporting period, is so comprehensive and multifaceted that there is insufficient room to go into all the details in this country report. However, certain specific studies are available.[183]

Over the last decade, the impact of European law on national law is most clearly illustrated by the ban on gender-specific discrimination in §611a of the Civil Code. This provision, which represents the ban on discrimination between men and women in simple (i.e. not constitutional) law, had to be amended several times after the European Court of Justice found that certain aspects of the national regulations were illegal under European law.[184] In the second *Gleichberechtigungsgesetz* (Equal Treatment Act) of 14.6.1994, which came into force on 1 September 1994, the legislator took a comprehensive approach. In cases of sexual harassment, those affected now have a right of complaint and the right to refuse to work. In the public sector, women's promotion plans must be drawn up and womens' representatives appointed. In line with the position of the European Court of Justice, victims are entitled to reasonable compensation of no more than three months' salary in the case of sex discrimination for which the employer is responsible. This reform also had to be amended following the guidance of the European Court of Justice, which had been referred to once again.[185] Like the previous law, the currently applicable version of §611a of the Civil Code, the *Gesetz zur Änderung des Bürgerlichen Gesetzbuchs und des Arbeitsgerichtsgesetzes* (Civil Code and Labour Court Act Amendment Act) of 29 June 1998, does not grant a right of employment, but it does dispense with the need for fault to be proved as a prerequisite for a

---

178 The latest from the broad debate, critical: Franzen, *RdA 2002*, p. 258 ff. and Willemsen/Lembke, *NJW 2002*, p. 1159 ff.; in favour: Wulff, *AiB 2002*, p. 594 ff.

179 Fundamentally ECJ 19.10.1977, ECJ 1977, 1753.

180 For the latest from France: Le Friant, *AuR 2003*, p. 51 ff.

181 This amendment does not lead to any significant amendments to German law: Hadeler, *NZA 2003*, p. 77 ff.; Rust, *NZA 2003*, p. 72 ff.

182 ECJ 11.1.2000, *NZA 2000*, 137-Tanja Kreil.

183 For a more recent and comprehensive overview, e.g. Wank in Hanau/Steinmeyer/Wank, *Handbuch des europäischen Arbeits- und Sozialrechts*, §16, note 22 ff., 194 ff., 209 ff.; Kilpatrick in Sciarra, *Labour law in the Courts*, 2001, p. 31ff.; Kretz, *Jahrbuch des Arbeitsrechts* (Labour law Yearbook), 2001, p. 29 ff.

184 ECJ 10.4.1984, *European Court reports 1984*, 1891-Colsen/Kaman.

185 ECJ 22.4.1997, *European Court reports 1997*, 2195-Draempael.

claim for compensation against an employer. The law now provides for unlimited damages to be paid to the best-qualified candidate if sexual discrimination can be proved in the recruitment to a position. If the candidate in question would not have been considered even if the selection procedure had not been discriminatory, the amount of damages is limited to three months' salary.

A source of controversy regarding the equality principle during the reporting period was whether the current **ban on night work for female workers** (in §19 of the *Arbeitszeitordnung* (AZO – Working Time Ordinance)) – which did not apply to female *employees* – should be lifted, as it may keep women out of certain jobs. The *Arbeitszeitordnung* dated from 1938 and continued to apply as federal law from 1949 onwards. At almost the same time, the European Court of Justice[186] and the *Bundesverfassungsgericht*[187] ruled that this rule violated the ban on discrimination at European and national level respectively. The *Bundesverfassungsgericht* declared §19 of the AZO unconstitutional and laid down principles for the legislator to follow in the amendment of the law concerning night work. The *Arbeitszeitgesetz* (ArbZG – Working Time Act) of 6.6.1994 laid down certain minimum standards for both sexes, such as medical examinations, the change from night shifts to day working under certain conditions, etc. (§6 of the ArbZG).

3.3. Equal opportunities in paid work and family life

The parts of labour law that aim to better reconcile paid work and family life have a wider impact than the ban on sexual discrimination. This is particularly the case following the birth of a child. New focuses were set out in particular in the *Elternzeitgesetz* (Parental Leave Act) of 23 October 2000, which came into force on 1 January 2001 This Act continues with the main thrust of the *Bundeserziehungsgeldgesetz* (Child Allowance Act) in the version of 1994.

The main reform is that parental leave can now be taken for a maximum of three years, not just *pro rata* but by both parents together. One year of the leave can be carried over until the end of the child's eighth year if the employer agrees.

Part-time work of up to 30 hours per week (previously 19) is also possible. Under certain conditions – similar to those in the *Teilzeit- und Befristungsgesetz*[188] – there may be an entitlement to change a full-time job into a part-time one. Child allowance is paid for a total of two years, in the first year EUR 460, in the second year EUR 307.[189]

The aim of these provisions is to help to ensure that parental leave is not predominantly taken by women, as has been the case so far. These provisions are modelled on the system in the Scandinavian countries, in particular Sweden.[190] Whether or not this succeeds will depend not least on the creation of an altogether **more child-friendly infrastructure** in Germany. This includes far more kindergarten places, whole-day schools and tax measures that do not put working married women (families) at a disadvantage, etc. The discussion is already under way,[191] although the practical results are still limited by the lack of public funding.

Some collective agreements for large companies (especially in the chemical and metalworking sectors) include further-reaching leave schemes, combined with training measures.[192]

3.4. Equality between manual and non-manual workers

The equality principle played an important role not only in the relationship between the sexes but also with regard to unfair discrimination between workers and employees. Decisive moves came from the courts on 30 May 1990, the *Bundesverfassungsgericht* ruled that provisions favouring 'employees' above 'workers' were, in most cases, anti-constitutional, as it was hard to find any difference in the work of these two groups. The legislator was therefore called upon to tackle the issue of longer periods of notice for employees than for workers in §622 of the Civil Code by 30 June 1993, because this would now constitute an infringement of the ban on discrimination.[193] Changes have now taken place. Since the introduction of the *Kündigungsfristengesetz* (Period of Notice Act) of 7 October 1993, the statutory basic period of notice for all workers and employees is four weeks as from the 15ᵗʰ of the month and rises gradually to seven months, depending on length of service.

186   ECJ 25.7.1991, *European Court reports 1991*, I-4047-Stoeckl.
187   Federal Constitutional Court 28.1.1992, *BVerfGE 85*, 191.
188   See Chapter II, section 2.1.4 of the German report.
189   This provision goes far beyond those in the Parental Leave Directive 96/34/EC, a result of the social dialogue.
190   Only just over 1% have been men so far: Government report BT-Drucks.10/6430, 11/8517 and 12/7778.
191   A new example: Schwerpunktheft, *WSI Mitt. 3/2002*, Konturen einer modernen Familienpolitik (Outlines of a modern family policy) with contributions by various writers.
192   Examples in Kempen/Zachert, *TVG*, §1, note 217 ff.
193   Federal Constitutional Court 30.5.1990, AP No 28 on §622 of the Civil Code.

Accordingly, the legislator amended the 1969 *Lohnfortzahlungsgesetz* (Sick Pay Act), which applied only to workers, whilst employees came under the old rules in §616 of the Civil Code, with some minor divergences. Under §1(2) of the *Entgeltfortzahlungsgesetz* of 26 May 1994[194] sick pay is now paid for six weeks for all workers and employees.

The most recent alignment of the status of these two groups in a single employment (protection) act took place via the reform of the *Betriebsverfassungsgesetz* of 27 July 2001.[195] According to the new version of §5 of the BetrVG, 'employees' within the meaning of the Act include both workers and employees, including apprentices, regardless of whether they work in the company itself, in the field service or as teleworkers.

Collective agreements are continuing and reinforcing the trend towards treating workers and employees equally. In certain sectors (e.g. chemicals, food and luxury goods, restaurants), joint remuneration agreements for both groups have already existed for some time. In the negotiations in the metalworking industry in the spring of 2002, the parties agreed to negotiate a uniform remuneration package to be worked out by 2003 by the individual regions.[196] A decisive contribution to evening out any remaining inequalities between workers and employees in German labour law will be made following the accession of the *Deutsche Angestelltengewerkschaft* (DAG), which predominantly represented white-collar employees,[197] to the service trade union *ver.di* in the spring of 2001, under the umbrella of the German Trade Union Confederation (DGB).

3.5. Equality of opportunity for disabled people

Over the last decade, the law relating to disabled people, highlighted in a European context by various initiatives,[198] has also been developed at national level.

First of all, an Article 3(2)(3) was added to the German Constitution on 27 October 1994 following German reunification, containing an explicit ban on discrimination against disabled people. The Red/Green government then overhauled

the 1974 *Schwerbehindertengesetz* (Severely Disabled Persons Act) with its *Gesetz zur Bekämpfung der Arbeitslosigkeit Schwerbehinderter* (Combating Unemployment among Disabled People Act) of 29 September 2000. Under this Act, companies in Germany employing 16 or more people were obliged to fill at least 6% of their posts with disabled people. If this obligation is not met, a monthly compensatory payment must be made. The quota of disabled people was then reduced from 6% to 5% and the maximum size of the exempted small businesses was increased to 20 employees. On the other hand, the level of the compensatory payment was increased substantially for companies that significantly failed to meet their legal obligation to employ disabled people. There are also new institutional measures, in particular in the interplay between corporate interest representatives and the employment office. Examples of these are integration agreements for the severely disabled, prevention obligations, integration projects, etc. A year or so later, on 1 July 2001, the revised *Schwerbehindertengesetz* was included in **Social Code IX.** This means that the labour law aspect and the rehabilitation entitlement under social law are now combined in a single legal code. The main change associated with this reform is an explicit ban on discrimination against severely disabled people, combined with an entitlement to compensation (§81(2) of Social Code IX).

The Federal Government is pleased with the results of these reforms and estimates that the unemployment rate for the severely disabled was cut by around 24% (around 45 000 out of around 190 000) between October 1999 and October 2002 (a 25% cut was originally sought).[199]

Again, about a year later, on 1 July 2002, the *Gesetz zur Gleichstellung behinderter Menschen* (Equality for Disabled People Act) came into force in the form of a (relatively complex) article law. This regulates a wide range of aspects, such as eliminating obstacles, the interests of disabled women (gender mainstreaming), agreed objectives between companies and associations, an initial association right of action, etc.[200] Fundamentally, all these changes to the law reflect a changing attitude towards (severely) disabled people: from care and welfare provision provided by the state to active participation and stakeholding in all aspects of life in society.[201]

---

194 More under Chapter II, section 2.2.3 of the German report.

195 See Chapter III, section 3.1 of the German report.

196 Peters/Schild, *GMH 2002*, p. 542, 549 f.

197 See Chapter I, section 1.2.2 of the German report.

198 Council Decision 1999/C 186/02 of 17.6.1999, Wank in Hanau/Steinmeyer/Wank, *Handbuch des europäischen Arbeits- und Sozialrechts*, §18, note 1078 ff.; also Article 1 of Directive 2000/78/EC of 27.11.2000.

199 Claevenger, *Bundesarbeitsblatt 12/2002*, p. 5 f.

200 Stähler, *NZA 2002*, p. 777 ff.

201 Stähler, *NZA 2001*, p. 777, 781 with reference to the conformity of these regulations with Directive 2000/78/EC.

3.6.   General equal treatment

Although, initially, European-level equality policy focused on gender equality, it has been interpreted more broadly since the mid 1990s to include equality of opportunity in all areas of policy.[202] This change is expressed in several amendments to European law. In addition to the amendment of primary legislation in Articles 3(2) and 13 of the EC Treaty (Treaty of Amsterdam) and Articles 20-26 of the Charter of Fundamental Rights, it is included in Directives **2000/43/EC** of 29 June 2000 implementing the principle of equal treatment between persons irrespective of racial or ethnic origin and in **2000/78/EC** of 27 November 2000 establishing a general framework for equal treatment in employment and occupation.[203] Although these Directives do not have to be transposed into national law until (at the latest) 19 July 2003 (2000/43/EC) and 2 December 2003 (2000/78/EC) – with the option of an extension – they have already led to an intensive debate on the consequences for German labour law. Concerns are being expressed about the impact of the ban on age discrimination, for example with regard to existing standards for making it easier to conclude fixed-term contracts for older workers (from the age of 58: §14(3) of the TzBfG – (Part-time Work and Fixed-term Employment Act)) and under the Hartz plan (from the age of 52).[204]

An intense and heated discussion, even touching on the principle of private autonomy,[205] has been caused by the **draft anti-discrimination act** of 13 December 2000,[206] intended to transpose Directives 2000/43/EC and 2000/78/EC. Following vigorous protests from business, the draft legislation was dropped and was replaced by the *Vereinbarung zur Förderung von Frauen und Männern in der Privatwirtschaft* (Agreement on the promotion of women and men in the private sector).[207] It remains to be seen how this area will develop in the future.[208]

---

202   See Chapter II, section 3.1 of the German report.; also Kretz, *Jahrbuch des Arbeitsrechts* (Labour law Yearbook), 2000, p. 29 ff.

203   Coen, *AuR 2000*, p. 11 f.; von Roetteken, *Der PersR 2002*, p. 12 ff.; Bauer, *NJW 2001*, p. 2672 ff.; Schiek, *AuR 2003*, p. 44 ff.

204   On the discussion: Kerwer, *NZA 2002*, p. 1316 ff.; Kohte, *BB 2002*, p. 11; Leuchten, *NZA 2002*, p. 1254 ff.; Schmidt, Marlene/Senne, *RdA 2002*, p. 80 ff.; Leber, Klaus, *AuR 2002*, p. 401 ff.; Wiedemann/Thüsing, *NZA 2002*, p. 1234 ff.

205   Critical e.g. Picker, *JZ 2002*, p. 880 ff. and Säcker, *ZRP 2002*, p. 286 ff.; in favour: Baer, *ZRP 2002*, p. 290 ff.

206   Extracts: *DB 2002*, p. 470 ff.; also Laskowski, *ZRP 2001*, p. 504 ff.; Braun, Stefan, *ZTR 2001*, p. 200 ff.

207   Laskowski, *ZRP 2001*, p. 504 ff.

208   Further reaching and in perspective: Kocher, *RdA 2002*, p. 167 ff.; Pfarr, *Ein Gesetz zur Gleichstellung der Geschlechter in der Privatwirtschaft* (A gender equality law in the private sector), 2001.

Chapter III:
Amendments to the labour law levels, assessment and outlook

1. Objective and focuses

The following section systematically presents once again the main amendments to the labour law levels (some of which have already been discussed above). They include the codification of extracts of individual labour law (section 2), reforms to corporate co-determination at national and European levels (section 3), selected issues from the broad debate on the general collective agreement (section 4) and the status of the discussion on the law governing industrial disputes (section 5). Once again, a link is made to the introductory Chapter I.

2. Partial codification of the employment relationship

2.1. *Nachweisgesetz (Employment Conditions Information Act)*

European Directive 91/533/EEC was transposed into German law by way of the *Nachweisgesetz* (NachwG – Employment Conditions Information Act) of 20 July 1995. The cornerstone of this Act is the employer's obligation to provide a written, signed document outlining the main terms and conditions of employment, such as the place of work, working time, remuneration, leave entitlement, etc. This document must be provided no later than one month after the agreed start date of the employment relationship. The main practical problem is how to penalise those employees who do not provide such a document or who provide one whose content is insufficient.[209] German case law in this area is reticent and sets out the distribution of the burden of proof – an issue that the European Court of Justice has left open[210] – not in terms of a reversal of the burden of proof, but rather in the sense of an alleviation there-

of.[211] The *Bundesarbeitsgericht* recently affirmed the obligation on employers to pay compensation, under certain conditions, in the event of a violation of the NachwG.[212]

2.2. Reform of the law of obligations in the Civil Code

Consumer protection legislation and the *Gesetz zur Regelung des Rechts der Allgemeinen Geschäftsbedingungen* (AGBG – General Contract Terms and Conditions Regulation Act) have been incorporated in the Civil Code. This has been done against the backdrop of the implementation of a number of European directives as part of the reform of the Civil Code in the *Schuldrechtsmodernisierungsgesetz* (Law of Obligations Modernisation Act) of 26 November 2001 – in force since 1 January 2001. The exception in the AGBG relating to employment contracts based on pre-printed forms was also deleted. Pursuant to §310(4) of the Civil Code, the law on general contract terms and conditions now also applies to individual contracts, whereby 'the applicable features of labour law should also be considered'. This has led to an intensive discussion about what this means in individual cases(e.g. preclusive periods, contractual penalties, revocation provisos) and about other problems of applying the new regulations.[213] It can be assumed that the courts, which in the past reviewed unfair provisions in model (form-based) contracts of employment, will increasingly pursue their monitoring role in the future.[214]

2.3. Revision of the Industrial Code

A final – somewhat surprising – reform introduced by the Red/Green government during the last legislative period was the *Drittes Gesetz zur Änderung der Gewerbeordnung und sonstiger gewerberechtlicher Vorschriften* (Third Act to Amend

---

209 Some 84% of all employment contracts are in writing, but in many cases do not meet the requirements of the NachwG: Walter, Thorsten, Bericht Europarechtliches Symposium, *AuR 2001*, p. 215, 216.

210 ECJ 2.8.2001, Lange, AP No 4 on §2 of the NachwG = *AuR 2000*, p. 108 with note by Buschmann.

211 LAG Köln 31.7.1998, *NZA 1999*, 545.

212 BAG 17.4.2002, *AuR 2002*, p. 467 with note by Rehwald.

213 Some examples from the broad debate: Däubler, *NZA 2001*, p. 1329 ff.; Reim, *DB 2002*, p. 2434 ff.; Richardi, *NZA 2002*, p. 1057 ff.; Hromadka, *NJW 2002*, p. 2523 ff.; Thüsing, *NZA 2002*, p. 591 ff. and *BB 2002*, p. 2666 ff.; Henssler, *RdA 2002*, p. 129 ff.

214 Reinecke, *DB 2002*, p. 583, 587.

the Industrial Code and other Industrial Law Provisions) of 24 August 2002. The Act came into force on 1 January 2003. The provisions do not really constitute a new approach to individual labour law. Instead they undertake some precisions regarding: standards on the general framework of contractual freedom; the definition of the employer's authority to give directions; the termination, payment and calculation of remuneration; as well as references and bans on working for competitors after the termination of the contract.[215]

3. Corporate co-determination and participation at national and European levels

3.1. Reform of corporate co-determination

One of the focuses of the Red/Green government's labour law reforms during the first legislative period (September 1998 – September 2002) was to modernise corporate co-determination. The legal basis for this is the 1972 *Betriebsverfassungsgesetz*. The new *Betriebsverfassungs-Reformgesetz* entered into force on 28 July 2001. Its aim was to better deal with shortcomings resulting from the sometimes far-reaching changes to company structures, organisation and management techniques which occurred in the 1980s and 1990s. A number of changes and additions to the existing legal situation were made to accomplish this aim.[216]

The structures of corporate co-determination itself remain. Those are dual representation of unions and works councils in the company; the dialogue and cooperation philosophy; and institutional dispute settlement 'around the table' using

a conciliation board in the largely extended co-determination rights for personnel and social issues.

The main changes relate to organisational aspects such as facilitating the voting procedure in small companies, integrating workers with 'non-standard employment relationships', the continuity of the works council's work in the case of restructuring,[217] and calling in external experts, etc. Material co-determination rights were extended in only a few areas, e.g. group working and further training.

Despite all the criticism made in advance, particularly from employers, we can therefore speak of a reform that maintained the existing system.[218]

3.2. The *Europäische Betriebsrätegesetz* (European Works Council Act)

The European Works Council Act (the EBRG) was brought in by the conservative/liberal government on 28 October 1996 as a result of the implementation of Directive 94/45/EC of 22 September 1994.[219] There are now more than 100 European works councils in Germany in transnational companies.[220] This Act will acquire an importance in the future which should not be underestimated.[221] This will be the case even though the powers of European works councils in this Act are limited to informing and advising[222] and are thus weaker than the traditional co-determination powers in Germany.[223] The practice of an internationally organised and institutionalised exchange of experiences can contribute to a greater European character of industrial relations in the future. This represents a learning process with regard to the challenges brought by globalisation and the internationalisation of markets for the representatives in the various Member States with their different traditions.[224]

215   Düwell, *ZTR 2002*, p. 461 ff.; Perreng, *AiB 2002*, p. 521 ff.; critical: Bauer/Opolny, *BB 2002*, p. 1590 ff.; Wisskirchen, Gerlind, *DB 2002*, p. 1886 ff.

216   Dieterich, *AuR 1997*, p. 1 ff.; WSI project group, *WSI Mitt. 1998*, p. 653 ff.; Bielinski, *WSI Mitt. 2000*, p. 697 ff.; Seifert, Hartmut, *WSI Mitt. 2001*, p. 65.

217   No definition of a 'company' was given, although the concept of a 'Community firm' was explicitly acknowledged; from the broad debate: Preis, Ulrich, *RdA 2000*, p. 257 ff.; Wißmann, *NZA 2001*, p. 409 ff.; Richardi, *FS Wiedemann*, 2002, p. 493 ff.

218   See Richardi/Annuß, *DB 2001*, p. 41 ff.; more forward-looking e.g. Däubler, *AuR 2001*, p. 1 ff.; on the election results in the spring of 2002, see chapter 1, section 1.3 of the German report.

219   On the implementation in the other Member States: Kolvenbach, *NZA 2000*, p. 518 ff.

220   Kittner, *Arbeits- und Sozialordnung*, p. 554 with references.

221   On other aspects and problems of the European Company and employee participation, recently only: Heinze, *ZGR 2002*, p. 67 ff.; Keller, Berndt, *WSI Mitt. 2002*, p. 203 ff.; Herfs-Röttgen, *NZA 2002*, p. 358 ff.; Wißmann, *FS Wiedemann*, 2002, p. 685 ff.; Kleinsorge, *RdA 2002*, p. 343 ff.; monographic: Mävers, Die Mitbestimmung der Arbeitnehmer in der Europäischen Aktiengesellschaft (Employee co-determination in the European Company), 2000.

222   On Directive 2002/14/EC of the European Parliament and of the Council of 11 March 2002 establishing a general framework for informing and consulting employees in the European Community: Weiler, *AiB 2002*, p. 265 ff.; Shahatit, *Bundesarbeitsblatt 4/2002*, p. 18 f.

223   On the difficulties of European company agreements: Schiek, *RdA 2000*, p. 218 ff.

224   Recently, only: Altmeyer, *Interessenmanager vor neuen Herausforderungen* (Interest managers faced with new challenges), 2001, p. 361 ff.; Lecher/Nagel/Platzer, *Die Konstituierung Europäischer Betriebsräte – vom Informationsforum zum Akteur?* (The constitution of European works councils – from information forums to actors?), 1998, p. 630 ff.; Eberweil/Tholen/Schuster, *Die Europäisierung der Arbeitsbeziehungen als politisch-sozialer Prozess* (The Europeanisation of employment relations as a politico-social process), 2000, p. 202 ff.; Weiss, *NZA 2003*, p. 177 ff.

4. Crisis and future of the group collective agreement and the *Bündnis für Arbeit*

4.1. Background

The broad debate on the crisis and future of (group) collective agreements is one of the main labour law issues during the reporting period. The debate can however not be described in detail here.[225] The core of this debate is which powers should be reserved for (general) collective agreements and what should be delegated to other levels, i.e. the company agreement or the contract of employment. Behind this legal controversy are different conceptions – sometimes unspoken – of the role of associations in a social democracy, the appropriateness of transferring competition principles to the labour market and the value of individual and collective freedoms. In other words, fundamental labour law principles.

4.2. The value of the favourability principle

One of the main aspects of the discussion was and still is the issue of how to interpret the **favourability principle** in collective agreement law. It is expressed in §4(3) of the TVG, according to which more favourable conditions than the standard ones are permissible. If this principle is interpreted broadly and it is assumed, for instance, that a 40-hour week laid down in a contract of employment in conjunction with a fixed-term job guarantee is more favourable than the collective agreement laying down a 37-hour week, the normative effect of the collective agreement is significantly reduced. In such a case, the collective agreement would be only a recommendation (with the effect of a gentleman's agreement) as in Anglo-American labour law. Such an interpretation would constitute a sea change for German labour law culture. The *Bundesarbeitsgericht*[226] has therefore rightly rejected this position.[227]

4.3. Controlled decentralisation through savings clauses in collective agreements or state intervention?

The parties have themselves used **saving clauses in collective agreements** to regulate many matters. Primarily this has been used for working time (working time accounts and corridors), but also for *Bündnisse für Arbeit* in times of economic difficulty (shorter working hours, wage cuts, short-term job safeguarding), and sometimes even for remuneration (remuneration corridors) in order to take account of the need for flexibility.[228] It is likely that the trend to decentralise and differentiate the general collective agreement will continue, i.e. transferring some of the powers to company level, with all the associated ambivalences. Where the openings are anticipated in the collective agreement itself with saving clauses, we can talk of **controlled decentralisation**.

The latest proposals from conservative and liberal elements, supported by some academic circles,[229] concern weakening or even scrapping the primacy of collective agreements under §77(3) of the BetrVG by changing the law to the benefit of company agreements.[230] The Red/Green government, however, wants to maintain the primacy of collective agreements over company agreements and is in favour of the reform being pursued by the parties to collective agreements themselves, also during the second legislative period.[231]

4.4. The relationship between collective agreements and national law

There are also reasons for thinking that we are about to see a realignment of not only the relationship between collective agreements and company agreements/contracts of employment, but also of that between collective agreements and national law.

---

225 See Chapter I, section 1.2.3 of the German report; by way of example, with various focuses: Rieble, *RdA 1996*, p. 151 ff.; Zachert, *RdA 1996*, p. 140 ff.; Richardi, *Report of the 61ˢᵗ German Juristentag 1996*, volume I/1, part B, p. 7 ff.; the papers given by Wendeling-Schröder and Reuter, volume II/1, part K, S. 9 ff. and 35 ff.; for the latest: Hanau, *FS Wiedemann*, p. 281 ff.

226 BAG 20.4.1999, AP No 89 on Art. 9 of the Constitution.

227 The position is still very controversial; recent contributions: on one side Kempen, supplement to the *NZA 3/2000*, p. 7 ff.; Zachert, *AuR 2002*, p. 41, 47 ff.; on the other side: Picker, *NZA 2002*, p. 767 ff.; Zöllner, supplement to the *NZA 3/2000*, p. 1 ff.; the latest is that Schliemann, *NZA 2003*, p. 122 ff., as the chair of the fourth division of the Bundesarbeitsgericht (collective agreement division) ruled against the ruling of the first division of 20.4.1999, see previous footnote.

228 For the details, see Chapter II, sections 1 and 2 of the German report; from the empirical studies, e.g. Oppolzer/Zachert, *Krise und Zukunft des Flächentarifvertrages* (Crisis and future of the general collective agreement); Höland/Reim/Brecht, *Flächentarifvertrag und Günstigkeitsprinzip* (General collective agreement and favourability principle).

229 E.g. CDU/CSU programme, see *AuR 2002*, p. 253; also Hanau, *FS Wiedemann*, p. 296 ff.; for the latest, e.g. Möschel, *BB 2002*, p. 1314 ff.

230 Constitutional concerns from Dieterich, *RdA 2002*, p. 1 ff.

231 Documentation: *AuR 2002*, p. 456, 457.

A contradictory development can be seen here. On the one hand, the *Bundesverfassungsgericht* has recently ruled that the legislator may intervene to the detriment of standards in collective agreements, thus limiting the autonomy of collective agreements provided for in Article 9(3) of the German Constitution.[232] On the other hand, it has acknowledged that minimum standards may be set with state assistance in areas which are insufficiently protected by collective agreements, for instance, the setting of a minimum wage in the building industry by ordinance.[233]

Another very controversial area is that of *Tariftreueerklärungen* (declarations of adherence to the collective agreement). The trade unions are demanding that the award of public contracts, e.g. in the building sector, be made dependent on the adherance to a relevant collective agreement, whether or not the company in question is bound by one. A bill to this effect has been presented. The case law of the European Court of Justice permits this in principle.[234] However, there is strong opposition to and criticism of this from political and academic circles.[235]

4.5. *Bündnis für Arbeit*

The *Bündnis für Arbeit* is a dialogue between the unions and employer associations, chaired by the State. There were eight meetings during the first legislative period of the Red/Green government and the dialogue was not considered to be very efficient.[236] The *Bündnis für Arbeit* should however be maintained but in a modified form (closer to models from the Netherlands).[237] The employers are insisting that collective agreement policy be discussed too. The unions, on the other hand, are refusing to do this, insisting that only concrete aspects such as employment should be tackled.[238] However, the most recent developments (as of March 2003) show that, in times when little can be distributed because of exceptional pressures on the public purse (EU stability criteria), this form of 'consensus democracy' has reached its limits. The discussions are not continuing for the time being.[239]

5. Industrial disputes/collective action/conciliation

5.1. The intensive debate about industrial action law

Whilst industrial action law was one of the hottest subjects in labour law in the 1970s and 1980s, it has proved less controversial during recent years.[240] The Supreme Court's rulings on lockouts in the 1980s and 1990s have obviously had a pacifying impact.[241] The regulation of so-called **cold lockouts** (§116 of the *Arbeitsförderungsgesetz*/§146 of Social Code III) is still controversial. In the case of a cold lockout, the question is who should bear the risk of the **indirect impact of industrial disputes** on other companies in sectors characterised by a high degree of division of labour (e.g. the automotive industry). Following an extremely serious conflict, the conservative/liberal government changed the legal situation in 1986 (§116 of the AFG/§146 of Social Code III). Since then, workers are, in principle not eligible for unemployment benefit or short-time allowance. The *Bundesverfassungsgericht* considers this provision to be 'constitutional, but only just' and a latent threat to collective bargaining freedom.[242] Despite the unions' criticism of the existing legal situation, the Red/Green government has also retained the relevant provisions on cold lockouts.[243]

5.2. Low frequency of strikes: some empirical data

The number of industrial disputes in Germany has traditionally been low. This was also the case during the reporting period. According to the latest survey into industrial disputes around the world (annual average for 1991-2000), Germany lost 11 working days annually per 1 000 employees. Only Austria (four days lost per year per 1 000 employees), Japan (three days) and Switzerland (two days) had lower figures than

---

232 See Dieterich, *AuR 2002*, p. 390 ff. with references.

233 Federal Constitutional Court 18.7.2000, *BB 2000*, 1768.

234 ECJ 26.9.2000, Commission/French Republic, *NJW 2000*, 3629.

235 From the broad debate: e.g. Scholz, Rupert, *RdA 2001*, p. 193 ff.; also Federal Supreme Court 18.1.2000, *NZA 2000*, 327: order for reference to the Federal Constitutional Court .

236 For the unions' position: Lang, Klaus, *WSI Mitt. 2001*, p. 194 ff.

237 *Bündnis-Debatte bringt Zündstoff für die DGB* (Bündnis debate brings controversy for the German Trade Union Confederation), Handelsblatt, 4.12.2002.

238 Documentation: *AuR 2002*, p. 417.

239 *Wenig Hoffnung vor neuer Bündnisrunde* (Little hope before new Bündnis round), Handelsblatt, 3.3.2003.

240 Recent, critical commentary with reference to European developments: Zachert, *AuR 2001*, p. 401 ff. with references.

241 Bundesarbeitsgericht 10.8.1980, AP No 64 on Article 9 of the German Constitution; Federal Constitutional Court 26.6.1991, *BVerfGE 84*, 212; also Däubler, *AuR 1992*, p. 1 ff.

242 Federal Constitutional Court 4.7.1995, *BVerfGE 92*, 365 ff.; on the ruling: Griese, *ArbRGgW. 1995*, p. 33 ff.; Heilmann/Menke, *AuR 1996*, p. 11 ff.; Rüfner, *RdA 1997*, p. 133 ff.; Schulin/Wietek, *ArbRGgW. 1995*, p. 29 ff.; Zachert, *ZRP 1995*, p. 445 ff.

243 See Zachert, *AuR 2000*, p. 53 ff.

Germany. In comparison Spain lost 327 days per 1 000 employees per annum during the same period (1991-2000), Italy lost 130 and France lost 77.[244]

5.3. The changing nature of industrial disputes

The nature of industrial disputes changed considerably between 1990 and 2000 and over the following years. The 1970s in particular were characterised by large-scale disputes with strikes and (hot) lockouts. In 1984, a six-week dispute occurred in the metalworking and printing industries to push for a 35-hour week. This dispute included strikes, hot lockouts and prolonged cold lockouts.[245]

IG Metall, still spearheading the implementation of worker demands, has carried out only **warning strikes** since then, with two exceptions. However, many workers were involved in these, and they generally ended in a (partial) victory for the union.[246]

5.4. The European dimension

With regard to **the European dimension**, it is important to meet the demand for the formulation of a legal framework for transnational (solidarity) industrial disputes.[247] Otherwise, Article 28 of the European Charter of Fundamental Rights of December 2001 could lead to an opening up of German industrial dispute law to European standards. This Article confirms that – in contrast to the traditional interpretation by case law in Germany – workers and employers, and not just the unions and employer associations, are entitled to negotiate and conclude collective agreements. Furthermore, collective measures are also permissible, including the right to strike not only in the case of disputes relating to collective agreements, but more generally in cases of conflicts of interests.[248]

5.5. Conciliation

Germany has a highly developed system of collectively agreed (voluntary) conciliation procedures that help to avoid or quickly end industrial disputes. In this context, it should be emphasised once again that, in contrast to most other countries, in Germany it is generally assumed that there is a peace obligation inherently included in collective agreements. This means, *inter alia*, that the peace obligation can be extended or indeed restricted, depending on how the conciliation procedure is organised. In practice, there are certain sectors that are very keen on solving disputes relating to collective agreements through conciliation (e.g. the chemicals industry). In other sectors, the conciliation procedure is structured such that the conflict resolution by collective negotiation is always in the foreground, even during the influence of the industrial dispute itself (e.g. the metalworking industry). This differentiated system of conciliation is also acknowledged in German labour law. State sponsored conciliation, such as the British 'Advisory, Conciliation and Arbitration Service' (ACAS), does not exist in Germany. The well-developed employment jurisdiction, with competences in collective labour law, should also play an important role here.[249]

6. Assessment and outlook

6.1. Assessment

It can be stated that, over the last decade, German labour law has remained remarkably stable in terms of its basic structures. Various legislative and collective initiatives have, however, led to significant changes and modernisation.

Since 1998, the Red/Green government has been trying, via various initiatives, to pay greater attention to the idea of minimum social protection, whilst at the same time guaranteeing companies the flexibility they need to cope with fluctuations in orders brought on by the state of the market. As demonstrated by the new provisions on economically dependent work and small-scale part-time work, these initiatives are often experimental. Obviously, it is often difficult in real life to draw the line between socially acceptable flexibility and abusive practice.

I will be not be summarising all the important results here, so as not to run the risk of arbitrarily boiling down the many

---

244   Institut der deutschen Wirtschaft, industrial dispute assessment, Globus-Infografik, 8.4.2002.

245   Overview in Gamillscheg, *Kollektives Arbeitsrecht* (Collective labour law), p. 918 ff.; Wolter in Däubler, *Arbeitskampfrecht* (Industrial dispute law), Note 852 ff.

246   On the major IG Metall strikes under the restrictive regulations on cold lockouts (§146 of Social Code III): Detje/Ehlscheid/Unterhinninghofen, *Perspektiven des Streiks* (Outlook for strikes), 2003, p. 130 f.

247   Clauwaert, *Haupt- und Sympathiearbeitskampf auf internationaler und transnationaler Ebene* (Main and sympathy strikes at international and transnational level), European Trade Union Institute, 2002, English version: Transfer 2002, p. 625 ff.

248   On the Charter of Fundamental Rights, most recently: Däubler, *AuR 2001*, p. 380 ff.; Weiss, *AuR 2001*, p. 374 ff. Zachert, *NZA 2001*, p. 1041 ff.

249   For a European perspective: Zachert, *Conciliation, mediation and arbitration in Germany*, in Valdés Dal-Re, ed. *Conciliation, Mediation and Arbitration in Europe*, European Commission Project, 2003; also Kocher, *The regulation of conflicts in the German industrial relations system: legal and extra-legal institutions and procedures*, Transfer 2002, p. 655 ff.

focuses, trends and facets over the reporting period to just a few points. However, with this proviso, I would like to highlight some of the results.

Firstly, it is clear that the **borders between labour law and social law** in particular have become more open. This is partly because structuring and prevention are playing a stronger role in social law than they did in the past. This is particularly the case with the law pertaining to employment promotion. At the same time it is important to see the impact of the difficulties faced by the social security systems (unemployment insurance, health, old age protection), which burden companies and workers with high incidental wage costs. Moreover, the dividing line between labour law and other legal fields, including that of (European) competition law, is becoming more vague.[250]

German labour law has remained relatively stable in terms of its basic structures over the last decade. However, a remarkable push towards modernisation has taken place in certain areas. In principle, state law and collective agreements must be seen in this perspective. Collective agreements still play a fundamental role, despite all the talk of a 'crisis of (general) collective agreements'. It is notable that, on the one hand, the flexibility and innovativeness of German labour law is often confirmed by empirical data, for example in terms of the rate of turnover on the labour market, or openings in collective agreements for company-friendly solutions. However, the debate is becoming more heated about whether the labour law structures are too rigid.

In political and academic circles, labour law is sometimes considered to have a key role in the solution of economic and labour market policy problems. However, well-founded comparative studies on labour markets in the USA and Europe (Germany) show that one-dimensional statements like this are too simplistic and look to the production and financial markets in particular for the necessary initiatives.[251] The Maastricht stability criteria set out narrow margins for an anti-cyclical economic policy. That could also play a role inasmuch as they contribute to labour law being underestimated in terms of its importance in the overall context of the necessary measures.

The **influence of EU law** on labour law was very important indeed during the reporting period. This applies both to European legislation, in particular directives, and to the case law of the European Court of Justice. The following could be cited as examples: the equality principle; industrial safety; European works councils; working time law; and employee claims in the event of transfers of undertakings. Acceptance and, above all, knowledge of European (labour) law have grown considerably in Germany. The implementation of European labour law does not bring any fundamental difficulties, despite the complexity of the interrelationship between European and national law.[252]

The associations, trade unions and employer federations are comparatively weak. There is therefore no need to dramatise the situation in Germany. However, there is a question that could become more pressing in future. This is the question of how to protect the representativeness and democratic legitimacy of the associations in order to continue to fulfil the protection function of labour law, and also to guarantee a high level of social integration through strong and reliable coalitions.[253]

6.2. Outlook

Notwithstanding all the future initiatives, measures and approaches, it would seem particularly important to create **cross-overs and bridges** between different types of contract and between paid work and other productive activities. Because, despite all the controversy about economic and labour market policy concepts, broad agreement exists that the pace of change on the labour market in particular over recent years has accelerated compared to previous decades. Labour market theoretical studies talk of 'high-speed labour markets' and 'transitional labour markets'.[254]

In principle, calculable rules and elementary protection standards in the sense of substantial guarantees – (*Habeas Corpus*) which must be met whatever the economic conditions – are needed,[255] if individuals are not to become mere objects of flexibility controlled from outside. Variety calls for regulation, otherwise it will be to the detriment of the weak. This relates to the **labour law protection principle,** which is a central

---

250 Bruun/Hellsten, *Collective Agreement and Competition Law in the EU*, 2001.

251 Most recently: Finken, *RdA 2002*, p. 333 ff.

252 Summary in Sciarra and Simitis in Sciarra, *Labour law in the Courts*, 2001, p. 1 ff. and 291 ff.

253 On this idea of Hugo Sinzheimer: Zachert, *RdA 2001*, p. 104, 109 = Herrera, Les *Juristes de Gauche sous la République de Weimar* (Left-wing lawyers under the Weimar Republic), 2002, p. 49, 59 ff.; on the European Commission's endeavours to develop the social dialogue: Com (2002) 341 final: *RdA 2003*, p. 54 ff.

254 Rogowski/Schmid, *WSI Mitt. 1997*, p. 568, 576 ff.; critical, however, with empirical references: Bosch, *GMH 2002*, p. 688, 690 f.; more under Chapter I section 2.2. of the German report.

255 Zachert, *FS Dieterich*, p. 699, 724 ff.

element of labour law and will remain so. The Danish and the Dutch debates led to the emergence of the term 'flexicurity' to describe a hybrid of flexibility and security. This idea is also being fleshed out in German labour law.[256]

As shown in this country report, we can already see attempts to reconcile flexibility and security. This means that the new labour constitution has already been set out in its current structures. Often this has happened in a fragmentary and ambivalent way, because the pendulum sometimes swings towards economic efficiency and then back again towards greater individual freedom. As this country report shows, there have been many examples over the last ten years to show that this does not have to represent a contradiction.[257]

However, the most recent developments, in particular since the end of 2002, have raised the question of whether models based on the neo-liberal political philosophy could become more influencial. That would entail the idea that the best way to improve companies' competitiveness and the labour market situation is to lower protection standards (flexibilisation) and cut (wage) costs.[258] A review of the past ten years shows that a radical change in policy is unlikely. Much will depend on economic developments and foreign policy unknowables, and whether the social security system (unemployment, health and pension insurance) can be successfully reformed, thus cutting the proportion of incidental wage costs.

---

256 Zachert, *WSI Mitt. 2000*, S. 283, with references.
257 See European Commission, 14.1.2003, *The future of the European Employment Strategy*, COM(2003) 6 final.
258 Most recently: Rüthers, *NJW 2003*, p. 546 ff.

Part 2: Austria

Chapter I:
The structure of labour law relations and how they have changed

1. Labour law structures: an overview

The labour law structures in Austria are broadly comparable to those in Germany. However, in the area of collective labour law relations, Austria has certain peculiarities, which will be described in more detail below.

1.1. Austrian labour law system

Austrian labour law can be divided into **collective** and **individual** labour law. Basically, collective labour law regulates relations between individual workers and the workforce and between individual workers and umbrella associations (statutory and voluntary representation bodies); the relations between these associations; between employers and their workforces; between employers and the employer associations; and finally the law relating to industrial disputes. Individual labour law can be divided into employment contract law, i.e. the legal standards relating to contractual relations between employers and employees; and employee protection law, i.e. all the legal standards which set out under public law the duty of employers to protect their employees. Austrian labour law is therefore covered by both a public-law regime and – especially in the area of contract law – the principles of private law.[259]

1.2. Hierarchical structure of Austrian labour law

In Austria, the labour law structures can be ordered in a **hierarchical system**, under which the possibility of invoking a subordinate statute depends in each case on the superordinate statute.[260] The hierarchical labour law structure can be represented as follows:

- Community law, constitutional law
- Binding act
- Ordinance, minimum wage, apprentices' wages
- Collective agreements, articles of association
- Company agreements
- Contracts of employment
- Dispositive law
- Employer's instructions.

The **favourability principle** is often applied to the relationship between collective agreements and their subordinate legal sources. This means that special agreements (e.g. via company agreements or contracts of employment) are valid only if they are more favourable for employees or they contain measures that are not dealt with in the collective agreement. However, the favourability principle can be overruled by the **order principle**, if the collective agreement specifies that it has a binding effect on both sides and therefore rules out the application of the favourability principle.

1.3. State law

1.3.1. Employee rights in the Constitution

There are just a few constitutional sources of labour law. The **freedom of association** is enshrined in Article 12 of the Basic Law on the General Rights of Citizens (StGG) and Article 11 of the Human Rights Convention, as both the right to join an employee or employer association (**positive freedom of association**) and the right to refrain from doing so (**negative freedom of association**). There is furthermore the freedom to choose and engage in an occupation regulated in Article 6 and Article 18 of the StGG. In contrast to Germany, Article 11 of the Human Rights Convention is not considered by Austrian academics as a constitutional guarantee of the right to engage in industrial disputes.[261] Moreover, **industrial dispute law** in Austrian is

---

259 See Schwarz, *Öffentliches und privates Recht in der arbeitsrechtlichen System-bildung* (Public and private law in the formation of the labour law system), 1973.

260 Schwarz/Löschnigg, *Arbeitsrecht* (Labour law), 2001, 71.

261 Marhold, *Kollektivarbeitsrecht* (Collective labour law), 1999, 108.

not guaranteed constitutionally.[262] This is because the right to strike as enshrined in Article 6(4) of the European Social Charter is not applicable because of an Austrian reservation. Instead, the Austrian legal system rejects any subjective right to engage in such disputes.[263]

1.3.2. State labour law

Austria has **no comprehensive labour code**. Efforts to codify Austrian labour law commenced in 1960. A codification committee was set up in 1967. However, the committee's work did not lead to overall codification, but rather to the adoption of several **partial codifications**, such as the 1973 *ArbeitsverfassungsGesetz* (Works Constitution Act) or the standardisation of holiday rights for most employees in the 1976 *UrlaubsGesetz* (Holidays Act).[264]

Austrian state labour law today is almost impossible for users to understand because it has been so fragmented. Looking systematically at the various acts, the user is first of all confronted by a categorisation by occupational group (e.g. employees and workers, agriculture and forestry workers, actors, journalists, pharmacists, domestic assistants and domestic employees). This is followed by a classification by group of persons (e.g. children and young people, pregnant women and mothers, disabled people, arduous night workers, and those undertaking military or civilian service). Finally, certain labour law issues are regulated for most – but by no means all – employment relationships by special laws conferring individual rights (e.g. holidays, technical employee protection, working time, insolvency wage guarantee, employee liability, company pension, employment of foreigners). The AVRAG (*Arbeitsvertragsrecht-Anpassungsgesetz* – Employment Contract Law Modification Act) served originally to implement all the various EU labour law provisions in Austrian labour law, but has recently been enhanced by specific Austrian provisions. The AVRAG defies any systematic classification.[265] A **codification** of Austrian labour law is therefore urgently needed.[266]

1.4. Collective labour law and professional corporations

1.4.1. Collective agreements

Collective agreements are written agreements between authorised employer and employee representatives. They regulate, in particular, working conditions (§ 2 of the ArbVG – Work Constitution Act). Austrian collective agreements have **normative effect** (§12 of the ArbVG) and regulate, in particular, the 'reciprocal rights and obligations of employers and employees arising from the employment relationship' (§ 2(2)(2) of the ArbVG). This means that the typical, fundamental or regularly recurring contents of employment relationships can be regulated by collective agreement.[267]

1.4.2. Bodies authorised to conclude collective agreements by law

It should be remembered that both employers and employees are covered by **statutory representation bodies.** Membership of such a body is compulsory. These statutory representation bodies are authorised to conclude collective agreements by law. On the employer side, they are the Chambers of Commerce, comprising the Federal Chamber of Commerce, with jurisdiction for the whole of Austria, and the nine *Land* Chambers of Commerce, each with jurisdiction for its own region.

1.4.3. Chambers of Labour – a unique feature of Austrian labour law

Employees are represented by the **Chambers of Workers and Employees**, with each *Land* having its own regional chamber and all nine regional chambers forming the *Bundesarbeitskammer* or Federal Chamber of Labour. As statutory representation bodies for workers are very rare in Europe (with the exception of Luxembourg and the German *Bundesländer* of Bremen and Saarland),[268] these will be described in more detail below.

---

262   Binder, *Kollektives Arbeitsrecht*, 58.

263   In particular: Tomandl, *Streik und Aussperrung als Mittel des Arbeitskampfes* Strikes and lockouts as methods in industrial disputes), 1965, 99 ff.; The industrial dispute.

264   Floretta/Spielbüchler/Strasser, *Arbeitsrecht I* (Labour Law) (73).

265   See Binder, *AVRAG* (2001), 24 f.

266   Floretta/Spielbüchler/Strasser, *Arbeitsrecht I* 73.

267   See, for more details, Strasser in Strasser/Jabornegg/Resch, (ed.) *Kommentar zum Arbeitsverfassungsgesetz* (Comments on the Arbeits-verfassungsge-setz), 2002, notes 27 ff.; Labour constitution law, 2000, 46 ff.; Commentary on the ArbVG.

268   Strasser/Jabornegg, *Arbeitsrecht II* (Labour law) (2001), 73.

In principle, all workers are compulsory members of the Chambers of Labour, although §10 of the *Arbeiterkammergesetz* (AKG – Chambers of Labour Act) has an exhaustive list of exceptions, including certain territorial authority workers, managers and directors of corporations and senior employees with permanent, significant influence on the management of their companies. The Chambers of Labour are funded by a charge on all the workers who are members, which may not exceed 0.5% of the basic contribution for statutory health insurance (§61(2) of the AKG).

The Chambers of Labour have many different roles. In general, they are called on to represent and promote the social, economic, professional and cultural interests of workers (§1 of the AKG) and to take all necessary, appropriate measures to represent the interests of workers, the unemployed and pensioners (§4 of the AKG). Since 1992, the Chambers of Labour have also been responsible for advising workers in labour and social law matters and providing them with legal protection via court representation (§7 of the AKG).

Given the wide range of duties of the Chambers of Labour, it should be emphasised that the membership rate of the Austrian trade union confederation (ÖGB)[269] demonstrates that the unions' concerns that compulsory membership of a representation body would deter employees from joining a union have not been borne out in Austria.[270] It should be underlined, however, that in practice the Chambers of Labour do not exercise their right to conclude collective agreements. Instead they leave that to the ÖGB. In addition to political reasons, this is because of the statutory principle of the **primacy of voluntary trade associations** (§6 of the ArbVG). If a voluntary trade association (such as the ÖGB) concludes a collective agreement, the relevant statutory representation body (in this case the Chambers of Labour) loses its power to conclude such an agreement.

1.4.4. The power to conclude collective agreements by appointment

In addition to *ex lege* powers to conclude collective agreements, the ArbVG also provides the option for the power to conclude such agreements to be conferred on coalitions of employees or employers, as well as on associations at the request of the *Bundeseinigungsamt* (Federal Conciliation Office)

(§5 of the ArbVG). Accordingly, a coalition may be granted the power to conclude collective agreements if (1) in accordance with the rules under which it is established, it has the objective of regulating working conditions; (2) it is active in a broad specialist and geographical area, according to its employee or employer representation objectives; (3) it has considerable economic weight because of the number of members and the scope of its activities; and (4) there are no conflicts of interest.

1.4.5. The Austrian trade union confederation

The Austrian trade union confederation (ÖGB) has a special position with regard to employee coalitions to which the power to conclude collective decisions has been granted. Although Austrian labour law recognises the principle of trade union pluralism, the ÖGB is, as it were, a unified trade union, the only umbrella union organisation in Austria, to which some 50% of employed workers belong.[271] The ÖGB is a non-partisan organisation. One of its founding principles was to avoid conflicts between rival unions.[272] It considers that it has co-responsibility in the State and has developed into an important economic and social policy force. The ÖGB is different in nature and significance from trade union organisations in other countries inasmuch as its posts are often filled by leading officials from the political parties and members of parliament. There is also a relatively high degree of interrelation between the ÖGB and works councils in companies.[273] The high membership rate and the de facto monopoly on collective agreements have already been mentioned.

1.4.6. The cartel effect of collective agreements as the product of the primacy of sectoral collective agreements and the outsider effect

Austrian collective agreement law is characterised by two other peculiarities: the legal primacy of sectoral collective agreements and the so-called outsider effect vis-à-vis employees. Both principles mean that the 'cartel effect' of collective agreements in Austria is very important. In addition they create a 'protection function' together, as all employment relationships in a specific sector have the same 'minimum labour costs' within the geographical field of application of the collective agreement.

---

269 As at 31 December 2001, 1 427 027 workers were members of one of the 13 ÖGB-affiliated unions (*Source:* Annual report of the ÖGB 2001, 70).
270 Tomandl/Schrammel, *Arbeitsrecht I*, (1999) 36.
271 Tomandl/Schrammel, *Arbeitsrecht I*, 31; Strasser/Jabornegg, *Arbeitsrecht II*, 51.
272 Tomandl/Schrammel, *Arbeitsrecht I*, 31.
273 Strasser/Jabornegg, *Arbeitsrecht II*, 50.

1.4.6.1. Legal primacy of sectoral collective agreements

In connection with the primacy of sectoral collective agreements, it should be pointed out that the limits of the actual field of application of collective agreements depend on the organisational affiliation of the owner of the business (industry association principle),[274] and the nature of the employer's activity is another determining factor.[275] This means that the ability to conclude collective agreements on the employer side – where the Chamber of Commerce acts as the representative, as is usually the case – depends on the categorisation by the Chamber of Commerce of the company in a particular professional group or association, in accordance with the wording of the business licence.[276] **Business collective agreements** or **single-company collective agreements** are very rare under Austrian labour law, occurring only in the case of non-profit associations, public corporations and certain other specific cases, such as the ORF (Austrian broadcasting corporation), Austro Control AG, the post office, Telekom AG and the universities. But even in the case of non-profit associations and public corporations, sectoral collective agreements have priority if the organisation in question belongs, in whole or in part, to another organisation with the right to conclude collective agreements.[277]

1.4.6.2. The 'outsider effect' in Austrian collective agreements

§12 of the ArbVG sets out the so-called '**outsider effect**' of collective agreements for employees, whereby the legal effect of the collective agreement applies also to those workers who are not members of the concluding employee association. This means that collective agreements concluded by the ÖGB apply also to non-members of the ÖGB. Moreover, the legal principle of the outsider effect means that the effect of a collective agreement does not depend on trade union membership.[278] Consequently there is no indirect pressure exerted by law on employees to join the voluntary trade associations. It also means that in times of economic recession union members are not undercut by non-members in terms of wages.[279]

1.5. The Austrian social partnership

The complex operation of the **Austrian social partnership** and its significance for the development of labour law and economic and social policy in Austria can be described only partially here, but should under no circumstances be left out. The almost total absence of industrial disputes and the high level of social stability in Austria are the direct result of the Austrian social partner system.

Strictly speaking, the only Austrian social partnership body is the **Joint Commission for Wages and Prices**, founded in 1957, and its four subcommittees: the wages subcommittee; the prices subcommittee; the international affairs subcommittee; and the advisory board for economic and social affairs. Each of these bodies comprises government representatives, as well as representatives of the ÖGB, the Federal Chamber of Labour, the Federal Chamber of Commerce and the Presidents' Conference of the Chambers of Agriculture. However, the key decisions are made in a so-called presidential preliminary discussion.

The **legal basis** for the Joint Commission is a gentlemen's agreement between all the parties. Decisions are made **unanimously**, and none of the bodies have any legal power to impose sanctions. Its original task – to dampen inflationary price and wage developments – has since been extended to include the entire economic and social policy area. The most important role of the Joint Commission has, however, always been to bring the leaders of the representation bodies and the government to discussions around the same table.[280]

Fundamentally, given the structure of the employer and employee representation bodies, the role of the social partnership can be said to be to bring together the production factors of capital and labour in strong, centrally controlled associations with a quasi-monopolistic position, whose joint decisions are considered to be applicable to and have authority for economic and social policy.[281] The underlying idea is to simplify the plurality of interests by combining them into two

274   Schwarz/Löschnigg, *Arbeitsrecht,* 96.

275   Marhold, *Arbeitsrecht II,* 74.

276   Schwarz/Löschnigg, *Arbeitsrecht,* 98.

277   Mazal, *Grenzen der Einräumung kollektiver Gestaltungsmöglichkeiten* (The limits of collective structuring possibilities), in Tomandl, (ed.) *Aktuelle Probleme des Kollektivvertragsrechts* (Current problems in collective agreement law), 2003, 1 (15).

278   See only: Marhold, *Arbeitsrecht II,* 75.

279   Schwarz/Löschnigg, *Arbeitsrecht,* 100.

280   Tomandl/Schrammel, *Arbeitsrecht I,* 39.

281   See Strasser/Jabornegg, *Arbeitsrecht II,* 82 with further references.

or, at the most, four large groups and replacing the competition principle by the agreement principle, in order to achieve the common goals of economic growth, stability of property and income distribution and securing jobs.[282] Labour negotiations in Austria therefore do not tend to be conflictual, but rather are characterised by the robust thrashing out of a compromise that can be accepted by both sides.[283]

1.6. Corporate co-determination

Like Germany, Austria has a legally regulated system of company co-determination by employees exercised via **works councils**. A company's employees form, together, the 'workforce', which is assigned certain tasks and powers under the ArbVG. Under the powers assigned to it, the workforce has partial legal capacity and therefore constitutes a partial legal person under private law. The works council, which must be elected in companies with at least five permanent employees, acts as the administrative and representative body of the workforce.

1.6.1. General tasks of the workforce representation bodies

In general, the workforce representation bodies must protect and promote the economic, social, health and safety and cultural interests of the workforce in the company (§38 of the ArbVG). The aim is to bring about a balance of interests to the benefit of both the workers and the company (§39(1) of the ArbVG). This means that, where possible, the workforce representation bodies must act without disrupting the business of the company. They are not allowed to intervene unilaterally in the management and activity of the company (§39(3) of the ArbVG obligation to keep the peace).

1.6.2. Individual powers of the works council

The works council has the following individual powers:

1.6.2.1. General powers

Their general powers include supervision and monitoring powers, the right of intervention, a general right to information and a comprehensive entitlement to be consulted and to make recommendations.

1.6.2.2. Social affairs and company agreements

The **company agreement** is a tool available to the works council in the area of social affairs. In Austria, however, company agreements – written agreements between the owner of the company and the works council – can be concluded only regarding matters specifically laid down by law or in the collective agreement as coming under the competence of a company agreement (§29 of the ArbVG). Whilst collective agreements regulate all matters forming the typical, regular content of employment contracts, company agreements are limited in scope to a range of matters laid down by law or in the collective agreement. This is because the works council, as part of the workforce, has only a 'diluted influence' on the necessary appropriateness and balance for the conclusion of contracts. For example, when it comes to **wages**, the works council may intervene only in certain areas (e.g. piece rates and performance-related pay, company pensions, profit-sharing schemes and special allowances) but may not take part in negotiations concerning the basic wage. Recently, the issue of whether greater powers should be conferred on company agreements has been discussed repeatedly,[284] but, so far, no relevant changes to the law have been introduced.

1.6.2.3. Personnel management and general protection against redundancy and dismissal

The powers of the works council are very well defined in the area of personnel management. The works council has a right of information when it comes to staff planning, collaboration and approval authority in the case of permanent transfers. In addition it has information and advisory rights for the allocation of works accommodation and for planned promotions. It should be pointed out in this context that general protection against dismissal and redundancy in Austria is shaped through collective agreements. Before dismissing or making redundant any worker in a company with a works council, the owner must inform the latter. The works council then has five working days to state its position on this step (§105 of ArbVG). If the works council approves the dismissal or redundancy, no challenge on the basis of socially unfair dismissal may be brought. This means that, in the event of unavoidable redundancies for business reasons, the workforce is itself in a position to take on joint responsibility for the choice of which workers to lose. In principle, a

---

282 Strasser/Jabornegg, *Arbeitsrecht II*, 83, with further references.

283 Tomandl/Schrammel, *Arbeitsrecht I*, 40.

284 See Mazal, *Grenzen der Einräumung kollektiver Gestaltungsmöglichkeiten* (The limits of collective structuring possibilities), in Tomandl (ed.) *Aktuelle Probleme des Kollektivvertragsrechts* (Current problems in collective agreement law) (2003) 1 (16); Firlei, *Flucht aus dem Arbeitsrecht* (The flight from labour law), DRdA *1991*, 221 (231 ff.).

dismissal or redundancy is considered socially unfair and therefore appealable to the labour court if it seriously affects the interests of the worker, unless the owner of the company can prove that his action was based on (1) circumstances rooted in the person of the worker which have a negative impact on the business, or (2) commercial reasons which make it difficult to continue to employ the worker in question (§105(3)(2) of the ArbVG). If the works council decides to lodge an objection to the proposed dismissal or redundancy, it may, at the request of the worker in question, challenge it in court. The worker him- or herself is not entitled to bring a challenge personally until the works council itself has dropped the case. If the works council decides not to take a position, it loses the right to challenge the proposal. The worker can him- or herself challenge the decision, but without recourse to the objection that the social impact on another worker in the same company and division (social comparison) would be less severe.

1.6.2.4. Commercial matters

In this area, the works council has commercial information, intervention and advisory rights, which provide for its collaboration in the case of corporate changes, and it has one-third joint representation on the supervisory board of corporations.

Chapter II:
The development of central labour law themes over the last ten years

The following chapters look briefly at the main developments in Austrian labour law between 1992 and 2002. For reasons of brevity, the author has had to make a personal choice of the main reforms. Moreover, he has had to make general comments in order to make the content and effects of the reforms transparent and understandable even for those who are not well versed in Austrian labour law. The focus is on the more recent labour law reforms, but particularly significant social law measures will also be mentioned. In addition, the author looks at Federal Government plans that are soon to be implemented at the time of writing, so as to ensure that this report is as up-to-date as possible.

1. Companies' responsibility towards their employees – new severance pay arrangements

The most important reform of Austrian labour law over the past two decades has been the **restructuring of severance pay** in the *Betriebliches Mitarbeitervorsorgegesetz* (Corporate Employee Provision Act) (Federal Gazette I No 100/2002), on the basis of a corresponding agreement between the social partners.[285]

The old arrangements continue to apply in principle to all employment relationships that began before 31 December 2002. This means that employees whose employment relationship has ended after at least three years' uninterrupted service are entitled to severance pay from their employer, calculated as a multiple of their monthly pay and increasing with length of service.[286] The increase in the entitlement goes up in 'steps', so that, after three years of service, employees are entitled to two months' pay; after five years,

three months' pay; after ten years, four months' pay; after fifteen years, six months' pay; after twenty years, nine months' pay; and finally, after twenty five years, the highest entitlement of twelve times the last monthly pay. However, this right to severance pay is lost in full if the worker terminates the employment relationship him- or herself[287] (with exceptions for maternity or paternity leave;[288] acceptance of a statutory pension; resignation as a result of significantly worse working conditions following a transfer of an undertaking), or is dismissed for misconduct or gets a summary resignation. This system fulfils several functions. It represents a **loyalty bonus**, provides **compensation** and acts as an **indirect disincentive for employees to terminate their employment relationship**.

The disadvantages of this system are that (1) employers are tempted to dismiss employees just before they reach the next 'step', (2) the loss of severance pay in the case of voluntary resignation impedes mobility, (3) SMEs can experience cash-flow difficulties if several high claims coincide, and (4) seasonal workers (with the exception of building workers) get no severance pay whatsoever. This means that, each year, only around 160 000 workers receive severance pay. That represents just 15% or so of all employment relationships ended each year.[289]

The *Betriebliches Mitarbeitvorsorgegesetz* applies, in principle, to all employment relationships that began after 31 December 2002. This law has been reformed so that workers are entitled to severance pay for any termination of an employment relationship. The old system has been replaced by a capital coverage-based contribution system. Under this system, the employee does not claim severance pay from the employer. Instead (from the second month of the employment relationship onwards) employers pay 1.53% of the employee's gross wages via the district health insurance board to specially licensed

285 See: Binder/Schifko, *Abfertigung Neu* (The new severance pay), 2002; Felbinger, *Abfertigung NEU,* 2002; Leutner/Achitz/Farny/Wöss, *Betriebliches Mitarbeitervorsorgegesetz,* 2003; Mayr/Resch, *Abfertigung Neu,* 2003; Ruf, *Abfertigung Neu,* 2002; Tomandl/Achatz/Mazal, *Abfertigung Neu,* 2003.

286 See: Martinek/Schwarz, *Abfertigung – Auflösung des Arbeitsverhältnisses* (Severance pay – dissolution of the employment relationship), 1980; Mayr/Resch, *Abfertigung* (severance pay), 1999; Migsch, *Abfertigung für Arbeiter und Angestellte* (Severance pay for workers and employees), 1982; Runggaldier (ed.) *Abfertigungsrecht* (Law on severance pay), 1991.

287 This is in line with EU law: Court of Justice 27.1.2000 (Graf case), 2000, 101 (Runggaldier).

288 Limited, see also Court of Justice 14.9.1999 (Gruber case) ARD 5009/8/99.

289 RV 1131 BlgNR 21. GP 46.

employee welfare boards. These boards invest the money in specific employee severance pay accounts. It follows that the entitlement to payment of severance pay vis-à-vis the board arises only in certain cases. Broadly speaking, the conditions that ruled out severance pay under the old system now merely make it less likely. In order to ensure provision for employees' claims, the boards have to provide a 100% capital coverage guarantee for the contributions paid, keep administration costs within legally laid down (but still very generous) limits, and comply with extensive investment conditions.[290]

Moreover, the restructuring of severance pay was also used to introduce a new element to the pension system, at least politically, as the opportunity was created to use this accumulated capital **tax-free** for **additional pension insurance** (§17(1)(4) of the BMVG). It is noticeable that the new Federal Government (formed by the same parties (ÖVP/FPÖ) following new elections) is making swingeing cuts to the statutory pension system just a few months after the creation of this new severance pay system. The argument that the BMVG has, in any case, strengthened the corporate second pillar of the pension system is not relevant, as severance pay was always considered as part of the employee's remuneration. This means that, if the severance pay system is restructured and the severance pay used as an additional pension, this should be attributed to employees' own contributions and thus to the third pillar of the pension system.

Finally, **voluntary transfer options** to the new severance pay system were created for employment relationships falling under the old system. These require a written agreement between the employer and the employee (§§46, 47 of the BMVG). Such transfers are rarely used in practice because of the unfortunate complexity of these provisions and the lack of protection mechanisms.

1.53% of gross wages represents a rather low contribution rate. That fact together with the expected investment results of the compensation boards, makes severance pay under the new system significantly lower than under the old system until around the 40th year of service. However, – and this reflects its socio-political significance – the new system is very attractive for young employees who can count on a long contribution period. The other clear winners in the new system are seasonal workers, who are now covered for the first time ever.

2. Family compassionate leave

One prominent social policy achievement is the introduction of family compassionate leave (Federal Gazette I No 89/2002). This closes a regrettable gap in the legislation relating to the granting of compassionate leave to care for dying or seriously ill relatives.[291] The starting point is the old legal situation, which will continue to apply in parallel.[292] According to the old system, employees were entitled to paid leave of up to one week's working time per working year to care for sick relatives living in the same household (§16(1) of the UrlG (Leave Act)). A further week's leave can be claimed without loss of pay when caring for a sick child below the age of 12 (§16(2) of the UrlG). Once the entitlement to paid leave is exhausted, employees are allowed to use their annual leave for this purpose (§16(3) of the UrlG). However, once the annual leave entitlement is exhausted, employees are dependent on the willingness of their employer to agree to (generally unpaid) leave. In the past, around 1 600 employees per year have taken advantage of this system.[293]

The introduction of family compassionate leave (§§14a and 14b of the AVRAG – *Arbeitsvertragsrechts-Anpassungsgesetz* (Employment Contract Law Amendment Act)) means that employees have a conditional entitlement to a reduction in their normal working hours; a change to the arrangement of their normal working hours, or a full release from their duties, in return for loss of earnings, to care for dying relatives or seriously ill children. Contrary to the old system, this entitlement can also be taken to care for siblings, and the condition that the relative in question lives in the same household no longer applies – except in relation to caring for seriously ill children.

Compassionate leave can be taken initially for a specific period not exceeding three months. An extension is possible, but the total period per leave may not exceed **six months**. The employee must inform the employer in writing that he or she wishes to take (or extend) family compassionate leave. If the employer does not approve the application, he has five days to appeal to the Labour and Social Court. This Court will then rule on the matter, having considered the interests of both parties (§14a of the AVRAG). The same applies to care for seriously ill children living in the same household, so that parents can look after their children who are suffering from cancer or leukaemia (§14b of the AVRAG). In order to safeguard

---

290   See Grün/Martinek, *Mitarbeitervorsorgekasse* (Employee compensation boards), 2002.

291   See Geist, *Begleitung sterbender und schwerst erkrankter Angehöriger: Gesetzliche Neuregelungen* (Caring for dying and seriously ill relatives: legal reforms), RdW 2002, 606; Jöst/Risak, *Aktuelle Neuerungen im Arbeitsrecht* (Recent innovations in labour law), ZAS 2002, 97; Ercher, *Fragen zur Famienhospizkarenz* (Questions about family compassionate leave), ASoK 2003, 74; Mazal, *Familienhospizkarenz, Fragen der Rechtsdurchsetzung* (Family compassionate leave, implementation issues), Ecolex 2003, 9; Ruhm/Petzl, *Familienhospizkarenz*, SoSi 2003, 173.

292   Also: Cerny, *Urlaubsrecht* (Leave entitlement), 2002, 203 ff.; Kuderna, *Urlaubsrecht*, 1995, 205.

293   RV 1045 BlgNR 21. GP 6.

the employee's job, a special protection against redundancy and dismissal has been created. It starts with the notification of the compassionate leave and lasts for up to four weeks after the leave period has ended (§15 of the AVRAG).

Finally, **social security support measures** provide that employees are covered during the period of compassionate leave (in particular, §§29 to 32 of the *Arbeitslosenversicherungsgesetz* – Unemployment Insurance Act). These persons thus continue to be covered by health insurance and they acquire pension contributions of at least the level of the compensation premium guidance rate (2003: EUR 643.54).[294]

3. Inclusion of all earned income for social security purposes

With the 1996 *Strukturanpassungsgesetz* (Federal Gazette 201/1996), Austria took the first steps towards making **all earned income** subject to statutory social security contributions. The aim was, firstly, to offer all wage and salary earners social protection and, secondly, to prevent a '**flight from social law**', as ever more services are being provided in 'social insurance-free' employment relationships. The Constitutional Court banned some of these arrangements as anticonstitutional.[295] Next the *Arbeits- und Sozialrechtsänderungsgesetz* (ASRÄG – Labour and Social Law Modification Act) 1997[296] brought a successful restructuring of compulsory social insurance for occupations with self-employment elements. Broadly speaking, compulsory insurance for **the self-employed** now comes under the *Allgemeines Sozialversicherungsgesetz* (ASVG – General Social Security Act). This

applies to workers and employees because, as they provide their services in the context of a permanent debt relationship, they are related to 'traditional' workers. One new feature was the creation of the category of the '**new self-employed**', who are closer to entrepreneurs and therefore came under the Social Security Act for freelance workers in the industrial sector (GSVG). For these groups of people, social protection under the statutory health, pension and accident insurance funds has existed only since 1998.

3.1. Social protection for economically dependent workers

By law, the self-employed are subject to social security contributions if (1) the services they provide to clients are in the context of the latters' business or their business licence or their occupational authorisation or field of activity as laid down by their statute, where (2) this activity yields an income, (3) the service is, in principle, performed in person, and (4) no significant own production facilities exist (§4(4) of the ASVG).[297]

3.2. Social protection for the 'new self-employed'

The 'new self-employed' (without a specific business authorisation, which would normally bring membership of the Chamber of Commerce and thus also compulsory insurance in the GSVG) were included in the GSVG.[298] The insurance obligation applies to all self-employed persons who, through their work,[299] earn income from self-employment and/or business activity, as long as no insurance obligation has already arisen in

---

294   See Müller, *Sozialversicherungsrechtliche Auswirkungen der Familienhospizkarenz* (Social security implications of family compassionate leave), ASoK 2003, 106.

295   Constitutional Court 14.3.1997 ZAS 1997/17 (see Aigner, 'Das VfGH-Erkenntnis zur sog Werkvertragsregelung' (the Constitutional Court's findings on Contracts for Work) ZAS 1997, 129) = ASoK 1997, 152 = ARD 4830/31/97; for the old legal situation, see A. Radner, *Sozialversicherungsrecht* (Social security law) – in brief 1999, 58.1.

296   Federal Gazette No 139/1997. See Grillberger/Mosler, *Sozialversicherung für Dienstnehmer und Selbständige* (Social security for workers and self-employed) (1998); Schrank, *Werkverträge und freie Dienstverträge* (Contracts for work and service contracts)2, 1998; Adametz/Schachinger/Sedlacek/Souhrada, *Handbuch Werkverträge* (Handbook of contracts for work)(looseleaf); Krejci, *Das 'Werkvertrags'-Erkenntnis des VfGH und der künftige Geltungsbereich des ASVG* (Contracts for work – findings of the Constitutional Court and the future scope of the General Social Security Act) VRdSch 1997, 78; Schrammel, *Vom 'Werkvertragserkenntnis' zur umfassenden Sozialversicherungspflicht* (From contracts for work to a comprehensive social security obligation), ASoK 1997, 333; Schrank, *Ausgewählte Rechts- und Praxisfragen zur neuen GSVG-Werkvertragsregelung* (Selected legal and practical issues associated with the new GSVG – 'Contract for work' regulations), ASoK 1997, 374 (376); Tomandl, *Rechtsprobleme einer umfassenden Sozialversicherung* (Legal problems with comprehensive social security), ZAS 1998, 9; Mosler/Glück, *Einbeziehung aller Erwerbseinkommen in die Sozialversicherung* (Inclusion of all earned income for social security purposes). Selected problems with the new arrangements, *RdW* 1998, 78, 141; Runggaldier, *Probleme der Einführung einer alle Erwerbseinkommen umfassenden Sozialversicherungspflicht* (Problems associated with introducing a comprehensive social security obligation for all earned income), ÖJZ 1998, 494; Pöltner, *Die Einbeziehung aller Erwerbseinkommen in die Sozialversicherung* (Inclusion of all earned income for social security purposes), DRdA 1998, 316.

297   See the table in A. Radner, *Sozialversicherungsrecht – kurz gefasst* (Social security law – in brief) 2003, 58.3 und 58.13; Grillberger, *Österreichisches Sozialrecht* (Austrian Social Law), 1998, 16.

298   See A. Radner, *Sozialversicherungsrecht* (Social security law – in brief) 2003, 58.15; Grillberger, *Österreichisches Sozialrecht* (Austrian social law) 17 f.; Binder/Radner, *Österreichisches Sozialrecht* 22.

299   See Schrank, *Ausgewählte Rechts- und Praxisfragen zur neuen GSVG-Werkvertragsregelung* (Selected legal and practice issues regarding the new GSVG contracts for work arrangements), ASoK 1997, 374 (376); Mosler/Glück, *Einbeziehung aller Erwerbseinkommen in die Sozialversicherung* (Inclusion of all earned income for social security purposes); Selected problems with the new arrangements, *RdW* 1998, 78, 141.

the corresponding insurance sector(s) (§2(1)(4) of the GSVG). The 'new self-employed' include psychologists, psychotherapists and physiotherapists, authors, speakers, ski and sports instructors, experts and persons running their own business without a specific authorisation, such as those working in the shadow economy. Since 2001, freelance artists have also belonged to this social security group.

However, certain insurance thresholds apply. If only income as a 'new self-employed person' is taken into account, the threshold is EUR 6 453.36 per annum. This threshold is EUR 3 712.56 if other income is earned (2003 figures).[300]

The current plan is to introduce voluntary unemployment insurance for freelance workers and the self-employed.

3.3. Social protection for small-scale part-time workers

If a person's income from one or more employment relationships as an employee or freelance worker is under the minimum threshold (2003: EUR 309.38 per month), there is no statutory social security obligation for health and pension insurance (§5(1)(2) of the ASVG). There is merely a partial inclusion in the accident insurance scheme. For this the employer has to pay social security contributions of only 1.4% of the pay. For this group of low income earners, the law assumes that their work is not their main source of income, but rather that their main source of income comes from someone else, normally a family member through whom social protection is also available.

However, this is not the case for employees or self-employed people who do several part-time jobs in parallel and whose total income exceeds this threshold. Moreover, employers were starting to employ several part-time workers in order to save on social security contributions. A serious lack of provision became apparent for the growing number of part-time workers (often with several part-time jobs)

who, up until the 1997 ASRÄG (Labour and Social Law Modification Act), had had little social protection.

The legislator therefore decided to restructure the social security system for part-time workers from 1 January 1998 with the 1997 ASRÄG (Labour and Social Law Modification Act). If the total amount of income from several part-time jobs exceeds the minimum threshold, health and pension insurance is compulsory under the ASVG (General Social Security Act) (i.e. no unemployment cover).[301] If the total income does not reach the threshold, employees resident in Austria can opt to insure themselves cheaply (2003: EUR 43.65 per month) for health and pension cover (§19a of the ASVG).[302] In this way, part-time workers obtain the same social security protection as those who are compulsorily insured. In particular they gain periods of contribution towards their pension insurance.

For part-time workers, the obligations on employers and workers to make contributions must be considered separately.[303] Workers pay their own social security contributions. Regardless of whether the insurance contributions are compulsory for the part-time worker in question or not, the employer must pay the 'flat-rate employer's contribution'[304] if he has employed several part-time workers whose total wages exceed 150% of the minimum threshold. In this case, the employer has to pay 17.8% of the monthly wages of his part-time workers as social security contributions.

4. Introduction of childcare allowance

Federal Gazette I No 103/2001 introduced a new family benefit, **childcare allowance**, for all children born after 1 January 2002.[305] This new benefit replaced the previous parental leave allowance,[306] which was designed as an insurance payment and paid in the event of the loss of earned income for childcare reasons. The new childcare allowance is in contrast not at all linked to previous employment.

---

300 §4(1)5 and 6 of the GSVG.

301 §5(1)2 in conjunction with §5(2) of the ASVG; see the table in A. Radner, *Sozialversicherungsrecht – kurz gefasst 2003*, 58.5; also Binder/Radner, *Österreichisches Sozialrecht* (Austrian Social Law) 21 f.

302 See also Runggaldier, *Probleme der Einführung einer alle Erwerbseinkommen umfassenden Sozialversicherungspflicht* (The problems of introducing a comprehensive social security obligation for all earned income), ÖJZ 1998, 494; Risak, *Das 'Opting-In' in der Sozialversicherung* (Opting into social security), Ecolex 1998, 336.

303 See the table in A. Radner, *Sozialversicherungsrecht – kurz gefasst 2003*, 58.15.

304 §53a of the ASVG; see Mosler/Glück, *Einbeziehung aller Erwerbseinkommen in die Sozialversicherung* (Inclusion of all earned income for social security purposes). Selected problems with the new arrangements, RdW 1998, 78 (83), 141; Karl, *Die Einbeziehung geringfügig Beschäftigter in die Sozialversicherung* (The inclusion of part-time workers in social security), ASoK 1997, 383.

305 See Ehmer/Lamplmayr/Mayr/Nöstlinger/Reiter/Stummer, *Kinderbetreuungsgeldgesetz* (Child Care Allowance Act) (2002); Mayr, *Offene Fragen zur Anspruchsberechtigung nach dem Kinderbetreuungsgeldgesetz* (Unresolved issues concerning eligibility for child care allowance), ASoK 2001, 276; Burger-Ehrnhofer, *Ab 1.1.2002: Das Kinderbetreuungsgeld* (Child care allowance), RdW 2002/27; Rauch, *Zur freiwilligen Verlängerung der Karenzzeit für Mütter bzw Väter* (Voluntary extension of parental leave for mothers or fathers), ASoK 2002, 106; ibid., *Dauer der Karenz und Kinderbetreuungsgeld* (Duration of parental leave and child care allowance), ARD 5379/3/2003.

306 See Dirschmied, *Karenzgeldgesetz* (Parental Leave Allowance Act), 2000.

Childcare allowance, which normally amounts to EUR 14.53 per day, is, in principle, open to all parents eligible for family allowance. However, only one parent is eligible – in cases of doubt, the parent who does the majority of the childcare. It can alternate between the parents, but may only switch twice per child, and the minimum period before a switch is allowed is three months. It can be drawn until the child is 36 months old, unless only one parent draws it, in which case it can be drawn only until the child is 30 months old. This provides an incentive for fathers to also take on childcare.

Compared to the old system, the scope of the new childcare allowance has been extended in several ways. Firstly, it has been extended with regard to the personal scope of the allowance. Now housewives, students and schoolgirls are entitled to it, whereas formerly they would have been excluded if they had not been in work beforehand. It also represents a bonus for the self-employed and farmers' wives, who, in the past, were entitled only to partial benefits of half the parental leave allowance. Moreover, the drawing period for the allowance has been increased from 16 or 22 months to 30 or 36 months, in order to increase financial security in the early stages of starting a family.[307] Finally, the extra earnings ceiling for the allowance was raised from the low-income threshold to EUR 14 600 per annum. The aim of this was to allow people greater freedom to structure their lives, in the interests of better reconciling work and family. In particular, the idea was to help people to stay in contact with their employer during the childcare period – through part-time working, for instance – in order to facilitate subsequent (gradual) reintegration into working or a first job, or to remain gainfully employed.[308]

The most important social security accompanying measures are health insurance, linked to the childcare allowance, and the decision to count the first 18 months of the childcare period as a pension contribution period. The main criticism of the new system is that the protection against dismissal and redundancy in the case of parental leave will still run out four weeks after the child's second birthday, so there is no harmonisation with the extended period for drawing childcare allowance. The same applies for parental leave under labour law for workers (several aspects of which are legally relevant), which can also be claimed only until the child's second birthday (§15 of the MSchG; §2 VKG).

5. Introduction of care allowance

In 1993, the Federal and State Governments agreed a new system of reimbursement for care expenses. This system was implemented by the *Bundespflegegeldgesetz* (BPGG – Federal Care Allowance Act; Federal Gazette 110/1993) and nine essentially identical regional Acts.[309] It was decided that the Federal Government would be responsible for all cases where the basic benefit (*Pension, Rente, Ruhegenuss*) is based on federal law. And the *Länder* would be responsible for those cases where no basic benefit exists or where the basic benefit is based on a regional law.[310]

According to §1 of the BPGG, the aim of care allowance is to ensure that people needing care are looked after properly and given the opportunity to lead an independent life in accordance with their needs. A flat-rate contribution to care-related expenses is to achieve this. The care allowance is intended to allow them to stay in their own homes and buy in the necessary care services, helping them to live an independent life.[311]

The allowance is granted at **seven levels**, depending on the degree of need and therefore the number of hours of care required. The eligibility criterion for the lowest level is that the person in question will probably require at least 50 hours' care per month for at least six months because of a physical, mental, psychological or sensory disability. Care allowance of EUR 145.40 per month is paid for this level. At the highest level, the allowance is EUR 1 531.50. The condition for this level is a need for at least 180 hours' care per month because of loss of functional movement in all four limbs or an equivalent situation.

The care allowance is funded not by contributions but from the Federal and *Länder* budgets. It is therefore not an insurance benefit in the narrow sense. It is however often granted as an addition to a social security basic allowance, whereupon it becomes an allowance based on social insurance.[312] In such cases, it is limited by law to persons whose normal place of residence is in Austria (§3(1) of the BPGG). This is however contrary to European law.[313]

---

307 RV 620 BlgNR 21. GP 55.

308 RV 620 BlgNR 21. GP 55; see also: Schäffer-Ziegler, Aspekte des *'Zuverdienstes' im neuen Kinderbetreuungsgeldgesetz* (The 'extra job' aspect of the Child Care Allowance Act), ÖJZ 2002, 16.

309 See Gruber/Pallinger, *Kommentar zum BPGG* (Commentary on the BPGG), 1994; Pfeil, *Neuregelung der Pflegevorsorge in Österreich* (New care system in Austria), 1994; ibid., *Bundespflegegeldgesetz und landesgesetzliche Pflegegeldregelungen* (Federal Care Allowance Act and regional care allowance schemes), 1996.

310 Tomandl, *Grundriss des österreichischen Sozialrechts* (Outline of Austrian social law), 2002, 240.

311 RV 776 BlgNR 18. GP.

312 See Resch, *Sozialrecht,* 2001, 156.

313 European Court of Justice, 8.3.2001 (Jauch case) DRdA 2001, 579 (Windisch-Graetz) = RdW 2001, 322 (Resch); Tomandl, *Grundriss des österreichischen Sozialrechts* (Outline of Austrian social law) 240; Resch, *Sozialrecht* 152; Binder, *Österreichisches Sozialrecht* (Austrian social law) 105.

6. Planned changes to pension insurance

The parliament is about to decide upon a radical shake-up of pension law, to the detriment of beneficiaries. The public discussion about the need for the planned cuts was very controversial. Indeed the government only toned down its original plans in the face of joint action by the social partners and intervention by the Federal President, accompanied by two days of strikes organised by the trade unions throughout Austria. Despite the most serious industrial action of the last forty years in Austria, employees and employers kept their heads and, thanks to their reasonableness, the social peace in Austria was not seriously undermined. It is worth noting that this comprehensive and extremely important pension reform (in terms of its impact and contents) will be decided upon as one of many points in the 2003 *Budgetbegleitgesetz* (Budget Accompanying Law), through which a total of 85 laws are to be amended!

6.1. Main points of the pension reform

The main points of the pension reform are likely to be the following:[314]

- A **replacement rate** of 80% on the basis of life income after 45 years' contributions, with a retirement age of 65 years for men and women.

- **Raising the early retirement age** (currently 61.5 years for men and 56.5 years for women), starting in 2004, in steps of four months, whereby the early retirement pension in the case of a long insurance period is to be scrapped in 2013 and 2017 for men and women respectively.

- **Lowering the amount of the increment** (currently, a person receives 2% of the calculation basis for each contribution year) to 1.78% per year in five annual steps beginning in 2004, so that, after 45 contribution years, 80% of the calculation basis is reached.

- **Extending the calculation period** for the calculation basis from the best 15 or 18 income years to 40 years. This brings the Austrian pension model more into line with the calculation method used for the German pension system. However, it should be remembered that Austrian pensioners – in contrast to German pensioners – have to pay income tax and that, until 1996, the total

income tax paid by ASVG pensioners was higher than the federal subsidy to these pensions.

- As it is usually women who take a **career break to care for children**, increasing the calculation basis to 40 years is disproportionately hard on them, as the pension contributions accumulated during the childcare period are only small. For this reason, the calculation period for periods over 15 years will be shortened by three years per child. Although the same problem exists for those working part-time for childcare reasons, no measures to help them were put forward.

- **Raising the calculation basis** for the maximum four-year imputation of childcare periods per child by a total of 50% by 2028 (current calculation basis: EUR 643.54 per month).

- **Deductions** of 4.2% of gross pension per year if the old-age pension is drawn early, before the standard pension age (65 for men, 60 for women), or bonuses of 4.2% if the old-age pension is drawn later.

- Capping of any losses caused by the reform, with a maximum **loss ceiling** of 10% compared to the current pension system. However, those now under 35 years old are not covered – they are hit by the full effect of the pension reform. A hardship fund is to be set up for those whose gross pension is less than EUR 1 000, in order to compensate for any individual cases of hardship caused by the changes.

- **Raising the pension-accumulating proportion** of the childcare period from 18 to 24 months. However, this measure applies only to periods when childcare allowance is drawn (see Chapter IV, from 1.1.2002).

- **Postponement of the pension increase** in the calendar year following retirement.

- Improved **revaluation of future contribution periods** from 2004, taking into account wage developments. One problem, however, is that the revaluation factors for the previous periods are completely insufficient,[315] which means that, if the calculation period is extended, there will be a further cut in pensions.

- The details of the politically controversial '**Hackler system**', i.e. the issue of different pension rights for people with 45 (men) or 40 (women) years of contributions

---

314   Taken mainly from the offer made by the Federal Chancellor and the Deputy Chancellor to the social partners on 27 May 2003.

315   See also Tomandl, *Die Vorschläge der Pensionsreformkommission* (The proposals of the pension reform committee), SoSi 2003, 96 (98).

(employed continuously for 45 or 40 years), will not be dealt with here, because of a lack of relevance with regard to the figures.

- Those just starting their working life and employed people under 35 years old are to be incorporated in a **new standard pension system** based on the ASVG framework conditions from 2004.

- Creation of a **contribution-based personal pension account** with performance-based components. However, the question of which performance-related components will be used has still not been decided. The *Bundesarbeitskammer* takes the view that the pension account should not be contribution-based, as this passes on the risks of demographic trends to each generation reaching pension age, but rather performance-based, in order to safeguard the living standards principle, whereby a demography-dependent federal contribution would be paid.

- Once the Barcelona objective on the employment of older workers has been reached, the idea of creating a **pension corridor with a 'no-claims bonus' system** to allow people to decide for themselves when to retire, using the standard pension age of 65 years as a baseline, should be considered.

6.2. Impact of the pension reform

The main effects of the pension reform can be summarised as follows: the worsening of the situation affects all three possible components of the pension calculation: (1) lower increments for calculating the amount of pension in percentage terms, (2) a longer calculation period and consequently smaller calculation basis, and finally (3) maintenance of the low revaluation factors for previous contribution periods (these were designed for a calculation period of the best 15 or 18 years). As the current average gross pension under the ASVG is EUR 1 076 and the highest amount possible is EUR 2 364.49 (both 14 times per year) and the loss for those retiring from 2028 onwards will be some 25% to 30%, according to the calculations of the *Bundesarbeitskammer*, there is a risk that a large proportion of the Austrian population will suffer old-age poverty.[316] Given that – as shown – the younger generation will bear the brunt of the losses, even if they make the same con-

tributions, the phrase 'pension reform' sounds euphemistic at best. Moreover, the bad experiences with corporate pension fund law (those with company pensions in contribution-based systems are currently facing significant pension cuts) clearly demonstrate that a pension model based on investments on the financial markets in accordance with the funding principle is completely insufficient for safeguarding pensions over the long term. Furthermore, many workers do not have the necessary capital to invest in a private pension scheme.

The scrapping of early retirement, meaning that everyone now has to retire at 65, is justified in the public discussion by claiming that, because of the low birth rate, sufficient jobs will be available even for older workers in the future and that, moreover, these older workers will be urgently needed in a few years. It goes without saying that claims of this kind are more accurate for the near future than for the more distant future. A look at the development of the Federal Government's contribution to pension insurance as a percentage of GDP shows that there is no need for the current pension reform - on this scale at any rate. The impact of the 2000 pension reform alone has led to a drop in federal funding for statutory pension insurance (measured as a percentage of GDP) from 3.1% in 2003 to 2.9% in 2007.[317] Assuming that the Federal Government were prepared to maintain this percentage, there would have been enough time to create labour market policy incentives to increase employment among older workers (for the current plans, see section 10.9 below) and subsequently implement a pension reform based on the impact of these incentives and more up-to-date demographic and economic forecasts.

Whilst the objectives of the Lisbon European Council (March 2000) and the Stockholm European Council (March 2001), to raise the employment rate for older workers, are welcome in principle and can be implemented by labour market policy measures, the socio-political aim of the objective of the Barcelona European Council (March 2002) to raise the average pension age by five years by 2010 is puzzling (in Sweden, it would mean raising the pension age from 63.4 years now to 68.4 years).[318] Raising the pension age does not affect the social budget at all if loss of income for people stopping work before pension age – as a result of old-age unemployment or ill health – is compensated for by other social benefits, such as unemployment benefit, income support or social assistance. The only way to sensibly raise the employment rate for older people is through employment incentives; linking it to pension law is not the right way to proceed.

---

316 For existing old-age poverty, caused by cuts in the income replacement rate of pensions, see: Kohmaier, *Pensionsversicherung: Unfinanzierbar oder doch nicht? Eine Begriffsklärung* (Pension insurance: unfundable or not? An explanation) SoSi 2003, 140; *Zum System der Nettoanpassung und der diesbezüglichen Reformmöglichkeiten* (On the net adjustment system and the related reform possibilities): Stefanits, *Überlegungen zu einer Neugestaltung der Pensionsanpassung* (Considerations on a restructuring of pension adjustment), SoSi 2003, 124.

317 Table 1, page 47 of the draft report of 31 March 2003, GZ 21.119/8-1/03.

318 See Pöltl/Spiegel/Stefanits, *Die europäische Dimension der österreichischen Pensionsdiskussion* (The European dimension of the Austrian pension debate), SoSi 2003, 56 (63).

7. Further steps towards equalising the legal position of blue-collar and white-collar workers

The 2000 *Arbeitsrechtsänderungsgesetz* (ARÄG – Labour Law Amendment Act, Federal Gazette I No 44/2000) took steps to equalise the legal position of these two categories.[319]

7.1. Towards equal sick pay and accident pay

In the area of **sick pay and accident pay**, most of the provisions of the *Angestelltengesetz* (Employees Act) were extended to also include blue-collar workers, through an amendment to the *Entgeltfortzahlungsgesetz* (EFZG – Continuation of Payment Act).[320] This represented an improvement for blue-collar workers. The previous 14-day waiting period was scrapped. The payment period was extended to six weeks (or eight weeks after an industrial accident) after five years' service, ten weeks after fifteen years' service and twelve weeks after twenty five years' service. Furthermore for the first time, there was an entitlement to half-pay for each further four-week period. However, two differentiating elements were maintained: the different method of calculation in the event of repeated inability to work within a year and – at least in practice – the non-eligibility for half-pay for four weeks and the limit of ten weeks on sick pay after fifteen years' service in the event of an industrial accident. Although the latter is covered by the wording of the Act, it leads to the perverse situation that, after fifteen years' service, a blue-collar worker is entitled to better sick pay for illness than for an industrial accident.

7.2. Dissolution of the sick pay reimbursement fund

Moreover, the **reimbursement fund** for sick pay in the event of workers' illness or accident was dissolved. Whilst the employers of white-collar workers have always had to pay sick pay from their own funds, blue-collar workers were covered until 30 September 2000 by a kind of statutory sick pay insurance. Up to this date, employers paid 2.1% of the ASVG contribution basis for each worker to the sick pay reimbursement fund. In return, they received from the fund a reimbursement of the worker's pay, plus a flat-rate sum to cover social security contributions and taxes. For large companies only, just 70% of sick pay was reimbursed.

Under the new rules, employers now have to continue to fund sick pay for blue-collar workers, as well as for white-collar workers, from their own resources. For small companies in particular, this can lead to financial problems, as they try to come up with both the sick pay for the worker in question and extra money to cover the cost of a replacement worker, so that their orders can still be met on time. Under Austrian law, employers who dismiss employees during a period of sick leave have to continue to pay sick pay beyond the termination of employment. In order to circumvent this continuing payment obligation it has become common, since the law was changed, to create mutual agreements between employers and sick workers to terminate the employment relationship (and then re-engage the worker when he or she has recovered. This leads to a further burden on the statutory sick pay system, which is already in the red. In principle, it does not have to pay sick pay under social security law as long as the employer is obliged to do so. However, the health insurance boards have started to refuse sick pay under these circumstances, on the grounds that a mutual agreement to end the employment relationship during the period of illness constitutes an illegitimate contract to the detriment of third parties. In such cases, workers receive no compensation for the loss of wages during their illness.

The resulting request by the employee representation bodies has so far not been met. They want the state to reinstate the sick pay reimbursement fund. Some employers also supported this request because private insurance policies providing the same cover charged not 2.1% but rather around 5% of wages.

8. Restricting claims in the event of an employment relationship ending

The ARÄG (Labour Law Amendment Act) 2000 also limited the rights of workers upon termination of their contract, in addition to the amendments described in section 7 above.

---

319   See Drs, *Neues aus dem Arbeits- und Sozialrecht: Das Arbeitsrechtsänderungsgesetz 2000* (Labour and social law news: the Arbeitsrechtsänderungsgesetz 2000), RdW 2000/453; Mayerhofer, *Arbeitsrechts-Änderungsgesetz 2000* (ARÄG 2000) infas 2000, 119; Kaun, *Änderungen im Arbeits- und Sozialrecht ab 1.1.2001* (Changes to labour law and social law from 1.1.2001), ASoK 2001, 2.

320   See Cerny/Kallab, *Entgeltfortzahlungsgesetz* (Continuation of Payment Act), 2001, 63 ff.

8.1. Loss of 'job-search days' where the employee gives notice

An employee's entitlement to job-search time during the notice period has been scrapped completely where it is the employee who has terminated the employment relationship. In the past, this entitlement was four hours per week for full-time employees. From now on, only employees whose employer has given them notice are entitled, if they so request, to take off a minimum of a fifth of their regular working time per week with no loss of pay.[321]

8.2. Restricting payment in lieu of unused leave

Furthermore, the abolition of *Urlaubsentschädigung* and the introduction of *Urlaubsersatzleistung* have, in many cases, significantly restricted the entitlement of employees to payment in lieu of unused leave at the end of an employment relationship. Under the old system, employees were entitled to payment for unused leave if the employment relationship had been terminated in particular ways (e.g. non-blame dismissal, justified resignation, notice given by the employer and – if more than half of the leave year had passed – lapse of time, mutual termination, employee resignation from the second year of service onwards). The new system, however, requires that the amount of leave taken be compared with the amount that should have been taken given the proportion of the leave year that has already elapsed. In the event of a dismissal for misconduct or an unjustified resignation, any excess leave taken must be 'refunded' (§10 of the *Urlaubsgesetz* (Leave Act) in the version published in Federal Gazette I No 44/2000).[322]

It should be noted that the reforms described in sections VII and VIII above are not related in substance but have still been linked by the legislator in financial terms. The bill, for example, states that 'When the extra burden on employers caused by the adjustment of sick pay rules is seen in the context of the unburdening of employers as a result of the new leave provisions and the scrapping of the job-search

days, it is evident that no additional burden on employers but rather an alleviation of incidental wage costs is to be expected.'[323]

9. Ban on discrimination and information obligation in the case of fixed-term employment relationships

The addition of §2b to the AVRAG (*Arbeitsvertragsrechts-Anpassungsgesetz* – Employment Contract Law Amendment Act) (Federal Gazette I No 52/2002) created a ban on discrimination and an information obligation for fixed-term employment relationships, according to which employees on a fixed-term contract should not be disadvantaged compared to those on a permanent contract, except on objective grounds (paragraph 1 of the ban on discrimination). Moreover, employers must inform fixed-term workers about any vacancies for permanent positions. This information must be provided through general announcements at suitable, easily accessible locations (paragraph 2: information obligation).

§2b of the AVRAG transposed Council Directive 1999/70/EC of 28 June 1999 concerning fixed-term work into Austrian law, although Jöst/Risak, in the light of the jurisprudence of the European Court of Justice, take the view that Austrian legislation demonstrates shortcomings with regard to the *pro-rata-temporis* principle (§4(2) of the Annex to Directive 1999/70/EC) and measures to prevent the misuse of successive employment contracts (§5 of the Annex to Directive 1999/70/EC).[324]

10. Labour market policy

The following section provides only a summarised, but by no means comprehensive, description of the many measures taken in the context of Austrian labour market policy.[325]

---

321   See Trattner, *Wann haben Arbeitnehmer Anspruch auf bezahlte Freizeit? Neuerungen aufgrund des Arbeitsrechtsänderungsgesetzes 2000* (When are employees entitled to paid time off? Amendments introduced by the Arbeitsrechtsänderungsgesetz), ASoK 2001, 144.

322   See Schindler, *Ansprüche bei Beendigung des Arbeitsverhältnisses* (Entitlements upon termination of an employment relationship), in Mazal/Risak, *Das Arbeitsrecht* (Labour law) (2002) 135 ff.; Kaszanits, *Das Arbeitsrechtsänderungsgesetz 2000 – ARÄG 2000: Soziale Gerechtigkeit am Arbeitsplatz* (Social justice at the workplace), ASoK 2000, 235.

323   RV 91 BlgNR 21. GP 14.

324   Jöst/Risak, *Aktuelle Neuerungen im Arbeitsrecht* (Current innovations in labour law), ZAS 2002, 97.

325   For the most recent detailed measures in unemployment insurance, which cannot be discussed here: Ch. Klein, *Abänderungsantrag zur 'Erhöhung der sozialen Treffsicherheit'* (Amendment to increase social precision) ASoK 2000, 441, gives an excellent overview.

10.1. Study leave

The 1997 *Arbeits- und Sozialrechtsänderungsgesetz* (ASRÄG – Labour and Social Law Amendment Act), Federal Gazette I No 139/1997,[326] gave employees the opportunity (under §11 of the AVRAG in conjunction with §§26 and 26a of the AlVG (*Arbeitslosenversicherungsgesetz* – Unemployment Insurance Act)), to take a course of vocational study funded by the public purse. As long as the employment relationship has lasted for a minimum of three uninterrupted years, **study leave** of between three months and one year can be agreed between the employer and the employee, with loss of pay. However, whether or not employees have a legal entitlement to study leave is unclear.[327] If the conditions of §11 of the AVRAG are met and employees prove their attendance at a course, they are entitled to a further training allowance under the unemployment insurance system.

10.2. Unpaid leave

The 1997 ASRÄG also created the legal basis for combining personal leave with the employment of a replacement member of staff funded by the public purse. Leave agreed for between six months and one year, with loss of pay (§12 of the AVRAG), may be eligible for support from the labour market service. The employee to whom leave has been granted receives a further training allowance from the unemployment insurance, as long as the employer recruits a replacement worker who was previously drawing unemployment benefit or income support for more hours than the part-time threshold. (§§26, 26a of the AlVG). Moreover, in this case the employer could also apply for support in the form of a recruitment grant.[328] In practice, this measure has very rarely been used.

10.3. The solidarity premium model

The 1997 ASRÄG also introduced the 'solidarity premium model', the general aim of which is to encourage a number of workers to **voluntarily** cut their working time for a given period in order to facilitate the recruitment of new workers. The labour market service reimburses some of the resulting loss of pay. The more detailed conditions for the solidarity premium model are set out in a collective agreement or in a

company agreement, if the collective agreement does not contain any relevant provisions or is not applied. However, actually cutting the hours of individual workers requires individual agreements between employers and employees within the framework of the collective agreement or company agreement. Originally, the workers involved would receive a solidarity premium equivalent to a proportionate amount of the corresponding unemployment benefit, depending on the number of hours lost. Since 1 January 2000, 'solidarity premium model allowances' have instead been paid to the employer, as long as he makes up some of the loss of wages and employs replacement workers (who were previously drawing unemployment benefit or income support) to cover the working time that has thus been released (§37a of the AMSG).

10.4. Enforceable claim to reduced working hours in the case of progressive retirement

The 1997 ASRÄG introduced an **enforceable right** to shorter working hours in the context of progressive retirement, taking into account the interests of the employee and of the business, in companies with more than ten employees (§14(1) of the AVRAG).

10.5. Reduction in normal working hours with 'severance pay protection'

A final reform introduced by the 1997 ASRÄG, pursuant to §14(2) and (4) of the AVRAG, is the possibility of an agreement between an employer and an employee to reduce the normal working time whilst maintaining the statutory severance pay protection. Such agreements can only be made if the employee is either (1) 50 years or older or (2) has to care permanently for a close relative. If the shorter working hours have applied for less than two years, the previous, effective working time (rather than the agreed shorter working time) must be used as the basis for calculating the relevant monthly wage for the severance pay. However, if the agreement lasted longer than two years, the average working hours over the relevant years of service are used. This provision applies also to the solidarity premium model and, similarly, to study leave.

---

326   For all the measures in the ASRÄG 1997 see: Jabornegg/Resch, *Rechtsfragen des ASRÄG* (Legal issues concerning the ASRÄG) 1997 (1998); Tomandl, *Neue österreichische Ansätze zur Flexibilisierung der Arbeitszeit* (New Austrian approaches to working time flexibilisation), FS Zöllner (1998) 965; Mitter, *Bildungskarenz, Freistellung gegen Entfall des Entgelts und Solidaritätsprämie* (Study leave, unpaid leave and solidarity premium), RdW 1998, 554; Ch. Klein, *Neues aus der Gesetzgebung* (New legislation), ASoK, 1999, 228; Schwarz, *Nochmals: Das AVRAG im Zwielicht!* (Once again: the AVRAG under suspicion) RdW 2000, 27.

327   See Binder, AVRAG 397.

328   See Binder, AVRAG 413 and 417; Holzer/Reissner, *Arbeitsvertragsrechts-Anpassungsgesetz* (218).

10.6. Old-age part-time allowance

The old-age part-time allowance was first introduced in Federal Gazette I No 179/1999 under the name *Altersteilzeitbeihilfe* as one of the measures to combat unemployment among older people.[329] The old-age part-time allowance received its current form in the *Sozialrechts-Änderungsgesetz* (Social Law Amendment Act) 2000, Federal Gazette I No 92/2000. According to §27 of the AlVG, the employer is entitled to old-age part-time allowance from the labour market service where an older worker reduces his or her working time and receives compensation for loss of earnings from the employer. This allowance can be paid for a maximum of 6 $\frac{1}{2}$ years for women aged 50 years or more and for men aged 55 or more, provided that they were employed and paid unemployment benefit contributions for at least 15 out of the last 25 years and their normal working time (which may not be less than 80% of the normal working time agreed by statute or collective agreement) is reduced to between 40% and 60%. The employer must furthermore pay compensation for at least 50% of the loss of earnings caused by the reduction in the number of working hours. Social security contributions have to be paid in accordance with the calculation basis before the reduction, and severance pay must also be calculated in accordance with the working hours before the reduction. The old-age part-time allowance reimburses the cost to the employer of paying compensation of half the difference between the wages before and after the reduction of working time and social security contributions based on the normal working time before the reduction.

This scheme has proved very popular in practice, as the reduction of working time required by law can also be realised over a particular calculation period. It is possible, for instance, to agree 'block leave'[330] (e.g. for a six-year old-age part-time agreement: three years full-time and three years off), which, in the final analysis, is the same as taking early retirement funded by the public purse, which, because of the continued full payment of social security contributions, does not even have a negative impact on pension entitlement. As the funding for this measure has now exploded, because of the high and ever increasing number of people taking advantage of it, certain restrictions are planned – to mention just the main ones: limiting the scheme to the last five years before pension age is reached; and introducing an obligation to employ a previously unemployed replacement in order to

allow the block leave model to be admissible and 100% reimbursement of the employer's extra costs.[331]

10.7. *Jugendausbildungs-Sicherungsgesetz (JASG – Youth Training Guarantee Act) and 'pre-apprenticeships'*

10.7.1. *The Jugendausbildungs-Sicherungsgesetz*

The *Jugendausbildungs-Sicherungsgesetz*[332] (JASG; Federal Gazette I No 91/1998) encouraged the placement of young people looking for an apprenticeship, as part of the **National Employment Action Plan** in Austria. Additional training is offered in regions with a particularly large imbalance between the supply of and demand for apprenticeships. This is done in the form of ten-month vocational training pre-apprenticeships as a labour market support measure for young people who find themselves at a disadvantage on the labour market and for those who could not find an apprenticeship.[333] *Land* project groups are responsible for setting and implementing policy in the individual *Bundesländer*. These training courses may not start before mid-November of any given year, so as not to compete with 'traditional' apprenticeships.[334] The conditions for participation are that; the young person in question must have completed compulsory education and be registered with the labour market service as looking for an apprenticeship; the labour market service sees no likelihood of finding an appropriate apprenticeship; or the young person has already made at least five independent applications and been unsuccessful (§5 of the JASG). The labour market service allocates the young people to training courses.

These courses are held over ten months and organised and implemented by parties who are not official employers of apprentices. The aim is to teach the skills and knowledge of the first year of an apprenticeship so that the young person can then switch to a proper apprenticeship in the second year. For any subsequent apprenticeship in the same trade, the initial training period is counted in full. In all other cases, a justifiable proportion is counted (§3(6) of the JASG). Participants can receive a special allowance of EUR 150 net per month.

The apprenticeship foundations gave courses in promising occupations organised by state-certified, licensed training

329   See Dirschmied, *Änderungen in der Arbeitslosenversicherung* (Changes to unemployment insurance), DRdA 2000, 189; Lutz/Gagawczuk, *Arbeitsmarktpolitische Begleitmaßnahmen zur Pensionsreform* (Labour market policy pension reform accompanying measures), infas 2000, 140; Höfle, *Altersteilzeitgeld* (Old-age part-time allowance), SWK 2000 S 776.

330   See Schrank, *Geblockte Altersteilzeit: Was heißt 'fortlaufende Entgeltzahlung'? Was gilt für den Urlaub?* ('Blocked' old-age part-time: what does 'uninterrupted payment of wages' mean? What about holiday leave?), Ecolex 2001, 79.

331   See RV 59 BlgNR 22. GP (Budgetbegleitgesetz 2003).

332   See Ch. Klein, *Jugendausbildungs-Sicherungsgesetz und Vorlehre* (Youth Training Guarantee Act and pre-apprenticeships), ASoK 1998, 278.

333   AB 1261 BlgNR 20. GP 2.

334   Löwe, *Jugendausbildungs-Sicherungsgesetz*, infas 1999, 35.

providers,[335] who were not official employers of apprentices. However, they were available only to youngsters who completed their compulsory education in 1998 and 1999. The aim was that, at the end of each learning year, at least a third of the participants should start a proper apprenticeship. Participants were eligible for a special training allowance of EUR 220 per month. This system was stopped in the end, as the employers were not keen on state-funded competition to traditional apprenticeships. This is all the more surprising as the lack of apprenticeships and the lack of skilled workers show clearly that employers are not doing enough to provide places for all those who want them.

10.7.2. Pre-apprenticeship

Pre-apprenticeships were also introduced by the amendment to the *Berufsausbildungsgesetz* (BAG - Vocational Training Act) (Federal Gazette I No 100/1998) on the basis of the **National Employment Action Plan**.[336] The aim of this measure is to better integrate disadvantaged young people who are difficult to place[337] in the world of work. A pre-apprenticeship is a paid employment relationship. The educational content of the first year of the pre-apprenticeship is imparted over a maximum of two years (with a possibility of an extension by one year), to facilitate disadvantaged young people's access or transfer to an apprenticeship (§8b of the BAG). If, upon completion of the pre-apprenticeship, the person concerned starts an apprenticeship in the same (or a related) trade, the pre-apprenticeship counts as six months' worth of credit towards the full apprenticeship. If the pre-apprenticeship is not finished but was followed for at least six months, the time spent in the company must count at least for 25%. Companies that are licensed to take apprentices and licensed training establishments, are entitled to provide pre-apprenticeship training. The obligation to take on the young person at the end of the pre-apprenticeship period applies only if the trainer does not inform him/her or his/her legal representative (in a way that can be proved) at least two months before the end of the contract that the pre-apprenticeship is to be terminated. Another feature is that unilateral termination of the pre-apprenticeship contract is possible for both parties during the first six months. A diploma listing the achievements of the pre-apprenticeship must be issued once it has been completed.[338]

10.8. Carrot-and-stick system for the recruitment and dismissal of older workers

Federal Gazette 153/1996 introduced a carrot-and-stick system for the recruitment or dismissal of employees aged over 50 via unemployment insurance contributions (§§5a and 5b of the *Arbeitsmarktpolitik-finanzierungsgesetz* – AMPFG – Labour Market Policy Funding Act). According to §5a of the AMPFG, the employer's contribution (3%) is not payable if the employer recruits someone who is older than 50 years (the carrot). There are just a few exceptions to prevent abuses. These are: a job with the same employer within the last three years; employment lasting less than a month; or change of jobs within the same group of companies.

Conversely, according to §5b of the AMPFG, employers have to pay higher contributions if a worker aged over 50 years, who has at least 10 years' service, is dismissed or made redundant (the stick). There are many exceptions here too. Broadly speaking dismissals are acceptable if the termination of the employment relationship is the employee's own fault; the employee has reached pensionable age; or is redeployed within a group; or the plant closes and no other employment is possible. The contribution itself must be paid as a total amount and rises with age and the number of years left until reaching pensionable age.

10.9. Current measures to increase the activity rate among older workers

The Austrian Federal Government's programme for the current 22nd legislative period includes measures to increase the activity rate for older workers. Under the 56/58 Plus project, there is a plan to reduce wage ancillary costs for over-56/58 year-olds of 3%, and for over-60 year-olds of around 10%. The idea is to scrap unemployment benefit contributions and, in some cases, accident insurance, Family Assistance Fund and insolvency insurance contributions for these workers. There are also plans for a training offensive for older workers and a legal entitlement to participate in training measures offered by the labour market service for unemployed people aged under-25 or over-50 who have not been offered suitable employment within eight weeks.

---

335   See §30 of the *Berufsausbildungsgesetz* (Vocational Training Act).
336   See, for more details, Berger/Fida/Gruber, *Berufsausbildungsgesetz*, 1994, 214a ff.
337   According to the Decree of the Federal Ministry of Economic Affairs and Labour of 13 July 2000, Zl 33.550/23-III/A/3/00, 'disadvantaged young people who are difficult to place' are those who are looking for an apprenticeship, have been registered with the labour market service for at least three months or have demonstrated that they have applied at least five times unsuccessfully for an apprenticeship. In addition, at least one of the following criteria must apply: (1) compulsory schooling entirely or partially at a special school or secondary school for pupils with special needs; (2) the young person has had to resit a class between grade 5 and 9 at least once; (3) school leaver with learning difficulties; (4) the young person has no school leaving certificate or a negative one; (5) the young person has already had to interrupt one course at technical college because of bad results.
338   See also Gittenberger, *Änderungen im Bereich der Lehrlingsausbildung und der Beschäftigung von Jugendlichen* (Changes in apprenticeships and the employment of young people), infas 2000, 149; ibid., *Novelle zum Berufsausbildungsgesetz*, infas 1999, 5.

Chapter III:
Summary

The main reforms since 1992 have taken place in the past six years. Essentially the reforms are confined, in accordance with the structures of Austrian labour law, to the legislation governing labour and social law. Like other Member States, Austria too has seen an increased focus on the interaction between labour law and social law. This can be seen particularly through measures taking into account the gainful income for social security matters and through measures to improve the employment rate of older workers. Reforms are often justified by considerations of fairness, but have mostly resulted in adjustments at the bottom or lower end (for example with regard to the new severance pay arrangements or to pension insurance) or an increase in contributions (e.g. obligatory insurance for all earnings).

Towards the end of the coalition between the Socialist Party of Austria (SPÖ) and the Austrian People's Party (ÖVP) (up to October 1999), the main emphasis was put on labour market reforms to promote the occupational integration of young people (Young People Training Guarantee Act, pre-apprenticeship) and the employment of older workers. More 'age-independent' labour market measures intended to encourage employment have hardly acquired any practical significance. Examples of these are 'educational leave', 'unpaid leave' and the 'solidarity premium model'. There has however been a very high acceptance of 'partial retirement'. This is presumably due to the fact that it in many cases amounts to a form of assisted 'pre-retirement model'.

The Austrian People's Party (ÖVP) and the Freedom Party of Austria (FPÖ), have a programme generally aimed at bringing about a 'turn-around' in Austria. Since the coalition of these parties there has been increasing intervention in existing substantive labour and social law. This has, however, led to little actual improvement in the legal position of employees. Improvements of the level of labour and social protection have been driven either by the requirements of European law (such as the prohibition of discrimination and the obligation to provide information in the case of fixed-term employment relationships) or considerations of family policy, as for example with family care leave or childcare allowance. However, even the childcare allowance has brought about only minor improvements compared to previous entitlements for female workers. The main beneficiaries are self-employed or non-active women. Equal status for manual and non-manual workers has not been properly implemented. A particular example of this is that the improvement to the law governing the 'entitlement to continued payment of wages in the event of illness' for manual workers has been offset by the negative practical impact of the abolition of the compensation fund. A result is that employers now often exert considerable pressure on sick workers to consent to termination of the employment relationship with a concomitant loss of entitlements (with re-employment when the illness is over). The abolition of job search days upon notice and further restrictions on compensation for unused holiday leave upon termination of the employment relationship were also detrimental to employees. Moreover, reductions in non-wage related labour costs to promote the Austrian economy only concerned costs borne by the employer.

More recently, attempts have also been made by the government to curtail the importance of Austria's tried and tested 'social partnership'. This is shown in particular by the current move to reform the pension system. This has led to the most significant industrial action and protest measures Austria has seen in the last 40 years. Nevertheless, the most significant reform of Austrian law in the past 20 years, i.e. the complete overhaul of the law governing severance pay in 2002, follows a model agreed by the social partners and consequently exhibits all the advantages of legislation based on the broadest possible consensus. This reform, while worsening the position of some individuals compared to the previous situation, introduces substantial improvements for both employees and employers, if it is considered globally.

A number of the (in some cases) very innovative reforms of Austrian labour and social law in the past decade clearly demonstrate that necessary legislative adjustments to changing economic circumstances are not necessarily associated with a deterioration in the level of labour and social protection. A prerequisite for this has been the sufficient involvement of both the labour and employer organisations in the legislative process and their readiness to arrive at a compromise acceptable to both sides of the industry, taking into account the legitimate interests of the other social partner. In precisely those areas where such an involvement has been absent, an increased trend towards a reduction of the level of social protection has recently become evident. In these cases, the social policy reforms are, together with an increase in the contribution burden particularly for employees, not providing any noticeable stimulus for development of the labour market and the economy. From a personal standpoint, this seems all the more regrettable as in recent decades the excellent competence exhibited by the Austrian social partners in resolving economic and social policy issues has constituted one of the foundations of the positive economic development and at the same time a guarantee for the preservation of social peace.

THE EVOLUTION OF LABOUR LAW
IN GREECE

1992-2002

Dr. Stamatina YANNAKOUROU
Attorney-at-Law, Adviser to the Economic and Social Council of Greece
myannak@hol.gr
Work Completed: June 2003
Last Update: January 2004

Table of contents

Executive summary

The aim of this report is to examine the evolution of Labour Law in Greece over the past ten years. This evolution is traced in four domains. First, the regulatory techniques of labour law, second, the possible transition from job protection to employability, third, the encouragement of adaptability of both workers and enterprises by labour law, and finally, the promotion of equal opportunities as far as employment and occupation are concerned.

1. The development of labour law in Greece from 1992 to 2003 appeared to be more active than at other periods in the past

A combination of **factors** (EMU,[1] EES[2] and OMC,[3] EC legislation, etc.) has influenced the development of Greek labour law during the 1990s. Among the aforementioned factors, two served mainly as a force to accelerating changes in the field of labour law and labour relations: the Greek preparation for the country's access to economic and monetary union on the one hand and the European Employment Strategy and the Open Method of Coordination on the other. The European Union and convergence with the other Member States became synonymous with **modernisation** and **normalisation**, i.e. the pursuit of a solution to the widespread hidden economy and the establishment of a controlled and disciplined system of regulating labour relations similar to that of other European systems.

The main trend in the evolution of labour law in Greece during the reporting period is **modernisation**, meant as the search for some flexibility, through changes mostly in individual labour law, related especially to new forms of employment and working time. Changes were instigated by the EU, but performed in a national way. As a whole, the 1990s were characterised by a lack of innovation and radical legislative reform in the field of labour relations. Changes focused on the creation or modernisation of structures, infrastructures, institutions and mechanisms, many of which did not actually function or fell into disuse.

Changes were much sounder as regards **employment policy**. The EES forced Greece to include its legislative policy on labour relations within a national employment strategy, which until then was lacking. However, even today there is no unified legislative planning, as there is still no comprehensive strategy embracing a partnership approach with the social partners aiming to step forward labour law.

Two points represent a radical reorientation of Greek employment policy. Firstly, the promotion of active and individualised employment policies, together with a tightening of the conditions for entitlement to unemployment benefits; secondly, the abolition of state monopoly in job placement and the decentralisation of powers and functions from the state to private actors.[4]

Another major influence of the EES is that Greek labour law has acquired a new content, adapted to more horizontal issues, such as quality at work, active ageing, vocational training and lifelong learning, which were completely foreign to its legal tradition. This larger scope tends to lead to interconnection between labour law and other legal fields, especially tax law, social security law and education law.

Besides these factors, the **need to adapt Greek labour law to EC legislation**, as a form of hard law and as a result of the classic community method of governance, also greatly influenced the development of certain parts of Greek labour law – **particularly in the fields of health and safety, sex equality and the restructuring of enterprises**. To this must also be added the contribution of EC legislation in covering legislative gaps (Directives 93/104/EC, 97/80/EC, 91/353/EC, 98/59/EC), in improving existing regulations on part time work (Directive 97/81/EC) and on parental leave (Directive 96/34/EC) and in protecting pregnant women (Directive 92/85/EC).

1   Economic and Monetary Union.
2   European Employment Strategy.
3   Open Method of Coordination.
4   i.e. Temporary Employment Agencies, private Labour Offices and other private agents, which were authorised to get involved either in the job placement or in providing vocational orientation services.

It must, however, be noted that the **incorrect transposition of Labour Council Directives** are a frequent phenomenon in Greece, reducing the level of protection awarded to the workers. Many times domestic legislation simply reiterates the provisions of the directive, without accompanying them with the statutory prerequisites that would allow for their effective implementation and without adapting them to the Greek legal order.

In parallel, one should stress that **other forms of 'non-binding' EU regulation ('soft law')**, such as Green Papers, Community Action Plans, as well as broader horizontal strategies such as mainstreaming, were also important. Actions of an educational and informative nature played a large part in heightening the awareness and responsiveness of the Greek judges to Community law on the equality of the two sexes. Although the implementation of EC labour law is a very complicated task, one should note that the possibility of challenging national labour law through preliminary rulings by the European Court of Justice (ECJ) was very rarely used.

II. Ongoing developments

The transposition of the Fixed Term Directive 99/70/EC, through Presidential Decree 81/2003, has actually become the most controversial issue of Greek labour law. Following an investigation, which resulted in official meetings of European Commission's officials with representatives of the Greek Ministry of Labour in January 2004, the Commission did not seem convinced that the Greek government had fulfilled its obligation to transpose the Fixed Term Directive into domestic law as regards the abuse in use of successive fixed term contracts in the public sector (Art. 5 of the fixed term Directive). At this time the Commission gave the Greek government formal notice by letter, in accordance to Article 226 of the EEC Treaty, allowing it a period of two months to respond and is likely to bring an action before the ECJ. The abuse in the conclusion of successive fixed term contracts in the Greek public sector is a legal question with high social and political implications, which involves almost 45,000 employees, employed under this kind of contract. A number of Greek court rulings issued in April-June 2003 converted workers' successive fixed-term contracts into contracts of indefinite duration, on the basis of direct application of the EU 1999 Fixed Term Contracts Directive. It is very significant that the Greek courts avoided addressing the ECJ for preliminary rulings on the correct or incorrect adaptation of Council Directive 99/70/EC and its compliance or not with existing Greek law.

A recent development of significance in 2003 was the effect of the legal engagements derived for Greece from international labour conventions, which after having been ratified are considered a part of national law (Art. 28 Para. 1 of the Constitution), and take precedence over any national provisions to the contrary. A November 2003 decision by the Committee of Freedom of Association of the ILO stated the non-compliance of the system of compulsory arbitration provided by the Greek independent service OMED (Art. 16 Law 1876/1990) with international labour Conventions 98 and 154, which have been ratified by Greek law. Therefore it recommended the Greek government to start consultations with the most representative organisations of trade unions and employers in view of measures which will restrain compulsory arbitration in cases involving companies providing goods and services covering substantial and vital needs of the population (mainly public corporations).

This decision, which is binding for the Greek authorities, requires Greece to review its legislation on mediation and arbitration, through extended social dialogue with the social partners. The fact that this extrajudicial legal mechanism of resolving conflicts of interest was a product of political compromise in 1990, which reflected also a balance of powers between social partners, is likely to have an impact on social peace in the near future. *A possible outcome of this change could be the individualisation of labour relations.* Concluding collective agreements in several sectors or enterprises of the private sector – where either trade unions have a weak bargaining power or are completely absent – will be impossible, if unilateral appeal to arbitration is limited in theory to very few conflicts involving mainly public corporations, which in practice rarely reach OMED.

We should also stress that discrimination in the workplace is another field in which Greek labour law **is expected to undergo drastic changes, under the influence of the Council Directive 2000/78/EC**. New draft legislation, which will probably pass before the Parliament after national elections take place, will cover important legislative gaps, as Greece lacks specific anti-discrimination regulations, especially in terms of age discrimination and of sexual orientation.

III. Overall assessment

There are two changes that are considered as the most significant **changes** to Greek labour law during the reporting period.

The **first** concerns the procedure of law-making. The way in which Greek labour law was formulated, changed. First, its drafting and content has evolved as an indirect effect of the EES and the OMC. Under pressure by changes instigated by the EU, labour law has become more the result of consultation and social dialogue with the social partners than it was in the past. Besides the foundation of an Economic and Social Council (OKE) in 1994, as a central forum for social dialogue, **the government introduced by law in 2003 two new social dialogue bodies: the National Committee on Social Dialogue for Employment and the National Committee on Social Dialogue for Social Protection**. However, even today, legislative changes in the field of labour relations and employment do not reflect a real partnership approach. They are neither a product of a wider employment strategy nor of central negotiation and agreement between the state, employers and workers. **For this reason, legislation remains fragmentary and not fully effective.**

The role of collective autonomy in the law-making process has been strengthened during the last decade, but has not reversed the primary role of state legislation. Collective bargaining manifested dynamism and innovation only on the national inter-sectoral level and as this did not permeate to other levels, more specialised regulations are still needed. Qualitative aspects of work have been completely neglected till now. What is needed is for the social partners to abandon the authoritarian state mindset which would have the state as the initiator of all regulations and for them to take on initiatives to regulate and deal with matters such as corporate restructuring, collective redundancies and their consequences, organising working time, the new forms of employment, life long learning, flexicurity, etc., through innovative and radical collective agreements. We should also note that no European directive on labour law was ever transposed into domestic law through collective agreements.

The **second** change concerns the progressive transformation of Greek labour law, both statutory and autonomous (collective autonomy), into **employment law,** which, among its other aims, seeks to facilitate the demand for employment, its management and the re-regulation of the labour market. This change in the function of labour law is still in the early stages. It coexists with the traditional function of Greek labour law, which is the protection of workers' rights and jobs both as to their substance (limits on termination and end of work relations see Chapter II) and as to their contents (forbidding the unilateral change in the terms of employment contracts). Because of this, and according to the findings of this study, **there is still no clear change in the function of Greek labour law from protecting workers' rights and jobs to regulating transitions from one status to another** (i.e. from unemployment to

active employment or from employment to training and career breaks) **and from one employment profile to another** (i.e. from dependent employment to self-employment or from stable employment to temporary and vice-versa).

One **major challenge** for Greek labour law is to tackle various forms of discrimination in the workplace and in employment in general, which go beyond the grounds covered by Council Directive 2000/78/EC. The most sound are those concerning blue-collar and white-collar workers, those employed in a private and a public law relationship (see Chapter IV) and those employed with standard and non-standard employment relationships (see Chapter III).

IV. Greek labour law

The picture of Greek labour law remains today one of an uncodified, pedantic and chaotic system of rules, without internal unity. Inflation and complexity of legislation are also a result of the large number of EU labour directives which need to be implemented. This bloated legal system, based mainly in statutory rules more than in collective autonomy rules, has produced a *de jure* over-regulation of the Greek labour market and at the same time it has encouraged its *de facto* deregulation. This has rendered the **Greek labour market intensely dichotomous in nature**. One part, which includes undeclared employment (particularly in small businesses), and is a part of the hidden economy (which accounts for approximately 33-35% of the GDP), is flamboyantly flexible and not necessarily regulated – a fact which creates conditions for unfair competition. The other part, that of the public sector and the 'law-abiding' part of the private sector, remains rigid and over-regulated, but organised, nevertheless, by rules that are not always adjusted to its real needs. Besides that, there exists also a flourishing of the so-called 'grey zones of subordination', which are on the fringes of salaried and independent employment and which serve as a means to circumvent labour law.

Thus, there is still an imperative need to support and enhance the state control mechanisms which monitor the enforcement of labour law and of collective agreements on the one hand and the proper operation of the labour market on the other. Measures need to be taken to reduce the hidden economy, convert illegal and undeclared employment to regular employment, and to drastically deal with the phenomenon of 'pseudo-independent' employment, which distorts the image of salaried employment and transgresses labour and social security law.

Chronology of legislation discussed

Law	Title	Government gazette issue
1876/1990	'On free collective bargaining'	A 27
1892/1990	'On modernisation and development and other provisions'	A 101
2232/1994	'Establishment of an Economic and Social Council and other provisions'	A 140
2224/1994	'Regulation of labour issues, union rights, health and safety of workers, organisation of the Labour Ministry and of monitored legal entities and other provisions'	A 112
2434/1996	'Policy measures for employment and vocational education and training and other provisions'	A 188
2525/1997	'Unified Lyceum, access of its graduates to higher education, assessment of teaching and other provisions'	A 188
2639/1998	'Regulation of labour relations and other provisions'	A 205
2640/1998	'Secondary technical vocational education and other provisions'	A 206
2643/1998	'Measures promoting the employment of people in certain categories'	A 222
2683/1999	'Ratification of code for civil administrative workers and workers of legal entities of public law and other provisions (Civil Service Code)'	A 19
2738/1999	(Chapter A: on 'Collective bargaining in public administration and other provisions')	A 180
2874/2000	'Promotion of Employment and other provisions'	A 286
2910/2001	'Admission and stay of immigrants in Greece. Acquisition of nationality with naturalisation and other provisions'	A 91
2956/2001	'Restructuring of OAED and other provisions'	A 258
3144/2003	'Social Dialogue for the promotion of employment and social protection and other provisions'	A 111
3191/2003	'The National System on Linking Vocational Education and Training with Employment (ESSEEKA)'	A 258
3174/2003	'Part-time employment and social services' (public services, local administration and public entities under public law)	A 205

Presidential decree	Title	Government gazette issue
17/1996	'Measures on the improvement of health and safety of workers during work in compliance with EU Directives 89/391/EC and 91/363/EC'	A 11
176/1997	'Measures for the improvement of health and safety during work for pregnant and breast-feeding women in compliance with Council Directive 92/58/EC'	A 150
88/1999	'Minimum provisions for organising work in compliance with Council Directive 93/104/EC'	A 94
160/1999	'Terms, conditions and procedure for the establishment and operation of Private Employment Agencies'	A 157
178/2002	'Measures on the protection of workers' rights in case of transfer of undertakings, establishments or parts of establishments or undertakings, in compliance with Council Directive 98/50/EC'	A 162
81/2003	'Measures for workers with fixed term contracts' (Compliance with Council Directive 99/70/EC)	A 77
105/2003	'Adaptation of domestic law to Council Directive 97/80/EC on the burden of the proof in cases of sexual discrimination'	A 96

Chapter I:
Introduction[5]

1. Brief overview of labour relations in Greece

1.1. The role of the state

The primary characteristic of the Greek system of labour relations is its *legal structure,* which arises from the interventionist role of the Greek state (Koukoules, 1998, Kravaritou, 1995). Its basic institutions, such as trade union freedom and democracy within the workplace, the structure and internal organisation of trade unions, collective bargaining and the right to strike, are areas regulated by statutory law. The intervention of the social actors, as well as their collective autonomy, has played a limited role in shaping the system.

Until the end of the 1980s, labour relations were confrontational, with both sides directing their demands to government. It is only recently that a climate of relative trust has been created between capital and labour on the one hand and these two and government on the other.

Extensive post-war intervention by the government (in 1990 the state owned or controlled two thirds of the assets and more than 40% of employment in large enterprises) contributed to the creation of an oversized public sector, which for years was the chief vehicle for the implementation of 'social policy'. The Greek state essentially became the nation's largest employer. At the same time, a strong trade union movement developed in the public sector. This movement became accustomed to extensive privileges, strengthened by a climate that favoured the trade union movement following the end of the seven-year junta (1967-1973). Trade unionists and workers in public sector enterprises and in the public utility corporations (what is called 'broad public sector') gradually acquired strong vested rights as a result of the clientelist capitulations of governments, which aimed to ensure either political support or 'peace' in labour relations.

A state of duality was thus created in labour relations in the private and in the public sector. As a result, labour within the broad public sector was clearly in a much more advantageous

position and workers became differentiated into the 'privileged' and the 'non-privileged'. Today, this duality has begun to find balance, or rather, to shift towards the relations of the newly hired, who have more flexible forms of employment, but less security, and the old workers who have significant rights as to job security.

At the same time, in addition to direct intervention the Greek state developed a form of *indirect* intervention in labour relations. Specifically, collective bargaining in the private sector depends on the various austerity programmes implemented by government at a given time and, more recently, nominal convergence and compliance with the National Stability Programme.

1.2. Social partners in Greece

The social partners are the most representative top-level organisations of employers and workers who are signatories to the National General Collective Agreement (EGSSE). They are comprised of the following:

On the part of the workers: The Greek General Confederation of Labour (GSEE), which was founded in 1918 and is the only tertiary level trade union. GSEE is a confederation of secondary level trade union organisations; i.e. 116 inter-sector or inter-professional federations and 82 Labour Centres, which are regionally based. The trade union movement, with approximately 4 500 primary level unions, reflects severe organisational fragmentation. The primary level unions are traditionally organised on the basis of occupation. Organisation based on an industry sector is an exception and enterprise-level unionism has only recently started to develop. Law 1876/1990 attempted indirectly to intervene in these primary structures by bolstering the sectoral and enterprise-level bargaining, as opposed to occupational-level bargaining (see section 1.3 below).

GSEE represents wage workers in private law employment relationships, who are employed either in the private or in the public sector. The trade union density 23-25%. In contrast,

---

5   The information in this study covers a period up to December 2003 and does not contain developments that have taken place since that date. Many points could not be analysed technically because of the limits set by the common outline of the study.

workers with a public law employment relationship (civil servants) are represented at the highest level by the Confederation of Civil Servants (ADEDY), which has 60 federations, approximately 1 300 primary level unions and 230 000 members. Civil servant union density is approximately 60%. These days, there are discussions[6] on the merging of the two high-level Confederations.

On the part of employers: The Federation of Greek Industries (SEV), which was founded in 1907, remains the main representative employers' organisation in manufacturing, the service industry and in the new economy. Along with the EGSSE, it negotiates and signs approximately 80 sectoral collective agreements a year. The General Confederation of Greek Small Businesses and Trades (GSEVEE) was founded in 1919 and represents a whole range of craftsmen, small business owners and merchants with 60 regional and sectoral federations and 1000 primary level union members. Finally, the National Confederation of Hellenic Trade (ESEE), which was established in 1994 as heir to the defunct Union of Commercial Associations of Greece, represents merchants through 12 federations and 132 primary level union members.

1.3. The structure of collective bargaining

1.3.1. Detailed provisions in Greek law [7] minutely regulate the organisation of trade unions and the legal categories of collective agreements

There are four *types* of collective agreements that are provided for by law and signed in practice:

1. National general collective agreements (EGSSE), which fix minimum wages and minimum working conditions for all wage workers in the country, regardless of whether they are members of a trade union. This minimum level of protection set by the EGSSE's also covers workers under private law labour relationships in the public sector, legal entities of public law and local government organisms. The EGSSE is signed by the so-called 'social partners', i.e. the GSEE, the SEV, the GSEVEE and the ESEE (see *above*).

2. Industry-wide collective agreements, which cover workers in similar industries (e.g. metal industry, commerce, food and beverages, etc.) in a particular city, region or in the whole country. These agreements are only binding to workers and employers who are members of the signatory organisations.

3. Enterprise-level collective agreements, which regulate the terms of employment of all the staff of a company. Only employers with a staff of fifty or more persons are obliged by law to enter into negotiations under such agreements.

4. Occupation-based collective agreements. National occupational collective agreements cover a certain profession in the whole country (e.g. the accountants of the whole country). They are binding only on those workers and employers who are members of the relevant signatory organisations. Local occupational collective agreements which cover a certain profession in a particular city or region (e.g. accountants in Thessaloniki) are binding only to those workers and employers who are members of the relevant signatory organisations.

1.3.2. The relationship among the collective agreements

Law 1876 abolished the hierarchical relationship among the various collective agreements. However, industry-wide, occupation-based and enterprise-level collective agreements are *not* permitted to create terms of employment and remuneration that are more or less favourable to workers than those under the EGSSE. When more than one collective agreement is applicable, workers are subject to the one with the most beneficial provisions. There is, however, one exception; if both an enterprise-level or an industry-wide agreement and an occupation-based agreement apply, the former shall apply even if its terms are less beneficial for the workers.

1.3.3. Binding effect for workers

Collective agreements in Greece act both as contracts and as laws. This means that some of their terms are only binding on the signatory parties (duration, way of termination, etc.), while others, e.g. the terms that fix remuneration and work conditions, are legally binding – directly and compulsorily for blue- and white-collar workers.

Directly binding means that the regulatory terms are automatically in effect in the individual work relationships, which must be in conformity with the terms of the collective agreement regardless of the terms of the individual contract. Compulsorily binding means that any contradicting agreement is void. Article 7, paragraph 2 of Law 1876/90 does allow for an exception whereby the terms of an individual contract of employment can deviate from the regulatory

---

6   Decisions of the extraordinary organising Congress of the GSEE held in Athens (23-24/11/02).

7   Law 1876/1990 'On free collective bargaining', *Government Gazette* A 27/8-3-90.

terms of collective agreements if they provide greater protection for workers (favourability principle).

According to a Decision of the Minister of Labour, it is possible to extend the regulatory terms of a collective agreement or to proclaim them obligatory for all branches or occupations, if employers who employ 51% of workers in a given branch or occupation are already bound to it. In such a case, the terms of the collective agreement are extended to the other workers in this branch or occupation.

1.3.4. Labour disputes and means envisaged for their solution (See in detail Yannakourou and Koukoules, 2003)

Individual labour disputes are those arising from the provision of dependent labour or from any other cause, between a working person(s) and his (her/their) employers with respect to the provision of such labour. These disputes are legal in nature and are primarily resolved by the competent courts, according to a special procedure (labour dispute procedure) that is foreseen by article 664 of the Civil Procedures Code (CivPC). Individual labour disputes can also be subject to the process of conciliation, which is an administrative process, but cannot be subject to mediation and arbitration.

Collective labour disputes are those arising from conflicts between employers and employees in the evolution of industrial relations. They come to light when working terms and conditions, remuneration, the company's hiring policy and other issues, labour-related and otherwise, are being discussed. These conflicts can be legal, in which case they are resolved either judicially or through the administrative procedure of conciliation. Collective labour disputes may also reflect a conflict of interests, in which case they constitute the object of mediation and arbitration.

In Greece there are three types of extra-judicial mechanisms for settling labour disputes: conciliation, mediation and arbitration, provided for by Law 1876/1990 (Yannakourou and Koukoules, 2003). Arbitration is also foreseen by the Greek Constitution of 1975 (Article 22 paragraph 2), which states that *general working conditions shall be determined by law, supplemented by collective labour agreements contracted through free negotiations and, in case of the failure of such, by rules stipulated by arbitration.*

Conciliation is of an absolutely voluntary character. Mediation includes mainly voluntary elements, while those of arbitration are mainly compulsory.

Arbitration awards issued by an independent arbitrator, a member of the Mediators-Arbitrators Corps, are assimilated by collective agreements in all respects. The Mediators-Arbitrators Corps functions as part of the independent Organisation for Mediation and Arbitration (henceforth referred to as OMED) with a view to resolving collective labour disputes when a negotiating stalemate has been reached.

1.3.5. Ultimate developments as to compulsory arbitration

In 2003, a significant development took place with the effect of the legal engagements of Greece that derived from international labour conventions, which after having been ratified are considered as part of national law (Article 28 paragraph 1 of the Constitution), and take precedence over any contradicting national provisions. A November 2003 Decision by the Committee on Freedom of Association of the ILO (see Gavalas, EErgD 2003.1457) noted the non-compliance of the system of compulsory arbitration provided by the Greek independent service OMED (Article 16 of Law 1876/1990) with international labour Conventions Nos 98 and 154, which have been ratified by Greece. It was therefore recommended the Greek government start consultations with the most representative organisations of trade unions and employers in order to introduce measures that will restrain compulsory arbitration only in cases involving companies providing goods and services covering substantial and vital needs of the population (mainly public corporations).

This Decision, which is binding for the Greek authorities, obliges Greece to review its legislation on compulsory arbitration through extended social dialogue with the social partners. The fact that this legislation was a product of a political and social compromise, reflected in Law 1876/1990, risks to undermine social peace in the near future. In addition, some of the employers' organisations are completely hostile to compulsory arbitration and took the initiative to appeal before the relevant Committee of the ILO.[8]

2. Facts on the Greek labour market

1. The Greek labour market has some peculiarities (Sabethai, 2000, Chletsos, 2002a, Chletsos, 2002b,

---

8   To follow the debate see mainly A. Vayas, *EErgD* 1996, 805 s., D. Papastavrou, *EErgD* 1996. 949 and *DEN vol. 1418*, January 2004, p. 1. Contra Kazakos, *EergD* 1997. 625, L. Dassios, *EergD* 1997, p. 1.

Chletsos, 2003) with regard to those of the other European countries:

- The rate of self-employment in Greece is the highest in the EU (44%) (Gavroglou, 2003). This rate could, however, be considered misleading, as it includes the large number of workers working under a work contract and contracts for independent services, which are often facades for dependent employment. This number also includes those who work freelance (e.g. doctors, lawyers), but also offer salaried services. Furthermore, the current recession is leading many self-employed persons to search for dependent employment.

- Businesses that employ up to 49 people account for 99.7% of the nation's enterprises and they employ 73.5% of those in employment. More specifically, according to Eurostat,[9] these numbers break down to: 53.7% self-employed enterprises (this includes the actual self-employed person and perhaps non-paid members of his family), 43.8% very small businesses (1-9 workers) and 2.2% small businesses (10-49 workers). The Greek Civil Code (AK 78) states that at least 21 persons are needed to form an enterprise-level union and thus excludes a large number of small and medium-sized businesses from collective agreements. The national collective agreement and sectoral collective agreements are thus particularly important for small and medium-sized businesses, but they are often violated.[10]

- A large number of women are employed as non-paid staff in family businesses. Such staff account for 1.3% of the employed and are more often found in small businesses in the primary sector, in hotels and in catering.

- The Greek labour market is characterised by *low mobility* (GSEE-ADEDY Institute of Labour, 2002): 84.3% of wage earners stay in the same business for more than two years and only 9.6% remain for less than a year. This low figure is accompanied by a small percentage (14%) of workers who take part in company training programmes to upgrade their skills compared to the European average (33%).

- Remuneration in Greece is particularly low at barely 65% of the EU average. More specifically, part-timers earn approximately EUR 245 per month, which is equal to unemployment benefit. According to figures (The GSEE-ADEDY Institute of Labour, 2002), the purchasing power of the lowest paid in Greece is the lowest in Europe, except for Portugal. For this reason, one third of the labour force works overtime and one fifth holds more than one job that is frequently not covered by labour law.[11] Extensive overtime work and the extended working time of the self-employed seem to account for the upward divergence (42.4% compared to 38.2% of the EU average) of the real working week. Violations of labour law on overtime work and on rest time are the most usual violations and often occur with the consent of workers for financial reasons.

2. As concerns the structure of employment *(PAEP, 2003)*, one could note the following:

- In 2002 the labour force of the nation stood at 4 369 010 out of a total of 6 760 323 of the economically active population. According to recent data[12] provided by the Social Security Foundation (IKA), the foreign labour force accounted for 11% of the country's legal labour force and for 15-20% of the country's total labour force.[13] For the most part, these labourers are unskilled and are employed in occupations that the Greek labour force avoids.

- The employment rate for women (42.7%) and for the young (26%) is low. The unemployment rate, which was the lowest in the EU in the 1980s, rose to a higher number (9.6%) than the EU average in 2002. The unemployment rate for women is double (15.6%) that of men. Long-term unemployment stands at 5.4%, which is much higher than the EU average.

- Although employment in the primary economic sector fell overall, the rate of employment in agriculture continues to be high (15.8% in 2002). In industry, the figure has remained steady over the last years (22.5% in 2002) and is rising in the service sector (61.7% in 2002), where many new jobs are being created.

---

9   Economic and Social Council of Greece (OKE), *Own-Initiative Opinion on 'SMEs: past and future'*, (no 62/2001), http://www.oke.gr.

10   A similar problem can also be seen in some service sectors (e.g. banking and the financial sector) or in businesses that have operational problems and consider the sectoral collective agreement a restraint and for this reason doubt its authority.

11   Labour Inspectorate's reports (2001, 2002) impressively state that there are workers who are employed at one job for the working week and at a second job on weekends.

12   Published in the newspaper *ELEFTEROTYPIA*, 30-12-2002, page 23.

13   From a demographic point of view, the 6.7% increase in the country's population noted between the censuses carried out by the National Statistical Service in 1991 (10 255 000) and 2001 (10 939 606) is exclusively due to immigrants.

3. Basic features of Greek labour law

Greek labour law today has the following features:

- It is not codified and is a mixture of regulations without internal unity. These regulations are mainly of legislative origin, but have also been derived from case law (particularly with regard to the forming of individual labour law). Collective autonomy has played a smaller role in forming Greek labour law.

- Greek labour law acquired its contemporary form after 1975, when the seven-year colonels' dictatorship ended and the period known as the 'changeover' began. Labour law was fundamentally influenced by the Constitution of 1975, which democratised labour relations. The 1975 Constitution extended and enlarged the list of fundamental rights, under the heading 'individual and social rights'[14] (Chryssogonos, 1998). We may note especially the safeguarding of human dignity (Article 2, paragraph 1), the free development of the individual (Article 5, paragraph 1), the right to work (Article 22, paragraph 1), the right to equal pay for work of equal value (Article 22, paragraph 1b), the recognition of collective autonomy (Article 22, paragraph 2), the right to social security (Article 22, paragraph 5), the right to association (Article 12), the protection of trade union freedom (Article 23, paragraph 1) and the right to strike (Article 23, paragraph 2). These constitutional rights have a special place in the development of Greek labour law. The interpretation of the rules of labour law, which in Greece is an autonomous branch of private law, must take place according to the Constitution.

- Until 2001, when the last constitutional revision took place, Greek constitutional theory accepted that fundamental rights might have only an indirect horizontal effect on the relationships between private parties. The reference to an indirect horizontal effect means that fundamental rights have a regulatory effect on relations between private parties through the provisions of civil law, i.e. the general clauses and the abstract concepts, which a judge should interpret and make more specific, thus shaping the law. The new Constitution of 2001 (Article 25 paragraph 1c) signalled a reversal of this position, providing for the direct horizontal regulatory effect of fundamental rights in the relationship between private parties (European Constitutional Law Centre, 2001). The same Article mentioned for the first time that the exercise of individual and social rights is limited by the principle of proportionality. This is a written confirmation of a constant position maintained both by scholars and by case law in Greece.

- As mentioned above, the 1975 Constitution has been amended two times thus far, in 1986 and in 2001 (Venizelos, 2001). In the last revision (Chryssogonos, 2001, Gogos, 2001), the right to collective bargaining in the public sector was provided for the first time (new Article 22, paragraph 3). In addition, the revision also provided for the opportunity to take affirmative action to promote equality between men and women (new Article 116, paragraph 2) for the first time. This very important Article will be discussed in Chapter IV.

- During the 1980s, union freedom and collective action developed, as did participatory rights within the workplace, as a result of the post-dictatorship history of the country and the rise to power of the socialists (1981-1989). In 1990, with the consensus of all of the political parties and the social partners, legislation on collective bargaining, mediation and arbitration (Law 1876) was voted in. This period signalled the promotion of social dialogue between the government and the social partners.

- From 1993 onwards, the influence of the EU began to show. This period coincided with the rise (after a three-year hiatus) of the Pan Hellenic Socialist Movement (PASOK),[15] which began to express a gradual tendency towards liberalisation and modernisation in labour relations. In any case, since 1995 there has been a growing momentum for institutional changes, which took place in a climate of continuity and political stability.

- One of the most important problems facing labour law in Greece is the lack of enforcement of regulations, whether they are contained in laws or in collective agreements. The unsatisfactory manner in which the state control mechanisms of the labour market function also contributes to this problem. Placing the Labour Inspectorates under the jurisdiction of the Prefectural Local Government as part of the decentralisa-

---

14   Since 1822, all Greek Constitutions contain a catalogue of fundamental rights. Under the influence of the Constitution of Weimar, social rights appeared for the first time in the Greek Constitution of 1927. In Greek constitutional theory there are also similar terms used, such as 'individual or constitutional liberties', 'fundamental rights', 'public liberties' and 'human rights'.

15   A. Papandreou (1993-1996), C. Simitis (1996-2000), C. Simitis (2000 until today). The next national elections will take place in March 2004.

tion efforts by law,[16] has led to their growing inertia. Following protests by employers' and workers' organisations, Law 2639/1998 returned the Labour Inspectorates to the jurisdiction of the Ministry of Labour and Social Affairs and they were reorganised into a unified Labour Inspectorate Corps (SEPE) under central state control. SEPE began operations in July 1999 and was divided in one central and 23 regional services with jurisdiction all over Greece. The main task of SEPE is to monitor the enforcement of labour law regarding work conditions (hours, remuneration), the legality of employment, ensuring that workers are insured and the conditions of hygiene and safety at workplaces are adequate. Furthermore, the SEPE can intervene to conciliate individual or collective disputes. Despite the fact that the SEPE has been given wide-ranging powers (it can sue, impose fines), and is even authorised to temporarily terminate work that does not comply with legislation on health and safety, violations of law and collective agreements are difficult to discern because of the prevailing conditions in the labour market discussed in section 2.

4. New challenges in labour law: protection of workers' personal data

The rapid development of the information society and of new technologies has created a new area for labour law, namely the protection of data in the realm of labour relations, a subject on which there is no specific legislation in Greece. There is only general legislation on the protection of the individual's personal data (Law 2472/1997) and the specific legislation in the realm of telecommunications (Law 2774/1999).

The horizontal nature of these general regulations, as defined within the framework of Law 2472/97 and Law 2774/99 respectively, do not take into account the specific aims, conditions and environment of labour relations. Because of this, problems of interpretation arise and are invariably used as an excuse to monitor and restrict the liberties of workers. There is a *de facto* legislative vacuum as there are no protective regulations regarding the workplace and labour relations.

For this reason, the Hellenic Data Protection Authority,[17] which is an independent body safeguarded in the Constitution (Article 9A), whose mission is to oversee the implementation of Law 2472, issued a Directive,[18] aiming at interpreting Law 2472/1991 and Law 2774/1999 as to their application in labour relations.

The Directive made clear that the existing legislative framework applies to workers in the private and public sectors, to applicants for work and to former workers. It also applies to data of a personal nature of employment agencies, of management consultants, of public employment offices (OAED), and of temporary work agencies. The Authority posits general principles of protection (e.g. exercising rights which have been provided for by law cannot lead to a worker's negative evaluation) and the conditions under which workers' personal data can be collected. It provides for the protection of workers from systems of control and surveillance; for workers' rights (right to information, access, objections and temporary judicial protection); it assigns civil liability to those responsible for processing the personal data vis-à-vis the worker; and it imposes administrative and legal sanctions (as provided for in Law 2472).

The Directive does not posit new regulations and therefore is not of a regulatory or directly binding nature.

In conclusion, the lack of specific legislation, as well as the complete lack of recognition of the institutional role of workers' representatives (even in the Directive) has left many legal and substantive questions unanswered, particularly with regard to the protection of and respect for private life in the workplace.

There is also a vacuum with regard to the role of collective bargaining. Only the National General Collective Agreement (EGSSE) of 2000-2001 for the first time stated that employers' organisations should remind their constituents of their obligations within the general legal framework of the protection of the individual's private information. This provision is just a recommendation and thus is not binding. The protection of workers' personal data did not become a matter for collective agreements at decentralised levels up until now.

16   Law 2218/1994 'Foundation of Prefectural Local Government, amendment of provisions on local government and Region and other provisions', *Government Gazette* A 90/13-6-94. This decentralisation was in defiance of the principles of International Labour Convention 81, which was ratified by Law 3249/55.

17   L. Mitrou, *Hellenic Data Protection Authority*, Athens; A. Sakkoulas, 1999, Donos, Mitrou, Mittleton, Papakonstantinou, *Hellenic Data Protection Authority and the reinforcement of the protection of rights*, Athens, 2002.

18   Protection of personal data in the field of labour relations (Directive of Hellenic Data Protection Authority 115/2001), *EErgD 2001*. 913.

5. New regulatory techniques of labour law

In Greece, the regulatory sources of labour law are: the Constitution; ordinary law; international labour treaties, which have been ratified by law (Art. 28 paragraph 1 of the Constitution); EU law (Article 28 paragraph 2 of the Constitution); collective agreements and arbitration awards that are equal to them in rank, company work rules, practice followed within a company, the individual's contract of employment and the managerial rights of the employer.[19]

Legal precedents also play an important role. Although they are not an independent source of law, the decisions of Greek courts have played an important role in forming labour law. The role of legal precedents have been decisive in creating law particularly concerning the termination of contracts of employment, the equality of the sexes and equal pay, the definition of salaried employment, the definition of the limits of managerial rights, fixed-term contracts, etc.

The most important development in the regulatory techniques of labour law in the decade in question has been a partial decline in statutory law and the increasing importance of autonomous law, produced by collective agreements.[20] This is also a result of the independent social dialogue between the social partners and the enhancement of the procedures of negotiation and communication between the social partners and the government.

The role of company work rules in the transformation of labour relations in the public sector has also been significant.

5.1. The dominant role of legislation in Greece

Since the inception of labour law, law has been the main source of regulating labour relations. Generally, Greek labour law is considered to be particularly protective of workers.

The provisions of statutory labour law may have an absolute compulsory character, in which case no derogation is allowed. They may also have a unilateral compulsory character, which means derogations by other sources of labour law are permitted only when they favour the workers.

Statutory legislation is frequently supplemented by administrative acts (Presidential decrees, decisions of the Minister of Labour) that are issued with legal authorisation and with which laws are made more specific or are implemented (e.g. extending collective agreements, regulating shop hours, defining a maximum for overtime, etc.). Intervention by public administration has generally been very significant for labour relations in Greece.

5.2. The role of collective bargaining and of collective agreements as a regulatory technique

5.2.1. Collective agreements in the Greek system

In the Greek system, collective agreements have traditionally played a secondary role in regulating labour relations. This can be explained by two facts. Firstly, there is a tradition of intense intervention by the state in labour issues and this has made law the main vehicle for regulating labour relations. Secondly, until 1990 the structure of collective agreements was centralised, hierarchical and their provisions were exceptionally limited (only remuneration issues) compared to those of other European countries.

In 1990, during the all-party government of Mr. Zolotas (November 1989 – April 1990), Law 1876 'On free collective bargaining', was passed by unanimous agreement of all political parties, the representatives of GSEE and the three employer organisations (the SEV, the ESEE and the GSEVEE).

This Law is wide in scope and covers those working in agriculture, animal husbandry, home workers and those who, although they are not salaried workers, work under the same conditions and need to be protected in the same way as others (economically dependent workers). Shipping workers were excluded from this Law.

5.2.2. Legal conditions for collective autonomy

Law 1876/1990 created the legal conditions for collective autonomy to become the dominant source of regulation in Greece:

- It replaced the centralised and hierarchically structured system of collective bargaining instituted by Law

---

19 On a hierarchical scale, the Constitution is first in rank, followed by international regulations, conventions and treaties (Article 28, paragraph 1 of the Constitution) and EU law (Article 28, paragraph 2 of the Constitution) and common labour law. Within the framework of these sources, the autonomous legislation of the collective agreements, arbitration awards and the company internal rules may also intervene. An individual's contract of employment should respect all the aforementioned sources and is followed in hierarchy by customary practice within a company. Finally, the employer's managerial rights cover gaps left by the other sources. If there is conflict amongst these sources, on the basis of the favourability principle a regulation that is hierarchically lower overrides a higher one if it provides more favourable treatment for the worker.

20 The relationship between law and collective autonomy in Greek labour theory has been traced back to the classical monograph of Prof. G. Leventis, *Collective autonomy and state interventionism*, Athens 1981.

3239/1955 with one that was decentralised. Free bargaining took on a more significance at all levels and the notion of collective autonomy was restored.

For the first time, two new levels of bargaining were legally recognised: the sectoral and the enterprise levels that were given priority above the occupation-based collective agreements that had dominated until that time. Nevertheless, it must be noted that existing law does not recognise a group of companies as a potential bargaining level.[21]

- It broadened the field of collective agreements. As a result, any issue regarding the terms and conditions of work (except for pension issues), exercising one's right to belong to a trade union within the workplace and the business policy could become subject to bargaining. Theoretically at least, this Law allowed a wide range of issues to be introduced in collective bargaining.

- It abolished arbitration tribunals and compulsory arbitration as the only method of resolving collective labour disputes. To replace this, a system of mediation/arbitration with optional as well as mildly compulsory elements, was introduced. In essence, this system is an extension of collective bargaining, since it comes into operation after free bargaining fails. A central position in the management of the new system is now held by the Organisation for Mediation and Arbitration (OMED) (OMED, 2001), in whose administration the social partners participate, and the Special Mediators and Arbitrators Corps, from which the mediators and arbitrators are selected.

5.2.3. Recent developments in the legal framework

Following the 1990 change in the legal framework, the following developments were observed (OKE, 2002):

1. The abolition of arbitration tribunals and compulsory arbitration of collective labour disputes brought about a liberalisation in collective bargaining. After 1992, the annual average of arbitration awards fell to 13.5% of collective regulations (collective agreements and arbitration awards), with the exception of 2003, in which it went back up to 18.9% (OMED, 2004). From 1992 to 2001, only 21.4% of all collective labour agreements signed nation-wide were concluded through the OMED. This confirms that the parties to those agreements have, as a

rule, the ability to reach an agreement without the necessity of mediation by third parties (OMED, 2001).

2. A variety of types of collective labour agreements came into being and collective bargaining has become more decentralised. After 1992, most collective agreements signed in the course of a year fell into the category of enterprise-level agreements.[22] Enterprise and sectoral collective agreements have consistently outnumbered the occupation-based agreements, which have gradually become marginal.

3. Despite the full freedom that the new Law gives, the terms of collective agreements in Greece continue to be poor compared to other EU countries. The social partners appear to be reluctant – even at the national level – to include current issues such as the social effects of corporate restructuring (social plans, retraining, etc.) flexicurity, new forms of work organisation and career breaks into the bargaining agenda. Other issues, such as protection against racism, vocational training and life-long learning, are only posited in EGSEEs as matters on which initiatives should be taken. In addition, no European directive has ever been implemented by means of collective bargaining in Greece. With the exception of part-time work, some aspects of which were regulated by EGSSEs, new forms of employment such as telework, temporary agency work, or even widespread fixed-term contracts have never been subject to collective agreements at any level.

4. The national general collective agreements (EGSSEs), which are inter-sectoral and which usually have a duration of two years, have proved to be more innovative than the other categories of collective agreements (OKE, 2002).

5. In Greece, sectoral and occupation-based collective agreements simply reiterate the regulatory terms of EGSSEs without any significant innovations. Enterprise-level collective agreements deal with a broader spectrum of issues, particularly by linking remuneration with productivity, individual or collective performance, company profits, or special prerequisites for workers (group insurance, etc).

6. Law 2738/1999[23] belatedly established the institution of collective bargaining in public administration. Until

21 Travlos-Tzanetatos, *Collective bargaining in company groups*, Athens, 1997.
22 The annual average of national collective agreements for 1992-2001 is approximately 47%. Industry-based collective agreements are approximately 28.5%, while occupation-based collective agreements are approximately 24.5% of all collective agreements.
23 Law 2738/1999 (Chapter A: on 'Collective Bargaining in public administration and other provisions'), *Government Gazette* A 180/9-9-99.

then, ILO Conventions 150 and 151, which provided for this possibility, and which were ratified by the Greek Parliament only in 1996, were not implemented. Law 2738 ensured the right and obligation to negotiate and to define the terms and conditions of work for civil servants. Two levels of bargaining were instituted; one central and one decentralised, at the level of ministries, prefectures, public entities of public law, independent public services, as well as a third level of simple dialogue in the workplace. The issues that were not the subject of bargaining at a higher level are referred to at each level.

Finally, provisions for mediation were created in the instance that bargaining should fail. In such a case, a relevant body is set up. Issues that may be the subject of collective agreements are defined in the Law, such as changes in the terms of employment, training, measures for health and safety at work, national insurance (except for pensions), the exercising of one's trade union rights, leaves, work hours and interpretation of the terms of collective agreements. Because of constitutional restrictions, matters such as salaries, pensions and methods of employment cannot be included in collective agreements but can be resolved as part of an informal agreement.

5.3. Social dialogue and social consensus as a new technique in forming Greek labour law

5.3.1. The introduction of social dialogue institutions

The introduction of institutions of social dialogue and their establishment in the consciousness of the various parties involved (the state, employers and workers) has been considerably delayed in Greece compared to other countries in the EU (Spyropoulos, 1998). This delay is due to the fact that there is no tradition of social dialogue – its philosophy, techniques and procedures – and because the state's autocratic behaviour created a prevailing climate of suspicion and conflict.

The effort to promote social dialogue in Greece began after the fall of the junta (1975) and has had three notable developments.

Firstly, the social partners have engaged in a steady quest for autonomy and the establishment of a climate of trust in their

relations, together with an attempt to extricate themselves from the oversight of the state in collective bargaining. Indicative of the improvement of what used to be relationships of conflict between management and labour is the impressive decline in the number of strikes, which previously put Greece at the top of the list in numbers of strikes (from 472 in 1980 to 38 in 1998 and 15 in 1999).[24]

Secondly, there has been a partial eradication of traditional political perceptions regarding the state's exclusive right to create and implement social and economic policy. The state's retreat from this position could be ascribed mainly to the implementation of institutional changes brought about by membership to the EU. As a result, the state now has an obligation to consult with the social partners and they can now take an active part – at both European and national levels – in the implementation of the European Employment Strategy (Luxembourg Process) and in the achievement of the Lisbon objectives (2000).

Thirdly, the 1990s have seen the development of consensual institutions which aim to seek commonly acceptable solutions and the creation of a modern institutional framework within which they can function in the 1990s. This development was a result of Greece's preparation for admittance to the EMU, which necessitated the incorporation of the Community *acquis*, which includes social dialogue.

5.3.2. Strengthening of the role of the social partners

These three factors led to a clear strengthening of the role of the social partners in the creation of social policy, employment policy and labour relations. The creation of permanent institutions that promote social dialogue, such as the Economic and Social Council (OKE), the National Committee on Dialogue for Employment and the National Committee on Dialogue for Social Protection is particularly indicative (see *below*).

The Economic and Social Council, (OKE), was established in 1994[25] as an advisory committee and as a central forum for social dialogue with the most representative social actors in Greece (18 tertiary level organisations) on matters of social and economic policy. OKE ensures, among other things, the organised and coordinated participation of the representatives of productive classes in shaping labour and social policy. From OKE's inception in 1996, the Ministry of Labour and Social Affairs has submitted all draft laws on labour law and employment to it for consultation. Despite the fact that this sort of dialogue seems to be the norm in most EU coun-

---

24   Man hours lost to strikes fell from 20 494 944 to 1 515 347 in 1998 (*Source*: Ministry of Labour). Official available data exist up to 1999.

25   Law 2232/1994, *Government Gazette*, 140A/31-8-94. See also M. Yannakourou, (2001) 'Function and evolution of institutional social dialogue at national level', in Chr. Deliyanni-Dimitrakou, (ed) *Social Dialogue and Collective Bargaining in the EU*, Athens, Komotini: A. Sakkoulas: 75-97.

tries, in Greece it is noteworthy for two reasons. The first is the delay in introducing it and the second is that it was the first time in Greece that such an institution was established without the institutional intrusion of the state (OKE is one of the few Greek organisms that remains exclusively managed by the social partners).

5.3.3. An original method of dialogue: the tripartite social consultation

Besides the OKE, in 1997 the government introduced an original method of dialogue: the tripartite social consultation between the state, employers and workers. This method aimed to ensure mid-term consensus so that political and legislative reforms could be adopted to allow Greece to meet the EMU criteria. These discussions, which were informally structured, were not three-way negotiations as none of the parties wanted to achieve the convergence of positions through mutual compromises.[26]

In May 1997 the government announced the start of a dialogue, which it divided into three parts: development, competitiveness and employment. Before the dialogue began, it was believed that labour issues would be the focus of discussions and that dramatic changes in labour law would be agreed upon. In the end, the issues that were put on the table for discussion and the way in which they were discussed were not bold, as compared to similar discussions in other European countries that took place at the same time (i.e. Spain).

In November 1997, following six months of discussions, the agreement known as the 'Confidence Pact Between the Government and Social Partners Towards 2000' was signed (Robolis and Kouzis, 2000). The Agreement was signed by the ADEDY and the GSEE (with a marginal majority) for the trade unions and by the SEV and the ESEE for the employers. The GSEVEE did not sign.

The impact of matters that were agreed upon in the Agreement on subsequent labour law was unequal. One of the most interesting points was the agreement of all parties that the long-term unemployed over 55 years of age would have full medical and medicinal coverage by the OAED. The social partners finally implemented this with stipulations in the EGSEE

(see *below*). The parties displayed timidity in discussing important issues such as working time and this was finally put off because of the GSEE's complete disagreement with the employer's organisations. In the end, the government unilaterally voted in favour of measures contained in Law 2639/98, which were never implemented (see Chapter III).

5.3.4. Conclusion

In conclusion, it must be noted that during the 1990s the way in which labour law was formulated changed, but not radically. Under pressure by changes instigated by the EU, labour law has become more the result of consultation with the social partners than it was in the past. However, even today, legislative changes in the field of labour relations and employment are neither a product of a wider strategy, nor of central negotiations and agreement between the state, employers and workers. For this reason, legislation remains fragmented and not fully effective.

It is hoped that this vacuum will be filled by the establishment of two new social dialogue institutions: the National Committee on Dialogue for Employment and the National Committee on Dialogue for Social Protection. These were introduced by a very recent Law of the Ministry of Labour[27] and it is foreseen that these Committees will have widespread participation.[28] The task of the National Committee on Dialogue for Employment will be promoting social dialogue in forming policies to increase employment and deal with unemployment, advising on, monitoring of, and evaluating the National Action Plan for Employment and involvement in labour policy and labour law.

The National Committee on Dialogue for Social Protection will deal with fighting poverty and social exclusion and developing a network for social protection and social integration. It will also have an advisory role in forming, monitoring and evaluating the National Action Plan for Social Inclusion.

5.4. Internal company regulations

In the broader public sector (public enterprises), regulations for the workforce have been the basis for privileges and the

---

26   Chr. Ioannou (2001), 'Les pactes sociaux dans les relations professionnelles en Grèce: Ulysse ou Sisyphe?' in G. Fajertag, and Ph. Pocher, (sous la dir. de), *Les Pactes sociaux en Europe*, Bruxelles: P.I.E. – Peter Lang: 225.

27   Law 3144/2003 on 'Social Dialogue for the promotion of employment and social protection and other provisions', *Government Gazette* A 111/8-5-2003.

28   The Minister of Labour as Chairman, relevant Ministers, General Secretaries of relevant ministries, representatives of the social partners (SEV, GSEE, ESEE, GSEVEE, agricultures) local and prefectural government (KEDKE, ENAE), representatives of public organisms, representatives of people with disabilities and other institutions and/or NGOs.

formation of an inflexible model of protected employment for years. Until recently, the formation of rules was subject to a special regime that was different from that of internal regulations in private enterprises.[29]

In 1996, the gradual removing of public utilities (e.g. Hellenic Telecommunications, Public Power Corporation, Hellenic Railway Organisation, Hellenic Post) from state control began. They became joint stock companies and with the provisions of law,[30] their statutes were gradually transformed to comply with the law on joint stock companies. The 1996 Law did not address labour relations in the particular companies and changes could only be made with the agreement of employee representatives.

In the two years that followed, there was no modernisation of labour relations – a fact that directly contradicted the very reasons behind the changes in legal status. In fact, the precarious financial position of most of the companies worsened. For this reason, an amendment to an irrelevant statutory law[31] stated that changes in the General Staff Regulations of the public utility companies, which had poor financial performance or were in a process of reform, should be completed within six months of the Law's passing through Parliament. If this had not been the case, the changes would have be imposed with special laws that could only be changed in the future through collective agreements. This amendment initiated a wave of strikes by the trade unions because they considered that this was unwarranted intervention in collective autonomy.[32] However, the General Staff Regulations that were amended under the pressure exerted by this Law became the regulatory tool that introduced important innovations in the public utility companies (e.g. flexitime work, abolition of some levels of the hierarchy, working time arrangements, new rules on relocation of workers, a restriction of benefits, introduction of part-time work, etc).

---

29   For private enterprises, in order of priority, internal regulations are written and formed through a collective agreement – if there is a company trade union – or by agreement with a work council, or by a unilateral decision of management, which must then be ratified by the Labour Inspectorate. In the last case, management must proceed to the preparation of internal regulations if the enterprise has more than 70 workers.

30   Law 2414/1996 'Modernising public enterprises and organisms and other provisions', *Government Gazette* A 135/25-6-96.

31   Law 2579/1998 Article 31, paragraph 8.

32   D. Travlos-Tzanetatos, (1998), *Collective autonomy, general interest and purification of public corporations*, Athens: A. Sakkoulas.

Chapter II:
Labour law and employability

I. The traditional function of labour law: protecting jobs and rights

I.I. Protection of jobs and law on dismissals

In Greek labour law, dismissals are not totally free. The need to protect the interests of workers, in order to ensure that employment is steady and constant, has imposed restrictions on the freedom to terminate contracts.

Laws 2112/1920 and 3198/1955 formally restrict the termination of contracts and aim to diminish its consequences. These Laws constitute the basis of the general law on termination of employment (Zerdelis, 2003). The restrictions comprise: firstly, the obligation to notify the worker of the termination of his employment contract in writing; secondly, the obligation to observe specific deadlines (only for white-collar workers); and thirdly, the payment of severance pay.

Besides the general law on the termination of contracts, there are special prohibitive legal provisions. For example, it is forbidden to dismiss a female worker during pregnancy and for one year after childbirth (Article 15 Law 1483/1984). Freedom to unionise implies that it is forbidden to dismiss a trade union officer (Article 14, paragraph 10, Law 1264/82) and it is also forbidden to fire workers while they are on their annual leave.

Contrary to what occurs in other European countries, Greek legislation has not imposed substantial restrictions on dismissals. This means that the validity of the dismissal is not connected to specific reasons (justification). Case law has covered this vacuum in Greek statutory law, highlighting its contribution to the making of law on dismissals.

On the basis of Article 281[33] of the Civil Code and the general clause on the prohibition of any abuse of rights, case law has imposed substantial restrictions on the freedom to dismiss. Thus, dismissals with ill intent, as well as those that are objectively unjustified, are considered invalid. Case law says that a dismissal *which is not justified by the well-meant interests of the employer is void* (i.e. reasons which have to do with a specific worker, e.g. incompetence, not meeting normal responsibilities, or economic dismissals arising from restructuring or abolition of a particular post).

While the managerial decisions of an employer that result in dismissals are not subject to judicial control, dismissals as a result of these decisions are subject to such a control. In other words, a cause-effect connection between these decisions and dismissals must exist and be proven before the courts, if it is challenged.

Thus a new form of protection arises in which the position of work is protected. According to some labour law specialists,[34] the worker's right to retain his position is recognised in the Constitution, as is his right to job stability and security.

I.2. Corporate restructuring: from job protection to reintegration in the labour market

I.2.I. Current situation

In Greece, mergers and acquisitions (M&As) have become an important form of restructuring. From 1987 to 1995, more than 250 M&As occurred in all sectors of the Greek economy, with significant social ramifications in the area of individual and collective labour relations. This phenomenon, which has continued up to the present, constitutes a basic strategic option for private companies, in an attempt to strengthen their position in both the international and domestic markets. Nevertheless, a large portion of M&As are part of state policy and coincide in time with the planning as well as the implementation of the policy of privatisation that began at the end of the 1980s.

---

33   Civil Code 281: 'The exercising of one's right is prohibited if it exceeds the level of good faith or of decency or of the social and economic aims of the right'.

34   D. Zerdelis, *EErgD 2001*.101.

Government policy on M&As, as a whole, consists mainly in interventions related to the future of the ownership status of the companies in the broader public sector of the economy. This policy was a key point of the economic policy of successive PASOK governments in the framework of Greece's integration in the EMU. In this framework, processes of liberalising companies under state control were set in motion, either through their acquisition by companies in the private sector (AGET-Iraklis, Syros Shipyards, Ionian Bank), or through their listing on the stock exchange market (Hellenic Telecommunications Organisation (OTE), Public Power Corporation (DEI), Water Supply and Sewerage Systems Company of Athens (EYDAP)),[35] or by seeking strategic alliances with Greek or foreign companies (Commercial Bank of Greece). The process of selling off a company under state control can be interrupted or reversed if it is established that the buyer does not meet the necessary requirements set by the state for the acquisition. In the case of private sector companies, the acquisitions and mergers process is not subject to restrictions imposed by the existing legal framework. In the case of small and medium-sized enterprises (SMEs), the state favours the merger of SMEs through tax incentives.[36]

It should be noted that, as regards the first period of privatisations up to 1995, most of the interest was centred on the companies of the Business Restructuring Organisation (OAE), the 'deeply in debt' companies of the private sector, which came under state control to prevent them from winding up.

1.2.2. Protecting jobs during restructuring

1.2.2.1. Developments in domestic law after Council Directive 98/50/EC

In the existing legal framework, the term 'restructuring' does not appear. Presidential Decree 178/2002,[37] with which Directive 98/50/EC was transposed in Greek law, regulated the protection of workers during a transfer of undertakings, as defined in the case law of the European Court of Justice (ECJ).[38] The main changes introduced in domestic law[39] were:

- With Article 2, paragraph 1b and c of the Presidential Decree, the positions, stated by ECJ case law, as well as by Greek case law, on the meaning of the word 'trans-

fer' in the wording of Directive 77/187, were transformed into the rule of law. Protection of workers is provided for in all cases where the employer changes, regardless of whether the employer is a public or private undertaking engaged in economic activities[40] or if he operates for gain. At the same time, the Presidential Decree states that the restructuring of public administration or a shift in responsibilities in the public sector cannot be considered a 'transfer'.

- The meanings of 'transferor', 'transferee' and 'representatives of employees' are redefined and the meaning of 'employee' is defined legally for the first time in the Greek legal order. An 'employee' whose rights are being safeguarded is any person who is in salaried employment at the workplace (either with a valid or invalid contract, fixed-term or not, flexible form of employment, etc.).

- 'Representatives of employees' are work councils, foreseen in domestic law (Law 1767/1988) and whose competencies are thus extended. For the first time it is stated that if the business employs less than 50 persons and there is no work council, representation is undertaken by a three member council which is elected in an assembly called by the union which has the most members in the business.

- Using the flexibility provided by Article 4a of paragraph 1.3 of Directive 98/50/EC, domestic law does not apply to cases of bankruptcy or insolvency, under the condition that the process has been completed with a judicial decision.

- More specifically, with regard to participatory rights during the decision to transfer the undertaking or part of it, existing domestic law (Article 8, Presidential Decree 178/2002) states that both the transferor as well as the transferee must inform the representatives of their respective employees affected by the transfer of the following: the date of transfer, the reasons for the transfer, the economic, social and legal implications for the employees, as well as the measures envisaged for them. It must be noted that if there are no representatives of employees, the employer must fulfil the above obligations in a timely manner vis-à-vis all workers at

---

35 Public Corporations.

36 Legislative Decree 1297/1972, Law 2386/1996.

37 Presidential decree 178/2002, *Government Gazette* 162A/12-7-2002. This decree abolished Presidential Decree 572/1988 with which Council Directive 77/187/EC had been incorporated into Greek law. There is very rich literature regarding the issue of transfer of undertakings under presidential decree 572/1988 having transposed Directive 77/187/EC. See Douka (1997), *Transfer of undertakings and individual labour relations*, Thessaloniki: Sakkoulas; Leventis, *DEN 1989.1169* and *DEN 1998.99*; Zerdelis, *DEE 1996.238*; Kamenopoulos, *EErgD 1996.1046*.

38 Kamenopoulos, *EErgD 1997.146* and *EErgD 1998.1105*; Kalamidas, *EErgD 1998.909* and *EErgD 1997.1105*; Syggeniotou, *DEN 2001.804*

39 Douka, *EErgD 2001.997*.

40 This was the fixed position of Greek case law.

the same time. This provision is very important in Greece where, because businesses are small, there are usually no works councils or enterprise-level unions. With a provision introduced for the first time (Article 8, paragraph 4), the responsibilities of a company that is being transferred and that is part of a national or multi-national group of companies, are defined for the first time. There is an obligation to information and consultation even if the transfer has been decided upon by the holding company and even if the latter refuses to disclose the necessary information.

1.2.2.2. The gaps in collective bargaining in the field of restructuring

The issue of managing restructuring and its consequences in labour relations is completely absent in the collective bargaining agenda at all levels.

1.2.2.3. Case law developments concerning the regulation of redundancies fo financial or technical/organisational reasons

According to Article 5, paragraph 1 of Presidential Decree 178/2002, the transfer of an undertaking or business or part of it does not in itself constitute grounds for dismissal by the transferor or the transferee. However, this provision does not impede dismissals for economic, technical or organisational reasons.

A decisive step in safeguarding jobs was the implementation of the principle of proportionality when terminating an employment contract for financial reasons as a criterion for the abuse of this right. This is the most recent position of Greek case law in defining a dismissal as abusive. It is a rule expressed in case law following the interpretation of Article 281 of the Civil Code.

According to this rule, dismissals must not only be an appropriate, but also a necessary measure taken to satisfy an employer's interests. Redundancies are allowed only when the organisational or operational needs of a company cannot be addressed by other, less injurious, means (e.g. moving a worker to another department or branch of the company). Redundancy is thus considered a last resort for the employer. A significant portion of case law has recently adopted the principle of proportionality in redundancy for financial reasons. In implementing this principle, case law

judged that termination of an employment contract must be a last resort (*ultima ratio*) when dealing with restructuring.[41]

1.2.3. Protecting jobs in collective redundancies: legislative developments and the implementation of law

1.2.3.1. Regulating collective redundancies

In Greece, collective redundancies were regulated for the first time by Law 1387/1983,[42] which attempted to adapt domestic law to implement Council Directive 75/129/EEC. According to this Law, collective dismissals are those that occur in companies employing over 20 people, for reasons unrelated to the employees per se, and exceed the following numbers each calendar month:

1. Five employees for companies that employ from 20 to 50 persons, and

2. 2-3% of the staff and up to thirty persons for companies that employ over 50 persons. The Labour Minister, taking into account market conditions, redefines this proportion every six months. Since Law 1387 was implemented, the Minister's decisions have set this proportion at 2%.

The basic change brought about by Law 1387/1983 was that for the first time in Greek labour law, it introduced participatory procedures to the law on collective dismissals. Thus, the employer must inform workers' representatives[43] in writing of the reasons for redundancies (even in restructuring), before they take place, and must disclose any information that could lead to constructive proposals.

A twenty-day period for consultation is provided for, which begins when the employer invites representatives of the employees for this purpose, notifies them of future redundancies and discloses written information. During this period – which is essentially a period of negotiation – mutually acceptable solutions are sought to avoid or minimise redundancies and their damaging consequences. This period ends when an agreement is reached or a dispute is decided upon. In the first case, redundancies must take place ten days later under the conditions agreed upon. In the latter case, the recognition of a dispute opens the doors for administrative intervention. The Prefect or Labour Minister decides within ten days whether to approve all or part of the redundancies to take place.

41   Supreme Court 279/1996, Supreme Court 902/1998, Supreme Court 1364/1999, Supreme Court 513/1998, Thessaloniki Court of Appeals 958/2001 and 3977/1966, Court of the First Instance 1881/1996. In detail see Zerdelis, 2003 (Selected Bibliography) and D. Zerdelis, (1991), *Dismissal as ultima ratio*, Thessaloniki: Sakkoulas.

42   Leventis, *DEN 1987.449*; Bakopoulos, *Elliniki Dikaiossini vol. 38*, p. 274 s.

43   Works councils are considered employees' representatives for the purposes of the law, only when there is no union in the workplace that includes 70% of the staff and the majority of staff that is to be dismissed, or if the union is not in a position to exercise its rights.

1.2.3.2. Directive 92/56/EC

Directive 92/56/EC did not lead to any amendment to Law no 1387. The Greek legislator seems to have thought that existing Greek law already addressed the contents of the new Directive.

1.2.3.3. Directive 98/59/EC

On the other hand, Directive 98/59/EC, which codified the contents of the previous two Directives into a unified text, led to changes in two points of domestic legislation. Firstly, a provision of a 1999[44] Law clarified that the right to information and consultation exists independently of whether the decision to proceed with the redundancies has been taken by the domestic employer or the holding company of a multinational group. Secondly, the Law included provisions stating that the procedure of collective redundancies contained in Law 1387/83 cannot be implemented on workers who are dismissed because their company closed following a decision of the Court of First Instance. However, the Directive does not state how and with what procedures such a decision should be issued. As Greek law does not demand a court decision for the closure of a company, both literature and case law determined that this provision could not be implemented.[45] Essentially, it is a direct transfer of the text of the Council Directive, which has not in any way been adapted to conform to domestic procedures.

Law 2874/2000 (Article 9, paragraph 3), under the pressure of the alleged transposition of Council Directive 98/59/EC, extended the application of Law 1387 on collective dismissals in the case of interruption of activities. This Law provided that the company or establishment which terminates operations is relieved only from the responsibility to observe administrative procedures on collective redundancies, and is not relieved from the responsibility of consulting or negotiating with the representatives of employees.[46]

1.2.3.4. Recent developments

New developments were brought about by law. An amendment[47] in Law 1387/1983 stated that the limit beyond which redundancies are considered collective is four workers for those companies that, at the beginning of the month, employed 20 to 200 persons. For businesses employing over 200 persons, the proportion of 2% still applies.

The aim was to rationalise the limit of collective redundancies. Until 2000, businesses with less than fifty workers could make five redundant every month without having to resort to the legal procedure for collective redundancies. However, in businesses with 50 to 199 workers, the 2% limit meant that one to four people could be made redundant depending on the exact size of a particular business. This distorted the competition between big and small companies and had a negative impact on job mobility. With the amendment, the government attempted to do away with the deterrents to enlarging a business and the reluctance of employers to hire more staff.

1.2.3.5. Implementing legislation

As for the implementation of legislation, restructuring in Greece has, up till now, not been accompanied by dramatic reductions in employment or mass redundancies as in other European countries. In particular, dismissals of 100 or more workers per unit of economic activity were a rather rare phenomenon in Greece. The basic reasons for this are the following:

- Most companies in Greece are small (they employ less than 20 workers) and therefore the law on collective dismissals does not apply to them.

- Employers avoid coming under the process of the law on collective dismissals, especially because at the end of this process the Damocles sword of administrative intervention is left hanging over them.[48] Thus, in order to avoid implementing the relevant process, they usually resort to voluntary redundancies and early retirement practices, or to the method of breaking up the dismissals over the course of the year, so that they lose their collective character and fail to come under the legislation governing collective dismissals.[49] It is also important to highlight a decision of a Court of Appeals,[50] which stated that law and procedure on collective dismissals must apply to separate dismissals on mutual agreement, which are assimilated to collective dismissals. The legal basis of this position was the alleged direct effect of Article 2 of Council Directive 92/56/EC (reiterated by Article 1, paragraph 1 of Council Directive 98/59/EC), which, according to the Greek Court, had not been transposed into Greek law.

---

44 Article 15 of Law 2736/1999, *Government Gazette* A 172/26.8.99.

45 Leventis, *DEN 1998.92*, Lixouriotis (1999), *Collective Dismissals in Greece*, Athens: Editions of National Labour Institute, p. 106.

46 See also recent case law: Decision of the Athens Courts of Appeal 2635/2003 (unpublished).

47 Law 2874/2000 (art. 9) 'Promotion of employment and other provisions' see section III below. For this amendment see Metzitakos, *DEN 2001.634*.

48 The Prefect or the Minister of Labour has discretion to approve or reject in whole or in part the collective dismissals requested by the employer.

49 http://www.eiro.eurofound.ie/1999/04/Feature/GR9904122F.html.

50 Thessaloniki Courts of Appeal 2198/2000, *EErgD 2001.416* and *DEN 2002/124*.

This position was criticised by labour law scholars,[51] who maintained that a Council Directive does not have a horizontal direct effect on private relationships (ECJ 152/84 Marshall) and that the direct effect of a Directive in such a case should only be invoked as a last resort, after having attempted an interpretation of existing national law in light of EC law.

• With regard to the effects of restructuring on ownership, neither in the case of M&As, nor in the case of privatisation, has there been a question of collective dismissals. In some sectors, such as the banks, there has not even been a question of significant reductions in employment. As concerns the banks in particular, the changes to employment are more qualitative than quantitative in nature (e.g. significant changes to the role and duties of executives). In the case of the Greek telecommunications public service's (OTE) capital sell-off, where the reduction in employment involved about 10 000 workers (from 26 000 in 1996 to 16 000 in 2000), a system of voluntary redundancies was implemented and the conditions were agreed upon in the framework of a special enterprise-level collective agreement. Similar methods were followed in the case of restructuring in the shipbuilding industry. To give some indication of this, we cite the cases of the two biggest Shipyards, Skaramangas and Elefsina. In the Skaramangas Shipyards case in particular, the redundancy of 1000 workers carried out in 1995 was accompanied by a package of social measures including: voluntary redundancies, early retirement and self-employment through the Labour Force Employment Organisation (OAED) with full compensation. Similarly, at the Elefsina Shipyards, the reduction of permanent staff from 1800 in 1992 to 750 in 1999 was carried out gradually and a significant number of workers resigned with accompanying social measures of three types: voluntary redundancy with incentives, early retirement and transfer to companies in the public and broader public sector.

1.2.4. From protecting jobs to promoting accompanying social measures: the dominant curative role of the state

While the concept of a 'social plan' for helping those affected by restructurings to re-enter the workforce and to re-integrate into the labour market is compulsory in counties such as Germany, France and Spain, as the result of consultations with workers' representatives it does not have grounds in Greek law. As stated above, this has not been a subject for discussion among the social partners. There are, however, some glimmerings of a social strategy by the government when reform is attempted for businesses that are perennially in trouble (e.g. subsidising those of an advanced age if they choose to become self-employed, etc.).

From 1992 to 2002 the presence of the state in dealing with the social consequences either of restructurings or of the closure of businesses was notable. In many cases the state provided general or specific legislative measures that placed the dismissed staff in other services of the public sector.[52] In most cases the government promoted special programmes to bolster self-employment, retraining or a special unemployment allowance for staff, which was dismissed. These legislative measures were fragmentary and adapted to particular situations.[53]

In 2003 there was a wave of collective redundancies, concerning 500 persons each, due to discontinuation of company activities and company shutdowns. Two of them, involving TVX Hellas – the Greek subsidiary of a multinational mining corporation – and Schiesser Pallas, a subsidiary of the German apparel multinational, Schiesser AG, were highly debated in Greek society.

These redundancies are typical of the trade unions' attitude. Instead of negotiating re-employment plans, they challenged the legality of planned redundancies and resorted to the High Administrative Authority, the Ministry of Labour. Redundant workers were included in state-funded training programmes, while older workers were offered early retirement and increased severance pay or participation in training programmes and state payment of social insurance contributions to ensure that those approaching retirement age would be entitled to full pensions.

---

51 Leventis, *DEN 2002. 113*, Bakopoulos, *DEE 2002. 157*.

52 e.g. Law 2224/1994, Article 9 of Law 2266/1994, Article 20 of Law 2515/1997, etc.

53 To illustrate the situation, we will mention Law 2302/95 for the Scaramanga and Eleusina shipyards, Article 6, paragraph 1 of Law 2338/1996, Article 19 of Law 2458/1998, Article 43 of Law 2956/2001 (Various Metal Working Enterprises and 'Peiraiki-Patraiki S.A.'), Law 2336/95 ('Kassandra Metal Works of Halkidiki'). Indeed many of these special unemployment subsidies have been continuously extended with new legislative measures. These measures are contrary to EU policy, which proposes abolishing extended benefits (passive measures) discouraging the unemployed from seeking work.

2. The new function of labour law: promoting employability

2.1. Modernisation and the creation of new structures to promote employability: the role of the legislator and the social partners

The changes in the institutional framework during the reporting period mainly aimed to create new structures, infrastructures and mechanisms to facilitate access to the workplace and to modernise the existing structures.

Legislative intervention focused on the modernisation of the public organisation for employment (2.1.1) and the concurrent delegation of a portion of state functions to the private sector (2.1.2). Structures were also created by national level collective bargaining and these continue to be particularly effective (2.1.3).

2.1.1. The modernisation of the Labour Force Employment Organisation (OAED)

Legislative intervention to improve the services offered by the public employment services was attempted in a two-pronged approach with Law 2956/2001. The first was the *managerial restructuring* of OAED. The second was the establishment of a methodology to handle individual cases of unemployment and to extend this geographically. This was done through the Centres for the Promotion of Employment (KPA), which were transformed, and renamed (by Ministerial Decisions) Regional Offices and Regional Services of the OAED.[54]

The Greek government had committed to the managerial restructuring of OAED in the National Action Plan on Employment (NAP) in 2000. The OAED was established in a 1954 law as a welfare organisation to combat unemployment. This basic function was later extended to promoting professional training for the unemployed (apprenticeship schools, training programmes for the unemployed and the self-employed and in-company training) and finding employment. Because of a bureaucratic and out-dated structure, the OAED was not in a position to adapt to the new circumstances that resulted from the move from passive to active policies on employment.

It was commonly known that the OAED did not perform well in promoting employment through intervention (training, benefits, placing in jobs), matching supply with demand and reducing long-term unemployment. Furthermore, the OAED did not keep statistical records on the progress of the unemployed following training or their job placement.[55]

Restructuring the OAED was thus judged necessary so that it could deal with the new demands placed on it by the Greek labour market.

With the new Law, the OAED's functions were redefined to cover three areas: facilitating the entry of the workforce into the labour market, insuring the unemployed and promoting professional training and, finally, linking professional training with employment. The key factor of reform was delegating important OAED functions to three non-profit joint-stock companies, whose sole shareholder would be the OAED. These companies were created with Law 2956 as parts of the OAED under the auspices of the Minister of Labour.[56]

2.1.2. The development of structures to facilitate access to the labour market: private employment agencies and temporary employment agencies

Private employment agencies (IGSE) and temporary employment agencies (EPA) aim to help those seeking work and to modernise the structures of access to the labour market.

The creation of private employment agencies (IGSE), as a private intermediary for finding work, was first provided for

---

54   It was Law 2434/1996 (*Government Gazette* A 188/20.8.1996) that for the first time established in Greece an 'Employment Card', which aimed to create an individualised approach to the unemployed. The law stated that every worker in a programme of continued training which was subsidised by the OAED, the EU or both organisations would obligatorily be provided with a card, while other categories of the employed or unemployed would be provided with a card at will. In addition, it was established that the card would be used for many purposes – from registration in an employment programme to receiving unemployment benefits. The aim was to be able to electronically monitor the employment situation of the workforce and to offer individualised support. Based on this system, unemployment benefits could be exchanged for or counterbalanced with the receiver's participation in subsidised training/employment programmes (within the framework of active employment policies). In practice, however, this measure was not implemented.

55   Only 1% of the unemployed were placed in jobs by OAED.

56   The aim of the first company, 'Manpower Support Services S.A.', was to form and run Centres for the Promotion of Employment (KPAs) and to provide individualised support for the unemployed and those who had undergone professional training. This company never actually worked. With Law 3144/2003 (Article 1, paragraph 7) it was legally dissolved and its assets were handed over to the OAED.

The aim of the second company, 'Professional Training S.A.', was to set up and operate training services. And finally the aim of the third company, 'Research – Information Observatory of Employment S.A.', was to study and conduct research into the labour market.

in Greek law in Law 2639/98 (Article 5).[57] Until then, offices that mediated in job seeking were forbidden in Greece because of a state monopoly on job placement and mediation in finding jobs.

Only particular categories of work are open to the mediation of private employment agencies. These are: performing artists, management positions, accountants, cleaning staff, construction or technical labourers, guides, models, private nurses, caregivers for the elderly and live-in staff.

In order to set up and run an IGSE, a special license must be issued by the Ministry of Labour and Social Affairs, which is given following a certification procedure by a committee. It was recently provided for that representatives of workers and employers would be included in these committees. The license granted can be revoked and cannot be transferred.

Workers are not charged for the mediation of IGSEs. The employer who hires an unemployed person through an IGSE is obligated to pay up to 10% of the first year's annual salary of each worker hired to an IGSE (if the contract is open ended) or 10% of the total of the salary if there is a one year fixed-term contract.

According to NAP 2002, the IGSEs have found 1795 jobs for the unemployed to date. These jobs mostly concerned foreign workers.

The creation of temporary employment agencies (EPA) was allowed for the first time in Greece with Law 2956/2001 (Articles 20, 21). In contrast with the IGSEs, the EPAs do not simply mediate to find employment, but actually hire unemployed people and then hire their services out to a third party (a user company). They aim to function as intermediaries to provide skilled labour to the market, thereby meeting the demand for those with particular skills more directly and effectively.

According to law, EPAs can be formed only as public limited companies with shared capital. Their establishment and operation requires a special license from the Minister of Labour and Social Insurance, following the recommendation of the Temporary Employment Control Commission. The participation of social partners in this Commission has recently been foreseen.

Penal and administrative sanctions are foreseen for IGSEs and EPAs that do not operate legally.

2.1.3. The contribution of the National General Collective Agreement (EGSSE): the establishment of LAEK

The Fund for Employment and Professional Training (LAEK) was established by Law 2436/1996 (Article 1) as an independent part of OAED, following the merging of two special funds: the Special Fund for Professional Training and Education Programmes (ELPEKE) and the Special Joint Fund for Unemployment (EKLA).

These two Special Funds had been formed with a 1994[58] Law that ratified the terms of the EGSSEs of 1991, 1992 and 1993.

It had been agreed in those collective agreements that employers and workers would pay an extra sum to the OAED to help fight unemployment, especially amongst the long-term unemployed, the young and the old and those who were in the last five years of their working life (EGSSE 1994 Article 8). It was also agreed that all employers, from both the public and private sectors, who employ salaried workers would have to contribute to an entity of private law that would be set up under the OAED to support programmes for professional education and training.

In both cases, the parties stated that they wished for the aforementioned Articles to be put into effect quickly by the Ministry of Labour and for the Ministry to submit new legislation to enable employers' contributions to be collected and managed (Article 9 EGSSE 1994).

The Ministry did indeed form two funds, ELPEKE and EKLA, and set up a seven-member permanent Managing Committee comprised of an OAED representative and equal representation of social partners' organisations.

In 1996 the two funds were combined to form LAEK, which now constitutes the most innovative and substantial intervention body of the social partners (the GSEE, the SEV, the ESEE and the GSEVEE) in promoting life-long learning and employability of the unemployed, as it was created not only at their initiative, but is also funded and managed exclusively by them.[59]

---

57 The law was put into effect with Presidential Decree 160/1999 'Terms, conditions and procedure for the formation and operation of Private Employment Agencies', *Government Gazette* A 157/3.8.99.

58 Articles 14 and 15 of Law 2224/1994 on 'The regulation of labour issues, union rights, health and safety of workers, organisation of the Labour Ministry and of the monitored legal entities and other provisions', *Government Gazette* 112 A/6.7.1994.

59 LAEK is funded by employers' contributions to ELPEKE and employers' and workers' contributions to EKLA. Contributions to EKLA are used to run employment and professional training programmes for the unemployed – particularly the long-term unemployed –, the young and those in danger of being socially marginalised. LAEK has a Managing Committee that decides on the allocation and use of funds. It also provides an annual evaluation of OAED's policies vis-à-vis subsidies for unemployment. The Managing Committee comprises employer representatives (including the SEV, the ESEE and the GSEVEE), four worker representatives (GSEE) and the Director of the OAED, who is also the chairman of the committee.

LAEK mainly funds in-company training for workers.[60] Funds given to companies for these programmes are not taxed. In addition, LAEK funds programmes to improve employability of the unemployed including subsidised programmes for older workers or for those close to retirement.

In later EGSSEs the social partners expanded the activities of LAEK to other fields. It was agreed in EGSSE 1998-1999 (Article 7) to provide medical and medicinal insurance for the unemployed that were under the age of 29 with LAEK funds, through an agreement with the Social Security Foundation (IKA) following a study of economic data. This agreement was put into effect in 1998.[61]

Furthermore, in EGSSE 2000-2001 (Article 12) there was a unanimous decision that outstanding social insurance contributions for the long-term unemployed who had five years until retirement would be covered by LAEK. The aim was to help the long-term unemployed exercise their right to a pension.[62]

2.2. Measures to support employability for special categories of the unemployed

Both the legislation and the EGSSEs have fragmentary provisions that do not allow for a common, unified legislative handling of the unemployed that are at risk of social exclusion. From the NAPs one can see that the long-term unemployed, young people, women, the disabled and older workers are the ones that are mainly included in OAED programmes aimed at fighting unemployment.

The state particularly intervenes to create jobs for the handicapped and for those with over three children. In 1986 legislation was voted in to compel businesses with over a certain number of workers to hire 2% of the former and 3% of the latter. The Law was amended in 1998,[63] but without radical changes. The amended Law ensured greater objectivity in hiring workers by enforcing a system of credits for candidates. At the same time, businesses that had had losses in the last two fiscal years were excused from having to hire a certain number of these two categories.

The credit system works by assigning a certain number of credits for one's qualifications, age, degree of disability, family and financial situation. It is important to note that those

aged over 40, who are considered more vulnerable in trying to get jobs, are given more credits depending on their age.

In this area we must also take note of Law 3174/2003, which provides for recruitment of specific target groups under a new type of public sector part-time contracts and which is developed under the heading of 'Part-time employment' (see Chapter III).

Another recent development is a draft Law on 'Measures to address unemployment and other provisions', presented in December 2003, providing for incentives for the recruitment of unemployed people and boosting employment among women, young people and older workers. In particular, a scheme will promote the employment of women with at least two children, with the state bearing the cost of social insurance contributions. Moreover, employers that hire workers under fixed-term contracts to replace workers that are absent from their jobs due to maternity or childcare leave will receive subsidies for the term of the leave equal to the employers' social insurance contributions for the recruits.

2.3. Active ageing

Policy measures in this field are implemented through the Labour Force Employment Organisation (OAED), which funds in-company training programmes in the public and private sectors in order to help workers adjust more rapidly to new requirements. Workers of all ages take part in these programmes. However, there is no specific legislative policy for active ageing, which explains why legal and other measures taken are fragmented:

- A draft Law on 'Measures to address unemployment and other provisions', presented in December 2003, introduces a subsidy for employers that recruit long-term unemployed people over the age of 55, equal to 50% of the employer's social insurance contribution. This provision applies only if the employer has not, in the six months preceding the recruitment, dismissed staff from the company without good reason. The concept of 'good reason' is borrowed from law on dismissals (fixed-term contracts) and its interpretation lies in the case law.

---

60   In 1999, LAEK funded small businesses for the first time.

61   Article 18 of Law 2639/98 (see Chapter II). In contrast, IKA provides two-year medical coverage under certain conditions for the long-term unemployed over 55 (Article 10 of Law 2434/96).

62   This agreement was implemented with Article 10 of Law 2874/2000 and Ministerial Decision 302/2001/B-323 'Duration of optional continuation of insurance for the long-term unemployed'.

63   Law 2643/98 'Measures promoting the employment of people in certain categories' (*Government Gazette* A' 222/28.9.98).

- There are state programmes aimed at finding employment for those who have been made redundant or have been dismissed and are over a certain age. A characteristic example is Athens Paper Factory S.A. (SOFTEX). The first programme was introduced by a Ministerial Decision and was put into effect by the Ministry of Finance and Economy on 13 January 2003. It included approximately 200 workers (men over 50 and women over 45 years old), who will be employed for four years in state organisms and private industry, but with monthly wages of EUR 750 and social insurance. The second programme, which was put in effect in November 2002, was an initiative of the Ministry of Labour and Social Affairs and included 450 unemployed people aged 18 to 64 who were made redundant by SOFTEX. This programme is a Special Programme of Intervention, which includes training for new jobs and grants for young self-employed people.

- For older workers, EGSSE 2002-2003 (Article 11) states that all the signatories agree to promote: a) their participation in all programmes of enterprise-level training and re-specialisation b) motivation for their admittance into programmes for new jobs (if they have not been dismissed) and into programmes which aim to fight unemployment.

2.4. Bridging the gap between school, education and training and the labour market

2.4.1. The Greek legal and regulatory framework for vocational education

The Greek legal and regulatory framework for vocational education was always fragmented and uncoordinated, providing for the involvement of various actors. This resulted in a lot of red tape and an inability to put laws into effect.

2.4.2. The 1990s

During the 1990s, the main characteristic was an emphasis on creating new structures and systems for vocational education – primary and secondary – and for its certification. The main bodies involved were LAEK (see above), the Organisation for Vocational Education (OEEK), the National Centre for Certification of Continuing Vocational Education and Complementary Support Services (EKEPIS) and the National Centre for Vocational Guidance (EKEP).

- OEEK was created within the framework of the National System for Vocational Education whose aim was to organise, develop and provide official qualifications in vocational training. It was also responsible for coordinating its efforts with the existing educational system. OEEK also had the responsibility to organise, establish and monitor public Institutes of Vocational Training (IEK) and to administer exams to certify graduates.

- EKEPIS was created in 1997[64] to develop and implement the National System for Certification of Continued Vocational Education and Complementary Support Services and to coordinate the system of continuing vocational guidance with the system of primary vocational training and guidance. In practice, however, it merely certified institutions of continued professional education and complementary services.

- EKEP was created in 1994 (Law 2224/1994). In 1997 it came under the auspices of the Ministries of Education and Labour, so that it could plan and implement the National Strategy on Vocational Guidance and contribute to vocational guidance in schools, thus linking schools and the labour market.

All the mechanisms and systems discussed above were established and developed in isolation and in a non-coordinated manner. The result is that Greece does not yet have a cohesive strategy for lifelong learning and initial vocational training has not yet been linked to continued education and employment. This strategy would presuppose a network of educational and training opportunities (general and vocational) and easier access for people throughout their lives.

In order to fill this fundamental gap, the current government passed a Law[65] providing for the foundation of an institution responsible for shaping a national policy on vocational training and for monitoring its implementation. The government has had extensive and substantive input from the social partners. The institution in question is the National Council on Linking Vocational Education with Employment (ESSEEKA), which will aim to link all the various systems and mechanisms that exist into a unified whole, so that there is no overlap and the labour market is taken into account. It is foreseen as a high level institution through which the state and the social partners will discuss and determine national policy in this area and whose work they will monitor with an annual report.

---

64   Law 2469/1997 and Presidential Decree 67/97.
65   Law 3191/2003, *Government Gazette* A 258.

2.4.3. Recent years

In the last few years there has been emphasis on preventing school drop-outs. A Law in 1997[66] created second chance schools. The aim of these schools is to face school drop-outs during the nine-year compulsory education attendance and even during elementary school attendance. They concern young people over 18 who, upon completing these schools, would receive a certificate equal to a junior high school or primary school diploma.

In parallel, Law 2640/1998[67] provided for flexible technical/vocational education in Technical Vocational Schools, as an alternative offered to pupils who accomplish the nine-year compulsory education programme and do not wish to continue the three-year Unified Lyceum. Those eligible to enter these schools, which are of a secondary, but post-compulsory level, must have completed the nine years of compulsory education. Those who complete the first course following two years of study may continue for one more year so that they can register in the second form of a Unified Lyceum or they can get jobs once they have received certification and a professional license. Those who continue on to the second course can enrol in a relevant course in a post-secondary Institute of Vocational Training. They can also get jobs once they have been certified and have obtained a license to practice their occupation, or they can enter a Technical Vocational Institute in a relevant field if they can prove three years of professional experience and pass the relevant exams.

---

66   Law 2525/19997 entitled 'Unified Lyceum, access of its graduates to High Education, assessment of teaching and other provisions', *Government Gazette* A 188 (Article 5).
67   Entitled 'Secondary technical vocational education and other provisions', *Government Gazette* A 206.

Chapter III:
Labour law and adaptability

The present section will examine developments from the point of view of the adaptability of workers (1) and the adaptability of businesses (2).

1. Adaptability of workers

1.1. Developments as to new forms of employment

For the first time, institutional interventions in this decade regulated or re-regulated specific forms of employment. These mainly concern part-time employment, fixed-term employment, temporary employment, and pseudo self-employment.

1.1.1. Part-time employment[68]

1. In Greece, the statutory legal framework has given particular emphasis to part-time employment as a means for dealing with unemployment, despite the fact that it is not the main form of labour flexibility that exists in the Greek labour market.

   Part-time employment was legally recognised in Greece in 1990[69] when a legal framework was first set up, based on the proportional safeguarding of labour rights for part-time workers. Part-time employment was defined as daily or weekly employment with fewer work hours than standard employment,[70] which takes place either with a fixed-term or an open-ended contract. The provisions of the law safeguard the basic rights of part-timers (e.g. the right to paid annual leave and its benefits).

2. In 1998, the existing legislation was amended[71] to cover the gaps left after Council Directive 97/81/EC, so that provisions included in EGSSE 1993 could be ratified and codified. It is notable that in EGSSE 1993, the social partners included measures for part-time employment for the first time, long before the Euro-

pean collective agreement was signed and issued as a Directive that implements it.

The basic innovation introduced by the 1998 Law was the extension of part-time employment to companies and organisms in the broader public sector, including the public utility organisations and banks − following the abolition of an existing prohibition on this. The Law also provided for the possibility to fill the companies' cyclical need for staff with six-month part-time contracts, which could not be transformed into open-ended contracts. This measure implemented the agreement between the government and the social partners as stated in the Confidence Pact Between the Government and Social Partners Towards 2000, which was signed in 1997 (see Chapter I, section 4.3.3).

Another important change introduced by the new Law is the extension of the definition of the term 'part-time employment' to include any employment with reduced working hours (compared to the standard), not only on a daily or weekly basis, as in the past, but also on a fortnightly or monthly basis. Expanding the meaning of the term now implies that 'job rotation' is also included in this category and, thus, those who work alternately are also safeguarded by the regulations governing part-time work.

In addition, there were statutory provisions for part-timers to be able to take part in vocational education and benefit from their employers' voluntary benefits. This right was originally provided for in EGSSE 1993 (Article 5) and it is also a part of Council Directive 97/81/ EC. Article 5 of EGSSE 1993, which stated that workers' representatives must be informed of the number of part-time workers and their prospects for full time work, was ratified. As for other issues related to the equalisation of the rights of part-timers with those of full-timers, common labour law is applied.

---

68 For general information see Christoforatos, 'The promotion of part time in Greece. Legislative regulations in the past decade', *EErgD 2001.1169*.

69 Law 1892/1990 'On modernisation and development and other provisions' (Article 38), *Government Gazette* A 101 /31-7-90.

70 Standard work hours are considered to be the full working hours in effect at a workplace, whether this is established by law, collective agreement, internal work regulations, the practices of a business or any other possible ways.

71 Article 2 of Law no 2639/1998 'Regulation of labour relations and other provisions', *Government Gazette* A 205 /2-9-98. See G. Stivaktakis, *DEE 2001.979*.

3. In 2000[72] two supplementary statutory law measures were taken, but they did not have such a wide scope. The first aimed at establishing incentives for the re-entry of the long-term unemployed into the work force. The second aimed to abolish the wage deterrents to extending part-time employment, as it was believed that part-time employment in Greece was not widespread because of the low level of remuneration. (See Chapter I, section 2).

    In the first case, an increment of 7.5% would be provided for part-timers working less than four hours daily and who are paid on a minimum wage basis established by the EGSSE. In the second case, the OAED would provide a monthly sum for up to twelve months for the long-term unemployed hired as part-timers on at least a four-hour daily work schedule. The latter does not seem to have been implemented.

4. In August 2003, a new Law[73] was passed. It provides for public sector organisations to recruit unemployed people and other groups in a difficult labour market position on part-time, fixed-term contracts in order to provide certain social services, such as home care. According to the Law, local government bodies and state law entities may conclude 'programmatic contracts' with non-profit private law entities regarding the provision of social services at national or local level. Such contracts for the provision of social services should specify their terms and scope, along with the number of people to be employed for their performance, the source of their funding, the supervision and control of the quality of services provided and the rights and obligations of the contracting parties.

    Employment under such contracts is fixed-term part-time employment, which may not exceed 20 hours a week and its term may exceed 24 months. After termination of the period, such contracts may be renewed for the same worker only after an interval of two months. This kind of employment contract may be used for social service jobs, such as provision of care in the home, caretaker services for school buildings, schoolchildren's road safety or the social integration of immigrants.

    Candidates must be selected from specific target groups, as follows:

- 35% of recruits must be unemployed people registered with the Labour Force Employment Organisation (OAED), including a certain proportion of persons that have been unemployed for over 12 consecutive months

- 25% must be unemployed people registered with the OAED who are in the 'pre-retirement' phase

- 20% must be young people under 30 years of age

- 10% must be mothers of children under 12 years of age

- 10% must be people with disabilities

- 60% of the recruits in the first three categories must be women.

The funding of the provisions of these social services will be provided by subsidies of the state budget, programmes and initiatives of the European Union, the budgets of the bodies drawing up the programmatic contracts, or from other sources.

1.1.2. Fixed-term employment

1.1.2.1. General

In Greek law, the main difference between a fixed-term and an open-ended employment contract is their different treatment as regards the protection of workers' rights when the employment contract is dissolved.

Statutory law and case law have created a protective net for those working with an open-ended contract. As seen above, (section 1.1.1) in open-ended contracts workers are protected when their contract is terminated (e.g. through the payment of compensation, written notification, observance of deadlines, etc.). Fixed-term contracts, however, are terminated when the predetermined time has passed. No severance pay is owed or other safeguards provided for – a fact that makes this sort of contract attractive for employers. Premature termination of fixed-term contracts is possible only for 'good reason' (Civil Code 675) and in this case payment of compensation is an exception. For this reason, there is a high risk that fixed-term contracts will be used to bypass regulations on the termination

---

72   Articles 7 and 8 of Law 2874/2002, *Government Gazette* A 286/29-12-00.
73   Law 3174/2003, *Government Gazette* A 205/28-08/03.

of open-ended contracts. This danger is more imminent when the duration of the contract has not been clearly agreed upon.

In order to face this risk, Greek law included a measure as far back as 1920,[74] according to which, when a fixed-term contract is agreed upon in order to bypass regulations on the termination of open-ended contracts, these regulations shall apply in any case. Objective criteria are used to judge whether regulations were being bypassed. According to case law, it is enough to prove that the fixed-term contract cannot be justified by the aims and the nature of the work, the needs of the business and other applicable conditions in each case.

This matter has been judged on a case-by-case basis in case law, which has ruled on when a fixed-term contract is permissible (e.g. for completion of a particular project, for seasonal work, due to the seasonal nature of a businesses operation, for a trial period of work or the replacement of a worker, etc.).

If the use of fixed-term contracts is being abused by drawing up successive fixed-term contracts, when the nature of the work and the needs of the business do not justify this, the worker is judged to have been working with an open-ended contract.

It must be noted that case law has been based on particular cases and has not developed a unified stance on this matter.

1.1.2.2. The legal problem with successive fixed-term contracts in the public sector

A problem arose in Greece when fixed-term contracts began to be widely used in public administration, by public entities of public law and local government authorities to cover permanent positions that were presented as temporary needs. Both Article 103 of the Constitution of 1975/1986 and subsequent legislation[75] stated that hiring workers with private law contracts in the public sector was allowed only under certain extraordinary circumstances,

such as filling in unforeseen, emergency or temporary needs that could only be covered by fixed-term or work contracts.

A legal issue arose as to the above contracts, which are frequently consecutive in the public sector. Would Article 8, paragraph 3 of Law 2112/1920 also be applicable in the public sector and could consecutive fixed-term contracts be qualified as open-ended on the basis of this rule? Supreme Court case law in the 1990s[76] answered in the negative, arguing that in this case, it was not so much the nature of the work that was important for the qualification of the contract, but the obligation to use a fixed-term contract that arose from specific legislation mentioned above. This position in case law raised discussion as to how a particular contract could be statutorily imposed, ignoring the nature of the needs (permanent and continuous) which were covered by a particular contract.

This legal issue had enormous political implications for all governments from 1980 onwards. Hiring under fixed-term contracts in the public sector was always used as a carrot during election times. Following renewal upon renewal of the contracts, the following government would vote in special regulations under which these workers would be dismissed without compensation.

Afterwards, there was legislation[77] that attempted selectively and within specific guidelines to transform the successive contracts of special categories of public sector workers into open–ended contracts.

The new Constitution, which followed the 2001 revision, supplemented Article 103 with a new paragraph (8), which forbade oblique methods of changing fixed-term contracts into open-ended ones.[78] However, the legislators responsible for the revision of the Constitution included a transitional clause (Article 118, paragraph 7) which provided for cases where the procedure to change fixed-term into open-ended contracts had begun before the new Constitution had been voted in and was put into effect (transitional cases).

---

74 Article 8, paragraph 3 of Law 2112/1920 'On compulsory termination of employment contracts for private sector workers', *Government Gazette* A 67/18-3-1920.

75 Article 103, paragraph 2 of the 1975/1986 Constitution. 'No one may be appointed to a position which has not been provided for by law. Exceptions may be provided for by special law, so that unforeseen or emergency needs can be covered with staff that will be employed for a fixed term under private law'. Law 993/79 was passed to give effect to this Constitutional provision. This law, together with subsequent supplementary and amending provisions, was codified into a unified text – Presidential Decree 410/1988 'Codification in a unified text of provisions of the existing law referring to staff with a private employment relationship in public administration, organisms of local government and legal entities under public law', *Government Gazette* A 191-30-8-88.

76 Supreme Court 1376/1999, *DEN 2000*, 852 and Leventis, *DEN, 56/2000*, p. 844.

77 Article 32 of Law 2508/1997 and Article 17 of Law 2839/2000.

78 Open-ended contracts or tenure in this case refer to permanent employment in a vacant position.

Today a legal issue has arisen both as to the theory and judicial practice as regards to the Greek law's compliance with Council Directive 99/70/EC.[79] This Directive was transposed into Greek law very recently, but is nevertheless in effect for the period between the deadline for its incorporation into national law and the issuing of the legislative act that officially put it into effect.

1.1.2.3. The legal problems arising from the incorporation of Council Directive 99/70/EC into Greek law

The existence of many workers with successive fixed-term contracts in the public administration, legal entities of public law and local government authorities, who have been used in pre-election periods, has important legal and social implications.

It is for this reason that Greece has faced problems in incorporating Council Directive 99/70/EC, given that this Directive is applied indiscriminately both to the private and the public sector. This is why Greece has exhausted every opportunity to draw out the deadline contained within the Directive. The final deadline for incorporation was 10 July 2002. In the end, the Directive was incorporated after the deadline had passed with the very recent Presidential Decree, which was issued in April 2003.[80]

The practical interest in the incorporation of the Council Directive into Greek law is to be found in the establishment of a framework, which does not allow the abuse of consecutive fixed-term contracts. In order to achieve this, the Presidential Decree made use of all three criteria set by the Council Directive (clarification of objective reasons which justify the continuous renewal of contracts, the delimitation of the longest possible total duration of a fixed-term contract and the establishment of a limit on the number of renewals of such contracts).

In principle, the establishment of criteria that will determine if consecutive fixed-term contracts are permitted is a positive move if it truly contributes to the creation of security and abolishes the ambiguity arising from the implementation of the general provisions of Article 8, paragraph 3 of Law 2112/1920.

However, the Presidential Decree in question has introduced a plethora of exceptions to the ban on the limitless renewals of fixed-term contracts. The result of this has been that it has limited application in the public and broader public sector. This has

occurred because of the wide applicability of the meaning of 'substantial objective reason', which justifies the ban on limitless renewals of these contracts. It also occurs because of the direct exemption from this rule of significant business sectors (e.g. audiovisual sector, air transport), financial services (e.g. banking) and professions, but without this exemption being clearly justified by the nature of the occupation.

In this case, a list of these activities set by law would allow a worker to reverse it before the courts. Furthermore, a preference for an open-ended contract has been established by the greatest permissible duration for renewal (three), the greatest possible duration of consecutive contracts (up to two years) as well as by the definition given by the Presidential Decree on when fixed-term contracts (or relations) are considered consecutive.[81]

This means that whether renewals of fixed-term contracts are permissible or not will once again be judged on a case-by-case basis in court, thus recognising the widespread right of judges to form law. Presidential Decree 81/2003 did not bring an end to the major political and legal dispute on consecutive fixed-term contracts as, I believe, it arbitrarily limits the implementation of Council Directive 99/70/EC both in the private and public sectors.

The transposition of the fixed-term Directive 99/70/EC through Presidential Decree 81/2003, has actually become the most controversial issue of Greek labour law. Following an investigation, which resulted in official meetings of the European Commission's officials with representatives of the Greek Ministry of Labour in January 2004, the Commission did not seem convinced that the Greek government has fulfilled its obligation to transpose the fixed-term Directive into domestic law as regards to the abuse in use of successive fixed-term contracts in the public sector (clause 5 of the European Framework Agreement). At this time the Commission gave the Greek government formal notice in writing, in accordance with Article 226 of the EEC Treaty. The abuse in the conclusion of successive fixed-term contracts in the Greek public sector is a legal question with high social and political implications, which involves almost 45 000 persons. A number of Greek court rulings issued in April-June 2003 converted workers' successive fixed-term contracts into contracts of indefinite duration, on the basis of direct application of the EU 1999 fixed-term contracts Directive. It is very significant that the Greek courts avoided addressing preliminary rulings to the ECJ on the

---

79   Th. Kamenopoulos, *DEE 2000. 464*; Ath. Papaioannou, *EErgD 2000.529*.

80   Presidential Decree 81/2003 (*Government Gazette* 77/2.4.2003), 'Measures for workers with fixed-term contracts'. The Presidential Decree was issued following OKE's negative Opinion 81/2002, http://www.oke.gr.

81   If they are drawn between the employer and the worker themselves, with approximately the same terms of employment and there is no intervening period of greater than 20 days.

correct or incorrect adaptation of Council Directive 99/70/EC and its compliance or not with existing Greek law.

1.1.2.4. The consequences of the ECJ Bectu decision for fixed-term contract workers in Greece

A section included in the recent Law 3144/2003[82] provided for the abolition of the waiting period[83] required for one to be granted annual leave. This occurred because of ECJ case law in the Bectu case (Decision of 26.06.01, which interpreted Article 7 of Council Directive 93/104/EC).[84] The provision of Law 3144/2003[85] has wider application than Council Directive 93/104/EC, as its generalisation covers all categories of workers in all sectors – even those who do not fall under the EC Directive.

The abolition of a time frame for the right to annual leave is particularly important for those working with fixed-term contracts (even those with contracts for a short duration, renewable or not, including those engaged in seasonal work). All of the abovementioned workers are henceforth entitled to a yearly leave proportional to the duration of their employment. This was a significant step towards the equal treatment of fixed-term and open-ended contract workers.

1.1.3. Temporary agency work[86]

A 2001 Law[87] regulated temporary agency work for the first time. It laid down specific rules on the establishment, operation and obligations of agencies on the one hand (already developed in section 2.2.1) and the employment rights of temporary agency workers on the other. The aim of this legislation was to increase job mobility, which is very low in Greece, and to provide incentives for companies to hire new, flexible staff to cover their needs, rather than resorting to overtime for existing staff.

A temporary agency work contract, which must be in writing, is signed between EPAs, as temporary employment agencies (direct employer) and the worker and regulates the provision of labour by this worker to a user company (indirect employer) in the form of temporary employment. Although it is not clearly stated, it appears that the Law allows for both fixed-term and open-ended contracts of temporary agency work to be concluded between the

worker and the agency, opening the door to transforming temporary employment work to occasional work.

Workers are then hired out to a user company (indirect employer). The contract must clearly define the terms, conditions and length of employment, the terms and conditions of the provision of labour to the indirect employer, the terms and conditions of pay and social insurance coverage.

According to the Law, the level of wages must not be lower than those provided for by sectoral, occupation-based or enterprise-level collective agreements that are applicable to the indirect employer's staff and it may in no case be lower than that provided for in the current National General Collective Agreement (EGSSE). Furthermore, the worker's remuneration for the period in which he is not providing labour to an indirect employer cannot be lower than that provided for in the current EGSSE.

The Law requires that the duration of employment for the same indirect employer must not exceed eight months and is renewable for another eight months; otherwise the contract becomes open-ended. In the event that the employee continues in the employment of the indirect employer after the contract with the direct employer expires, and the contract is renewed for a period of more than two months, the employee's contract with the agency shall be deemed to have been converted *ipso facto* into an open-ended employment contract between the employee and the indirect employer.

The agency and the user company are jointly and separately liable vis-à-vis the temporary worker with regard to safeguarding his or her rights regarding pay and the payment of social insurance contributions. This liability on the part of the indirect employer shall be suspended if the agreement stipulates that the direct employer shall be liable for paying the emoluments and insurance contributions, and the rights of the temporary employee regarding pay and social insurance may be met by forfeiting the agency's 'indemnity bonds' (with subsidiary liability of the indirect employer) provided for in Article 23 of the Law.

With regard to health and safety at work, employees under temporary agency employment contracts enjoy the same level of protection as the indirect employer's other staff. The indirect employer, notwithstanding contractual provision for

---

82   Article 6 of Law 3144/2003 'Social dialogue for the promotion of employment and social protection and other provisions', *Government Gazette* A 111/8-5-2003.

83   The period in which one must have been employed with the same employer in order to acquire the right to vacation time for the first time.

84   Theodossis, *DEE 2001.749*; Sigalas, *DEE 2002.977*.

85   Lixouriotis, *DEE 2003. 740*; Sigalas, *EErgD 2003.961*; Metzitakos, *EErgD 2003.1137*.

86   Leventis, *DEN 2001. 1505*; Lixouriotis, *DEE 2002.43*; Vayas, *EErgD 2002.951*.

87   Law 2956/2001 'Restructuring of OAED and other provisions', *Government Gazette* A 258-6.11.2001 (Article 22).

the cumulative co-liability of the agency, is liable for the conditions in which the employee's work is performed and for accidents at work.

Employment by an indirect employer under a temporary agency work contract is not permitted:

*   When it replaces workers who are exercising the right to strike

*   When the user company had carried out collective dismissals of workers with the same qualifications in the previous year and

*   When the user company is subject to the provisions of legislation[88] regulating recruitment in the public sector, which enters into special procedures and rules.

1.1.4. 'Pseudo-independent' employment (economically dependent workers)

As noted in the Introduction (section 2), 'pseudo-independent employment' is a widespread phenomenon in the Greek labour market. It implies the conclusion of contracts for independent services or work contracts, while in reality it is salaried employment that is being offered. This phenomenon is injurious to the basic labour and insurance rights of workers (e.g. the right to compensation upon dismissal and employers' national insurance contribution) and creates unfair competition for businesses whose observance of law is assiduous. Influenced by the French Madelin Law of 11.2.1994, legislation sought to address this problem in 1998.[89]

This 1998 Law established a negative presumption of non-salaried (independent) employment for those workers who provide services as self-employed people, particularly those who do piecework, teleworkers, or home workers. There is a negative presumption of non-concealed salaried employment if:

1. The agreement has been invested in a written form and the Labour Inspectorate has been informed within 15 days and

2. The alleged self-employed person does not offer his services exclusively or mainly to the same employer.

This presumption is arguable in that either the worker or the national insurance institution involved can prove other-wise, but has the burden of proof to show that the worker has a salaried relationship to the employer.

1.1.5. Assessment – remaining challenges

1. The Greek institutional framework – both legislative and within collective agreements – treats the new forms of employment as exceptional and not as alternative forms of regular, stable and full-time employment. As a result, there are gaps in regulating these types of employment and workers offering their services in this way are treated unequally with regard to certain rights and/or prerequisites, such as those that the employer offers voluntarily.

    As a result, non-standard forms of employment are regarded with disfavour in Greece. Standard (stable and full-time) employment continues to be the main form of employment, accounting for 80% of waged work. This situation reflects a particular view of the security and quality of professional life, which is identified with permanent and standard employment. However, in the last two years one out of two new jobs has not been of the stable kind.

2. Part-time employment is the most fully regulated type of the new forms of employment. However, Greece has a low rate of part-time work (4.3% in 2002 compared to the EU average of 17.7%). The rigidity of the existing legal framework limits accessibility to this kind of employment. It should also be noted that part-timers in the private sector are not entitled to receive OAED unemployment benefits (of a maximum duration up to 12 months).

3. There is no statutory provision in Greece for on call labour or job sharing.

4. Temporary agency work represents a very low proportion (0.1%). Despite the guarantees afforded by the current Law 2956/2001 regarding the labour, social insurance and trade union rights of temporary agency workers, only some of the issues arising from temporary agency work are dealt with by existing law. Temporary agency workers are not entitled to the rights emanating from company work rules or company customs for the company staff and are excluded from the benefits that the indirect employer offers voluntarily to its permanent workers. According to the positions of some scholars (Leventis, 2001) the temporary agency workers work for the agency and are not counted among the

---

88 Law 2190/1994 regarding 'Establishment of an independent authority to select staff and regulate management issues' amended by the provisions of paragraph 3 of Article 1 of Law 2527/1997, as applicable.

89 Article 1 of Law 2639/1998 'Regulation of labour relations and other provisions', *Government Gazette* A 205/2-9-98.

employer's permanent staff with regard to legal consequences, such as the right to union representation. The issue of the equal treatment of agency and permanent staff thus arises.

5. Temporary employment (particularly fixed-term and seasonal work) accounts for approximately 15% of overall employment rates. Another 2.2% is employed under OAED fixed-term programmes (usually of an 11-month period) that cover the costs (stagiaires, subsidised unemployed, etc.). It is evident that fixed-term employment contracts (along with work contracts and independent services) constitute the prevailing and most widespread form of making work relations more flexible in Greece. However, the framework within which they operate continues to be made up of few, fragmentary regulations of a general nature, which have left the field wide open to case law interpretation. The legal framework governing fixed-term contracts is regulated by general provisions in the Civil Code (669, 671, 672) and by stray regulations that have no internal cohesion. Besides creating a state of legal uncertainty, this contributes to the belief that fixed-term contracts are treated as exceptional rather than alternative forms of open-ended work contracts.

Furthermore, it must be noted that the Presidential Decree by which Council Directive 1999/70/EC came into Greek law was not applicable to fixed-term contracts concluded for the first time, and thus did not substantively change the fragmentary legal framework of contracts. Also, it did not stave off the danger of using fixed-term contracts to bypass the regulations governing open-ended contracts, which continue to be considered the regular and desirable form of employment.

6. The concept and content of telework have not been defined by Greek legislation. The phenomenon of telework, which represents approximately 1.1% of the Greek labour force, has not developed due to the limited use of new technologies in comparison with other countries and the lack of a special regulatory framework that would encourage its expansion.

7. Although recent regulations seek to extend labour legislation to those who seem to be self-employed but actually resemble salaried workers, their effectiveness is limited since the Labour Inspectorate does not effectively monitor businesses in Greece. Furthermore, provided that the employer observes the procedure for notification laid down in the law, the employed person himself has to take on the burden of proof of the 'subordinate' content of his contractual relationship. The presumption set by law that those employed in atypical employment (telework, piecework, etc.) are working under a contract for services or a work contract, which means that they are not covered by labour law, clearly amounts to indirect discrimination against women.

8. The meaning of the term 'group of companies' or 'company networks' does not appear in Greek labour law. Commercial law recognises the existence of associated companies (Article 42e, paragraph 5 of Law 2112/1920), which it only accepts for the implementation of the specific law and only with regard to drawing up balance sheets.

Labour law has only dealt with groups of companies, as an exception, in the law regarding workers' councils in the enterprise.[90] In these cases, the law allows the formation of a common workers' council, with common representatives that deal with common issues.

Generally, a group of companies does not have legal rights and obligations and is thus not recognised as one employer. Internal worker mobility within a group of companies is a fundamental technique in organising work and managing human resources. However, this can only be legally carried out through employee leasing, when one enterprise (that is the original, regular employer) subcontracts workers for a fixed or open period to another enterprise. Greek law considers this kind of subcontracting/leasing 'authentic' and contrasts it with subcontracting through agencies (temporary agency employment contract).[91] Authentic staff leasing is when the worker is employed by the original employer and is conceded for a period to another company. Given that a group of companies is not considered to be one employer, subcontracting brings about a change in the terms of the individual employment contract, for which the worker's consent is necessary. Recognising the length of service within a group and the obligation of placing a worker in another company within the group if his position is abolished remain open issues.

---

90   Article 16, paragraph 1 of Law 1767/1988, 'Works councils and other labour provisions – Ratification of ILO 135', *Government Gazette* A 63/6-4-88.
91   Leventis, 'Staff leasing', *EErgD 2001.1112*.

Consequently, it appears that the existing legal framework does not favour mobility of workers within a group.

1.2. Developments with regard to working time

1. Greek labour law defines both the daily and weekly limits of work hours. The eight-hour working day was established in 1932 as the maximum permissible period of daily employment under compulsory law regulations. The same Law defined the maximum weekly hours of employment as 48 (legal working hours). EGSSE 1975 began with the gradual reduction of working hours that, with EGSSE 1984, stood at 40 hours a week (contractual working hours). These working hours were established as 'regular', despite the fact that there was divergence between different sectors (for example, banks have a working week of 38 hours and 20 minutes) and the fact that law provides for derogations in particular cases (e.g. companies which work around the clock). Fewer hours can be agreed upon in an individual employment contract or can be part of staff regulations or the practice of a particular enterprise.

The Law did allow contractual hours to be exceeded by up to five or eight hours per week, depending on whether there is a five or six day week. This was called *hyperergasia* and additional wages were paid. There is no equivalent term for *hyperergasia* in English, but this form of extra working hours is different to overtime and is peculiar to Greece.

The contractual reduction of work hours did not alter the eight-hour working day as the legal working day. The eight-hour day is the basis for defining additional work (over eight hours) as overtime, the legality of which is judged by a mesh of legislative rules (e.g. the need for authorisation, notifying the Labour Inspectorate, keeping within the maximum limit, etc.).

In the traditional regulation of work hours, flexibility was achieved through the use of overtime, *hyperergasia*, and shift work.

2. The incorporation of Council Directive 93/104/EC into Greek labour law[92] filled the gaps in labour law with regard to daily time off (at least 12 continuous hours), work breaks (15 minutes at least every six hours), weekly time off (24 hours at least, in which Sundays and the 12 continuous hours of daily time off are included), the maximum working week (48 hours on average), and working time arrangements of four months which, according to law, can be extended through a collective agreement.

3. Statutory law intervention was carried out in the field of working time during the 1990s, aimed at discouraging the use of overtime and not calculating working time on a daily or weekly basis.

The first measure taken was Law 2639/98 (Article 3),[93] which provided enterprises with the opportunity to sign their own collective agreements or to agree with workers' councils on increased working hours. More specifically, through working time arrangements,[94] it allowed for the increase in the legal working hours to nine hours per day for a period of up to six months, while in cases where objective, technical or organisational reasons applied, a working day of up to ten hours daily was allowed for a period of up to six months. In any case, weekly working hours could not exceed 48 hours on average. In this way, workers were not considered to be working overtime or *hyperergasia*, as they had the right to proportionally reduce their working hours, take time off or augment their annual leave in the three or six month period directly following. Based on the above, the average working time for the period in which the arrangements were in effect, which did not exceed six months in the first case and twelve months in the second case, should not exceed 40 hours a week. At the same time, a special case of working time arrangements was provided for in Law 2639 for enterprises employing up to 20 workers that cannot form an enterprise-level union or workers' council.

These provisions were abolished with Law 2874/2000,[95] which contained new provisions for working hours.[96] The above provisions were, in fact, abolished without ever having been implemented, since no enterprise-

---

92 With Presidential Decree 88/1999 'Minimum provisions for organising work in compliance with Council Directive 93/104/EC', *Government Gazette* A 94/13-5-99.

93 Leventis, *DEN 1999.467*.

94 Working time arrangements were introduced for the first time in a legislative text in 1990 with Law 1892 but never implemented in practice.

95 Law 2874/2000 'Promoting employment and other provisions', *Government Gazette* A 286/29-12-00.

96 Douka, *EErgD 2001. 289*; Lixouriotis, *EErgD 2001. 1127*; Ntotsika, *EErg D 2001. 625*.

level or other collective agreement was entered into on this matter.

4. The new Law in principle abolishes the worker's obligation to provide *hyperergasia* five hours a week at the employer's discretion in businesses where there is a 40-hour working week. In this way, the worker's obligation is limited to three hours per week of overtime, which is called 'peculiar overtime'[97] in Greek law.

Overtime is henceforth only each additional hour of work beyond 43 hours for which incremented pay is provided.[98]

The abolition of *hyperergasia* and deterrents for overtime work through the imposition of increased costs were aimed at motivating companies to hire new staff and thus contribute to fighting unemployment.

5. Besides the above, new measures with regard to working time arrangements are being introduced. Following an agreement at the collective level (with an enterprise-level collective agreement) or through an agreement between an employer and an enterprise-level union or an employer and a worker's council or an employer and a workers' association (*enosis prosopon*)[99], it is possible for 138 hours of the annual working year to become the object of working time arrangements. For a certain period annually (which is agreed in the collective or other agreement) it is possible for workers to work more than their contractual working time, up to 138 extra hours per year. To counterbalance this, workers may, for an equal period, work on a reduced working day or get days off or get a proportional addition to their yearly annual leave.

When the system of working time arrangements is in effect, the average working week must not exceed 38 hours. Consequently, workers who are included in this system benefit from a reduction of the working week (from 40 to 38 hours) for up to 92 hours annually.

Businesses included in the above measures are those that have a 40-hour working week and/or a less than 40-hour working week as a result of a collective agreement. In this case, work time arrangements are allowed only by a collective agreement. This condition is inflexible because it excludes businesses that have a regular working week of less than 40 hours arrived at by other means (e.g. internal practice). Small businesses employing up to five people are also excluded, as there are no statutory law provisions for their representation in negotiating a collective agreement.

6. Social partners' initiatives in the direction of reducing regular working hours. The sectoral collective agreement 1999-2001 between the Greek Federation of Bank Workers and the banks included a pilot programme for a 35-hour week without a reduction of salary. However, following the end of the pilot plan in two branches of each bank that ended in March 2000, it was decided that the plan had failed and it was abolished. Isolated capital-intensive enterprises also introduced the 35-hour working week in 1998 and 1999.

7.1. **Assessment** – Studies, opinions and research converge in the belief that the provisions of Law 2874 and particularly those provisions on working time (discouraging overtime and working time arrangements) have only minimally contributed to increasing employment.[100] As for the aim of discouraging the use of overtime, the Law failed completely. From 2000 to 2001, permits for overtime increased three-fold.[101]

---

97   For each of the three hours, a worker receives his hourly wage with a 50% increment. The necessary procedures to make overtime legal are not implemented in this case.

98   For each hour of overtime (up to 120 hours annually) the worker is allowed remuneration equal to his hourly pay increased by 50% (as opposed to the 25% allowed for in previous legislation). For more than 120 hours overtime, the existing 75% over hourly wages continues to apply. So-called 'illegal' overtime is also augmented (by 150% as opposed to the pre-existing 100%). Illegal overtime is yet another Greek peculiarity. It is overtime which is worked without the procedures provided for by law having been carried out (e.g. announcement to the Labour Inspectorate, keeping an overtime book, workers signing the book, etc.). Despite the fact that this overtime is illegal, Greek law provides that it is remunerated by an extra increment, which implies compensation for the worker for the hours worked. The maximum limits for overtime work for the whole country and for particular regions are set by ministerial decisions biannually or annually.

99   A workers' association can be set up with at least 10 workers. As a rule, it cannot negotiate a collective agreement. Exceptionally, such rights are legally recognised for the purposes of the present law; that is for the achievement of a working time agreement.

100   According to the nationwide survey on 'Employment and industrial relations in Greece: reality – trends – prospects' conducted by the Institute of Labour (INE) of the Greek General Confederation of Labour (GSEE) in October 2002, only 6% of companies, responsible for the 12% of all recruitment over the period examined were directly influenced in the direction of new job creation by the new regulations on increasing the cost of overtime exceeding maximum working hours, 'abolishing' overtime and reducing employers' social insurance contributions.

101   Labour Inspectorate Report of Proceedings of 2001 http://www.ypergka.gr.

Moreover, no working time arrangements were implemented by the legal framework of Laws 1892/1990 and 2639/98. In addition, only four agreements[102] have been reached using the legal framework of Law 2874/2002.

Flexibility of working hours in the Greek labour market is still achieved mainly through overtime and shift work. It is estimated that one third of manufacturing companies or 86% of businesses implemented this sort of flexibility in the last few years.[103]

The reason why working time arrangements are not widespread, despite insistent legislative interventions, is mainly due to the unwillingness of employers and representatives of the workers to make collective or other agreements on this matter. Businesses do not wish to introduce collective working time arrangements as the inability to sign or renew a collective or other agreement immediately creates the right to seek arbitration from the OMED. There is an evident preference for individual working time arrangements and flexible working time where the managerial rights of the employer are prevalent. Workers' representatives are also unwilling to enter into collective working time arrangements, which would reduce overtime – a regular source of additional income for workers in the private sector.

7.2. **Career breaks** – These are not regulated by labour law or by EGSSEs,[104] the provisions of which are binding for all businesses and all workers working under a private law contract. In contrast, the Civil Service Code (Article 59) provides for leaves of a shorter or longer duration for educational or scholarly reasons (such as participation in conferences, seminars both within Greece and abroad, participation in tests for scholarships, etc.). It also provides for professional education leaves of three years for enrolment in a two-year graduate programme or up to four years to complete a doctoral dissertation. The worker receives his pay with an increment of 15% to 75% for studies within Greece and with a 100% increase for studies abroad.

In the private sector, there are fragmentary measures in the internal company regulations of public utility corporations or other big companies or advanced in

content collective agreements (e.g. banks), which provide either unpaid leave or leave for educational purposes. Unpaid leave is granted for private reasons at the employer's discretion. The legal framework deals with such leave in a favourable manner for the worker, as if it is included in the length of service and is taken into account when defining a worker's rights, which are linked to length of service (including the allowance for the length of service and the amount to be paid as severance pay). Leaves for educational purposes are, as a rule, given with pay and full coverage of transport costs abroad and back and tuition fees. These leaves are given according to the staff policy of each enterprise or business. The worker using such a leave must continue to work for the company for a period stated in the internal regulations (usually five years), or return the money received during the leave compounded by an agreed upon amount (punitive clause).

The gap in legislation and the lack of provision for working time in the EGSSE has subjected career breaks to the internal policies and initiatives of companies that are primarily safeguarding their own financial interests. A generalised provision for this matter is necessary.

2. Adaptability of businesses

2.1. Quality at work: health and safety in the workplace[105]

Even as early as 1911, there was an abundance of special legislation for protecting the life and health of workers in Greece. These regulations have come to be seen as inadequate or have become outdated by rapid technological developments.

The first significant step taken to modernise the legislative and institutional framework of health and safety at work was in 1985,[106] following a 1978 report by a panel of experts 'on the improvement of working conditions and the working environment' (PIACT) of the ILO. Law 1568 was a landmark in workers' health and safety as it established a general system of prevention for work accidents for the first time. This Law systemised existing law, which did not contradict its terms, and created a series of public law obligations for the employer.

---

102   They either reiterated the law, or were misleadingly called 'arrangements'.

103   Annual Report on the Greek Economy for 2002 conducted by Institute of Labour (INE) of the Greek General Confederation of Labour (GSEE) p. 137.

104   The EGSSEs only provide leave for up to 30 days per year to participate in exams and the OAED pays for this.

105   Spyropoulos (general editor), 2000; IYASE, (1992), 'The implementation of the Community Framework Directive on the improvement of health and safety at work '(in Greek), *EErgD v. 51: 1013*.

106   Law 1568/1985 'Health and Safety of workers', *Government Gazette* 177.

It is this Law that created participatory bodies on a national level (the Council on Health and Safety in the Workplace) and on the level of enterprises (committees on health and safety in enterprises employing over 50 people)[107]. Three years after it was voted in, the state took the important step of extending[108] the Law to workers in the public sector, in legal entities of public law and the local authorities. Thus, an important legislative gap was filled for the first time in Greece.

From 1992 to 2002, Greece was intensely influenced by the EU in health and safety (Spyropoulos, 2000). The influence was dual in nature. On the one hand, it was informative with seminars and events held within the framework of EU initiatives (European Year for Health and Safety in the Workplace). On the other hand, it was legislative with the incorporation into Greek law of more than 20 EU directives. The most important of these was Council Directive 89/391/EC, which was incorporated into Greek law with Presidential Decree 17/1996.[109] Compliance with these EU directives was a matter of the highest importance in Greek law, as they supplemented the 1985 Law, introducing innovations, the extent and nature of which is difficult to assess. Indicative features are the employer's obligation to have a written report on professional dangers, to adapt work practices to people, to consult with workers' representatives in a timely manner and the extension of the responsibility of employers (which in the 1985 Law applied to those employers with a staff of over 150 people) occupying over 50 people to hire safety experts and a doctor.

2.1.1. Initiatives of the social partners

In EGSSE 1991-1992 it was decided that a Greek Institute of Health and Safety in the Workplace (ELINYAE) would be set up. It would be run exclusively and equally by the social partners without the participation of the state. According to the founding act, the Institute would be funded by LAEK through a special fund for vocational training, ELPEKE, to which employers contributed (see Chapter II, section 2.1.3), and possibly by the EU programmes.

The establishment of ELINYAE in 1995, with the agreement of the social partners, meant that for the first time Greece had a research, informative and consultative body on a national level in the fields of health and safety and working conditions.

2.1.2. Assessment

The barrage of legislative and institutional changes (both of national and EU origin) of the last 15 years in the field of health and safety in the workplace contributed to the modernisation of the legislative framework for protection from and prevention of dangers at work.[110]

However, the operation of these institutions and the implementation of law in practice revealed gaps and problems. The result was that the laws remained to a large extent inapplicable and the technical infrastructure was at best inadequate, at worst non-existent. Even the punitive procedure is problematic as, when violations are found at on-site inspections by the Labour Inspectorate, only inadequate fines are imposed where a cessation of work could be ordered. Although the accident rate has decreased significantly in recent years,[111] the inadequacy of preventive inspections has led to an increase in fatal accidents at work suffered mostly by foreign workers.

Despite the fact that the social partners seem to be more sensitised to this problem than they were in the early 1990s, their initiatives remain on the highest level, the second and first level organisations remain inert, and specific issues are not dealt with in any collective agreements, except in the EGSSEs.

In EGSSE 2000-2001, the social partners agreed on the necessity to observe health and safety measures in the workplace according to existing law and on the necessity to continuously inform employers and workers of their rights and obligations. However, they did not go on to specific measures, confining themselves to inviting ELINYAE to carry out systematic studies on the causes of work-related accidents and professional diseases.

2.2. Quality at work: reconciling of family and working life

2.2.1. Institutional developments

In Greece, the only legal text that plainly refers to family and professional life is Law 1483/1984 entitled 'Protection and

---

107   With Presidential Decree 17/1996 (see footnote 31), the minimum was lowered to 20 workers.

108   Common Ministerial Decision 88555/3293/88 'Health and safety of staff in the public sector, in public entities of public law and in local authorities', *Government Gazette* 721 B which was ratified by Article 39 of Law 1835/89 'Promotion of employment and vocational education and other provisions', *Government Gazette* 79 A.

109   Presidential Decree 17/1996 'Measures on the improvement of health and safety of workers during work in compliance with EU Directives 89/391 and 91/363', *Government Gazette* A 11/18-1-96.

110   I. Nikolakopoulou-Stefanou, 2001, *The modernisation of standards for health and safety at work* (in Greek), DEE, p. 814-827.

111   According to the SEPE's annual report for 2002 (www.ypergka.gr), which includes statistical data collected by the Social Insurance Foundation (IKA) on the insured people between 1977-1999, the general accident rate has fallen from 3.81% in 1977 to 0.91% in 1999.

facilitation for workers with family obligations', which implemented ILO Convention 156.

In the private sector, the EGSSE plays an important role as its provisions have a regulatory effect and define the minimum protection for the workers of the whole country. During the reporting period, the subject of leaves for family reasons appeared for the first time on the agenda of collective negotiations in 1993, and significant measures were taken in the 1993 EGSSE. It is important to note that the EGSSE 1993 provided for protection for pregnant women and breast-feeding women long before the transposition of Council Directives 92/85/EC and 96/34/EC[112] into Greek law. Since then, there has been no clear positive impact of the above directives on collective bargaining (Petroglou, 2000).

Since then, this subject was relegated to a drawer and only reappeared on the agenda of collective bargaining on a national level in 2000. EGSSEs 2000-2001 and 2002-2003 extended existing leaves for family reasons. These are frequently improved within the framework of industry-wide collective agreements in those industries whose union representation is powerful.

Important changes also took place for civil servants with the new Civil Service Code.[113]

2.2.2. Chief forms of leave related to the conciliation of family and professional life developed from 1992 to 2003

2.2.2.1. Maternity leave

Maternity leave was first created in the 1980s and was significantly extended during the period in question.[114] It is obligatory for the employer to grant this leave to women who work in the private sector, the public sector or public organisations, whether they are employed part-time or full time, whether they are married or not, regardless of length of service, nationality or occupation.

The duration of this leave and the financial and other arrangements differ in the public and the private sectors (see Chapter IV).

2.2.2.2. Marriage or childbirth leave

In the public and private sectors both men and women are entitled to a marriage leave of five paid days.[115] Following EGSSE 2000-2001, fathers are entitled to two days paid leave upon the birth of a child.

2.2.2.3. Leave for breast-feeding and care of children

This applies to both public sector workers (Article 53 of Law 2683/1999) and private sector workers who were provided for under EGSSE 1993 (Article 9) for the first time. This leave takes the form of a reduction of daily working hours. It is an indisputable right for all workers, even part-timers, who reduce their hours proportionately. This leave is paid. As to duration, there is a differentiation between private and public sector workers (see Chapter IV).

Other than leave for breast-feeding, there are no other statutory provisions for a reduction of working hours to take care of family.

2.2.2.4. Parental leave for care of children

In Greece, parental leave was granted for the first time in 1984[116] in private businesses with at least 100 workers and later, in 1988, it was extended to the public sector.[117] With EGSSE 1993, parental leave was extended to enterprises and services in the private sector and to public enterprises and banks with at least 50 workers. The prerequisites related to the size of the business were abolished in 1998,[118] as a result of full compliance with Council Directive 96/34/EC. These forms of leave are unpaid.

The duration of leave and the conditions under which it is given are much more favourable for civil servants than for those in the private sector (see Chapter IV).

---

112   Presidential Decree 176/97 'Measures for the improvement of health and safety during work for pregnant and breast-feeding women in compliance with Council Directive 92/58/EC', *Government Gazette* A 150/15-7-97 and Article 25 of Law 2639/98 (see above) respectively.

113   Chapter 6 Law 2638/1999, 'Ratification of code for civil administrative workers and workers of legal entities of public law and other provisions', *Government Gazette* 19 A.

114   Article 52 of Law 2683/1998 (Civil Service Code), Article 12 (1) of Law 1469/1984, Article 8.11 of Presidential Decree 176/1997 implementing Council Directive 92/85/EC (see above) and collective agreements in banks and public organisations.

115   Article 6 of EGSSE 1993 established the marriage leave and Article 10 of EGSSE 2000-2001 states that those that work a six-day week are entitled to six days marriage leave.

116   Article 5 of Law 1483/1984.

117   Article 3 of Presidential Decree 193/1988.

118   Article 25, Law 2639/1998 (see above), which amended Article 5 (1) of Law 1483/1984 (see above).

2.2.2.5. Parental leave for illness of family dependents

This is an annual unpaid leave, which was established for the first time in 1984[119] for workers in a private law relationship.

The duration is up to six working days a year, consecutive or not, for one child, up to eight days for two children and up to twelve days for three or more children. The increment for three or more children was established with EGSSE 2000-2001.

2.2.2.6. Special parental leave for children's schooling

This is provided for by law.[120] In the private sector it applies only to full-time workers who have children born either within or without a marriage or were adopted, who are up to 16 years of age and are in primary or secondary education. These workers can take some hours or up to four working days off every calendar year in order to visit their children's school to be informed of their performance. Parents with children in kindergarten are also entitled to this leave.

It is not clearly stated whether this is paid or unpaid leave. Supreme Court (Full Court) case law[121] (decision 4/2000) helped to establish this as paid leave.

2.3. Assessment: remaining challenges

Generally, for private sector workers there is a lack of substantive measures to facilitate the conciliation of family and work responsibilities, while the duration of existing leaves is exceptionally short.

Complying with Council Directive 96/34/EC significantly improved the matter of leaves for family reasons. It increased the maximum age of children from 2.5 to 3.5 years, abolished prerequisites as to the size of the business and increased parental leave from 3 to 3.5 months. At the same time, it provided that termination of employment contracts arising from these reasons is invalid.

However, the fact that this leave is unpaid and is not covered for by national insurance discourages workers in the private sector from taking it. The same applies for leave for a child's illness or other family members. The right to leave to check on a child's performance at school is, in any case, only an entitlement for full-time workers.

The nursery-school system is also inadequate (NAP 2003). On the one hand there are not enough public or local government nursery centres, and on the other hand there is no monthly supplement to help defray the costs of private school nursery centres, except for the collective agreements of banks and some public utility corporations. Despite the fact that this expenditure is not considered as a presumption of income, it is not tax deductible either.

119   Article 7 of Law 1483/1984 (see above).
120   Article 9, paragraph 1 of Law 1483/84 and Article 53 (5) of Law 2683/1999 (Civil Service Code).
121   Deltio Ergatikis Nomothesias (DEN) vol. 56/2000, p. 225.

Chapter IV:
Promoting equal opportunities

1. General institutional framework

1.1. Statutory provisions

The Greek Constitution has, since 1975, provided for many provisions to combat discrimination. Article 5.2 states that *all persons within the Greek state enjoy full protection of their life, honour and freedom, irrespective of nationality, race, language, religion or political conviction.* Furthermore, it provides for equality before the law (Article 4, paragraph 1) and equal rights and obligations for men and women (Article 4, paragraph 2) and postulates equal pay for work of equal value irrespective of sex or any other distinction (Article 22, paragraph 1, section b).

At present, there is no specific legislation in Greece aimed at tackling discrimination in the workplace, with the exception of sex discrimination. Council Directives 2000/43/EC, implementing the principle of equal treatment of persons irrespective of racial or ethnic origin and 2000/78/EC, establishing a general framework for equal treatment in employment and occupation, are in the process of being incorporated into Greek law. A draft transposition law is expected to pass before the Parliament soon after the national elections take place. Innovations brought by this draft legislation concern the introduction of new legal concepts into domestic law, such as 'harassment' and 'indirect discrimination'. In addition, general reversal of the burden of proof in cases of discrimination – including sex discrimination, as the transposition of Council Directive 97/80/EC has already taken place – is a wide-scale exception to the general rule that the burden of the proof in civil cases falls on the plaintiff. This is a major evolution for Greek law and ensures the implementation of the principle of equal treatment since, in most cases, discrimination takes the form of indirect discrimination which is difficult to prove before the courts.

1.2. Measures in collective agreements

1. No collective agreements are reported on the issues covered by the Framework Directive 2000/78/EC. However, the social partners have included special provisions on equal treatment in the framework of their intersectoral National General Collective Agreements (EGSEEs), which are not directly related to this Directive.

2. For the first time, EGSSE 2000-2001 stipulated that independent workers (employed under a work contract or a contract of independent services) have the right to similar or proportional treatment as salaried workers when this is imposed by the conditions under which they offer their services. Equal treatment is mandatory mainly in: health and safety, protection against any discrimination on the basis of sex, ethnicity or race, beliefs, previous service, protection of maternity, access to education or training, respect for the freedom of collective organisation or action, facilitation of access to national insurance and educational systems.

3. In addition, for the first time, EGSSE 2000-2001 stipulated that workers that are employed under similar conditions of dependence as salaried workers (economically dependent workers) have the right to treatment that is equal to that of salaried workers. Equal treatment must be safeguarded particularly in the fields of education, equality of sexes, employment and health and safety.

4. EGSSE 2001-2002 included for the first time an agreement between the social partners which stated that respect for racial, national, religious and cultural differences is a goal that should be put into effect for every worker. The need to facilitate adaptation to the working environment for every worker was also enunciated in this agreement.

2. Issues of equality of treatment for special categories of workers

2.1. Blue-collar and white-collar workers

The legal distinction between white-collar and blue-collar workers, set in a 1920 Law, has remained extant. The latter have less favourable treatment with regard to the sum received as severance pay upon dismissal, as well as with regard to the termination of their employment contracts. In fact, this can be done without having to follow notification deadlines.[122] A judicial decision stated that this anachronistic distinction is unconstitutional.[123] EGSSE 1989 (Article 7), EGSSE 1994 (Article 6), EGSSE 1998-1999 (Article 4), EGSSE 2000-2001 (Article 5) and EGSSE 2002-2003 (Article 4) have taken steps to diminish the differentiation between the two categories with regard to severance pay. The GSEE continues to place negotiations for national collective agreements on the complete equalisation of blue-collar workers and white-collar workers with regard to severance pay on its agenda.

2.2. Workers in a public or private law relationship

According to the prevailing view in case law, one reason that could justify differentiation in matters of pay for workers offering the same services under the same conditions is whether they are serving under a public or private law relationship.[124] This differentiation was deemed to be in line with Article 22, paragraph 1, section b of the Constitution and Article 119 (now 141) of the EC Treaty. As of 1983, the Special Supreme Court[125] determined that the principle of equal pay for work of equal value (Article 22, paragraph 1, section b of the Constitution) refers only to workers who provide their services in a salaried relationship to natural or legal entities on the basis of private law and does not apply to those who are working in a public law relationship.[126]

This distinction between workers in a public or private law relationship had a direct impact on the matter of family allowances. Contrary to what was stated above with regard to private law, where it was accepted that family allowances are included in remuneration, in public law, the family allowance was considered by the case law of the Council of the State to be an authentic family allowance which could not be affected by the principle of equality, as payment was not dependent on the sex of the beneficiary.

Following an ECJ decision in 1999,[127] which stated that family allowances are contained within the definition of remuneration of Article 119 section b (now 141) of the Treaty, and because of contradictory decisions on this issue by the highest courts (the Council of the State and the Court of Auditors), the whole matter was handed over to the Special Supreme Court. It ruled[128] that family allowances are an increment on salaries for married workers in the public sector, in legal entities of public law and local government. The Special Supreme Court did not change its previous position as to the extent of the implementation of Article 22, paragraph 1, section b of the Constitution. Based on the general constitutional principle of equality, as stated in Article 4 paragraph 1, it ruled that the establishment of distinctions which are not in themselves linked to employment, but to the employment or not of the other spouse or the working relationship of the latter in the private or public sector, and results in depriving the public worker of the allowance, is contrary to the constitutional principle of equality and the constitutional provisions on safeguarding the family.

There are significant differences between those in a public and private law relationship with regard to the provision of leaves for the conciliation of family life and career.

2.2.1. Maternity leave

In public administration, the duration of this leave, based on the Civil Service Code, is five calendar months (two months in pregnancy and three after childbirth). Furthermore, women civil servants are entitled to special additional maternity leave[129] if they need special treatment at home for a period that is not to exceed normal paid sick leave.

---

122 Leventis, *DEN 2001*, p. 65.
123 The One-member Court of the First Instance with decision 77/1994, *EErgD 1994.1012* stated that this distinction is contrary to Article 4, paragraph 1 and Article 22, paragraph 2 1 section b of the Constitution.
124 Supreme Court (Full Court) decision 3/1997, *EErgD 1999.585*, Supreme Court 1328/1997, *EErgD 1997.19*.
125 Supreme Special Court Decision 16/83, The Constitution 1985, p. 369.
126 Because the contents of the Constitutional provision are a transfer of identical regulations from EU and international labour law regulations (Article 119, *EC Treaty*, ILO convention 100/51), which are applied in all work relationships, the position of the Special Supreme Court has been criticised as theoretically unsound. For this reason, in later decisions the Supreme Court accepted the view that the principle of equal pay for work of equal value covers workers in a public law relationship based on EU and international labour law regulations (see Supreme Court 432/92, *Nomiko Vima* 41, 880).
127 [Case 187/1988 of 28.10.1999, *DEE 1999,1310*].
128 Supreme Special Court Decision 3/2001, *EErgD 2001*, p. 398. See Comments by Lixouriotis *DEE 2002.1270*.
129 Article 52 (3) of Law 2683/1999 (Civil Service Code).

In contrast, in the private sector, the duration of leave is 17 calendar weeks (eight weeks before childbirth and nine after). The seventeenth week was only added with EGSSE 2000-2001. Some sectoral collective agreements (e.g. those of banks) are more favourable, as are some staff regulations in public enterprises and organisms.

In public administration, maternity leave is fully paid. In the private sector, on the other hand, a worker who has worked for at least one year for the same employer is entitled to receive benefits equal to one month's salary. Otherwise, she receives the equivalent of half a month's pay. For the remaining period of maternity leave, the worker receives maternity benefit from her national insurance organisation if she can prove that she has been employed 200 days in the last two years before the expected childbirth date. The difference between the amount provided by the national insurance organisations and the worker's monthly salary is covered by the OAED.

2.2.2. Leave for breast-feeding

Civil servants: The beneficiaries of this leave are mothers who are civil servants (except if their husband is also a civil servant and is on leave). Use may be made of this leave until the children are four years of age. Working hours are reduced by two hours daily if children are up to two years old and by one hour if children are from two to four years old. If the civil servant does not take advantage of her reduced working hours, she is entitled to paid leave of nine months to raise the child. This leave may begin directly after her maternity leave ends, bringing the total to 14 months paid leave. There is no such right in the private sector.

In the private sector: EGSSE 2002-2003 increased the duration of leave for breast-feeding to 30 months after delivery. For this period, the working mother or the working father is entitled to reduced working hours by one hour daily. Upon agreement with the employer, daily work hours can be reduced by two hours for the first twelve months and by one hour for the next six months.

2.2.3. Leave for care of children

Civil servants are entitled to this until their children are six years of age. The duration of the leave is up to two years for each parent who is a civil servant and must be given upon request. The leave can be taken as a continuous period or in portions. The period of leave is not considered a period of employment, but the right of the civil servant to return to the same position is recognised. This is unpaid leave and, unlike in the past when there was insurance coverage on the condition that the worker pay the contributions him or herself, the present Civil Service Code has no such provisions.

In contrast, workers in a private law relationship in the public enterprises, banks and in the private sector are entitled to this leave until the child reaches 3.5 years of age. In all cases, the provision applies to every child.

The duration of leave is up to 3.5 months for each parent and is given on a priority basis to those who have submitted applications to their firm on a yearly basis. The worker must have been in service for at least one year and is entitled to return to the same or a similar position, but not to a lower one. The period of absence is considered to be a period of employment. Leave is unpaid. Those who take this leave may choose to pay their own and their employers' insurance contributions in order to maintain their national insurance coverage. In this case, the period of leave is taken into account for the purposes of retirement and the calculation of one's pension.[130]

2.3. Immigrants

In 2001 a new Law[131] was voted in for non-EU immigrants, regulating the conditions of entry and residence of foreigners in Greece and appointing the bodies responsible for drawing up and applying immigration policy. The aim was to maintain order, avoid illegal immigration, guarantee respect for foreigners' human rights and their social integration and maintain social cohesion in Greece. According to this Law, immigrants who permanently reside in Greece are to be insured in national insurance organisations and enjoy the same insurance rights and social protection as native Greeks. The Law further established the right to compulsory nine-year education for immigrant minors.

The initial draft Law submitted to the social partners was much more daring and progressive. It had provisions on the treatment of legally residing immigrants which would be equal to that of native Greeks with regard to social welfare, national insurance, health, vocational training, trade union freedom, the right to associate, access to employment and to independent professional activity. These provisions were withdrawn from the document that was voted on.

---

130   Article 6 of Law 1483/1984.
131   Law 2910/2001, 'Admission and stay of immigrants in Greece. Acquisition of nationality with naturalisation and other provisions', *Government Gazette* 91A/27.4/2.5.2001.

2.4. Age discrimination

There is no specific statutory provision that explicitly prohibits age discrimination in the workplace or any other place. The result is that this category of workers has significant problems both in access to the labour market and in the conditions and terms of their employment.

Wherever there are more specific provisions, these refer exclusively to pensioners. Generally, a pensioner's right to work depends on the statutory provisions of his or her national insurance organisation. Most organisations are averse to their pensioners working and oblige pensioners to withdraw from their profession in order to get their pension. Some organisations allow pensioners to continue working or to seek new work if their salary is not above a certain limit. If the pensioner's work is above a certain level (set by the insurance organisation), they postpone the payment of a pension.

In collective negotiations there is no substantive link between collective employment contracts and measures against age discrimination in work. The few initiatives that exist are confined to the national level (see Chapter II – Active Ageing) with no applicability on an industry-wide or enterprise-level.

There is a lack of substantive statutory and non-statutory intervention, which would facilitate the access of the older population to the labour market. Furthermore, the social partners have not taken initiatives within the framework of social dialogue. They have confined themselves to general statements on the necessity to remove obstacles to employment for older people.

3. Equal opportunities between men and women at work[132]

3.1. Statutory provisions

3.1.1. Constitutional amendments and the promotion of substantive gender equality

Among the amendments of the Greek Constitution in April 2001, one in particular replaced the provision of Article 116 (2), which allowed derogations from the constitutional principle of the equality of the sexes,[133] with a provision on affirmative action. Thus, the new Constitution that entered into force on 17 April 2001 no longer allows any derogation from the principle of the equality of the sexes. Now Article 116 (2) reads as follows:

Affirmative measures for the promotion of equality between men and women do not constitute sex discrimination. The state shall take measures in order to abolish inequalities which exist in practice, in particular those which are detrimental to women.

The amendment was, to a considerable extent, the result of a long campaign by Greek women's NGOs and inspired by Article 4(1) of the UN Convention on the Elimination of all Forms of Discrimination against Women (CEDAW), ratified by Greece in 1983. The Council of the State's (Full Court) 'historic' Decision No 1933/1998[134] supported the proposal to introduce a provision on affirmative action. It was the first time that a Greek Court had dealt with affirmative action and was quoted in the parliamentary debates on the revision of Article 116(2). The Council of the State clearly stated that:

insofar as discrimination against a category of persons is ascertained as having been applied in practice, the application of the principle of equality would result in a mere superficial equality, while, in fact, a situation of inequality would be consolidated and perpetuated; in this case it is not contrary to the Greek Constitution that for a certain period of time, statutory or administrative affirmative action in favour of women is taken so that de facto equality between men and women can be accelerated.

---

132 'Monitoring, implementation and application of Community Equality Law' (1999), General report 1997 and 1998 of the Legal Experts' Group on Equal Treatment of Men and Women, European Commission V/D.5 and Information about Greece (by Sophia Spiliotopoulos) collected in the *Bulletin of the Legal Expert Group on the Application of European Law on equal treatment between men and women* (2000, 2001, 2002), http://europa.eu.int/comm/employment_social/equ_opp/rights_en.htm.

133 Article 4(2) of the Constitution: 'Greek men and women have equal rights and obligations'.

134 Council of the State (Full Court) 1933/1998, NoB, 1998.1610; A. Maragopoulou, 1998, 'The historic shift of the Council of the State towards real equality', To Syntagma [The Constitution], v. 4, p. 773-801.

3.1.2. Law 1911/1990

Under Law 1911/1990 a 10% quota system was established for the admittance of women into certain sections of the military academies, while they were completely excluded from sections that trained for combative functions within the military. According to well-established case law from the Council of the State (Full Court),[135] unjustified maximum quotas for the admission of women to police and military academies are invalid and inapplicable, and candidates should be admitted according to merit, irrespective of sex. Although it did not refer to it explicitly, the Council of the State was clearly influenced by the ECJ case 318/86.[136] Upon the entry into force of the new Constitution, Parliament adopted Article 6 of Law 2913/2001, by which the quotas were abolished and undifferentiated access was provided to all sections of military academies for both women and men.

Nevertheless, discriminatory provisions to the detriment of women have been maintained in recent legislation concerning access to the Police Academy.[137] In addition, case law stated that the discriminatory provisions of this legislation were not unconstitutional. The Council of the State[138] failed to examine the grounds of annulment that were submitted, based on Community law, and entirely disregarded the claimant's request that the case be referred to the ECJ for a preliminary ruling and its own obligation to make such a referral.

3.1.3. Presidential Decree 105/2003

Presidential Decree 105/2003[139] has attempted to adapt domestic law in relation to Council Directive 97/80/EC on the allocation of the burden of proof in cases where there might be sexual discrimination. The Presidential Decree simply reiterates the provisions of the Directive. It should have made them more specific through references to the civil procedure law provided for by existing law and, if necessary, adapting them with amendments or supplements.

The allocation of the burden of proof in cases of sexual discrimination is particularly important in Greek law. Case law on wage discrimination continues to be limited. This leads indirectly to the belief that women, either because they do not know they are being discriminated against, for reasons

of caution, or because they worry about the safety of their jobs, do not bring their cases to the courts. In addition, the difficulty in proving indirect discrimination, especially with regard to salary, contributes to this and is the most usual form of discrimination that women are subjected to. It is worth noting that there is no decision of the Greek courts on the matter of indirect discrimination.

3.2. Collective agreement regulations

The issue of sex equality entered collective bargaining in the 1990s. The term 'equal opportunities' appeared for the first time in the EGSSE 1993 text. The EGSSE of 1993 is the most advanced collective agreement on the issue of equal opportunities between women and men. After this agreement was signed at national level, it stimulated a strong movement in specific sectors (banking, insurance), which in the last few years has retreated to a subordinate position because of the important restructuring which has taken place in the labour market.

Issues of sexual discrimination are dealt with at sectoral level. Enterprise-level agreements completely lack provisions against sexual discrimination, as there is no tradition of dealing with this issue. Whenever collective agreements are entered into that have provisions against sexual discrimination, these are supplementary and improve existing law. The provisions are poor and limited in content and focus either on the creation of organisations or committees on equality, which frequently remain inert, or on the conciliation of family and professional life.

In no case have we seen reparative provisions in collective agreements, substantively promoting the equality of the sexes in the workplace.

3.3. Case law developments

3.3.1. Council Directive 76/207/EC

For twelve years after Greece entered the EC, there was not one Supreme Court decision implementing Council Directive 76/207/EC and Law 1414/1984 which transposed it into

---

135 Council of the State (Full Court) judgements No 1917-1929/1998, Elliniki Dikaiossini 1998, p. 1050.

136 Commission v. France, Judgement of 30-06-88.

137 According to Article 12 of Law 2713/1999, non-transparent and non-justified quotas are maintained due to the nature of the mission of the Greek police and other factors which require 'increased levels of muscular strength, speed and endurance; requirements which, according to common sense and experience, are typically possessed by men, due to their specific biological characteristics'.

138 Council of the State 1850/2002.

139 Presidential Decree 105/2003, 'Adaptation of domestic law to Council Directive 97/80/EC on the burden of proof in cases of sexual discrimination', *Government Gazette* 96A/23-4-2000.

Greek law. It was only in 1992[140] that the first historic Supreme Court decision was made, which interpreted the letter and the spirit of Directive 76/207. This, like many subsequent decisions of the Supreme Court,[141] deemed that drawing up separate lists of successful men and women candidates in examinations taken for employment in a bank is against the principle of the equality of sexes. Such discrimination was deemed invalid, but did not affect the status of the examinations and the subsequent employment contracts that arose from these exams based on the conditions set by the call for applications. The candidates were considered successful based on their rank on the list of those that passed, without taking sex into account.

3.3.2. Equal pay constitutional provisions

Despite the constitutional provisions for equal pay when work of equal value is being carried out, collective agreements, arbitration awards, and staff regulations continued to contain unfavourable discrimination against women with regard to pay. The Greek civil courts considered this discrimination justified and indeed ignored ECJ case law.

The case law of Greek courts was reversed only in 1995 with two Supreme Court (Full Court) decisions. Decision 3/1995 is considered seminal. This decision was on a provision of the staff regulations of the Public Power Corporation. The Court decided that the family allowance is an element of pay and ruled that all regulatory provisions (collective labour agreements, company work rules, etc.) existing up until that time which discriminated against women became void as of 1975, when ILO convention 100 was ratified.

After this historic decision of the Full Court, Part B of the Highest Court has been fully compliant and amenable to this position taken in 1996 through a series of decisions which reiterated that arbitration awards which make the provision of the family allowance dependent on prerequisites (e.g. spouse without work and without a pension) are void, as such prerequisites are not set for working men.[142]

The preservation of such unfavourable terms until recently led to Greece's condemnation by the ECJ.[143] The European Court ruled that Greece failed to fulfil its obligations under Community law by not retroactively abolishing collective regulations that made the payment of family allowances dependent on prerequisites that discriminated against married working women. As to the scope of autonomy enjoyed by the social partners during collective negotiations, which the Greek government used as an argument, it is significant that the ECJ noted that implementation of the principle of equal pay is mainly the responsibility of the social partners. However, the state must intervene in any case where there is a lack of effective protection, especially if there is no collective agreement in effect or if the person who takes his case to the ECJ is not covered by a collective agreement or, finally, if a collective agreement does not safeguard the principle of equal pay in all its scope.[144]

3.3.3. Article 35 of Law 2956/2001

After this ruling, a ruling[145] was adopted which retroactively abolished as of 1/1/81, terms in all provisions of laws, decrees, Ministerial Decrees, collective agreements, arbitration awards, internal regulations of enterprises as well as terms in individual employment contracts. The terms abolished were those which set special prerequisites for married working women with regard to payment of marriage or child allowances by employers in the private or public sectors to workers in a relationship of private law. These terms were also abolished as unfavourable for the purposes of calculation of pensions, which were provided to married women after 23/12/84, given that the specific allowances were not taken into account in calculations for a social security pension.

---

140   Supreme Court Decision 1360/1992, *EErgD 1993.32.*

141   Supreme Court Decision 79/1993, Elliniki Dikaiosyni 1993.354, Supreme Court Decision 1095/1998 Elliniki Dikaiosyni 1999.281.

142   For example Supreme Court 356/1996, *DEE 1996.977*, Supreme Court 720/1996, *DEE 1996.1192.*

143   Case 187/98 Commission v the Hellenic Republic.

144   See also Case 143/83 Commission v. Denmark.

145   Article 35 of Law 2956/2001 'Restructuring of OAED and other provisions', *Government Gazette* A 258/6.11.2001.

Chapter V:
Conclusions

1. The plethora of statutory provisions and their *de facto* neutralisation: the Greek oxymoron

The picture that Greek labour law presents today is one of a complicated and chaotic system of rules that is difficult to enforce in practice. This bloated legal system has produced a '*de jure* over-regulation' of the Greek labour market and at the same time it has encouraged its '*de facto* deregulation'.[146] However, it can be argued that this deregulation was not the result of the content of labour law reforms, which we believe were rather timid compared to what happened to other European countries (e.g. the Netherlands).

The main reason for this situation is the fact that the Greek labour market is intensely dual in nature. One part, which includes undeclared employment particularly in small businesses, and which is a part of the hidden economy (which accounts for approximately 33-35% of the GDP), is flamboyantly flexible and not regulated – a fact that creates conditions for unfair competition. The other part, that of the public sector and the 'law-abiding' part of the private sector, remains rigid and over-regulated, but ordered, nevertheless, by rules that are not always adjusted to its real needs. The market's widespread flexibility outside the legal framework is also encouraged by illegal immigration, a high percentage of youth and female unemployment and parasubordination.

In parallel, there is a flourishing of the so-called 'grey zones of subordination', which are on the fringes of salaried and independent employment and which serve as a means to circumvent labour law. Rather than concluding open-ended employment contracts, Greek companies frequently resort to the use of successive fixed-term contracts, outsourcing, contracting out (which applies to a quarter of Greek businesses), work contracts and contracts for independent services. The three last forms are used to bypass labour law and

often conceal salaried employment and fulfil permanent functions within a business.

The picture of the labour market based on official figures is not adequate, because it does not reflect the rate of undeclared employment amongst Greeks and immigrants and its real impact on the labour market. It is estimated that widespread undeclared employment contributes to the evasion of national insurance contributions, reduces even further the already low costs of labour and is a delaying factor in modernising enterprises (in terms of the introduction of new technologies, new organisational structures, new methods of production, in-company training, etc.) which, in the mid-term, is necessary to important sectors of the Greek economy.

An understanding of this picture is a *sine qua non* to the discernment of the development of Greek labour law, which, in effect, is applied to only one part of the labour market.

The inability to improve the efficiency of those mechanisms, which have been assigned the task of controlling the labour market, and to properly implement labour law, has encouraged an anarchic flexibilisation in labour relations. At the same time it has also created the impression of a peculiar tolerance on the part of the state, the responsible institutions and of the social partners vis-à-vis the systematic breaking of the law.

Significant challenges for Greek labour law remain. Firstly, the legal and institutional framework must be simplified, made functional and codified in an accessible manner, so that it is clear which regulations are in effect. Regulations which are not implemented or which have fallen into disuse must be eliminated.

Secondly, there is an imperative need to support and enhance the state control mechanisms, which enforce law and collective agreements and monitor the proper operation of the labour market. Measures need to be taken to do away with the dual nature of the labour market, reduce the hidden

---

146   The expressions are borrowed from the article of E. Gazon, St. Gavroglou, A. Mouriki, (2001), 'Social dialogue and company renovation', *Epitheorissis Ergasiakon Shesseon*, vol. 23: 34-49.

economy, convert illegal and undeclared employment to regular employment, and to drastically deal with the phenomenon of 'pseudo-independent' employment that distorts the image of salaried employment and transgresses labour law.

2. The effect of the EMU in the development of Greek labour law[147]

The 1990s saw the start of a slow modernisation in labour law. Preparing the country to meet the convergence criteria for inclusion into the EMU had an effect on the institutional framework of labour relations and brought about changes.[148]

In Greece these preparations included the incorporation of the Community *acquis* into areas in which Greece was behind, such as the creation of institutions and procedures for social dialogue. The European Union and convergence with the other Member States became synonymous with modernisation and normalisation, i.e. the pursuit of a solution to the widespread hidden economy and the establishment of a controlled and disciplined system of regulating work relations similar to that of other European systems.[149]

The attempts at modernisation also included discussions on making laws on forms of employment, working time and, to a lesser extent, remuneration, more flexible. This discussion dominated in the latter half of the decade, bringing the state, the government and employers into conflict. This conflict and the lack of long-term strategic planning led to attempts at equilibrium and timid changes (Laws 2636/98 and 2874/00), the implementation of which was notable for delays and backsliding.

Greece's path towards the EMU mainly affected the policy on remuneration in collective bargaining and, to a lesser extent, perhaps, its structure.[150] On a national level, where minimum wages for unskilled workers in industry are set and where EGSSEs are compulsory for all employers and workers, there is a policy that is still in force today of constraining salaries as a result of the effort to be part of the EMU. Also, a partial shift in bargaining on the enterprise and local levels was observed, as well as differentiation of wages based on a company's profitability and the individual performance of workers.

3. The effect of traditional EC legislation on the development of labour law in Greece

The need to adapt Greek labour law to EC legislation, as a form of hard law and as a result of the classic Community method of governance,[151] also greatly influenced the development of certain parts of labour law, particularly in health and safety, sex equality and the restructuring of enterprises (see Chapters III, IV and II respectively).

In addition, the contribution of EC legislation in covering legislative gaps (Directives 93/104/EC, 97/80/EC, 91/353/EC, 98/59/EC), in improving existing regulations on part-time work (Directive 97/81), in protecting pregnant women (Directive 92/85/EC) and on parental leave (Directive 96/34/EC) is also significant.

However, it must be noted that the government tends to simply replicate the contents of Directives (e.g. 97/80 burden of proof or 98/59 on the condition of closure following decision of a Court of First Instance) without accompanying them with the statutory prerequisites which would allow for their effective implementation and without adapting them to the Greek legal order. To give an example, the official transposition (with Presidential Decree 17/1996) of the regulations in Directive 91/383 on the health and safety of fixed-term and temporary workers, did not lead to a substantive implementation for temporary workers, as temporary work was not, until recently, legal in the Greek system and temporary employment agencies were prohibited. Therefore, although Greece proclaimed that it had incorporated Directive 91/383 in a correct manner, this was not accurate because the issue of health and safety for temporary workers could not have been regulated independently of the legalisation of this kind of work relationship. Finally, Greece safeguarded this form of work in a recent Law (2956/2001).

Also, it must be noted that the incorrect transposition of directives is a frequent phenomenon. As a result, illegality, client-oriented relations and inequality between the public and private sectors continue (see, for example, the problems arising from the incorporation of Directive 99/70/EC on the issue of consecutive fixed-term contracts in the public sector).

147   S. Yannakourou, (2003), 'European Union Social Regulation in the Greek context' in D. Dimitrakopoulos and A. Passas, (ed.), *Greece in the European Union: explaining the sources and pace of change*, London: Routledge: 61-74 (in English).

148   Y. Koukiadis, (2001), 'Problems and perspectives of labour law in the framework of the EMU', *EErgD*, p. 1067.

149   K. Featherstone, (2001), 'The Political dynamics of the Vincolo Esterno: the emergence of EMU and the Challenge to the European Social Model', *Queen's Papers on Europeanisation no 6*.

150   I. Kouzis, (1998) 'The consequences of EMU for industrial relations: the case of Greece' in T. Kaupinnen (ed.), *The Impact of EMU on industrial relations in the EU*, Helsinki: FIRA, pp. 111-121.

151   European Commission (2001), *European Governance. A White Paper*, COM 428 final, 25.7.2001.

Finally, with regard to the development of collective bargaining, EC legislation has had no influence. The opportunity provided by the Social Protocol of 1992, later incorporated into the Treaty of Amsterdam – namely the ability to transpose Community directives into domestic law through collective agreements – was ignored.

4. The effect of non-binding intervention by the EU in the development of labour law in Greece

Besides Community legislation that is directly binding, other forms of 'non-binding' intervention were also important. Examples include the Green Paper on European Social Policy: Options for the Union, (COM(93) 551, 1993) or the Third Community Action Plan for health and safety during work, as well as broader horizontal strategies such as mainstreaming.

Actions of an educational and informative nature played a large part in raising the awareness and responsiveness of the Greek judges to Community law on the equality of the sexes.[152] As was noted above (see Chapter IV), in the early 1990s Greek case law seemed to refuse to implement both Community and domestic sex equality law. Actions taken in this field include seminars for lawyers, judges, labour inspectors and other professionals in the legal system. The EU also funded scientific events/meetings, which aimed to make Community law more accessible.

5. The effect of the European Employment Strategy (EES) and the Open Method of Coordination (OMC)

The EES forced Greece to include its legislative policy on labour relations within a national employment strategy, which had previously been lacking. However, even today there is no unified legislative planning, as there is no comprehensive strategy that embraces a partnership approach with the social partners in order to modernise labour law. The Greek government's awareness led it to establish National Committees on Employment and Social Protection in order to continue social dialogue on the formation of a national

strategy with the participation of all the interested actors and the relevant ministries (see Introduction).

The EES also led to a greater decentralisation of powers and functions within the state, between the social actors (the establishment of LAEK by EGSSE – Chapter II), as well as with private actors (e.g. the creation of Temporary Employment Agencies and of private labour offices and the abolition of the state's monopoly on job placement – L. 2956/2001).

In addition, it led to a more horizontal integration among separate, but interdependent administrative and policy areas (such as the labour market, pensions, social assistance and taxation). In 2000 and again in 2003 this led to a restructuring by law of the administrative services of the Ministry of Labour. The Directorate for Social Protection was founded with the aim of covering the needs created by the EES.

Responsibility for drawing up the National Action Plans on Employment (NAPs) and the recent coordination of the National Action Plan on social inclusion (NAPIncl) generated the need to create more strategic bodies. The Ministry of Labour expressed this need by establishing (Article 2 No 2874/2000) an advisory-consultative body named the 'Council of Experts on Employment and Social Security' whose task is to draw up and monitor employment and social policies. In practice, this body has no obvious role. The law provides also for the creation of an 'Analysis and Documentation Unit' to provide scientific and administrative support for the Council.

The Open Method of Coordination reoriented Greek labour law towards employment and the unemployed person, and had an impact on its penetration into policy fields such as active and preventive measures to deal with unemployment, and the redefinition of the role of the public employment services. At the same time, labour legislation has become more targeted and can deal with a) specific parts of the population that are thought to be vulnerable (such as long-term unemployed people, the unemployed below the age of 29, women, immigrants, etc.), b) specific areas of economic activity in which employment can be increased (such as culture, environment and tourism) and c) regions with high unemployment rates (with the support of territorial employment pacts).

In effect, Greek labour law has acquired new content and has been adapted to more horizontal issues, such as quality at work, active ageing, vocational training and lifelong learn-

152   Tr. Mitsou (1996), 'The impact of economic integration on labour and employment. Adjustment and harmonisation of individual labour law' (in Greek), *EErgD, 55: 1-11* (in Greek).

ing, which were previously completely foreign to it. This larger scope has led to interconnection between labour law and other legal fields, especially tax law, social security law and education law, because it necessitates statutory actions in order to adapt law in these areas.

6.   Overall assessment

The development of labour law in Greece from 1992 to 2003 appeared to be more active than during other periods in the past. This is the result of many factors (EMU, EES, EC legislation, etc.), as examined above. The 1990s were, however, also characterised by a lack of innovation and radical reform in the field of labour relations. Changes focused on the creation or modernisation of structures, infrastructures, institutions and mechanisms, many of which did not function or fell into disuse. However, the activity mentioned above did signal changes in labour law, of which two are particularly important.

The first concerns the procedure of law making; the way in which Greek labour law was formulated changed. First, its drafting and content has evolved as an indirect effect of the EES and the OMC. Under pressure by changes instigated by the EU, labour law has become more the result of consultation and social dialogue with the social partners than it was in the past. However, even today, legislative changes in the field of labour relations and employment do not reflect a real partnership approach. They are neither a product of a wider employment strategy nor of central negotiation and agreement between the state, employers and workers. For this reason, legislation remains fragmentary and not fully effective.

The role of collective autonomy in the law-making process has been strengthened during the last decade, but has not reversed the primary role of state legislation. Collective bargaining manifested dynamism and innovation only on the national inter-sectoral level and, as this did not permeate to other levels, more specialised regulations are still needed. Although bipartite relationships with social partners have progressed, they have not abandoned the authoritarian state mindset, which perceives the state as the initiator of all regulations. Social partners face the challenges to take on initiatives to regulate and deal with matters such as the restructuring of businesses, collective redundancies and their consequences, organising working time, the new forms of employment, life-long learning, etc., through innovative and radical collective agreements at all levels.

The second change concerns the progressive transformation of Greek labour law, both statutory and autonomous (collective autonomy), into employment law, which, among its other aims, seeks to facilitate the demand for employment, its management and the re-regulation of the labour market. This change in the function of labour law is still in the early stages and coexists with the traditional function of Greek labour law, namely the protection of workers' rights and the protection of jobs both as to their substance (including limits on termination and end of work relations; see Chapter II), as well as to their contents (unilateral changes in the terms of employment contracts are forbidden).[153] Because of this, and according to the analysis of this study, we believe that there is still no clear shift in the function of Greek labour law from protecting workers' rights and jobs to regulating transitions from one status to the other (i.e. from unemployment to active employment or from employment to training and career breaks) and from one employment profile to another (i.e. from dependent employment to self-employment or from stable employment to a temporary one and vice-versa), through the promotion of employability, adaptability and equal opportunities.

One major challenge for Greek labour law is to tackle various forms of discrimination in the workplace and in employment in general, which go beyond the grounds covered by Council Directive 2000/78/EC. The most sound are those concerning blue-collar and white-collar workers, those employed in a private and a public law relationship (see Chapter IV) and those employed with standard and non-standard employment relationships (see Chapter III).

---

153   The protective nature of Greek labour law is as old as the first labour legislation, which emerged in 1911-1920 during the government of Eleftherios Venizelos, who was an outstanding politician. See *National Research Foundation 'Elefterios Venizelos'* (2003), Elefterios Venizelos as Jurist and his contribution to the reform of the Greek Law (in Greek), Athens: A. Sakkoulas.

Selected bibliography

P. Agallopoulou, (2000), *Introduction to Labour Law*, Athens: A. Sakkoulas.

Association of Jurists of Northern Greece (ENOBE) (1995), *The principles of European law of Contracts. Sex equality in labour relations* (in Greek), Thessaloniki: Sakkoulas.

M. Chletsos   (2002a), *Labour Market in Greece: what statistics tell us about labour supply*, PAEP Employment Observatory Research – Informatics S.A., Working Paper no 1.
(2002b), *Labour Market in Greece: what statistics tell us about unemployment*, PAEP Observatory Research – Informatics S.A, Working Paper no 2.
(2003), *Labour Market in Greece: what statistics tell us about employment*, PAEP Observatory Research – Informatics S.A, Working Paper no 3.

K. Chryssogonos   (2000), *A confirming revision of the Constitution* (in Greek), Athens: A. Sakkoulas.
(1998), *Civil and Social Rights* (in Greek), Athens: A. Sakkoulas.

V. Douka, (1997), *Transfer of undertakings and individual labour relations* (in Greek), Thessaloniki: Sakkoulas (in Greek).

T. Doulkeri, (1994), *Sex Equality in Labour Relations*, Athens: Papazissis (in Greek).

Economic and Social Council of Greece (OKE), Own Initiative Opinion on '*Social Dialogue in Greece: evaluation, trends, prospects* (in English), (No 86, December 2002), http://www.oke.gr.

EDEKA and Peiraias Bar Association, (1998), *Contemporary trends of labour law and social security* (in Greek), 6th Panhellenic Congress on Labour Law and Social Security, Athens: A. Sakkoulas (in Greek).

European Constitutional Law Centre, (2001), *The new Constitution. Acts of Congress* (14-15/06/01), Athens: A. Sakkoulas (in Greek).

European Employment and Industrial Relations Glossary: *Greece* (1994), Y. Kravaritou (ed.), with contributions from G. Koukoules, N. Karasavidou, A. Stergiou, London: Sweet and Maxwell and Office for Official Publications of the European Communities.

S. Gavroglou, (2003), *Flexibility and organisation of work: empirical data from Greece and the EU*, PAEP Observatory Research – Informatics S.A, Working Paper no 9 (in Greek).

K. Gogos (ed.), *Towards an European Constitution and the recent revision of the Greek Constitution: Thoughts, trends and perspectives*, (Preface: V. Skouris), Athens: A. Sakkoulas (in Greek).

J. Iliopoulos-Strangas and G. Leventis, (2000), 'La protection des droits sociaux fondamentaux dans l'ordre juridique de la Grèce', in Iliopoulos-Strangas, (ed.), *La protection des droits sociaux fondamentaux dans les Etats membres de l'Union Européenne* (in French), Athènes, Bruxelles, Baden-Baden.

Institute of Urban Environment and Human Resources, (2002), *Labour 2002,* Collective Tome, Athens: Editions of University Pantheon of social and political sciences (in Greek).

A. Karakatsanis, St. Gardikas, (1995), *Individual Labour Law,* 5th edition. Athens: A.Sakkoulas (in Greek).

Ath. Kardaras, (1995), *Regulation of labour conditions on the company level,* Athens: A. Sakkoulas (in Greek).

Th. Koniaris, (2002), *Labour Law in Hellas,* Athens: A. Sakkoulas (in English).

I. Koukiadis
(2000), *Social Europe* (in Greek), Thessaloniki: Paratiritis (in Greek).
(1995), *The impact of community law on greek private law,* Thessaloniki: Sakkoulas (in Greek).
(1999), *Collective Labour Relations,* Volume 2, (1997), Volume 1, Thessaloniki: Sakkoulas (in Greek).
(1995), *Labour Law. Individual Labour Relations,* 2nd edition, Thessaloniki: Sakkoulas (in Greek).

G. Koukoules, (1998), Collective Labour Relations, in Petrinioti, Koukoules (eds), *Labour Year Book,* Athens: Panteion University Editions, pp. 101-115 (in Greek).

Y. Kouzis, (2001), *Labour relations and European unification. Flexibility and deregulation or revalorization of work?* (in Greek), GSEE-ADEDY Labour Institute, Studies no 14 (in Greek).

Y. Kravaritou, (1995), 'Main trends of the Greek labour relations system '(in Greek), *EErgD,* v. 54:289-306.

Labour Inspectorate Corps, *Reports Activity 1999, 2000, 2001, 2002* (in Greek).

Labour Institute of GSEE-ADEDY, (2002), *Employment and labour relations in Greece* (nation-wide research), INE GSEE-ADEDY Editions (in Greek).

G. Leventis, (1996), *Collective Labour Law,* Athens: Bulletin of Labour Law (in Greek).

I. Lixouriotis, (1998), *The legal status of the immigrant worker in Greece,* Athens: A. Sakkoulas (in Greek).

I. Lixouriotis, (1999), *Collective redundancies in Greece,* Athens: Editions of National Labour Institute (in Greek).

Ministry of Labour and Social Security, (2002), *Evaluation of the labour market policies and assessment of the influence of EES in Greece during the period 1997-2001,* Final Report (in English) Athens, February.

A. Mouriki, M. Naoumi and G. Papapetrou, (ed.) (2002), *The social portrait of Greece 2001,* Athens: National Centre of Social Research (in Greek).

CDE (2001), *Regulatory reform in Greece,* OCDE Reviews of Regulatory Reform (in English).

OMED
(2004), Report Activity 2002-2003, Athens: OMED's editions (in Greek).
(2002), *Codification of Provisions of Collective Regulations,* Vol. I and II (in Greek).
(2001), *Report Activity 1992-2001,* Athens: O.M.E.D's editions (in Greek).
(1996), *The institutional framework of collective bargaining, mediation and arbitration,* Athens: O.M.E.D.'s editions (in Greek).

PAEP (2003), *Yearbook of the Labour Market,* http:www.paep.org.gr (in Greek).

A. Petroglou, (2000), *Good Practices for reconciliating family life and the career*, Greek Report, Athens: Research Centre on Gender Equality, http://www.kethi.gr (in English).

S. Robolis and Y. Kouzis, (eds) (2000), *Social Dialogue issues*, Athens: Gutenberg Editions (in Greek).

I. Sabethai, (2000), 'The greek labour market: trends, problems and policies', *Financial Bulletin of the Bank of Greece*, vol. 16, December (in Greek).

G. Spyropoulos, (1998), *Labour relations. Developments in Greece, in Europe and in the international field* (in Greek), Athens: A. Sakkoulas (in Greek).

G. Spyropoulos (general editor), (2000), *Health, safety and working conditions in Greece. Developments and perspectives*, Athens: A. Sakkoulas (in Greek).

Studies in memory of Professor Alexandros Karakatsanis (2001), EErgD, vol. 60: 946-1180 (in Greek).

E. Venizelos, (2001), The Constitutions of 1975/1986/2001. The revised text of Constitution. Introduction. Index. Athens: A. Sakkoulas (in Greek).

S. Vlastos   (2003), *Codification of Labour Legislation: Labour Laws from 1912 to 2002*, Athens: A. Sakkoulas (in Greek).
(2001), *Individual Labour Law*, Athens: A. Sakkoulas (in Greek).
(2000), *Individual Labour Law*, Vol. III (second edition), Athens: A. Sakkoulas (in Greek).
(1999), *Individual Labour Law*, Vol. II (third edition), Athens: A. Sakkoulas (in Greek).
(1999), *Individual Labour Law*, Vol. I (third edition), Athens: A. Sakkoulas (in Greek).

M. Yannakourou and G. Koukoules, (2003), 'Labour conciliation, mediation and arbitration in Greece' in Valdes Dal – Re (Ed.), *Labour conciliation, mediation and arbitration in the European Union countries*, Madrid: Ministerio de Trabajo y Asuntos Sociales (in English).

S. Yannakourou, (2003), 'European Union Social Regulation in the Greek context' in D. Dimitrakopoulos and A. Passas, (eds), *Greece in the European Union: explaining the sources and pace of change,* London: Routledge (in English).

D. Zerdelis, (2003), *The law on termination of dependent employment contract*, Athens: A. Sakkoulas (in Greek).

D. Zerdelis, (1999), *Individual Labour Relations*, Athens: Sakkoulas (in Greek).

Law Review (in Greek)

Epitheorissis Ergatikou Dikaiou (EERgD)

Deltio Ergatikis Nomothessias (DEN)

Dikaio Epiheirisseon kai Etaireion (DEE)

Nomiko Vima (NoB)

To Syntagma (The Constitution)

Elliniki Dikaiossyni

Epitheorissis Ergassiakon Shesseon

THE EVOLUTION OF LABOUR LAW
IN SPAIN

1992-2002

Miguel C. Rodríguez-Piñero Royo
Labour Law Faculty
University Carlos III, Madrid

Table of contents

Chapter I:
Introduction: Labour law and industrial relations in Spain

Despite its unusual history, the industrial relations system in Spain today has all the attributes of an advanced and democratic model. The long periods of authoritarian government that the country suffered, some of which coincided with crucial moments in the development of labour law, exercised such a profound influence that traces of them still remain in its dynamics and structure. For this reason, some of the distinctive features of working life in Spain can only be explained as being the remnants of practices introduced under the previous regime and adjusted to the requirements of the current democratic government. These are, as it were, echoes of a past that has been overcome. However, these practices remain as a result of inertia or because they are in the interest of decision-makers that regard them as both permissible and sustainable. Some of the unique features of the Spanish system of industrial relations are due to this past, setting it apart from other countries.

I. Ten years of legal reform

For Spanish labour law, the ten years that have elapsed since 1992 constitute one of the most unsettled periods in its entire existence. The series of changes and trends it has experienced over this period are testament to the social, economic and production-related upheavals in the country.

The 1980s were a very difficult time for Spanish law, as many different challenges had to be faced simultaneously: the consolidation of a democratic system of industrial relations, which had begun in the second half of the 1970s; the integration of Community law after Spain's accession to the European Economic Community in 1986; and, above all, the struggle against unemployment which had been exacerbated by the opening and restructuring of the Spanish economy and a series of international economic crises. The basic instruments of Spanish labour law date from this decade: the Statute of Workers' Rights (*Estatuto de los Trabajadores*) of 1980, the Law on Trade Union Freedom (*Ley Orgánica de la Libertad Sindical*) of 1985, the Law on Infringements and Penalties in the Social Order (*Ley de Infracciones y Sanciones en el Orden Social*) of 1988 and the Law on Employment Procedure (*Ley de Procedimiento*

Laboral) in successive versions between 1980 and 1990. By and large, these were the outcome of a legislative programme aimed at reforming labour legislation or reactions to a series of employment crises that arose in Spain from 1980 onwards.

After this decade of upheaval, Spanish legislation should have benefited from a certain amount of stability since the major structural elements of both the the labour market and industrial relations had already been established. However, this was not the case. The 1990s were also a period of major reform in which, without changing the basic elements of the Spanish model, key aspects of its substance were modified. There were several reasons for this:

- **Firstly**, the measures adopted during the 1980s had failed to deal with the persistent problem of unemployment

- **Secondly**, some of the measures started to create problems that required a series of new solutions

- **Thirdly**, the Spanish economy was suffering from the effects of a changing global production system and economic structure that had heavy repercussions on the functioning of the labour market

- **Fourthly**, the European institutions started to produce legislation faster, with a wider scope and higher standards, making it difficult for Spanish law to keep up.

For these reasons, the decade between 1992 and 2002 was a period of more change and transformation than might have been expected.

Moreover, the year 1992, where this analysis begins, is a particularly pertinent date for a study on the evolution of Spanish labour law, as it was precisely at this time that one of the most important processes in Spanish history began. This process was a consequence of the economic and unemployment crisis the country faced following two major international events in Spain that year, namely the World Fair in Seville and the Olympic Games in Barcelona.

The first reaction to this crisis came at the end of 1993 with Royal Decree-Law 18/1993, which contained far-reaching measures governing the labour market and terms of employment. In 1994, the most important reform of the period came into force, transforming the Statute of Workers' Rights with regard to the legal provisions governing contracts of employment and the legal bases. This reform was implemented by Laws 10 and 11 of 1994 and brought about fundamental changes in the legislation on industrial relations in Spain and the labour market. In the same year, Law 14/1994 was adopted, which legalised temporary work agencies in Spain, along with Law 42/1994, which affected provisions on part-time work and other aspects of individual working relations.

The subsequent reforms were on a much smaller scale, frequently in the form of selective intervention through laws accompanying the budget law. In 1995, Law 31/1995 on the prevention of risks at work was adopted, which was intended to implement various directives in this area. In the same year, Law 4/1995 on parental and maternity leave was enacted to transpose the relevant Community directive.

Two main thrusts can be identified in the development of Spanish labour law during the first half of the 1990s: the advance of flexibility measures mainly in the regulation and management of employment relationships, and the liberalisation of the labour market by steadily opening it up to a wider circle of operators.

In 1997, a process of nation-wide social consultation culminated in the social partners signing various inter-confederal agreements, including agreements on remedying shortcomings in collective bargaining and on stability in employment. To give effect to these agreements, the Government undertook a new legislative reform, enacted initially via Royal Decree-Law 18/1997 and later via Law 63/1997. These laws, *inter alia*, introduced contractual arrangements for promoting permanent employment contracts.

In 1998, an agreement on part-time work was signed between the State trade union confederations and the Government. This resulted in the amendment of the Statute of Workers' Rights, as justified by the need to implement the 1997 Directive. In 1999, the Law on Temporary Work Agencies (*Ley de Empresas de Trabajo Temporal*) was also amended to establish a more stringent and controlled regime after serious dysfunctions had been found in the sector. This reform covered the agreements that had been made by the social partners of these enterprises through collective bargaining, in previous years.

The reforms of the second half of the 1990s must be understood in the context of the political changes of the times. In 1996, the socialist Government was replaced by a conservative Government with a very different labour policy. From 1996 to 2000, this Government struggled to achieve consensus on its labour policy, perhaps because it was concerned by the Spanish conservative parties' traditional lack of credibility with regard to social matters. As a result, some major inter-confederal agreements were signed over the course of these years, sometimes with the direct participation of the executive, which produced major labour reforms. This policy had two main effects: there was a resurgence of social consultation, which had been abandoned in Spain since the mid-1980s, and there was a reconsideration of the flexible labour policies that had determined the evolution of Spanish labour law since the transition to democracy. For the first time, legal instruments which partly reversed the trend towards flexibility and refocused attention on the situation of wage-earners, were created by introducing aspects related to the quality of employment. The aim of improving working conditions is to be found in all the 1996-2000 reforms – with regard to temporary work agencies, part-time work and the promotion of permanent employment – in what constitutes one of the most interesting attempts to restore the balance of labour law in Europe.

The second conservative Government, from 2000 onwards, undertook a radical reappraisal of this policy. Having gained an absolute majority and thereby resolving its problems of legitimacy, the Government did not wait for social dialogue agreements, as it had done previously, to undertake reform. In fact, when the inter-confederal agreements of 1997 expired in 2001 and the attempts to repeat the process of social consultation failed, the Government adopted a significant reform which affected contractual arrangements and the legal regime governing the inheritance of companies and subcontracting. This reform altered many aspects of the legislation governing contracts of employment and implemented some Community directives, introducing provisions that are ambivalent with regard to labour flexibility.

The following year (2002), a new reform was introduced, this time focusing on aspects of the functioning of the labour market and protection for the unemployed, obviously reflecting the new thrust in labour policy. The 2002 reform introduced by Royal Decree-Law 5/2002 increased jobseekers' obligations and restricted their protection in a bid to motivate people to actively seek employment. These measures gave rise to widespread social protest that culminated in a general strike. With elections approaching, the Government's need to regain the support of trade union organisations obliged it to modify its stance and amend the bill substantially. The instrument finally adopted in December 2002, Law 45/2002, was a much-revised version of the original bill and had done away with many of the measures initially introduced.

In general, the second conservative Government's labour policy aims to differ from the labour policy of the first conservative Government. It is thus geared almost exclusively towards measures promoting employment, in many cases via flexibility arrangements, without any concern for issues related to the quality of employment.

In summary, the legislative changes that were made from 1992 to 2002 demonstrate that a fairly significant process of change has taken place.

2. The parties to the system

When it comes to trade unions, the Spanish model has been described as 'an attenuated trade union duopoly', since there are two major trade union confederations that represent the vast majority of Spanish workers, if not in terms of membership then in terms of trade union support. However, other trade union players have also played important parts in their specific fields of action.

First of all, there are national trade unions which operate in certain Autonomous Communities and are normally linked to political parties with the same aims, such as ELA in the Basque Country and CIGA in Galicia. Secondly, there are occupational trade unions, some of which are strongly represented. In fact, the law obliges certain professions – such as the police, airline pilots, engine drivers, etc. – to have occupational trade unions and prohibits them from being affiliated with larger confederations. Thirdly, some important sectors have their own trade unions, such as public health, civil service, banks, etc.

But this does not mean that the description of the Spanish system as a duopolistic model is not entirely valid: UGT and CC.OO are the authorities' negotiating partners and the ones which conduct collective bargaining and represent trade unions to the outside world.

Unlike in other countries, Catholic trade unions have not been and are still not major players.

These trade unions do not constitute a traditional element of industrial relations in Spain, since they did not exist before or during the Franco era. In fact, of the two large trade union confederations, only one, UGT, could consider itself 'historical'

in as much as it is over a century old. The other, CC.OO, originated during the Franco era. The other large historical trade union, the Confederación Nacional del Trabajo (CNT – National Labour Confederation), plays a very marginal role today.

The reason for this unusual configuration of trade union influence can be found in the transition from the Franco era to democracy from 1975 onwards and the evolution of the trade union landscape from that time. The first years of democracy saw a greater number of trade unions, with older trade unions coexisting alongside others that had emerged during the Franco era or had just been created. These were gradually thinned out as workers concentrated their support on fewer organisations, leaving the others stranded. Some of the decisions made by the labour legislator also contributed to this process of trade union concentration. It favoured a trade union model based on a few very strong and representative organisations to facilitate management of the system and social dialogue. So the decisions to maintain trade union elections – elections to the bodies legally representing workers in the enterprise – as a basic indicator of their representativeness, and to use the most representative trade union, had a fundamental impact on the final composition of the system.

A peculiarity of the Spanish system is the low level of trade union membership, with the exception of some specific occupations. However, the representativeness of the major confederations cannot be questioned once they have obtained a majority vote in the trade union elections that are held periodically. Although these elections do have another aim, namely to provide members for the legal bodies representing workers in companies – work councils and workers' delegates in the private sector, and staff delegates and councils in the civil service – they are also used to calculate the level of representation of the trade unions taking part. The results determine who obtains the status of the most representative trade union under the Law on Trade Union Freedom of 1985, which brings a whole series of advantages in all aspects of trade union activity, particularly with regard to collective bargaining and financial support from the public authorities.

The representation of employers' interests is even more highly concentrated since, to all intents and purposes, the Confederación Española de Organizaciones Empresariales (CEOE – Spanish Confederation of Employers' Organisations) is the only relevant employers' organisation. There is also a regional CEOE organisation where some regional confederations have a certain amount of independence, as with the FTN in Catalonia. The Confederación Española de la

Pequeña y Mediana Empresa (CEPYME – Spanish Confederation of Small and Medium-sized Enterprises) is affiliated to the CEOE and has the special status of a confederation that represents small and medium-sized enterprises. In addition to the employers' organisations proper, there are also other channels for representing enterprises' interests, such as the chambers of commerce and the professional associations.

The third player in the system, the State, has a key role in Spain and is one of the identifying features of Spain's industrial relations. The State's involvement in industrial relations and in the labour market as a whole – through regulations, inspections and various policies – is considerable. This is a tradition that dates back to the previous regime, which developed a very extensive role in the labour market and assumed powers of regulation and guarantee that, under normal conditions, would have been wielded by collective bodies. This tradition has been upheld by the current social State, and the State has even developed new means of intervention.

Another peculiarity of the Spanish system with regard to public intervention is the process of transformation undergone in these areas since the Constitution of 1978, which introduced the State of Autonomous Communities as a new organisational model for the country. Spain is constituted as a quasi-federal State where a number of powers are exercised by territorial bodies, the Autonomous Communities. Although the Constitution grants the State exclusive powers in labour legislation and social security, the Governments of the Autonomous Communities now have basic powers with regard to labour affairs and the labour market, including the implementation of State labour law, labour administration, employment policies and meso-scale social consultation.

3. Labour market

The reforms that Spanish labour law underwent from 1992 to 2002 cannot be understood without a rudimentary knowledge of the labour market in Spain, since this has been both the cause and the explanation for the majority of the legislative changes that have occurred. Other factors inducing change that were important at the time, such as the construction of a democratic system of industrial relations or the adaptation of the acquis communautaire, were less relevant between 1992 and 2002. In some cases, this was because they were processes which had already been completed and in others because of the dearth of Community legislation. All the reforms of this decade, barring some exceptions, are justified in terms of employment irrespective of the subject and legislative technique used and irrespective of the Government that was responsible for them. In fact, the majority of the important labour reform laws contain in their titles a mention of the labour market and some substance related to it.

The demographic factor is one of the keys to the behaviour of the labour market in Spain. As in the majority of developed countries, it is faced with a process of gradual ageing due to a combination of declining birth rates and a considerable increase in life expectancy. Although this is a phenomenon that is common to all developed countries, the way it has been experienced in Spain has been unusual. As in other southern European countries, it has been characterised by the speed with which the ageing process has set in. The fall in the birth rate has been conspicuous in the last few decades: while in 1975 the birth rate was 2.5, it has been close to 1 during the 1990s. There has also been a gradual decrease in the average size of households. With the turn of the century, it picked up slightly, moving to 1.24 in 2001, although much of the increase can be attributed to immigration.

The first defining feature of the Spanish labour market is a high level of unemployment over the entire decade. Despite the improvement in employment over the past few years, with steady decreases in unemployment since 1994, the current levels are still above the Community average: in 2002 it was 11.4%. And this is after practically a decade of progressive reduction of these figures.

A second feature of the Spanish labour market is temporary work and the high incidence of all types of fixed-term contracts. Once again, the figures here indicate that Spain has one of the most insecure labour markets in Europe. In a relatively short period of time, the Spanish labour market went from having virtually no temporary work to a proportion of 31% of the entire economy in the year 2002, and this after a significant reduction of this percentage over the last five years, with an even higher incidence in some sectors and areas.

The above feature is primarily a result of the labour policies implemented throughout the 1980s to combat unemployment. These were based on more flexible arrangements for entering the labour market, making it easier to offer workers fixed-term contracts without altering the rules for managing the employment relationship or the cost of dismissals. In the 1990s, fixed-term work started to be regarded as a problem in itself due to the speed with which it had increased. So the decade saw the progressive introduction of legislative reforms restricting the possibilities for offering fixed-term contracts and providing incentives for permanent or stable employment. From the middle of the 1990s, the aim of employment policies in Spain shifted from simply creating more jobs to seeking better quality jobs.

By contrast, part-time work has always been of very marginal importance, despite successive attempts to promote its use by means of legal reforms and all manner of incentives.

Another feature of the Spanish labour market during this decade is the uneven impact of unemployment on the different groups of persons and professions. Unemployment affects certain groups of workers more than others, especially young people, women and elderly workers.

The case of female workers is fairly unusual. In 2002, over 57% of all Spanish unemployed persons were women and this figure has been increasing over the past ten years. Unemployment is starting to be thought of as a strictly female problem with a rate of 16.4% for women and 8% for men, together with a rate of female employment that is one of the lowest in Europe.

In the case of elderly workers, there is a clear tendency for them to be excluded from the labour market. This is a result of practices deployed by companies to restructure the workforce that mainly affected the over-fifties, namely early retirement schemes which were intended to rejuvenate the workforce. In view of the problems that this raises for the dynamics of the market and the financial equilibrium of the system, measures are already being taken to prevent premature exclusion, promoting an extension of working life by means of flexible retirement schemes, incentives to employ older people, etc.

Finally, a trend towards regional segmentation can also be discerned, with a reduction of internal migratory flows as a result of a variety of factors, including the creation of the State of Autonomous Communities, linguistic plurality, housing prices, etc. This means that, at a given time, there are employment vacancies in some regions and very high levels of unemployment in others.

The Spanish labour market is thus highly fragmented, with deep structural imbalances and serious problems. The different measures taken over the past few years to cope with the most serious problems – unemployment and insecurity – have had some effect, but have not been sufficient to cope with the scale of unemployment and fixed-term work.

As in the rest of Europe, immigration has become a key factor in terms of both demographic structure and the functioning of the labour market, although it should not be forgotten that in absolute terms there are still far fewer immigrants in Spain than in other European countries. What is striking is the speed at which the size and composition of the immigrant population are changing. In approximately two decades, Spain has gone from being an emigrant country to one that is a host to immigrants. According to data from the 2001 Population Census, a total of 1 572 017 foreigners now reside in Spain, which is 3.85% of the total population. In addition, the composition of this population is changing rapidly: whilst in 1985 some 70% of all the foreigners living in Spain came from developed countries, the same percentage now comes from developing countries. A peculiarity of the migrant population in Spain is the large number of Latin American nationals as a result of the cultural and linguistic affinity. The other major sources of immigration, Maghreb, sub-Saharan Africa and the countries of the former Eastern Bloc, are common to the rest of Europe.

The past few years have also seen a sharp increase in the female population in this group, rising to 48% of the total in 2001. Women account for the majority of Latin American immigrants and, what is more, they tend to come to Spain independently, without their spouses already being in the country – as is the case with female immigrants from other geographical areas. The potential importance of immigration as a factor of demographic change must be underlined: despite the fact that female immigrants account for only 3.6% of the female Spanish population, they account for 8% of the total national birth rate.

4. Sources of labour law

4.1. The sources of labour law from 1992 to 2002

As in all developed and democratic States, Spanish labour law is marked by the existence of a variety of legal sources, both public and private, which distinguish it from other sectors of the legal system. Article 3.1 of the Statute of Workers' Rights (ET) lists these sources, stating that '*the rights and obligations relating to the employment relationship shall be regulated by:*

1. *Legal provisions and regulations of the State*

2. *Collective agreement*

3. *That which is freely agreed upon by the parties and written into the contract of employment, constituting its legitimate aim and ensuring that in no case may less favourable conditions or conditions contrary to the legal provisions and collective agreements cited above, be established to the detriment of the worker*

4. *Local and occupational practices and customs.'*

The above comes from the original wording of the ET in 1980, which has survived 20 years of successive reforms unchanged. However, the fact is that the sources of labour law have changed radically during this period and strikingly over the course of the decade that we are looking at. Although the sources are logically still the same as the ones mentioned above, the role played by each one and their interaction have changed substantially. In particular, the 1994 reform had a direct impact in this area, aiming to make the labour market more flexible in two ways: by directly introducing more flexible regulations for managing labour and by increasing the regulatory powers of collective bargaining, particularly with regard to the law, since this was considered a more suitable source to be adapted to the specific needs of enterprises.

The result of all these changes is an enormously complicated situation with a variety of sources, particularly of collective origin, and different relationships between them depending on the subject matter covered and the situation of the enterprise. The labour legislator establishes the role of each source in each case, which means that the level of State intervention in the system of sources has increased, as can clearly be seen in the regulation of collective bargaining.

4.2. State legislation

The tradition of forceful State intervention in the labour market in Spain has led to the primacy of legal instruments as regulatory mechanisms. This is something that has been upheld in the constitutional regime, which gives legislation a priority as a fundamental instrument of the constitutional State, and which uses the restriction to cases provided for by the law in typical labour matters. As we have seen, the main legal instruments that make up the nucleus of labour law were adopted at the end of the 1980s, with some significant exceptions. Much of what was adopted in the 1990s resulted from the implementation of Community directives, and over the course of the decade Community law proved to be an important force of change for Spanish law.

At present, labour law as a whole is very extensive, combining wide-ranging texts with laws on specific subjects. The Statute of Workers' Rights, which directly governs contracts of employment, the representation of workers in an enterprise and collective bargaining, has an important role as a benchmark in this sector of the legal system. Other laws have the same importance in specific areas, such as the Law on the Prevention of Risks at Work (*Ley de la Prevención de Riesgos Laborales*) with regard to safety and health and the Basic Law on Employment (*Ley Básica de Empleo*) with regard to the labour market. In general, the decade under study was, above all, a time when specific laws on specific subjects were adopted, such as Law 45/1999 on the posting of workers for cross-border services, Law 14/1994 regulating temporary work agencies and Law 10/1997 on rights to information and consultation of workers in enterprises or Community-wide groups of enterprises.

Of the laws adopted between 1992 and 2002, the one with the greatest scope is indubitably Law 31/1995 on the Prevention of Risks at Work, which, as pointed out above, constitutes the core regulation on safety and health at work. This was the last of the major instruments of labour law to be adopted and, as it was adopted a considerable time after the others, it provided an opportunity to implement a number of employment directives, including the 1989 Framework Directive. This delay was accounted for by the problems in organising such complex subject matter and the resistance from some sectors. Although a revised version of the Statute of Workers' Rights was adopted in 1995, this was actually confined to updating the Statute to include the reforms that had taken place at the beginning of the 1990s.

Regulations, the standard instrument of labour law during the dictatorship, have lost some of their importance for a series of reasons: the development of collective bargaining (in the Franco era conditions of work in sectors and large enterprises were governed by means of regulations and employment ordinances); the predilection for laws in the democratic constitutional State, and the preference for laws as instruments for implementing the *acquis communautaire*. The introduction of laws has become something of a fetish, to the extent that when the social partners decide on any measure which should be put into practice by means of an act of the State, they demand that this should be done by a law, although a regulation would be a more logical option given the substance of the measure. Even so, there is still an important role to be played by regulations, which still have their own particular scope and functions:

- **Firstly**, to develop legal provisions in some areas, such as fixed-term employment contracts, temporary work agencies, prevention of risks at work and collective redundancies, to name only a few

- **Secondly**, in the field of employment policy

- **Thirdly**, in relation to organising the labour market

- **Fourthly**, as a mechanism for transferring responsibility for labour affairs from the State to the Autonomous Communities.

Over the course of this decade, various changes have been observed in the legislative technique used in Spanish labour law. First of all, the rate at which State instruments are changing has picked up considerably as a result of abandoning the traditional technique of adapting labour regulations. Until a few years ago, the normal procedure was to update labour rules and regulations by spreading their weight across statutory, regulatory and collective instruments. Laws were presumed to have a certain degree of permanence as benchmarks for the entire legal labour system, although they were increasingly subject to change as in other sectors of the legal order. Regulations could be amended more frequently and one of their functions was to adopt and develop what was provided for by law. Collective instruments were intended to create a perfectly calibrated framework in terms of both space and time for each negotiating sphere or unit, which means that they are, by their very nature, temporary. This system is underpinned, of course, by ongoing legal reforms that were introduced when it was thought necessary, but without being planned at specific times or intervals.

In the decade under study we can see that the pace of reform of the basic legal instruments has changed radically and hence:

• Major reforms occur at short intervals, affecting a large number of basic legal principles; during the reference decade alone. The reforms of 1994, 1997, 2001 and 2002 can be termed 'major' reforms.

• There are institutions that are constantly undergoing change: part-time work regulations, for example, have been amended at least six times in 20 years.

• There is now a stream of continuous change in legislation, often via laws accompanying the Law on the General State Budget (*Ley de Presupuestos del Estado*). It is rare for the Statute of Workers' Rights and the General Law on Social Security (*Ley General de la Seguridad Social*), the two fundamental laws of Spanish labour law, not to be amended in any given year, and they are now losing their role as the benchmark and core of the system.

• Instruments with a fixed duration and an actual expiry date have appeared. The most striking example was in 1997, when a legal reform was adopted and accorded the same period of effect as the agreement that it covered. This form of legislation has been particularly common in the case of employment law, fundamental aspects of which are governed by regulations valid for one year implemented by programmes or plans.

In order to give an idea of the volume and pace of change, the best example is probably the Statute of Workers' Rights, which constitutes the basic instrument governing labour affairs. This has undergone more than 20 reforms of all types in its 22 years of application. In fact, at this not particularly old age, fewer than 30% of the original articles remain in force, it has gained and lost an entire chapter, and it has had to be recast completely.

Another significant factor during this decade was the breakdown in the interaction between laws and regulatory instruments, with a tendency to incorporate regulation in laws and to disregard the developmental role of secondary legislation. Frequently we find very detailed laws, the substance of which belongs in a regulation. There is no systematic development of regulatory instruments, resulting in regulations that are as important as laws and areas that are in need of regulation. In general, the legislative process is riddled with doubts and uncertainties, causing a general deterioration in the quality of legal texts. This also leads to a loss of focus on the basic body of legislation such as the Statute of Workers' Rights, whose link with specific labour laws does not follow a predetermined pattern.

These factors — more regulations, higher levels of complexity and accelerated change — accumulate to produce a process of legislative inflation which makes it more difficult to implement labour regulations. Inflation brings insecurity and problems in determining what regulations are currently applicable to a given legal relationship. In general, it signals a loss of quality in labour legislation that limits its effectiveness as a mechanism for regulating industrial relations and the labour market.

4.3. Collective agreements

Article 37 of the Spanish Constitution recognises the workers' rights to collective bargaining and obliges the State to guarantee 'the binding force of the agreements'. This is an explicit acknowledgement of this right in addition to the freedom to form trade unions which, in principle, encompasses it and which was developed by the legislation in Chapter III of the ET that was specifically intended to foster collective bargaining.

In Spanish labour law, collective autonomy gives rise to various types of negotiated instruments which develop different aspects of the system. This variety has been a typical phenomenon of the decade that we are analysing, since the reform of 1994 used company agreements extensively as a mechanism for adaptation and flexibility.

Social consultation played an important part in Spain since the transition to democracy, when it was a basic instrument for introducing a democratic model of industrial relations. There was an initial phase of major inter-confederal agreements, which ended at the beginning of the 1980s, and no new agreements were produced for over ten years. However, from 1992 to 2002, there was a resurgence of social consultation, particularly after the first conservative Government came to power. This reached its peak in 1997, when four major inter-confederal agreements were signed that launched several important legal reforms through 'negotiated legislation'. At the end of the period under review, there was another breakdown in the process of social consultation in response to the labour policy of the second Government, which even gave rise to a general strike in 2002.

The absence of inter-confederal agreements does not mean that there was a lack of social consultation. On the contrary, negotiating forums, which remained functional throughout the period, provided another channel for social consultation in agreements on specific subjects, such as vocational training or the future of the public social security system. In addition, these were accompanied by a very important process of social consultation, with inter-confederal agreements being signed within the remit of the Autonomous Communities that are normally promoted and supported by the regional Governments. These agreements have been vital in securing the involvement of the Communities in labour affairs, in addition to developing systems for settling disputes out of the courts and the employment policies of the Autonomous Communities during this decade.

As regards collective bargaining in the strict sense of the word, the paradigm of collective agreements used in Spain is very unusual and different to that of the other European systems. Here we see once again a carryover from the model of the Franco collective agreement, a unique instrument which is heavily influenced by the public authorities during the negotiation process and bears the hallmarks of an administrative regulation with regard to drafting and application. The salient feature of a collective agreement governed by the Statute of Workers' Rights is its universal scope; because it is signed and negotiated in accordance with the procedure laid down in the Statute, it applies to all the workers and employers within its purview, irrespective of whether they are affiliated to the organisations which are signatories. In the majority of the European systems where this universal applicability exists, it is the result of an administrative act of extension or a similar operation. In Spain, an agreement that meets the requirements of the ET – or a 'statutory' agreement – has this universal scope without needing such an instrument. For the purposes of implemen-

tation, it is accorded the same effect and application as a legal instrument, irrespective of its contractual origin. Once again we can see that a template designed during the Franco era, inspired by regulations and applied as such, has survived. The ET has upheld it because it is useful in a system with low trade union membership, as is the case in Spain.

The need to increase levels of flexibility in managing the labour force in this decade has also had its effects on the legal regime of the statutory agreement. On the one hand, it has increased in importance because the law has accorded it new regulating powers, particularly in governing individual working relationships. However, on the other hand, its legal effectiveness has been reduced with the introduction of several institutions from the 1994 reform, such as:

- Article 82.3 of the ET provides for a 'pay opt-out', the possibility of one enterprise not applying the pay scales established in the agreement. This is only possible if there is an agreement with the workers' representatives and if the circumstances of the enterprise require it.

- Article 84 of the ET offers the possibility of 'decentralised competition', which is when a negotiating unit, which comes within the scope of an agreement currently in force, regulates certain aspects of it differently. This is only possible by agreement with the workers' representatives and for units which are larger than enterprises.

- Article 41 of the ET provides for a procedure to modify working conditions on the initiative of the employer, which may affect conditions, agreed upon in the collective agreement.

On the whole, a statutory collective agreement of 2002 has less legal force than one of 1992 as a result of these mechanisms, even though it retains the unusual Spanish character that makes it so similar to State legislation.

Together with the statutory collective agreements, negotiations have created a variety of collective regulatory instruments, which have been gaining acceptance, first of all by social and then by labour jurisprudence. One of the first is the 'extra-statutory' collective agreement, which is basically a collective agreement that does not meet the requirements of the ET, usually because it has not obtained a majority for approval. In principle, this type of agreement does not have *erga omnes* force, although in many cases employers apply them as if they do. The extra-statutory agreement has been used to resolve situations where it was difficult to comply with the legal requirements as a result of the characteristics of the sector or the circumstances of the negotiating parties. While it featured in the Spanish industrial relations system in the 1980s, it was in the 1990s that it reached its peak. Although it is difficult to calculate how many there are – since many are not registered publicly – they are clearly in the minority compared with the statutory agreement, which is still the predominant model.

Another typical instrument for governing industrial relations in the era of flexibility is the company agreement, which was used widely in the 1994 reform. There are a number of different company agreements, which are provided for throughout the ET. These meet various requirements, depending on the subjects they govern, such as:

• Subsidiary or supplementary agreements, which are only possible in the absence of a collective agreement (22.1, 24.1, 29.1, 31, 34.2 and 3)

• Agreements on the restructuring of companies on economic, technical, organisational or production grounds (40.2, 41.2 and 4, 51.4, 47)

• Agreements amending the collective agreement (41.2 referring to working hours, shift work, pay systems and performance-based work, 41.4, 82.3 and 85.3.c on a pay opt-out)

• Agreements that terminate a strike or dispute.

However, the legal status of these company agreements or pacts remains fairly vague in the ET inasmuch as there is no specific regime for them. As a rule, they are negotiated by the legal representatives of the workers in the enterprise and this tends to be their natural scope of application. They also apply to all of the workers in a company.

4.4. The structure of collective bargaining

One of the most controversial aspects of collective bargaining in Spain is its structure, to which particular attention has been given throughout the decade. This has therefore been examined separately.

This structure has attracted widespread criticism from all of the parties to the industrial relations system, since they regard it as irrational, inefficient and unduly fragmented. It is true that Spain has a very large number of agreements – over 5 000 – and a highly decentralised structure, with two major types of agreement, in terms of the number of workers affected, the State sector and the provincial sector. There are many company agreements, but these do not play

a leading role since they apply to a relatively small number of workers. Other more modern models for agreements, such as for a group of enterprises, are still very rare.

As an example, one of the most important areas is the provincial sector, i.e. Agreements that apply to a sector of activity in a province. This means that there can be more than 50 agreements throughout the country that are very similar to one another. This type of agreement has no precedent in other countries and stems from the trade union organisation that emerged under Franco, which, like any administrative organisation, was based on the provinces. Many other agreements still have the same scope as the labour ordinances under Franco, which were administrative regulations governing working conditions in enterprises and activities. For years, the social partners have endeavoured to replace these agreements with nation-wide sectoral agreements in line with other European systems, but have failed to do so.

One highly relevant regulatory aspect needs to be borne in mind. The provisions on collective bargaining in the ET promote the stability of the negotiating units and give priority to a preceding agreement. This is compounded by the reluctance of the local trade union and employer structures to renounce control over the collective negotiation that they enjoy under the current negotiating structure.

Criticism of this structure is therefore based on the fact that some of the negotiating units are not equipped for their task in terms of specialisation or suitability, and are merely a consequence of the system's inertia – as is the case with the provincial sectoral agreements. Furthermore, there are so many of these units that large numbers of negotiating procedures run in parallel, increasing all of the costs involved in negotiating an agreement. Finally, Spanish collective agreements tend to cover all areas of activity with a single – exclusive – agreement generally applying in each unit. There is a lack of coordination between agreements, which implies that more than one agreement can be applied in the same area, each regulating different activities.

One of the best known diagnoses of the situation of collective bargaining is the preamble to the 1997 Inter-confederal Agreement on Collective Bargaining: *in our country there are multiple units of competing collective bargaining bodies. The majority of the existing units deal with the same matters which are subject to negotiation from the most general to the most detailed level, giving collective bargaining considerable scope for complexity, since no collective agreement has any reason to bow to a previous agreement or to one with a wider scope, which may deal with any matter it chooses and does not have to comply with any specialisation criterion.* The preamble calls for action designed to *streamline the collective bargaining structure to remedy the current state of fragmentation.*

There are therefore two aspects which attract criticism: the negotiating structure, which is considered unsatisfactory because it is fragmented, irrational and, to some extent, anachronistic; and the lack of coordination mechanisms, which results in agreements being applied independently and exhaustively. The combination of these two shortcomings means that negotiating effort is wasted, the substance of agreements is impoverished and the system is generally inefficient.

Despite the time which has elapsed since the introduction of the right to free collective bargaining and the considerable degree of consensus between the social partners in diagnosing and criticising these rights, these problems have persisted and have prompted a series of reform initiatives throughout the decade under review.

The first serious attempt to modify the negotiating structure took place during the 1994 labour reform, when substantial amendments were made to the legal regulations covering it. The clause providing that all agreements have the same value was amended; the law thus accorded certain regulatory powers to different types of agreements in specific matters or circumstances. By the same token, the clause stating that one agreement could not be affected by another during its period of validity was also reformed, enabling subsequent agreements to be applied, in certain cases, in units already covered by an agreement which was still in force. Although there was no clear model for a negotiating structure in the 1994 reform, there was clearly a will to promote decentralisation, attributing considerable authority to company agreements and agreements which did not cover the whole country. This was consistent with the general aim of the reform of increasing flexibility in the labour market, which, for the labour legislator in 1994, was more practicable with agreements closer to enterprise level.

However, the labour legislator upheld the basic premise underlying all regulation of the structure of collective bargaining: as collective bargaining is a matter for the social partners, they should be free to choose the level of negotiation that they prefer. In fact, Article 84.1 of the ET was not amended and still provides that agreements will have the scope of application that the parties to them agree upon. This means that the intervention, in terms of legislation, is conducted indirectly, by way of facilitating or promoting certain negotiating units, and does not therefore impose a specific blueprint for the negotiating structure.

The second attempt to reform the negotiating structure took place in 1997, at the same time as the process of social consultation in that year. One of the major agreements signed at the time was the Interconfederal Agreement on Collective Bargaining (Acuerdo Interconfederal para la Negociación Colectiva) (AINC). Through this agreement, the social partners at State level undertook to establish negotiating procedures to set up a new structure which was more rational and more in-keeping with modern times. The AINC model for the negotiating structure was based on two techniques. The first, which became the rule as agreements were coordinated with each other, was that at least one State agreement and one company agreement should be applied in every negotiating unit. In effect, the AINC distributed the powers of negotiation between the various negotiating levels, identifying the subject matter that was to be negotiated upon at each of these levels.

The second technique was to promote the State sectoral collective agreement as a basic agreement throughout the negotiating system. This covered all essential aspects and determined what powers were to be delegated to the lower levels.

This agreement therefore aimed to centralise collective negotiation in order to break the current pattern of decentralisation. The idea was to reduce the number of negotiating units at lower levels, especially provincial level – for which there is no room in the model – and strengthen the central trade union structures' control over the entire negotiating process.

A model for an ideal structure of collective bargaining therefore exists. However, the negotiators in every sector and at every level have the last word on coordinating the various matters to be negotiated, and they therefore have an overriding influence. According to the preamble to the AINC, the entire system must be put into practice *whilst respecting the principle of independence of the social partners at every level of negotiation.* As a result, the legal authority accorded to the AINC under Article 83 of the ET – which states that, according to clause II of the agreement on its 'juridical nature', all of the provisions *are legally binding* – is undermined. Furthermore, while the existence of *several different models for collective bargaining* is always alluded to, no specific one has been imposed.

Once the initial term laid down for this agreement had elapsed, its results became evident in the practice of collective bargaining in Spain, as different techniques for coordinating agreements started to appear regularly. From this point of view, the AINC has had a beneficial effect on the practical side of industrial relations in Spain. Even so, there is still a certain amount of discontent with regard to the AINC, which has not had as direct or palpable an effect as was claimed. Although this lack of impact may be questionable, it led various bodies to seek more direct and incisive action, imposing changes on the negotiating structure by reforming the articles of the Statute of Workers' Rights on this matter. The Government's initiative last year, set out in a *Discussion paper of the Ministry of Labour on collective bargaining* in July 2001 and in the *Bill for a law reforming the Statute of Workers Rights with regard to collective bargaining* in October of the same year, should be interpreted in this light. These documents should be mentioned here, if only because they appeared during the period under review. The model which the Government intends to introduce is much more interventionist, in which the labour legislator indicates what subjects are to be negotiated upon at each level and priority is given to company agreements.

This course of action is justified by the need to establish legal instruments that have a scope beyond that of the agreement-based AINC and represents a fundamental change in Spain's negotiating landscape within a short period of time. Apart from the considerations in terms of industrial relations, there was another economic deliberation: the Government's experts believe that the current negotiating structure has an inflationary effect and therefore needs to be changed. Given the changes in the Spanish political landscape, it remains to be seen whether these proposals will be approved or whether the slow process of transforming the negotiating structure offered by the AINC, which is still supported by the social partners, will be maintained.

4.5. The employment contract and the individual independence of the parties to it

The employment contract is mentioned in the legal bases that govern working relationships, although strictly speaking it is a source of obligations rather than a legal regulation as such. It is of very little importance in contemporary Spanish labour law, merely formalising the consent of the parties to commit themselves to a working relationship. The employment contract is even referred to as a contract of affiliation, a mere form to be filled out by the workers and the employers, which does not impose any new or uncommon conditions but is required by both the law and collective bargaining. This must be understood in the context of a legal system which systematically places little value on individual autonomy, both in terms of the legal definition of rendering services and in determining the composition of these services.

The process of the 'individualisation of industrial relations', which gives greater regulatory power to individual autonomy than to the State or any other collective authority, has had relatively little impact in Spain. This is a result of the model of flexible employment pursued in Spain, which does not involve the deregulation of employment relationships, but, on the contrary, has given rise to greater regulation, covering differentiated treatment on a case-by-case basis through exceptions, transitional situations, the proceduralisation of decisions, etc. The result has been a process of legislative inflation that has increased rather than reduced state regulation and has not provided any fresh scope for individual autonomy.

Two factors have contributed to this lack of individualisation in employment relationships: on the one hand, resistance to change in labour tribunals that uphold the traditional view of the role of individual autonomy; on the other, the technique used by the labour legislator which has recourse to company agreements as a source of flexibility for enterprises. Even so, there is no doubt that over the course of the decade the regulatory role of the individual employment contract has become more important, if only as a reflection of the changes that have taken place in company management and the functioning of the labour market.

One of the areas in which individual autonomy has perhaps acquired greater force is where a contract of services has been defined as a contract of work or other type of contract. In traditional Spanish labour law, there was a systematic preference for the employment contract, to the extent that any exchange in return for services was, in principle, made on the basis of a contract of this type. This preference was even formalised by introducing a presumption of the existence of an employment contract. This was accounted for by the legislator's desire to make the employment contract the prototype for a service contract and because there had been a number of cases of fraud in defining these. There was therefore a lack of confidence in the way the parties defined their service contracts, and as a result this was replaced by the legal title of an employment relationship. Over the course of the decade, the employment contract has gradually lost its status as a benchmark or priority contract. It has become one of several contractual options available for the rendering of services, for a number of reasons.

Firstly, labour jurisprudence progressively abandoned its traditional interpretations, becoming more disposed to accept non-labour, civilian or commercial options. Secondly, the legislator introduced selective reforms that overturned the interpretation of certain services as employment, as happened with the agency contract in the case of some independent transport companies. These changes took place in the context of an economic system characterised by a general decentralisation of production, where the means of organising the rendering of services in enterprises were multiplying. At the end of the decade in question, little remains of the traditional pre-eminence of the employment contract. Even so, the fundamental rule is maintained that it is not the *nomen iures* of a contract of services which is the defining factor, but the actual substance of the exchange of services. Controversies on the legal definition of the remunerated rendering of services continue to be a major factor in labour litigation in Spain.

4.6. The relationship between the various sources

In 1992, when the period under review started, the relationship between these various sources followed a 'conventional' pattern based on the technique of minimum legislation combined with the principle of relative non-exemption of labour regulations. This implied that a lower-ranked regulation could override a higher one, as long as it brought better conditions for the workers affected. The order of precedence was determined by a progressive improvement in conditions, except in the case of State legislation, which, although ranked higher, was strictly bound by this principle.

The reform of the Statute of Workers' Rights of 1994 radically altered this situation by establishing completely different rules governing the relationships between the various sources. It did not, however, establish any new general rules or principles, but rather introduced new mechanisms regulating each specific field throughout the Statute. In most cases, these rules granted the collective bargaining system the power to amend state regulations that had been imperative hitherto. In the case of fixed-term contracts, for example, considerable authority was delegated to collective bargaining in order to fine-tune and supplement the juridical regime. However, this authority remained within the limits laid down by the law, which also contained a supplementary regulation that applied in the event of an agreement not dealing with a given matter. On other occasions, the employer was allowed to adopt certain decisions on the condition it was done via an agreement with the workers' representatives and not unilaterally. There are also situations in which exemptions are permitted, but only within the ambit of a company agreement. By the same token, it is possible for the corresponding collective agreement not to be applied if an agreement to the same effect can be reached with the workers' representatives. And, of course, the possibility of impro-

ving legal conditions by an agreement, or the conditions of an agreement by individual or collective pacts, remains. There are many possibilities and the relationship between them has been made much more complex.

5. Settling industrial disputes

The identifying feature of industrial relations in the Franco era was the considerable degree of public control over the labour market and the permeation of the law throughout the entire system of labour affairs. In an authoritarian regime that denied even minimum collective rights, the absence of alternative dispute-resolution channels meant that practically the only way to settle disputes at work was in court. This led to the creation of specialised labour courts, with labour magistrates who were very efficient and well suited to a model heavily regulated by the public authorities. During the transition to democracy these labour tribunals were kept in place, becoming perfectly integrated in the judiciary as social courts and retaining much of their operational identity by using, for example, rapid verbal procedures.

These tribunals operated reasonably well, were available free of charge for workers, and were highly specialised from a technical point of view. As a result they continued to be the preferred instrument for resolving industrial disputes in Spain. Apart from the successive procedural reforms, the only changes over the last four years have been with regard to their organisation and procedures, as a result of the development of the State of the Autonomous Communities and the subsequent need to set up higher courts of justice in the Autonomous Communities. Today, they are still highly functional courts by any standards, although there are stirrings of criticism about their operations and even complaints of a procedural crisis. This crisis is said to be the result of a variety of factors, including: overuse, which limits the speed and quality of judgements; a chronic shortage of resources in the administration of justice; inadequate procedural laws, particularly for executing judgements; problems in determining the scope of legal authority as a result of the new judicial structure; and, above all, inadequate legal remedies in the context of a highly insecure labour market where fixed-term workers do not have recourse to the courts to defend their rights.

For many years, systems for settling disputes out of court played a very marginal role in Spanish working life because there was no tradition of such mechanisms, because those which did exist were not very efficient and, above all, because the legal channels were fairly rapid and economical.

Despite pressure from the labour legislator, which made their use obligatory before having recourse to the courts, they never got off the ground as an authentic alternative to the labour tribunals.

Curiously enough, it was the Autonomous Communities that eventually managed to develop these mechanisms for settling disputes out of court, creating or supporting the creation of systems of mediation and arbitration within the framework of regional social consultation processes. These systems appeared in the 1980s and are now widespread throughout all 17 Autonomous Communities in the Kingdom of Spain. They are public or semi-public, have a territorial scope which is restricted to the Autonomous Community and vary considerably with regard to both the techniques they deploy for resolving disputes and the disputes they deal with. In general, they have been very efficient and have obviated the need for a large number of court proceedings. They tend to include mediation as an obligatory phase as well as arbitration, access to which is only available on the basis of an agreement between the parties.

The labour legislator has contributed to the development of these systems by means of selective reforms. For example, these systems have been given the power of prior conciliation before court proceedings, which the law on labour procedures still imposes, and the decisions of arbitration have been granted the same effectiveness as court judgements, by virtue of being executed by courts of law.

Finally, and once the systems had been consolidated in the majority of the Autonomous Communities, the social partners at State level signed an Acuerdo Solución Extrajudicial de Conflictos (ASEC – Agreement on the Extrajudicial Resolution of Conflicts), by which a State system was created in 1997. To this effect, the Servicio Interconfederal de Mediación y Arbitraje (SIMA – Interconfederal Mediation and Arbitration Service) foundation was set up to provide administrative and technical aid to the process of settling disputes. This system is voluntary and it is up to the various sectors and levels to sign up as members. It supplements the autonomous systems, since it comes into play only when a dispute exceeds the territorial scope of an Autonomous Community. At present, ASEC–II is in force, which is much along the same lines as its predecessor.

Despite the fact that they have only relatively recently become widespread in Spain, the systematic use of mechanisms to settle disputes out of court constitutes a salient feature of industrial relations in Spain today.

As regards the use of collective pressure mechanisms to settle industrial disputes, the most striking feature of this decade is the gradual decline in the number of strikes and workers affected by them. Labour statistics clearly show that, with the exception of an occasional resurgence, direct conflict has gradually been abandoned as a result of the insecurity in employment and other factors. This is in the context of fairly inconsistent legislation on the right to strike. In fact, this legislation is enshrined in the Royal Decree-Law on Industrial Relations of 1977, a law dating back to the transition, which predates the Constitution and is interpreted in agreement with it by the judgement of the Constitutional Court 11/1981. The lack of consensus between the political parties and the social partners, as well as the need to regulate strikes by establishing an organic law by a constitutional mandate, has disrupted the various attempts at approving a law on strikes.

Chapter II:
From employment security to employability

1. Protection against dismissal

As in other countries, one of the most controversial aspects of labour law in Spain is unquestionably the regime governing dismissals. This is a very delicate subject, where the interests and preferences of those involved in the labour market come into direct conflict. Furthermore, in Spain, the point of departure is very unusual, since the regulations on dismissal are fairly restrictive with regard to causes, procedures and costs. This rigid dismissal regime has its roots in the Franco era, but it was during the transition to democracy that it was consolidated. The Statute of Workers' Rights maintained its essential features in 1980.

The Spanish system drastically curbed employers' powers to terminate employment contracts unilaterally. Justification for a dismissal was required and the failure to provide it resulted in the dismissal being termed 'unfair dismissal'. It was also a system of compulsory legal stability in which, in the event of an illegal dismissal, there was no obligation to reinstate the worker, but merely to compensate him. However, the compensation could be fairly high, since it depended on the worker's seniority in the company.

The case law of the Constitutional Court introduced the concept of invalid dismissal, which, by way of exception, obliged the employer to reinstate the worker in a system of *de facto* stability. However, this only applied to dismissals when fundamental rights were violated or where the legal procedure had not been followed. The type of dismissal determined the calculation of compensation since, even in the case of legal dismissal, there was an obligation to compensate a dismissed worker.

In terms of collective dismissals, there was no separate regime linked to the number of workers affected. Instead the choice of regime to be applied depended on the reason given for the redundancies. So, the regime covering dismissals on economic grounds was considered to adequately implement the 1975 Directive on collective dismissals, but this was applied even to dismissals that affected only two workers. It was also compulsory, as was then common in

Europe, to obtain administrative authorisation for the termination of employment contracts on these grounds. The administrative practice of making this authorisation contingent on the existence of a previous agreement with the workers' representatives led to a considerable increase in the costs of dismissals and lengthened and complicated the processes of restructuring companies.

This regime was in force throughout the 1980s, coinciding with rising rates of unemployment and the conversion of entire sectors of the Spanish economy. The authorities did not opt to make dismissals more flexible or less expensive, but they did seek other means that were less costly in terms of social impact. In practice, the option taken systematically during these years was to make it easier to award fixed-term contracts, advocating flexibility of entry into the labour market. The idea was that enterprises could adjust their workforces to cope with changing requirements by not renewing fixed-term contracts rather than dismissing employees. Terminating a fixed-term contract did not, barring exceptions, oblige the company to compensate the worker affected. The regime governing dismissals, and in particular the costs thereof, therefore became something of a taboo for the labour legislator.

In the 1990s it became evident that the approach adopted in the previous decade was not working. Recourse to fixed-term contracts as a mechanism for guaranteeing flexibility of workforces was generating very considerable costs for all those involved. For enterprises, the constantly rotating employees depleted the skills of their workforces. In addition, the fixed-term contracts did not provide an effective means of adjusting the workforce immediately, since employers often had to wait up to three years for the contract to expire. For workers, it led to a segmentation of the market that left many without any possibility of developing a career in an enterprise and obtaining a permanent job. The insecurity of employment that had been the reason for fixed-term contracts became a source of insecurity for workers, with very serious social consequences. In fact, the exponential increase in fixed-term contracts ended up worrying the labour authorities themselves. It was therefore clear at the beginning of the 1990s that flexibility of entry to the labour market, without adjusting other aspects of the legal regime for managing the workforce, caused more problems than it solved.

Yet the authorities did not opt for an in-depth reform of the regulations on dismissals, which would have altered the foundations of its juridical regime. This might have seemed excessive at a time in which a far-reaching flexibilisation of Spanish labour law was underway. During the first half of the decade, and particularly at the time of the 1994 reform, internal flexibility within enterprises was promoted without enhancing flexible arrangements for leaving the labour market. In return, the scope for fixed-term contracts was reduced by the virtual elimination of the most flexible and harmful contractual model – the contract for promoting employment that could be used systematically without any justification.

The options pursued in a bid to make dismissals more flexible were indirect, including the adoption of a series of selective measures intended to make dismissals easier and cheaper under certain circumstances and for certain groups.

In 1994, the reform of the Statute and the Law on Labour Procedure restricted the scope of invalid dismissals, whose regime henceforth applied only to dismissals where fundamental rights were violated. It was only for these dismissals that a regime of *de facto* stability existed in Spain. Subsequently, and in compliance with Community directives, this protection was extended to cover the dismissal of workers during periods in which the employment contract was suspended on grounds of maternity, risks during pregnancy, adoption and child placement, and for pregnant workers from the date the pregnancy started till the beginning of the period of suspension.

In 1994 there was also a major reform of the regime for collective dismissals regulated in Article 51 of the ET, which, before the entry into force of the ET, had required recourse to the 'procedure for issuing notices of dismissal' with the intervention of the workers' representatives and authorisation of the administrative authorities. The reform was fairly subtle and indirect, like all those with regard to dismissals in Spain. Formally, it was a minor change because the compensation to be paid to workers remained the same, as did the need for administrative authorisation to terminate a contract – the two most controversial issues with this type of dismissal. However, the procedure was eased and the legal conditions for dismissals on economic grounds were redefined. Perhaps most interestingly, a collective element was introduced into the definition, applying the system of numerical thresholds featuring in the Community Directive. As a result, many dismissals on economic, technological, organisational or production grounds remained outside the scope of Article 51 of ET, which applied solely to those that were

genuinely 'collective' within the meaning of the Directive. All other grounds remained subject to a separate regime with a lower level of guarantee. In other words, from 1994 onwards, Spanish law made a distinction between two types of dismissal for the same causes, depending on the number of workers affected: those coming under Article 52 – objective dismissals – and those coming under Article 51 – collective dismissals. This arrangement, which is fairly common in Europe, was, however, unusual at the time in Spain, since the traditional system had made no distinction in terms of number or time, and the same regime applied for all dismissals on these grounds.

It was interesting that reference was made to the Community Directive to justify reducing the scope of the procedure for issuing dismissal notices and the guarantees it offers. In reality this had a detrimental effect on workers' rights and left many without the above guarantees because they did not meet the minimum threshold under Article 51 of the ET. Indeed, this reduction would have been dubious if the Directive had had a non-regression clause like the more recent Community instruments. What is more, the opportunity was taken to use the same technique for the differentiation of legal regimes according to the number of workers affected by other actions taken by the enterprises, such as postings (Article 40 of the ET) and changes to working conditions (Article 41 of the ET).

Also during this decade, a very selective legal reform took place with a considerable practical repercussion on the application of the regulations for dismissal. Explicit definitions were laid down of the causes that could justify economic and collective or non-collective dismissals, which under Spanish law were called 'dismissals on economic, technical, organisational or production grounds'. By defining the situations in which workers could legitimately be dismissed, it was no longer necessary for the situation in the enterprise to be critical for such dismissals to be considered legitimate.

The most direct intervention in the matter of dismissals took place in 1997, when the Acuerdo Interconfederal para la Estabilidad en el Empleo (Interconfederal Agreement for Stability in Employment) was signed. In this agreement the partners paved the way for reducing the costs of dismissals, placing their faith in the original consensus and legitimacy of this measure. This was something that the labour legislator would probably not have dared to do alone. Because of the symbolic value of the regulations governing dismissals, the statutory arrangements governing this matter were not amended indiscriminately – an indirect and much more subtle approach was adopted. A new contractual model was created, granting lower levels of compensation for dismissal. If the levels of compensation were not reduced universally, this was only because it was a special type of contract with a special regime for dismissals.

The labour legislator adopted this solution and, in a law of 1997, introduced the notion of a contract for promoting permanent contracts in the Spanish labour laws. The main feature of this contract was that the level of compensation in the event of invalid dismissal was lower – 33 days for each year of service – than that generally established by the Statute – 45 days for each year of service. Because the objective of the agreement was to curb the increasing insecurity in the Spanish labour market, the contract had to be a permanent one and could only be signed by unemployed workers who had particular problems finding work.

Since this measure stemmed from an inter-confederal agreement with a duration of four years, the law governing this contract was also adopted with the same fixed duration. In 2001, as a result of the breakdown in negotiations to renew the agreement, the Government opted to undertake a legal reform that made the contract to promote permanent employment perdurable. In fact, this contract is still in force *sine die*. It also extended its scope, including new groups of workers as possible targets for the contract. Currently this type of contract can be used to employ, on a permanent basis, unemployed workers with problems finding work and, specifically, the following groups:

- Young workers aged between 16 and 30

- Workers over 45

- Disabled workers

- Long-term unemployed workers, i.e. workers who have been registered as jobseekers for at least six months without interruption

- Female workers, if they are employed in professions and occupations where women are under-represented.

This type of contractual arrangement can be entered into by *workers who, on the date of signature of the new contract to promote permanent employment, were employed in the same enterprise under a fixed-term contract or temporary contract, including training contracts*, which meant that the process of converting temporary employment into permanent employment – one of the objectives of all the labour reforms of that decade – was not geared to this type of contract.

Since its appearance in 1997, this type of contractual arrangement, which is no more than an ordinary contract with a spe-

cial regime for dismissal, has gained ground, becoming a permanent feature of the labour market and applicable to an increasing number of people. Any worker may experience the wide range of conditions applicable under its regime. For example, anyone can be employed under such a contract if they have been registered as unemployed for six months. And as women are under-represented in the majority of sectors and activities, they can easily be employed under such a contract too. The widespread opinion is that this is a disguised reform of the dismissal regime that aims to gradually replace contracts with higher compensation by the standard type of permanent contract. Indeed, since 1997 there has been a marked increase in unlimited contracts and the majority have been under the contractual arrangements for reduced compensation for dismissal.

The result of these selective reforms is that, in one way or another, the dismissal regime has become more flexible, making it easier for enterprises to reduce the costs thereof in many instances. But the taboo effect of the regulations on dismissals is obvious: despite the evident relaxation in the rules, the corresponding principles of the Statute of Workers' Rights continue to recognise the same compensation as hitherto, although for many workers they no longer apply because they are employed under contracts for promoting permanent employment. For the majority of Spanish workers, termination of the employment contract does not entitle them to any compensation because their contracts are temporary. Administrative authorisation is still required for issuing notices of dismissal, but this is not the case for many dismissals on economic grounds and, what is more, the labour authorities are now more inclined to give their authorisation.

Added to this, enterprises continue to have at their disposal a variety of fixed-term contracts with which they can streamline their workforce. In addition, they can resort to temporary work agencies in order to manage minor fluctuations. The result is that, by one means or another, enterprises have a number of instruments to adapt their labour force to their production requirements. And they have managed this in an indirect manner, without an in-depth formal reform of the legal regime governing dismissals that retains the axiom of the traditional regulations.

2. Training at work

The Spanish Constitution acknowledges the right to vocational training in Article 40.2 where it states that *the public authorities shall promote a policy guaranteeing vocational training and retraining*. There are three levels or types of vocational training in Spain:

- Statutory training, which forms part of the public education system, to prepare young people for entry into the labour market.

- Occupational training for unemployed workers, to increase their employment prospects.

- In-service training, to help employed workers increase their qualifications or, if necessary, to enable them to be redeployed.

The Statute of Workers' Rights contains a variety of instruments to put this into practice, starting with contractual arrangements to enable workers to acquire or improve training. Two of these contracts are classified as training contracts and are regulated by Article 11 of the Statute. They are:

- The work experience contract for workers who have a qualification to carry out an occupation, in order to enable them to practice it and to obtain occupational experience. This is contingent upon holding the necessary qualification.

- The training contract, which is intended to enable workers without training to be trained whilst working, and to pursue specific supplementary training activities. This is the modern-day equivalent of an apprenticeship.

The regulations governing these training contracts also encourage job creation, since the legal regime is fairly favourable for the enterprise using them. In effect, the aim is to encourage enterprises to use these contracts so as to create more training opportunities for young people, one of the groups hit hardest by unemployment. The main element that makes them attractive to enterprises is their temporary character, undoubtedly an advantage in a system with such an expensive system for dismissals. They also have a legal regime which is fairly flexible, allowing various options which, as a rule, are fairly relaxed, for meeting the training obligations under the contract. In addition, they provide for lower contributions than for the other workers in the enterprise. It is hardly surprising that the current arrangements governing these training contracts largely came about under the 1994 labour reform.

Together with these training contracts, the Statute attempts to facilitate access to training for workers under Article 4.2.b of the ET, which states that *workers are entitled to vocational qualification and training at work*. Article 23 of the ET takes this further, giving workers the right to:

- Have the necessary leave to take part in exams and to have priority in choosing which shift to work, if that is the regime in the company, when they have regularly pursued studies to obtain an academic or professional qualification.

- Adapt their daily working hours to enable them to attend vocational training courses or to obtain the necessary time off to pursue vocational training or upgrading with their job being kept open.

Collective bargaining is not particularly innovative with regard to training at work. It tends to improve the legal regulations, widening the scope for educational leave and the conditions for granting it. At times, it obtains guarantees from enterprises to set aside certain amounts for training, to offer specific training programmes or conditions for access to them, etc. Sectoral agreements also tend to regulate specific aspects of the legal regime of training contracts, with regard to the matters delegated to them by the State.

An essential factor in the dynamics of vocational training in Spain is the concerted management of this area, with tripartite bodies responsible for devising and monitoring courses. Inter-confederal agreements on vocational training are also signed periodically.

Another equally significant factor during virtually the entire decade under review is the generous funding available to finance vocational training. This funding comes primarily from Community sources, since much of the aid from the European Social Fund earmarked for this purpose is spent in Spain.

3. Progressive retirement

As in many other countries, retirement was linked directly with employment policy in Spain. Alongside its original or direct aim of providing pensions to replace salaries when a worker leaves the labour market for reasons of age, it was also used as an instrument to meet a series of labour market-related objectives. In fact, retirement policies were based on several basic assumptions, taken for granted in the 1980s but now seen as somewhat questionable. The first assumption is that there is a given volume of employment that the economy can generate and the aim is to distribute it between workers. If some workers are made redundant, others will be able to take on the jobs that they occupied. Secondly, enterprises that retire workers will maintain the volumes of employment since they will use this means as an instrument for renewing and not reducing their workforces. Thirdly, it was assumed that elderly workers suffer less if they lose their jobs because they are protected by the public social security system. This implies that when the time comes to decide who to give jobs to, they can be sacrificed without too much expense. All kinds of schemes were organised on the basis of these assumptions, all of which had the same objective – to get rid of elderly workers as soon as possible in order to make their jobs available to younger workers.

Back in 1980, the ET was approved with an additional provision, No 10, which allowed collective agreements to set an age for the compulsory retirement of the workers they covered. The Constitutional Court accepted the validity of this system as long as safeguards were introduced to maintain the volume of employment in the enterprise and forcibly retired workers had access to retirement benefits from the public social security system.

Of the various retirement measures put to the service of employment policy – imposition of compulsory retirement, changes in the retirement age – the main instrument used in Spain, as in other countries, was the relaxation of the rules on the retirement age, particularly by means of progressive retirement.

The first time that this was put in practice was in Law 32/1984, where flexible retirement was put forward in the guise of the handover contract, a model copied from other countries. Although this regulation does not fall within the time frame of this study, it deserves to be mentioned for two reasons: firstly, the regime that it established remained in force during most of the period we are studying and, secondly, the context of the regulation helps to understand its significance and aims. It was this law that introduced the option of entry flexibility typical of Spanish labour law in the 1980s, definitively ushering in fixed-term contracts. It was quite clearly an 'emergency law' and all of the measures it involved were geared towards creating employment. This law introduced job-sharing, an idea that is not at all unique to Spain and is intended to create employment by occupying two workers in the same job. With job-sharing, a worker who is close to retirement age can go into partial retirement for up to three years before the statutory age. This worker shares his daily working hours 50:50 with another worker who is seeking employment and who will take over when the first worker retires.

As in the rest of Europe, the handover contract did not work. In the case of Spain, this was probably because the way it was regulated was too rigid so it could not be adapted to the individual enterprise or worker. In statistical terms it was a total failure, resulting in a derisory number of contracts without ever being regarded as a genuine option by the employers.

Despite the fact that they were a failure, handover contracts remained unmodified in the catalogue of atypical contracts until the end of the 1990s. In fact, even the major labour reform of 1994, which affected virtually all regulations governing employment contracts and brought sweeping changes to the legal regime for fixed-term contracts, did not lay a finger on handover contracts. It was not until the key reform of the part-time employment contract in 1998 that any substantial change was made to this model. One of the main aims of this reform, which stemmed from an agreement between the Government and the trade union confederations, was to promote the use of handover contracts, relax the rules on their use, eliminate inflexibility and remedy the technical shortcomings which had come to light. Amongst other things, the options for job-sharing were extended. The period of time before retirement age in which it could be used was extended to five years, the job that was freed no longer had to coincide with the one handed over, and the possibility of a full-time handover contract was accepted. This flexibility was designed to encourage its use. The philosophy was still the same: to gradually get rid of workers from the labour market early and to ensure that jobs were not lost since they were already occupied by the beneficiary of the handover.

Now that we have entered into the 21st century, flexible retirement has acquired a different philosophy and different aims. Although basically the same techniques and legal models are used – in essence, partial retirement and handover contracts – the aim is now different because the priorities of the labour legislator have changed. It is no longer about safeguarding the distribution of employment, but rather the financial stability of the public social security system. This system is feeling the effects of the trend in the country's population – which is starting to age quite appreciably – and is bearing the costs of the policy pursued to date of removing workers from the labour market and paying them retirement pensions from a very early age. This is how the reform of this institution in Law 12/2001 is to be interpreted.

Apart from more flexible arrangements for using this model, the key innovation was that the handover contract could be used beyond the retirement age of the worker. This means that the worker does not have to bring forward his retirement date in order to retire progressively, as previously was the case, but can also set it back. Gradual access to retirement may thus be turned into a partial deferment of it, which is basically what is needed now since a slight increase in the retirement age would assure the financial equilibrium of the system for one more decade.

In any case, we will have to see how the new model – which now offers real progressive retirement – works. The predecessors of the handover contract are not promising and the reality of the Spanish labour market is that very few workers employed in the private sector reach retirement age whilst still employed. On the contrary, there is a very marked tendency to exclude workers from the labour market early by a variety of legal arrangements. This has been harshly criticised, not only because it is irrational in terms of human resources or because it is an unjust and discriminatory measure, but above all because it has come at a very high price for the public social security system during the decade which we are analysing. The public social security system has responded to this situation by contriving various mechanisms for protecting these workers, including systems for linking unemployment benefit with retirement, and a new pre-retirement model that provides protection under the system before retirement age is reached. These measures have not only come into play when enterprises were in difficulties, but have also been used by competitive and successful companies to rejuvenate their workforces.

4. Occupational integration

In Spanish labour law there was no tradition of occupational integration contracts that justified offering little protection for the worker and lower costs for the enterprise. In fact, an attempt by the Government to introduce a contract of this type for young people – the 'contract to promote youth employment' – at the beginning of the decade met with such resistance from the trade unions that the proposal was dropped after a general strike.

A different approach was used in Spain. Different types of fixed-term contracts were devised whose main incentive, as far as the employers were concerned, was their temporary nature in the context of a labour law with rigid and costly regulation of dismissals. At the beginning of the decade there was even a type of temporary contract – a fixed-term contract to promote employment – that was made temporary precisely in order to support job creation since it could be used without any need to justify the temporary nature of the occupation. However, the use of this contract was severely curtailed in 1994 because it was the principal cause of insecurity in the Spanish labour market. Employment policy in the 1980s and 1990s was very largely based on fixed-term contracts of one type or another. When required, incentives were provided for offering contracts to certain groups of workers, normally in the form of reductions in social costs or direct subsidies. For young workers there are

also the training contracts referred to above, which also have a strong component of employment policy in their design and dynamics. From 1994 onwards, fixed-term contracts were no longer an option for employers, and as such they became a less effective mechanism of integration.

Spain's experience from 1992 to 2002 made it clear that the technique of flexible entry used by the labour legislator fragmented the labour market and hit some groups particularly hard, namely people who had problems of employability. Even when fixed-term contracts enabled these persons to find jobs, they mainly did so within a secondary labour market that offered few opportunities to make the transition to the primary market. Enterprises' obsession with not offering permanent contracts obliged them to constantly rotate their fixed-term workers, since they could legally acquire the status of permanent employees if they were kept in the enterprise for a given period. This meant that many of these workers had irregular careers, with constant changes of employers and periods of unemployment, making it difficult for them to progress and gain access to vocational training. As a result, there are doubts concerning the usefulness of fixed-term contracts as a mechanism of integration. In addition, as their legal regime – which is virtually identical to that for permanent workers except with regard to the termination of the contract – provides no great incentive for enterprises, workers with a higher risk of exclusion are not employed under such conditions.

If fixed-term contracts had any effectiveness as a mechanism of integration, it was mainly for younger workers. They enabled them to find their first jobs, acquire a certain amount of experience at work and improve their position in the labour market. Furthermore, fixed-term contracts were frequently used by enterprises as extended probation periods, after which they employed workers who had performed well during the temporary phase on a permanent basis.

By and large, if we look at the behaviour of the labour market during the decade, it is clear how fragmented it has become and how unemployment and inferior-quality contracts are rife amongst the same groups.

From 2001 onwards, there was a fourth type of fixed-term contract, which was called an 'integration contract'. The beneficiaries of these contracts were unemployed workers registered at the labour exchange, although it was pointed out that employing them *was in keeping with the State's priorities to comply with the guidelines of the European employment strategy*. The possibility of the same worker being contracted in this way several times in succession was restricted, with a moratorium of three years being imposed between one integration contract and the next. The only employers in question were public administrations or non-profit organisations and the object of the contract was *to perform work or services of general or social interest as a means of acquiring occupational experience and to improve the employability of the unemployed person participating*. These contracts were concluded under public programmes and the public employment services financed the attendant wage and social security costs. Thus, these integration contracts are far removed from the market. Companies cannot use them to take on labour under favourable terms. Even if the work is not necessarily 'non-productive', the priority is clearly given to the social aspects of the contract.

The restrictions on potential employers, the need for a public programme and the availability of public funds to pay the workers suggests that this is a contractual model of very limited scope without any impact on the labour market.

However, this is perhaps too simplistic a view and distorts the real picture. It is true that the integration contract has very limited scope because it can only be used in very specific situations. However, it is also true that since 2001, when it was finally introduced in the legislation, the contract for training has opened up considerably and the scope for its potential beneficiaries has widened substantially. This contract, which was originally aimed solely at young untrained workers, was modified in the reforms of 2001 (Article 11 of the ET) to allow the age limit – between 16 and 21 years – to be waived to provide training contracts for unemployed workers from the following groups:

•   The disabled

•   Foreign workers during the first two years in which their work permit is valid

•   Workers who have been out of work for over three years

•   The socially excluded

•   Workers who enrol as student workers in craft workshops, work and training centres and employment workshops.

At the time of the 2001 reform, the integration contract was widely viewed as a smokescreen to divert attention towards the widening of the scope of the training contract. In the course of this widening process, which integrates the tradi-

tional institution of apprenticeships into contemporary legislation – and was thus known for some years as an 'apprenticeship contract' – it has actually become an instrument to facilitate the employment of people from the most disadvantaged groups in the labour market. For this group the opportunity to work is more important than the training they can receive during the time they are working. As a result, the Government took the disingenuous option of surreptitiously incorporating a low-quality contract at low cost for enterprises, aimed at persons under threat of social exclusion.

Chapter III:
Labour law and flexibility

1. Atypical work and the labour market in Spain

1.1. Fixed-term contracts and insecurity in the labour market

We have already said that one of the salient features of the Spanish labour market is the segmentation caused by the preponderance of fixed-term contracts, resulting from the labour legislator's focus on entry flexibility as the key mechanism to promote employment during the 1980s. However, in the 1990s it became obvious that this was a problem rather than a solution.

The best way to understand why fixed-term contracts were used excessively is to analyse the imbalance between the costs of terminating permanent and fixed-term contracts. We have already seen how the regime governing dismissals, which did not restrict the power to dismiss workers but made it more expensive, remained practically unchanged during the decade. Redundancies were a very costly way of adjusting workforces. However, if workers were on fixed-term contracts, employers only had to wait until the contracts came to an end for them to be terminated at no cost. Furthermore, in most cases the fixed-term workers, who were younger and had less seniority in the company, generally received lower wages. It was this excessive difference in costs between permanent and fixed-term contracts that provided the incentive for the latter, particularly in periods of economic uncertainty and systematic downsizing.

For this reason, reforms in the legal regime covering fixed-term contracts during this period can be interpreted as an effort to restore the balance in the labour market and bring the costs of permanent and fixed-term employment closer together. We have already seen how attempts were made to gradually lower the costs of dismissals, albeit in an indirect and subtle manner. At the same time, the reforms sought to make it more difficult and more expensive to hire people on fixed-term contracts, but the employment crisis prevented this second course of action from being pursued vigorously. Although fixed-term contracting was considered dangerous

and ill-advised, it was the only way of creating or at least maintaining jobs in the context of the economic crisis at the beginning of the decade under review.

The first attempt to change the situation came with the reform in 1994, which had a profound effect on fixed-term contracting. The first step was to do away with the contract to promote permanent employment. Vestiges of this contract, which had been a major factor of insecurity throughout the 1980s, remained in force, extending its validity from one year to another through programmes to promote employment for specific groups. As regards the regulation of structural and training fixed-term contracts, the changes were contradictory: on the one hand, the legal regime was relaxed considerably in some respects, but on the other hand, the authorities attempted to control its use by restricting the maximum duration of fixed-term contracts, and making it difficult to use them systematically and award a series of contracts to the same worker. Collective bargaining was also given considerable authority to regulate these contractual arrangements. This made for a certain degree of deregulation of fixed-term work, but only in the sense that it was then up to the collective bargaining system to decide how it functioned in many important respects. On one hand, a greater degree of control was obtained over fixed-term work since the social partners established more rigid rules for its use, but on the other hand contractual arrangements were adopted reflecting the peculiarities of each sector. Normally this task was undertaken solely by sectoral collective bargaining, which in practice did not put too many restrictions on the use of fixed-term contracts in the respective areas of activity.

With this reform too, temporary work agencies were introduced in Spain and, although there were relatively few of them, this brought another factor of insecurity into the Spanish labour market. At that time, the priority was still to create jobs, even if they were of low quality, which explains why the measures adopted with regard to fixed-term contracts were ambivalent and certainly far from incisive.

The first serious attempt to get to grips with fixed-term work in the labour market was made in 1997 through the

Acuerdo Interconfederal para la Estabilidad en el Empleo (Interconfederal Agreement on Stability in Employment). Rather than changing the regime governing fixed-term contracts, it focused on the regime governing permanent contracts in a bid to make them more flexible and reduce their costs. The real problem – the vast difference in costs between fixed-term and permanent employment – was addressed by making it less costly to dismiss persons who had permanent contracts. As has already been seen, this was done surreptitiously to avoid any overt reduction in the costs of dismissals. It introduced a new contractual arrangement – the contract for promoting permanent employment – characterised by compensation for unfair dismissal that was substantially lower than for legitimate dismissal.

This harmonisation of costs continued in the final years of the 1990s, when an attempt was made to penalise fixed-term work by increasing the social security contributions. However, this was done only under certain specific conditions and for a very limited number of contracts. The idea of increasing the costs of fixed-term contracts, in order to make them less attractive for enterprises, was good. However, employment problems prevented more incisive measures from being adopted.

The reform of 2001 focused directly on the issue of fixed-term contracts, which was justified *inter alia* by the need to implement the relevant Community directive. With regard to fixed-term contracts in general, four sections were introduced under Article 15 of the ET in order to promote stability in employment.

- **Firstly**, it was made explicit that sectoral collective agreements should make provisions for additional requirements geared to preventing abuses in the uninterrupted use of fixed-term contracts. This was possible given the scope that the law attributes to collective agreements.

- **Secondly**, the principle of equal treatment for fixed-term workers was expressly acknowledged in application of the Community Directive. In cases where it was not possible to provide equal treatment, the principle of equality was to be applied *pro rata* depending on the time worked.

- **Thirdly**, and most originally, the employer was obliged to inform fixed-term workers of vacant permanent posts in the enterprise so that they could take part in the relevant selection procedure. This was an obligation provided for by the Community rules but it did not appear to be accompanied by a commensurate obligation to give priority to these workers in the selection procedure.

- **Fourthly**, provision was made for collective agreements to establish means of facilitating the access to continued training for fixed-term workers, again in application of the 1999 Community Directive.

This attempt at restoring the balance included the new drafting of Article 49.1.c of the ET, also introduced by the reform of 2000, which provided for compensation when the term of a fixed-term contract expired, another instance of 'compensation for insecurity' which was familiar from other ordinances. Compensation was now to be paid at the end of fixed-term contracts as a means of combating the temporary nature of employment and making this type of contract more expensive. In any event, this measure was unsatisfactory for three reasons.

- **Firstly**, it did not apply to all fixed-term workers and excluded workers with interim, integration and training contracts.

- **Secondly**, the amount paid – eight days for each year of service – was very small given the short duration of fixed-term contracts in the labour market.

- **Thirdly**, this amount was not guaranteed in every case, but could be lower if this was agreed upon in collective negotiations or any other specific regulation which applied.

- **Finally**, the contract for promoting permanent employment was also made permanent and its scope was broadened, virtually making it the standard type of permanent contract from then on.

The outcome of these measures has been to bring the costs of adjusting a fixed-term and permanent workforce closer together, making it more difficult to offer fixed-term contracts and making permanent ones less expensive. Statistics on the labour market illustrate the results of these measures: authorities have managed to halt the continuous decline in permanent employment and even reverse it over the past few years.

1.2. The introduction of temporary work agencies

One of the most relevant innovations from 1992 to 2002, in terms of the structuring of the labour market and contractual arrangements, was the legalisation of temporary employment agencies, which had originally been prohibited by Article 43 of the ET banning any form of provision of labour. By 2002, temporary employment was a flourishing, well-established sector with high volumes of activity.

Spain was one of the last of the Member States of the Union to legalise temporary work agencies. It did not do so until 1993, when these enterprises were well-established throughout most of Europe. Against the background of a severe employment crisis and a policy aimed at liberalising the labour market, Royal Decree-Law 1993 exempted temporary work agencies from the general prohibition on detachment of labour that had been in force up to then. From then on, temporary work agencies were considered the only exception to the ban on the provision of workers established by Article 43 of the ET, as long as they had been duly authorised. In the following year, Law 14/1994 was adopted, governing the activity of these enterprises, which started operating from that time onwards.

The first version of Law 14/1994 introduced a relatively liberal regime for these agencies, making them simple to set up and relatively easy to manage. User enterprises could enlist the services of temporary work agencies under the same conditions as those for which fixed-term contracts and there were no sectors in which this activity was banned. Law 14/1994 was not only liberal and flexible, but also contained some errors and loopholes that allowed abuses to take place. Prevention of occupational risks was the only matter that appeared to be dealt with effectively both in Law 14/1994 and in Law 31/1995 on the Prevention of Occupational Risks and in an implementing regulation. Clearly, this was the consequence of Directive 91/383, which was concerned solely with the protection of health and safety of workers in temporary work agencies.

In particular, there was no general principle of equal pay for temporary workers and those in the user enterprises, and the task of guaranteeing a suitable economic and legal status for such workers was entrusted to collective bargaining in temporary work agencies. During the drafting period, it was thought that the agreements in the sector would be negotiated by the most representative trade union organisation and, to this end, the most representative trade unions were even accorded authority for these negotiations by means of a special rule. In practice, however, the system did not work because the special rules on collective bargaining in the temporary work agencies were applied only as supplementary rules and other negotiating arrangements were allowed. Temporary work agencies started the practice of negotiating company agreements with very poor working conditions

and pay scales, effectively excluding the most representative trade unions in the sector.

The company agreements had the effect of imposing a very specific model of temporary work. Temporary work agencies offered their services very cheaply because they operated with very low wage costs. As they applied their own agreements, which were much less costly than in the user enterprises, the latter could reduce their wage costs by having recourse to temporary work agencies. This led to the paradox that hourly pay for temporary work agencies was frequently cheaper than for workers employed directly by the company, even allowing for the temporary work agency's operating costs and profit. In this context, temporary work agencies were competing almost exclusively on costs instead of other factors, such as the quality of the services rendered.

Another error made by the legislator in 1994 was to introduce extremely ineffective entry barriers to the sector. Although the same techniques were pursued in other countries – administrative authorisation, registration, financial guarantees, etc. – the way in which this was regulated in Spain meant that, in practice, it was very easy to set up a temporary work agency and operate in the sector. The number of temporary work agencies multiplied and there was a proliferation of small companies ill-equipped to meet their legal obligations. The ease of entry into the temporary work market also had an effect on the way in which this activity developed, since competition was very keen and forced the temporary work agencies to offer their services at lower and lower prices, putting downward pressure on their employees' pay.

In practice then, temporary work agencies (ETT) went from being an instrument of flexibility for workers – as the legislator had intended – to a means of cutting labour costs. The practices of the temporary work market reflected those adopted by the agencies: contracts of very short duration which increased the insecurity of the Spanish labour market even more, jobs with very low skills and pay levels, no opportunities for advancement and the systematic contracting of the most disadvantaged groups in the labour market. The cheap, poor quality temporary work came at a high price for the workers employed by these agencies.

The development of this ETT model generated considerable resentment against the agencies, which were considered to be poor employers and exploiters of their workforces. Within a very few years, two contradictory trends emerged. While the operating volume of ETTs increased sharply and they were very successful, they drew criticism from all of the social sectors and political parties. The issue of the working conditions of ETT workers also made itself felt in public opinion, formed part of electoral manifestos and even gave rise to attacks on the offices of some ETTs. There was a general consensus on the need to improve conditions for their employees and parallel reform processes were launched. These included a popular legislative initiative, under the auspices of the UGT trade union, various proposals by regional parliaments to the national parliament to the same effect, and a proposal for a law by the Socialist Party that had approved Law 14/1994.

The aim of the Socialist Party's proposal was to amend Law 14/1994 to introduce the principle of equal pay for temporary workers. However, in the course of the parliamentary proceedings, the proposal turned into a comprehensive overhaul of the 1994 legislation, affecting key elements of the legal regime governing ETTs. As evidence of the widespread criticism these enterprises attracted, the reform law, 29/1999, was approved virtually unanimously, obtaining the support of all political groups.

The salient features of these large-scale reforms of 1999 included the following:

- A system for calculating the pay of temporary workers was established, so they earn more or less the same as the workers in the user companies, without this being a principle of complete and absolute equality.

- New requirements were imposed for setting up an ETT, clarifying the aspects for which they needed to obtain administrative authorisation.

- An attempt was made to reduce the temporary nature of employment in these enterprises. However, this was done in an unusual way, obliging them to hold a minimum number of permanent posts for the staff in the agency – those who work at the ETT itself – and not for the people who are on assignment.

- Several technical aspects were clarified, such as the consequences of providing services without administrative authorisation.

Once these reforms had been put into practice, they led to a radical change in the model of temporary work in the Spanish labour market. ETTs were no longer useful for cutting costs, because the pay of a worker on assignment went up considerably. Since they were now more expensive, user enterprises found themselves obliged to make more selective use of their services, using them only when they provided a solution to their workforce requirements. The role of ETTs

in human resource policy was defined more clearly in order to optimise a form of employment that was no longer cheap.

The labour market statistics show that from 1999 onwards there was a gentle but steady decline in the number of ETTs operating in Spain and the number of contracts signed. Many small companies were put out of business and, as concentration intensified in the sector, a very large percentage of all the contracts were signed with a very small number of large enterprises, usually multinationals. However, there is still a certain amount of resistance to these companies, which have yet to gain social acceptance.

The process of legal reform of the ETT model in Spain is certainly interesting, if only because it goes against the general trend for regulating these enterprises in the whole of Europe. Its legal regime was relaxed to the extent that, in some cases, it dispensed with the need for administrative authorisation. In fact, the legislator had actually pursued the same course as collective negotiators in this sector, implementing many of the measures instituted by Law 29/1999.

In this sector, sectoral State negotiation started as a reaction against the proliferation of company agreements, which were directly responsible for the poor working conditions in the ETT, and against the wishes of some Autonomous Communities that wanted to have their own regional agreement for ETTs. Today only Catalonia has its own agreement. This negotiating unit was successfully set up, in apparent contradiction to the interests of the enterprises, as a result of a strategic alliance between the trade unions and the large enterprises in the sector, which were the only ones capable of meeting the costs of higher pay and better working conditions. After a first agreement on a small scale, the second Collective State Agreement set in motion the 'convergence process', which comprised a progressive harmonisation, over the course of three years, of the pay of workers on assignment and in user enterprises. This was calculated in percentage increments, which meant that temporary workers received 80% in one year, 90% in the second and 100% in the third. All in all, the idea was to establish the principle of equal pay over an extended transitional period, a principle that was not provided for in the law. However, before the convergence process was complete, Law 29/1999 enacted this principle directly. It was also collective bargaining that obliged the ETTs to have a minimum number of permanent employees among their structural staff.

In this way, the legal model for ETTs in Law 14/1994 was amended by collective negotiation. Because this negotiation was at sectoral level, it had the same scope as the law and the agreement hence operated as the real regulating legislation for this activity. The legal reform of 1999 brought about acceptance of the reform and incorporated it in the law. This was a very interesting experiment for at least two reasons. Firstly, it was a legal reform running counter to the mainstream in European labour law, which was definitely on course for greater flexibility and deregulation. It was thus a step backwards in terms of flexible labour law, replacing a flexible regime with one that was far less so. Secondly, it was an unusual type of cooperation between collective bargaining and the law, unlike the model of negotiated legislation common in Europe. Here, it was an agreement that assumed a regulating role that, in principle, ought to be played by a law, occupying its legislative space and correcting the legal model.

The introduction of ETTs in the Spanish labour market also gave rise to changes in the traditional substance of collective agreements, many of which – especially at State level – started to include clauses on the use of ETTs by enterprises coming within their scope. These regulations came to be highly restrictive in some cases, even prohibiting recourse to ETTs, which posed major problems as to the legality of these agreements from the point of view of competition law. In other cases, the clauses on the use of ETTs turned out to be a genuine instrument for trade union pressure, because there were some which obliged enterprises to enlist the services of only those ETTs that were signatories to the State agreement or which guaranteed the principle of equal treatment for its workers. These clauses, which are normal in other systems of labour relations, were completely new in Spain. In fact, it was the fear of losing market shares as a consequence of these restrictive clauses that convinced many enterprises to abandon their own agreements in favour of the State sectoral agreement.

There were only a few small reforms subsequent to Law 14/1994, the most important being Law 45/1999 on the posting of workers in the framework of the transnational provision of services. This covered cross-border fixed-term work and incorporated a new *ad hoc* chapter in the 1994 law.

1.3. Part-time contracts

Spain also differs from the rest of Europe with regard to part-time work. Although there is a high incidence of atypical work, it is virtually all linked to fixed-term employment, and Spain is, by far, the country that makes least use of part-time work in Europe. Furthermore, this phenomenon has been impervious to change over the years, and policies to promote part-time work have had very little impact. It is surprising given that successive Governments have been promoting the use of part-time work for virtually 20 years, using all types of measures with scant success. The most important of these

measures was the amendment of its legal regime to make it more attractive and convenient for enterprises and workers. There have been six in-depth reforms of the regulations on part-time work in Article 12 of the ET. These reforms have been of all types and have used all kinds of measures but none of them has produced any tangible results. This is called the 'mystery of part-time work' – a reluctance to sign a contract and to be contracted for part-time work – a very Spanish phenomenon that is difficult to explain. All kinds of explanations have been offered, such as cultural factors, the lower proportion of women in the labour market, the low activity rate amongst students, premature exclusion from the labour market on grounds of age, etc.

The period that we are studying started with a part-time work regulation that was fairly rigid and anchored in the mentality of the 1980s. The 1994 reform introduced a much more flexible regime, which regarded part-time work as any contract for fewer working hours than in a collective agreement and which was generally fairly convenient for enterprises. However, it was severely criticised by the trade unions, since they regarded it as a very low-quality form of employment that was not attractive for workers.

One of the labour policy priorities set by the first conservative Government was to promote the use of part-time work, particularly permanent or stable part-time work, in order to increase employment and reduce the temporary nature of the Spanish labour market. To this end, the Government concluded an agreement on part-time work with the trade union organisations and against the explicit opposition of the employers' associations. This agreement translated into a redrafted Article 12 of the ET, in which almost every aspect of its legal regime was new.

Under this regime, the definition of part-time work was fixed and was calculated as a percentage – 77% – of normal full-time working hours. This was a departure from the norm at that time in Europe, where there was generally a variable rather than a fixed threshold. The regulation introduced was very protective of workers and was intended to promote open-ended part-time work contracts. Working hours had to be stipulated in full at the time when the contract was signed, leaving the employer little room for unforeseen circumstances. The peculiarity of this regime is that it is a regulation of a flexible form of employment devised by the trade unions themselves. This means that it reflects a model of flexibility that the Spanish trade unions considered suitable, i.e. one that did not amount to deregulation or the attribution of unlimited powers to an enterprise, but, on the contrary, was full of guarantees and checks.

The main problem with this model was its complexity. It resulted in a highly complex regulation full of limitations and restrictions that was enormously cumbersome and difficult to manage. The clearest example was overtime, which was prohibited in part-time work in order to avoid this exceeding the maximum working hours for this type of employment. However, additional hours were introduced which fulfilled the same function but were subject to an entirely different regime that was much more complicated. These additional hours were only allowed for open-ended part-time work if they were agreed upon explicitly, in a separate document, at the time when the contract was signed. In addition, only a limited number of additional working hours per year were allowed, calculated as a fairly small percentage of the agreed part-time working hours. The additional hours had to be spread evenly over the quarters of the year and if they were worked repeatedly they needed to be consolidated, increasing the part-time working hours originally agreed. The management of this system was an enormously complex task and, while the idea of the additional working hours was to introduce a degree of flexibility in regulating this form of employment, this was clearly not the result.

The 1998 reform, like so many others in this area, was a failure and did not achieve its objective of increasing stable part-time work in the labour market. This failure was the argument used by the Government to introduce a new reform in 2001, establishing the regime that is currently in force. The real reason for the reform was actually that, since the Government had an absolute majority and was in dispute with the trade unions for other reasons, it did not value the social partners' consensus in the same way it had in 1998. The pressure from the employers' associations to achieve more flexibility in this type of employment obviously had an impact as well.

The model for part-time work approved in 2001 differed radically in its objectives and its basic features from that of 1998 and catered far more for the employers' than the trade unions' wishes. However, the new model did not openly replace the previous one and Article 12 of the ET was not completely redrafted as it had been in 1998. Although the reform was much more subtle, it amended fundamental aspects of the regulations on part-time work. Some sections were replaced, some words or clauses in others were deleted, but ultimately the legal regime for this model was completely overhauled without any major changes appearing to have been made. It should not be forgotten that the 1998 regime had been the result of an agreement between the trade unions and the same Government and it did not wish to be seen breaking its own promises or undermining its own work. What the reform amounted to was a controlled demolition of the 1998 part-time regulations. Technically speaking, the 2001 reform was a fairly disingenuous piece of legislation.

As regards the substance of the reform, a new definition of part-time work was introduced. Henceforth *the employment contract is regarded as a part-time contract when it has been agreed upon that service should be rendered during a number of hours per day, week, month or year less than the working hours of a comparable full-time worker.* The fixed limit of 77% of full-time working hours that had been used since 1998 was abandoned and the legislator returned to the system in force from 1994 to 1998. Furthermore, the obligation to state in the contract *the distribution of working hours and the specific monthly, weekly and daily working hours, including a specification of the days on which the worker must work,* which RDL 15/1998 had introduced, was also removed. This made working additional hours much more flexible, at least compared with the previous regime. But the aspect of part-time work where the desire for flexibility in the reform can best be appreciated is the regime for additional working hours, which was one of the key aspects of the part-time work regime established by RDL 15/1998. RDL 5/2001 claimed to make the use of these hours more flexible by doing away with the consolidation mechanism and the statutory requirement to distribute the working hours throughout the quarters of the year. Moreover, the maximum number of additional hours that could be established by collective agreement was increased to 60% of the working hours agreed upon, whereas previously it had been 30%.

There is one peculiarity which may be of particular interest for this study: the two major reforms of part-time work in 1998 and 2001, which had virtually diametrically opposed philosophies and objectives, were both presented as implementing the 1997 Community Directive. In both cases the reform was justified by the need to comply with European standards. This shows the complex and ambivalent nature of Community legislation resulting from both of its consensual character and of the need to design a regulation that is workable in all the Member States. We can perhaps now see how clarity suffers as a result.

2. Labour law and the decentralisation of production

Like all the European economies, the Spanish economy experienced a marked process of decentralisation of production throughout the decade that we are studying. The subcontracting of works and services became the standard way of organising production of goods and services, affecting the internal and central functions of an enterprise.

Spanish law found itself ill-equipped to cope with the consequences of this phenomenon in terms of labour. The existing regulations in the Statute of Workers' Rights actually predated it considerably, since they came directly from the legislation of the 1970s, which in turn was adapted from Italian legislation dating from 1960. The legal regime for subcontracting works and services was therefore restricted to making the main contractor jointly liable for wage and social security debts incurred by the contractor during the contract and, what is more, enabled him to be absolved of this in certain circumstances. Furthermore, the regime did not apply to all subcontracts, but only to those for the enterprise's own activity. Any contract that did not come under this heading was excluded, as was any contract for the account of, say, a head of household for home repairs. Not only was the regime inadequate, it was also confusing. There was no definition of the 'contract and subcontract' that Article 42 of the ET referred to and it was not clear what the main contractor's 'own activity' was, leading to extensive and complex jurisprudence. In conjunction with Article 42, Article 64 of the ET acknowledged the right of the legal representatives of the workers in the company to be informed of the company's plans for subcontracting, but without any further indication. The legislation on social security also contained a reference to this phenomenon in similar terms to those in the Statute of Workers' Rights.

This was a regime which was inadequate by any standard and which attracted widespread criticism for two main reasons. The first was the enormous increase in subcontracting and outsourcing that was gradually affecting all enterprises and sectors, including public administrations. The second was the link that gradually emerged between subcontracting and accidents at work, particularly in the construction sector, where this was most common.

However, the fact that the provisions governing subcontracting of works and services were obsolete did not produce a legal reform establishing a new regime. On the contrary, the only reform that had any bearing on it during most of the decade was the adoption of the Law on the Prevention of Occupational Risks, which contained some mention of work under a subcontracting regime.

In the absence of any legal remedy for the labour consequences of subcontracting works and services, collective bargaining was used to deal with these questions in those services where this form of decentralisation was most common. The measures that feature in the agreements are very varied and include the following:

- The employer's obligation to inform his workers about the subcontracting to be undertaken in the enterprise, which has now been adopted by the Statute of Workers' Rights

- A ban on outsourcing some of the enterprise's services

- The obligation to maintain jobs for workers in the event of contracts being ceded

- The guarantee of working conditions for the persons employed by the contractors.

The 2001 reform sought to get to grips with the problem of subcontracting and appeared to tackle it with determination, introducing a new version of Article 42 of the ET. Nonetheless, this is not borne out by the facts, since it merely imposed obligations to provide information both to the workers in the contracting companies and to the representatives of the workers in the main contracting company. This information may make it easier to use legal mechanisms to safeguard labour rights, such as joint and several liabilities, but these mechanisms are no longer adequate. Indeed, the provisions of Article 42 of the ET are much older than the 20 years of the Statute, and were drafted at a very different time. Today, in the throes of the quickening process of the systematic decentralisation of production and outsourcing, more effective mechanisms are required.

Section 1 of Article 42 virtually reiterates the previous text with some minor innovations. A final paragraph in section 2, restricting the joint and several liabilities of the main contractor to *what would have been the case if it had been the company's permanent workforce in the same category or job*, has been dropped. This must be interpreted as meaning that liability extends to the entire wage and social security debts of the contractor during the period of the contract without any limit. This measure could be interpreted as a minimum extension of the effect of the protective mechanism of Article 42 of the ET governing subcontracting of work.

The new section 3 of Article 42 of the ET obliges the contracting company to inform workers of the main contractor. This should be done in writing and should include the name or title of the main contractor, the domicile and the tax identification number. This obligation is accompanied by the need to identify the main contractor to the General Social Security Treasury.

Section 4 of Article 42 of the ET, which is also new, obliges the main contractor to inform the representatives of the workers of any subcontracting done, without prejudice to the provisions of Article 64.1.1 of the same Statute. The information to be provided is fairly comprehensive and is set out in detail.

Finally, section 5 of Article 42 of the ET obliges the contractor or subcontractor to provide their workers' representatives with information on the contracts to be performed before work is started on them. The substance of this information is determined by reference to the previous sections of the same article.

The 2001 reform certainly improved the legal regime for the subcontracting of works and services, but offered no solutions to the many problems that it poses for workers and for industrial relations. Many have therefore called for a law on subcontracting to be drafted that is capable of regulating this phenomenon properly and comprehensively.

Among the many problems raised by subcontracting today is that of distinguishing it from another form of decentralisation of production with which it has clear similarities, namely the posting of workers. Another peculiarity of Spanish labour law is that it upholds a ban on any form of hiring out of workers, with the single exception of ETTs, whose activity is legally defined as a provision of workers in Article 43. This is only permitted for legally constituted ETTs and is prohibited otherwise. In many European systems, however, the legality of other – non-profit making – forms of detachment of workers or employee-leasing is starting to be accepted. However, a classical problem of labour law in the 20th century has been to distinguish between two practices, one of which was legal and the other not. Normally the difference is that one offers an organised service and the other merely supplies workers. This criterion is now inadequate as subcontracting is on the increase and subcontracting work is starting to lose its material and organisational basis. The main component of many contracts for services is the know-how of the contractor's workers. This is clearly the case with many IT contracts.

There is also the special Spanish case of the 'service enterprise', an entrepreneurial organisation that provides services of all types to their customers from cleaning to security. In many cases, the services mainly involve supplying workers to perform these services. These service enterprises are often constituted around the major ETTs, which are the only ones that can legally provide workers on a temporary basis. Sometimes they are ETTs that were constituted before the 1999 reforms that left the temporary work sector to operate as service enterprises without their activities undergoing any major changes in practice. There is a fine line between ETTs and service enterprises, which has to be drawn by reference to the fact that only the former are legally entitled to provide workers.

Finally, it should be pointed out that the provision of workers has been a perennial problem in the Spanish labour market since the legalisation of the ETTs, as many forms of these still exist although, in theory, they are all prohibited under the terms of Article 43 of the ET. Specific types of services, forms of workforce mobility within groups of enterprises, and workers placed at the disposal of other enterprises, are still common phenomena in a decentralised economy and in enterprises that are organised in the form of networks. The only response to these phenomena that labour legislation has to offer is prohibition, which the courts are still enforcing, although some cases do raise questions. Spanish labour law quite clearly has work to do to fully regulate all aspects of the decentralisation of production, particularly in relation to its effects on industrial relations.

3. Labour law and teleworking

Despite its relative youth, Spanish labour law has so far shown little awareness of the impact of new technologies, especially information and communication technologies (ICT). The legislative prototype for enterprises and labour relations is still the Ford prototype, with industrial technology predating the informatics revolution.

Throughout the decade under review, various problems have arisen because the Statute of Workers' Rights is ill-equipped to cope with ICT. The courts have not always been up to the task and collective bargaining is therefore becoming the principal regulatory benchmark, as Spanish agreements are starting to get to grips with these issues and plugging the legal gaps.

The Statute of Workers' Rights only contains rules to protect a worker's privacy against searches of his person or his locker, but says nothing about checks on his computer, his e-mail accounts or surfing on the Internet. The courts were first uncertain, but now generally accept the legitimacy of such checks and do not see them as violations of the worker's right to privacy. To safeguard this right, some collective agreements now establish guarantees for these checks. Some courts have also applied the same guarantees that govern searches of lockers under the Statute to searches of employees' computers and e-mail accounts by enterprises, and companies have also reacted by drawing up codes of conduct on the use of informatics equipment by their employees.

The law also says nothing about the consequences of improper non-work-related use of these technological resources, such as private e-mail and Internet surfing. In the absence of any regulations, the judges of industrial tribunals endorse decisions to dismiss workers on the grounds that they have not acted in good faith. To prevent this, collective agreements include a codification of such behaviour with more suitable consequences in their disciplinary regime.

The legal shortcomings with regard to trade union use of ICT, or 'on-line rights' as the unions call them, are even more patent. The Statute still talks about notice boards, the distribution of paper-based information and assemblies with the physical presence of workers, but says nothing about virtual notice boards, on-line assemblies or the dispatch of trade union information through the company Intranet. The courts have refused to interpret the Statute's provisions as extending to these new forms and formats of trade union action. It has therefore once again been made the task of collective bargaining to regulate these matters and there are already agreements which cover them fairly comprehensively. These include, among other, electronic notice boards on the BtoE portal, free access to the e-mail accounts of members (for the trade unions) or of all employees (for the legal representatives), virtual assemblies, chats on matters of interest for workers. Various parliamentary initiatives have also been presented to amend the Statute and the Organic Law on Trade Union Freedom in order to allow access to trade union members and other workers' representatives to the working networks of the enterprises, but they have had little success so far.

One of the many areas in which the obsolescence of Spanish labour law with regard to ICT can be seen is teleworking, a special type of remote work using electronic resources. There is no mention of this form of employment in the labour legislation currently in force, and attempts to bring it under the ambit of existing models of work have failed for various reasons:

* Article 13 of the ET, which deals with work at home, offers a very unsubstantial and incomplete regulation of this model.

* The type of home working covered by Article 13 of the ET is industrial work in small workshops in workers' homes, using equipment from the company. It has nothing to do with teleworking that has very different characteristics and poses very different problems too.

* Not all teleworking is done at the worker's home since there are also telecommuting and telecentres.

Once again it has been up to collective bargaining to address the issues raised by teleworking and there are already some agreements that cover it very fully, of which the Telefónica agreement is an outstanding example.

The signing and implementation of the European Agreement on Teleworking is outside the time frame of this report, so we will limit ourselves to pointing out that the Agreement for Collective Bargaining for 2003 incorporates the text of the European Agreement as an annex, in which the social partners at State level, who are signatories, undertake to do what is necessary to ensure that it is put into practice.

In any event, it should be borne in mind that there is very little teleworking in the Spanish labour market, according to the few studies available.

4. Organisation of working time

The legal organisation of working time is one of the aspects that have changed the most during this decade and where the effects of Community labour law on Spanish law can be seen. It is, of course, the 1993 Directive on certain aspects of the organisation of working time that served as a guide for the profound transformation this regulation underwent during the 1994 labour reform.

The regime in force in 1992 was essentially the same as that established by the original version of the Statute of Workers' Rights in 1980. It was not particularly rigid, since it permitted instruments of flexibility such as flexible working hours, shift work and relative freedom for overtime, but it left little space for adjusting its rules and regulations to the peculiarities of each enterprise.

In 1994, the legal regime on working time was adapted as part of a reform process heavily geared towards flexibility, as the changes to this specific aspect of labour law show. In this area, unlike others, there was some justification for change, namely the need to implement the 1993 Community Directive, which was adopted as a guide and a pretext for the majority of the changes that were introduced. All of these changes were aimed to permit more varied and flexible ways of organising working hours.

The maximum weekly working hours laid down in the Directive were therefore reduced from 48 to 40, but annual computation was allowed, which in practice meant that many more hours could be worked in some weeks. The same happened with the breaks, which could be organised in various ways in addition to that provided by the Statute in general terms. The only hard-and-fast rule was the minimum break of nine hours between the end of one working day and the start of the next. Exceptions to all the others were permitted. The rules and regulations on overtime were relaxed, allowing many hours to be worked and at a lower cost than under the previous regime.

In the majority of cases, the use of flexible working hours was dependent on the approval of workers' representatives in company or collective agreements. However, there was no deregulation of the daily working hours, but a reorganisation of the sources of regulation.

Although the Directive was mentioned occasionally as a justification for the reforms, the Spanish legislator showed little enthusiasm for its implementation, as can be seen in Article 36.5 of the ET that transposes the article on patterns of work. Instead of establishing a regulation that ensures compliance with the Directive, this article virtually reproduces the provisions of the Directive verbatim, making the State responsible for the way employers organise patterns of work.

The other major debate on the reduction of working time during this decade had little practical impact in Spain. While it attained some strength at the end of the 1990s – at a time that coincided with the reforms in France – it met with strong resistance from the employers' organisations and little support from the Government. Only in some Autonomous Communities were measures to reduce weekly working hours to 35 introduced, but only for their own employees, since they did not have the authority to enact labour legislation. What happened was that there was a gradual reduction of annual working hours in collective bargaining, leading to an average of 37.5 hours a week. Over the past few years of the decade, however, this process appears to have stalled.

Chapter IV:
Equal opportunities at work

The field of equal opportunities at work is one where the fault line between democratic labour law and the dictatorship's is most visible. This is not only because the previous regime did not recognise the principle of equality as a general and fundamental legal value, but because the regime had a view of social, family and working life which was very detrimental to the position of women in the labour market.

The Spanish Constitution made equality a supreme value and a fundamental right for all citizens. Article 14 of the Constitution affirms in its first clause referring to equality under the law and before the law that *Spaniards are equal before the law*, whilst the second clause prohibits any discrimination *on the grounds of birth, race, sex, religion, opinion or any other personal or social condition or circumstance.*

In keeping with this constitutional remit, Articles 4 and 17 of the Statute of Workers' Rights are geared specifically to prohibiting discrimination. However, in light of the most recent Community legislation, both articles are inadequate from a conceptual point of view. They fail to define basic concepts such as direct or indirect discrimination or discriminatory harassment, although these concepts have been the subject of legal interpretation by the Constitutional Court.

Article 4 c) of the ET under the heading *occupational rights* establishes workers' rights to non-discrimination *for the purposes of employment or once employed on the grounds of sex, civil status, age within the limits laid down by the law, race, social circumstances, political or religious beliefs, membership of a trade union and language within the Spanish State.*

Article 17 of the ET specifies or develops the ban on discrimination contained in Article 14 of the Constitution within the specific context of industrial relations. In the first section, it stipulates that any regulatory principle, clause of a collective agreement, individual agreement or unilateral decision by an employer that could be described as discriminatory, is null and void. In other words, no outcome of collective bargaining, of private individual autonomy or the entrepreneur's own authority may discriminate for the purposes of access to employment on the grounds prohibited in Article 17 of the ET, on pain of being declared null and void.

Under Article 17 of the ET, discrimination exists when, in any of the instruments mentioned above, there exists unfavourable differentiation on the grounds of age or either favourable or adverse differentiation on grounds of sex, origin, civil status, race, social circumstances, religious or political beliefs, membership of trade unions and subscription to their agreements, links of kinship with other workers of the enterprise and language within the Spanish State. Although the list in Article 17 is longer than in Article 14 of the Constitution, there is no open clause as in the constitutional law. This prevents discrimination on, say, the grounds of sexual orientation mentioned in the derived Community legislation from being interpreted as included, unless it is interpreted as discrimination on the grounds of sex. However, this is something that, on the basis of the judgment of the European Court of Justice in *Grant,* appears to be at least questionable.

In addition to the prohibition of discrimination as a legal restriction, there are possible exclusions, reservations or preferences relating to free contracting which, under Article 17.2 of the ET, can only be established by law: *exclusions, reservations and preferences relating to free contracting may be established by law.* This is, for example, the legal basis on which LISM, Law 13/1982 of 17 April on Social Integration of the Disabled (amended by Law 66/1997), was adopted.

The third section of this Article stipulates that:

Notwithstanding the provisions of the previous section, the Government may lay down measures governing reservations, duration or preferences for the purposes of employment which are intended to make it easier for jobseekers to find work.

By the same token, the Government may grant subsidies, relief and other measures to promote employment of specific groups of workers who are having particular difficulty in finding work. This will be done after prior consultation with the most representative trade union organisations and employers' associations.

The measures to which the above paragraphs refer will mainly be geared to promoting stable employment for unemployed workers and converting temporary contracts into permanent contracts.

With this in mind, the Government can grant tax subsidies, relief, allowances and other forms of positive action favouring access to employment for certain vulnerable groups after prior consultation with the most representative trade union organisations and employers' associations. Many of the measures adopted in the programmes to promote employment are intended to achieve this aim and provide incentives to take on certain vulnerable groups, including the disabled, the unemployed who are 45 years or older, young people (between 16 and 30) without occupational experience, women in sectors where they are underrepresented, and the long-term unemployed who have recently given birth or are aged between 16 or 45.

With regard to the guaranteeing and safeguarding of fundamental rights to equality and non-discrimination recognised in Article 14 of the Constitution, it should first be pointed out that, according to Article 53 of the Constitution, these rights enjoy maximum protection under the law. This precept is binding on all public authorities, including the judicial bodies, with regard to compliance and implementation, and the restriction to cases provided for by law applies with regard to its essential substance. By the same token, these rights are to be protected before the normal courts by means of summary and emergency proceedings that are designed to safeguard equality and non-discrimination and, with regard to employment and under the terms of Article 181 of the Law on Employment Procedure (hereinafter LPL), are conducted using procedural arrangements to 'safeguard trade union freedom and other fundamental rights'. These proceedings come under Articles 175 *et seq* of the LPL and have been recognised as the most appropriate to deal with any discrimination which may have existed prior to the working relationship, such as access to employment. At the same time, it should be noted that, with regard to certain conditions set out in Article 182 LPL, preference is to be given to other procedural arrangements than those mentioned above. Specifically, this procedure is used to handle actions concerning *dismissal and other causes for terminating the employment contract, entitlement to holidays, electoral matters, challenges to the statutes of trade unions or their amendment and challenges to collective agreements invoking violations of trade union freedom or other fundamental rights*. However, these specific procedural channels must respect the procedural guarantees laid down in Articles 175 *et seq* for the protection of fundamental rights. For the purposes of emergency and summary proceedings, the public prosecutors must be involved, as must the trade union, which, on occasion, acts as intervener. The instrument under challenge can also be suspended and judgments enforced provisionally, immediately and automatically. In the course of these proceedings, the burden of proof may be reversed, which is specifically provided for in Article 96 LPL with regard to discrimination on the grounds of sex.

There was also a reform of the Penal Code in 1995 with regard to safeguarding these rights. The new Penal Code, the first during the democracy, includes a safeguard mechanism in Article 314 of Chapter XV, where offences against workers are dealt with. This law, which was amended by LO 11/1999 of 30 April 1999, provides that *persons guilty of serious discrimination in public or private employment against any person on the grounds of ideology, religion or beliefs, ethnic, racial or national origin, sex, sexual orientation, family situation, disease or disability or because that person is a legal or trade union workers' representative, is related to other workers in the enterprise or on the grounds of the use of official languages in the Spanish State and does not restore the situation of equality before the law after an administrative order or penalty, making good the economic damage stemming from the discrimination, shall be punished by a prison sentence of between six months and two years or a fine of between six and twelve months' pay.*

Once the normal and secondary channels have been exhausted, an appeal on fundamental rights may be lodged with the Constitutional Court under Article 53.2 of the Constitution, if violations of Article 14 of the Constitution persist. This body also rules on appeals of non-constitutionality which, under Article 162 of the Constitution, can be made against any law or provision with legal effect which contravenes this article.

In the course of an appeal, the equality clause of Article 14 of the Constitution cannot be invoked directly, but the non-discriminatory clause can be relied on with regard to decisions or actions taken by private enterprises and, in this specific case, with regard to access to employment. This circumstance is not an obstacle, because an appeal could be made indirectly for infringing the effective judiciary safeguards of Article 24 of the Constitution if it is shown that, in the course of the normal judicial channels, no scrutiny of the possible arbitrariness or irrationality of the unfair measure has been made.

As part of the safeguards and guarantees existing in Spanish legislation, the LISOS or the Ley de Infracciones y Sanciones del Orden Social (Law on Infringements and Penalties in the Social Order) (RD 5/2000 of 4 August) provides for administrative sanctions by means of fines against employers who discriminate with regard to access to employment. In this context one very serious infringement stands out, as codified in Article 8 section 8, which, with a clear reference to the above-mentioned Article 17 of the Statute of Workers' Rights, established that *unilateral decisions taken by the employer which involve unfavourable discrimination on the grounds of age or favourable or adverse discrimination with regard to daily pay, training, promotion and other working conditions, on grounds of* sex, origin, civil status, race, social circumstances, religious or political beliefs, membership of trade unions and subscription to their agreements, links of kinship with other workers in the enterprises, language within the Spanish State or on the grounds of physical, mental or sensory disabilities will be regarded as such.

In the same way, Article 15.3 of LISOS identifies the non-fulfilment of the legal obligation to reserve jobs for the occupational integration of the disabled as a serious infringement. Article 16.2 classifies setting conditions of access to employment that constitute discrimination on the above grounds, as a very serious infringement.

The development of legislative instruments to combat sexual harassment also forms part of this protection against discrimination in employment. These instruments were mainly designed and implemented during the decade that we are analysing. Although sexual harassment is a type of conduct which can impinge on a number of rights, from the right to health to the right to dignity at work, it is generally included as a part of discriminatory behaviour on the grounds of sex, since it is the sex of the victim which is the key to identifying this behaviour as an offence.

Article 4.2e ET states explicitly that *workers are entitled to respect of their privacy and consideration for their dignity, including protection against offensive physical or verbal behaviour of a sexual nature.* The scope of this article is very wide and it is not worded very clearly, as it does not contain a definition of sexual harassment. In order to identify behaviour as sexual harassment, the definition in the 'Code of Conduct on measures to combat sexual harassment', which accompanies the Recommendation of the Commission of the European Communities of 27 November 1991 on the protection of the dignity of women and men at work, is therefore used. This affords workers in Spain protection from both sexual blackmail and a hostile working environment, the latter condition of sexual harassment having served as a basis for labour tribunals to defend workers against moral harassment.

After recognising the right of workers not to suffer sexual harassment, Spanish labour law introduced a variety of methods to effectively protect this right. First of all, LISOS sanctions this conduct, stating in Article 8.11 that *sexual harassment is a very serious infringement when it occurs within the sphere of responsibility of an enterprise's management.* What is more, the 1995 Penal Code contains a criminal offence which is designated 'an offence of sexual harassment' specifically for the purposes of sanctioning and is defined by Article 184 as follows: *Soliciting favours of a sexual nature for oneself or a third party, taking advantage of a position of superiority in a working, teaching or similar environment with the explic-*

it or tacit intention of disappointing a victim's legitimate expectations of a relationship shall be punishable as sexual harassment on pain of imprisonment for between 12 and 24 weeks or a fine of between 6 and 12 months' pay.

Chapter V:
Conclusions

If we look at the changes in Spanish labour law as a whole, we can draw some conclusions that, in the author's view, identify how it has developed over the reference period.

In the first place, throughout the past few decades what might be termed the 'Spanish flexibility model' has emerged as a result of a continuous process of reform that has affected virtually all occupational institutions. This model is characterised *inter alia* by the following:

- The widespread use of fixed-term contracts as an instrument of flexibility, enabling workforces to be adjusted at a low cost, albeit to the detriment of the quality of employment.

- The use of laws as the fundamental instruments of reform.

- Successive use of various types of flexibility, opting initially for flexibility on entry to the labour market and only years later for internal and management flexibility. However, use of flexibility techniques for wages and employees leaving the labour market have not been made so far.

- Transfer of costs of restructuring of enterprises to the State, above all through the benefits of the public social security system.

Secondly, the hallmark of Spain's experience has also been its very special relationship with flexibility. Starting from a type of labour law which was based on traditional techniques of legal guarantees, mechanisms of entry flexibility and internal flexibility were gradually accepted in the course of successive and cumulative legal reforms until the level of flexibility of the system was very high. This was responsible for a series of dysfunctions in the labour market and caused some problems that were as serious as unemployment itself.

Once these problems were identified and the attitude of the social partners to requests for reform changed, the time was ripe for a different course to be adopted in the final years of the 20th century, when a series of legislative measures were geared to different objectives from those of the previous reforms. Attention was once again focused on the qualitative aspects of working relationships, enhancing protection for specific groups of workers and seeking a new balance in the labour market. This new phase was also characterised by the use of techniques of negotiated legislation, which meant that there was solid social consensus behind the reforms. These years saw an increasing role for social dialogue and collective bargaining, returning to the autonomous nature of traditional labour law. This is a type of labour law that is inherently flexible. It uses original techniques in which requests to adapt the system of production are not met with deregulation or the systematic and generalised reduction of the legal status of paid workers. Instead, they are dealt with by means of differentiation, complexity, subtlety and checks and balances. This means that labour law becomes much more complex, but also fairer, more balanced, and more efficient in macroeconomic terms.

This process of abandoning and returning to flexibility is not exclusive to Spain, although it is true that it has perhaps been seen earlier in this country. It was also in Spain that the progress towards a flexible type of labour law was most rapid and inconsistent, which is why the effects were felt more intensively. The special and almost unhealthy relationship between labour law and employment revealed itself with particular clarity, as it did in other national systems that pursued the same flexibility course.

Thirdly, the values and techniques of flexibility have provoked different responses, further complicating the labour legislation that has become more extensive, more varied and more complicated in technical terms over the years. Rather than opting for deregulation as the most direct and rapid mechanism for putting their flexibility aims into practice, the authorities opted to do so on the basis of laws, resulting in a change in the traditional techniques of drafting and implementing labour law. The relationship between the sources, their respective roles, legislative technique and the period of validity of legislation have all undergone changes and have generally contributed to an increase in the complexity of all facets of labour legislation, including legislative inflation, hasty and poorly coordinated legislation, the fragmentation of legal statutes, transitory rights, etc. This makes it more difficult to get to grips with and administer labour law and is detrimental in terms of both access to the law and legal certainty.

Annex:
Latest reforms to Spanish labour law during 2003

The first couple of years of the 21ˢᵗ century were most productive in terms of legislation, with two major and highly controversial labour reforms – the reform of 2001 and, more importantly, the unemployment protection reform of 2002. However, the first few months of 2003 passed with no major new developments, with the most important reforms taken in the last quarter of the year. Among others, special attention should be given to Organic Law 14/2003 on the rights and freedoms of foreigners, which among other things amends various provisions on work by foreigners and Law 51/2003 of 2 December 2003, on equal opportunities, non-discrimination, and universal accessibility for the disabled. Also significant are Law 52/2003 of 10 December 2003, laying down specific provisions in the area of social security, Law 54/2003, of 12 December 2003, reforming the legislative framework of the prevention of workplace risks and Law 55/2003 of 16 December 2003, on the framework statutes for statutory health service personnel. This period also saw the adoption of Royal Decree 1326/2003 of 24 October 2003, adopting the Research Grant Statutes, a rather special regulation in Spanish labour law. This Royal Decree does not contain an actual Statute for grant holders, who are still not considered as employees and are therefore not subject to labour laws. The only thing it does, in fact, is make it possible for them to be covered by a social security system with a status similar to that of persons in active service. The interest of this regulation lies in the fact that it marked a move towards developing 'semi-employed' status for staff such as these through social protection, using the same technique used for self-employed workers.

One major legislative milestone was the adoption of the Employment Act, Law 56/2003 of 16 December 2003. This law, which had a very long gestation period, replaces the Basic Law on Employment of 1978, which was previously the fundamental labour market regulation. However, the importance of the scope of this legislative substitution must be qualified. Firstly, the Basic Law on Employment had been amended several times while it was in force, and had already been partially repealed, meaning that very little of the regional 1980 regulation remained. Secondly, the placement model included in the Employment Act is basically the same as the one that was previously in force, particularly follow-

ing the labour reforms of 1994. The Employment Act incorporates an employment placement model that had already been put into practice by successive reforms throughout the 1990s. Nonetheless, this is an important regulation that deserves particular attention.

The process of placement reform in Spain, which involved a shift away from the traditional public employment services monopoly model, started in 1993 with Royal Decree-Law 18/1993. Among other things, this law did away with the monopoly of the Instituto Nacional de Empleo (INEM – The National Employment Institute), making it no longer compulsory for companies to use it, accepting non-profit placement agencies and legalising temporary employment agencies. After 1993, the reform process continued with:

* The transfer of responsibility for placement to the Autonomous Communities, which was already partly complete

* The nationalisation of non-profit placement agencies, the vast majority of which had been established or financed by public bodies

* A major reform of the legislation governing temporary employment agencies.

The Employment Act was intended to put some order into this process, devising a new legislative framework to encompass all of the reforms that had taken place over the previous decade.

This law comes across as a highly complex text, given its far-reaching nature and the range and difficulty of the matters it deals with. This complexity also stems from its objective of serving as a basis for a wide range of labour market-related policies and ensuring their consistency and compatibility. In fact, in many cases these policies are no longer the responsibility of the State but have been transferred to the Autonomous Communities.

This is the first difficulty encountered by the bill – it is an extemporaneous regulation, required to bring order to a process of transfer of responsibilities that has already taken place. The second is the complexity resulting from the absence of employment from the list of responsibilities established in Articles 148 and 149 of the Spanish Constitution. This has forced the Constitutional Tribunal to define its limits wholly on the basis of an unfinished case law construction.

According to Article 1 of the Employment Act, *employment policy is made up of all of the decisions adopted at State and Autonomous Community level intended to develop programmes and measures geared towards attaining full employment, matching demand for employment with supply both in terms of quality and quantity and reducing unemployment and providing appropriate protection for the unemployed.* The role of the two administrations, the State and the Autonomous Community, is thus expressly recognised.

Article 5 defines the National Employment System, a central element in implementation of this policy. It comprises *all of the structures, measures and actions necessary to promote and develop employment policy* and it emerges as a result of the interaction of different administrations. According to the same Article, *the National Employment System is made up by the State Public Employment Service and the Autonomous Communities' Public Employment Services.* Its objectives are defined in Article 6 and include:

• Offering a public employment service to workers and employers free of charge

• Providing the information required to enable jobseekers to find work or improve their possibilities of finding it

• Enabling employers to recruit the workers best suited to their needs

• Promoting employment and supporting job creation, particularly jobs intended for persons with greater difficulty entering the labour market.

Incidentally, its remit also includes – as stated in Article 9 – responsibility for *applying the European Employment Strategy, within the framework of its powers, through the National Employment Action Plans.* This is an attempt to overcome one of the main shortcomings of the existing model: the incongruence between a European strategy that is based on an active role of the State and the implementation of the employment policies by the Autonomous Communities. The same Article also extends its remit to *ensuring the coordination and cooperation of the State Public Employment Service and the Public Employment Services of the Autonomous Communities.*

As to the rest, the Employment Act skims over essential labour market issues such as placement, which it does not define. Neither does it provide a clear and precise definition of the role of other bodies in the labour market.

The adoption of the law results in a situation similar to the current one, unchanged apart from the replacement of the Basic Employment Act with the Employment Act, and with its implementing provisions remaining in force. This continuity demonstrates that the placement model, around which the Employment Act is constructed, is the same as the decentralised and partially liberalised model that currently exists in Spain. Along with public placement, as brought about by the activity of the State and Autonomous Community services, room is made for private placement, subject – as was already the case – to the control of the public authorities. The basic premise is practically complete State responsibility in this area, but the model presupposes the transfer of this responsibility to the Autonomous Communities, limiting the role of the State Public Employment Service (PES) to coordinating and establishing a legal framework for the network of Autonomous Community placement agencies. The agents that were already involved in placement remained, and the current organisational model of the National Employment Institute, handed down to the State Public Employment Service, was maintained. As the first transitional provision of the draft states, *until the organic structure of the Ministry of Labour and Social Affairs is amended, references to the State Public Employment Service will be understood to be references to the National Employment Institute.*

The Employment Act was not particularly well received for many reasons, the first being the mistrust of the Autonomous Communities towards a regulation that appears especially centralist in their eyes. More specifically, it is based on the perception of employment policy as being the exclusive responsibility of the State. In light of recent Constitutional case law, this should be re-thought given that the Constitution does not view what we now term employment policy as a single concept, since it is not listed as an area of responsibility in Articles 148 and 149 of the Constitution, nor could all of its components fit into any one of these. In reality, employment policy is a combination of various issues, each one of which falls into different areas of responsibility and can therefore be the responsibility of both the State and the Autonomous Communities. It is partly employment legislation, but it is also vocational training and the promotion of economic activity, meaning that the Autonomous Communities' responsibility in this area cannot be ignored.

The lack of detail in the text of the Employment Act has also been criticised, as it reduces the possibility of such a regulation attaining its objectives. In the words of Economic and Social Council, *as to the contents of the Bill, the Council takes the view that the text in question does not correspond to a complete conception of employment policy.* Criticism is aimed in particular at its failure to include unemployment protection; the insufficient treatment of objectives, such as linking active employment policies and unemployment benefits or the coordination of the PES with other placement bodies; and the failure to deal with problems such as the high rate of unemployment, regional imbalances, excessively high levels of temporary employment, the low rate of participation by PES in labour mediation or the difficulties faced by particular groups in entering the labour market. These deficiencies prevent the Employment Act from fulfilling its role as a reference that brings order to the series of regulations governing employment-related issues.

The end of 2003 saw the approval of an important regulation with direct repercussions on one of the main areas of interest of this research project. This was Law 62/2003 of 30 December 2003 on Tax, Administrative and Social Measures. This is the Law that accompanies the General State Budget Act each year, as it did in 2004. For some time now Spanish legislators have adopted the habit – criticised by the Constitutional Tribunal – of taking advantage of the adoption of the Budget by accompanying it with a wide range of measures in an 'omnibus law'. In this case, Law 62/2003's Title II 'social affairs' contains labour and social security reforms. Chapter III of this Title bears the heading 'Measures for the application of the principle of equal treatment'. Among other things, this Chapter adopts measures for the implementation of the most recent Directives in the area of equality.

The first section of Chapter III contains general provisions and states that its objective is to *lay down measures for the real and effective application of the principle of equality of treatment and non-discrimination, particularly on grounds of race or ethnicity, religious beliefs or convictions, disability, age or sexual orientation.* This chapter applies to all persons, both public and private. This first section defines the basic concepts in this area, taken from Community Directives, such as 'the principle of equality of treatment', 'direct discrimination', 'indirect discrimination' and 'harassment'. The second section contains specific measures covering equality of treatment and non-discrimination on grounds of a person's race or ethnic origin, implementing the corresponding Directive.

The third section of Chapter III is devoted to *measures in the area of equality of treatment and non-discrimination in the work-place,* and is intended, according to Article 34, to *lay down measures ensuring that the principle of equality of treatment and non-discrimination is real and effective in access to employment, membership of and participation in trade union and employers' organisations, working conditions, professional promotion and vocational and ongoing training, as well as in access to self-employment and professional activity and the inclusion and participation in any organisation of which the members exercise a specific profession.*

Article 35 provides for positive action measures: *in order to guarantee, in practice, full equality on grounds of race or ethnic origin, religious beliefs or convictions, disability, age and sexual orientation, the principle of equality of treatment will not exclude the maintenance or adoption of specific measures in favour of specific groups intended to preclude or compensate for any disadvantage affecting them in respect of the matters included in the scope of the section.*

Law 62/2003 amends various articles of the Workers' Statute. First of all, it re-words some paragraphs of Article 4, which covers the basic rights of workers. The point relating to non-discrimination is therefore worded to protect the following rights: c) *to not be subject to direct or indirect discrimination in recruitment, or once employed, on grounds of sex, marital status, age within the limits fixed in this Law, racial or ethnic origin, social status, religious beliefs or convictions, political ideas, sexual orientation, membership or non-membership of a trade union, or for reasons of language, within the State of Spain. Neither can they be discriminated against on grounds of disability, provided that they are fit to perform the work in question.* The point relating to the protection of privacy and dignity, for its part, defines the following rights: e) *to respect for their privacy and due consideration of their dignity, including protection against verbal and physical abuse of a sexual nature, and against harassment on grounds of racial or ethnic origin, religion or convictions, disability, age or sexual orientation.* The original version of this last paragraph already included protection against sexual harassment as one element of a worker's right to the protection of his or her privacy. It now includes not only sexual harassment, but also harassment in general, for numerous reasons. The only difference is that this new wording includes discriminatory harassment as established in Community Directives, which is probably more closely related to the right to non-discrimination than to the right to dignity. The fact that the concept of discriminatory harassment is based on the concept of sexual harassment explains this debatable position.

Amendments were also made to Articles 16 – on placements – and 17 – on non-discrimination in employment – of the Statute. These are precepts which already prohibited discrimination, and in both cases the wording is now adapted to that of the Directive by the express inclusion of the list of prohibited grounds for discrimination as contained in the Directive. Apart from this change to the wording, the content of both precepts remains essentially unchanged. Article 54, listing the reasons justifying the dismissal of workers on disciplinary grounds, has also been amended to include, in addition to the traditional reasons such as lack of discipline or failure to act in good faith, *harassment of the employer or the persons working in the undertaking on grounds of racial or ethnic origin, religious beliefs or convictions, disability, age or sexual orientation.* Harassment in the workplace thus becomes grounds for the dismissal of the harasser; it remains to be seen whether collective bargaining will include this widened concept of harassment, as a form of discrimination, in undertakings' penalty clauses.

Amendments have also been made to various precepts of Law 13/1982 of 7 April 1982 on the social integration of the disabled; to Law 45/1999 of 29 November 1999 on the posting of workers in the framework of the provision of services; to the revised version of the text of the Law on Employment Procedure, approved by Royal Legislative Decree 2/1995 of 7 April 1995, and the revised text of the Law on Infringements and Penalties in the Social Order, approved by Royal Legislative Decree 5/2000 of 4 August 2000. Of these reforms, perhaps the most interesting is that made to Article 96 of the revised Law on Employment Procedure, which inverts the burden of proof in cases where discrimination is alleged. While its previous wording only referred to cases dealing with sexual discrimination, the new wording states that *in those cases where the claims made by the plaintiff clearly demonstrate the existence of discrimination on grounds of sex, racial or ethnic origin, religious beliefs or convictions, disability, age or sexual orientation, the defendant will be asked to provide objective and reasonable justification, with sufficient evidence, of the measures adopted and their proportionality.*

I shall conclude with two provisions worthy of particular attention. The first is Article 42 of Law 62/2003, dedicated to the promotion of equality in collective bargaining, according to which *collective bargaining can include measures intended to combat all types of discrimination in the workplace, to support equal opportunities and to prevent harassment on grounds of racial or ethnic origin, religious beliefs or convictions, disability, age or sexual orientation.* This measure accompanies various recent initiatives undertaken by both the public administrations and the social partners in Spain that use collective agreements as a tool to fight discrimination in the workplace. The second is Article 43, on the promotion of equality plans, which states that *the public authorities will promote the adoption by the undertakings and by trade union and employers' organisations of equality plans in favour of persons with disabilities, using the incentives and support measures established for this purpose.*

THE EVOLUTION OF LABOUR LAW
IN FRANCE
1992-2002[1]

This report presents an analysis of changes in labour law in France during the period 1992-2003 in line with the significant interaction between the employment guidelines drawn up as part of the European Union employment strategy and French labour law.

In addition, the overall background, marked by the legal changes that have occurred during this eleven-year period will be presented in a preliminary chapter. The changes throw light on developments in labour law in France concerning the flexibility of employees (Chapter II), employability and job security (Chapter III), and equal opportunities (Chapter IV).

Marie-Ange MOREAU
Professor at the European University Institute (Florence)

[1] Carried out in relation with the major employment policy trends. This report is intended to be a comparison between Member States and thus keeps to a common framework. From a technical point of view, a number of points could not be developed due to the limits set for the report.

Table of contents

Chapter I:
Significant changes between 1992 and 2003

In France, the period between 1992 and 2003 is characterised by profound change in the field of labour law.[2] It is therefore important to examine the causes of change before assessing what they have contributed.

1. Causes of change

The changes were brought about by a combination of economic, political and, of course, legal factors.

1.1. Economic

Like other G8 countries, France is caught in the whirlwind of globalisation characterised by the move to a global economy that is poorly understood and poorly managed in terms of its legal consequences.

In 1992, a change in the approach to labour law could only just be detected in discussions centred particularly on the risks of company relocations and the risks of social dumping. These issues led to mobilisation in 1993 and, in particular, as a result of the 'Hoover affair' (a factory was closed in Dijon and relocated to Scotland), but there was still no real questioning of the State's ability to govern labour relations.

However, as from 1995 (following the shock of closures in France of companies belonging to international groups), rules emerged that were adapted to international social developments, in response to the phenomenon of globalisation.

Changes involving the sources of labour law were due to the impacts caused by economic difficulties in France that led to widespread structural unemployment and the need to consider legislative changes to fight unemployment directly and structurally.

The vast majority of the reforms undertaken therefore had the direct or indirect aim of fighting unemployment (and in particular through reduced working hours in 1996, 1998 and 2000 and reforms relating to redundancies and restructuring).

From 1992, the Court of Cassation also used creative and much-disputed case law to fight unemployment through labour law (especially by interpreting laws relating to redundancy). A very strong concern for the fight against exclusion and the search for ways to reintegrate unemployed and other non-working groups into the labour market were combined with the fight against unemployment.

The end of the reference period saw a return to growth, which led to very short-lived improvements in the unemployment figures before a return to virtual recession in 2002-2003. This brief improvement was not enough to change the direction of a labour law focused on improving the employment situation. Alternate periods of growth and non-growth reinforced debate about the balance that French labour law needed to find between security and flexibility, and this led to incessant reforms.

Obviously, there was a great deal of opposition to the political expression of the legal and economic means used.

1.2. Political

France continues to alternate between victories for left- and right-wing parties. As the social debate (particularly clearly since 1986) – and more precisely the labour law debate – is part of the political remit, major legislative changes have taken place in two areas: redundancy and the reduction of working time (RTT).

---

2   Preference has been given to the overall view in this report. It was also agreed that only a summary documentation list would be given. Articles giving preference to analysis in terms of overall view or development are referred to.
We shall refer in the main to the various editions of the Dalloz summary of *Droit social*, of 1992 to 2002, by G. Lyon-Caen and J. Pelissier, then by G. Lyon-Caen, J. Pelissier and A. Supiot, then, since the 20th ed., A. Jeammaud, J. Pelissier and A. Supiot (21st ed. 2002), also the various publications by G. Couturier, *Droit social*, vol.1, *Relations individuelles*, vol.2, *Collective relations*, PUF, Fundamental law, over the last ten years, J.E. Ray, *Droit social, droit vivant*, published annually by Liaisons since 1993. Concerning social policies and employment, the various editions of *Récapitulatif du Droit Social Dalloz*, by J.J. Dupeyroux, then 13th ed. J.J. Dupeyroux and R. Ruellan, then 14th ed. (2001) by J.J. Dupeyroux, M. Borgetto, R. Lafore and R. Ruellan. Concerning the social welfare law of the European Union, P. Rodière, LGDJ, two editions.
This report is also drawn up using an analysis of the eleven-year period by the monthly review *Droit social*, directed by J.J. Dupeyroux.

The debate has been passionate. This has led the legislator to re-evaluate the reforms after each change of power. For example, the reduction of working time came up for technical and political reform in 2002, although analysis of the Act of 19 January 2000 could not provide an accurate impact assessment; the reform of the so-called social modernisation act in January 2002, covering restructuring and the increasing number of restructuring plans, was 'suspended' in January 2003 despite the fact that the disastrous effects of restructuring were still strongly felt. On 6 January 2004, a law to carry out a wholesale reform of collective bargaining and 'modernise' labour law was passed on its first reading. This happened despite strong opposition from the unions, who wanted to increase social dialogue using new foundations based on majority participation and encouraging more flexible agreements, as expressly requested by employers.

Between 1992 and 2003, a great deal of legislative activity continued to change the face of labour law, showing the predominance of the law and a labour law system controlled by the State. The result has been an explosion of complex legislative techniques.[3]

Opposition and conflicts of interest remain very strong in France and have given rise to an attempt at radical social reform ('Refondation sociale'):[4] the objective sought by employers since 1998 has been to create a sharing of competence between the government, unions and employers, which would restrict the legal domain to the basic principles, with labour law being entirely contract-based. From 2000, negotiations were opened on the great themes of 'Radical social reform' between MEDEF (the employers' federation) and France's five nationally representative unions. The aim was to try to modernise labour relations in France and adapt joint institutions, especially those involved in managing the risks of unemployment and sickness.

These discussions on the main themes of social reform were not a complete failure as, in fact, the unions agreed, sometimes under threat from the employers, to discuss important issues such as the terms of collective bargaining, restructuring, the management of social welfare bodies, etc.

But this did not lead to a contract-based modernisation of labour law. The blurred concepts of 'modernisation', and 'radical reform' are mainly used to conceal objectives to modify labour law in order to adapt it to the demands of competition, which, for the employers, means flexibility and deregulation.

A significant interprofessional agreement on vocational training was however signed by all the unions on 20 September 2003. Previously, a programme-based agreement had been signed in 2000 on health at work and, especially, unions and employers had adopted a 'common position in July 2001' setting the foundations for a reform of collective bargaining.

This common position served as a basis for the 'Fillon' reform of collective bargaining, which was passed on its first reading on 6 January 2004. Another law on restructuring is likely to follow in 2004 due to the failure of negotiations following the 'suspension' by the Act of 17 January 2003 of the provisions passed in January 2002.

In fact, due to the major political issues underlying the discussions, the right-wing majority in Parliament has managed to persuade the legislator to significantly reform the laws governing collective bargaining.

Until 2003, the labour relations system therefore did not change through agreements reached between unions and employers, but within the framework of the law. As a result of the reform passed in January 2004, it is likely that there will be a move towards introducing greater decentralisation into collective bargaining and greater flexibility into negotiated social rules.

Apart from this reform, it should be pointed out that the government, unions and employers have refused to accept any form of tripartite consultation.[5]

But there appears to be a strong move towards extending the competences of the social partners.

The key issue is whether a contractual basis for labour relations, which is what the employers want, is desirable in France. It was not permitted by the Act of 6 January 2004, as passed at the first reading. Following a major discussion of the place of the law and contracts in the normative French system a certain number of protective controls were maintained (see below).

1.3. Legal

There have been several causes of change: first of all, **the influence of Community law became greater over the decade**. Even though France was slow to transpose social directives, over the ten-year period it realised the need to incorporate European social policy.

---

3   A. Supiot, *Critique du droit social*, Essay, PUF, 1994, publ. by Quadrige, 2002, 'Du bon usage des lois en matière d'emploi', *Droit social 1997*, p. 229.
4   G. Adam, 'Refondation sociale, quelle deuxième étape?', *Droit social 2003*, p. 44, January 2003 special issue 'Un nouveau droit social?'.
5   See below for sources.

The last eleven years have been a 'forced learning' period. It was through the impact of health and safety directives on French law that the government in 1991 started to realise the extent of the changes brought about by Community social law.

The government gradually implemented a policy of transposing social directives, but systematically blocked any transposition bills if they were likely to run contrary to internal policy objectives.

An excellent example of this can be seen in the legislation relating to night-time work for women. In 1991, the CJEC acknowledged in the Stoeckel ruling (25 July 1991)[6] that French law went against the principle of equality between male and female workers. The government was condemned for one breach after another in 1997. This was accompanied by the threat of a high financial penalty, before the law incorporating an identical night-time working system for men and women was adopted on 9 May 2001.

But sometimes, French law adapts within the deadlines (e.g. for the European works council) or is even the leading figure in bringing about changes to Community law (e.g. The posted workers directive, adopted in 1996, where the French system dated back to 1993).

Since 2001, the French government has tried to accelerate the transposition of social directives.

This change in labour law brought on by Community pressure has also been very noticeable in the case law of the Court of Cassation.[7]

The Court asked for very few preliminary rulings but did have some answers to them (very slow change).

Over this eleven-year period there has been a slow but sure acceptance by the authorities involved of the need to take European developments into account.

Faced with the pressure to deregulate labour law and make it more flexible, Community law was a vital asset in France in the fight to preserve guarantees for workers on issues relating to redundancy and the reform of working time.

In the area of employment policies, the 'employment' strategies introduced since the Treaty of Amsterdam created much less reticence than the directives as it was clear that economic problems, and especially the question of unemployment and exclusion, were felt right across Europe. Above all, the plans were national plans; they left the authorities involved with their reference framework and usual concepts, even though the indicators were standardised across Europe.

The reluctance caused by the special features of binding European rules and the arguments of the ECJ were therefore not present with regard to employment policy.

In addition, due to the fact that French policies leaned heavily in favour of employment, whatever the political make-up of the government, French national plans were generally along the same lines as those drawn up at a European level and were even a major source of reference.

At this precise moment it is difficult to gain a clear view of the impact of the European employment strategy on changes in the workplace due to the influence of proposals put forward in French national plans on the European process and to the many factors leading to changes in French labour law.

However, during the most recent period, it is clear that changes have been brought about by the influence of the EES. By the force of its proposals, the EES has forced the government, unions and employers to enter discussions on new issues. In 2001, for example discussions on the regions, the quality of employment, lifelong training and the extension of working life took place in the permanent discussion body set up for employment (CSDEI – Committee for social dialogue on European and international issues). These were quite new issues at the time for unions and employers.[8] In late 2003, these discussions had progressed and led to measures of varying importance. A very clear turning point was reached with decisions involving incentives to preserve employment for older workers in the retirement reform act of 23 August 2003. It may be said with confidence that the EES had a direct influence on this. Concerning the interprofessional agreement of 20 September 2003 on lifelong training, the agreement was primarily the result of changes decided by the French authorities. On issues as crucial as restructuring, it was noted that the positions taken at a European level were never referred to in the discussions that took place during 2003.[9] Only the French unemployment situation and national policy decisions were presented as part of

---

6   M.A. Moreau, *Droit social 1992*, p. 174.

7   See below.

8   Study carried out by Gilles Raveaud, for the 'Délégation générale à l'emploi et à la formation professionnelle', not published, November 2001, 'The European dimension in French employment policies, an analysis of the involvement of government, unions and employers in the drawing up of the 2001 National Employment Plan'.

9   It should also be said that the 'reference orientations' finally decided on by government, unions and employers in July 2003, due to an inability to reach a collective agreement, were not accepted by the ECS in October 2003 and constitute a 'soft' law, a very, very soft law...but the key point to emphasise is probably that government, unions and employers in France are only concerned by the French situation (G. Raveaud's study also tends towards this conclusion).

the various technical measures for employment that were introduced for young people, the unemployed and women. The EES was never referred to as a source or justification for a reform. This was both for political reasons and because, in the eyes of the political and social authorities involved, the EES does not present an efficient cause for reform.

The participation of unions and employers in CSDEI, a body founded at the express request of Brussels, has increased over the years. It is however still the case that the national plan is the responsibility of government, something which severely restricts the involvement of unions and employers.[10]

It could be said that it is only due to the combination between purely national objectives (as they arise out of economic analyses of the French employment situation) the government's political orientations and the position of the EES that a convergence can be seen that leads to changes in labour law on the ground.

To take just one example, the introduction of 'flexibility' into labour law is due not only to the influence of the EES, but to decisions made by the legislator depending on the majority at the time.

Though the EES is certainly a source of learning and proposals, its influence on law construction mainly depends on **how its proposals may be adapted**[11] **to national circumstances** according to purely national political imperatives.

From a legal point of view, apart from the impact of restrictive Community law, the main cause of change is without doubt linked to an intrinsic movement based on a demand for flexibility in labour law rules and, at the same time, to that of a reinforcement of the fundamental social rights of workers.

The movement, which may at first sight appear paradoxical, is in fact consistent.

It stems on the one hand from a need to compete internationally and across Europe, which leads to a strong demand from employers for flexibility and, on the other from the key role of ECHR case law.

In 1992, the French legislator introduced Article L 120-2 into the Labour Code. This Article allowed judges to carry out checks on infringements of the fundamental social rights of workers. However, these checks incorporated a need to ensure that the interests of the company were upheld, which may justify an infringement of the rights of workers.[12]

Fundamental protection is therefore relative and included the tendency of French law to justify and develop mechanisms to make labour law more flexible.

Obviously, over this eleven-year period, the two demands mentioned above will have a profound influence on the labour relations system in France, being the starting point for changes in normative sources, the balance between the law, the contract and the collective agreement, and the source of changes in the attitudes of the groups involved, particularly unions and employers, in a context of changes in collective bargaining.

2. Changes relating to sources of labour law and the groups involved

Changes with regard to the sources of labour law are obviously closely linked to changes in union and employer attitudes, as the advancement of collective bargaining is at the heart of this double chapter of change.

2.1. The sources of labour law

It is important to point out the changes in each area.

2.1.1. The increase in references to fundamental social rights and changes in the control of constitutionality

In addition to reference to Community law, we can see a surprising increase in the number of references to the ECHR, with regard to both Articles 8 and 14, every time an employee's personal life is threatened, or to Article 6 in order to give workers strong jurisdictional guarantees.[13]

---

10   The above study makes this point very clearly after interviews with union and employer representatives at CDSEI.

11   G. Raveaud talks of 'portmanteau words' used by the EES (as, for example, 'quality of social dialogue'), which are fulfilled in the French method by unions and employers.

12   T. Aubert-Montpeyssen, 'Les libertés et les droits fondamentaux dans l'entreprise: brèves remarques sur quelques évolutions récentes', Mél. Despax, 2002, P.U. Toulouse, p. 261.

13   Most recently on Article 6-1, Appeal Court 10/06/03, working hours in the health sector, Droit social 2003, p. 1017, obs. by J. Mouly.

The Court of Cassation has not hesitated to use every legal source allowing it to invoke the fundamental rights of workers. Where the Court has deemed it useful to emphasise the essential place of the respect for the fundamental social rights of workers in French law, it has referred to the ECHR and/or the Constitution and/or internal law (art. L 120-2 of the Labour Code).

However, even though we are seeing a dramatic increase in the number of references to workers' social rights, proclaimed by national or European sources, these are not implemented until they have been weighed with regard to other constitutional principles or the legitimate interests of the company.

We can, however, confirm that no labour law legal source is excluded from these jurisdictional checks on the respect for the fundamental social rights of workers. This marks considerable progress compared to the situation 1992.

In addition, this reinforcement of workers' social rights is guaranteed by the intervention of constitutional terms in labour law in the 1990s.[14]

Every time a major law on labour relations is passed, it is automatically referred to the Constitutional Council for both political and legal reasons. This relatively common use of the 'Constitutionality Block' (consisting of the text of the Constitution, the 1789 Declaration of Human and Citizens' Rights, the Preamble to the Constitution and the way in which the Court of Cassation may, at the moment of judicial control, refer to constitutional principles) shows the cardinal importance of the social rights acknowledged for workers, 'particularly necessary in our times', in the French legal order. Thus, insofar as these rights are constitutionally recognised, the right to oppose them is guaranteed.[15]

The Constitutional Council is keen to reconcile constitutional rules and ensure that 'the fundamental rights and freedoms acknowledged for employers and workers' are respected. Each decision is therefore a work of reconciliation, which nevertheless shows that the principles of freedom of association (to join a union), the right to strike, the right of workers to participate, including the right to collective bargaining, have a confirmed, guaranteed constitutional value.[16]

Though the right to work and the right to obtain employment are a 'constitutional requirement', they generally give way to the freedom to run a business.

The principle of equality is at the heart of most appeals but the Council considers that it does not automatically lead to censure, due to the differences that may exist between different situations.

Contractual freedom, the monopoly of the unions with regard to negotiation and the principle of favour have not been recognised as having constitutional value.[17]

In recent years, the Constitutional Council has issued 'interpretational reservations'[18] that bind the judicial judge. These reservations show the Council's wish to check that the legal authorities are adhering to the spirit of the Constitution.[19] The Council has also agreed that certain laws may be promulgated as an experiment, even where certain principles were concerned (employee representation in particular).

The influence of the checks carried out by the Constitutional Council has certainly increased during the reference period. These checks are a political weapon serving the issues linked to changes of government, but they remain limited, due to the competence conferred by Article 34 on Parliament, which is authorised to make decisions about the place of the law and the balances chosen between guaranteed rights and freedoms in the practical manifestations of the latter.

Furthermore, these checks are much weaker than those that exist in other countries in the European Union, due to the Council's referral mechanisms.

2.1.2. Changes in the role of the law between 1992 and 2003

These changes are difficult to define. The law is still the predominant source for drawing up rules in France, which is why, up to now, it has been the only means by which directives have been transposed.

The number of labour regulations contained in the Labour Code continue to increase, containing a huge number of implementing rules that are often excessively technical.

---

14   A. Jeammaud, J. Pelissier, A. Supiot, op. cit., no.52 et seq , V. Ogier-Bernaud, 'Les droits constitutionnels des travailleurs', *Economica*, P.U. Aix-Marseille, 2003.

15   In the absence of a direct right of referral to the constitutional principles courts.

16   M.L. Morin, 'Le Conseil constitutionnel et le droit à la négociation collective', *Droit social 1997*, p. 25, B. Mathieu, 'Précisions relatives au droit constitutionnel de la négociation collective', D. 1997, p. 152.

17   Which allowed the legislator to remove the principle of favour from the Act of 6 January 2004.

18   For example, in 2002, through a requirement that, in cases of mental harassment, concrete, matching evidence should be gathered to constitute proof of the acts that may be considered to be a form of harassment.

19   See below.

Two features combine to make labour law rather opaque:[20] the profusion of legislation and the complexity of the wording.

In this respect, the period 1992-2003 was almost a caricature if we look at the changes in the laws on redundancy (with, in particular, the 'Loi Fillon' in January 2003 which 'suspends certain articles in that of January 2002') and on the reduction of working time, for which laws were produced in 1996, 1998, 2000 and 2002, of a rare complexity, making it a nightmare to analyse these transitory positions.

The problem is made worse by the increase in the interpretation of texts by case law, which professionals see as a source of insecurity.

This complexity probably had the positive effect of leading to a change in the roles of the various bodies involved, and, in particular, of opening the way for an increased amount of collective bargaining. It has also allowed established case law to be integrated into the law for the purposes of clarification.

The heavy political issues, to which we have already referred, encouraged this complexity through the use of amendments during parliamentary discussions.

There is nothing to suggest that legislative texts will become any simpler or clearer in the near future.[21] However, in 2003, the Employment Minister set up a Commission (the Virville Commission) made up of experts (whose political leanings corresponded to those of the majority in Parliament) to make proposals for simplifying labour law.

This complexity is an obstacle that makes it more difficult to comply with labour law in companies and in SMEs in particular. It also acts as an indirect brake on employment in France.

The biggest changes between 1992 and 2003 involved the use of new or renewed legislative techniques;[22] the negotiated law technique, which left unions and employers to negotiate the content of rules between them; the experimental law technique, where the text's impact on labour relations was assessed after two or three years; and the suspended law technique, used so that any decision that was taken did not look too final.[23]

We also note that the legislator sought to lean heavily on negotiations with unions and employers, even when it was not likely in practice that agreements would be reached (the retirement and restructuring issues).

There was a great deal of doctrinal discussion in France about what room should be left for law or contract,[24] in the face of strong claims, mainly from employers, that all rules surrounding labour relations should be dealt with by negotiation, except for the fundamental principles of labour law.

For the time being, the balance is set by Article 34 of the Constitution, which is relative to the domain of the law. This means that the growth of collective bargaining must remain dependent on legislative principles. In 2002 the Council of State noted with regard to the agreement on unemployment insurance that unions and employers may innovate in an agreement, but, if it does not comply with the law, the agreement may not come into force until it has been modified by law.

2.1.3. Changes to collective bargaining

In the past eleven years, there have been changes in methods of negotiation and levels of negotiation that have been closely connected with the profound changes that have affected the bodies involved in negotiation.[25]

- **Concerning methods of negotiation**, an initial negative comment is required.[26] The labour relations system in France has not managed to take on board the tripartite consultation method that has been adopted in other neighbouring countries with a tradition of multiple unions and government centralised control of labour rules. Major efforts were undertaken in 1995, where a tripartite negotiation was set up to renew collective bargaining and introduce new working-time arrangements to combat unemployment. A national interprofessional agreement (ANI) was signed on 31 October 1995. This negotiation had been made possible as a result of a more open attitude on the part of the employers, due to the personalities of Mr Gandois (CNPF), Mrs Aubry, Employment Minister and Mrs Notat (CFDT). The agreement came in for heavy criticism from the 'grass roots' and afterwards the CNPF performed a spectacular change of direction, the high point of which was the failure in 1997 of negotiations on the reform of working time. The CNPF transformed itself into MEDEF, and all moves towards genuine tripartite consultation were henceforth blocked.

20   G. Borenfreund, 'Le droit du travail en mal de transparence', *Droit social 1996*, p. 461.
21   A Commission was set up in 2003 at the request of the Ministry of Labour. Its task was to make proposals for clarifying the texts.
22   A. Supiot, 'Critique du droit du travail', op. cit. and loc. cit.
23   The 'Loi Fillon' of 2003 suspended texts and referred suspended issues to interprofessional negotiation.
24   A. Supiot, 'Un faux dilemme: loi ou contrat?', *Droit social 2000*, p. 59.
25   M.A. Souriac, G. Borenfreund, 'La négociation collective entre désillusions et illusions', Mel. Verdier, Dalloz, 2001, p. 383.
26   M.L. Morin, 'La loi et la négociation collective: concurrence ou complémentarité', *Droit social 1998*, p. 419.

The 'radical social reform' negotiations were not properly tripartite and ended in failure.

This lack of a possibility of tripartite negotiation could be seen particularly clearly when national employment plans were drawn up. Following the comments from Brussels, France introduced an ongoing consultation structure to draw up these national plans, but this did not give rise to genuine negotiation.[27]

• **Concerning levels of negotiation**, it is clear that the interprofessional level was far from abandoned, but these agreements never came to anything during this period, apart from in the area of vocational training and, more recently, unemployment. These failures were due to the deep divisions between unions and employers. All attempts to introduce a policy to reduce working time via an interprofessional agreement failed, though some of the negotiated changes were not abandoned and were taken up by the legislator in the Act of 12 November 1996.

The most striking change was the very clear move towards decentralising collective bargaining to the company level. The traditional level of negotiation in France had been the branch. This was still the preferred level for negotiating collective agreements of general significance.

Now, however, began a vast movement towards using company-level negotiations and agreements in the area of salaries and reduced working time. The legislator encouraged this move towards company level negotiation by approving the signature of 'derogatory agreements' in these two areas first in 1982, and then 1987.[28]

The five-year Act of 1993 gave unions and employers the benefit of 'deregulated' negotiation.[29]

It may be said that collective bargaining, which, until 1992, had been confined to a form of 'give and take'

negotiation, became a form of deregulation negotiation through the extension of derogatory agreements.

After a well-noticed case law saga (Basirico rulings) the Act of 31 December 1992 also played its part in leading to the revision of collective agreements under conditions that allowed for change. The agreement could be revised on the signature of a single union body, which may be different from the union bodies that signed the original agreement. If the content is different (often unfavourable to workers or to some of them), the majority unions can oppose the agreement.

In other words, starting in 1992-1993, a large number of agreements that were signed through company agreements, substantially changed workers' rights by introducing useful forms of flexibility to increase the competitiveness of companies (and sometimes to safeguard employment). In a context of multiple unions and crisis in the union movement, it was enough for one representative union to sign the agreement. This permitted the other union organisations to form a right of opposition that rendered the agreement null and void, provided that they could prove the presence of a criterion that was restrictive for the majority, something very hard to do.

This derogatory agreement and agreement revision process became an excellent lever for moving negotiation towards the company level and developing new flexibilities controlled by the law. It allowed discussion to begin about introducing rules relating to the majority principle into the French system.[30] This took concrete form in the Act of 6 January 2004, which passed in the first reading. The legislator wanted to extend the right of veto given to the majority unions and use a series of mechanisms to reinforce democracy in the company environment by forcing the unions to be closely linked with 'grass roots' employees in the company. The law also sought to achieve better representation for employees in small companies and to allow negotiation to take place at company level, whatever the size of the

---

27   See above.

28   The agreement is derogatory if the law states that unions and employers can provide for measures different from the law within the agreement, bearing in mind that this difference may end up in the agreement being more unfavourable than the law as far as the employee is concerned. A special system was introduced, in which the union organisations that had registered the majority of votes cast by voters registered in the last workplace elections could object to the agreement coming into force, thus rendering it null and void (Article L 132-26 of the labour regulations for company agreements). On overall trends, M. Bonnechère, 'Les tendances de la déréglementation et leur incidence sur la théorie des sources en droit du travail', *Droit social 1990*, p. 48 and 'La loi, la négociation collective et l'ordre public en droit du travail', *Droit ouvrier 2001*, p. 419 et seq.

29   Special Droit social of February 1994 issue on the five-year law, especially J. Barthelemy, 'L'aménagement conventionnel de l'organisation et de la durée du travail', *Droit social 1994*, p. 156, F. Favennec-Hery, 'Le travail à temps partiel', *Droit social 1994*, p. 165.

30   See about this change, most recently, G. Borenfreund, 'L'idée majoritaire dans la négociation collective', Mel Despax, P.U. Toulouse, 2002, p. 429, M.A. Souriac, G. Borenfreund, 'Les rapports de la loi et de la convention collective, une mise en perspective', *Droit social 2000*, p. 72, Joint position of 16 July 2001 on the ways and means of improving collective bargaining, *Droit social 2003*, p. 92.

company. However, there was a great deal of concern about these proposals, since there was a risk that they would not guarantee the independence of the negotiators if they were not part of a union organisation.[31]

During the reference period, there was an even greater increase in flexibility in the area of reduction of working time (RTT).[32] This was because the agreements that introduced the 35-hour week after the Acts of 1998 and 2000 were generally accompanied by a calculation of working hours on the basis of an annual reference period. In addition, the legislator made use of the majority principle to allocate government grants to companies that applied an RTT agreement.[33] Finally, in 2003, the 'Loi Fillon' increased overtime to give greater management flexibility to companies operating the 35-hour week.

In these laws, the legislator favoured the company level and, at the same time, the restoration of the company level as a useful negotiating level.[34] It also changed the legal framework surrounding the bodies involved in collective bargaining. The change was extended in the Act of 6 January 2004. In future, company negotiation is no longer likely to be subject to the traditional principle of the hierarchy of rules that states that it is subordinate to the branch agreement unless it is more favourable.

We may expect that, once the law is passed, there will be an appeal to the Constitutional Council due to the size of the reform and the questioning of the founding principles of collective bargaining in France.[35]

Alongside this movement towards the decentralisation of collective bargaining, the Court of Cassation acknowledged in a ruling of 30 April 2003[36] the validity of group agreements and group negotiation. This has helped to modernise the collective relations system in France. The group level negotiation should also be confirmed by law in 2004.

2.1.4. Changes in non-negotiated professional sources: weakening and flexibility

It is useful to note that, from 1989 onwards and definitively after 1992, the Court of Cassation has constructed a legal status for non-negotiated collective rules including customary practices, so-called 'atypical' agreements concluded by employee representatives or works councils,[37] and unilateral commitments by the employer that have a collective impact. The employer can, at any time, go back on his commitment for the future as long as he informs his employees both individually and collectively via their representatives and gives them reasonable warning calculated according to the nature of the benefit that is to be lost.[38]

This procedure therefore gives the employer a very easy opportunity to challenge collective benefits,[39] and provides greater flexibility for management of benefits, extra days off and bonus payments.

As long as the employer abides by the warning procedure mentioned above, the reference period is marked by the Court of Cassation's approval of the employer's use of these unilateral rules and the flexibility that they give employers, who can use it as a management tool for coping with cyclical factors.

2.1.5. The role of the employment contract: a tool for flexibility and resistance

The change in the role of the employment contract was particularly interesting, as the contract became both an instrument for greater flexibility for the employer and a legal instrument for employee resistance.[40]

The contract is an **instrument for greater flexibility** for the employer to the extent that the employer can insert clauses into the contract to provide flexible management of

---

31   The issues relating in particular to appointment and the guarantees that this gives had already been examined when the RTT (reduction of working hours) scheme was introduced.

32   There was a great deal of doctrinal debate in France from 1993, see in particular the work of A Supiot, cit., 'Temps de travail: pour une concordance des temps', *Droit social 1995*, p. 947.

33   A. Jeammaud, J. Pelissier, A. Supiot, *Droit du travail*, Dalloz, op. cit. no.918 et seq.

34   See below for the bodies involved.

35   Previously, however, the Constitutional Council stated that the favour principle was not a constitutional principle, see above.

36   B. Gauriau, 'La consécration jurisprudentielle de la représentation syndicale de groupe et de l'accord de groupe', *Droit social 2003*, p. 732.

37   [text missing in original], not having the legal nature of a collective agreement. Collective agreements must, in principle, be signed only by union organisations. However, see changes in bodies involved, below.

38   A. Jeammaud, J. Pelissier, A. Supiot, op. cit. no. 79 et seq., G. Borenfreund, 'L'articulation du contrat de travail et des normes collectives', *Droit ouvrier 1997*, p. 514.

39   If we compare with the termination of benefits contained in a collective agreement, Article 1 132-8 of the labour regulations.

40   The contract is still the leading basic mechanism for legal regulation, A. Jeammaud, Ph. Waquet, 'Le renouveau du contrat de travail', RJS 5/99, p. 383, A. Jeammaud, 'Les polyvalences du contrat de travail', Mél. Lyon-Caen, Paris, Dalloz, p. 299, C. Radé, 'La figure du contrat dans le rapport de travail', *Droit social 2001*, p.802, concerning the general issue of the use of contracts, Ph. Gerad, F. Ost, M. Van de Kerchove, 'Droit négocié, droit imposé?', Brussels, Pub. by the Saint Louis university faculties, 1996, p. 696, see especially M.L. Morin, 'Droit négocié, droit imposé, regards à partir du droit des salariés à la négociation collective en France', p. 643.

the labour force. Mobility, non-competition, training default, flexibility concerning working hours, versatility, objectives and salary variations clauses have systematically been used in this way.

In a period of high unemployment, employees cannot, in most cases object to these clauses. Instead they are imposed as part of a joining contract.

Aware of the employer's supremacy at the moment when the contract is signed, the Court of Cassation has, in the last eleven years, sought to guarantee employees a nucleus of protection, while at the same time allowing the employer to manage his workforce with the flexibility demanded by the competitive international context.

In 1992, the Court first set out to check that these clauses had been agreed in the legitimate interests of the company. Next it checked that the infringement of personal rights, individual and collective liberties were justified by the objective that the company had to achieve (Article L 120-2 of the Labour Code),[41] and that the conditions for implementing these clauses were neither arbitrary nor discriminatory. In 2002, the Court of Cassation required that non-competition clauses contain an element of financial compensation. This control is in addition to the absence of an unjustified infringement of the employee's freedom to work.

Lastly, objective clauses have to be the subject of a contractual agreement with the employee in order to enable him to object to it as a contractual obligation and to take account of the economic environment (2002). Salary variation clauses have also got to be based strictly on objective information external to the employer (2002).

The employee may therefore object to improper, discriminatory or arbitrary use of these clauses and in all cases demand that his fundamental rights should not be affected in an excessive or unjustified way. The introduction of widespread legal controls on the employment contract clearly showed the Court of Cassation's wish to use general rules to supervise the employer's leadership and management powers.

It is however still the case that as long as he can prove that they are in the legitimate interests of the company, the employer can introduce flexibility clauses to allow him to impose significant changes to an employee's contract, agreed in advance, concerning his place of work outside his geographical sector, his rhythm of work, his job definition and – though this is more difficult – his salary.

The employment contract thus becomes a real **instrument of resistance**[42] with regard to changes to its status imposed by the conclusion of derogatory collective agreements or revised collective agreements. Collective agreements, even if they are unfavourable to the employee, apply to all employees (irrespective of whether they are a member of the signing union).

But when it came to concluding agreements relating to the 35-hour week, which included salary decreases or changes in the rhythm of work, employees were able to use their contract, which was more favourable than the collective agreement, as an individual bulwark against the change in collective status.

The Court of Cassation confirmed the 'principle of favour',[43] in application of Article L 132-4 of the Labour Code, not only to guarantee that collective agreements (apart from the exceptions mentioned above) should be more favourable to employees than the law and the regulations, but also, in application of Article L 135-2, to guarantee that the contract should be applied whenever it is more favourable than the collective agreement.

In this period of increasing flexibility, the employment contract became a means of protecting the employee.

2.1.6. The central role of case law

Over the last eleven years, the Court of Cassation has asserted its central role of regulating labour relations. The Court has established itself as the guardian of the employees' fundamental rights and of an essential, justified control mechanism overseeing management power through the introduction of procedures (especially for the termination of employees' collective benefits, in cases of redundancy, for the conditions surrounding the form of fixed-term contracts, etc.).[44]

The Court of Cassation has not hesitated to give rulings that change the balance of power in companies, by: establishing greater rigour when identifying the powers of the employer (in

---

41   J.E. Ray, special issue of Droit social, 'Les réformes I et II', February, March 1993, p. 103, and 215. Article L 120-2 allows the employee to object to any decisions taken by the employer that unjustifiably infringe the rights of individuals, individual freedoms and collective freedoms, P. Waquet, op. cit. 2003, lastly, concerning the prohibition against wearing Bermuda shorts, (justified by the constraints of the company), Court of Appeal 28 May 2003, *Droit social 2003*, p. 813.

42   G. Borenfreund.

43   A. Jeammaud, 'Le principe de faveur, enquête sur une règle émergente', *Droit social 1999*, p. 119, M.A. Souriac and G. Borenfreund, loc. cit.

44   See below.

particular, since 1996, by differentiating between the change in working conditions imposed on the employee on pain of gross misconduct and changes to the contract, which he can refuse to accept); by accepting the reversibility of collective benefits, introducing very severe sanctions (cancelling redundancies declared as part of a null and void restructuring plan – 1997-); or by broadening the scope of the employment contract to include new obligations implicit in the contract (flexibility obligation, redeployment obligation, etc.).[45]

In most of its innovative, creative rulings, the Court of Cassation has sought to give case law a regulatory social function by contributing directly to the fight for jobs and against unemployment. It has conducted a real jurisprudential policy.[46]

Over the last eleven years, the Court of Cassation has helped to transform the role of the company into that of a 'responsible company' – sometimes against its wishes – by imposing strong obligations to protect jobs.

However, by not challenging the employer's right to make timely economic decisions (SAT ruling – Ch. soc. 8 December 2000),[47] it has also sought to allow the company some economic freedom. It is not restricted, but controlled by procedures.

The Court of Cassation has proved particularly strict in ensuring that these procedures are complied with.

To establish a general guideline, it refers to the legitimate interests of the company, a standard that shows remarkable flexibility.

This regulatory role, specifically with regard to the protection of fundamental rights and employment is particularly strongly contested and is the subject of lively debate. This is particularly so because of the negative effects on companies of intervention after the event.

The courts, and in particular the Court of Cassation, have become fully involved in grass roots labour relations strategies. Over the last eleven years, both unions and employers have used the law as a normative battle ground likely to change the existing balance of power in labour relations. Issues such as anti-union discrimination (2000-2001), economic redundancies (1996: possible interim proceedings in cases of restructuring, 1997: restructuring plan declared null and void), redeployment obligations (1992), are notable examples of this.

2.2. Changes relating to the groups involved in labour relations

Despite this review of changes in the sources of labour law, it is useful to note the following:

1. The Government is still a key player in the field of labour relations in France and does not appear to have lost any of its powers. The government has however accepted the concept of flexibility in certain limited areas. But this flexibility is limited (the restricted area of derogatory agreements up to 2003), and is controlled and surrounded by non-discretionary legal constraints.

2. Judges have become fully involved in labour relations and union/management strategies.

3. The company has acquired a role as a 'social enterprise', at least in areas such as employment and the health and safety of workers.

We should therefore look at the changes that have affected unions and employers between 1992 and 2003, as these throw light on changes that have occurred in collective bargaining.[48]

French law has been based on the dual representation of workers, formed by an elected representation (employee representatives, works council) legitimised by the elections and a union representation, characterised by a large number of unions and based on the representativeness of union organisations.

Collective bargaining has always been a union monopoly for important reasons which have to do with the autonomy and independence of union representation. In the 1990s, the obvious crisis in the union movement could no longer be denied. Only around 5% of private sector employees were union members. There was also a lack of union activity in small companies, restricting collective bargaining to large companies. In addition there were strong objections to the methods of representation used by the unions, which were often detached from the professional interests of employees.

Negotiations became riddled with trouble both in quantitative and qualitative terms. This was demonstrated by a number of factors: defence committees were formed outside the unions (e.g. The 'nurses' conflict in 1994-1995); new union movements emerged (in particular the 'Sud' union) emphasising the lack of representative unionism nationally; and the number of 'negotiations' with elected representatives, works councils or employee representatives increased dramatically.

---

45   See developments below concerning all these issues.
46   See all authors mentioned. A. Jeammaud, J. Pelissier, A. Supiot, G. Couturier, J.E. Ray, see mentioned manuals.
47   A. Jeammaud and M. Le Friant, 'Du silence de l'arrêt SAT sur le droit à l'emploi', *Droit social 2001*, p. 417.
48   M.A. Souriac and G. Borenfreund cit.

At the same time, and in particular after the five-year Act of 1993, the employers realised that it was possible to achieve more flexible arrangements through signing of derogatory agreements. This meant acknowledging new forms of negotiation, especially in companies with less than 1000 employees.

The turning point came in 1995. First, the Court of Cassation decided that a union could mandate an employee (not a union representative) to negotiate with the employer.[49] Then the ANI agreement (National Interprofessional Agreement) of 31 October 1995 provided more openness in the professional branches, subject to an express contractual provision that elected representatives could negotiate collective agreements, and that the content being checked by a joint branch committee.[50] Similarly, more widespread use was made of mandating procedures.

This opening up to new forms of negotiation under strict controls was incorporated into the Act of 12 November 1996 for an 'experimental period'.

The Act was therefore the first to step outside the union monopoly that was highly controlled by the representative unions at branch level.

The Acts relating to the reduction of working time, known as the 'Aubry I' and 'Aubry II' Acts of 13 June 1998 and 19 January 2000, provided even more freedom of choice in the negotiation of agreements relating to RTT by allowing employees who have been given an express mandate by their unions, or representatives elected in the branches that have authorised them, to negotiate these agreements.[51] Even if they have not been mandated, employee representatives could also negotiate if they hold the post of union representative.

In addition to this limited opening up to new types of negotiators, there was also a move towards simplifying elected representation. After the Act of 20 December 1993, single representation between employee representatives and works councils in companies with 50 to 200 employees, 60% of works councils were targeted. There was also a move to claim legitimacy. The opening up to new types of negotiators for RTT was accompanied by special provisions aimed at reinforcing participative democracy in companies and the emergence of a majority criterion for unions.

The Act of 19 January 2000 required that a referendum had to be organised to validate the RTT agreement in cases where a company wanted to benefit from government grants but where the agreements had not been signed by the unions that had obtained the majority of votes in the last elections.

In companies with less than 11 employees, the arrangements drawn up by the employer for introducing the 35-hour week could also be validated by referendum even if there was no extended branch agreement or union mandate.

The use of the referendum in the process of negotiating agreements has obviously changed union strategies. Referendums were also organised by majority organisations for consulting employees prior to signature. Though it was strongly contested by the unions, the referendum found a new home in French labour law.[52]

A great deal of discussion took place about the very notion of representation, the mechanisms of representativeness and the legitimacy of representatives. This gave rise to a 'common position' expressed by the unions on 16 July 2001, which asked the legislator to give the majority criterion a new place in the system.[53]

There is no doubt that the new mechanisms introduced by the 35-hour week were the start of a profound change in collective bargaining in France, which led to the major reform undertaken in early 2004.

Anyway, it seems established that the unprecedented increase in the number of agreements signed, at company level in particular, was caused by the fact that the system had been broadened to include other types of representatives (a third of RTT agreements signed by appointed employees and up to two thirds in SME sectors).

However, a large part of doctrine points to the lack of independence of appointed employees confronting employers and the latent danger of extending a negotiation method that operates without the vital contribution of a properly-constructed labour relations system.

It appears that the unions were also aware of the need to re-establish their legitimacy in the eyes of the employees. The extension of a right of objection, based on a majority principle, as put forward in the bill passed at first reading on 6 January 2004, should, if the government's objectives are adhered to, lead to a strengthening of social democracy in companies.[54]

49   'Comité contre la faim' ruling, Soc. 25 January 1995, loc. cit.
50   F. Favennec-Hery, 'L'accord interprofessionnel du 31 October 1995 sur l'emploi', Droit social 1996, p. 20.
51   For more on this development, see the special issue of Droit social April 1998, 'Négociation collective et emploi, de l'accord interprofessionnel du 31 October 1995 sur l'emploi à la loi Aubry de 1998'.
52   B. Gauriau, 'Le referendum, un préalable nécessaire?', Droit social 1998, p. 338, J.E. Ray, 'De l'individuel au collectif', Droit social 1998, p. 347.
53   Droit social January 2003, cit., p. 92, review by A. Supiot, loc. cit. p. 65.
54   As the Act is still being voted on, it cannot be analysed in detail here. The promulgated text should be referred to in a few weeks' time.

3. Changes relating to the impact of Community law

As has already been pointed out, Community labour law has had little impact in France. The attention paid to the European legal context and the normative decisions taken by other European Union countries is not of central importance – indeed, it is very subordinate.

French labour law is still drawn up on a national basis according to internal objectives and the national political context. To take one significant example, the reform relating to the 35-hour week took place despite the fact that such reforms had not been undertaken in other European countries and that competitive conditions needed to be assessed in the context of the European market and against the general background of a globalised economy and a single currency.

Community labour law only plays a role when the government is forced to take an interest in it.

Social directives are better transposed now, but the government has never used a Community directive to carry out a reform in France. The provisions are incorporated (satisfactorily at best) but no more.

To give a typical example, the directive of 14 October 1991 was transposed without any overall discussion of the arrangements for concluding an employment contract. France is left with a succession of provisions that are more or less consistent but give a rather 'patchwork' impression.

However, the period between 1992 and 2002 has certainly seen concerned parties in France adapting to Community law, which is no longer foreign to the Ministry of Employment or to the judges.

There is still considerable reluctance to pay attention to the arguments of the ECJ; to the ignored concepts of French law (particularly on the part of some unions); to the risk of social dumping arising out of the confrontation between labour law and competition law; and to the risk – often imaginary – of deregulation through Community labour law.

3.1. Community law's significant contributions

The first of these significant contributions[55] is discrimination law. French law has finally agreed to incorporate the notion of indirect discrimination and has above all, incorporated some highly fundamental additions through the directive of 16 December 1997 relating to proof of discrimination between male and female workers. The Court of Cassation used these types of presumption of fault in cases of union discrimination. The Act of 16 November 2001 then extended it to other areas of discrimination. In the Act of 17 January 2002, known as the Social Modernisation Act, this method of proof also led to the emergence of a method of proof adapted to moral harassment. In fact, the mechanism for reversing the burden of proof, which came from Community law, was applied to issues affecting the rights of individuals and violating their dignity, thus spreading the Community law mechanism far and wide.[56]

With regard to health and safety, French law has fully incorporated the often highly technical directives. These now make up most of the current regulations.

However, it took ten years before the framework directive of 12 June 1989, transposed by the Act of 31 December 1991, was properly applied.[57] It was not until the decree of 5 November 2001 that employers were obliged to draw up a statement of risks and the chosen means of preventing them. For the first time, in its rulings on asbestos on 28 February 2002, the Court of Cassation applied Articles L 230-1 and 230-3 of the labour regulations, which gave life to the general obligation on employers and employees to become involved in risk prevention themselves.[58]

The possibility that Community law opened up for an employer to challenge an employee for not complying with safety measures or the obligation to prevent accidents (Article L 230-3 of the labour regulations) had never been used in France. The provision was highly contested in 1991 due to the historical background in France, dating back to the 1898 Act relating to workplace accidents. We can see from this that, ten years later, the joint responsibility approach chosen by the Community directive has now been incorporated into French law.

---

55   P. Rodière, *Droit du travail de l'Union européenne*, LGDJ, see both editions for changes.

56   M.T. Lanquetin, 'Discrimination à raison du sexe, commentaire de la directive 97/80 du 15 décembre 1997', *Droit social 1998*, p. 688, M. Miné, 'Les discriminations dans l'emploi', *La semaine sociale,* Lamy suppl. no. 1055, 17/12/2001, M.A. Moreau, 'Les justifications des discriminations', *Droit social 2002*, p. 1112.

57   M.A. Moreau, 'Pour une politique de santé dans l'entreprise', *Droit social 2002*, p. 817.

58   P. Morvan, 'Le "déflocage" de la faute inexcusable', RJS 6/02, p. 495, R. Vatinet, 'En marge des affaires de l'amiante: l'obligation de sécurité du salarié', *Droit social 2002*, p. 533, B. Gauriau, 'Obligations du salarié et performance de l'entreprise en matière de sécurité', *Droit social 2002*, p. 1054.

Concerning transfers of undertakings, the French Court of Cassation was, up to 1990, very slow to align itself with Community law. During the period 1992-2003, it agreed to align itself with definitions given by the ECJ.[59] The Court even applied provisions incorporated since the latest modification to the directive in 2001 concerning the application of the principles to public undertakings. It is still very slow, however, to apply the contract continuity principle to temporary employment agencies.

Since the Perier ruling of 18 July 2000,[60] it has also provided an original, and restrictive interpretation of the definition of 'autonomous business' every time transfer has been linked to parts of the business, or if parts of the business are to be outsourced (e.g. manufacturing of wooden pallets to carry mineral water, or catering activity in a clinic).

The Court does not choose the notion of an autonomous business through an interpretation of the facts in order to avoid that employees faced with outsourcing are transferred to an employer who offers fewer guarantees, especially in terms of their collective status. Without opposing the Community interpretation, the Court of Cassation uses its power of applying the law to circumstances to avoid the more perverse effects of the directive, particularly where large companies set up an outsourcing process. It adapts the rights of the employee, offering him the chance to refuse to pursue the contractual relationship with the company purchaser if the latter changes the working conditions.[61]

It is clear that the French Court of Cassation wants its case law to send 'signals' to the ECJ or to the Community legislator: Should the objective of maintaining employment contained in the directive not also lead to the EES' objective of quality of employment?

3.2. The reluctance of French law to embrace Community law

As has already been stated, French law remains highly reluctant concerning the issue of night working for women. The French text was condemned in 1991 as being contrary to the principle of equal treatment between male and female workers, and legislative changes were made in the Act of 9 May 2001. It took ten years and a strong threat of condemnation with a financial penalty to calm emotions that had run high on this issue.

Until 1996 there was a strong refusal to introduce the notion of indirect discrimination in France.[62] The legislator referred to this in the Act of 16 November 2001.

1992-2003 was a pivotal period for reciprocal influences between Community employment law and French labour law, acceptance and refusal, autonomy and submission.[63]

However, it is clear that it was the restrictive nature of the directives that led to significant changes in French law.

As has been emphasised above, the influence of the EES was widespread. New directions in terms of objectives were more easily in phase with French policy as several of these objectives had already been fully incorporated, especially those concerning: the level of employment of women; professional qualification initiatives, particularly for the young; and initiatives to provide individual monitoring for the long-term unemployed.

Since 2003, the government and the legislator have committed themselves to a policy aimed at lengthening the working life of employees over the age of 55, but company policies do not appear to be moving in the same direction.

A revision of the tax and social security systems has been introduced with the appearance of employment allowances, reduced social security contributions on low salaries and reform of the pension system (against a background of strong opposition). Lastly, improvements to the conditions for starting a new company (which were already the subject of measures in 2003) are amongst the reforms to be introduced in 2004 as part of a major employment Act that is in the pipeline. The aim is to make the process of setting up a company easier and more efficient.

It should also be noted that a major report proposing changes to many of the provisions of the labour regulations was requested from a high-level Commission known as the Virville Commission. In a report in early 2004, which attracted considerable attention, the Commission made proposals for simplifying and modernising the labour regulations, incorporating

---

59   P. Morvan, 'Le "déflocage" de la faute inexcusable', RJS 6/02, p. 495, R. Vatinet, 'En marge des affaires de l'amiante: l'obligation de sécurité du salarié', Droit social 2002, p. 533, B. Gauriau, 'Obligations du salarié et performance de l'entreprise en matière de sécurité', Droit social 2002, p. 1054.

60   Droit social 2000, p. 850, chr. G. Couturier.

61   Latest view Court of Appeal 11 March 2003, no choice however if the buyer informs the employee that he no longer wishes to alter the contract during the notice period, P. Bailly, 'Le salarié peut-il refuser les effets du transfert d'entreprise?', Droit social 2003, p. 474, et comm. A. Mazeaud, Droit social 2003, p. 482.

62   M.T. Lanquetin, loc. cit., M. Miné, loc. cit.

63   See above.

demands for flexibility on the part of employers and the EES. In addition, again due to the influence of the EES, a report (the Marimbert Report) was requested and published in early 2004 on the reform of key labour market institutions (ANPE, ASSEDIC).

Of course, these proposed reforms are controversial. However, they show that there is an open debate about the issues put forward by the EES.

But it may be that the EES will not have the authority to bring about practical changes on issues such as equal opportunities that have come up against strong sociological inertia, or redundancy practices involving employees over the age of 55.

But it does seem that a turning point was reached in 2003 with the government's determination to take on board the guidelines for employment and translate them into labour law, as the current reforms of early 2004 show.[64]

4. Special features of the French labour market

Over this 11-year period, the labour market has been characterised by high, structural unemployment. The period has also seen an increase in the working population, which rose from 21.8 million in 1975 to 26 million in 2001.[65]

Starting in 1990, unemployment rose to 12.5% of the working population. Apart from a few years of respite between 1997 and 2001, the whole period, was marked by increasing unemployment and a difficulty in moving from a policy of fighting cyclical unemployment to a fight against structural unemployment.

During the 1990s, indicators clearly demonstrate a change. The average length of time that people remained unemployed rose from 13.9 months in 1990 to 16 months in 1996.

A clear improvement was seen from 1999, with a return to growth and lower unemployment. The level of unemployment began to fall from its peak of 1996 (12.5%) to 11.8% in 1998. In 2002 it stood at 8.2% as a result of growth and

probably also the introduction of the 35-hour week. In 2003, four employees out of five were working 36 hours a week, according to a recent survey.

The period is also remarkable for the continued increase in the proportion of women in the working population. Between 1975 and 2001, this rose from 55.7% to 78.7% in the 30-54 age group. In the 25-49 age group, 57% of women were working full-time and 22% part-time.

Women continued to represent the vast majority of part-time workers at the end of the reference period. In 2002, 5.1% of men worked part-time and 29.1% of women. Together they represented 16.2% of the working population.

During the reference period there was a fall in the number of young people in work due to the fact that the young were spending more time in school and higher education. Similarly, there was a fall in the number of older employees, since less than half of private sector employees were still working at the age of retirement.[66]

Lastly, it is important to emphasise that it is women who are hit hardest by unemployment. In 1992, 8.32% of men were unemployed, compared to 12.84% of women. In 1996, men represented 10.59% of unemployed people, while women represented 14.33%.

Similarly, unemployment affects young women (30.5% in the 16-25 age band) more than young men (25%). Overall, the under-25 age group is more affected by unemployment (28%) than the 26-49 age group (11%). Unemployment has continued to increase for the over-50s during the last eleven years. All these trends are pronounced and can be seen throughout the period.

Finally, it should be stated that, over this period, immigration policies, which have been very fluctuating, have been aimed at maintaining 'zero immigration'. It was not until 2002 that people realised that certain sectors of the economy were short of labour.

The fight against illegal immigration and the management of illegal immigrants were at the heart of many debates between 1992 and 2002.

---

64   As part of the report drawn up by Dares (Ministry of Employment) relating to '(Les) politiques de l'emploi et du marché du travail', published in 2003, by *La Découverte*. It is stated on p. 32: 'French employment policy is now very much in line with that of the EES, which it explicitly aims to implement. In accordance with the provisions of the Treaty of Amsterdam and in line with other Member States, the policy will be implemented with the inclusion of arrangements specific to France'.

65   Dares report, 'Les Politiques de l'emploi et du marché du travail', 2003, cit, p. 11.

66   Dares report, cit. p. 12.

While the period was strongly marked by the fight against unemployment, it was also a time in which huge numbers of jobs were created. It is estimated that over 2 million jobs were created between 1997 and 2002. This included creating 600 000 jobs in 2002, thanks to the combined effects of an unexpected, short-lived upturn and the introduction of the 35-hour week.[67]

5. The issue of the outlines of the labour market

From the early 1990s, new forms of work developed. These were most often subject to restrictions and limits of subordination. They were generally linked to independent forms of activity. There was also an increase in the number of self-employed workers operating on the margins of companies, often involved in outsourcing activities. Two questions therefore arose: on a practical level, how do we react to the 'false self-employed', and, on a theoretical level, how do we re-draw the outlines of labour law.[68]

These questions became very important over the next decade. Over these years, the Labour Inspectorate carried out a great deal of inspection work to crack down on the most obvious abuses (particularly in the transport sector). The Court of Cassation also gave innovative rulings concerning taxi drivers, in which it tried to adapt subordination criteria to the actual, practical, economic conditions in which these workers operated. Doctrine also worked hard to put forward the idea of a status for active employment that was broader than that of legal subordination.[69] The idea of acknowledging a firm nucleus of essential fundamental rights continued to make its way without however giving rise to legislation.

These questions arose in a different guise with regard to companies organised into networks or systematically using subcontractors.

In 1991, the legislator started to intervene to gain a legal grasp of subcontracting relations, as part of a fight against illegal employment.

During this period, the legislator became involved on several occasions, forcing project managers to check that subcontractors were employing their workers legally (responsibility of the project manager), and, in the area of safety (in 2003, Act of 30 July)[70] in companies where there was a high technological risk.

In the Social Modernisation Act, subcontractors began to be taken into account in cases where the project management company fell into financial difficulties (right to information, but these measures were suspended in January 2003).

However, these measures are timid and isolated. They did not lead the legislator to challenge the autonomy of legally distinct companies in order to give greater protection to workers who are suffering due to the outsourcing of activities, even in matters concerning worker safety. As a result, the subcontracting and outsourcing of activities generally leads to a deterioration in the status of workers.[71]

The only really effective policies have been the ones that have fought against illegal employment. These have led to a gradual strengthening of cooperation in the fight against all forms of illegal employment.[72] In the last eleven years, the legislator has regularly intervened to reinforce and adapt ways of fighting illegal employment to the new forms of activity. A major dispute is developing regarding the redefinition of employment contracts.

---

67   Dares report, p. 14.

68   F. Gaudu and R. Vatinet, 'Les contrats de travail', *Traité des contrats*, (dir. J. Ghestin) LGDJ 2001 et ref., F. Gaudu, 'Travail et activité', *Droit social 1997*, p. 119, A. Supiot, op. cit.

69   A. Supiot, 'Au-delà de l'emploi, Transformation du travail et devenir du droit du travail en Europe', Flammarion, 1999.

70   OJ of 31 July 2003.

71   Which explains why, in its interpretation of Article L 122-12, the Court of Appeal attempts to limit the transfer of workers in cases of outsourcing.

72   T. Aubert-Montpeyssen, 'Le renforcement de la lutte contre le travail illégal', *Droit social 1997*, p. 915.

Chapter II:
Changes in employee flexibility

The period between 1992 and 2003 was dominated by the constant concern on the part of the legislator and the legal authorities to improve economic competitiveness and to fight unemployment.

This was the result of lessons learned from the major restructuring plans of the 1980s, especially in the metallurgical, mining and shipyard sectors.

It appears that, from 1990s, firms had also fully understood the need to train employees in the new technologies (e.g. systematic, wide-ranging training in the banking and insurance sectors).

Adapting employees to changes in employment was thus at the heart of policies led by the public authorities and organised in occupational groups and a large number of companies.

After the interprofessional agreement of 3 July 1991, which set out the principle of joint investment (company/employee), a wide range of highly complex mechanisms were developed to encourage and increase employee flexibility.

Some very useful legal innovations arose out of case law due to the appearance of the employment contract redeployment and adaptation obligations (2-1), and also the legislator intervened to adapt and diversify employee training policies (2-2), and to introduce practical policies, against a background of unemployment, to improve qualifications and adapt employees to changes in employment (2-3). In the latter period, the reform of vocational training was sanctioned by an interprofessional agreement, signed on 20 September 2003, which marked the acknowledgement of an individual right to lifelong training (2-4).

Training is, in turn, an obligation on the employer and a right for the employee; the latter can take time off to adapt his skills to economic changes and, in return, the employer can impose training on his employees as part of the employment contract.

However, from 1992, French law considered that the employer loses his right to terminate the employment contract if he has not beforehand made any attempt to help the employee adapt to requirements for change within his company.[73]

Major efforts were made on the contract front, particularly in the occupational groups, to ensure that training required by changes in the job should help to maintain workforce numbers in companies.

In the 1990s, 'forward-looking labour market management agreements' gave way to 'skills management agreements', sometimes as a way of masking the negotiation of job losses. Training programmes aimed at providing employee flexibility in the face of changing employment conditions took a further hold in occupational groups and companies, through either collective agreements or training plans drawn up by the employer in collaboration with the works council.

Employee flexibility was therefore both a strong requirement of legislative, contractual and legal employment policies introduced by the legislator, contracts and the law, and an obligation within the context of individual labour relations.

This was therefore a major change, as it was not just a case of offering employees opportunities to develop their skills; it was also a matter of forcing the employer to introduce them collectively and individually.

---

73   Soc. 25 February 1992, D.1992, 390 note by M. Defossez, A. Bouilloux, 'L'adaptabilité du contrat de travail', *Droit ouvrier 1997*, p. 487.

1. Adaptation and redeployment obligations

With its rulings of 25 February 1992 and of 1 and 8 April 1992, the Court of Cassation ensured that adaptation and redeployment obligations entered the realms of the employment contract.

Based on the obligations of the employment contract, the supreme court identified these obligations as being implicit to the employment contract: they were therefore imposed on the employer by the very conclusion of an employment contract.[74]

This double offshoot of case law was justified by the Court of Cassation's wish to contribute to the policy of preserving jobs and to the fight against unemployment. They were strictly imposed by the courts with great regularity from 1992 and were incorporated by the legislator, firstly within the RTT mechanisms (Act of 19 January 2000) and then in the Act of 17 January 2002, known as the social modernisation Act.

The development of the adaptation and redeployment obligations was probably the most innovative case law addition to the case law policy in operation during the period 1992-2002.

1.1. The content of the adaptation obligation

The employer is bound by the employee's job definition in the employment contract and provides the employee with an appropriate job. He is bound to help the employee adapt to changes in his job. The courts have clarified that the employer simply has to provide the employee with training to enable him to keep up with changes in his job. Consequently the employer is not obliged to train the employee in new skills different from his original skills, or to help him to acquire basic knowledge that was not useful in his original job (Court of Cassation 3 April 2001),[75] or to redefine his qualification.

Employee flexibility implies a continuity in the acquisition of knowledge on the part of the employee, provided by short bouts of training.

The adaptation obligation is imposed on the employer during the employment contract. A dismissal is without effective, genuine cause if an employer dismisses an employee for a reason connected to his lack of professional competence or ability, and the employer has not first tried to adapt the employee's skills.[76]

Various factors ensure that employers adhere to this adaptation obligation properly, at least in companies with over 500 employees. For example: the low cost of the adaptation obligation; the company's economic needs; the scope of the technological changes imposed by rising international competitiveness; and the existence of training plans in the company.

It remains that, in small companies, compliance with the obligation, as with all the other obligations imposed by labour law, is more erratic. However, measures have been taken to extend employee flexibility. Since 2000, flexibility initiatives must take place during working hours and be paid as such (Article L 932-2 of the Labour Code). The interprofessional agreement of 20 September 2003 and the Act that extended the agreement (in the process of adoption in late 2003) differentiate between three categories of initiatives. The first type is flexibility initiatives, which are carried out during working hours. The second type is training sessions linked to changes in the jobs, which take place during working hours. Unless the training exceeds normal working time with over 50 hours it may not be considered as overtime (this means no cost for the employer if they exceed normal hours). This type of training may be carried out outside working hours if a company agreement or the employee's written agreement authorises it.

Lastly, the new law provides for an initiative of 'skills development'. This consists of training sessions outside actual working hours, which require the employee's express agreement. The plan is that, after a year's skills development training, the employee may be given priority access to a job that matches the skills he has acquired.

---

74   In particular, M.J. Gomez-Mustel, 'Formation et adaptation dans la jurisprudence sociale', *Droit social 1999*, p. 801, F. Gea, 'Licenciement pour motif économique: l'obligation de reclassement' RJS 7/2000, B. Lardy-Pelissier, 'L'obligation de reclassement', D. 1998, ch. 401, F. Heas, 'Les obligations de reclassement en droit du travail', *Droit social 1999*, p. 504, 'Droit au reclassement et sauvegarde de l'emploi', *Travail et Protection sociale*, special issue, June 2002, p. 127.

75   B. Reynes, 'Limite à l'obligation de formation de l'employeur', D. 2001, J., 3010.

76   It should be mentioned for the record that the employee can only obtain damages, which are a minimum six months' salary after two years' service. The employee can only be re-integrated into the company if the redundancy is nullified, see below. The courts estimate damages according to the actual prejudice suffered. Damages may exceed a year's salary in some cases, particularly for employees over the age of 50. The employer must also repay unemployment benefits, but the legislator has limited this reimbursement to 6 months' salary.

In 2003, the agreement and the legal mechanism have led to a sophisticated set of mechanisms and obligations that are the responsibility of both the employer and the employees. This creates strong incentives for the employer to provide more training for his employees (compulsory financial obligations of 1.6% of payroll, to be spent even if it is not used in the company). It also creates strong incentives for the employee (payment for training, guarantees in terms of training outside working hours and priority in terms of career development).

1.2. The outlines of the redeployment obligation

The redeployment obligation is imposed on the employer in two situations: where the employee is declared physically unsuited to his job due to incapacity as declared by the company doctor (not discussed here), and in the event of redundancy. Since 1992, the employer must, **prior to** the notification of the redundancy, conduct a search for jobs that may be available to the employee. This obligation applies whether the dismissal concerns an individual or a collective redundancy and regardless of the size of the redundancy.[77]

1. The employer is obliged to look for available jobs. This means that he is obliged to conduct a proper search in application of the principle of loyalty. The employer may not simply present the employee with possibilities (Court of Cassation 15 May 1995, Everite ruling), and cannot prove that his search has been valid if, at the same time, he employs temporary workers (Court of Cassation 4 April 2001) or recruits other employees.

   The judges are very strict in checking the seriousness of the employer's search for redeployment jobs.

2. The employer must carry out the search not only within the various parts of the company but also in all the companies in the group. The Court requires the search to be carried out in companies in the same business sector, insofar as the activities, organisation and operating methods mean that employees can be readily interchangeable (Video-color ruling, 5 April 1995).

   The possibilities of the group are assessed according to the criterion of employee interchangeability, which means that the redeployment obligation is not just aimed at companies located inside France but also at companies located abroad.

3. The employer is obliged to offer the employee available jobs which match as closely as possible the job previously occupied by the employee.

   In other words, the employer must redeploy employees who have been made redundant before making use of his career development plan.

   He may offer employees redeployment to jobs which, for the employee, mean a change to his employment contract. This could mean jobs outside the geographical area, jobs with fewer contractual or collective benefits (if there is a change of company), or a job with a different definition.

   In the redeployment proposals, the employer must demonstrate good faith and must, of course, exclude any discriminatory or arbitrary proposals.

4. The employee can choose whether or not to accept the redeployment proposals. He is not committing any offence if he turns down a redeployment that might change his contract. If he turns down the proposed redeployment, the redundancy procedure begun by the employer will carry on, the next step being a notification of the decision. If the employee accepts his redeployment, the employer must help him adapt to the new job. Adaptation and redeployment obligations are thus combined to achieve the required job objective.

5. Non-compliance with the redeployment obligation is punished by the payment of damages, as the redundancy is now deemed to be without effective, genuine cause. The fine is not applied when the redeployment plan is part of a restructuring plan (null and void in this case, see below).

During the ten years since the redeployment obligation was introduced it has been developed and companies have gradually learned, according to their size and means, to accept the obligation and deal with it.

It is certainly effective in large companies and groups. Its effectiveness in restructuring plans has been guaranteed by the risk that the restructuring plan may be cancelled if the redeployment plan is not good enough.

The redeployment obligation has helped to bring about a change of mentality with regard to the type of mobility required by economic changes.

---

77 Concerning changes, see manuals cit., G. Couturier, 'Vers un droit du reclassement', *Droit social 1999*, p. 497 latest view, P.H. Antonmattei, 'L'obligation de reclassement préalable au licenciement pour motif économique: nouvelles dispositions', *Droit social 2002*, p. 274.

It is very difficult to know the precise impact of the redeployment obligation on labour relations in France. Reasons for accepting or refusing redeployments vary greatly.

From a legal point of view the redeployment obligation is, like the adaptation obligation, a vital development with regard to changes in general contract theory. That is the reason why the legislator extended the life of the redeployment obligation in 2002, in Article L 321-1 of the Labour Code. This requires that every effort should be made in terms of training and flexibility before an employee's redundancy can be considered, and that every effort should be made to redeploy the employee, with appropriate training, before the redundancy can be pronounced.

These obligations are therefore the linchpin of the legal rules surrounding employee flexibility.

2. Company training policies

The primary objective of the increase in vocational training is to adapt employees to changes in jobs.

2.1. The features of the training policy

The training policy is based on a set of superimposed regulations that make up a dense, complex law. Some of these regulations are part of legal obligations, in particular where financial obligations are imposed on the employer and where employees are granted training leave rights. Other regulations form part of the contractual obligations of the company or occupational branch. In addition, there are obligations that impact on the company through training plans drawn up by the employer after consultation with the works council.[78]

As well as a large number of sources, there are a large number of measures, people, and rights involved. A number of measures are also introduced as part of unemployment policies, or legislation on redundancy, or reduction of working time.

Whatever the legal framework in which it is planned, access to all training measures is encouraged by offering the employee and unemployed person a 'skills evaluation', which helps to point up the individual's training needs. The evaluation may be requested by the employer, but it must be formally accepted by the employee, who is the only person to receive the results.

The widespread use of the skills evaluation is part of a policy to make the employee's training path increasingly individual. At the same time, if there is an agreement between the employee and the employer, it is used to develop employment in the company. The unemployed person also needs it, as the skills evaluation is used to organise training courses and adapt methods of reintegration.

The most important foundations of the right to vocational training were introduced before 1992 (particularly in 1990 and 1991). However, a number of key dates should be mentioned over the last eleven years:

1. The interprofessional agreement of 3 July 1991 (followed by the Act of 31 December 1991) which allowed the introduction of long-term training based on the sharing of vocational training time between the employer and the employee.

2. The five-year Act of 20 December 1993, which re-cast the rules relating to organisations responsible for collecting funds for vocational training and for their distribution.

3. The interprofessional agreement of 3 July 1994 on the negotiation of training measures in the occupational branches.

4. The Act of 6 May 1996, creating training time capital.

5. The Act of 19 January 2000 on defining the time needed to adapt the employee in terms of actual working time and the possibility of negotiating agreements on the time savings account in the company.

6. The unemployment insurance agreement of 1 January 2001 and the Act of 17 July 2001 instituting 'PARE' (return-to-work assistance plan), which was combined with a personalised action project, making the payment of unemployment benefits conditional on the completion of integration initiatives, especially training if it is negotiated in the unemployed person's plan.

7. The Act of 17 January 2002 legalising a number of provisions relating to vocational training, creating redeployment leave and imposing the validation of employees' vocational skills.

---

78 M.J. Mustel, 'Le rôle des acteurs dans la formation professionnelle continue', septentrion thesis, 2000, J.M. Luttringer, 'Le droit de la formation continue', Dalloz, 1986.

8. The organisation of interprofessional negotiation as part of 'radical social reform' in 2003,[79] which led to the signature of the interprofessional agreement of 20 September 2003.[80] This agreement is considered to be historic as it was signed by all the unions, including the CGT. It creates a subjective right to training for the employee. The mechanism was due to become law in late 2003 (Act discussed in Parliament from 11 December 2003).[81]

It may be said that employees in France enjoy a wide range of opportunities of access to vocational training in companies.[82] These stem from a certain number of rights that are connected to their contractual status (individual training leave and training during working hours), the fact that they belong to the company (beneficiary of training plans) and collective agreements (negotiation compulsory within the occupational branch every 5 years).

But, since the agreement of 20 September 2003, this right to training has become, for the future, an individual right belonging to the employee (Article L 933-1 of the Labour Code), and is open to employees with a year's service in the company or holding a fixed-term contract of over four months (open formation *prorata temporis*). Unless there is a company agreement, training should be focussed on promoting, acquiring, maintaining or improving knowledge and skills, or on actions leading to a diploma or vocational qualification. This individual right to training allows the employee to build up a fund of 20 hours of training per working year (on a *pro rata* basis for part-time) and he obtains a right to 120 hours after six years, which may be more if it has been increased by a collective agreement. The employee must carry out the training outside working hours, using an allowance equalling 50% of his salary. If his employment contract is terminated (except in the event of a serious offence or gross misconduct) the employee receives the acquired training allowance if he has not used it, which will enable him to finance skills evaluations or training sessions, or an initiative to develop his skills.

The 2003 reform shows that, within the outlines required by the EES, French law has created a full individual and collective right to training, which aims to develop synergies at the individual employee level and at the level of the company

and the profession, via the occupational branch. The Act adopted in late 2003 makes the negotiation of vocational training in the branch compulsory every three years (previously it was every five years).

It has been noted that there is a very clear tendency to place vocational training on a contract basis. The interprofessional agreement of 20 September 2003 is worthy of note in this regard as it led to legislative reform. It develops mechanisms to encourage the negotiation of training at company and branch level, or through 'social dialogue', so that the works councils could be involved in implementing the individual right to training.

In late 2002, major inequalities could be seen in the access employees had to training. The aim of the 2003 reforms is also to fight these inequalities.

2.2. The most significant changes

It is not possible, in a summary analysis of the changes, to describe in detail the many measures that helped to make employees more flexible through changes in employment. The following will nevertheless highlight the most striking changes that have occurred over the period.

It should be stated first that **training is possible whatever the size of the company.**

Thanks to all the superimposed normative mechanisms, employees can in fact benefit from genuine training, whatever the size of their company.

Even if the company is not covered by a collective branch agreement or it is not negotiated in the company, training is organised within the company via the training plan, which is introduced unilaterally by the employer, in collaboration with the works council.

This large number of mechanisms thus allows the employer and the unions to develop mechanisms in the company that are appropriate to changes in employment in the sector in which the company operates. These mechanisms are combined with the employee's individually acknowledged rights.

---

79 For more information on these changes, see 'Toute la vie pour apprendre, un slogan ou un véritable droit pour toutes et tous?', by Y. Baunay et A. Clavel, FSU Institute of Research, publ. by Nouveaux regards, 2002.

80 *Liaisons sociales*, Legis.soc.D1-no.8415, 9 October 2003.

81 *Liaisons sociales*, no.82/2003, 4/12/03.

82 It is important to note that the employee is protected by a specific legal status: that of vocational training course member, which allows him to keep or acquire social security cover during the training period.

2.2.1. The right to individual training leave and the individual right to training

The employee enjoys individual training rights via training leave, the cost of which may be paid by the financial bodies overseeing vocational training (Fongecif). During individual training leave, the employee's employment contract is suspended for a maximum of 12 months.

The training course is chosen by the employee. The employer is not bound to offer the employee another position at the end of the training course, but he is bound to guarantee the same job or a similar job on his return. This right to training leave is confirmed by the recognition of the individual right to training since the agreement of 20 September 2003 (see above).

2.2.2. Training time as actual working time

Training time may be allocated to the employee's free time or to actual working time.[83] The legislator has intervened to encourage the training of employees, seeking to increase the number of incentives for developing vocational training. For example, in 2000 the legislator stated that the training time required to adapt an employee to changes in his job should be paid as for actual working time.

Also, as part of the RTT scheme, the legislator has sought to favour the negotiation of time-saving accounts, which, subject to there being a collective agreement providing for them, allows the employee to 'store' reduced-working-hour days and turn them into training days so that these can be remunerated.

The time-saving account may therefore be used if it is provided for in the agreement that the employee can allocate set-aside days to skills training. The problem of whether the employee can transfer the time-saving account when he has professional mobility has not been settled.

Where training courses are provided for in the company training plan, the employer can force the employee to follow a training course.

The course is therefore a method of performing the employment contract and is paid as working time. When the course takes place outside working time, the employee must agree to this joint investment.

Since the Act of 19 January 2000, these opportunities for training by joint investment no longer concern only training

leading to a qualification. The joint investment training has been aimed at all vocational skills, thus extending the opportunities for creating employee flexibility. To make sure that the acquisition of these training courses, which interfere in the personal lives of employees, do not become the subject of pressure on the part of employers, a collective agreement has to be signed at either occupational branch level or company level. As mentioned earlier, the system has been refined by the reform of 2003. This means that the employee can acquire all the training required for adapting to changes in his job during his actual working time. In addition, he can undergo all the skills development training he wants outside working hours with payment, and with a fund-building and transferability mechanism to enable him to spread training throughout his life.

2.2.3. Validation of skills learned from experience

The greatest step was taken in 2002 with the 'acknowledgement of skills learned through experience' (Article L 900-1 and L 934-1 of the Labour Code): all the skills learned in working life should be validated by joint committees in the occupational branches or by authorities put in place by the Ministry of Employment or Education to give employees access to training leading to diplomas.[84]

It is still too soon to assess the effects of this reform but it may be assumed that the validation of skills learned through experience will be an excellent springboard for accelerating the training of employees and acknowledging their expertise.

3. Unemployment and reintegration policies developed to encourage flexibility

Without exception, governments are all looking for measures to significantly improve the employment situation. For over twenty years, they have been using social security contribution exemptions to encourage growth in employment.

The same can be said for the joint management of unemployment. It should be noted that, in France, unemployment risk is guaranteed by a voluntary joint insurance mechanism, administered by Unedic (Assedic at local level). Agreements are renewed every three years in a climate of high tension due to the structural imbalances caused by the increase in the number of unemployed. With each agreement, new bal-

---

83   M.J. Mustel, 'La construction des normes', in *Toute la vie pour apprendre*, op. cit. p. 133.

84   *Toute la vie pour apprendre*, op. cit. p. 321-350.

ances are negotiated between the allowances and the rights made available and Unedic's resources, and brought into force by a series of highly technical measures.

Here again, policies have been marked by a profusion of measures 'targeting' specific objectives (reintegration/training) and selected beneficiaries (e.g. 'young unskilled workers' or 'long-term unemployed over the age of 50').

Firstly, the key directions for change will be presented. This will be followed by the broad outlines of measures adopted that encourage the unemployed to flexibility and employability.

3.1. Key directions for action

A number of directions for action were used during the period between 1992 and 2003:

1. Introducing measures and administrative support to personalise the path followed by the individual unemployed, to help him to reintegrate by offering useful, individual support. This individualisation was brought about by the use of appropriate training, retraining and even vocational retraining measures.

2. Fighting unemployment in its various categories, starting with increasingly precise identification and, in particular, a series of mechanisms to favour the long-term unemployed, whose special professional and psychological problems have been recognised and treated.

3. Developing incentive measures based on exemptions from social security contributions. Between 1992 and 2000 exemptions to encourage part-time work led to significant growth in this type of employment (35% of part-time work is evaluated to be imposed and not chosen).[85] An original mechanism was adopted in 2001 to encourage an upturn in employment through the 'employment allowance', which reduced income tax (or gave a tax credit) on incomes close to Smic (minimum wage), similar to the kind of negative tax mechanisms found in the Anglo-Saxon countries. In 2003, the allowance mechanism was made more favourable to part-time workers.

4. Organising the end of working life for the over-50s. During the period between 1992 and 2000, there was considerable use of early retirement policies which provided unemployed people over the age of 55 with cover mechanisms and allowances that lasted until retirement.

From 2000, these policies were stopped to end the financial haemorrhage and the disastrous consequences on the economy from this loss of expertise.

In 1997, however, an early retirement policy was introduced for people who had completed their contribution years before the age of 60 (legal retirement age). In 2003, as part of the pensions reform, measures were adopted (improved pension rights, exemption from social security contributions) to encourage the over-55s to stay at work, which constitutes a complete turnaround in the policy for that age group.

However, there is, in France, a considerable difference between the decisions taken by companies to exclude employees aged over 50 on a massive scale (32% of employees aged between 50 and 60 are still working in France) and the turnaround made regarding policies for the same age group.[86]

5. Simplifying back-to-work assistance measures. This objective, which was introduced in 1997, was only partially achieved, though an effort was made to give greater visibility to the employment assistance offered to employers.

6. In 1997, a system of graduated benefits was brought in as an incentive to the unemployed to find work. The aim was to create a form of financial motivation for the long-term unemployed. In 2001, PARE was introduced (return-to-work assistance plan) which created an obligation to seek work that could lead to the removal of benefits. It was based on the construction of a personalised path to help reintegrate the unemployed person into the labour market. This was linked to a contract based on the negotiation of commitments between the employment authorities and the individual. These commitments were accompanied by objectives that had to be met. Integration therefore became a contractual obligation within the unemployment benefit system.

3.2. The broad outlines of policies to encourage flexibility and employability[87]

It is not the intention of this report to go into detail on measures concerning allowances for the unemployed. These were aimed at providing replacement income and were coordinated with measures to encourage reintegration.

---

85 See Dares report on these changes, cit. p. 45.
86 Y. Moreau, 'Avant ou après les retraites, reformer le travail', *Droit social 2003*, p. 684, F. Jeger, 'L'exclusion des plus de cinquante ans: conséquence inévitable de l'évolution du chômage ou problème culturel majeur?', *Droit social 2003*, p. 686.
87 These issues are developed in all the general works quoted.

Though the primary objective was reintegration into the labour market, many measures included a requirement for the employee to be flexible within the same labour market. To be 'employable', the individual had to adapt his qualifications and individual skills to the demands of the labour market and then to the demands of job changes within the company.

Flexibility is evaluated over time, unlike employability, but at the reintegration stage they were often dealt with via global measures.

Three major directions were chosen: aids to redeployment, employment and early retirement.

1. **Aids to redeployment** were, up to 2001, organised using two mechanisms: the contractual training-redeployment mechanism and retraining leave. The training-redeployment mechanism linked replacement income and training courses over one year (maximum three years) with training offered by the unemployment services (ANPE – 'Agence nationale pour l'emploi').

   Retraining leave, which was introduced in 1986, allowed employees who had been made redundant to undergo training with a view to redeployment, after a skills evaluation. Retraining leave was organised using tripartite financing (Government, company, employee giving up certain allowances).

   Since 2001, training grants have been granted individually with the aim of encouraging redeployment or, where training is a prerequisite, recruitment. The ANPE is solely responsible for prescribing who enters training courses.

   These forms of aid are coordinated with support for employment and geographical mobility in such a way that training can lead directly to the possibility of a job. The link with labour market demand is strengthened by efforts to provide individual measures and organise relevant training.

2. **Aids to employment.** These are very varied and are mostly based on incentives offered through exemption from social security contributions. They are often in favour of 'targeted' beneficiaries. Many measures aim to create a link between professional integration and training. These policies have been diversified for the com

mercial and non-commercial sectors[88] and contain aid initiatives in every sector, measures for providing personalised monitoring of the unemployed, training initiatives and financial incentives for employment. These combined measures have had positive effects, which were particularly visible between 1997 and 2001.[89]

There has been, in particular, the very important development of the 'qualification contract' and the 'flexibility contract', two alternating training options aimed at integrating young people without qualifications. In 1998, these qualification contracts were also opened up to adults over the age of 26, every time the contract could lead to a return to work. Special aids were also introduced for the long-term unemployed, who benefit from accompanying measures for their return to work (consolidated employment contract) or even have training at the same time. A number of other measures were introduced simply to integrate young people into working life (employment initiative contract, youth employment 1997-2002) without offering training to encourage flexibility. Simple immersion in the job was supposed to help achieve this objective. In addition, policy changes concerning the young ended up in 2002 with young beneficiaries finding themselves out-of-work, due to the removal of financing, despite the fact that many of them had integrated successfully into jobs that were of benefit to the community. These youth employment schemes were replaced by contracts enabling young people without qualifications to obtain an assisted job in 2002.[90]

These open-ended, part-time 'youth in enterprise' contracts, which were introduced in 2002, were part of an extension of measures exempting employers from social security contributions if they took on young people. A one-off grant was allocated to employers in the commercial and associative sectors. This was not accompanied by any specific training obligations. Of the 400,000 people recruited in late 2003, three-quarters were men between the ages of 19 and 21. Half of them had a level equal to the 'CAP' (vocational training certificate) and had previously been in work.[91] These early figures explain why the measure was strongly criticised. It is seen as a mechanism that may lead to a deterioration in the quality of jobs, an increase in inequality between men and women with no qualifications, and a lack of improvement in qualifications for this population of young people.

---

88   See Dares report, p. 55 et seq for greater detail.

89   See above: job creation and reduced unemployment with the effects of growth and the 35-hour week.

90   C. Willmann, 'Une jeunesse en droit de l'emploi (concerning the youth employment scheme, Act of 16 October 1997 and the youth in enterprise scheme, Act of 29 August 2002)', *Droit social 2003*, p. 10.

91   Dares report, p. 62.

Apprenticeship contracts also became more prominent. The legislator created strong incentives. Apprenticeships are organised in a decentralised way. New apprenticeship opportunities have since 2001, been offered in the occupational branches in the manufacturing sector, who were experiencing recruitment problems. The 2003 reform refined the apprenticeship mechanism to make it simpler and extend it to people over the age of 25, making it easier to create apprenticeships within higher education diplomas.

These very diversified aids show the French concern with finding measures that combine protection for the unemployed, reintegration and training for redeployment. But the policies that were put forward were not always a result of consistent political change, especially on the issue of the integration of young people.

However, it can be said that the unemployment situation allowed people, and particularly young, unqualified people, to find aid to make them more employable. The main problem was in keeping checks on the training that was being offered: was it of sufficient quality, and quite simply, was it actually happening?

Employers have become used to the idea of taking on assisted employees and do not always meet the training and reintegration obligations that accompany them. Judges are very strict in matters of an employer's non-compliance with assisted contract rules, when cases are referred to them.

3. **Early retirement mechanisms** have changed, but were until 2001 characterised by the exclusion of the over-55s from the labour market. Such exclusion also exists for the over-50s.

Despite special taxation imposed on employers if they make employees over the age of 50 redundant ('Delalande contribution'), the rule is one of exclusion (generally involving compensation mechanisms) and there is certainly no attempt to improve their employability.

A certain consensus is operating here. Employers prefer a labour force trained for less onerous intellectual and technological developments and there is a strong social demand to limit unemployment for young people. These ideas suggest that excluding employees over

the age of 50 will improve employment conditions for the young (especially where there are restructuring plans). There are also strong claims for early retirement from employees who started work very young (hence the system known as ARPE, retirement before 60 after 40 years' social security contributions). Since 2001, these ideas have been challenged.

The government has put a stop to overall early retirement measures. The National Employment fund (FNE) encourages gradual early retirement measures in companies where job losses are required. But a clear turning-point was reached in 2003 with an attempt to reverse the trend, not only by putting a stop to the exclusion of employees aged over 55 but also by encouraging them to carry on working after the age of 60. The Act of 21 August 2003 encouraged employees to extend their working life beyond the age of 55.[92] Early retirement or premature cessation of work became subject to a special contribution. Except in special cases, the employer could no longer retire an employee automatically at 60 – the age was now 65. If not all the conditions for retiring an employee are met, termination of the employment contract is considered to be a dismissal (confirmed by case law).[93] The employee can obtain extra pension rights if he extends his working life (provided he has paid his contributions for the period required for obtaining a full pension). There is therefore a political will to encourage so-called older employees to carry on working.

4. Lifelong training

Until the interprofessional agreement of 20 September 2003, the employee had no subjective right to lifelong vocational training. This right is now recognised and was due to be made law and extended to a broad population by late 2003.

During the reference period, French law has therefore gradually constructed: a right to development in employment, via a right to flexibility; a right to individual leave; collectively guaranteed rights to training; and a mechanism that provides continuity of training throughout the employee's life. It is also to be noted that these individual rights are available in independent legal and social organisations through state education, companies and the unemployment system, which presupposes belonging to the system.

---

92 *Liaisons sociales*, Legis. soc. 11-no.8411 of 12/09/03, analyses incentives to keep older employees in work, *Liaisons sociales 5/12/03*, no. 8428.
93 J. Pelissier, 'Age et perte d'emploi', *Droit social 2003*, p. 1061.

The principle of validating skills acquired by experience in 2002 is, without doubt, an important stage, as it means that a person's changing skills can be taken into account in different environments.

Contractual provisions in a large number of RTT agreements mean that part of an employee's free time can be allocated to training, either via the joint investment scheme or by using the time savings account.

Links have been created between these environments (school/company, unemployment/company) but there is no simple, linear mutualisation scheme to provide continuity of training rights. Even with the reform of 2003, and the recognition of the transferability of training rights, there is still no full mutualisation of individual rights.

Over this eleven-year period, there has been a strong doctrinal trend for suggesting that the whole issue of company time and the need for the different groups to share training rights needs to be discussed (cf. Alain Supiot, 'special drawing rights'). The idea is to get away from the concept of belonging (to the company, to the unemployment insurance scheme) and to allow employees to acquire rights at various points in their lives that might be used appropriately during their working lives and the changes that occur in them. This trend was very broadly established in the interprofessional agreement of 20 September 2003.

The construction of a right to lifelong training now has a future.

Chapter III:
Employability and job security

Employability implies that, when an employee is in or on the labour market, he can reposition himself because he has relevant skills and qualifications, whatever economic changes are taking place in jobs and companies.

These adaptations are increasingly difficult to organise, both in the practical world of running companies, due to the pressures of competition, and to legal obligations.

Over the eleven years between 1992 and 2003, the adaptation between European pressure on competitiveness (demanding an increase in the 'employability' of employees) and traditionally strong demands for 'job security' has given rise to major debates and a succession of legislative changes, mostly in the field of redundancy, RTT and restructuring.

However, if we attempt to stand back from these changes, we can see that a number of rights have been guaranteed or established during the last eleven years:

1. It is established that contracts of a temporary nature (fixed-term contracts/temporary employment contracts) are necessary in companies but that they must be strictly limited, controlled and checked (section 1.1).

2. It is established that the works council is the employer's main negotiating partner in the event of redundancies and that it is essential to have procedural rules for limiting the number of job losses and appropriate support measures in the event of redundancies (section 1.2).

3. It is established that the judge must have the power to keep a check on the redundancy procedure and to intervene in the procedure (section 1.2).

4. It is also established that a reconciliation between working life and private life should be encouraged by measures offered to employees, using combined actions of the legislator and unions (section 1.3).

5. It also appears to be established that Community law is empowered to govern cross-border restructuring

plans or perhaps more generally that the issue is of community interest (section 1.4).

As we can see, most of these established privileges are linked to the contribution of Community labour law or are related to it.

1. Job insecurity

After some ten legislative changes between 1979 and 1990, French law relating to fixed-term and temporary employment contracts focussed on a few strong principles: strict limitation of the use of fixed-term and temporary employment contracts in order to prevent a sustainable job from being taken by a temporary worker; strong protection of the job during its limited period; equality of treatment between workers with permanent contracts and those with temporary contracts; and termination of these contracts by their term, with no other procedural constraints.

It is important to emphasise first of all the direction that these changes have taken over the last eleven years, before discussing the scope of the controls placed on temporary contracts and the problems linked to the status of employees in insecure jobs.

1.1. Overall changes in the status of workers in insecure jobs

It should be pointed out that, in 1990, after a long period of legislative turbulence, French law passed an Act that set a legislative framework for fixed-term contracts and temporary employment contracts, which had a number of points in common. In France, temporary work is considered to be an exception to the prohibition from offering labour force to obtain a financial gain, which is justified by the strict controls placed on temporary employment agencies (authorisations, financial guarantees). The triangular relationship between the temporary employment agency, the user company and the employee is strictly regulated to prevent abuse and bargaining.

Regulations for precarious contracts have been altered over the last eleven years to:

- Reinforce the security of temporary workers (1994, 2001)

- Widen their use (2001-2002), organise trial periods for short-term assignments (2002), to give companies a bit more flexibility

- Reinforce works council control over temporary employment by introducing a warning procedure (2002)

- Make it easier to recruit temporary workers on a permanent basis (2002).

Between 1992 and 1999-2000, there appeared to be a certain social consensus regarding non-compliance with the rules relating to the limitation of use despite strict regulations and rigorous legal controls surrounding the use recourse to precarious contracts.[94] Employers used fixed-term employment contracts to give themselves lasting flexibility in their management of the labour force (e.g. contracts for more than 18 months were generally accepted, as was increased renewals of contracts, and continually calling on extra temporary work during normal periods). At the same time, due to the high level of unemployment and particularly of youth unemployment, the unions considered that it was better for an employee to work in conditions of doubtful legality rather than to be unemployed.

Similarly, the government accepted implicitly that inspections by the heavily overworked Labour Inspectorate should concentrate on other matters, especially job losses.

The level of unemployment, which rose continuously until the year 2000, also encouraged the government to close its eyes to irregularities in the training of these temporary workers.

During the period 1999-2000, the voluntary introduction in 1999 (imposed in 2000) of the 35-hour week changed the attitudes of unions and employers and of the Labour Inspectorate, and led to a reinforcement of controls and increased severity on the part of judges (as a result, more cases were referred to them).

The legislator accepted a few new cases where temporary contracts could be used. This was a result of lobbying by certain professions (e.g. pharmacists) and a certain attitude linked to occupational usage (in the agricultural sector) without significantly increasing the flexibilities granted to employers.

From 1994, security at work for temporary workers was central to the actions and policies put forward by the legislator and by works councils, unions and employers.

1.2. Controls operated to supervise insecure employment

The period between 1992 and 2003 has been marked by difficulties in checking the increase in unemployment against an economic background of increased competition and an increased search for competitiveness.

This explains the steady increase in the number of precarious contracts, which has been accompanied by a widespread demand from employers for greater flexibility in managing the labour force. In early 2004, there was a proposal to introduce a new contract known as the 'assignment contract', which will be for a period of five years, giving companies a new form of flexibility via the contract.[95]

This flexibility stems not just from the legal framework, but also from the use of illegal, unauthorised contracts, which in turn leads to several reactions: strict legal controls and increased powers for worker representatives.

- **Legal controls** have been reinforced over the last eleven years.

The use of temporary contracts has increased, despite the obvious difficulty temporary workers have in taking out legal proceedings. Judges check that the imposed law is strictly complied with (thus giving protection to the employee) and also that the usage in question is actually justified. The existence of the replacement or the increased temporary activity is checked.[96] So is the fact that the position occupied by the temporary worker is not a sustainable one. This form of control covers most situations. Until the rulings of 26 November 2003, it also covered sectors or professions in which it was 'customary' to use a fixed-term contract (a restrictive list is provided for in the Labour Code). In three fundamental judgements, the Court ordered that the judge should note whether there was 'customary' use of fixed-term contracts, and should

---

94   For the large amount of case law, see the regular columns by Mrs Roy-Loustaunau in the review *Droit social* and in the general works quoted.

95   As proposed by the Virville Commission, this contract would be created by branch agreement and would be limited to skilled jobs. It is presented by the unions as a new form of structural job insecurity. Some, however, make the point that it is better to have job security for 5 years than to be on a permanent contract and achieve job insecurity rapidly by being made redundant.

96   The most frequent uses. Also, the completion of dangerous works, contracts abroad, seasonal contracts, 'customary' contracts and contracts that fall within employment policy.

no longer check whether the employment was permanent.[97] The effect of this re-focussing of case law has been to increase recruitment flexibility for employers.

However, contracts concluded as part of employment policies (e.g. qualification contract, youth employment contracts) are excluded. Although they come within the legal framework applied to employment by fixed-term contract, they have a status adapted to occupational integration and may therefore be concluded to fill sustainable positions.

Judges are also very strict in checking that employers meet the training obligations as part of assisted contracts concluded under policies to encourage employment.

Possibilities for terminating these contracts are limited by the legislator to professional misdemeanour and *force majeure*. Case law is strict in its interpretation of these notions so that employees' jobs are not threatened for the period of the contract.

The change in economic circumstances justifying the use of temporary workers (e.g. A major contract suddenly terminated by a customer) is not considered to be a case of *force majeure*. It is therefore extremely difficult to terminate a fixed-term contract (professional inadequacy or financial grounds are not acceptable).

As a result, where contracts are for a long period (maximum 18 months for a fixed-term contract) or where an employee is absent for a long period (replacement of an individual until he returns, with no fixed term), the precarious contract is better protected during the contract period than the permanent contract.

This rarely happens, as the average period for a fixed-term contract is two to three months, and two weeks for a temporary job. However, the paradox is well worth mentioning.

Sanctions for these irregularities are generally of a financial nature as the employment contract is redefined as a permanent employment contract (since 2001 without the employee loosing his insecurity allowance). The employee is then awarded damages for the prejudice suffered (no minimum). Compulsory reintegration is not provided for.

The recourse to penal sanctions, which was introduced to limit abuses in the use of illegal precarious contracts is very seldom used. It is a potential, effective weapon that may be used by the unions acting instead of the employee (the latter's agreement is required) where practices are totally illegal and deemed to be improper, or where, after a report from the Labour Inspectorate, abuses are found to be repeated.

The status of the employee with an insecure job therefore offers solid guarantees during the contract period, though it does not, of course, avoid the problem of insecurity when the contract comes to an end.

- **Reinforced powers for worker representatives.** This has been significant in recent years.

It is stipulated that, during compulsory annual negotiation of effective salaries and the length and reform of working hours, the employer and the unions must look at changes in the number of fixed-term contracts and temporary assignments in the company (Article L 132-27 of the labour regulations). The same is stipulated for the occupational branch (Article L 132-12). The works council must also be sent figures relating to these contracts at regular intervals.

Worker representatives may therefore report to the Labour Inspectorate if these contracts are used too frequently. They often conceal the illegal use of contracts that might give rise to an infringement report from the Labour Inspectorate (with the possibility of proceedings being pursued by the Public Prosecutor).

In 2002, the social modernisation Act created a right of warning in favour of the works council. It can alert the employer to increases in the number of contracts, demand, justified responses and alert the Labour Inspectorate.

This provision is sufficient in itself to create pressure on the company to restrict the number of temporary employees, if the employer is concerned that employee representatives will take action on the issue of job insecurity.

Worker representatives have therefore been given a monitoring task that may help to limit the use of workers employed on short-term contracts.

1.3. The status of workers in insecure employment

The legislator has intervened in a piecemeal way to react to the most flagrant abuses of working practices. Similarly, unions and employers have helped to improve the collective status of these workers, particularly in the area of temporary work.

The most sensitive aspects of the status of temporary workers are as follows: the safety at work of temporary workers, their integration through a move to a lasting job, their training, their collective defence and new situations of poverty.

- **Safety at work,** the employer is obliged to give the worker safety training when he arrives at his workstation (taken from Community law). Worker representatives are careful to ensure that this provision is complied with in a large number of sectors and companies. A list of dangerous jobs has been published to prohibit these from being offered to temporary workers.

But working practices show that potentially dangerous jobs are more easily given to temporary workers.

Risk increases even further when a subcontracting company employs temporary workers. This is because although controls of the organisation of work on site are stipulated in the labour regulations, there are many gaps. Following the factory explosion in Toulouse (September 2001), measures were to be taken to improve safety. If the company managing the project recognised the risks it would be an important step as it would prevent pressure on subcontractors from leading to increased risk at work, which weighs particularly heavily on temporary workers. The draft bill only concerns chemical risks.

- **Occupational reintegration.** Measures have been taken to improve occupational reintegration, but they are still insufficient. Workers who have been given an assisted job to help them integrate into the world of work and temporary agency workers can now (since 2002) interrupt their contract if they are offered a permanent contract.

Workers in insecure employment who are in vocational training are obviously only assisted to maintain their flexibility between contracts via unemployment assistance mechanisms. Employees who move from one fixed-term contract to another have no opportunity to complete their training as they do not remain unemployed and, due to lack of time, do not receive training in the company. Recognition of the right to lifelong training is therefore vital for temporary workers.

However, in the temporary employment sector, major collective agreements have been concluded since 1992, as the profession has fully understood that it could offer quality services to companies if it offered them workers with relevant qualifications. As a result, workers who belong to large temporary employment agencies can benefit from training to adapt their skills, even while they are working on short-term assignments with users.

The working practice involving temporary, so-called 'pre-recruitment' assignments has developed considerably since 1995. It now allows companies to try out employees over a different period from that of the permanent contract trial period. In addition they avoid direct recruitment costs and enable themselves to find a prospective employee with the required skills.

This 'pre-recruitment' practice is not always carried entirely in line with the usages imposed by the law, but it does fall in with the drive for integration that all the parties concerned want.

- **The collective defence of temporary employees** is difficult in practice due to the short time they spend in a specific company. However, collective agreements have been concluded to specifically set up union rights in temporary employment agencies.

The legislator has also allowed unions to go to court to defend temporary employees and act in their place. This is a very useful provision in principle. But practice shows that, even with this opportunity, temporary workers rarely take action to defend their rights. Litigation has nevertheless increased during the reference period.

- **Poverty amongst temporary workers** was first considered in 1999-2000. It is the result of insecurity linked to the opportunities for workers to find a job at the end of the contract, and also of the conditions of employment offered to employees.[98]

Many part-time employees are in a situation of poverty, even while they work. It should also be said that most of these poor employees are women working part-time.[99] Women make up 80% of those with salaries below the SMIC (minimum wage).

Provisions have been made as part of unemployment legislation to encourage employees to accept low-paid jobs as a

---

98   M.L. Morin, 'Partage des risques et responsabilités de l'emploi', *Droit social 2000*, p. 730.
99   M. Maruani, 'The working poor', *Droit social 2003*, p. 696.

means of moving towards integration and to ensure that they do not suffer financial loss during their reintegration period.

Similarly, provisions in the 'Loi Aubry' of 2000 prohibited companies from dividing up working time for part-time workers more than once in the day, to enable these workers to possibly obtain another part-time job.

In France these employment and poverty situations are not analysed accurately enough[100] as the reactions of the legislator are only in terms of benefit transfers (lost if the person returns to work) or unemployment benefit, which is not appropriate.

2. Redundancy and the procedure for safeguarding employment

The regulation of redundancies and company restructuring plans is a highly controversial subject in France and is at the centre of political debate.[101]

The Community directive of 1975, revised in 1992, gave the reference framework. A wide-ranging debated followed upon the Act of 17 January 1993 relating to the content of the restructuring plan, which provided for accompanying measures where jobs were lost. This debate concerned legal controls on redundancies and also the role of the works council, unions and employers during the redundancy procedure, especially every time negotiation is organised concomitantly with works council consultation and every time a restructuring plan with a site closure is concerned.

The legislator intervened in 2002 via the Social Modernisation Act (17 January 2002) to give new guarantees to employees and to the works council in the event of a restructuring plan. Some of these measures were 'suspended' by the 'Loi Fillon' in January 2003 due to the political issues surrounding the question.

The period between 1992 and 2002 was marked by the strong wish on the part of the judiciary to control redundancies in order to safeguard jobs by increasing the strategic role of the works council, and by the difficulty in organising consultation and negotiation with the unions to improve the safeguarding of jobs.

2.1. Strict legal controls to safeguard employment

The Court of Cassation introduced very rigorous case law aimed at helping to safeguard jobs. All the case law was focussed on creating a limitation, within the legal framework, of the interpretation of the notion of redundancy, and the interpretation of the content of the restructuring plan. The idea was to encourage redeployment and its accompanying measures, and the reinforcement of sanctions against employers so that they introduce restructuring plans that are relevant in the fight against unemployment.

2.1.1. The notion of redundancy[102]

The Court of Cassation checks the causes related to job transfers and to the financial grounds underlying redundancy. It also checks that the reasons are not connected with the employee personally (taken from the 1975 directive) but this point does not take on any specific feature.

2.1.1.1. The causes of threats to jobs

First of all, the Court interprets concepts such as job losses, job changes and technological changes by searching for the reality behind the events. From 1995, it considered that the relocation of jobs abroad is equivalent to job losses, which opens up the right for the employer to invoke redundancy[103] (with, however, a redeployment obligation, even abroad, see above).

With regard to contract modifications on economic grounds the Court changed its approach in 1996 by giving an objective interpretation of the notion of modification:[104] what is 'objectively essential' was to be considered the essential components of the contract and not what was considered by the parties at the moment of signature of the contract. For example, working hours for a mother who wants to take her children to school before going to work – which was considered to be essential when the contract was concluded – may be changed by the employer as, since 1996, changes to working hours are considered to be a 'change to working conditions', not a modification.

The issue of a definition between 'contract modification' and 'change to working conditions' comes from the legal system. This means that if the employee refuses to accept a 'change to

---

100 A. Ratouis, 'Précarité et vie quotidienne des ménages actifs, de quoi parle-t-on?', *Droit social 2000*, p. 717, special issue 'Minima sociaux, revenus d'activités, précarité' and M. Maruani, loc.cit., P. Concialdi and S. Ponthieux, 'L'emploi à bas salaires: les femmes d'abord', *Travail, genre et société*, 1/1999.

101 There is a lot of literature available, but we shall refer here to general works, cit., which all deal in detail with changes in redundancy law.

102 For a summary, 'Le licenciement pour motif économique après la loi de modernisation sociale', special issue of the review *Travail et Protection sociale*, June 2002.

103 'Videocolor' affair, relating to a business relocation to Brazil, Court of Appeal 5 April 1995, Bull.V no. 562.

104 Ph. Waquet, RJS 12/96, p. 793, 'Le renouveau du contrat de travail', RJS 5/99 p. 383.

working conditions', the employer can dismiss the employee for serious misconduct. It also means that if the employee has a legitimate reason, particularly a family one, the employer can dismiss the employee for a misdemeanour. In the latter case, the employee has the right to a notice period and redundancy pay, which is granted according to his length of service in the company.

In the case of a 'contract modification', the employee has the right to refuse to accept the modification. The employer may then dismiss him if, for a legitimate economic reason, he has to impose the modification (e.g. decrease in salary due to financial difficulties). The employee then benefits from the whole redundancy procedure and especially from the redeployment obligation.

But in both cases he is still dismissed, which means that the employer currently has total flexibility in managing the organisation of the company and its workforce, the procedure and the cost change. Due to the flexibility given to the employer, legal checks on definitions and procedures are merciless for the employer.

This case law is extremely harmful to the reconciliation of working life and family life (see below). The following are considered as contract modifications that the employer cannot change without the employee's agreement:[105]

- Modifications affecting salary, if they refer to the amount or the methods used for calculating salary.

- A change of place of work outside the geographical sector. The geographical sector is a *de facto* notion that is generally interpreted by judges according to the availability of public transport. The employer may therefore change the place of work at will within the geographical sector, even if travelling time is significantly increased for employees.

- The job definition modification, which leaves the employer free to change the tasks performed by his employees, even when the new tasks are much more demanding.

- A change in the rhythm of work, day/night, or in the days worked (week/Sunday).

All other decisions taken by the employer are changes to working conditions. A number of issues still remain unclear.

This objective approach gives employers considerable room for manoeuvre, which is considered to be necessary to the company's ongoing adaptation to the demands of competition.

It also means that all employees who are subject to the same changes are treated in the same way. The employees can have clauses inserted into their contract to protect their private life and to avoid changes that upset family life. Then the situation is contractually organised on agreed objective bases. But the employee must have some capacity for negotiation. The employer therefore introduces flexibility clauses.[106] These are subject to strict legal controls as they must fit in with the company's interests and must not unjustifiably violate individual rights and individual and collective freedoms (L 120-2).

But the scope for clauses have grown considerably over this eleven-year period to arrive at a totally flexible form of management. If contract modifications are accepted at the outset, they are imposed on the employee.

The move since 1996 from a subjective approach to an objective approach has been an important step towards making labour law more objective. It leads directly and indirectly to an increase in the employer's reorganisation options, which are deemed to be useful from a financial point of view. They are, however, harmful to job security.

2.1.1.2. Economic causes

The Court of Cassation has had to interpret the legal text (Article L 321-1-1 of the Labour Code) stating that economic grounds are 'in particular' financial difficulties or technological changes. It has added cessation of activity by the employer due to his age and, above all, the reorganisation of the company. Faced with the systematic use of this cause by companies to justify, in particular, all their contract modifications, it stated from 1995 that reorganisation must 'be required to safeguard the company's competitiveness'.

In 2002, in the Social Modernisation Act, the legislator wanted to place stricter controls on the definition by deleting the 'in particular'. The provision was however censured by the Constitutional Council as the over-strict limitation on the definition was a violation of the freedom to run a business.

The phrase 'safeguard the company's competitiveness' is a notion greatly appreciated by judges looking into the merits of the case. The reference framework is however stipulated

---

105   Concerning the lack of clarity in this case law and its developments, F. Favennec- Hery, 'Modification du contrat de travail: le glissement de l'objectif vers le subjectif', RJS 6/03 p. 459.

106   See below.

by the Court of Cassation. It refers to the group's sector of activity, which is obviously an important stipulation in groups of companies and international groups.[107]

This reason is very easy to invoke in the latter situation as, where an activity is being relocated to a country with low labour costs, safeguard of competitiveness is always guaranteed due to the resulting comparative benefits. Legal controls have been shown to be strict. The economic grounds must be real and serious. The controls have been considerably reinforced over the last eleven years.

However, where the company is making a profit and makes employees redundant to increase profitability, the judges generally refuse to uphold economic grounds. There is however, a certain lack of clarity in situations in which a restructuring plan is required to safeguard company competitiveness.

2.1.2. The contents of the restructuring plan and sanctions against inadequate measures

The Act of 27 January 1993 stipulated the compulsory content of the restructuring plan. The restructuring plan should provide for an internal redeployment plan and actions other than simple retraining agreements that must be offered to employees faced with redundancy. From 1995, a Court of Cassation case law developed that required measures in the plan to be relevant, appropriate, precise and in proportion to the size of the company.[108]

The Court of Cassation also required that the jobs offered under the internal redeployment plan should be identified by professional category and place of work. Failure to meet these requirements was sanctioned by a declaration that the procedure was null and void in line with Article L 321-4-1 of the Labour Code. The nullity of the procedure led, after the Samaritaine rulings of 13 February 1997 to the nullity of redundancies.[109]

This nullity therefore forces the employer who has drawn up a restructuring plan, deemed to be inadequate and therefore null and void, to reintegrate the employees. 130 people were concerned in the Samaritaine affair.

The strictness of the sanction had the effect of forcing companies to construct intelligent, relevant, and appropriate restructuring plans to avoid the risk of nullity. From 1997, real improvements could be seen in the quality and the diversity of measures for redeployment and restructuring plans. After 1999, the conditions for taking action to have restructuring plans declared null and void have largely opened up. This has caused fury amongst employers due to the resulting legal insecurity. The works council or an employee can take action until five years after the event. A major almost systematic dispute started developing in 1993 bearing on all aspects of the redundancy procedure. This procedure was facilitated in particular from 1993 by strict controls on the conditions in which the restructuring plan should be introduced (as soon as modifications on economic grounds were proposed, the Framatome and the Majorette rulings) and the right for the works council to bring in summary proceedings, i.e. very rapidly, while the procedure is underway.

This right to bring summary proceedings[110] from 1996 gave the works council a central role, protected by the possibility of a timely intervention by the judge on the redundancy, before the redundancies are announced to employees.

2.2. The increased strategic role of the works council

The role of the works council continued to grow, as, within the framework of legal procedure, it became the legislator's chosen negotiating partner and received a full range of economic information.[111]

The increase in the works council's strategic role was brought about by the opportunity offered to the council, in the event of collective redundancies, to bring legal proceedings between the two consultation meetings provided for by Articles L 321-1 and following of the Labour Code.

If the works council is unable to persuade the employer to fully negotiate the restructuring plan or even to enter into a dialogue 'with a view to an agreement', as the directive stipulates, it can, at any time, refer the matter (within 24 hours) to the emergency interim judge (President of the High Court) to ask him to appoint an expert or suspend the procedure due to the inadequacy of the measures set out in the restructuring plan.

---

107   Court of Appeal 5 October 1999, Bull. civ. V no.366.

108   See in particular, G. Couturier, *Droit social 1993*, p. 219, 2002, p. 279, *Special issue of Droit social*, May 1994, 'Les plans sociaux', J.E. Ray, 1994, p. 444, Ph. Waquet, 'Les plans sociaux', RJS 5/96, p. 303.

109   Soc. 13 February 1997, RJS 3/97, no.269, G. Couturier and J. Pelissier, SSL 1997, no. 829, p. 3, F. Favennec-Hery, 'La jurisprudence Samaritaine et la prescription des actions en justice', *Droit social 1997*, p. 341, T. Grumbach, 'Encore une fois sur les arrêts Samaritaine', *Droit social 1997*, p. 331.

110   Emergency procedure to obtain a legal ruling within 24 hours in the event of a manifestly illegal disorder or emergency. The Court of Appeal acknowledged that works councils have this right of action in its Sietam rulings of 16 April 1996.

111   R. Vatinet, 'De la loi sur les nouvelles régulations économiques à la loi de modernisation sociale: une montée en puissance du comité d'entreprise ?', *Droit social 2002*, p. 286.

Thereafter, it can also seek within five years to have the restructuring plan declared null and void, allowing time to prepare an effective legal action.

These opportunities for legal action are set out in a series of Court of Cassation rulings between 1995 and 2000[112] and demonstrate that the Court wishes to impose a specific obligation on the employer to do his utmost to maintain workforce numbers by reinforcing the measures contained in the restructuring plan (renamed 'job safeguard plan' in 2002).[113]

The rigour of the legal regime imposed by the judges forced companies to enter into proper dialogue with works councils. This dialogue may lead to consultation to improve the restructuring plan or to acceptance by the employer of alternatives to redundancy. It may also be combined with genuine negotiations with the unions (see below).

This legal involvement in redundancy was heavily criticised by the employers. It was reinforced by the Social Modernisation Act of 17 January 2002, which legalised certain concepts established in case law (redeployment and adaptation obligations, see above), and extended the powers of the works council, in particular with regard to restructuring. However, the Acts of 3 January 2003, known as the 'Loi Fillon', suspended a number of these provisions, preventing works councils from acquiring the right to present alternative proposals.

It is important to emphasise that, during this period, the increase in the strategic role of the works councils was based not only on this strategy developed for restructuring plans, but also on certain financial prerogatives that were granted to them from 1982. The works councils fully 'appropriated' the very extensive rights that they had with regard to information and the use of experts. These were at the heart of a number of actions, allowing works councils to obtain relevant, useful information from employers that could be looked at by experts.

The conjunction of this right of information, guaranteed by judges, and the use of experts, enabled them to put forward alternative proposals to those presented by employers which were also based on a financial argument.

The works council's right to present alternative proposals for restructuring was recognised in the Social Modernisation Act of 17 January 2002 and immediately suspended ('loi Fillon', 3 January 2003),[114] due to strong opposition from the employers to this change in the role of the works council.

However, the Act of 3 January 2003 legalised the possibility of concluding method agreements for managing restructuring.[115] These agreements were derogatory and experimental.

Since 1996, the Court of Cassation had forced employers, in cases of restructuring with the closure of a site, to comply 'concomitantly' with both the general obligations to provide works councils with information and consult with them, and with obligations relating to redundancies (strict deadlines, use of an expert).

From 1996, the people who had to put these obligations into practice had to solve the problems of concomitance between the two procedures and, to resolve conflicts and for practical reasons, had to develop 'method agreements'. These agreements were generally aimed at setting out the procedural arrangements for working procedures, and to avoid hold-ups caused by legal appeals.

This possibility of concluding method agreements was recognised by the law in 2003. But the right to put forward alternative proposals, which, if they were opposed by the employer, were submitted to a mediation procedure, was 'suspended'.

We therefore note that there was strong opposition to the idea of the works council becoming a real negotiating partner with the employer in economic matters.

In addition, in a SAT ruling of 8 December 2000,[116] the Court of Cassation clearly asserted that the employer was still in charge of economic decisions and the decisions taken to face up to financial difficulties. The judge controls the reality and gravity of the financial grounds, not the appropriateness of decisions concerning the safeguarding of jobs. In other words, the employer is not obliged to choose the financial route that best preserves jobs. Within these parameters, he simply has to limit the number of redundancies.

With the indisputable prerogatives that it has acquired, the place of the works council depends on the forces that it can mobilise within the company.

In large companies, it can present genuine alternative proposals. Method agreements can also be concluded to set out

---

112   Soc 30 March 1999, RJS 5/99, no.564, Soc. 28 March 2000, RJS 5/2000, no. 519.
113   G. Couturier, 'Du restructuring plan au plan de sauvegarde de l'emploi', *Droit social 2002*, p. 279.
114   OJ of 4 January 2003.
115   P.H. Antonmattei, 'Licenciements économiques et négociation collective: un nouvel accord collectif est né', *Droit social 2003*, p. 486.
116   A. Jeammaud and M. Le Friant, cit. Above.

restructuring procedures. But this obviously concerns only a very limited number of companies.

There is therefore a great deal of unrest over the position of employee representatives, and this can also be seen in the link between consultation and negotiation in employment-related issues.

Negotiations took place with unions and employers after the suspension of the provisions relating to restructuring during the year. In late 2003 it was difficult to envisage an agreement being signed between representatives of MEDEF and the unions, bearing in mind the clash of interests against a background of increasing job losses in France.

2.3. The link between consultation and negotiation in issues relating to employment

The distinctive feature in France is double representation: elected (works council) and appointed (union representatives). Works councils receive all financial information, while the unions only receive it during negotiations and in particular during the compulsory annual negotiation.

The link between consultation and negotiation does not necessarily pose problems, but it is evident that areas of competence are superimposed, especially with regard to employment.

Since an ECJ ruling on 5 May 1998, the Court of Cassation has ordered that the works council should be consulted before any agreement is signed concerning its area of competence, and in particular all issues concerning employment.

In addition, when agreements relating to the 35-hour week were being concluded, the unions had to consult employees and the works council concerning both the rules relating to the allocation of aids for reduced working hours, and to establish their legitimacy.

Furthermore, a strong controversy started in 1999 regarding the obligation to impose the conclusion of an RTT agreement before any restructuring plan. In 2000 the Constitutional Council censured the provision, which was eventually reinserted (known as the 'Michelin amendment') in 2002. Now that the RTT scheme has been introduced (and then made more flexible in 2002) this obligation to introduce RTT before any restructuring plan is only a means of checking that the law is being complied with.

However, the provision is part of a more general movement to create a link between consultation and negotiation procedures. The provision encourages potential synergies in favour of employment between the action of the works council and negotiation by the unions.

The method agreements that appeared during the restructuring of large companies to regulate the way in which consultation procedures, and even dialogue between the employer and the works council took place, point in the same direction.

This link is usually the result of concerted action between the unions and the works council, which is encouraged by the union leanings of members of the works council. Inasmuch as the judge or the legislator contribute, it encourages the resolution of problems relating to employment via consultation and negotiation.

It is very difficult to evaluate the strength of these synergies. They are mostly found in large companies rather than in small ones. Although the negotiation of RTT agreements has greatly increased company negotiation, even in small companies, it is difficult at the moment to assess how negotiation of other employment-related issues (other than RTT) is moving.

As a result of this change, a large number of controls, covered by sophisticated legal procedures, have been placed on the employer's right to modify and axe jobs in companies. These procedures provide relative job security.

With regard to redundancy, the balance between the employer's power to manage and the prerogatives of unions and government is provided by strict legal controls. These are to ensure that procedural obligations are complied with. Compliance is imposed via strict sanctions that demonstrate the will of the judges and the legislator to promote a coordinated policy for fighting unemployment by limiting redundancies and their effects, while at the same time allowing the employer to make financial decisions if they are justified.

3. Job protection and family life

Clearly, the objectives put forward in France help to favour both working life and family life. The overall trend is to enable employees of either sex to reconcile the two.

In practice, the situation is much more delicate. The reference period is obviously marked by both a considerable increase in the proportion of women in the working population and by high unemployment figures. Regular political changes have shown that there is a great deal of controversy about the role of women and maternity, and these give rise to provisions that do not always favour women's search for employment. Nor are company demands for competitiveness necessarily reconciled with this overall objective. Economic and political objectives do not therefore enable us to identify a totally consistent line.

It is therefore important to look carefully at the influences of the use of flexibility clauses on employment contracts, the effect of the reform of working hours on family life, the reinforced protection of maternity and parental rights and, lastly, the effects on family life of teleworking and new technologies.

3.1. Flexibility clauses in the employment contract and family life

We will simply state here the possible consequences of the increased use of clauses that introduce flexibility into the employment contract.

As has already been mentioned, the move towards objectivising modifications to the employment contract has allowed the employer complete freedom to impose changes to working conditions on the employer. In theory the employer must, however, obtain the employee's agreement to any modifications concerning the basis of the contract, which is made up of the four pillars: salary, job definition, place of work outside the geographical sector, and working hours.[117]

To avoid the inconvenience arising from the obligation to obtain the employee's agreement (and then, if he refuses, to avoid the cost of a possible redundancy),[118] employers offer employees contracts when they are taken on, which, over the years, have become increasingly sophisticated and adapted to the needs of the company. These clauses are subject to legal controls with regard to their legality in respect of the application of Article L 120-2 of the Labour Code. This is also to ensure that there is no misuse of right and discrimination in their implementation.

A practical effect of the widespread use of these clauses is to provide greater flexibility in labour force management. This has also reduced employees' opportunities for reconciling their family life and working life.

This is particularly clear in the case of mobility clauses.[119] Once an employee has accepted a mobility clause, he can be transferred outside the geographical sector. However, the judge checks whether this is in the company's legitimate interests, whether it is precise (especially if the clause is international) and whether the employer is not using it too precipitately (to give the employee time to organise his private life) or for arbitrary or discriminatory purposes.

These legal controls are important to prevent abuses. In periods of crisis and unemployment, employees cannot object to mobility. Very often, the mobility decision is imposed on the spouse, and one or the other of the partners loses his/her job as a result. Again, very generally, it is the woman who either refuses the mobility and is dismissed for misdemeanour or resigns to follow her spouse.

However, mobility support allowances in favour of the spouse are often negotiated in large companies. In addition, there are unemployment insurance mechanisms to compensate the spouse who follows the transferred employee.

It is considered as progress that the Court of Cassation has revised its case law, which used to describe the refusal of an accepted mobility as serious misconduct. It has now decided to describe this refusal as a misdemeanour where there are family reasons.[120]

Except for part-time work, which is protected by the Community directive, it is still the case that family life is not a sufficient reason for blocking the flexibilities imposed by the employer.

It should also be emphasised that these clauses are even more dangerous for employees as their effects take their course over time. A mobility clause may be looked at favourably by a young single person, but will still be in the contract when the same person has two or three children to look after and a working spouse.

However, a number of collective agreements adapt mobility conditions for employees. The most frequently used clauses are statements about the notice period and the employee's right to turn down a number of proposals by the employer.

The widespread use of mobility clauses where both spouses work is actually a new difficulty that, for sociological reasons,

---

117   See above, F. Favennec-Hery, RJS 6/06 cit.

118   See above.

119   For information of the law before the Court of Appeal development, I. Daugareilh, 'Le contrat de travail à l'épreuve des mobilités', *Droit social 1996*, p. 128, then, Ph. Waquet, 'Le renouveau du contrat de travail', loc. cit.

120   See, for a refusal to change working hours after 25 years of not working on Saturdays, not described as serious misconduct, Court of Appeal 21 January 2003, *Droit social 2003*, p. 536, note Escande-Varniol.

usually affects women, who are generally less qualified and less well paid than men.

Allowances, which are regularly adapted to favour the birth rate, are combined with the types of female unemployment that is linked to the man's mobility. These allowances are to encourage women to 'take advantage of' a period of non-employment to have children.

3.2. The impact of the reform of working time on family life

One of the objectives of the laws on the reduction and organisation of working time (1996, 1998, 2000) was to enable employees to create free time and thus achieve a better reconciliation between working life and family life.[121] RTT's 'compensation' to employers was to allow them to negotiate agreements to calculate working hours on an annual basis and introduce working rhythms to increase the company's competitiveness.

The impact of RTT agreements on family life stems initially from the content and conditions of the agreements and also from the personal situation of the individual.

It is therefore impossible to make a single judgement as to whether the reforms relating to working time make it easier or harder to reconcile working life and family life.

It is therefore necessary to separate those measures that generally make it easier to reconcile family life and working life from those that make it harder, in the knowledge that it is usually a combination of several factors that contribute to this result.

3.2.1. Measures contributing to an improved reconciliation between family life and working life

First of all, when free time is organised in a constant, regular manner, it allows employees to organise their lives better. All the surveys show that women use this new free time first and foremost for household and family tasks, which helps to reduce the stress created by the need to reconcile working life and family life. After sport, men give more time to their children.

Here, the use of free time is very clearly based on gender and is almost a caricature of the traditional distribution of roles between men and women in our society.[122] However, it can be said that this free time offers the potential for a re-equilibration of the sharing of tasks related to the family, especially for the youngest couples.

Concerning the organisation of part-time work,[123] there are measures that allow employees to choose part-time work in order to reconcile working life and family life.[124] Examples of this are the introduction of a stipulation that allows the employee to refuse changes to working hours for reasons connected with family life, and the obligation to plan the distribution of working time at the moment of conclusion of the contract.

The legislator has also intervened to prevent working time from being split more than once in the day for part-time workers.

The introduction of time savings accounts can also greatly facilitate reconciliation between working life and family life, offering special leave arrangements (e.g. long-term illness of a child) or allowing parents who have been on parental leave to finance long-term training and re-qualification to help them re-train. It should be pointed out that agreements must set out the reasons for using the time savings account and that they do not usually stipulate freedom of use or reasons linked to family life.

The generalisation of flexible working time, already fairly widely used in 1992 (following the reform of working time) is probably the most important right in the attempt to reconcile family life and working life. Variable working hours offer invaluable flexibility, especially when it comes to dealing with the time demands of children.

It is difficult to assert that the introduction of annual hours 'packages' for managers, where they are free to organise their work, is always a factor that favours this reconciliation, as the annual package is generally accompanied by an increase in workload, which can lead to exhaustion. However, the allocation of RTT days to school holiday periods is an obvious gain in the struggle to organise family life and to respond to unforeseen events.

---

121   P.L. Remy, 'Réduction du temps de travail et vie familiale', Aubry II bill, *Droit social 1999*, p. 1012, see special issues of *Droit social: La réduction du temps de travail*, September-October 1998, 'Le projet de loi Aubry II', December 1999, 'Le temps après la loi Aubry II', March 2000.

122   D. Meda, 'Les femmes peuvent-elles changer la place du travail dans la vie?', *Droit social 2000*, p. 463.

123   F. Favennec-Hery, 'Les trente-cinq heures et le travail à temps partiel', *Droit social 1998*, p. 382, 'Mutations dans le droit de la durée du travail', *Droit social 2003*, p. 33.

124   F. Favennec-Hery, 'Le temps vraiment choisi', *Droit social 2000*, p. 295.

Organising work over four or four-and-a-half days can be helpful towards reconciliation. Even outside the conclusion of an agreement, the employer can impose it on employees if the works council accepts his proposal. Whether this is an asset or a burden depends on the individual context.

Some negotiations have been organised out of a constant concern for employees management of free time. This is especially the case in those sectors in which business depends on employee creativity.

However, this concern is not reflected in a considerable number of agreements which, instead, emphasise the flexibility required by competition.

3.2.2. Measures contributing to a deterioration in the reconciliation between family life and working life

The measures that contribute most to this deterioration are those that increase flexibility by changing working rhythms: changes to working time, changes to days and changes to periods worked. The time that is freed up is in those cases used simply for recovering from fatigue. It is not possible to organise family life or adapt to unforeseen events, which are frequent when employees have children. The law has stipulated a notice period of seven days for changing working time, but branch agreements may cut this period down to three days.

When both parents are under a flexibility regime, these incessant changes prevent life from adopting a consistent pattern. We are not at present in a position to measure the damage to family life caused by these new working conditions, but it is likely to be highly significant (divorce, juvenile delinquency, etc).

Obviously, due to the risk of redundancy, the employee cannot object for family reasons to these forms of flexibility, which result from collective agreement. Apart from part-time work, the preservation of family life is not considered to be a legitimate reason for refusing a change.

The introduction of night-time and Sunday working is only seen as a factor leading to a deterioration of family life if it is imposed by the employer.

In most companies, changes are based on 'voluntary' choices (also the requirement for higher wages due to the disappearance of overtime in large companies).

The law, which finally modified the norms relating to night-time work in 2001, after condemnation by the ECJ in respect of night work for women, makes the introduction of this form of work conditional on the conclusion of a collective agreement at either branch or company level.

Unions and employers are sensitive to the family aspect. We can only hope, therefore, that strong guarantees will be systematically negotiated to ensure that these forms of work are chosen on a voluntary basis.

It is especially important to note that the legislator has intervened to allow the employee to refuse to move from day-work to night-work where this is incompatible with compelling family obligations, particularly looking after a child or a dependent person (Article L 213-4-3).

A number of sociological studies are currently being carried out into working time. For the time being, assessments of the consequences of the 35-hour week in France are still dependent on political issues.

3.2.3. Maternity protection and parental leave

France traditionally gives strong protection to maternity, with social security provisions that guarantee a minimum of 16 weeks' leave with an allowance.

The employer is prohibited from dismissing the employee for any reason related to her pregnancy when he becomes aware of it. He must reverse his decision if he becomes aware of her condition within two weeks. However, a pregnant woman may be dismissed for serious misconduct or for another reason that obviously has nothing to do with the pregnancy (especially economic grounds).

Redundancy pronounced during maternity leave is null and void. The employee can therefore be reintegrated at the end of her maternity leave. Since 2001 the Court of Cassation has reinforced these forms of protection so that the nullity of the woman's redundancy during her maternity leave is treated in the same way as other cases of nullity.[125]

The protection was enhanced when a new rule of proof was introduced in 1993. This rule stated that, in the event of a dispute, the employee had the benefit of doubt. The protection improved further in 2001 by the introduction into the labour regulations of job adaptation or temporary assignment guarantees for pregnant women throughout their pregnancy and on their return from leave.

---

125   B. Gauriau, 'Licenciement nul et droit à réintegration: la salariée enceinte est un salarié comme les autres', C. Court of Appeal 30 April 2003, *Droit social 2003*, p. 827.

If it is impossible to find a temporary assignment appropriate to the woman's state of health, the contract is suspended but pay is maintained. The employer must obviously listen to the advice of the company doctor.

Lastly, case law has reinforced the sanctions. Since 1997, the case law allows a woman in a maternity situation to petition the emergency interim judge to demand her reintegration, or where the woman does not wish to be reintegrated, compensation, particularly since 2001. She is paid the salary due up to the pronouncement of nullity, and notice and redundancy pay and damages to compensate for the illegal nature of the dismissal, based on a minimum six months' salary.

Paid paternity leave of 11 days following the birth of a child was introduced in 2001. The measure was given an enthusiastic welcome by young fathers (Article L 122-25-4 of the labour regulations).

Parental leave was introduced in France in 1977, before the Community directive, but was modified thereafter. A parent with at least a year's length of service can ask for his contract to be suspended or for his activity to be reduced for the first three years of the child's life. The request must be sent by recorded delivery, but case law has toned down this formal condition so as not to deprive the employee of his right to leave. Social security pays a parental education allowance that acts as an incentive for employees on low salaries.

The employer must assign the employee to an equivalent or similar job on his return from leave and, of course, meet his adaptation obligations.

This form of leave is open to both father and mother but is still mainly used by mothers. Parental leave constitutes a break in career development, both during the leave period and after. As a result, it is more used by women on low pay and with few qualifications. But there are signs of a gradual change due to an evident search on the part of young employees for quality of life.

Lastly, there are various kinds of leave for family events that lead to the one-off absence of the employee. Since 1994, employees can take unpaid leave if their children are ill or have an accident. The family dimension is therefore very much a part of the leave system.

Obviously, the consequences of these various types of protection are felt in companies, in areas such as the recruitment of young women of childbearing age and the course of careers.

For the time being, though disputes over anti-union discrimination have developed in France since 2000, it has not yet developed **significantly** in the area of discrimination linked to maternity. This is the case despite changes in the law of proof because of application of the Community directive on proof of discrimination.

However, it should be noted that a significant number of companies are seeking to implement policies to reconcile working life and family life by introducing aid measures, often via collective agreements or benefits introduced by the works council in respect of social and cultural works. Examples of this are child-minding assistance, child-minding assistance in the event of illness, organising home help services accessed through the company, holidays for the children, etc. However, there is no special incentive to allow these contractual policies to develop more widely.

3.2.4. Teleworking, new technologies and their impact on family life

Technology has invaded the world of work and is posing a number of problems in France and other European countries. The employer's obligations to adapt means that job security is not threatened solely by issues concerning technological changes (cf. Above).

However, the adaptation of employees' individual and collective rights is in question.[126] The use of technology is directly linked to the issue of boundaries between working life and personal/family life.

The issues most clearly raised are:

- **Working time**. How do we define the time that employees spend linked to their company by mobile telephone or some other form of technology? Working time? Rest time? This is a grey area, and a clear answer from the ECJ would be helpful. Currently, on-call time is not defined as working time except when the employee is required to intervene in some direct way, and is counted as rest time, which is highly questionable in view of the health protection objectives in the directive of 23 November 1993, relating to the reform of working time.

- What is the **legal definition of time spent on work** by managers, during free time and in particular at weekends, due to work overload? Intrusion into family life is made much easier when people work with mobile telephones.[127]

---

126   J.E. Ray, 'Le droit du travail à l'épreuve du télétravail. Une nécessaire adaptation', *Droit social April 1996*, p. 351, Special issue of Droit du Travail op. cit.
127   F. Favennec-Hery, 'Temps de travail des cadres, temps de travail de demain?', *Droit vivant*, publ. by Liaisons, 2003.

- **Teleworking** is not growing at the expected rate and is still subject to the same rules as working at home. Specific problems arise, however, in organising collective rights for 'itinerant' employees. The Labour Code may need to be adapted on this issue.[128]

- Similarly, the relocation of work via **teleworking abroad** poses the problem of the rules that apply to this type of working relationship and of compliance with the fundamental rights of employees working abroad for a company situated in the European Union.

- Lastly, the use of the **Internet** by employees raises some delicate issues. In its Nikkon ruling (2 October 200)[129] the Court of Cassation gave its verdict on the principle of the protection of e-mails sent personally to an employee in respect of the protection of correspondence and private life. As the overall question of the delimitation of the employer's use of the Internet and Intranet has not been settled by law or case law, it is the subject of a great deal of consultation and negotiation in companies. A great number of charters and collective agreements have been drawn up recently, though there have been no clear statements regarding their legality. There could be a considerable amount of litigation on this issue in the future.

4. Community restructuring and its impact on employment

Employee rights during restructuring are mainly dealt with by national law relating to redundancies for economic reasons. The national law is supported by the 1975 Community directive relating to the same subject, which was modified in 1992.

As a result of moves towards mergers linked to the globalisation of the economy, company restructuring often takes place on a European and even worldwide scale.

The question of Community law's grasp of restructuring and employee rights issues has been raised at three levels during the period 1992-2002: the control of mergers by the Commission (section 4.1), the collective rights of employees during the Renault affair (section 4.2) and compliance with the 1977 directive relating to the transfer of undertakings (section 4.3).

4.1. Employee rights and controls on mergers

Since 1995, the French unions have taken legal action to try to have the rights of employee representatives recognised during merger operations. The ECJ has held that the merger regulation did not allow for any specific action on the part of the unions and that workers' rights were covered by Community law in the framework of the transfer of undertakings.

Despite the ECJ's clear position, action was repeatedly taken at the European Commission over major merger schemes, particularly Total/Fina/Elf and Schneider/Legrand in recent years.

The unions have asked to be allowed to automatically represent the views of third parties in the merger authorisation proceedings.[130]

These actions have not led to changes in the texts, and the unions represented in companies involved in restructuring are still not considered to be specifically involved due to the competition concepts.

However, the Commission has agreed to hear the unions informally as part of the authorisation procedure.

Since 2001, the question has arisen as to whether employee representatives could be considered as company representatives or parties directly involved in community employment policies. The French unions are particularly active on this issue.

However, in the area of employment, it should be noted that, in 2002, Community law had not yet transversely implemented the requirements of employment protection.

4.2. Restructuring and the Renault affair

In 1997, the Renault affair became a major turning point. For the first time a case focussed on the right to information 'in productive time' of Renault's European works council, which was not informed before the announcement of the closure at Vilvoorde.

The ruling of the Paris Court of Appeal on 7 May 1997[131] established the following:

1. The principles for interpreting Community law and in particular that of *effet utile* of the directives should apply

---

128   J.E. Ray, op. cit.

129   G. Lyon-Caen, A. Mole, 'Débat autour de l'arrêt Nikkon France', 15, SSL /10/01, p. 8, A. Mole, 'Mails personnels et responsabilités, quelles frontières?', *Droit social 2002*, p. 84.

130   Regular columns in *Liaisons Sociales Europe*.

131   M.A. Moreau, 'A propos de l'Affaire Renault', *Droit social 1997*, p. 493, obs. A. Lyon-Caen, p. 509.

to the interpretation of an agreement relating to the European works council.

2.   The principles for interpreting Community law and in particular that of *effet utile* of the directives should apply to the interpretation of an agreement relating to the European works council.

3.   Renault management should suspend its procedure since the procedure has not been carried out properly. The Renault affair was also a significant turning point with regard to union coordination in the face of Community-wide restructuring plans.

After 1997, agreements establishing European works councils became much more precise with regard to the rights of the works councils.

4.3.   Individual employee rights in cases of Community-wide restructuring

Community law has incorporated employee rights in the case of transfers of undertakings, but there are no specific provisions for cross-border restructuring.

To the extent that all countries have transposed the directives, differences between the laws that apply tend to bear only on non-standard issues.

There are two particularly difficult issues to deal with in the area of employment protection where restructuring takes place in several countries; contract modifications imposed on the employee during the transfer, which are dealt with by national law in each place of work; and the employee's right to refuse the transfer, an issue that had still not been settled in 2002.

It should also be noted that, though French case law has taken up the legal definitions set out by the ECJ and the directive of 12 March 2001, its interpretation is not in the spirit of Community case law, which is that of protecting the jobs of employees who are the subject of outsourcing. In its case law, the Court of Cassation emphasises that the application of the directive raises new issues concerning employment protection and job security.

These various questions, which are highlighted by French labour law, show the urgent need for Community law to carry out a full examination of Community-wide restructuring so that every aspect relating directly or indirectly to employment can be dealt with consistently.

With regard to job security, the period between 1992 and 2003 was therefore marked by the search for a legal balance to limit the effects of the economic crisis. This balance was found through continuous, controversial adaptation of the procedures surrounding the employer's management powers.

The social policy put forward by the judiciary is remarkable in this respect, as it demonstrates the determination of institutions, at all levels (above and beyond political differences) to contribute to the development of society by supporting the fight against unemployment and preserving jobs, while at the same time accepting that companies must be given greater flexibility – an impossible balancing act, as changes in labour law show.

Chapter IV:
Equal opportunities and the protection of individual rights

The period between 1992 and 2003 saw fundamental rights taking a much greater place in labour law. This was caused by the Court of Cassation's use of international norms (ECHR), reference to fundamental principles recognised in Community law (equal treatment in particular), and the use, from 1999, of Article L 120-2, which extended legal control to compliance with individual rights and individual and collective freedoms in labour relations. French law was greatly influenced by Community law in the fight against discrimination.

However, it should be noted that the chosen approach was a functional one, as the Court of Cassation did not protect the fundamental rights of employees in labour relations in absolute terms. This approach was relative as the legitimate interests of the company may justify restrictions of these fundamental rights. But the restrictions must also be proportional.

French law thus developed a new approach to the principle of balance, which allowed the judge to be the arbitrator of the interests present in each case.

Within this overall protection, there were highly significant developments in the field of equal treatment and non-discrimination, and also regarding the individual rights of the worker.

However, though approaches relating to professional equality between men and women (section 4.1) and discrimination (section 4.2) were reinforced, provisions concerning equal opportunities were only indirect and were put forward in priority programmes rather than in specific legal rules (section 4.3).

On the other hand, there was an increased will to protect the individual worker, particularly against violations that may occur as a result of new technologies (section 4.4).

1. Professional equality between male and female workers

The general legal framework relating to professional equality in France dates back to 1983 (Roudy Act). As has been pointed out, the major problem during the reference period has been linked to regulations surrounding night-time work for women. Between 1991 and 2001, the legislator remained silent on provisions relating to equality in order to avoid reforming the provisions relating to night work.

The Act of 9 May 2001 intervened to improve the mechanism by extending the rules relating to equal treatment and non-discrimination for job applicants, and opening up possibilities for union action on the issue. The Act of 9 May 2001 also introduced identical status for men and women as far as night-time work was concerned.

In addition, equality between male and female workers became subject to compulsory negotiation. The same Act instituted compulsory negotiation at branch level every three years (Article L 132-12). Negotiation must focus on catch-up measures to try to compensate for professional inequalities in the branch. Negotiation should also include examination of a report highlighting the differences in the situations of the two sexes.

Similarly, compulsory negotiation relating to salaries and qualifications should include the question of equality. Since 2001, as part of compulsory annual negotiation at company level, the employer must also negotiate equality objectives and measures to be taken to achieve them. Negotiation is also based on a comparative report (Article L 132-27).

On the expiry of a 12-month period, the unions may demand that negotiations be opened. Annual negotiation of salaries, effective working hours and working time, especially part-time work should also include the equality aspect. The legislator's intervention in 2001 aimed to force unions and employers to grasp the issue of professional equality.

The period 1992-2001 was marked by a lack of enthusiasm amongst unions and employers to tackle the issue of professional equality in any more than in a theoretical manner. In addition, equality plans that had been introduced in 1983 have not produced any significant results.

It appears that the professional equality issue is not a priority. It was not a priority in negotiations of agreements on the 35-hour week, even though unions and employers made efforts to protect certain forms of more female-orientated work such as part-time and occasional work.

It is very difficult to imagine that the effect of introducing an obligation to negotiate 'catch-up issues' will give any practical boost to the question of professional equality. An obligation to negotiate does not mean an obligation to conclude.

However, French labour law does demand a high degree of clarity on issues relating to working conditions that are differentiated between men and women. All the information given to the works council relating to employment is set out by sex. Compulsory negotiation reports must show up inequalities and figures on non-typical or part-time forms of work are set out by sex. Labour law therefore provides for clear visibility in the area of inequality.

However, if we examine the practical initiatives that have taken place, we can see that the issue is still not a priority for the unions. The legislator assumes that a new boost to professional equality will take place through collective bargaining, which of course depends on the commitment of the unions to the issue.

Hopefully the challenge set in 2001 will bear fruit. But, by the end of 2003, there had been no perceptible moves in that direction, though a major agreement on the fight against discrimination between men and women was concluded at PSA Peugeot Citroën on 4 November 2003.[132]

The French mechanisms appear to be comprehensive: monitoring of parity been men and women; professional equality commission and collective bargaining commission to monitor changes in agreements on equality issues; reports to the works council; and reports to the unions.

And yet, in a period of economic crisis, no major action has been taken, apart from targeted initiatives in favour of certain employees (e.g. The long-term unemployed) to ensure that the consequences of the crisis do not increase professional inequalities.

Social inertia is still strong in France, even though indicators point to a slow move towards reducing inequality in pay and improving the position of women in company and institutional organisation charts (except at management level). Change is still slow and inadequate, but it is nevertheless moving towards a reduction of inequalities.

This social inertia is combined with the ambiguity that exists in certain areas that have been catalogued in other countries as sources of indirect discrimination:

- Ambiguity concerning women returning home to bring up their children, good for the birth rate but harmful to career development. It is more or less encouraged depending on whether the government is right- or left-wing. An illustration of this during the period is the fluctuation in the portion of tax that can be deducted for looking after children.

- Ambiguity concerning part-time work, which is seen as being either a form of work that the individual has to put up with or as one that he/she can choose. The result is a complex set of provisions in the law governing the 35-hour week, but against a background of equal treatment.

- Ambiguity concerning the general opinion about women's access to higher positions, which is not followed up by practical action or appointments, against a general background of fierce opposition to measures for positive action.

At the other end of the scale, a strong line has been taken in the fight against discrimination.

2. Reinforcing the struggle against discrimination and the various forms of harassment

Since 1990, French law has continually reinforced its mechanisms for fighting discrimination. First of all, it extended the causes of discrimination (Article L 122-45 of the Labour Code). Next it made far-reaching changes to methods for proving discrimination. Since 1999, practical changes in the area of proof are, without doubt, the result of Community influence.

Between 1992 and 1999, Community law was not a welcome guest. The French legislator refused to acknowledge the notion of indirect discrimination, and judges hesitated to ask for preliminary rulings (the first in 1995).

With regard to progress in labour law on harassment, French law showed itself to be in advance of the rest of Europe, as the law on sexual harassment was passed on 2 November 1992 (Article L 122-46 of the Labour Code). It punished sexual harassment as abuse of authority.[133]

---

132   *Liaisons sociales* no. 14013, 18/11/03.

133   M.A. Moreau, 'A propos de l'abus d'autorité en matière de harcèlement sexuel', *Droit social 1993*, p.116, A.L. Martin-Serf, 'Harcèlement sexuel: huit années d'application des Articles L 122-26 à L 122-48 du code du travail', *Droit social 2001*, p. 610.

French law reinforced its mechanisms for fighting discrimination. This was done by an anticipated application of the rules relating to proof of discrimination from 2000, reinforcing provisions through the Act of 16 November 2001 and adopting a significant law on moral harassment in the social modernisation Act of January 2002.

Commencing with a set of rulings given in 2000, the Court of Cassation decided that victims of anti-union discrimination should provide proof of differences in treatment, then it was up to the employer to prove that this difference in treatment was justified and unconnected with union activity. A highly significant dispute arose in 2001 and 2002 in the area of anti-union discrimination, which showed the determination of the Court of Cassation to apply the rule of proof introduced by Community law in respect of discrimination to all forms of discrimination.

The Act of 16 November 2001 transposed the two directives of 29 June 2000 and 27 November 2000 to French law.[134]

The domain of protection was extended to job applicants, trainees and individuals in vocational training. The causes of discrimination are more numerous than those found in Community law, as they are aimed at origin, sex, customs, genetic features, real or assumed belonging to an ethnic group, nation or race, political opinions, union activities, religious beliefs, physical appearance, belonging to a family, health or handicap.

The unions can take action based on Article L 122-45 without needing to show a written mandate (just like the anti-discrimination associations can) unless the employee objects. The rules of proof have been reversed in line with the model imposed by Community law, witnesses are protected and the sanction is still nullity. Over this three-year period, case law has also reinforced compensatory sanctions whenever the victim does not wish to be reintegrated.

With the Act of 17 January 2002, the legislator acquired a law to protect employees who are the victims of moral harassment.[135] The Act also revised the law on sexual harassment, which was no longer looked at from the point of view of abuse of authority but as an offence in itself ('acts of harassment by any person, the aim of which are to obtain favours of a sexual nature for that person or for a third party' L 122-46). French law thus acquired a significant mechanism for fighting all forms of harassment, based on the fact that the victim simply needs to report proof of matching, relevant evidence. With regard to moral harassment, it is the defendant's task to provide justification for repeated acts of harassment that violate the employee's dignity or damage his/her health.

The Constitutional Council introduced an interpretative reserve creating an obligation on the judge to verify the material evidence of harassment.

As in 1992 for sexual harassment, the provisions of the Social Modernisation Act relating to moral harassment[136] created considerable turbulence in legal circles (some criticised the new method of proof as being anti-democratic…) and amongst employers. There was a fear of resort to legal action for all kinds of actions and gestures that was based on the 'American example'.

It may be said that, as for sexual harassment, moral harassment litigation was confined to flagrant situations of abuse. However, there is no doubt that the move towards an effective fight against discrimination was made thanks to the efforts of all the parties involved (legislator, judges, unions and associations). The progress is mainly the result of the legal construction work carried out by Community law since 1975.

3. Equal treatment and equal opportunities

With the Ponsolle ruling by the Court of Cassation in 1996, an equally important turning-point was reached in the move to extend the principle of equal treatment to all employees.

It was accepted, long before agreements were concluded by European unions and employers, that the principle of equal treatment should apply to temporary and part-time workers. This was extended to all workers who should receive equal pay for an equal job.

The Court of Cassation therefore required that differences in statutory treatment should be justified objectively and

---

134 M. Keller, 'La loi du 16 novembre 2001 relative à la lutte contre les discriminations', D.2002, 1355.

135 S.Licari, 'De la nécessité d'une législation spécifique au harcèlement moral', *Droit social 2000*, p. 492, B. Laperou-Schneider, 'Les mesures de lutte contre le harcèlement moral', *Droit social 2002*, p. 313, A. Mazeaud, 'Harcèlement ente salariés: apport de la loi de modernisation sociale', *Droit social 2002*, p. 321.

136 See special issue of *Droit du Travail*, March 2002, cit.

should have no link with any form of discrimination.[137] However, it accepted that, because different unions negotiated agreements, the application of establishment agreements could lead to differences in treatment within the same company. It refused to allow the principle of equal treatment to limit that of the collective bargaining.

There was a clear movement towards making the law more objective. This became part of a significant move on the part of labour law to limit the scope of arbitrary decisions.

It is therefore of interest to note that – while French law was being considerably reinforced in the area of discrimination and the promotion of equal treatment between employees – equal opportunities did not have full legal cover, only a few isolated measures. The legislator encouraged non-typical employees to return to the permanent employment contract, and part-time workers to return to full-time work; it gave employment priorities to the disabled and re-employment priority after redundancy. With regard to equality between men and women, it encouraged the negotiation of catch-up measures.[138]

Unions and employers were given the task of producing specific measures to improve the equal opportunities situation as part of their branch or company negotiations, whether these were compulsory or not, annual or running over several years.

No legal mechanism was introduced for affirmative action. In a number of employer and doctrinal circles there is strong opposition to the technique of quotas.

Using financial incentives to guide employers in their decisions is a preferred option. For example, between 1990 and 2000, there was a significant increase in part-time work in France (from 8% to 18%), not because companies wanted to encourage their employees to choose part-time work, but because part-time work was exempt from social security charges.

The same technique could be used to encourage equal opportunities, but it would come up against the principle of formal equality.

The principle of formal equality was well entrenched in French law. Only a change emanating from Community law could lead to progress in France on the principle of equal opportunities.

Above and beyond these principles of non-discrimination and equal treatment, French law has developed a series of measures that contribute to the protection of the individual.

4. The protection of the individual

Since 1992, French law has moved clearly towards reinforcing the protection of the individual. In 1982 the legislator intervened to protect the citizen, and between 1992 and 2002, it intervened tentatively and in limited ways to protect the individual, and in particular his dignity and individuality.

- **The protection of dignity.** In addition to the Act of 2002 relating to moral harassment, a right of warning was offered to employee representatives when they came across situations that violated individual rights, or individual and collective freedoms. The employer had to carry out an enquiry and take all steps to stop these violations. In the event of a dispute, the employee representative could refer the matter to the emergency judge for an interim ruling. This procedure is still not often used, but it has the advantage of protecting the worker via both the company representative and rapid legal support.

  Since the Act of 31 December 1992, major steps have also been taken to protect individual workers against technological innovations used by employers.[139] The employer is obliged to inform employee representatives and the employees themselves of any technological equipment that may infringe their freedom: cameras, computer surveillance, use of files, etc. This obligation is combined with the obligation to declare all computer systems used to CNIL (Commission Nationale Informatique and Liberté [National Data Protection Committee]) since the Act of 6 January 1978.[140] CNIL's control aims to protect individual rights and freedoms, including those of workers. It is proving to be very effective.

  Since 1991 the Court of Cassation has refused to accept any proof against employees when it has been acquired through the use of a form of technology about which employees have not been informed (e.g. hidden camera). Employees must be warned that they are under surveillance.

---

137   M.A. Moreau, 'Les justifications des discriminations', loc. cit.

138   A. Jeammaud, J. Pelissier, A. Supiot, op. cit. no. 103 et seq.

139   See special issue of *Droit social*, 'Droit du travail et nouvelles technologies de l'information et de la communication', January 2002.

140   J. Frayssinet, 'Nouvelles technologies et protection des libertés dans l'entreprise', *Droit social 1992*, p. 596, A. Mole, 'Au-delà de la loi informatique et libertés', p. 603, P.H. Antomattei, 'NTIC et vie personnelle', *Droit social 2002*, p. 37 et seq. (special issue, 'Nouvelles technologies et droit du travail'), and on all recent aspects, J.E. Ray.

- **The protection of individuality:** again, this is the Act of 6 January 1978, known as the 'Loi Informatique et Libertés' [Data Protection Act] which provided for the protection of workers' personal data, as the employer must make a prior declaration to CNIL concerning all computer files containing information about named individuals. The employee must be informed of the content of the information in the employer's files.

  Progress was also reached when the directive of 24 October 1995 was transposed into French law.[141] It was submitted to Parliament during 2002 (though the deadline for transposition was 1998). CNIL's powers are to be reinforced for the future.

In conclusion, this eleven-year period between 1992 and 2003 has been marked by unemployment and economic difficulties that led the legislator and the judges to introduce procedures that were constantly in need of overhaul.

The balance was found in the acceptance of new forms of flexibility for companies, which was counterbalanced by the reinforcement of the fundamental rights of workers and a strict approach to compliance with procedures that protected employees' jobs.

Finally, we have seen that, over these last eleven years, the impact of Community law has become increasingly significant (even though there is still some reluctance to embrace it in France). This impact concerns areas that have been subject to restrictive norms and which have given rise to firm case law on the part of the Court of Justice.

However, there does not appear to be any change in the way labour law is created. The approach is still a national one, based on purely French considerations. The groups involved find it very difficult to incorporate the European dimension as an obvious dimension that that has risen out of the impact on the labour market of changes in the structure of Europe.

---

141   S. Simitis, 'Quatre hypothèses et quatre dilemmes, à propos de l'état actuel de la protection des données personnelles des salariés', *Droit social 2002*, p. 88.

Annexes

1. List of the main Acts quoted in chronological order

- Act of 31 December 1991: transposal of framework directive 89/391 (Articles L 230-1 and following)

- Act of 2 November 1992 relating to sexual harassment (Article L 122-48 CT)

- Act of 31 December 1992 relating to public freedoms (Article L 120-2 CT)

- Act of 27 January 1993 relating to restructuring plans

- Five-year Act of 20 December 1993 relating to employment

- Act of 5 July 1996 modifying parental leave (Article L 122-28-1 CT)

- Act of 6 May 1996 relating to working hours

- Act of 12 November 1996 relating to employee representation (including the European works council)

- Act of 13 June 1998 relating to the reduction of working time, known as the 'Loi Aubry I'

- Act of 19 January 2000 known as the 'Loi Aubry II' relating to the reduction of working time (RTT)

- Act of 9 May 2001 relating to professional equality (including the law relating to night-time work for women)

- Act of 17 July 2001 relating to the integration of unemployed people, instituting the PARE (return-to-work assistance plan)

- Act of 16 November 2001 relating to discrimination

- Act of 17 January 2002 known as the social modernisation act

- Act of 3 January 2003 known as the 'Loi Fillon', relating to redundancy

- Act of 17 January 2003 relating to the reform of working time (RTT)

- Act of 23 August 2003 relating to retirement

- The Act of 6 January 2004 relating to collective bargaining was passed on its first reading

2. Summary

The period between 1992 and 2003 saw a great deal of change in labour law. Regular changes in political power led to frequent changes in the law on sensitive issues such as redundancy and reduced working time.

The economic crisis and high unemployment figures led to efforts by all the parties involved to tackle the issue of defending jobs and fighting unemployment.

Over this eleven-year period, judges had a central role in developing labour law. This was partly because the judges reinforced the control of constitutionality and the fundamental rights of workers in companies, and partly because the judges introduced a genuine social policy via a consistent creation of jurisprudence, guided by a concern for safeguarding jobs and fighting unemployment.

The result has been a certain legal uncertainty (which employers have strongly opposed) due to changes to labour law on issues which have the most important market interaction. Legislators and social partners had to resort to 'experimental' techniques demonstrating the difficulty that exists between reconciling the need to adapt labour law to economic developments, and the essential need for legal security.

A number of guiding principles can be seen with regard to the sources of labour law. There is a clear reinforcement of the protection of fundamental rights, along with a preference for flexibility mechanisms that favour the management of the company with regard to both individual labour relations within the framework of the employment contract and to collective relations. Where flexibility is imposed by the employer, it is procedurally defined and controlled if it removes benefits or results in a move towards a form of insecure contract. When it is negotiated, it gives rise to a derogatory type of negotiation that is strictly controlled from a procedural point of view so that the majority union organisations have the right to object.

There has been a movement towards diversification of forms of labour, a preference for the flexible management of the employment contract, and a strong movement by companies towards outsourcing to encourage management flexibility.

This movement has tended to increase insecurity and lead to the development of new forms of poverty that have mainly affected women. However, the move towards greater flexibility and job insecurity has been accompanied by measures aimed at making the works council responsible for monitoring the employment policy chosen by the employer.

The need to rethink collective bargaining has arisen in a context where both the number and quality of the negotiation partners involved (these are no longer only unions) have increased. There has also been an effort to give greater legitimacy to the unions.

During this eleven-year period, the unions had to introduce, in the context of derogatory agreements and the revision of collective agreements, strategies based on the possibility of exercising a right of objection for the unions who were in the majority at the last elections.

This majority-based principle was also applied during the implementation of agreements relating to the reduction of working hours. A profound change took place, affecting all the parties involved and the conditions of negotiating legitimacy, while at the same time company negotiation increased. These changes led to a major reform of collective bargaining in 2004, causing this form of negotiation to be considerably decentralised and giving greater autonomy to company negotiation in important areas of labour relations.

Labour law increasingly included mechanisms aimed at increasing employee flexibility both through the individual employment contract (adaptation and redeployment obligations) and through a number of complex mechanisms organ-ised within the context of continued vocational training and unemployment. A strong movement towards individualising the legal instruments covering the flexibility and reintegration of the unemployed can be seen.

In 2003, a right to lifelong training was introduced as part of a major national interprofessional agreement.

The balances leading to a position of relative job security are created by a strict procedural supervision of the powers of the employer: checks on the use of short-term contracts; strict controls over the redundancy procedure, and the reinforcement of sanctions against employers not complying with the requirements of the restructuring plan.

Over this eleven-year period, the Court of Cassation has rigorously developed these requirements qualitatively, which has greatly upset employers due to the legal uncertainty created by the evolving nature of the rules imposed on them with regard to jobs, especially as part of the plan to safeguard employment. It is very clear that, throughout this period, there has been a strong demand on employers to try to reduce the dimension of their restructuring plans. This demand has been translated into strict controls on the redundancy procedure imposed by judges. Despite the severity of sanctions introduced since 1997 (restructuring plan rendered null and void), this demand will not stop huge numbers of jobs from being lost and will make the restructuring issue highly controversial.

A response to unemployment was given by the reforms of working time, known as 'RTT' or 'the 35-hour week', in 1998 and 2000. These reforms forced companies to negotiate, allowed them to introduce new forms of flexibility and made them adapt to market demands within a negotiated framework. In 2003, the development of RTT in small companies was stopped. The results of RTT are highly controversial and contrasting.

Lastly, concerning equal treatment, French labour law effectively reinforced all its mechanisms: extension of the principle of equality of treatment, reinforcement of the fight against discrimination and all forms of harassment (sexual and moral). The French legislator has however not introduced an equal opportunities policy.

The introduction of an equal opportunities policy comes up against the barriers of formal equality and clear political and social inertia.

It can be concluded that, over this eleven-year period, the influence of Community law increased in terms of both legislation and jurisprudence. There has been a great deal of learning about techniques, reasoning and procedures in every sphere of drawing up and applying labour law. There is however still some reluctance about applying social directives.

The approach to labour law is still a national one. In France, there is still no thought of developing labour law rules on a European scale, though it should be noted that the European Employment Strategy (EES) is starting to have an effect. The EES has forced the government to introduce permanent consultation with unions and employers over employment (but without tripartite negotiation), the guidelines are taken into consideration when reforms are envisaged (reform of the labour market envisaged in 2004, extension of working life in 2003), and exchanges of 'best practices' are opening up to new ideas about ways to fight unemployment.

It appears that France is slowly opening up towards Europe, as can be seen by the analysis and taking into consideration of employment policies followed by other European countries.

However, the significant advances made in France as a result of Community influence have been brought about by 'hard law'. Certain domains have only changed in France due to the creativity of Community social law (equal treatment between men and women, burden of proof in cases of discrimination, European works council and health policy).

It is also very difficult to analyse the extent of existing convergences with other countries in the European Union.

It appears that these convergences can be seen when they are the result of both the market (pressure linked to competitiveness) **and** government decisions. This is the case with: the general move to find new forms of flexibility in contracts; the move to decentralise collective bargaining; the diversification of initiatives to help the unemployed; and the individual treatment of the latter. Similarly, it seems that the move to reinforce fundamental rights is a response to the insecurity generated by the market and the globalisation of the economy.

But if we look carefully at the techniques chosen, we can see the limitations of this approach in terms of convergence. For example, the very notion of flexibility expresses itself very differently because of the counter-balances that are organised and introduced.

At the heart of its paradoxical changes, labour law in France shows clearly that the balance between job security and flexibility is the outcome of forms of arbitration that are constantly being questioned, linked to the rules and techniques chosen.

It is important to emphasise that social directives have acted as a base to allay fears of deregulation when political changes led to reforms in the areas of redundancy and working time.

THE EVOLUTION OF LABOUR LAW IN IRELAND

1992-2002

PART ONE

Professor Alan C. Neal
(Employment Law Research Unit, University of Warwick, United Kingdom)
Main Report Completed: May 2003
Annex Completed: February 2004

PART TWO

Anthony Kerr
Faculty of Law – University College
Belfield – Dublin 4

Table of contents

PART ONE

Executive summary

This report traces the development of labour law in Ireland during the period 1992-2002 (with an Annex note on further developments during 2003). It draws upon a wide range of material and includes statistical data derived from both official and non-governmental sources. The framework for presentation reflects agreement in the Group of Experts upon key themes and issues.

CHAPTER I sets out the historical background to the development of labour law in Ireland, leading to the emergence of a uniquely Irish framework of regulation. After identifying an important period of legislation between 1941 and 1976, dealing with detailed regulation for the conduct of trade unions and industrial relations, modern developments since dramatic fundamental reform in 1990 are presented.

The institutional framework is outlined, with a preference for 'non-juridical' conflict resolution in relation to the largely voluntary system of Irish collective labour relations, while regulation of other matters, such as minimum notice, dismissal, holidays, redundancy payments and employment equality is provided for in legislation. A particular focus upon mediation and conciliation in employment dispute matters (including in relation to discrimination issues) is identified.

Some areas of concern are indicated, including a growing trend towards litigation over employment matters, a narrowing of the scope for 'industrial relations' in the face of increasing 'hard law' measures (many of which involve implementation into domestic labour law of provisions adopted at the European level). However, the trends since 1992 are identified as having been remarkably consistent, until sudden setbacks to the Irish economy following the turn of the millennium. That turnaround has stimulated a substantial move for reform of the institutions and the substantive content of Ireland's labour law. The system has thus been responding in most recent years to a number of pressures, with a keen questioning of the sustainability of the 'Irish model' for conciliation and dispute resolution through the institutions settled in 1990.

The dramatically fluctuating economic performance between 1987 and 1998 is outlined, by way of a context for

a note on 'partnership' the Irish way. This model of social partnership has been associated with particular problems, identified in 1997 as including (i) the limits of 'consensus'; (ii) the limited terms of inclusion; (iii) the difficulty of linking national representation to local action; (iv) a limited effectiveness in achieving real change; (v) problems of monitoring; and (vi) the relationship between social partnership and representative democracy.

After a survey of the main elements of the Irish labour market, a description is offered of collective bargaining arrangements and the levels at which this takes place. This is followed by a comment on Irish regulatory techniques, in the course of which it is observed that, since 1990, an important shift of emphasis has occurred towards a statutory framework for industrial relationships – notwithstanding the significant scope still provided for voluntary activity. The section is completed with an outline of the current Irish mechanisms for dispute resolution and the enforcement of labour law rights.

CHAPTER II, which looks at the interaction of Irish measures providing for job security and the modern trend towards 'employability', sets recent developments in the context of the European Union's Employment Strategy after 1997.

The issue of workforce skills is considered in a number of contexts. Mention is made of the consistently high historical levels of Irish youth unemployment, and in the context of low pay, a new measure to introduce a national minimum wage in 2000 is reported. The problem of poverty is seen as one of the more significant issues in relation to social exclusion, while a number of underlying social problems are seen to have been taken into the Irish social policy framework through the route of 'equal opportunities'. A specific mention is made of problems touching ethnic diversity (including the peculiarly Irish issue of the traveller community) and concerning disability. This section then ends with consideration of some of the measures taken by the Irish government to assist employability – drawing upon material prepared in the context of the most recent Irish National Action Plan.

CHAPTER III reports on various developments of adaptability in the Irish situation, and notes dramatic changes in the Irish labour market over the period under consideration. In particular, part time work (recently regulated in legislation from 2001) increased significantly after 1997, while the social partners have introduced various actions to promote 'family-friendly' practices at the level of the firm. At the level of government, it is noted that Ireland has introduced a series of innovative measures in both the tax and social welfare systems to reduce the 'tax wedge' and to ease the transition of unemployed people (particularly the long-term unemployed) back to work.

CHAPTER IV takes up the area of equal opportunities, in relation to which the Irish experience has been at the 'cutting edge' of European developments. The modern framework in this field – introduced through legislation in 1998 and 2000 – replaced older, more fragmented, protections, and with its nine 'prohibited grounds' of discrimination, the Irish model is commonly held up as an example of 'best practice' in relation to such issues. In order to set the Irish experience in context, detailed material is presented in respect of the demographic features of national origin and gender.

CHAPTER V offers a concluding comment on developments in Ireland since 1992. It is acknowledged that the 'Irish model' of partnership has been widely acclaimed as having underpinned a remarkable transformation of the country's economic fortunes and stability over a period of fifteen years, and that, at the same time, a groundbreaking framework for addressing issues of discrimination and equal opportunities has been established. However, by the turn of the millennium, the 'storm clouds' had gathered over the Irish economy, and a variety of underlying structural problems had become increasingly apparent. The views of various commentators are presented in relation to where the root of the problems might lay, while a number of negative phenomena – an increase in inequality, the more widespread incidence of low-paid employment, and a lack of state support for childcare – are highlighted.

A relative breakdown in the closeness of the 'social partnership' after 2000 is noted, with growing 'conflictualism' between the social partners. At the same time, doubts are voiced as to whether new legal mechanisms for delivering trade union recognition and ensuring a minimum wage floor can contribute to continued industrial harmony.

The trend towards increasing normative intervention by the legislator (in common with much of Europe), with an ever-increasing reliance upon the mechanism of 'hard law' statutory regulation, is identified as a factor undermining the traditional Irish 'abstentionist' approach. So, too, does the growing stream of social policy measures adopted to implement European Union directives serve to diminish the national sensitivity of the regulatory framework for labour law.

Nevertheless, Ireland has introduced reforms for its underlying 'floor of rights' – especially in relation to dismissal protection – although concern for some of the newer areas of regulatory policy, such as data protection and privacy regulation in relation to employment, has only recently begun to develop.

The areas of equal opportunities and anti-discrimination are identified as having received a significant boost through the measures adopted in 1998 and 2000. By contrast, the continued problem of divided jurisdiction between a wide range of regulatory and enforcement bodies has been identified as a significant weakness in the Irish structures dealing with labour law issues.

The report concludes by linking labour law development in Ireland with the changes in economic fortunes at the national level. It is observed that the underlying economic and labour market position is likely to dictate the continuing direction and pace of developments in Irish labour law. Consequently, it is suggested that, if labour law in Ireland is to be anything more than a 'side-show', the remarkable post-1999 economic decline has to be arrested, the structural shortcomings in the Irish labour market and its administration have rapidly to be addressed, and a new 'Irish model' has to be developed out of the phoenix of the 'miracle' of the 1990s.

Chapter 1:
Introduction

1. Historical background

The historical background to the development of labour law in Ireland is rooted in the British governance experienced before independence, together with what has now become a uniquely Irish framework of regulation. Unlike the British situation, however, Ireland is founded on formal constitutional rights, and the Irish Constitution guarantees the right of citizens to form associations and unions, while also allowing the State to enact legislation for the regulation and control of this right in the public interest.

In the early phase, which saw statutory intervention established, Irish labour law very much reflected the equivalent United Kingdom provisions – with legislation from 1871 onwards, giving rise to a variety of provisions familiar to all British commentators. Thereafter, the framework was established (particularly with the highly influential Trade Disputes Act 1906) for trade union legislation over the following three-quarters of a century. Thus, legislation gives immunity from civil legal proceedings to acts legally done in contemplation of furtherance of a trade dispute. However, nowadays, this immunity is confined to trade unions holding negotiation licences from the Minister for Enterprise, Trade and Employment.[1]

Historically, although there was an important period of legislation between 1941 and 1976 dealing with detailed regulation for the conduct of trade unions and industrial relations, it was not until the beginning of the modern period – ushered in by fundamental reforms in 1990 – that the current framework for Irish industrial relations and labour law was eventually completed.

The 1990 reforms were dramatic, with an Industrial Relations Act 1990 standing at the centre of the modern structure. This Act deals with a variety of collective labour matters, including procedures for industrial action, picketing, and rules of procedure in relation to the obtaining of injunctions, etc. It also includes provisions for the establishment of negotiating arrangements, through a form of registration with the Irish Ministry for Enterprise and Employment. All of this is set in an institutional context which places prominence on a Labour Court, established in 1946. Its task has primarily been conflict resolution of a 'non-juridical' nature in relation to collective labour relations.

The point is regularly made that, while a variety of basic rights covering such matters as minimum notice, dismissal, holidays, redundancy payments and employment equality are provided for in legislation, the State's involvement in industrial relations is mainly confined to assisting in the prevention and resolution of disputes. This, it is maintained, leaves the labour relations system largely voluntary, with pay and conditions of employment normally being agreed through free collective bargaining between employers and employees.

2. The institutional framework

It is important to recognise that the nature of the institutional framework plays a significant part in the operation of the mechanisms for resolving disputes on various fronts. The institutional pattern which has emerged has, however, given rise to widespread concern about the fragmented manner in which employment-related disputes fall to be dealt with – with particular causes of action being allocated to the jurisdiction of one institution, while other matters which might arise in the course of the same employment relationship may come within a different jurisdiction. This, in great measure, reflects the mixture of 'voluntarism', institutionalised mediation, and traditional legal dispute resolution

---

1   The Minister grants a licence once certain legal conditions are met, the most important of which are the maintenance of a substantial deposit of money in the High Court and a minimum level of membership.

mechanisms which are to be found within the Irish arrangements. The basic pattern in Ireland has developed as follows:

- The principal mediation bodies are the Labour Relations Commission and the Labour Court. Of these, the Labour Relations Commission,[2] which was set up under the Industrial Relations Act 1990, works generally to promote good industrial relations in the Irish economy, with a primary purpose to prevent and resolve disputes. The Labour Court,[3] however, which was established under the Industrial Relations Act 1946, normally investigates disputes only if either (i) it receives a report from the Labour Relations Commission that no further efforts on its part will help resolve the dispute or (ii) the Commission waives its function of conciliation in the dispute.[4]

- For a limited number of industries and trades Joint Labour Committees operate to draw up minimum rates of pay and other conditions of employment. These rates can be made legally binding where they are ratified by the Labour Court in the form of Employment Regulation Orders.[5]

- Meanwhile, the Employment Appeals Tribunal, which is established independently of the Labour Relations Commission and the Labour Court, hears disputes over entitlements under legislation, including dismissal, notice, redundancy payments, payment of wages and maternity entitlements.[6]

- Dealing with the field of anti-discrimination and equal opportunities,[7] the Equality Tribunal – which was established on 18 October 1999 under the Employment Equality Act 1998 – is an independent quasi-judicial statutory body whose core function is to investigate and mediate in relation to complaints of unlawful discrimination which have been referred to it.[8]

Where an Equality Tribunal investigation is carried out, this will be conducted by an Equality Officer, and where discrimination is found to have occurred, redress will be awarded.[9] If both parties consent to mediation, the matter will be referred to an Equality Mediation Officer within the office of the Director of the Equality Tribunal, and the process of mediation will be conducted in private.[10]

Should a mediated agreement be reached, this will be reduced to writing and becomes legally binding upon the parties, with enforcement, in the event of non-compliance, through the Circuit Court. In the event that mediation is attempted but proves unsuccessful, the matter may be re-submitted for an investigation to be undertaken.

2   The Commission comprises equal numbers of employer and trade union representatives as well as independent representatives. Note should also be taken of the office of Rights Commissioner, which was set up under the Industrial Relations Act 1969 and, since 1991, has been operated by the LRC. Rights Commissioners – whose decisions are non-binding – investigate disputes or make recommendations under the Industrial Relations Acts 1969 and 1990, the Unfair Dismissals Act 1977, the Maternity Protection of Employees Act 1981 and the Payment of Wages Act 1991.

3   The Labour Court consists of a chairperson, deputy chairpersons and ordinary members representative of employers and workers. As emerges from its *2002 Annual Report*, the Labour Court experienced a significant increase in activity in 2002, both in terms of referrals received and cases completed. Referrals increased by 6% on 2001 and the number of cases completed by the Court during the year increased by 13%. The increase in the number of referrals under equality legislation was particularly marked – 19% up on the previous year – thereby continuing a trend observed over a number of years (particularly since the coming into operation of the Employment Equality Act 1998). One particularly interesting observation in the Labour Court's *2002 Annual Report* offers a good indication of the tension which arises in relation to involvement of 'the Law' in the field of industrial relations: 'On the industrial relations front, 2002 was a relatively calm year, with fewer days lost to industrial action than in over 30 years. There was, however, an increase (of 5.7%) in referrals to the Court under industrial relations legislation. The Court has voiced its concern in the past that its role as court of last resort be respected in the interests of the orderly conduct of industrial relations generally. Previous annual reports have referred to an unwelcome tendency to view the Court as a staging post rather than the terminus. Unfortunately, the revolving door phenomenon re-emerged in 2002. A small number of cases, having gone through the procedures and been the subject of Court Recommendations, returned to the Labour Relations Commission's conciliation service. The Court has on many occasions expressed concern at the damage being done to the industrial relations procedures by this practice.'

4   Once the Court has investigated a dispute, it usually issues a recommendation giving its opinions on the merits of the dispute and the terms on which it should be settled. Such recommendations are not legally binding, except in certain limited cases. The Court also exercises an appellate function in areas such as working time, part-time and fixed-term working regulation, and equality matters.

5   Another minimum pay enforcement procedure arises when the Court registers an employment agreement. A Registered Employment Agreement is binding on all employers for every worker of the class, type or group to which it is stated to apply. The Court registers voluntary Joint Industrial Councils – negotiating forums within particular industries.

6   This body – which started out in 1967 as the Redundancy Appeals Tribunal – is composed of employer and worker nominees with an independent chairperson and vice-chairperson.

7   Under Irish equality legislation, discrimination is unlawful on the following nine grounds: gender, religion, marital status, age, family status, disability, sexual orientation, race (including colour, nationality or national or ethnic origin) and membership of the 'Traveller community' in relation to employment. The same applies in relation to the disposal of goods and property, the provision of services and accommodation, and in certain aspects of education. It may be noted that the scope of the Equality Tribunal's remit was extended to cover discrimination outside employment under the Equal Status Act 2000, with effect from 25 October 2000.

8   Formally, this is the Office of the Director of Equality Investigations, which has informally renamed itself as 'The Equality Tribunal'. This body replaced the former Equality Service, which had been set up in 1975 as part of the Labour Court, and then transferred to the LRC.

9   The remedies available may be one or more of (i) compensation, (ii) an order for equal pay, (iii) an order for equal treatment and/or (iv) a direction of a specific course of action.

10   For details of the mediation process, and an overview of the first two years of operation, see ODEI – The Equality Tribunal, *Developments in Alternative Dispute Resolution (ADR) – The Equality Tribunal's Mediation Service: 2 Years On* (Dublin 2002).

3. Key issues as at 1992

If one looks at the issues facing Ireland's labour law system in 1992, one may identify the following as having been particularly significant:

1. The maintenance of a coherent regulatory structure under the umbrella of the 1990 reforms, such as to separate clearly the 'industrial relations' approach to regulating labour market matters, and the 'labour law' approach to resolving disputes (particularly those concerning individual employment rights claims) as a 'court of last resort'. This desire also reflected the concentration upon conciliation and non-legalistic approaches to dispute resolution, inherent in the institutional structures developed before 1990, and embedded in the structures established for the new system by the reforms of that year.

2. An increasing number of individual employment rights disputes making their way to the Employment Appeals Tribunal and the Rights Commissioners and a growing number of issues relating to discrimination of various forms within and throughout the Irish labour market. The increasing caseload of complaints to the Employment Appeal Tribunal reflected very much the operation of the rules on unfair dismissal, emanating from the 1977 legislation. The concern with matters of discrimination received a strong impetus in the framework of developing equal opportunities and anti-discrimination measures at the level of the European Union, but also involved a number of particular issues of direct concern to the Irish context (in particular, the treatment of certain groups such as 'travellers', of a very specific Irish nature).

3. A concern that, notwithstanding the broadly successful model of dispute resolution and 'non-legalistic' institutions for regulating both collective and individual labour law, the scope for 'industrial relations' was beginning to narrow in the face of increasing use of 'hard law' techniques in the form of statutory interventions. This was particularly problematic given the increasing volume of measures from the European level requiring implementation into domestic labour law.

4. The recognition, associated with the point before, that EU membership, and loyal adherence to the measures adopted under the Union's social policy arrangements, involved a shift in emphasis to implementation of European-wide norms, as opposed to specific legislation for domestic circumstances (particularly in relation to individual rights).

It should also be noted that Ireland was party to the arrangements agreed at Maastricht in 1992, involving the new route for social policy legislation at EU level through social dialogue and partnership methods.[11]

4. Broad trends from 1992 to 2000

In relation to those key issues, the trends since 1992 were remarkably consistent, until the sudden setbacks to the Irish economy following the turn of the millennium.[12] That pessimistic backdrop has stimulated moves for reform of the institutions and the substantive content of Ireland's labour law, and includes the following pressures:

1. The coherence of the institutions for regulating labour law and industrial relations in Ireland has been severely questioned in recent years, and a strategic review of the Labour Relations Commission has been undertaken. At the same time, the Labour Court has been reflecting upon how it might be modernised to take account of the increasingly limited room for manoeuvre left by labour law for 'traditional industrial relations'.

2. The increase in caseload of individual employment rights complaints to the Employment Appeal Tribunal has continued apace. Indeed, in 2001 the number of complaints rose by a staggering 56% to over 5 000. This mirrors trends in other countries (in particular the United Kingdom) where the dramatic spread in the scope of individual employment protections whose enforcement lies through variants of 'labour courts' has triggered a massive rise in litigation and severe pressure upon the institutions called upon to resolve the disputes involved. A further push in this direction has been evident through the arrangements in place to promote equal opportunities and to deal with matters of discrimination (both work-related and more generally). This is an area where Ireland has been in the vanguard of developments – particularly in relation to the scope of the anti-discrimination measures and to matters such as combating 'harassment'.

---

11 This placed the Irish situation in stark contrast to that prevailing in the United Kingdom, where an 'opt-out' was in operation following the failure of the government to agree to the terms of the proposed new 'Social Chapter' included with the Maastricht revisions to the Treaties.

12 Some caution needs to be exercised in respect of how dramatic the Irish downturn has really been. Although domestic characterisations are (perhaps surprisingly) pessimistic, it remains the case that Irish GDP growth remains amongst the highest of the European Union Member States. What is undoubtedly problematic, though, is the state of Irish competitiveness.

3. As elsewhere, the resort to 'hard law' techniques of delivering domestic employment protection and of implementing EU measures in the form of statutory regulations has highlighted the 'legalistic' path to dispute resolution. The role of labour law has been seen to be squeezing out more traditional forms of industrial relations regulation and dispute resolution, with a consequent shift to judicial procedures and practices. This has given rise, in particular, to a keen questioning of the sustainability of the 'Irish model' for conciliation and dispute resolution through the institutions settled in 1990. At the same time as the government's *Programme for Prosperity and Fairness* has been taken as a framework for developing social partnership on the successful foundations laid in Ireland since 1990, there have been important moves to facilitate 'union recognition' in the face of employer hostility, and a number of other initiatives which bear more than a semblance of similarity to experience 'across the water' in the UK.

In what follows, a picture is drawn of the dramatic changes which have been taking place in the Irish context during the period since Maastricht.

5. The changing face of the Irish labour market

A 1999 study on Ireland, prepared for the ILO in the wake of the Declaration and Programme of Action of the World Summit on Social Development in Copenhagen in 1995, observed that:

The period since 1981 has seen dramatic fluctuations in trends in employment and unemployment. Total employment contracted by about 6% between 1981 and 1985 and unemployment increased from less than 10% in 1981 to a peak of almost 18% in 1987. While impressive growth has been achieved over the 1987-98 period as a whole, the rate of growth was uneven, and three sub-periods are identified.

1. *Recovery, 1987-1990, aided by strong export growth and public sector cutbacks. Total employment increased by 4% over the sub-period and unemployment fell to 13% of the labour force in 1990.*

2. *Sluggish growth, 1991-93, reflecting the downturn in international activity. Employment grew by about 1.5% over three years, and with strong labour force growth, unemployment climbed again to almost 17% in 1993 and*

3. *Very rapid growth, 1993-1998. Since 1993 the Irish economy has expanded very rapidly, with annual rates of growth in excess of 8% averaged over the 1993-1997 period. Total employment grew by 25% between 1993-1998 and unemployment fell to less than 12% in 1997. By 1998 the standardised unemployment rate had fallen to less than 8% – below the EU average. Continued growth is forecast in the medium term.[13]*

In like vein, the Irish Department of Enterprise, Trade and Employment, looking at the period up until 2001 has opined that:

Over the last decade, unprecedented economic growth has seen Ireland's GDP almost double in size. This growth could not have been sustained without a parallel expansion of the workforce arising from inflows from education and rising female participation rates, along with a reversal in the trend of net migration... The latter half of the 1990s saw the most pronounced growth in both economic activity and employment levels, with average annual growth rates of 8.5% and 5% respectively. The rapid expansion in employment enabled many of those who were previously unemployed to find jobs. Between 1993 and 2001 the unemployment rate fell by 12 percentage points, from 15.7% to only 3.7%. There was an even more dramatic reduction in long-term unemployment, with the percentage of the labour force unemployed for more than one year falling from 8.9% in 1993 to only 1.2% in 2001.[14]

This development, however, was not all viewed in a positive light, since:

Unfortunately, the success of the economy created new dilemmas for the labour market. Skill, and subsequently, labour shortages became an important feature of the latter years of the Irish economic boom. These shortages had implications for a number of areas including employers' ability to expand their business, confidence in investment decisions, and more rapid wage growth.[15]

Furthermore, a marked downturn in the buoyant Irish position was noted, in terms that:

13   P. O'Connell, 'Astonishing success: Economic growth and the labour market in Ireland', *ILO Employment and Training Papers 44*, 1999.

14   Department of Enterprise Trade and Employment (FAS), *The Irish Labour Market Review 2002*.

15   Ibid. In relation to wage development, FAS points out that: 'The tightening labour market precipitated rapid growth in earnings levels with non-agricultural real wages rising by an annual average of 5.5% between 1996 and 2000. However, productivity growth increased at an even faster rate over the same period, with average increases of 8.4% per annum. The market services sector witnessed the fastest increase in real wages over the latter half of the decade (7.3% per annum) compared to an annual average increase of 4.8% in the industrial sector. All sectors experienced their most rapid earnings growth in 1999 and 2000, as the labour market tightened considerably.' Nevertheless, the point was made that, 'Irish labour costs have risen vis-à-vis all the larger continental EU countries over the latter half of the decade. Yet despite the considerable wage growth that occurred in the latter part of the 1990s, only Spain had lower labour costs than ourselves come the year 2000', something which, it was maintained, 'should not be surprising, given that Irish labour costs had been extremely competitive in 1996 relative to the rest of the EU'.

The phenomenal rate of growth experienced in the Irish economy in recent years began to subside in the latter half of 2001. While Gross National Product (GNP) in 2001 is still estimated to have increased in real terms by 5.5%, this belies the full extent of the slowdown given that much of last year's growth was propelled by momentum generated in the year 2000 and aided by the persistent weakness of the Euro. That said, the continued increase in the labour supply was an important factor in ensuring economic growth remained well above the EU average of 1.7%… Less favourable economic conditions have led to an inevitable slowdown in the demand for labour and this is reflected in the latest employment data… In the first quarter of 2002 there were a total of 1.75 million people employed in Ireland. Although this was 2.1% higher than a year earlier, it is lower than the growth rate of 3.6% recorded a year previously.

Other commentators have identified this dichotomy between a period of high growth and a number of more worrying consequences developing against that bullish background. In particular, growing wage inequality among workers has been reported,[16] while it has been noted that the share of output going to capital, as opposed to labour, has also risen substantially.[17] Both of these developments have given rise to concern on the part of the Irish government to step up efforts aimed at combating social exclusion through direct intervention in the labour market, including introduction of a national minimum wage; reform of the unemployment benefit system with tighter controls being placed on those receiving benefits in return for greater assistance in obtaining work and restrictions on the working week.[18]

The spread of problems in the Irish context would appear to be continuing, as evidenced by quarterly statistics issued by the Irish Central Statistical Office (CSO). Thus, writing in June 2002, *The Irish Times* commented, in relation to the most recent data from the CSO's *Quarterly National Household Survey*, that:

According to the latest survey, overall employment growth in the economy slowed to just over 2% year-on-year in Q1, from 2.5% in the previous quarter and an annual average of almost 3% for 2001 as a whole. Economy-wide employment growth has been on a more or less uninterrupted decelerating trajectory since the middle of 1999, when it peaked at 7% year-on-year… More

tellingly, private non-agricultural employment in Q1 was just over 1% above its year- earlier level. This marks the continuation of an even steeper deceleration that dates from mid-1999, when it was growing by 7.6% year-on-year… At a sectoral level, the change has been especially marked in the case of construction, where employment was growing at an annual rate of 15% three years ago, and has since slowed to less than 2%. Even more notable is the case of the manufacturing industry where mid single- digit growth in numbers engaged has given way to a contraction: in Q1 industrial employment was down 2.5% from its year-earlier level… Most remarkable of all is the pattern of public sector employment. In the 12-month period to Q1 of this year, public administration, health and education accounted for 21 000 of the 36 000 increase in economy-wide employment that took place. Over this period, public sector employment rose by 6.5%, or six times the rate achieved in the non-farm private sector.[19]

Nevertheless, progress on stabilising the Irish situation within the framework of EU employment policy has been positive, as confirmed in the most recent report prepared within the terms of the Luxembourg Process arrangements:

Employment grew by 2.9% in 2001, with 49 000 jobs created. This represented a decrease on the rate of job creation in the boom years of 1999 (6.3%) and 2000 (4.7%)… The average overall employment rate for 2001 was 65.7%, compared to 65.1% one year earlier and a European average of 63.3%. The target under the Employment Strategy is to achieve an EU employment rate of 67% by 2005 and 70 % by 2010… The female employment rate reached 54.9%, compared to 54.1% in 2000 and an EU average of 54.0%. The EU has set targets of 57% in 2005 and 60% in 2010… Unemployment averaged 3.9% during 2001… Long-term unemployment fell to 1.2% from 1.4% one year earlier.[20]

6. A note on 'partnership' the Irish way

Trade unionism first emerged in the larger cities of the island (Dublin, Belfast and Cork) during the 18th century, despite legislation against combinations of workers.[21] The Irish Congress of Trade Unions (ICTU), established in 1959,

---

16   A. Barrett, T. Callan & B. Nolan, 'The Earnings Distribution and the Returns to Education in Ireland', *ESRI research paper*, 1997.

17   P. Lane, 'Profits and Wages in Ireland, 1987-1996', 1998, *27 Journal of the Statistical and Social Inquiry Society of Ireland 223.*

18   D. O'Neill, *Evaluating Labour Market Interventions*, NUI Maynooth, March 2000.

19   *The Irish Times*, 'Public sector growth slows jobless rise', 14 June 2002.

20   *Ireland's Employment Action Plan 2002.*

21   The first association of trade unions, representing thirty crafts and industries, was formed in 1863 and in 1894 the Irish Trades Union Congress, representing most Irish and British unions in the country, was established.

is now the main co-ordinating body of Irish unions and includes unions in Northern Ireland. At the beginning of 2000 there were 46 trade unions representing some 562 000 workers. About 47% of all employees are union members.[22]

On the other side of the relationship, eleven employers' associations hold negotiating licences. The main representative organisation of the management side of industry and business is the Irish Business and Employers Confederation (IBEC), with a membership of approximately 7 000 companies.[23]

Before proceeding further, however, a word should be said about the nature of 'partnership' – which initially constituted a response to fiscal crisis in 1987, before being extended to wider social policy areas during the 1990s – as this is understood in the Irish context. Thus, in its 1996 report, *Strategy into the 21st Century*, the Irish National Economic and Social Council offered the following characterisation of social partnership, as it had developed in the preceding decade:[24]

(i) The partnership process involves a combination of consultation, negotiation and bargaining; (ii) The partnership process is heavily dependent on a shared understanding of the key mechanisms and relationships in any given policy area; (iii) The government has a unique role in the partnership process. It provides the arena within which the process operates. It shares some of its authority with social partners. In some parts of the wider policy process, it actively supports formation of interest organisations; (iv) The process reflects inter-dependence between the partners. The partnership is necessary because no party can achieve its goals without a significant degree of support from others; (v) Partnership is characterised by a problem-solving approach designed to produce consensus, in which various interest groups address joint problems; (vi) Partnership involves trade-offs both between and within interest groups; (vii) The partnership process involves different participants on various agenda items, ranging from national macro-economic policy to local development.

The broad principles set out there were carried over into the subsequent agreement of 2000. However, at the same time as renewal arrangements were being put into place, a fundamental reconsideration of the strengths and weaknesses of the Irish social partnership arrangements was undertaken by the National Economic and Social Forum, which published its analysis in the 1997 report *A Framework for Partnership – Enriching Strategic Consensus through Participation.*[25] That report identified a number of specific problems, including what it indicated as arising out of (i) the limits of 'consensus'; (ii) the limited terms of inclusion; (iii) the difficulty of linking national representation to local action; (iv) a limited effectiveness in achieving real change; (v) problems of monitoring; and (vi) the relationship between social partnership and representative democracy.

Most recently, discussions over a new agreement to succeed the three-year *Programme for Prosperity and Fairness* of 2000 have taken place in a tense context, in contrast to the previous decade and a half of national partnership accords. Nevertheless, at the end of 2002, the social partners were still continuing these discussions with a view to entering a new agreement in 2003.

7. Key characteristics of the Irish labour market

There has been a significant increase in the Irish labour force since 1997. According to the latest figures from the CSO, out of a total employment figure of 1 749 900 in May 2002, there were 157 000 employees in the health sector, 89 200 in public administration and defence, and 110 000 in education. Total public sector employment at that date was approximately 390 000, leaving a figure of approximately 1 359 900 employed in the private sector.

---

22   The Services, Industrial, Professional and Technical Union (SIPTU), formed in 1990 through the amalgamation of the Irish Transport and General Workers Union and the Federated Workers Union of Ireland, is the largest trade union with 227 000 members. Other large unions are MANDATE – The Union of Retail, Bar and Administrative Workers (38 000 members), Irish Municipal Public and Civil Trade Union (35 000 members), the Technical Engineering and Electrical Union (29 000 members), the Irish Nurses Organisation – (27 000 members) and the Irish National Teachers Organisation (21 000 members). (All membership figures are for 1 January 2000).

23   Other major associations include the Construction Industry Federation (2 700 members), the Society of the Irish Motor Industry (1 700 members), and the Irish Pharmaceutical Union (1 400 members).

24   NESC, 'Strategy into the 21st Century: Conclusions and Recommendations', *NESC Report No 98*, Dublin 1996, at p. 66.

25   NESF, *A Framework for Partnership – Enriching Strategic Consensus through Participation,* Dublin 1997.

Table 1: Ireland, Employment and Unemployment (ILO defined) (in thousands) – Source: CSO

Economic Sector (NACE Rev.1)	Jun-Aug 2001	Sep-Nov 2001	Dec-Feb 2002	Mar-May 2002	Jun-Aug 2002	Sep-Nov 2002
Agriculture, forestry & fishing	127.3	124.4	121.7	120.7	122.7	119.8
Other production industries	330.8	318.0	310.4	302.9	314.0	302.2
Construction	186.4	184.8	183.2	181.1	190.0	190.8
Wholesale & retail trade	253.4	245.6	249.1	245.9	257.1	250.3
Hotels and restaurants	116.3	109.1	108.7	104.8	116.6	112.4
Transport, storage & communication	112.6	100.9	108.9	110.2	114.2	112.3
Financial & other business services	230.7	228.2	226.4	229.1	229.1	225.3
Public administration & defence	84.2	81.4	82.0	89.2	90.0	87.1
Education & health	248.1	255.7	260.0	267	262.7	272.7
Other services	96.9	94.9	94.9	99.0	98.6	97.7
Total in employment	**1 786.6**	**1 752.9**	**1 745.5**	**1 749.9**	**1 794.8**	**1 770.7**
Total unemployed	**79.5**	**72.6**	**80.0**	**77.2**	**86.7**	**84.1**
Total labour force	**1 866.1**	**1 825.5**	**1 825.4**	**1 827.0**	**1 881.5**	**1 854.7**
Not in labour force	1 168.0	1 232.5	1 245.6	1 247.6	1 203.7	1 254.4
Population 15 years & over	**3 034.0**	**3 058.0**	**3 071.1**	**3 074.7**	**3 085.3**	**3 109.1**

8.   The actors on the Irish labour law stage

The Irish Congress of Trade Unions (ICTU), established in 1959, is now the main co-ordinating body of Irish unions (and, interestingly, includes unions in Northern Ireland). At the beginning of 2000,[26] there were 46 trade unions in Ireland, representing some 562 000 workers. About 47% of all employees are union members.[27] These bodies are licensed and undertake bargaining functions on behalf of their members.

On the other side of the social partnership, eleven employer associations hold negotiating licences, of which the main representative organisation of the management side of industry and business is the Irish Business and Employers Confederation (IBEC), with a membership of approximately 7 000 companies.[28]

As of 1999, there were 561 800 union members in Ireland, which, at the time, constituted a membership density of 44.5% of those in employment. Significantly, during the recent economic boom, the rate of membership growth has failed to keep track with a very strong rate of employment growth. Therefore, union density levels, and collective bargaining coverage, have decreased as a proportion of the total number of workers in employment. Some data on the trend between 1994 and 1999 is presented in Table 2.[29]

Women constituted 42% of the total union membership of 561 800 in 1999. Recent growth in union membership has been quite marked amongst unions representing professional and white-collar workers.

---

26   The following data is for 1 January 2000.

27   The Services, Industrial, Professional and Technical Union (SIPTU), formed in 1990 through the amalgamation of the Irish Transport and General Workers Union and the Federated Workers Union of Ireland, is the largest trade union with 227 000 members. Other large unions are MANDATE – The Union of Retail, Bar and Administrative Workers (38 000 members), Irish Municipal Public and Civil Trade Union (35 000 members), the Technical Engineering and Electrical Union (29 000 members), the Irish Nurses Organisation – (27 000 members) and the Irish National Teachers Organisation (21 000 members).

28   Other major associations include the Construction Industry Federation (2 700 members), the Society of the Irish Motor Industry (1 700 members), and the Irish Pharmaceutical Union (1 400 members).

29   Taken from P. Gunnigle, M. O'Sullivan & M. Morley, 'Trade Unions Under Bargaining Corporatism: The Case of Ireland', Paper presented to the 2nd International Conference, *Human Resource Management in Europe: Trends and Challenges*, Athens, 17 October 2002, p. 4, Table 2.

Table 2: Trade Union Membership and Density (1994-1999)

Year	Total Union Membership	Total Employed	Total Labour Force	Employment Density	Workforce Density
1994	499.7	1 221 000	1 432 000	54.3%	41.7%
1995	518.7	1 282 000	1 459 000	53.2%	41.5%
1996	539.1	1 329 000	1 508 000	52.4%	41.1%
1997	538.4	1 380 000	1 539 000	50.2%	40.6%
1998	545.3	1 494 000	1 621 000	46.5%	38.9%
1999	561.8	1 591 000	1 688 000	44.5%	38.5%

Importantly, the fact that a union is recognised in Ireland does not necessarily mean that collective bargaining takes place, although this is usually the case.[30] Collective bargaining coverage and trade union recognition have been a major issue of debate in Ireland in recent years. Irish unions felt that the difficulty experienced in gaining recognition from recalcitrant employers was a key factor contributing to a decline in membership density. These difficulties prompted the unions to seek a new procedure designed to promote recognition for collective bargaining purposes, although they faced opposition from employers. Eventually, following changes introduced by the Industrial Relations (Amendment) Act 2001, with effect from 1 June 2001, there is a new power of the Labour Court to make binding decisions in relation to trade union recognition (but not, it may be noted, in respect of collective bargaining arrangements).[31]

9. Collective bargaining coverage and levels

In contrast to some other European countries, Ireland does not have any widespread procedures for the extension of collective agreements, at whatever level, to cover parties who were not originally signatories to the agreement. However, certain procedures for the extension of agreements and the imposition of binding terms and conditions of employment do exist. First, there are Registered Employment Agreements (REAs), whereby the parties to an agreement can register it with the Labour Court and, depending on the nature of the agreement in question, the effect of such registration may be to make the agreement binding on non-signatories. In addi-

tion, Joint Labour Committees (JLCs) set minimum rates of pay and terms and conditions of employment for workers in certain low-paying sectors.[32]

Since 1987, all union members have been covered by national-level collective agreements, such as the *Programme for Prosperity and Fairness*. However, there are no precise figures on the number of employees covered by local-level collective agreements in Ireland. As regards the coverage of collective bargaining arrangements, therefore, the best estimate of the situation has been summed up as being that:

Although union membership has increased in recent years, employment density levels have decreased as union membership has failed to keep pace with strong employment growth during the recent economic boom. Thus, it is reasonable to assume that the overall coverage of collective bargaining may have decreased slightly.[33]

10. Regulatory techniques

The important shift of emphasis in 1990 towards a statutory framework for industrial relationships in Ireland has already been noted. Even though the period 1941–1976 saw significant activity on the part of the legislator, the Industrial Relations Act 1990 was an important landmark. Subsequent developments have followed the path of many other European systems towards a growing dominance for the statutory norm.

This is the case notwithstanding the significant scope provided for voluntary activity – especially in relation to dispute

---

30   See data prepared by T. Dobbins for the *European Industrial Relations Observatory* (EIRO).

31   The Labour Court has also issued Guidelines on the operation of that procedure. See C. Higgins, 'Union Recognition – Labour Court Issues Guidelines', 2001, *47 Industrial Relations News 19*.

32   T. Dobbins, op cit.

33   See footnote 32.

resolution – and the establishment of a variety of institutions which undertake both mediation/conciliation functions and more 'legalistic' dispute resolution decision-making. Thus, for example, mention has been made of the recent arrangements providing for a statutory route to trade union recognition – coming in the wake of recommendations put forward in 1999 by the High Level Group on Trade Union Recognition, which was set up under the 'Partnership 2000' agreement.

Ireland does not have any widespread procedures for the extension of collective agreements, at whatever level, to cover parties who were not originally signatories to the agreement. However certain procedures for the extension of agreements and the imposition of binding terms and conditions of employment do exist.[34]

11. Dispute resolution and enforcement of labour law rights

Matters of individual labour law and employment protection under statutory arrangements have been dealt with in Ireland by various different routes involving District Courts (which deal primarily with matters relating to payment of wages, and which hold formal – rarely used – powers relating to gender discrimination), and the very important Employment Appeal Tribunal (which deals with matters of notice and dismissal).[35] The Labour Court also plays a role in relation to discriminatory dismissals as well as acting as an appellate level in respect of certain other issues.[36] However, it is generally accepted that the interface between the various institutional bodies is far from clear, indeed, this matter has recently been the subject of growing calls for reform.

On the collective labour law front, a statutory framework is in place which provides a procedure for resolving disputes where negotiating arrangements are not in place and the parties are not engaged in talks. This arrangement, which is conducted by the Labour Court under the provisions of the Industrial Relations (Amendment) Act 2001,[37] sits alongside the facilities for voluntary dispute resolution, contained, in particular, in a Code of Practice.[38]

The Irish model for conciliation – and, generally, for dealing in non-legalistic ways with employment-related disputes – has been regarded in various parts of Europe and further afield as a framework to be admired and copied. That system – relying upon a number of institutions whose primary objective is to bring the parties together and to seek dispute resolution without the formalities of legal and judicial intervention – is considered to have thrived during the period since 1992, at a time when the Irish economy was booming. However, with the advent of serious problems in the Irish economy more recently, a number of strains have begun to appear in the institutional framework for labour law and industrial relations regulation, giving rise to various significant calls and proposals for reform.

The institutional framework, as has already been noted, is very particular.[39] Thus, the Labour Relations Commission, which was established in 1991 under the Industrial Relations Act of 1990, carries out its specialist functions by providing an industrial relations conciliation service, an industrial relations advisory, development and research service, and a Rights Commissioner service. It also furnishes assistance to Joint Labour Committees and Joint Industrial Councils in the exercise of their functions.[40]

One indicator of the extent to which 'social partnership' delivers a stable context for the relationship between the

---

34   First, there are Registered Employment Agreements (REAs), whereby the parties to an agreement can register it with the Labour Court, and, depending on the nature of the agreement in question, the effect of such registration may be to make the agreement binding on non-signatories. The Industrial Relations Acts 1946 to 1990 provide for the extension of collective agreements to non-signatories through the Registered Employment Agreement system. In addition, Joint Labour Committees (JLCs) set minimum rates of pay and terms and conditions of employment for workers in certain low-paying sectors. JLCs are bodies established under the Industrial Relations Act 1946, and may be established by the Labour Court on the application of (i) the Minister for Enterprise, Trade and Employment; or (ii) a trade union; or (iii) any organisation claiming to be representative of the workers or the employers involved.

35   The Employment Appeals Tribunal is composed of employer and worker nominees with an independent chairperson and vice-chairperson. The Tribunal hears disputes over entitlements under legislation including dismissal, notice, redundancy payments, payment of wages and maternity entitlements.

36   The Labour Court, established under the Industrial Relations Act, 1946, consists of a chairperson, deputy chairpersons and ordinary members representative of employers and workers. The Court normally investigates disputes only if either (i) it receives a report from the Labour Relations Commission that no further efforts on its part will help resolve the dispute or (ii) the Commission waives its function of conciliation in the dispute. The Court, having investigated a dispute, usually issues a recommendation giving its opinions on the merits of the dispute and the terms on which it should be settled. Except in certain cases, the Court's recommendations are not legally binding.

37   The President of the Labour Court has issued Guidelines for trade unions and employers in relation to referrals to the Court under the statutory provisions.

38   Issued under the Industrial Relations Act, 1990, *Code of Practice on Voluntary Dispute Resolution* (Declaration) Order, 2000 (SI No.145 of 2000).

39   Supra.

40   The Commission also undertakes other activities of a developmental nature relating to the improvement of good industrial relations practices including the review and monitoring of developments in the area of industrial relations; the preparation, in consultation with the social partners, of codes of practice relevant to industrial relations; industrial relations research and publications; and the organisation of seminars/conferences on industrial relations/human resource management issues.

Table 3: Industrial Disputes, 1994-2002

Year	Disputes which began	Number of disputes	Disputes in progress		
			Number of firms involved	Workers involved	Total days lost
1994	28	29	238	5 007	25 550
1995	34	34	34	31 653	130 300
1996	30	32	30	13 339	114 584
1997	28	28	33	5 364	74 508
1998	33	34	62	8 060	37 374
1999	32	32	127	36 505	215 587
2000	39	39	41	28 192	97 046
2001	24	26	58	32 168	114 613
2002	27	27	43	3 553	21 257

respective partners is the incidence of industrial disputes. The pattern of Irish experience in this regard between 1994 and 2002 is set out in Table 3.[41] From this, it can be seen that during 2002 there were 21 257 days lost to industrial disputes. This is the lowest annual total going back as far as 1970, and represents a sharp fall from the 114 613 days lost in 2001. Indeed, the total of days lost in 2002 remains significantly less than in 2001, even if allowance is made for the impact of a major teachers' dispute in 2001.

41   Published by the Central Statistics Office, Ireland (CSO).

Chapter II:
From job security to employability

1. The context of the EU Employment Strategy

The loyal adherence by Ireland to post-Maastricht social policy within the framework of the EU directives in this field has been followed by a similar commitment to active participation in, and compliance with, the post-1997 'Luxembourg Process', which constitutes the context for the European Employment Strategy. Consequently, the most recent *Ireland's Employment Action Plan 2002*, setting out the measures taken and steps to be implemented within that supra-national framework provides the clearest picture of developments in this context.

A few words are offered, however, in relation to particular components within that larger picture. Thus, note may be taken that the focus of statutory employment rights can be found in the Unfair Dismissals Act 1977 (amended in 1993), which forms part of a network of basic individual rights reflecting substantially the same areas of concern as United Kingdom developments in the same area – from a Redundancy Payments Act 1967 (shortly to be superseded by new provisions in 2003) through to a modern period of implementation for EU directives as a consequence of Irish membership of the EU.[42]

2. Upgrading workforce skills: towards a higher 'quality' workforce

As reported in *Ireland's Employment Action Plan 2002,*

Under the Programme for Prosperity and Fairness, a Taskforce was established to examine the adequacy and coverage of lifelong learning opportunities. The report… represents a compre-hensive and coherent framework for providing education and training on a lifelong basis, covering aspects including: The national qualifications framework; Literacy and other basic skills; Information and guidance; Delivery access and funding and Workplace Training.[43]

3. Young people

The particular problem of youth unemployment has haunted the Irish labour market for decades. Trends between 1983 and 1997 can be seen in Table 4.[44] Thus, as total unemployment soared over the course of the 1980s and again in the 1990s, so did unemployment among young people. In 1981, almost 15% of labour force participants in the 15-24 year age group were unemployed, compared to about 9% of those aged over 25. The unemployment rate among young people reached its peak in 1993, when, at over 27% of the young labour force, it was almost double the rate among older participants (14%). This sharp increase occurred despite a fall in the numbers of young people participating in the labour force.

4. The national minimum wage

For a limited number of industries and trades, Joint Labour Committees, which draw up minimum rates of pay and other conditions of employment, operate. These rates become legally binding when ratified by the Labour Court in the form of Employment Regulation Orders. Another minimum pay enforcement procedure arises when the Court registers an employment agreement. A Registered Employment Agreement is binding on all employers for every worker of the class, type or group to which it is stated to apply. The Court registers voluntary Joint Industrial Councils – negotiating forums within particular industries.

---

42   The details of the framework in relation to dismissals can be found in the 1997 report prepared for the European Commission, 'Termination of employment relationships: Legal situation in the Member States of the European Union', Luxembourg 1997. The earlier operation of the regime from 1977 is described by N. Butler, 'Statutory Employment Protection', in T. Murphy & W. Roche (eds), *Irish Industrial Relations in Practice,* Dublin 1994, Chapter 11.

43   *Ireland's Employment Action Plan 2002.*

44   Source: *Labour Force Surveys,* 1983 and 1997. Drawn from P. O'Connell, 'Astonishing success: Economic growth and the labour market in Ireland', *ILO Employment and Training Papers 44, 1999,* at p. 32.

Table 4: Labour force and population trends among those aged 15-24, 1983 & 1997

Principal Economic Status	1983		1997	
	(1000s)	%	(1000s)	%
At Work	287	47.0	224	33.6
Unemployed	72	11.8	51	8.6
Labour Force	359	58.8	276	42.2
Education	220	36.0	346	54.5
Other Non-Active	32	5.2	22	3.3
Population 15-24	610	100.0	643	100.0
Unemployment Rate		20.1		18.6
Youth Employment as a Percentage of Total Employment		25.5		16.8

The introduction by the Government of a national minimum wage in April 2000 has had an impact on the Joint Labour Committee system in Ireland. Prior to the introduction of the minimum wage, many employees protected under the JLC system failed to receive the minimum rates specified, with greater enforcement being needed. A problem with the JLC system is that, in many cases, the minimum rates specified are low, limiting the potential of the system to act as an obstacle to competition based on low pay and conditions.[45] From 1 October 2002 the minimum wage rate was set at €6.35 per hour.

5. The problem of social exclusion

In terms of social exclusion, the Irish situation differs little from its neighbour the United Kingdom when it comes to identifying the potential for exclusion and the concern of the government to take steps to combat this. The problem of poverty associated with low pay has been touched upon by the introduction of the national minimum wage since 2000 (*supra*), while a number of underlying social problems are taken into the Irish social policy framework through the route of 'equal opportunities', as can be seen below.

Two areas may be mentioned here: that deriving from an increasing ethnic diversity in Irish society and the labour market, and that concerned with disabled workers.

5.1. Ethnicity related

Although problems relating to the ethnic harmony of Irish society have only been highlighted recently, the phenomenon of the traveller community has stood out as a particular national characteristic. Indeed, a remarkable number of cases involving this group are dealt with by the Equality Tribunal.

The national make-up of the Irish population is presented below in Table 6, and a comment on the changing pattern in this regard is set out *infra* in Part IV, when dealing with equal opportunities. In this context, the *2002 National Action Plan* for Ireland points out that the increased number of migrant workers in Ireland raises the need for a programme of public awareness and education measures to prevent the emergence of racism in the workplace.[46]

---

45   A significant number of the pay rates specified by the various JLCs were below the then national minimum wage rate of IEP 4.40 per hour (€5.59). This minimum wage rate represented approximately 56% of median earnings in 2000.

46   See *Ireland's National Action Plan 2002*, at section 3.6.4. The important point is made that 'foreign workers are entitled to the same rights as Irish/EEA workers'. The comment continues by pointing out that a variety of initiatives have been undertaken with a view to dealing with this emerging issue. Thus, 'ICTU (the Irish Congress of Trade Unions) operates a training programme in the area of anti-racism in the workplace. A public awareness programme was launched in 2001 in partnership with the Equality Authority and the Social Partners to combat racism in the workplace. Anti-Workplace Racist Week was initiated in November 2000 and repeated in November 2001, with additional funding from Know Racism (the National Anti-Racism Awareness Programme).'

5.2. Disability related

According to the *Quarterly National Household Survey* for the second quarter of 2002, over 10% (271 000) of all persons in Ireland aged 15-64 indicated that they had a long-standing health problem or disability. Approximately 11% (142 700) of males reported having a health problem or disability, compared to 10% (128 300) of females. The prevalence of health problems and disabilities varied by age, with a quarter (84 400) of all persons in the 55-64 year age group suffering from a long-standing health problem or disability. This compares to less than 5% (30 600) of persons in the 15-24 year age category.

Just over 40% (108 600) of all persons aged 15-64 with a disability/health problem indicated that they were in employment, which compares to an overall rate of 65% for the total population in the same age category. In relation to people reporting a disability/health problem, the 25-34 year age category had the highest percentage in employment, at 55.6%. The lowest rate, 27.0%, was reported in the 55-64 age group. The equivalent figures for the total population in employment also showed the 25-year age group having the highest rate, at 81.3%. The lowest rate was found in the 15-24 year age group, at 45.3%.[47]

6. Measures to assist employability

Leaving aside the temptation to highlight the 'political spin' which might be perceived in the comment, the Irish Minister for Enterprise Trade and Employment, in her 'Foreword' to Ireland's *Employment Action Plan, April 2002*, declared that:

The period of office of the current Government coincides with that of the EU Employment Strategy. Europe, having experienced a period of jobless growth in the early and mid-1990s and with unemployment running over 10% needed new strategies to address these challenges. At the end of 1997, as we prepared the first Employment Action Plan, Ireland had an unemployment rate of 10% and long-term unemployment was at 5%. The transformation in the Irish labour market in the interim has been remarkable and as a result we are facing a new set of short- and medium-term challenges.[48]

The *Irish National Employment Action Plan*, adopted by the Government as its response to the European Employment Guidelines, included a commitment to a more systematic engagement of the Employment Services with the unemployed. Implementation of this commitment commenced in September 1998.

From that date, all persons under 25 who were six months on the Live Register (LR) were referred by the Department of Social and Family Affairs (DSFA) for interview by FÁS. As the Employment Action Plan progressed, the programme was extended to include other groups crossing nominated thresholds of unemployment. At present, all individuals under 25 are being referred when they cross the six months unemployment threshold as before. The timing of intervention (previously 12 months) by FÁS into all other age groups was reduced in July 2000. From this period all persons in the 25-54 years age bracket are being engaged with as they cross the nine month threshold.[49]

---

47 See Central Statistics Office, Ireland, Quarterly National Household Survey. The CSO goes on to observe that 'Of the 108 600 persons in employment suffering from health problems/disabilities, over three-quarters (81 700) were in full-time employment. The majority of those in employment were employees (87 600) with just over 20 000 falling into the self-employed and assisting relatives categories.'

48 The Minister went on to claim that: 'In summary since mid-1997: We have created 350 000 jobs – an increase of 26%; Almost 180 000 women – an increase of 33% – have taken up employment; Unemployment has more than halved from 160 000 to just over 70 000 – and despite the recent increase it is still among the lowest in the EU at 4.0%; Long term unemployment has fallen from 86 000 to 21 000; Emigration has been reversed: Over 100 000 Irish people have returned since 1997... There are several factors – in both supply and demand terms – which contributed to this success: We have strongly supported the development of enterprise and the creation of jobs through sound macroeconomic policies, political certainty, a competitive economy and progressive social partnership; The decrease in Corporation Tax from 40% to 16% has greatly encouraged new start-ups and re-investment; Investment in infrastructure – both physical and human – to meet current and future needs as provided in the National Development plan will amount to almost €29 billion over 2000-2006... To tackle both the tightening labour supply situation and address social inclusion issues we have provided incentives and supports for different groups wishing to join the labour market, including: lower taxes and taxation reforms (personal tax rates have been reduced from 48% and 26% to 42% and 20%. Over 380 000 people have been taken out of the tax net); training and education, where educational attainment for under-35s is now at the EU average and many new targeted initiatives such as the Education Welfare Act and training for people with disabilities have been introduced; direct intervention with the unemployed (68% of persons referred to FÁS have signed off the Live Register); increased childcare provision (€436m to 2006) and the introduction of flexible work permit arrangements for workers from third countries... These measures have encouraged many unemployed or disadvantaged people to take up employment opportunities, encouraged women outside the workforce to avail of jobs and facilitated workers from outside the EEA to fill available vacancies... In devising and delivering on these strategies we have engaged in a comprehensive set of agreements with the Social Partners. We have also targeted higher investment in the Border Midlands and Western Region to ensure that the skills and jobs are shared across the country.'

49 Department of Enterprise, Trade and Employment, *Tackling Youth Unemployment and Preventing Long-term Unemployment – Employment Action Plan: Monthly Progress Report No.52,* January 2003.

Chapter III:
Labour law and adaptability

In its most recent 'mission statement',[50] the Irish Department of Enterprise, Trade and Employment sets out its activities as being designed,

To promote quality employment, meet the labour supply and skills needs of the economy, foster social inclusion, protect the welfare of workers, facilitate industrial peace and promote social policy as a productive factor.

This focus is set against the recognition that:

The Irish labour market has changed dramatically over recent years. The challenges to be faced over the foreseeable future are vastly different to those of the past ten or even five years. Notably, Ireland will have to mobilise labour supply from all available sources and increase skill levels to meet the needs of a rapidly developing economy. FÁS, with an annual expenditure of €800 million..., is the Department's principal agency for labour market interventions. Increasingly too, developments in employment strategy at EU level, aimed at achieving a more integrated and flexible European labour market, are impacting on national employment policies.

By way of example of such change, *...part time work has increased by 13.3% since 1997, the vast majority of which is voluntary. New legislation – the Protection of Employees (Part-Time Work) Act – was introduced at the end of 2001, implementing measures introduced at the level of the European Union, and giving part-time workers the same rights as full time workers. Recognising the trends in work practices, the social partners have put in place a framework and a range of actions to promote family friendly practices at the level of the firm.*[51] This growth in part-time working emerges from the data in Table 5.

In recent years, the Irish authorities have been very innovative in introducing measures in both the tax and social welfare sys-

Table 5: **The incidence of part-time working, 1983-1997 (ILO basis)**

Year	Men	Women	All (%)
1983	2.7	15.6	6.7
1990	3.4	17.6	8.1
1993	4.8	21.3	10.8
1994	5.1	21.7	11.3
1995	5.4	23.1	12.1
1996	5.0	22.1	11.6
1997	5.4	23.1	12.3
1998	7.8	30.1	16.7

Source: Eurostat *Labour Force Survey*, and Central Statistics Office

tems to reduce the 'tax wedge' and to ease the transition of unemployed people (particularly the long-term unemployed) back to work. These have included both tax breaks to the long-term unemployed and the 'Back-to Work Allowance' scheme, which withdraws income support on a gradual basis over three years from the long-term unemployed returning to work, as well as allowing continued access to important secondary benefits, such as free medical care.[52]

---

50   Developed primarily in the context of Strategic Goal 2 of the Department's *Strategy Statement 2001-2003*.

51   *Ireland's Employment Action Plan 2002*.

52   See Department of Enterprise and Employment, *Growing and Sharing our Employment*, Dublin 1996. Commenting on such measures, O'Connell observes that 'These carefully targeted measures can have the effect of mitigating unemployment traps and the numbers making the transition from unemployment to employment has grown rapidly in recent years. The success of these programmes serve to highlight the importance of further progress in reducing the tax burden on the low paid, and the potential of tax reforms targeted specifically at the lower paid for further reducing unemployment.' See P. O'Connell, 'Astonishing success: Economic growth and the labour market in Ireland', *ILO Employment and Training Papers 44*, 1999, at pp. 78-79.

Chapter IV:
Promoting equal opportunities

1. Introduction

Unlike many countries, Ireland does not have a specific Bill of Rights and for many years did not have comprehensive anti-racial discrimination legislation. However, unfair dismissals legislation did specifically prohibit race, colour and religion as acceptable reasons for dismissing workers. Furthermore, the Irish Parliament enacted legislation in 1989 designed to prohibit incitement to hatred on the grounds of race, colour, nationality, religion, ethnic or national origin, membership of the travelling community, or sexual orientation.

That framework for combating discrimination has undergone dramatic revision and modernisation in recent years, to the point where the 'Irish model' is commonly held up as an example of 'best practice' in relation to such issues. At its heart is the Equality Tribunal, which operates on the basis of nine 'prohibited grounds' of discrimination.

The Equality Authority is an independent body set up under the Employment Equality Act 1998.[53] It replaced the former Employment Equality Agency, and has a greatly expanded role and functions. The Employment Equality Act 1998 and the Equal Status Act 2000 outlaw discrimination in employment, vocational training, advertising, collective agreements, the provision of goods and services and other opportunities to which the public generally have access on nine distinct grounds. These are: gender; marital status; family status; age; disability; race; sexual orientation; religious belief; and membership of the Traveller Community.

2. Demographic features: national origin

Even though the total number of foreign nationals in Ireland is small when compared with other European countries, it has been growing. The statistics for April 1997 show that,

out of a total population of 3 660 000, an estimated 114 000 were foreign nationals (3.1%). Nearly 81 000 (over 70%) were from European Union countries (mainly the United Kingdom), while, among the remaining 'non-EU' group amounting to 33 000 persons, about a third were nationals of the United States. The comparison between 1988 and 1997 is set out in Table 6.[54]

In overall terms, these figures represent a significant increase when compared with the beginning of the decade. Thus, the total number of foreign residents in 1990 was 81 000, or 2.3% of the total population. Among the various groups distinguished, those classified as 'non-EU' and not from the United States exhibited the most rapid increase – rising from 11 000 in 1990 to almost 22 000 in 1997.

Table 6: Total population by nationality, 1990 and 1997 (in 1 000s)

Nationality	1990	1997
Irish	3 422.0	3 546.2
EU	62.3	80.8
UK	-	64.6
Other EU	-	16.4
Non-EU	18.4	33.1
USA	7.1	11.3
Other	11.3	21.8
Total	**3 502.7**	**3 660.1**

3. Demographic features: gender

The gender split in the Irish labour force between 1988 and 1998 is indicated in Table 7.[55]

---

53   The 1998 Act repealed the former Anti-Discrimination (Pay) Act 1974 and the Employment Equality Act 1977.

54   Source: *CSO Labour Force Surveys, 1990 and 1997*. Taken from Jerry Sexton, 'National Labour Market Policies – Trends', *European Employment Observatory, InfoMISEP*, updated regularly.

55   Taken from P. O'Connell, 'Astonishing success: Economic growth and the labour market in Ireland', *ILO Employment and Training Papers 44, 1999*, at p. 17.

Table 7: Total employment by gender, 1981-1997

Year	Total	Men	Women	Female Share
	(1 000)	*(1 000)*	*(1 000)*	%
1988	1 111.8	747.0	364.7	32.8
1993	1 183.1	749.4	433.7	36.7
1998	1 494.5	899.9	594.6	39.8
Annual percentage change				
1988-93	1.3	0.1	3.8	2.4
1993-98	4.9	3.8	6.9	1.6
1988-98	3.3	1.9	6.0	2.0

Source: Central Statistics Office, various years, *Labour Force Survey*

Note: In order to render the 1998 data comparable with earlier years, annual percentage changes are estimated on adjusted data, which reduce the total number employed in 1998 by 20 000 (8 000 men and 12 000 women) to take account of changes in measurement.

The Irish Congress of Trade Unions' response to the 2002 National Action Plan for Ireland made the critical point that, *While the causes of segregation are debated there is no dispute that the labour market in Ireland continues to be highly segregated by sex.*[56]

Particular attention has been drawn to the gender wage gap, and research published in relation to the impact of the EU Employment Strategy in Ireland suggests that:

...the gender wage gap across the economy as a whole is narrower than that reported in the manufacturing sector. In 2000 the mean gross hourly wage for men was IEP 10.29 while for women it was IEP 8.77, which was 14.7% less. The results also show that (despite a significant increase in the hourly wages) there was a very small decrease in the gap between average male and female wages between 1997 and 2000 of 0.3 of 1%.[57]

However, of some concern in this context is the additional revelation that:

Prior to the introduction of the Employment Strategy in 1998 the male/female wage gap was already on the decline, and if anything the pace of this reduction has slowed since its introduction.

At the time of writing, a major study is being undertaken into the extent of the gender wage gap in Ireland and its underlying causes.[58]

---

56 The ICTU observation continues to remark that: 'Gender segregation within the labour market can result from a variety of undesirable practices, and the view that occupational segregation is largely because of 'choice' is by now largely discredited... The gender divide is particularly noticeable in the apprenticeship system where women represent approximately less than 300 of the 25,000 apprentices.' See *Ireland's National Action Plan 2002*, at p. 78.

57 See H. Russell & B. Gannon, 'Equal Opportunities Between Men and Women: The Male/Female Wage Gap in Ireland', Section 4 of the ESRI report, *Impact Evaluation of the European Employment Strategy in Ireland*, Dublin 2003.

58 According to the 2002 National Action Plan for Ireland, 'A Consultative Group Established under the PPF will report to Government by end 2002 on proposals to address the issues raised following research conducted by the Economic and Social Research Institute in the report: *How Unequal – Men and Women in the Irish Labour Market*. This Group is also overseeing sectoral studies on the gender wage gap in the following areas: IT, electrical and electronic, retail, food and local government. This research project is being carried out in partnership with Finland, Sweden and Northern Ireland under funding provided by the EU Gender Equality Programme 2001-5.' See Section 3.8.2, at p. 68).

Chapter V:
Overview and comment

The 'Irish model' of partnership has been widely acclaimed as having underpinned a remarkable transformation of Irish economic fortunes and stability over a period of fifteen years. At the same time, a groundbreaking framework for addressing issues of discrimination and equal opportunities has been established. Both of these phenomena have developed in a context where a major shift in regulatory policy was heralded by legislation in 1990, and with increasing influence being felt from the level of European Union social policy initiatives.

Against that background, it is tempting to look at progress over the past decade as highly positive in terms of competitiveness and economic stability at the national level. Thus,

According to the EU Commission's European Competitiveness Report 2001, GDP per capita caught up with the EU average in 1997. Ireland built its remarkable catching up process on its attraction of foreign capital, but has ingeniously connected inward investments with local strengths. It has attracted dynamic high-tech industries, developed programmes to upgrade qualifications and to cluster firms around the subsidiaries of multinational firms. The supply of skilled labour was a contributing factor...

The output share of manufacturing is rising and, at 32%, is now by far the highest in Europe. The ratio of exports to production is the highest of all the Member States. Value added per employee is also the highest among EU countries. The share of production in marketing-driven and technology-driven industries is high...

Business R&D is moving closer towards the EU average, even though multinational firms still perform a larger share of research in their home country, as compared to production. Skills are highly rated, due to an efficient education system and the supply of new graduates in science and technology is the third strongest. Ireland has a large share of ICT-producing industries. Average innovation expenditures (compared with a fast increasing turnover) are complemented by higher rates of innovation based on co-operation and on continuous research at firm level, as expressed by the capabilities indicators...

The National Competitiveness Council 2001 Report gives Ireland a rank of 1st out of 18 countries in terms of economic performance in 2001, reflecting strong economic growth over the last five years, rapid capital formation, rapid export growth, positive current account and extremely rapid expansion in the numbers at work. ...

As regards the human resource dimensions there has been strong employment growth and labour force participation rates for males and females are around the average compared to other EU/OECD countries. Only five developed countries had lower unemployment rates.[59]

Yet, as the same document proceeds to point out, the 'storm clouds' have already gathered over the Irish economy, and a variety of underlying structural problems have become increasingly apparent. As the 2002 Employment Action Plan puts it:

However in 1999, Ireland's score for Education ranks it 16 out of 20. Ireland is fourth lowest as regards the proportion of 25 to 64 year olds participating in continuing education. In 1998 Ireland ranked 23 out of 29 in terms of the 25-64 year olds with at least upper second level education. ... In terms of Productivity, Labour Compensation and Unit labour Costs, Ireland ranks 11 out of 16 countries. During the 1990's, productivity was growing at over 3% per annum (the best of comparator countries). Wages for the economy in general ranked 16th lowest out of 28 countries, using 2001 estimates. Wages for production workers are lower at 7ᵗʰ out of 23 (1999 data). However, labour costs had been rising rapidly, reflecting the tightness of the labour market.

In like vein, this 'Janus quality' in the Irish situation is identified by O'Connell, writing in 1999:

...the Irish variant of social partnership provided the institutional framework to achieve the combination of policies which transformed a failing economy into one of the fastest growing in Europe over the course of a decade. The Irish solution represents one approach to economic steering – one that carries with it the advantage of preserving greater levels of social cohesion than

59   *Ireland's Employment Action Plan 2002.*

other solutions to economic crisis and declining competitiveness, such as the liberal market oriented experiment conducted in Britain over the past two decades.[60]

That having been said, however, the same author goes on to comment that,

...rapid economic growth has coincided with an increase in inequality. The incidence of low-paid employment has increased over time. So also has the incidence of poverty. Moreover, despite the dramatic increase in women's paid employment, married women and women with children face a series of interrelated obstacles to entering the workforce, including low wages, the lack of state support for childcare, and disincentives in the taxation and welfare systems.

The blame for this apparent paradox is laid squarely at a key 'trade-off' in the Irish government's strategy during this period – what is described as *the trade off between incomes restraint and tax cuts achieved through public sector cut backs.*[61]

In consequence, looking at the trends over the period since 1992, the key question has to focus upon whether the 'model' and approaches which delivered the period of 'Very rapid growth, 1993-1998' (see *supra*), is suited to the challenges which have now begun to make themselves so sharply felt in Ireland since 2000.

A partnership agreement entered into for only 18 months, and a break from the 'tax reduction trade-off', along with growing 'conflictualism' between the 'social partners' do not bode well for the coming years. Nor do the trends in union density and collective bargaining coverage since the early 1990s.

Whether the new legal mechanisms for delivering trade union recognition and ensuring a minimum wage floor can contribute to continued industrial harmony must be open to doubt, while pressures towards 'individualisation' of Irish industrial relations have been pointed to as influencing the Irish context in broadly similar ways to experience 'across

the Irish Sea' in the United Kingdom.[62] Meanwhile, migration pressures – only recently impacting upon the Irish economy to any significant degree – and an increasing 'rights-aware culture' within society are placing pressure upon even the highly-regarded Irish institutions and mechanisms for addressing issues of discrimination and equal opportunities.

A move towards normative intervention by the legislator (in common with much of Europe in recent years) has also turned the spotlight upon the role of labour law in Ireland, and upon the adequacy and suitability of the institutions which served that system well during the 1990s.

Nevertheless, against that background, the development of labour law in Ireland since 1992 displays quite strong similarities with developments elsewhere in the European Union. Thus, there has been an ever-increasing reliance upon the mechanism of 'hard law' statutory regulation, with a substantial proportion of newer measures owing their origins to social policy enactments in the form of directives passed at EU level. This 'hard law' emphasis has progressed apace, notwithstanding that use has been made, from time to time, of Codes of Practice and similar instruments.

At the same time, however, the Irish legislator has taken the opportunity to update the existing basis of the individual 'floor of rights' – particularly with the modified regime for unfair dismissal since 1993, and with moves to amend the framework dealing with redundancy.

Issues such as data protection and privacy regulation in relation to employment have come to the fore only relatively recently in Ireland,[63] although a Freedom of Information Act has been in place since 1997 and steps are being taken to amend and update both this and the Data Protection Act.[64]

Meanwhile, the growing importance of employment-related protections being delivered through frameworks for 'equal opportunities' and 'anti-discrimination', rather than by way of

---

60   P. O'Connell, 'Astonishing success: Economic growth and the labour market in Ireland', *ILO Employment and Training Papers 44, 1999,* at p. 76.

61   As the author notes, 'The persistence of these social problems is not unrelated to successful economic and employment growth. A central element in the strategy to boost international competitiveness, the essential spur to growth in a small open economy, was the trade off between incomes restraint and tax cuts achieved through public sector cut backs. Table 5.1 compares public expenditures and receipts in Ireland in 1987 and 1994 with those in Britain and the other European cases of labour market success. Here also Ireland represents an exceptional case... Averaging across the 15 EU countries, both total general government expenditures and spending on social security transfers increased as a proportion of Gross Domestic Product, and so also did government receipts, mainly from tax revenue. In Ireland, however, total government spending fell by 9 percentage points, and both spending on social security transfers and receipts also fell somewhat over the period... Moreover, in terms of spending on either social security or total government expenditure, Ireland lags well behind the other European examples of labour market success.'

62   See the analysis contained in W. Roche, 'The Individualization of Irish Industrial Relations?', 2001, *39 British Journal of Industrial Relations 183.*

63   As can be seen in the comparative sections of the report prepared for DG Employment by Mark Freedland. See *Data Protection and Employment in the European Union: An Analytical Study of the Law and Practice of Data Protection and the Employment Relationship in the EU and its Member States,* Oxford 1999.

64   Instruments such as the Communications Regulation Act 2002 confirm the developing need effectively to regulate such important areas, while it should be noted that this is not a field in which Ireland has been entirely inactive – see, for example, a measure such as the Interception of Postal Packets and Telecommunications Messages (Regulation) Act 1993.

more traditional labour law provisions, has been evident since 1998. Although the Irish legislator had long made provision to combat gender-related discrimination,[65] the enactment of the Employment Equality Act in 1998, together with the Equal Status Act 2000, has given a significant impulse to this aspect of employment regulation.

However, it is arguably in relation to the institutional framework for administering and dealing with employment rights and disputes related to these that Ireland faces particular problems. The characteristic Irish mixture of judicial involvement, mediation, and 'light' state intervention has given rise to a 'model' which has attracted widespread positive attention in the past decade. Yet, at the same time, the uneasy division of jurisdiction between the Labour Court, the Employment Appeals Tribunal, the Rights Commissioners serving the Labour Relations Commission, and the Equality Tribunal – not to mention the possibility of involvement by the Circuit Court – leaves too much potential for both overlap and 'black holes'. This continues to present pressing problems for the ministries concerned – whether or not explicitly recognised.

Whatever the success in addressing such issues, however, the fact remains that the underlying economic and labour market position is likely to dictate the continuing direction and pace of labour law development for Ireland. As *The Irish Times* has noted:

Economy-wide employment growth has been on a more or less uninterrupted decelerating trajectory since the middle of 1999.[66]

Consequently, if labour law in Ireland is to be anything more than a 'side-show', that perceived economic downturn has to be arrested, the structural shortcomings have rapidly to be addressed, and a new 'Irish model' has to be developed out of the phoenix of the 'miracle' of the 1990s.

---

65   With, for example, the Anti-Discrimination (Pay) Act 1974 and the Employment Equality Act 1977 (both since repealed), and later measures such as the Maternity Protection Act 1994 and the Adoptive Leave Act 1995.

66   *The Irish Times*, 'Public sector growth slows jobless rise', 14 June 2002.

Annexes

1. Selected bibliography

Barrett *et al* 1997	A. Barrett, T. Callan & B. Nolan, *The Earnings Distribution and the Returns to Education in Ireland,* ESRI research paper, 1997.
DEE 1996	Department of Enterprise and Employment, *Growing and Sharing our Employment,* Dublin 1996.
DETE 2000	*Programme for Prosperity and Fairness,* Dublin 2000.
DETE 2002(a)	Department of Enterprise, Trade and Employment (FAS), *The Irish Labour Market Review 2002.*
DETE 2002(b)	*Ireland's Employment Action Plan 2002.*
DETE 2003	Department of Enterprise, Trade and Employment, *Tackling Youth Unemployment and Preventing Long-term Unemployment – Employment Action Plan: Monthly Progress Report No. 52,* January 2003.
Higgins 2001	C. Higgins, '"Union Recognition" – Labour Court Issues Guidelines', 2001, 47 *Industrial Relations, News* 19.
ICTU 2001	Irish Congress of Trade Unions, *Migration and Immigration: Changing the Face of Irish Society,* Dublin 2001.
Irish Times 2002	*The Irish Times,* 'Public sector growth slows jobless rise', 14 June 2002.
Labour Court 2002	The Labour Court, *Annual Report 2002,* Dublin 2003.
Lane 1998	P. Lane, 'Profits and Wages in Ireland, 1987-1996', 1998, 27 *Journal of the Statistical and Social Inquiry Society of Ireland* 223.
LRC 2002	The Labour Relations Commission, *Annual Report 2002,* Dublin 2003.
Murphy & Roche 1994	T. Murphy & W. Roche (eds), *Irish Industrial Relations in Practice,* Dublin 1994.
NESC 1996	NESC, *Strategy into the 21ˢᵗ Century: Conclusions and Recommendations,* NESC Report No 98, Dublin 1996.
NESF 1997	NESF, *A Framework for Partnership – Enriching Strategic Consensus through Participation,* Dublin 1997.
Nolan *et al* 2003	B. Nolan, J. Williams & S. Blackwell, 'New Results on the Impact of the Minimum Wage on Irish Firms', 2003, *Quarterly Economic Commentary,* ESRI, Dublin 2003.
O'Connell 1999	P. O'Connell, 'Astonishing success: Economic growth and the labour market in Ireland', *ILO Employment and Training Papers 44,* 1999.
O'Neill 2000	D. O'Neill, *Evaluating Labour Market Interventions,* NUI Maynooth, March 2000.
ODEI 2002(a)	ODEI – The Equality Tribunal, *Annual Report 2002,* Dublin 2003.
ODEI 2002(b)	ODEI – The Equality Tribunal, *Developments in Alternative Dispute Resolution (ADR) – The Equality Tribunal's Mediation Service: 2 Years On,* Dublin 2002.
Roche 2001(a)	W. Roche, 'Accounting for the Trend in Trade Union Recognition in Ireland', 2001, 37 *Industrial Relations Journal* 37.
Roche 2001(b)	W. Roche, 'The Individualization of Irish Industrial Relations?', 2001, 39 *British Journal of Industrial Relations* 183.
Sexton 2001(a)	J.J. Sexton, 'Interpreting Recent Developments in the Economy and Labour Market', ESRI, Dublin 2001.
Sexton 2001(b)	J.J. Sexton, 'Some Important Changes in the Structure of Irish Society. A Review of Past Developments and a Perspective on the Future', ESRI, Dublin 2001.
Sexton (EEO)	Jerry Sexton, *National Labour Market Policies – Trends,* European Employment Observatory, InfoMISEP, updated regularly.

2. Principal Irish legislative measures

2.1. Primary legislation

Industrial Relations Act 1946
Industrial Relations Act 1969
Employment Agency Act 1971
Redundancy Payments Act 1971
Minimum Notice and Terms of Employment Act 1973
Protection of Employment Act 1977
Unfair Dismissals Act 1977
Worker Representation (State Enterprises) Act 1977
Protection of Employees (Employer's Insolvency) Act 1984
Labour Services Act 1987
Industrial Relations Act 1990
Payment of Wages Act 1991
Worker Protection (Regular Part-Time Employees) Act 1991
Unfair Dismissals (Amendment) Act 1993
Maternity Protection Act 1994
Terms of Employment (Information) Act 1994
Adoptive Leave Act 1995
Protection of Young Persons (Employment) Act 1996
Transnational Information and Consultation of Employees Act 1996
Organisation of Working Time Act 1997
Employment Equality Act 1998
Parental Leave Act 1998
Equal Status Act 2000
National Minimum Wage Act 2000
Carer's Leave Act 2001
Industrial Relations (Amendment) Act 2001
Protection of Employees (Part-Time Work) Act 2001
Employment Permits Act 2003
Protection of Employees (Fixed-Term Work) Act 2003
Redundancy Payments Act 2003

2.2. Secondary legislation

European Communities (Safeguarding of Employees' Rights on Transfer of Undertakings) Regulations 1980
Safety, Health and Welfare at Work (General Application) Regulations 1993
European Communities (Safeguarding of Employees' Rights on Transfer of Undertakings) (Amendment) Regulations 2000
European Communities (Protection of Employment) Regulations 2000
Industrial Relations Act 1990 (Code of Practice on Voluntary Dispute Resolution) (Declaration) Order 2000

3. A note on further Irish developments in 2003

This annex, indicating further developments in Ireland during 2003, follows the pattern of the main report covering 1992-2002.

Undoubtedly, the most important development during 2003 has been the effort invested in establishing a renewed equilibrium between the social partners at the national level. Following difficult discussions over the preceding months, on 26 March 2003, the Irish Congress of Trade Unions (ICTU) and the Irish Business and Employers Confederation (IBEC) formally ratified Ireland's latest national partnership agreement, *Sustaining Progress*, which covers the period 2003-2005.[67] However, it has been highly significant that the pay agreement component runs for just 18 months, which means that the social partners will have to negotiate the second 18-month period of the three-year programme during 2004. It may also be noted that the new agreement includes no formal commitment to further tax reductions (a key departure from the previous five agreements), and involves the introduction of a variety of 'compliance measures', as well as commitments to improved statutory redundancy pay provisions, an increase in the level of the national minimum wage in 2004, and amendments to statutory provisions on workers' representation.

In the wake of the renewed social partnership agreement, new legislation on statutory redundancy payments – the Redundancy Payments Act 2003 – came into force on 25 May 2003, increasing the statutory severance terms, as well as introducing a number of other important changes based on provisions in the national tripartite agreement.

Also on the legislative front – and underlining the continuing influence of normative statutory regulatory mechanisms – a new Industrial Relations (Amendment) Bill 2003 was published in July 2003. The draft of this proposed measure was judged to have been at least partly in response to growing disillusionment among trade unions and their members in relation to the existing procedures for resolving union recognition and representation disputes.

Nor has the statutory tool been confined to immediate labour law measures. Thus, following publication of a report – commissioned by the Health and Safety Authority (HSA) and the Office of Tobacco Control (OTC) – on the adverse health effects of passive smoking in the workplace, the Minister for Health and Children announced that Ireland was to ban the smoking of tobacco products in the workplace with effect from 1 January 2004.

With respect to the implementation of EU social policy measures in Ireland, the Minister for Labour Affairs published a consultation paper on 11 August 2003, outlining how Directive 2002/14/EC on information and consultation should be transposed into Irish law. An Information and Consultation of Employees Bill is scheduled for publication in the summer of 2004, with a view to enactment by March 2005.[68]

Meanwhile, in relation to the requirements introduced by Directives 2000/43/EC and 2000/78/EC, much of the basic equality legislation and institutional supports required by the new Directives have already been in place for Ireland – and, indeed, in many areas the Irish legislation goes considerably further than the strict requirements of the Directives.[69]

Meanwhile, the end of year statistics for 2003 indicate that the Equality Tribunal (ODEI) published 144 decisions (up 20% on the previous year), and resolved some 61% of the 105 cases referred for mediation (up 64% on 2002). A total of 1078 individual complaints were referred during 2003, with both race and gender complaints recording significant increases over previous years. As in earlier years, over half of the equal status complaints which were referred during the year related to the traveller community – although the overall figure was nearly half of the previous year's total.[70]

Finally, it may be noted that, in the context of preparing the 2003 National Action Plan under the EU Employment Strategy, the Irish government consulted a wide range of organisa-

---

67 This is the sixth successive agreement of its kind since the original negotiation of the *Programme for National Recovery* (PNR) in 1987, and overcame – at least temporarily – the threat of a lapse in what had been 15 unbroken years of national partnership deals.

68 The indication that transposition might take place by this date – the 'normal' transposition deadline set by the Directive – is interesting, given that transitional arrangements are in place for Member States, such as Ireland, which currently do not have 'general, permanent and statutory' information and consultation systems (providing that such countries may elect to phase in the application of the Directive for smaller undertakings over a period up until March 2008).

69 For details of the situation as of August 2003, see *EIRO Online*, 'Thematic feature – implementation of the EU framework equal treatment Directive', published by the European Foundation for the Improvement of Working and Living Conditions (Dublin, regular updates – note prepared by T. Dobbins).

70 See, Equality Tribunal (ODEI), *End of Year Report 2003*, Dublin 2004.

tions when preparing the plan for the period 2003-2005.[71] Much of the policy content is drawn from the recent national tripartite agreement *Sustaining Progress*, which complements the National Action Plan and applies over the same time frame. This provides some considerable overlap between the level for national agreements and the level touched by the NAP – with evident advantages in terms of co-ordination and consistency for the social dialogue in Ireland.

---

71   These included the Irish Congress of Trade Unions (ICTU), the Irish Business and Employers Confederation (IBEC), the Construction Industry Feder-
      ation (CIF), and the Community and Voluntary Pillar (CVP). The CVP encompasses a wide range of organisations, including the Conference of Reli-
      gious of Ireland, the Congress Centres for the Unemployed, the Community Platform, the Irish National Organisation of the Unemployed, the Nation-
      al Women's Council of Ireland, the National Youth Council of Ireland, Protestant Aid, and the Society of St. Vincent de Paul. All of these organisations
      are also involved – to some extent – in the current national agreement, Sustaining Progress, and the overall national social partnership process. The
      2003 consultation process involved the government meeting the social partners to outline the Employment Guidelines, receiving views, and giving the
      parties the opportunity to comment on the draft NAP in advance of its submission to the European Commission. Individual government departments
      also consulted with the social partners on specific elements of the Plan where necessary. The NAP has also been submitted to parliament.

PART TWO

Industrial relations in Ireland has to a large extent been characterised by a commitment to legal abstention, sometimes referred to as 'voluntarism'. The system in the main is a voluntary one in the sense that the parties to the industrial relations process are free to agree or not on the substantive principles governing their mutual rights and obligations and to regulate or not their behaviour without the intervention of the State.

The role of the State is primarily one of facilitating the relationship between trade unions and employers by providing both the legislative framework within which unions can operate and the machinery to assist the parties in resolving trade disputes that may arise. The State also provides and safeguards the individual employment rights of workers by enforcing a range of protective legislation and providing specialist bodies (such as the Labour Court and the Employment Appeals Tribunal) for the resolution of disputes arising there under.

Upon independence from Britain in 1922, Ireland (then known as the Irish Free State) inherited a body of labour legislation consisting of the Trade Union Act 1871 (as amended in 1876), the Conspiracy and Protection of Property Act 1875, the Trade Disputes Act 1906 and the Trade Union Act 1913, all of which had been passed by the UK parliament. In addition there were the Truck Acts 1831-1896 (which required payment of wages in the 'current coin of the realm'), a 1743 Act of the pre-union Irish parliament (17 Geo. II c.8) which required payment of wages 'in ready money' and the Trade Boards Acts 1909 and 1918.

The first labour legislation enacted in the new Irish State were the Conditions of Employment Act 1936 and the Shops (Conditions of Employment Act 1938) which regulated the working hours of those employed in industrial work and retail distribution by providing for a working week of 48 hours and six days paid annual leave (extended to seven in 1939, ten in 1961 and 15 in 1973) together with certain public holiday entitlements (six in 1936, seven in 1974, eight in 1977 and nine in 1994). It might be noted that the designation of New Year's Day as a public holiday in 1974 was intended to mark Ireland's entry to the EEC.

The 1940s saw the enactment of two significant pieces of legislation: the Trade Union Act 1941 and the Industrial Relations Act 1946. Both Acts were subsequently amended (the former in 1942, 1947, 1952, 1971 and 1975; the latter in 1969 and 1976) before major changes were made to both with the enactment of the Industrial Relations Act 1990. The 1946 Act was further amended in 2001 and 2004.

The trade union legislation sought to reduce the number of unions operating in Ireland by establishing a licensing system, thus making it more difficult for new unions to become established, and by improving the procedures whereby two or more could merge. The Industrial Relations legislation concerned the institutional arrangements for the promotion of harmonious labour relations, namely the establishment of machinery for the prevention and settlement of trade disputes. It might be noted that the 1946 Act (and its amendments in 1990, 2001 and 2004) was preceded by prolonged discussions and negotiations with the trade union and employer bodies over its content.

As regards individual employment rights legislation, the first significant enactment since the Conditions of Employment legislation of the 1930s was the Redundancy Payments Act 1967 (based on the British legislation of 1965). The 1967 Act has been amended on many occasions, most recently in 2003, when statutory redundancy pay was increased. The 1970s then saw the enactment of a significant body of legislation following the election in 1973 of a Fine Gael/Labour government with the Minister for Labour being drawn from the Labour Party (Michael O'Leary T.D). The Holidays (Employees) Act 1973 increased the annual leave entitlements of employees from two to three weeks; the Minimum Notice and Terms of Employment Act 1973 gave employees a right to a minimum period of notice before dismissal and to receive a written statement of the main particulars of their employment; the Anti-Discrimination (Pay) Act 1974 and the Employment Equality Act 1977 implemented the 1975 Equal Pay and the 1976 Equal Treatment Directives; the Unfair Dismissals Act 1977 (as amended in 1993) gave employees (with one year's continuous service) a right not to be unfairly dismissed; and the Worker Participation (State Enterprises) Act 1977 (as amended in 1988) provided for the election of worker directors to certain state-owned companies. At this point it should be noted that the equality legislation aside, the aforementioned statutes did not apply to part-time workers (effectively defined as those working less than 20 hours a week). 1977 also saw the enactment of the Protection of Young Persons (Employment) Act and the Protection of Employment Act, as amended in 1996 and 2000, (implementing Council Directive 75/129/EEC).

Following the return to government of the Fianna Fail party, two *National Understandings for Economic and Social Development* were negotiated in 1979 and 1980 by the Government, the Irish Congress of Trade Unions and the employer associations. These provided not only for national wage increases but also for more general areas such as employment legislation. One measure to emerge from this process was the Maternity Protection of Employees Act 1981 which provided for 14 weeks unpaid maternity leave (together with a right to return to work), with ancillary changes to the social welfare legislation providing for the payment of a maternity allowance to those on statutory maternity leave.

The 1980s also saw the implementation in 1980 of Council Directive 77/187/EEC and in 1984 of Council Directive 80/987. The 1984 Employers' Insolvency legislation also reduced the weekly hours threshold from 20 to 18.

Following a period of political instability, the first of a series of social partnership agreements was negotiated in 1987. This committed the Minister for Labour to holding discussions with the social partners about changes to the trade union and industrial relations legislation which would provide 'a better framework for collective bargaining and dispute settlement and help create conditions for employment generating investment'. In February 1988, a set of proposals – described by the Minister as a 'pragmatic package' – was published addressing the major issues which the Minister believed needed to be tackled. Extensive consultations with both sides of industry took place and ultimately arrangements were devised considered to be workable by both sides. The position in relation to secondary picketing was clarified; there was a requirement for trade unions to include pre-strike ballot provisions in their rule books and linked to this were restrictions on an employer's ability to obtain injunctive relief in trade disputes. Additionally, there was a major change in the dispute settlement machinery with the creation of a Labour Relations Commission with the primary responsibility of promoting better industrial relations.

The period 1991-2003 has seen the enactment of a considerable body of legislation, much of which stems from Ireland's EU obligations. Significant pieces of legislation, however, have been dictated by domestic considerations. In chronological order this legislation is as follows:

1. **Payment of Wages Act 1991**, the purpose of which was to provide further protection for employees in relation to the payment of wages and to facilitate the payment of wages otherwise than in cash. Its enactment followed the commitment in the Programme for Economic and Social Progress (the second social partnership agreement) to finalise legislation facilitating the move towards cashless pay. Three basic rights are enshrined in this Act: the right to a readily negotiable mode of wage payment; the right to protection against unlawful deductions; and the right to a written statement of wages and any deductions therefrom.

2. **Worker Protection (Regular Part-Time Employees) Act 1991**, the purpose of which was to ensure that regular part-time employees (defined as those normally expected to work not less than eight hours per week and had so worked for a continuous period of 13 weeks) enjoyed the same protection under the redundancy, minimum notice, unfair dismissals, maternity and holidays legislation as did full-time employees. This Act was repealed in 2001 (see below).

3. **Terms of Employment (Information) Act 1994**, the purpose of which was to transpose Directive 91/533/EEC.

4. **Maternity Protection Act 1994**, the purpose of which was to transpose Directive 92/85/EEC.

5. **Adoptive Leave Act 1995**, the purpose of which was to give effect to one of the recommendations in the Report of the Second Commission to the Status of Women, namely the introduction for adoptive mothers of a scheme similar to that for natural mothers.

6. **Protection of Young Persons (Employment) Act 1996**, the purpose of which was to transpose Directive 94/33/EC. The Act repeals the 1977 Act.

7. **Organisation of Working Time Act 1997**, the purpose of which was to transpose Directive 93/104/EC. The Act also contained provisions concerning Sunday work and 'zero hours' contracts.

8. **Parental Leave Act 1998**, the purpose of which was to transpose Directive 96/34/EC.

9. **Employment Equality Act 1998**, the purpose of which was to outlaw discrimination in employment on nine separate grounds (gender, marital status, family

status, sexual orientation, religion, age, disability, race and membership of the Traveller Community) thus further implementing Directives 75/117/EEC and 76/207/EEC and anticipating Directives 2000/43/EC and 2000/78/EC. The 1998 Act is due to be amended to more fully comply with the latter directive.

10. **National Minimum Wage Act 2000**, the purpose of which is to give effect to the recommendations of the National Minimum Wage Commission. The minimum hourly rate of pay was initially set at €5.59. As and from February 1, 2004 the rate is €7.00.

11. **Carer's Leave Act 2001**, the purpose of which is to confer a right on employees to take temporary leave from their employment for up to 65 weeks to look after persons in need of full-time care and attention. It is designed to complement the carer's benefit scheme introduced by the Minister for Social, Community and Family Affairs in October 2000.

12. **Protection of Employees (Part-Time Work) Act 2001**, the purpose of which was to transpose Directive 98/81/EC and Directive 96/71/EC. The Act repeals the 1991 Act.

13. **Protection of Employees (Fixed-Term Work) Act 2003**, the purpose of which was to transpose Directive 99/70/EC.

14. **European Communities (Protection of Employees on Transfer of Undertakings) Regulations 2003**, the purpose of which was the transposition of the mandatory requirements of Directive 2001/23/EC.

15. **European Communities (Protection of Employees on Transfer of Undertakings) Regulations 2003**, the purpose of which was to transpose the mandatory requirements of Directive 2001/23/EC.

The period also saw the enactment of the Transnational Information and Consultation of Employees Act 1996, transposing Directive 94/45/EC.

The position of agency workers

The rights conferred by the above legislation are confined to employees, that is persons employed under a contract of employment. Because of court decisions suggesting that agency supplied workers were not employees, the Govern-

ment decided, in 1993, to amend the unfair dismissals legislation. This provides that, where an individual agrees with another person, who is carrying on the business of an employment agency, to do or perform personally any work or service for a third person, then the individual is *deemed* to be an employee employed by the third person under a contract of employment. Subsequent legislation then defined a 'contract of employment' as meaning:

1. A contract of service or apprenticeship, and

2. Any other contract whereby an individual agrees with another person who is carrying on the business of an employment agency, to do or perform personally any work or service for a third person.

'Employer' is accordingly defined as the person with whom an employee has entered into a contract of employment subject to the qualification that the person who, under a contract of employment referred to in paragraph (b) 'is liable to pay the wages of the individual concerned', is *deemed* to be the individual's employer.

A recent decision of the Labour Court under the Part-Time Workers Act 2001 questions the thinking behind these developments by holding that a worker supplied by an agency to a client company was employed by that latter company under a contract of service.

Family-friendly labour law

In this context, the relevant provisions of the Organisation of Working Time Act 1997 should be noted. These provide that, in determining the times at which annual leave is granted, the employer must take into account:

1. The need for the employee to reconcile work and any family responsibilities, and

2. The opportunity for rest and recreation available to the employee.

It should also be noted that, although a social welfare benefit is available for working mothers taking maternity or adoptive leave, no such benefit is available for working parents who take parental leave. Research commissioned by the Working Group on the Review of the Parental Leave Act 1998 showed that only 20% of eligible employees were estimated to have taken parental leave with the majoriy of those taking such leave being women (84%).

THE EVOLUTION OF LABOUR LAW
IN ITALY
1992-2002

Silvana Sciarra
Professor of Labour Law
University of Florence Law School

Table of contents

Legislation quoted in the Report

L. 12 June 1990, n. 146
L. 23 July 1991, n. 223
D. lgs. 3 February 1993, n. 29
L. 19 July 1993, n. 236
L.19 July 1994, n. 451
L. 28 November 1996, n. 608
L. 23 December 1996, n. 662
L. 24 June 1997, n. 196
D.lgs. 4 November 1997, n. 396
D.lgs. 23 December 1997, n. 469
D.lgs. 25 July 1998, n. 286
L. 12 March 1999, n. 68
L. 17 May 1999, n. 144
D.lgs. 26 November 1999, n. 532
D.lgs. 25 February 2000, n. 61
L. 8 March 2000, n. 53
L. 11 April 2000, n. 83
D.lgs. 21 April 2000, n. 181
D.lgs. 23 May 2000, n. 196
L. 23 December 2000, n. 388
D. lgs. 2 February 2001, n. 18
D.lgs.26 February 2001, n. 100
D.lgs. 26 March 2001, n. 151
D.lgs. 30 March 2001, n. 165
D.lgs. 6 September 2001, n. 368
L. Cost. 18 October 2001, n. 3
D.lgs. 2 April 2002, n. 74
L. 30 July 2002, n. 189
L. 9 December 2002, n. 222
D.lgs 19 December 2002, n. 297
D.lgs. 9 July 2003, n. 215
D.lgs. 9 July 2003, n. 216
L. 14 February 2003, n. 30
D.lgs. 8 April 2003, n. 66
D.lgs. 10 September 2003, n. 276

Chapter 1:
Introduction: Essential features of the industrial relations system

In the attempt to sketch out the evolution of Italian labour law in the decade running from 1992 to 2003, we must first of all consider the essential characteristics of the system. This will allow us to place this evolution in a context and to be aware of the relevance that collective actors, courts and labour market institutions may have.

1. The main actors

Data on employers' associations and trade unions are based on figures made available by the associations themselves. Since they are private associations, no duty to register membership is provided for.

In the year 2000, Confindustria, the largest association of private companies, reported 112 000 members, employing 4 600 000 workers. In 1998, Confapi, the association of small and medium enterprises, reported 65 094 members, with 1 130 631 workers. In 1998, Confcommercio associated 750 000 companies and Confesercenti 315 000 in commercial enterprises. In agriculture, Confagricoltura associates the largest number of members (in 1997 there were 685 000).

Quite a large number of associations can be counted in the area of co-operative work. They serve different purposes and are often organised along political lines, as well as by area of activity.

ARAN is the representative of public administrations acting as employers. It is not a voluntary association, but was granted legal personality. Its five members are all nominated through Ministerial Decree. The Minister for Labour and Welfare appoints three members, whereas the other two are appointed by an organisation of regions and local authorities.

In the public sector, unlike in the private sector, there are legal criteria to measure trade union representativeness. Unions with at least 5% of membership (measured as an average between trade union membership and results achieved in the elections) are recognised by ARAN as bargaining agents.

In June 1995, following the results of a referendum, a partial abrogation of Art. 19 of the Workers' Statute – dealing with union representatives at plant level – introduced new criteria for granting union rights. It is now established that workers can take the initiative to elect representatives at plant level among members of associations which have signed collective agreements enforceable in that particular workplace. The Constitutional Court specified[1] that being signatory to a collective agreement implies being a real bargaining agent and not to have adhered to agreements negotiated and signed by other organisations. Furthermore, the agreement must be of a binding nature and to have a direct impact on the regulation of economic and working conditions in individual contracts of employment.

As for trade unions, in the year 2000 CGIL reported 5 354 472 members; CISL 4 083 996; UIL 1 786 879. The total of unionised workers is 11 225 347; also including retired workers. The total number goes down to 5 458 232 if we consider active workers only. These unions are described as confederations, since they associate individuals and also associations active in specific sectors of economic activity.

There are also unions of quadri (middle-managers) and dirigenti (managers) and a union of school teachers. These are exceptions to the Italian tradition of associations based on the economic activity performed, rather than on craft and individual occupations. Organisations lacking specific characteristics and having a rank and file basis were created in response to the centralised structure of traditional confederations (COBAS, RDB) and are active especially in transport and in secondary schools.

One of the most interesting recent phenomena has to do with the emergence of new actors on the scene of organised interests. Non-standard workers are represented within the three main confederations by special associations.[2]

*   I am very grateful to Prof. Giovanni Orlandini, who read a first draft of this Report and commented on it. I am solely responsible for omissions and mistakes.

1   *Corte Costituzionale,* 27 June 1996, n. 244.

2   NIDIL, ALAI and CPO are respectively associated to CGIL, CISL and UIL. The names are indicative of a new reality. NIDIL stands for 'New work identities', whereas ALAI stands for 'Association of atypical and temporary workers' and CPO for 'Co-ordination for employment'.

The idea, introduced in the 1993 Protocol of agreement signed by all major organisations (see *infra* 3), was to include such workers in the scope of traditional unions, which is in itself a challenging, albeit debatable, choice.

These associations have also signed agreements with the counterpart association representing temporary work agencies, mainly on training programmes for temporary workers, sometimes followed by the monitoring of such experiences.

2. The system of collective bargaining

The Italian labour law system is characterised by a several forms of regulation of individual employment contracts and collective agreements. The latter, though, are still lacking specific legal regulation.

Freedom of association is covered in the 1948 Constitution (Art. 39). It provides for a special procedure, whereby only registered unions can sign collective agreements with an *erga omnes* effect. The fact that no registration ever occurred for the absence of a constitutional law on this matter, created an original set up. Abstention of the law meant that collective agreements, grounded in the constitutional norm on freedom of association, are only *de facto* binding for those who do not fall within the scope of the agreements themselves, not being members of the signatory associations.

Collective agreements traditionally cover all relevant industrial sectors; their scope is nationwide within each sector. Plant agreements also have a long-lasting tradition in Italy. They are somehow linked to the national level of bargaining, which is traditionally considered as a higher source in the hierarchy of bargaining levels. Subject matters to be bargained at plant level are frequently specified in the national collective agreement, thus creating a more specialised level of negotiation, closer to specific patterns in work organisation and to specific individual needs of the workers concerned.

As for the centralised, cross-industry level of bargaining, agreements signed by employers' associations and the most representative trade unions (*accordi interconfederali*) were an important resource for Italian labour law in the immediate post-war period and later on, when issues of broad relevance were at stake. There have also been centralised agreements

dealing with issues of internal organisation of the bargaining machinery, in the attempt to rationalise levels of bargaining and the mandate of bargaining agents. Such agreements create an obligation on bargaining agents at lower levels to implement the indications provided for. They do not, however, give rise to individual enforceable rights within individual contracts of employment. This is a typical example of clauses of a 'procedural' nature, not binding on a normative ground.

Recently, there has been a return of large inter-sector agreements, as a result of remittals to collective bargaining in the recent 2003 reform. A first agreement intervenes on the transition from the old regulation of contracts of employment for professional training to the new one, provided for in the Decree.[3] A second agreement[4] deals with special contracts of employment for marginalised groups of workers to be brought back into the labour market, such as the long-term unemployed, or people who have ceased to be self-employed (*contratti di inserimento*).

A third recent agreement, covering the artisan sector,[5] is worth mentioning for the attempt it makes to regulate two levels of bargaining – national and regional.

Finally, collective actors have been frequently active in negotiations with the government on matters of political and economic relevance, including the adoption of legislation on very sensitive labour law areas. This practice, known as 'concertazione' and/or 'legislazione negoziata', indicates the urgency felt at particular times in history to include the social partners in a decision-making process, both for reasons of recognition of their institutional relevance and in order to acquire social consensus. These forms of tripartite bargaining do not give birth to a collective agreement in strict technical terms. Legal implications may, nevertheless, be very relevant.

It should be underlined that social consensus, reached through consultation of trade unions and employers' associations, has been an important component of the Italian labour law system. Initially an objective of governments favouring the inclusion of social partners in important stages of the law-making process, it then became a technique, useful to approach broader economic policy issues. Compliance with the Maastricht criteria, in view of Economic and Monetary Union, has played a substantial role in employing this technique.

Political scientists have observed that 'since 1992 no major interest group has withdrawn support from the Euro-goal,

---

3   Accordo interconfederale (as for art. 86 of D.lgs. 10 September 2003, n. 276) signed on 13 November 2003.
4   Accordo interconfederale (as for art. 54 ff. of D.lgs. 10 September 2003, n. 276) signed on 11 February 2004. This agreement is defined by the parties as transitory and subsidiary to other levels of collective bargaining. This implies that when other agreements will come into force, this broad and preliminary definition of the implementation of *contratti di inserimento* will cease to be effective.
5   Accordo interconfederale signed on 3 March 2004.

although there has been debate as to whether Italy would have been better off joining the single currency in the second wave'.[6] The most relevant feature of such political choices is that the social partners have been part of that crucial decision and have been converted to a European strategy, particularly through a re-discovery of social pacts.

It should also be briefly mentioned that the Italian labour market is still dominated by a North-South divide, visible in the rate of unemployment (a difference of up to 25% has been measured between the rates in Trentino and Calabria). In addition, the underground economy continues to be larger in Italy than elsewhere, almost twice as big as in other industrialised countries.[7]

3. Centralised negotiation and social pacts

The most relevant examples of centralised pacts were the Amato and Ciampi *accordi*, so called after the prime ministers who promoted them, respectively in 1992 and 1993. They re-designed the whole system of collective bargaining, with special attention to income policies, and the rationalisation of bargaining levels.[8]

In the 1993 Protocol of Agreement, signed by the social partners and the Ciampi Government, attention was also paid to one of the most controversial issues in Italian collective labour law. The lack of specific legal indications on how to measure trade unions 'representativeness' was counterbalanced by a voluntary initiative of the unions. The agreement reached by the main confederations for the election of RSU, namely unitary union representatives, was incorporated into the 1993 Protocol. The latter provides for union representatives' elections to take place at plant level. All workers are entitled to vote, choosing from lists presented by associations with at least 5% membership at the workplace or presented by representative unions at national level. The election grants two-thirds to representatives elected with a secret ballot and one third to lists presented by associations which are signatories to collective agreements enforceable at plant level.

A similar criterion is applied for the election of members of European Works Councils, in line with a 1996 national agreement signed by the main confederations.[9]

In 1996 the Prodi Government continued what Ciampi started in his administration and launched labour reforms as part of the *Patto per il lavoro*. It was the then Minister of Labour Tiziano Treu who signed significant reforms, known in the jargon as *Pacchetto Treu*, to be dealt with further on.[10]

The D'Alema Government followed and consolidated this trend in 1998, signing *Patto di Natale* or the 'Christmas Pact' with a large number of representative organisations, involving also regions and local authorities. This pact mentions all precedent agreements, thus underlining a strong element of continuity in a consolidated practice of consensual approach to labour and economic issues. The EU is also mentioned, not only with regard to the fulfilment of macro-economic policies, but also in relation to the Luxembourg Council, which expanded co-ordinated strategies to employment policies.

It is interesting to note that the *Patto di Natale* indicates the yearly meetings on income policies as the occasions in which National Action Plans (NAPs) on employment should be discussed and drafted, with a full participation of the social partners.

In the approach taken by the Italian centre-left governments in the 1990s, *concertazione* becomes an overall philosophy, a guiding principle both for facing internal domestic priorities and for getting closer to European targets. Born as a national practice of problem-solving, through the inclusion of representatives of economic, social and political interests, it then becomes a technique for the Europeanisation of Italian policies.

This makes a national model of multi-level governance, which maintains in full its domestic characteristics, a comparable model within Europe and one which can be exposed to the challenges of supranational institutions.

It is not insignificant that such a consensual climate also allowed innovative and original thinking in the contested terrain of welfare reforms. They were started by the Amato and Ciampi governments and found an exceptional outcome in 1995, with the Dini reform of the pension system, launched by the centre-right Berlusconi Government and yet agreed upon with the unions, due to an open and transparent bargaining mechanism, which allowed for some concessions to the interested parties.

During the Prodi Government, a most interesting and complete analysis on the feasibility of welfare reforms was pro-

---

6   The latter was the position expressed by C. Romiti, then a leading figure in Fiat. See M. Giuliani and M. Radaelli, 'Italian Political Science and the European Union', *Journal of European Public Policy 1999*, p. 522.

7   C. Dell'Aringa, 'The Italian Labour Market: Problems and Prospects', *Quaderni dell'Istituto di Economia dell'impresa e del lavoro*, Febbraio 2003, n. 33, p. 17 and p. 5-6.

8   G. Giugni, *La lunga marcia della concertazione*, Bologna 2003, p. 57 ff. in particular.

9   See also D.lgs. 2 April 2002, n. 74.

10 In his book *Politiche del lavoro*, Bologna 2001, T. Treu describes and analyses his own contributions in law and policy-making in the 1990s.

duced by a governmental committee (named after its chair – the *Commissione Onofri*). The main indication given in the report issued by this committee was to try and find a new balance among expenditures, rather than to simply try and pursue cuts in the budget.[11]

It has been suggested that the Italian road to Europe has been paved by two categories of actors. On the one hand there was a restricted circle of 'architects', who favoured economic recovery, due partly to their professional and institutional links with the Ministry of Treasury and the Bank of Italy. On the other hand, there was a wider circle of 'constructors', made up of political leaders, representatives of interest groups, members of parliament and politicians, who concretely guided the enactment of some reforms. The relevant innovation is the interaction between the two categories and the achievement of the proposed reforms on a step-by-step basis, typical of a 'learning' process.[12] The transversal nature of such a coalition, combining together actors of different political orientations, makes it possible to get closer to European targets and to appreciate their relevance for the development of domestic institutions and policy-making.

A recent inquiry, concentrated on the years 1997-2000, revealed that 71% of the population thinks that consulting the social partners is a positive approach when important decisions are at stake. These results must be framed within a growing awareness on the side of the working population that union membership is falling.[13]

Regional – or even sub-regional – collective agreements should also be mentioned. They fall within the logic of *concertazione*, aiming at forms of consensual local planning. They are often tripartite agreements, since they involve local public authorities in the definition of projects for local development (*patti territoriali*) or in active employment policies (*contratti d'area*), the latter with specific EU funding.

In the years 1993-1996, CNEL, a national council dealing with economic and labour issues, provided for by the Constitution, launched – in agreement with government – a series of initiatives to promote local development. A large number of pro-

posals were then transformed into agreements signed and formalised at CNEL, dealing with new investments, the creation of new jobs and training. Monitoring *patti territoriali* should have been the function of central authorities and, particularly after 1997, it should have been related to the allocation of public funds. This led to a more bureaucratic phase, which somehow reduced the original enthusiasm.[14]

Contratti d'area had a different geographical origin and was designed to promote employment in areas of Italy hit by economic decline. With the support of European funds, social partners and local authorities were bound together towards the achievement of better economic performances.

The evaluation of the bargaining system agreed upon in the 1993 Agreement was the task of a committee appointed in 1998 and chaired by a leading labour lawyer and former labour minister, Gino Giugni. The committee also gave recommendations on how to further improve the system. The most current evaluation is that decentralisation of the bargaining system did not occur to the extent that was expected, because of the non-availability of large parts of the employers' associations, fundamentally hostile towards a double level of negotiations. There is a slight contradiction in the fact that the linking of wage increases to productivity, which was also pursued by most employers, can only find its optimal solution at a decentralised bargaining level.[15]

It is expected that the 1993 Protocol will be subject to evaluation and possibly to changes in the near future.

4. Reform of the labour market under the Berlusconi government: A controversial time for centralised pacts

Soon after the start of the Berlusconi Government, a so-called 'White Paper on Labour Market Reforms' saw the light in October 2001. Prepared by a group of academics and collaborators of the Labour and Welfare Ministry,[16] this document

---

11   Further references to this and to subsequent measures in the fight against social exclusion are in S. Giubboni, 'Diritto della sicurezza sociale e lotta all'esclusione sociale', *Giornale di diritto del lavoro e delle relazioni industriali 2003*, p. 578 ff.

12   This is the opinion of M. Ferrera and E. Gualmini, *Salvati dall'Europa*, Bologna 1999, p. 131 ff.

13   M. Dau, *Oltre la concertazione*, Firenze 2001, p. 100 ff.

14   M. Dau, op. ult. cit., p. 76-77; B. Caruso, 'Decentralised Social Pacts, Trade Unions and Collective Bargaining. How Labour Law is Changing', in M. Biagi (ed), *Towards a European Model of Industrial Relations*, Kluwer 2001, p. 208; M. Giaccone, 'Fra settore e territorio', in *Quaderni di rassegna sindacale 2002*, p. 157 ff.

15   L. Bellardi, 'Dal Protocollo del 93 al Libro Bianco: nodi critici e ipotesi di riforma della struttura contrattuale', *Economia e lavoro 2003*.

16   Among these, the leading figure was Marco Biagi, a well-known labour lawyer who had generously contributed to the elaboration and the drafting of legislation even under previous administrations and was then killed by the terrorist group Red Brigades in March 2002. His work, as an advisor to the Labour Ministry is acknowledged in T. Treu, *Politiche del lavoro*, Bologna 2001, p. 269 ff.

provoked the criticism of CGIL in particular, mainly because of the potential danger it posed to the consensual climate established by national centralised pacts and collective bargaining.[17] This document also gave rise to widespread discussions in academic circles, resulting in an ideological confrontation.

One issue, more than others, was at the centre of opposite views with regard to the evolution of labour law. A proposed reform of Article 18 of the 1970 Workers' Statute, dealing with the regulation of individual dismissals, attracted the opposition of the unions and of CGIL in a most explicit way. The threatened intervention on one of the main pillars of Italian labour law was somehow instrumentally used in the presentation of a very aggressive labour law agenda, attributed to the 'White Paper' as the new manifesto of an overall deregulatory philosophy of reforms.

Article 18 – and, more specifically, its strong apparatus of sanctions, including reinstatement as the final outcome for unjustified dismissals – was not so central in the theories of labour market regulation put forward in the 'White Paper' and was certainly not considered by the drafters of this document as the absolute priority. Nevertheless, it polarised the attention of commentators and of the social partners as the emblem of individual guarantees not to be dismantled.

CGIL called a general strike in March 2002, which saw an impressive turnout of participants. However, the climate among the main confederations deteriorated, mainly because of differences over how to handle negotiations with the government. The result was that in July 2002, leaving CGIL alone in its harsh opposition, two confederations (CISL and UIL) and the main employers' association Confindustria signed a pact with the Berlusconi Government, called the Pact for Italy (*Patto per l'Italia*).

This new version of a centralised pact – with the main confederation left out of the picture – started a new phase in the long and well established tradition of wide and uniform consensus. This can either be attributed to the delicate nature of the issue put at the centre of political negotiations, or, more generally, to a new interpretation of what a bipolar democracy should be like, when a strong majority is guaranteed in parliament.[18]

This interpretation must be read in conjunction with a peculiar characteristic of the Italian system. The social partners acquired over the years a most relevant role in the shaping of policy-making and law-making, either at times of widespread social unrest, as in the late 1960s, or when most political parties had undergone a deep crisis, as in the 1990s. What used to be interpreted as a way to replace political parties (*supplenza sindacale*), then became a correct and quasi-institutional means to attribute a consultative power to private – and yet highly representative – organisations. This practice brought about, as previously indicated, better economic stability and consequently, a more qualified presence in the EU.

The symbolic – and yet highly technical – relevance of Article 18 was at the roots of a referendum called by several parties of the left in June 2003. The purpose was to expand the scope of individual dismissal law beyond the existing limits set in the Workers' Statute, namely companies employing more than 15 workers. The attempt to respond to a non-consensual governmental campaign with a different agenda, not fully shared by all unions and parties of the centre-left, proved to be a mistake. The result of the referendum – which in Italy can only be used for the repeal of existing laws – was void, due to the low number of citizens voting and, therefore, the failure to comply with the minimum turnout required.

The confrontation once again became political and gave rise to a complex – and perhaps less visible – negotiation between the social partners and the government, ending up in a compromise. The reform of Article 18 became a separate issue from the enforcement of other reforms outlined in the 'White Paper' and now rests in the hands of parliamentary committees.[19] The other proposals were dealt with in a *Legge Delega*, later transposed into a Decree.[20]

5. A constitutional reform: Title V revisited

An interesting open question is whether proper bargaining functions should be delegated to regional bargaining agents, thus adding yet another level to the already complex bargaining machinery. This discussion is now very relevant in the light of a reform of the Constitution, which is still in the process of being fully implemented. Such a reform,[21] which will almost certainly be subject to further adaptations, must be acknowledged as a relevant – albeit complex and often unclear – change in labour law perspectives.

---

17   A. Lo Faro, 'Fairness at Work? The Italian White Paper on Labour Market Reform', *Industrial Law Journal*, 2002, p. 290 ff.

18   The latter interpretation is offered by M. Ferrera and E. Gualmini, *Rescued by Europe? Social and Labour Market Reforms in Italy from Maastricht to Berlusconi*, Amsterdam University Press forthcoming. This is an updated translation in English of the Italian version of the book quoted earlier on.

19   Ddl 848-bis.

20   *Legge delega* (L. 23 February 2003, n. 30), followed by Decree 10 September 2003, n. 276, G.U. n. 235, 9.10.2003, suppl. ordinario n. 159.

21   L. Cost. 18 October 2001, n. 3.

It will suffice to say that the distribution of competence between the state and the regions appears has now been significantly altered, and the constitutional reform implies major revisions within certain areas of law.

One contentious point has to do with maintaining fundamental labour law rights within the exclusive national competence and delegating to regional competence only very specific legislative interventions.

The Constitutional Court has already intervened in these matters, ruling that the State remains responsible for a 'unitary' exercise of administrative powers and of uniformity in the discipline of fundamental rights.[22] The implications for labour law are that whenever regions have competence to legislate 'concurring' with the State and even when an 'exclusive' competence is indicated, the scope of regional legislation is rather limited.

According to the Court, the State's competence expands in controlling the concrete enforcement of administrative powers, so that their organisation at a decentralised level can still respond to unitary legal criteria. The Court's case law shows that labour law at a regional level can only deal with the regulation of different and varying forms of connection established among individual citizens and the public administration. One example of a unitary competence is the organisation on the whole State territory of services to promote employment.[23]

6. Privatisation of contracts of employment in the public sector

The so-called 'privatisation' of the public sector brings about a major reform which has to do with the transposition of private law principles into the regulation of contracts of employment in the public sector.[24]

For reasons of clarity, it should be pointed out that what has been said before (Section 1.2) about levels of bargaining and the legal nature of collective agreements does not automatically apply to the public sector. Through a mechanism of legal representation of all branches of the public sector which become parties to collective agreements, the latter

have been given an *erga omnes* effect. ARAN, the bargaining agent, has legal personality and operates following the government's guidelines, having gained more autonomy in 1997, in a reform of the original 1993 Law.[25]

7. Industrial conflict

As for industrial conflict, the **right to strike** is recognised as an individual right in Article 40 of the Constitution. No right to lock out is expressly mentioned in the Constitution, thus establishing the employer's responsibility to pay wages, even when he refuses the employees' offer to work.

Industrial conflict has been one of the most intangible areas of labour law for decades, due to the opposition of the main trade unions to legislation limiting the recourse to strikes. A law on strikes in the so-called essential public service sectors was passed in 1990 and revised in 2000.[26]

These are remarkable examples of legislation, combining the protection of fundamental freedoms covered by the Constitution and the exercise of the constitutional right to strike. The previous well-established tradition of the Constitutional Court in balancing such rights represented an inspiration for the legislature and so did the attempt of the main unions to regulate these matters by making recourse to codes of conduct.

The 2000 reform extended the philosophy of the 1990 Law – namely the introduction of legal limits to collective action – to areas of non-subordinate employment and also to small business. Even in such areas, concerted collective actions must not interfere with individual fundamental rights, protected by the Constitution. Voluntary codes must be adopted, providing for the announcement of the action within a given time, the length of the same and the reasons behind it.

They must also indicate the essential services to be delivered to users while exercising the right to strike.

The 2000 Law also reformed sanctions. Procedural limits were set, so that the agency supervising the correct implementation of the law (*Commissione di garanzia*) must evaluate the behaviour of the parties. The procedure can start *ex officio*, or on request of one of the parties. The other party must be heard (*principio del contraddittorio*).

---

22   Corte Costituzionale 19 dicembre 2003, n. 359; Corte Costituzionale 19 dicembre 2003, n. 361; Corte Costituzionale, 19 dicembre 2003, n. 363.

23   Corte Costituzionale 19 dicembre 2003, n. 363.

24   The reform of employment in the public sector started with D.lgs. 3 February 1993, n. 29, which was several times modified during the 1990s and then consolidated in D.lgs. 30 March 2001, n. 165 (Testo Unico).

25   D.lgs. 3 February 1993, n. 29, artt. 50 e 51, modified by D.lgs. 4 November 1997, n. 396 (now consolidated in D.lgs. 30 March 2001, n. 165, artt. 46-47).

26   L. 12 June 1990, n. 146; L. 11 April 2000, n. 83.

8. Labour courts

Labour law disputes are handled by labour courts. A significant reform introduced in 1973 specified the competence of such specialised judges and opened up the field to the inclusion in such a jurisdiction of quasi-autonomous contracts of employment. The above mentioned 'privatisation' of contracts of employment in the public sector expanded the jurisdiction of labour courts to also cover controversies in that area of employment.

With the exception of cases dealing with the employer's anti-union activities, no 'collective' representation in labour law cases is provided for under Italian law. Unions can appear in labour courts only for the defence of a collective right, namely that infringed by anti-union hostile behaviour.

9. Immigration

Italy has only recently dealt with immigration, as a social, cultural and economic phenomenon. 754 000 immigrant workers have requested and obtained a regular permit to work in the space of sixteen years (legislation on *regolarizzazione* was introduced first in 1986 and subsequently changed several times). Figures have risen drastically (almost 700 000 requests) under a recent law (L. 9 December 2002, no. 222) which introduced new forms of legalisation of immigrants already working in Italy. Up to December 2001, there were 1 362 630 third country immigrants.

In 1998,[27] the legislature attempted to deal with the phenomenon of immigration from third countries. The leading principle is to try and regulate employment contracts, so that immigrants should not become part of the black economy. Quotas of third country nationals are decided by ministerial decree. For each immigrant entering Italy, a special permit is issued if a guarantee is provided by an Italian citizen or a foreign legally resident citizen, offering housing, healthcare and of course salary. Equal treatment and equal rights were provided for immigrants.

Legislation changed under the current government and is at the centre of acute disputes, even within the centre-right coalition. The *Bossi-Fini* Law[28] is named after two well-known political leaders, the former active mainly in the North of Italy (*Lega Nord*), the latter a representative figure of the right-wing *Alleanza Nazionale* party.

The *Bossi-Fini* Law introduced a contested new regulation, by which each immigrant must enter a *contratto di soggiorno*, which means showing evidence of a contract of employment in order to become a legal resident. The law has not yet been fully enacted. Regulations on asylum seekers are still expected.

Equal treatment should be provided in Italian law, regardless of the national origin.

Recent research undergone by Fondazione Agnelli (results given in a conference in June 2003) shows that second generation immigrants have in some cases been fully integrated and even started entrepreneurial activities of their own.

27   D.lgs. 25 July 1998, n. 286.
28   L. 30 July 2002, n. 189.

Chapter II:
From job security to employability

1. Reforms of the placement system: Abolition of the public monopoly and decentralisation, Measures on disabled people, Third country immigrants

One of the traditional functions of labour law in Italy, from the post-war time onwards, has been to promote participation in the labour market through a public placement system (*colloca-mento*). The system is based on the assumption that weaker parties need to be assisted by objective criteria to enter the labour market. The individual freedom to work is therefore accompanied by individual guarantees, which do not give rise to proper subjective rights to be hired, except in cases for which special provisions are laid down. This is the case of the *assunzioni obbligatorie*, namely cases in which the employer is under the obligation to hire. One leading example is legislation on disabled people, improved in 1999, as we shall see further on.

The protection of employment – and consequently the fight against unemployment – is either assigned to collective means of action, or to legislation tuned in with economic policies aimed at promoting the creation of new working opportunities, through new investments or fiscal policies. Labour market regulation, particularly in the field of public placement mechanisms, is oriented towards the correction of potential unbalances in the equilibrium between supply and demand. The underlying rationale is that in order to protect employees against the risk of unemployment, obstacles which might prevent individuals from entering the labour market or moving from one occupation to the other should be removed.[29]

In the original set-up of Italian legislation in this field, the employer's freedom to choose and select the workforce was in a sense limited by legal provisions indicating numerical cri-

teria, such as the hiring of a certain number of employees falling within a certain category or having certain occupational qualifications. This attitude of the legislature showed, on the one hand, attention to the protection of the weaker party. On the other hand it was consequential to a vision of work in which the hiring of a specific employee (*assunzione nominativa*) with specific skills would represent the exception rather than the norm. Anonymous work would prevail over personalised employment, thus confirming the picture of alienated work within large companies. Exceptions were to be found in the hiring of highly specialised workforce, or in employment within the employer's family.

Certain parts of this legislation came to be perceived as potential barriers both to labour mobility and to new employment. In particular, the gradual abolition of the 'numerical' hiring has transformed the function of placement offices from mediation – to be considered a public function – into a public service.[30]

In 1991 the numerical hiring system began to be eroded and finally collapsed in 1997, thus opening the way to a new approach to placement mechanisms. In 1991, the legislature removed the ban on hiring 'by name' (so called *fasce deboli*).[31] In subsequent amendments to the law the principle of direct hiring, without being bound to lists of workers seeking employment, became central to the whole mechanism.[32]

In 1997,[33] following legislation which had empowered the government to act by decree and decentralise certain administrative functions to the regions, placement offices ceased to be governed by the centre and became the responsibility of local authorities. Regional legislation assigns tasks to sub-regional authorities – such as provinces – and indicates active employment policies among the aims to be pursued. Provinces have the task of setting up *centri per l'impiego*, namely local institutions substituting all previous decentralised branches of the central administration.

---

29   E. Ghera, *Diritto del lavoro*, Bari 2002, p. 542-543.

30   F. Liso, 'Collocamento e agenzie private', *Giornale di diritto del lavoro e delle relazioni industriali 2002*, p. 597.

31   L. 23 July 1991, n. 223, art. 25, abrogated by art. 8, D.lgs 19 December 2002, n. 297, giving to the Regions the possibility to reserve quotas in the hiring of 'particular groups of workers, at risk of social exclusion'.

32   L. 28 November 1996, n. 608, art. 9 bis sect. 2, amended by art. 6 sect. 2 D.lgs. 19 December 2002, n. 297, simply putting on the employer the obligation to communicate to the placement centre the decision to hire.

33   D.lgs. 23 December 1997, n. 469.

The State maintains responsibility for the promotion and the co-ordination of placement policies, and an exclusive competence for issues related to immigration, conciliation of labour disputes, co-ordination with international organisations and the EU.

The 1997 Decree uses the word *mediazione* to indicate the role of the regions in facilitating the placement of employees, including the disabled and socially excluded. It opens up the possibility for private companies and even co-operatives to fulfil such tasks, provided they are authorised by the Labour Ministry (Art. 10.2).

In 2000,[34] further modifications were introduced, which also expanded the competence of local placement centres. They were needed in order to comply with EU recommendations on the prevention of youth and long-term unemployment and facilitating the re-entry of unemployed women into the labour market (Art.1). A definition of unemployment is given (Art.2). Removal of unemployed status may follow non-compliance of the individual in question with the relevant obligations (such as the duty to take part in regular interviews, the availability to accept work, etc.).

Furthermore, *mediazione* has been specified by the legislature in 2000[35] as the activity which allows the encounter of supply and demand, but functions also for the research and selection of personnel, as well as for outplacement.

It is useful to recall that the gradual reform of the system took place under the threat of an ECJ decision in *Job Centre II*.[36] Following a preliminary ruling procedure, the Court had been asked to evaluate whether the public nature of placement offices in Italy would exempt them from competition rules. The Court found that such offices did not satisfy market demands. Furthermore it added that statutes prohibiting the placement of workers by private companies made it impossible to perform placement within or outside the state. The Italian legislature won its battle to approve the reform of the placement system before the Court's decision, thus establishing a symbolic principle of autonomy of the parliament. One of the protagonists of the time wrote that the introduction in the Italian system of legislation on

temporary work[37] – which was also in the spectrum of the ECJ's ruling – combined with the reform of the placement system in 1997, represented an historical landmark in the abolition of the state monopoly in the hiring system.[38]

Part of the active employment policies assigned to the new public placement offices is the so-called right to work of disabled people.[39] Employers, both private and public with 15 or more employees have to hire a certain percentage of disabled people. They include people affected by physical or mental handicaps, people with a certified invalidity and a reduced capacity to work, blind, deaf and dumb people, people with an invalidity from military service, etc.

These placement services are offered by regional specialised offices, working in close contact with social and health services. Agreements can be reached between the employer and such offices in order to set up a programme for the inclusion of disabled people, following a training programme. This solution offers more flexible possibilities to the employer, who can hire on a personal basis and not a numerical one, and include fixed term contracts and longer probation periods.

The 2003 reform of the labour market provides that the employer can also stipulate an agreement with specialised social co-operatives in order to move out of his own business the quota of disabled to be hired, thereby having work performed elsewhere, but in compliance with the basic statutory obligation.[40]

This is an interesting case of legal contracting out, since the employer has the obligation to provide work which is organised outside of the company. A regional fund, to be created by regional laws, covers the financing of such targeted placement services.

On the whole, legislation on disabled people aims to go beyond a merely protective attitude of public services and to promote the social inclusion of disadvantaged people. A 'collective remedy'[41] such as the one envisaged by this statute is based on principles of solidarity. This forces the legislature into a different pattern, whereby traditional punitive sanctions make way for positive measures.

---

34 D.lgs. 21 April 2000, n. 181, modified by D.lgs. 19 December 2002, n. 297. This decree is part of broader legislation aimed at rationalising public funding of unemployment and support to groups hardly hit by unemployment and at risk of being excluded from the labour market.

35 L. 23 December 2000, n. 388, art. 117.

36 C-55/96 Job Centre Coop [1997] ECR I-7119. Comments to the case in S. Sciarra, *Job Centre: an illustrative Example of Strategic Litigation*, in S. Sciarra (ed), *Labour Law in the Courts. National Judges and the European Court of Justice*, Oxford 2001.

37 See section III.3.

38 T. Treu, *Politiche del lavoro. Insegnamenti di un decennio*, Bologna 2001, p. 45. Treu was the Labour Minster when the Court decided Job Centre.

39 L. 12 March 1999, n. 68.

40 D.lgs. 10 September 2003, n. 276, art. 14.

41 As indicated by A. De Felice, *Le sanzioni nel diritto del lavoro*, Napoli 2003, p. 209-210.

2. Contracts of employment and professional training

Contracts of employment dealing with professional training were first introduced in the Italian legal system in the 1980s. They continued to have a significant success in the 1990s, due to their combination of traditional contractual obligations with the employer's duty to offer the worker training opportunities. For such contracts a fixed-term is traditionally indicated and lower contributions are due.

A first significant reform occurred in 1994,[42] with the aim to specify the employer's obligation to train for medium to high-level jobs, reducing the recourse to such contracts for jobs implying very low skills.

The ECJ (C-310/99, 7 March 2002) contributed to the decline of this particular employment contract. It ruled that laws which did not aim at a permanent increase of employment were to be considered an infringement of European law on state aid.

In 1997, in the framework of *Pacchetto Treu* reforms contributed to improving the regulation of another type of contract named *apprendistato* or apprenticeship. In the expansion of training obligations for young people up to 18 years of age, the access to training external to the company was also improved.[43]

The 2003 Decree innovates significantly on such matters. It introduces a complex system of sources, which all interact in the regulation of contracts with the aim to favour the employment of marginal groups, including young people. Decentralisation to regions, together with the recourse to other means of regulation, including the orientations coming from so-called 'bilateral bodies', does not seem to indicate training as a first priority.[44]

3. Collective dismissals and measures against unemployment

In 1991,[45] the Italian legislature conducted a very complex reform of an area traditionally criticised by the ECJ. This is why account is given of this law.

In 1982 and in 1985 the Court ruled against Italy, finding that the 1975 Directive on collective dismissals had not been correctly transposed, since legislation was lacking and the collective agreement in existence did not have an *erga omnes* effect. It has been argued that the Court's position was only partially correct, since Italian laws in this specific field are intertwined. The Court only looked at the agreement on collective dismissals, but legislation on *ammortizzatori sociali* (measures to soften the impact of unemployment and to aid the re-inclusion of workers) was in force, which also provided for supportive measures addressing workers displaced from the productive system.[46]

The rationale of the 1991 Law is precisely to co-ordinate these two sides of the same phenomenon. On the one hand, *cassa integrazione guadagni* (a support equal to 80% of the salary) can be required whenever mass dismissals due to economic difficulties can otherwise be avoided. The employer must submit a programme to the unions and to the public administration. On the other hand the law envisages situations of 'mobility' of workers whose individual contracts of employment are terminated. In this second case it so happens that the employer finds it impossible to bring workers back to work, after having started a procedure assisted by *cassa integrazione guadagni*, which should have made it possible for the employer to recover from the economic crisis. Workers are placed on a 'mobility' list, with the intention to move them to a different occupation from the original one. Employers hiring workers included in such lists are encouraged by economic incentives. Workers fired by the employer and in 'mobility' are assisted by an unemployment benefit different from *cassa integrazione guadagni*. The latter is kept alive for situations in which economic recovery of the enterprise is considered feasible. Choices left in the hands of the employer are in all cases difficult ones, since in both cases he participates in financing the benefits due to displaced workers.

---

42   L.19 July 1994, n. 451, art. 16.
43   L. 17 May 1999, n. 144, art. 68.
44   G. Orlandini, 'Contratti formativi e competenze normative delle Regioni', in R. De Luca Tamajo, M. Rusciano and L. Zoppoli (eds), *Mercato del lavoro, riforma e vincoli di sistema*, Napoli 2004, p. 515 ss.
45   L. 23 July 1991, n. 223.
46   O. Mazzotta, *Diritto del lavoro*, Milano 2002, p. 637.

Collective dismissals are dealt with in the 1991 Law, which, in taking care of a variety of issues, also transposes the European Directive. The crucial notion is that of 'reduction or transformation of activities or work', very similar, as it clearly appears to most commentators, to the notion of 'objective motives' developed in the case law on individual dismissals. It is, therefore, the numerical relevance (at least five workers to be dismissed) and the fact that dismissals take place within 120 days that indicate the scope of legislation. Changes in the employer's activities include cases of dismissals due to technological innovations.[47] Situations of complete and irreversible cessation of activities also give rise to collective dismissals. Legislation applies to undertakings with more than 15 employees (Art.24).[48] Certain employers (such as unions, political parties, co-operatives) are excluded. On this specific point, the ECJ ruled against Italy once again, claiming that there was non-compliance with Directive 1998/59 (C-32/02, 16 October 2003).

The complex statute under examination also provides for inclusion in a collective agreement of provisions to reconcile the interest of the employer in reducing the workforce and the desire of workers not to be dismissed (Art.4.11). Examples are: allowing a derogation from the law banning the downgrading of workers; moving temporarily one or more employees to another enterprise. This interesting example of collective agreement running parallel to a legal solution follows the Italian tradition dating from the 1970s of using voluntary sources as means to 'proceduralise' management prerogatives, namely to limit them by way of consensus with representative unions.

A collective agreement may also be used for the criteria in the selection of workers to be included in 'mobility' lists. This is yet another example of the disputed legal nature of collective sources, made enforceable *erga omnes*, because of the special subject matters they deal with. The Constitutional Court[49] found this solution not to be in conflict with Art. 39 of the Constitution (see above Section 1.2) since it deals with the possibility of applying a consensual regulation of criteria, instead of a unilateral legal one, which is also provided for by the law. In both cases the employer's prerogative is limited *ab initio* and is correctly exercised towards all workers affected by the same prerogative, namely all those potentially redundant.

When criteria for the selection of workers 'in mobility' are not followed, the dismissal may be rendered void; whereas in cases of lack of consultation of the unions and non-compliance with the requirement that dismissals should be communicated in writing, there can be grounds for considering the same as not producing effects. In all cases Article 18 of the Workers' Statute can operate and give rise to the most effective protection of all, namely reinstatement of workers illegally dismissed.

This is not a marginal result. Following the 1991 reform that we have been describing so far, it has been suggested that collective dismissals become in Italian labour law yet another case of justified dismissal, to be added to the ones covered by individual dismissals legislation. No structural difference can be proclaimed, but simply a difference in the 'articulation of protected interests'.[50]

4.   Transfers of undertakings

The evolution of labour law in this field has been influenced by European law. In 2001, the legislature reformed Art. 2112 of the Civil Code,[51] adopting the wide notion of 'organised economic activity' for each segment of the productive activity involved in the transfer. The notion of *ramo d'azienda*, namely a branch of the undertaking, has been added to the civil code, specifying that it is to be considered as 'functionally autonomous' before the transfer took place.

The rationale behind this innovation is to try and avoid instrumental recourses to transfers of undertakings, in particular when the intention is to outsource significant activities, avoiding the recourse to mass dismissals and failure to observe consultation requirements.

On this specific issue, the legislature intervened in the 2003 Decree, with the intent to simplify managerial strategies in externalising productive activities. The new version of Art.2112 c.c. leaves to the two parties – transferor and transferee – the definition of the 'branch' of the undertaking at the time of the transfer, thus implying the possibility of creating a 'branch' for the specific purpose to transfer it.

This is yet another example of liberalisation of the labour market in the direction of significantly reducing individual guarantees, notwithstanding the right of workers' representatives to be consulted.

---

47   R. Del Punta, 'I licenziamenti collettivi', in M. Papaleoni, R. Del Punta and M. Mariani, *La nuova cassa integrazione e la mobilità*, Padova 1993.

48   L. 19 July 1993, n. 236, art. 8 extends procedures for the inclusion of workers in mobility lists also to co-operatives, subject to the approval by the assembly of a 'programme for mobility'.

49   Corte Costituzionale 30 June 1994, n. 268.

50   O. Mazzotta, *Diritto del lavoro*, Milano 2002, p. 667. Also the public sector is now covered by very similar measures. See arts 33 ff. D.lgs. 30 March 2001, n. 165 with a specific cross reference to L. 23 July 1991, n. 223.

51   D.lgs. 2 February 2001, n. 18.

Chapter III:
Labour law and adaptability

1. Working time

The regulation of working time is a significant example of how European law can create a lively debate among national policy-makers, asked to adapt national law and yet to have elements of continuity within the national legal system.

In 1997, the three main confederations and Confindustria – the association of private employers – signed a joint opinion dealing with criteria for the transposition of the Working Time Directive. The 1996 *Patto per il lavoro* indicated that the Directive should be transposed subject to an agreement between the social partners. The opinion – technically not a collective agreement – touched upon significant issues, such as the principle that the confirmed 40 hours as a weekly maximum could also be the result of an average in hours, calculated within periods of more than one week and over 12 months. A relevant role was also maintained for collective bargaining, leaving to the legislature the task to fill in gaps left empty by the collective parties.

The issue of working time regulation has also been at the centre of political disagreement within the left, part of which was in favour of reducing working hours to 35 hours a week. The *Pacchetto Treu*[52] included measures which took into account the contents of the joint opinion and declared 40 hours the legal 'normal' weekly working time, previously set at 48 hours. The most important consequence of this legal innovation was the calculation of over-time. From the 41st hour onwards, provided there was agreement between the parties, overtime was paid with an increase not inferior to 10% and could not go beyond 12 weekly hours.

In 2003 the transposition of the Working Time Directive gave rise to a series of new controversies in its interpretation.

The Decree in question[53] does not specify the notion of normal daily working time. Overtime must be calculated on the basis of the 40 hour week, regardless of the daily limit. Maximum working hours are measured, as in the Directive, on average weekly hours, which cannot go beyond 48 hours.

Four months is the time within which to measure average working time, but collective agreements can expand this limit for organisational reasons.

Despite the fact that the legislature does not specify the notion of daily maximum working hours, we find indirect indications when compulsory daily rest time is set at 11 hours. The discussion, on this point and on other controversial passages of the Decree, deals with the fact that the transposition of a Directive should not lower existing standards in national law.

Even the new regulation of overtime may be considered disadvantageous. The previous double limit – 250 yearly hours and 80 hours within three months – has been substituted by the 250 yearly hours only. Collective agreements can derogate from this limit; they can also define the extra remuneration to be given to the workers, now that this issue is no longer covered by law.

The Decree leaves to collective agreements the possibility to adopt flexible arrangements (*orari multiperiodali*), whereby within a day or a week working hours can go beyond the agreed maximum if technical or market reasons so require, without the employer having to pay overtime. A reduction of working time must follow, to compensate for the overtime and to be within the average.

Night work has not been subject to significant changes since the 1999 Decree[54] which transposed the Directive on this issue. However, even in this field one can notice the very flexible nature of the rules to be applied. The 'absolute priority' to offer night work to workers who required it is no longer there. The right of workers who, for health reasons, asked to be moved to day work is not completely guaranteed with regard to the automatic return to the same job. If an equivalent job is not available, downgrading should be deemed legal.

If one takes a broader perspective on the new regulation of working time, one can see that derogation from the law is the relevant technique adopted. National and local collective agreements, following the rationale of the Directive, can

---

52   L. 24 June 1997, n. 196, art. 13.
53   D.lgs. 8 April 2003, n. 66.
54   D.lgs. 26 November 1999, n. 532.

derogate in matters such as night work, daily rest and work interruptions. Should the collective parties fail to reach an agreement, a ministerial decree can intervene.

2. Fixed-term contracts

The 2001 reform of fixed-term contracts was the first step taken by the centre-right government as far as labour law measures are concerned. The Decree in question, which also transposes the 1999/70 EC Directive,[55] was enacted without the consent of CGIL, the largest and most representative union, and marked the beginning of a non-unitary style among the unions.

The main aim of the reformers was to expand significantly the recourse to fixed-term contracts. Instead of following the previous legal technique of specifying the cases in which to allow the recourse to such contracts, it is now possible to do so when 'technical, productive, organisational and substitutive' reasons occur. Such wide options for the employers do not exempt them from the duty to give reasons behind their decisions, thus allowing judges to intervene on this point. In choosing to offer a generic and ample definition, the legislature has taken the risk of creating a potentially contentious terrain around this reform.

One of the most controversial aspects of the 2001 reform has to do with its relationship with the 1999/70 Directive, particularly with regard to the so-called *clausola di non regresso*. The latter states that the transposition of European law should not result in a lowering of existing national standards. The Italian reform we have analysed has significantly reduced the limits previously set for the recourse to fixed-term contracts. Furthermore, no indication is given for the obligation, present in the Directive, to set a limit on the maximum number of renewals of fixed-term contracts.

In the overall structure of the 2001 Decree, collective agreements simply have the role of indicating quotas of fixed-term workers within the company. Since the Directive states the employer's obligation to give reasons for the stipulation of fixed-term contracts, it seems debatable that full compliance with the Directive's aims has been achieved.

3. Agency work

The previously mentioned *Pacchetto Treu* was the relevant source for other labour law innovations falling under the heading of adaptability.

Law 1997/196 introduced in the Italian system the regulation of temporary agency work, with rather strong characteristics of rigidity, if compared with other European countries. This was true both for the requirements for temporary work agencies to be able to operate and for their purpose, which was limited to meeting 'temporary' needs of the user enterprise, with the exception of managers, who could respond to an unlimited demand of the user.

Articles in this law dealing with agency work have been repealed by the 2003 Decree.

Agency work is now described as *somministrazione di lavoro* and substitutes previous legislation on temporary agency work. Article 20 presents a list of activities for which open-ended contracts can be stipulated between the user company and the agency. Temporary agency work can take place when 'organisational, technical and productive' reasons are put forward by the user, even within the user's 'ordinary' production process.

In both cases collective agreements have wide margins for manoeuvre. For open-ended contracts, collective agreements can expand the Art. 20 list of activities, thus expanding the recourse to agency work beyond the letter of the law. In temporary agency work, collective agreements can set quantitative limits to the user company, thus partially limiting managerial prerogatives.

Several formalities are provided for in the Decree. Agencies must be authorised to perform their activities; the contract with the user must be in writing and include detailed information, even with regard to possible risks for health and safety. Art. 21 states very clearly the agency's obligations with regard to the payment of wages and the subsequent user's obligation to reimburse. In case of non-compliance in the obligation to pay wages and social security, the user is responsible for this and will then have to request compensation from the agency.

The Decree attempts to balance the principle of equal treatment between agency workers and workers employed by the user against a very clear separation of typical managerial prerogatives from the concrete control exercised by the user. It is, for example, specified that the recourse to disciplinary powers is an agency's prerogative, following the user's communication of the reasons why disciplinary measures should be taken. The managerial prerogative to move workers from one job to another appears similarly split and implies the user's obligation to inform the agency in case of changes in the content of the job. Even the exercise of collective rights should be made possible for agency workers in the user's premises.

---

55   D.lgs 6 September 2001, n. 368.

It is difficult to predict whether the 2003 Decree will favour differentiation in the services provided by agencies. Article 29 deals with *appalto,* or contracting-out of activities different from the ones performed by agencies.

The contractor takes full risk for the work to be performed, has its own organisation and exercises managerial prerogatives. Equal treatment does not apply to workers involved in contracting-out, due to the abrogation of the previous relevant norm. This relaxation of a previous legal limit might represent a 'competitive advantage', when compared to agency work. The delicate point for those interpreting the legislation will be evaluating the true entrepreneurial nature of contractors and their status as employers.

4. Part-time work

Measures on part-time work reflect a very slow adaptation of the legal system to changes both in the organisation of work and in individual needs. Part-time work is, in fact, often chosen by workers to satisfy specific demands in a limited period of their working life. The question as to whether some groups of workers are then made marginal as part-timers and actually constrained in such a choice still remains an open one, and may even be at the origin of indirect discrimination.

The first legal interventions on part-time work date back to the 1980s and also included minimum hourly wages, with important consequences on indirect costs. In 1996, some measures on part-time work were included in a financial law (*Misure di razionalizzazione della finanza pubblica*). These deal with the regulation of part-time work in the public sector (Art. 1 Section 57).[56]

The introduction of part-time work in the public sector has been recognised by the Constitutional Court[57] as a landmark in the approximation of public and private 'models' of employment and as a sign of increased efficiency of the administration. It has been maintained that through part-time, a better transparency of work performances could be guaranteed and a closer monitoring of external illegal activities could also be achieved. It can also be maintained that such innovation meant the introduction of a proper individual right to part-time working, namely by amending the previous contract of employment, albeit with some exceptions, such as university professors and schools.

In 2000, Italy implemented Directive 97/81; further changes were introduced in 2001 and the 1984 Law was expressly abrogated.[58] Essential definitions of 'normal' full-time working time are to be found in the previously mentioned Decree 2003/66, together with the notions of horizontal part-time (on the basis of a daily working time) and vertical part-time (during weeks, months, or years). These two types of regulation can also be mixed together, thus giving rise to a whole range of possibilities for both parties of the employment contracts.

The impact of the Directive is visible in the principle of non-discrimination, which means equal treatment with full-time workers, both for individual and collective rights, following the principle of *pro-rata temporis*.

The new regulation of part-time work is in Article 46 of the already mentioned 2003 Decree, which modifies – and not completely substitutes – previous legislation. The complex and often unclear legal ground created by so many different layers of legal intervention needs to be addressed as a serious challenge to the coherence of labour law.

In the legislation pre-dating the 2003 reform, collective bargaining played a role in dealing with various modalities for entering part-time work and also in approaching rather complex and controversial issues, such as overtime work. The most representative unions had in this field quite a large variety of options to intervene even in derogation from the law and were regularly informed by the employer about the number of part-time workers and the amount of overtime.

The so called *clausola elastica*, or elastic clause, allowed the employer to modify unilaterally the modalities of part-time work, provided that there was a collective agreement indicating the recourse to such a clause. One can see how this clause represented a compromise between collective guarantees and managerial prerogatives. Individual workers could, however, ask not to observe such a clause, if they produced evidence that it was impossibile for them to accept the employer's unilateral decision on the organisation of working hours. The employer had to give at least 10 days notice and to provide for an increase in remuneration. Health and family reasons, as well as the need to work elsewhere on a different contract of employment or even as self-employed, were deemed acceptable.

'Elastic clauses' are now in force even in the absence of collective agreements. This implies that individual workers have to give their consent; dismissals for refusing to consent are still illegal. The right to exit 'elastic clauses' has been repealed.

---

56   L. 23 December 1996, n. 662.

57   *Corte Costituzionale* 18 May 1999, n. 171.

58   D.lgs. 25 February 2000, n. 61; D.lgs.26 February 2001, n. 100.

Even the regulation of 'supplementary' work has changed after the latest Decree. A previous role of collective agreements, thought of as 'filters' for the admissibility of such additional work, has been swept away by the rule by which it is necessary to seek individual consent.

Individual guarantees are still visible, as they were in previous legal regulation of part-time work. For instance, the refusal to work part-time cannot by itself be a ground for dismissal. This does not mean that justified dismissals for objective reasons may not occur. Furthermore, the transformation from a full-time to a part-time contract is always done in writing, on the worker's request and with the assistance of a union representative. There is also a right of part-timers to apply for full-time jobs should the employer decide to hire new workers.

As for overtime, there is now a much too strict assimilation of vertical part-timers to full-timers when it comes to allowing the recourse to extra working hours.

Part-time work has been analysed as a leading example of 'instrumental use'[59] of the Directive, particularly of the clause (5.1.a) which places an obligation on Member States to identify and possibly remove all obstacles for the recourse to part-time. It is on the basis of such a clause that some observers justify all possible changes in national legislation, even downgrading existing levels of legal guarantees. The debate is open on the compatibility of such measures with the clause in the Directive (clausola di non regresso) stating that lowering existing standards should not be a direct result of the transposition of European law.

5. 'Lavoro intermittente': The Italian zero hours contract

A complete novelty in the Italian system is represented by the introduction of lavoro intermittente,[60] an extreme form of part-time, whereby the employer can, in a very discontinuous way, request that work is performed in areas of production indicated by collective agreements. In an experimental way, it is indicated that such contracts will be favoured for young unemployed people under the age of 25, and unemployed over 55 who were made redundant.

The contract of employment must be stipulated in writing, with all necessary details of the parties' obligations. It may provide that, if workers declare their availability even when work is not requested, an indemnity for this time of non-work is due. Refusal to work can only occur in case of illness or any other serious impediment. Even in such cases of refusal to work for legitimate reasons, workers will lose their indemnity. In all other cases, refusal to work may lead to the termination of the contract for just cause and will also imply the payment of compensation for damages caused to the employer.

In this last example of intermittent work and in the regulation of part-time work we find one of the most controversial parts of the new Italian reform. The legislature has, as one can see, expressed a precise philosophy of individualisation in employment contracts. This choice may give rise to a disequilibrium, particularly in those contracts characterised by a significant disparity in exercising bargaining powers.

6. 'Lavoro a progetto': A new approach to economically dependent work

The new definition of self-employment proposed by the 2003 labour market reform is lavoro a progetto e a programma.[61]

While leaving untouched some forms of genuine self-employment, the reform aims to tackle hidden forms of subordination. It does so by suggesting that a project or a programme – rather than a continuous and co-ordinated collaboration, as in the previous legal definition – helps to specify the content of the obligation carried by the self-employed. A first – and still vague – interpretation proposed by commentators is to view a project as a well-defined obligation, undertaken by a fairly skilled person with a very clear time limit. It is more difficult to detect what a programme should be, since in each job description, even the simplest one, such a content should be implicit.

The legislature is very cautious in specifying that the principle of remuneration related to quality and quantity of the work performed should be measured with relation to similar types of self-employment, thus intending to exclude assimilation to collective agreements and to wages for dependent workers.

59   A. Lo Faro, 'Adaptable Employment and Private Autonomy in the Italian Part-time Reform', forthcoming in S. Sciarra, P. Davies and M. Freedland (eds), Employment Policy and the Regulation of Part-time Work in the European Union: A Comparative analysis, Cambridge 2004; B. Caruso, 'Riforma del part-time e diritto sociale europeo: verso una teoria dei limiti ordinamentali', Diritti lavori mercati 2003, p. 301.

60   D.lgs. 10 September 2003, n. 276 artt. 33-40.

61   D.lgs. 10 September 2003, n. 276 artt. 61-69.

For people working *a progetto o a programma*, health and safety measures apply and a very timid attempt is made to provide entitlement to other rights. It is specified that work be suspended – with no remuneration – for reasons of pregnancy, illness and injury. Suspension due to pregnancy implies that a minimum of 180 days will be added to the duration of the project or of the programme, whereas for other reasons work will terminate as originally stipulated.

The newly enacted 'certification'[62] should serve to intervene in the gaps between subordinate work and self-employment, with a view to punishing abuses and reducing court cases. Certification is an administrative act and has *erga omnes* effects; rather than qualifying the nature of the contract, it indicates all legal consequences attached to it, be they civil, administrative, fiscal, or related to social security.

---

62   D.lgs.10 September 2003, n. 276 artt. 75-84.

Chapter IV:
Promoting equal opportunities

The example of night work is illustrative of the evolution of labour law from protection of women workers to gender-neutral equal treatment. It is also illustrative of the impact that a decision of the ECJ can have on national systems and of the necessary role of the national legislature in bringing about 'positive integration'.

It is well known that the ECJ ruled in *Stoeckel* (C-345/89, 25 July 1991) that banning night work for women represented a violation of the principle of equal treatment between men and women, regarding access to work. The Court also ruled against Italy for non-compliance with this principle (C-207/96, 4 December 1997). It was only in 2001[63] that the legislature intervened to eliminate the ban on night work for women (Art. 53), thus specifying a previous intervention in the 1999 *legge comunitaria*. This was a long and controversial process, in which a struggle took place between national judges enforcing directly the Court's ruling, and the legislature trying to find the necessary consensus to pass legislation.

Article 53 deals with a ban on night work for pregnant women, from the beginning of pregnancy up to one year of age of the child. It is not compulsory to work at night for women (or, for that matter, fathers or partners) with children up to three years; for single parents with children up to 12 years; or for workers, both male and female, with responsibility for the care of disabled people.

The regulation of parental leave is also part of a previous and indeed very ambitious statute, also dealing with leave for permanent training and flexible working time arrangements.[64] It must be underlined that the evolution of labour law measures in this field completely changes the approach followed in previous legislation, dating back to the 1970s. There is now a clearer indication that both parents are addressed by supportive measures, but it is difficult to establish the concrete impact of the Parental Leave Directive, given the fact that Italian labour law has traditionally been more advanced in this field.[65]

An interesting example of a legal reform which takes into account both the criticism that emerged in national academic work – aimed at improving the 1991 legislation on positive action – and the need to comply with European indications on gender mainstreaming can be found in a 2000 decree.[66] Although this piece of legislation is essentially meant to introduce new and more efficient norms on the appointment and the functioning of *consiglieri di parità* – national, regional and sub-regional bodies monitoring the enforcement of the equal treatment and non-discrimination principles – it also serves the purpose of introducing important innovations.

One of them is the power the Minister for equal opportunities has to appoint such bodies directly, should the lower levels of the administration not proceed in due time. There is also a wider role for the same bodies to intervene in court cases; a clear definition of their conciliatory powers in collective discrimination cases; and a duty on the public administration to adopt positive action schemes and seek for funding for these. The latter point is of some relevance, if one considers that the law explicitly mentions the duty to promote women's occupation in areas in which they are under-represented. Positive action plans must create an equilibrium where there is more than two-thirds gender imbalance in work activities and in the hierarchy of jobs. Both in the case of hiring and of promoting workers, when there is equal professional qualification, the administration must provide specific motives for choosing a man.

It is considered that this law follows the ECJ's rulings in *Kalanke*, *Marschall* and *Badeck*, thus showing an unusual and rather sophisticated attitude in the drafting and in the adaptation of European sources to specific national peculiarities, such as the multi-level organisation of monitoring bodies.

The Decrees[67] transposing the 2000 EU Directives (2000/43 and 2000/78) opened up the system to the new concept of harassment, not regulated before. They also included among

---

63   D.lgs. 26 March 2001, n. 151, a comprehensive decree dealing with supportive measures for working parents, protection of health and safety for women, also in compliance with EU law, maternity leave, parental leave. A reorganisation (Testo Unico) of various previous legal interventions is put forward.

64   L. 8 March 2000, n. 53, which is also at the origin of the re-organisation of parental leave occurred in the previously mentioned Decree.

65   R. Del Punta, L. Lazzeroni and M.L. Vallauri, *I congedi parentali*, Milano 2000.

66   D.lgs. 23 May 2000, n. 196.

67   D.lgs. 9 July 2003, n. 215; D.lgs. 9 July 2003, n. 216.

discriminatory acts those based on religion, personal conviction, handicap, age and sexual orientation. These two recent Decrees have been criticised for the unnecessarily wide derogations set to the principle of non-discrimination. For instance, some requisites for the hiring of workers in the army and the police, as well as in jails, even related to the above mentioned areas of anti-discrimination law, are considered genuine qualifications for employment. Furthermore, a very wide derogation from the principle of non-discrimination is introduced, with no link to specific cases, but simply based on 'objective justifications'.

Finally, it appears completely out of context in a text devoted to anti-discrimination measures to include an article stating that people found guilty of pornography and other sex related crimes can be refused employment in several places, including schools, centres for care and social assistance.

Chapter V:
Conclusions

In the attempt to improve the methodology introduced at Lisbon and to consolidate its success, the European Commission issued a series of national studies on the impact of employment strategies and of the Open Method of Coordination (OMC). The results of the comparative research promoted by the Commission are visible in later documents they have produced.[68]

Research on the Italian case was assembled by ISFOL, on the basis of a large number of papers written by researchers and academics.[69] Some of the results put forward in the ISFOL Report can be usefully recalled in the concluding section of this paper and be compared with the opinion of the present writer.

The overall impression one receives from looking at research carried by ISFOL is that flexibility measures introduced in the Italian system, up to 2001, had not drastically undermined the quality of jobs. The example taken was part-time work. Voluntary part-time seemed to prevail, thus showing a significant feature of a modern system of labour law. This observation must be linked to the impression, manifested in several research papers, that the *pacchetto Treu* the most European oriented of all labour reforms enacted in the recent past in Italy, was in fact following domestic priorities, while being in compliance with European goals.

This evaluation may change, once the concrete impact of the new 2003 Decree is measured. Part-time work is perhaps one of the most visible cases of a changed perspective of the legislature. An evaluation of the new Italian reform cannot be given at the time of writing; its compliance with the European Employment Strategy (EES) will be subject to future research.

A major theme, often recalled by European institutions when evaluating national responses to employment guidelines, is the reform of placement systems. The abolition of public monopolies and the creation of *centri per l'impiego* did not prove very successful in promoting active employment policies. A balance between decentralisation of the hiring mechanisms and correlation of the same with local development strategies still needs to be found. It was even insinuated by the ISFOL Report that the EES could have been an obstacle to the inclusion of labour policies in local development plans, since it tends by definition to ignore the peculiarities of sub-national levels of policy-making, such as, for instance, the *Mezzogiorno* region. This evaluation too would need to be updated through field research, in view of establishing whether the previously mentioned reform of Title V of the Constitution is proving effective in the enhancement of more efficient placement mechanisms.

One further point highlighted in the ISFOL Report is that the social partners were not sufficiently involved in the preparation of National Action Plans and might not have considered them too important. No clear evidence of such a lack of involvement is given. However, if we link this observation with the fact that – as the Report assumes[70] – there is very little practice of monitoring in Italian policy-making and that no clear rules are shared by the many actors involved in the process, we should conclude that the EES and the OMC could have an even more beneficial impact on the system if they were taken more seriously.

In this regard, the attitude declared by the 2003 legislature to enhance transparency in the reform of the labour market, in order to be fully in compliance with EES, may, nevertheless result in use of obscure legal language. The jargon of employment policies[71] does not always coincide with the formal and prescriptive style usually adopted in drafting legislation. The result is the combination of procedural and normative messages, at times combined with detailed indications which would best be placed within secondary or administrative sources.

---

68   Communication 'Taking stock of five years of the EES', *COM* (2002) 416 final, 17 July 2002; Communication 'The future of the European Employment Strategy. A Strategy for full employment and better jobs for all', *COM* (2003) 6 final, 14 January 2003.

69   ISFOL, 'Impact evaluation of the European Employment strategy. La politica del lavoro italiana negli anni recenti: valutazione e impatto', Final Report May 2002, co-ordinated by C. Dell'Aringa.

70   ISFOL Report, cit., p. 21 and p. 81.

71   See, for instance, art. 17 on statistical monitoring of employment policies. This long article instructs several branches of the administration on how to gather data and, at the same time, refers to lower sources – such as Ministerial Decrees – for the creation of specific committees charged with the evaluation of the impact of the new law.

If we look at the way the OMC is developing, mutual learning is indeed the first and most important achievement of a procedure based on what we can describe as institutional or moral accountability. It should be equally highlighted that no particular expertise is required in the many branches of the administration working on specific programmes and aiming at specific objectives.[72]

If we look at some recent research on the 'Europeanisation' of policies in the area of social inclusion, we see that the impact of guidelines has been useful to create a European culture within the administration, mainly because of the creation and the functioning of specialised committees, working groups and agencies.[73] Even the imposition of a deadline and the request to write a national report on anti-poverty measures – as it happened in 1993 – put branches of the national administration in contact with a supranational dimension of the problems at stake.

If 'Europeanisation' means exposure to other national experiences, as well as compliance with specific objectives, the role of expertise becomes once more crucial in ascertaining the independence of scientific evaluation and in describing future scenarios of policy-making.

Research on social inclusion is receiving new impetus through the OMC and through the creation in the Nice Treaty of the Social Protection Committee. This is an area of potential innovation in the evolution of labour law. Not only is labour law rediscovering its origins and linking up its individual and collective components with social security legislation. It is also forced to define the notion of 'protection', which is so central to European policies on social inclusion. Rather than discussing simply in terms of protection of workers already in employment, labour law must seek new forms of protection for those who have never been included in the labour market, or who are present in it, but in a very marginal position.[74]

The overall analysis on the evolution of labour law in Italy put forward in this report shows the solidity, at least up to the time of writing, of a system of norms which has positively – albeit at times slowly – reflected changes in the composition of social forces, as well as in the organisation of work and in productive systems.

The stereotype whereby Italy is an enthusiastic supporter of Europe which nevertheless remains rather weak in influencing policies and in assuming a relevant position among other Member States, is not to be confirmed.[75] This was the image suggested in the early days of the Communities, when Italy acted diplomatically in the areas left free by France and Germany, without having an independent dominant role of its own.[76] In recent years – but even when the Single European Act was approved – Italy has been in the front row to combat unanimity as a dominant rule in decision-making, a reform which has in the past opened new spaces for labour and social law legislative initiatives and could even more positively affect the evolution of such a subject at a supranational level.

There are many reasons to fight such an old stereotype and to propose an image of Italy as an active and dynamic Member State, with its own character and peculiarities in the approach to European integration. Labour law – both in its legislative evolution and in the contribution given by scholarly work – brings evidence for combating such a stereotype.

It has previously been underlined how the attitude of enlightened groups of bureaucrats is slowly pursuing changes inside the administration. The new climate of mutual learning brought about by the OMC is challenging with respect to 'old' styles of policy-making and demands that expert contributions be given for the drafting of NAPs both in the field of employment policies and in social inclusion.

In the late 1990s, when this process started to be visible, we witnessed the combination of high level experts, often recruited in ministerial or governmental committees, with occasional groups set up for ad hoc purposes and, in some cases, not present in later stages of the process.[77]

If we look at significant reforms of Italian labour law in the 1970s, we notice that legislation was drafted in a very rigorous way by a restricted number of experts, led by a legal adviser – frequently a labour lawyer – working in close contact with the Labour Minister. Those were also the years in which labour law took advantage of the evolution of collective bargaining in leading areas of the economy, incorporating in legislation what was the result of a collective practice of enforcement at the shop-floor level.

---

72   ISFOL Report, at p. 81.

73   T. Alti, 'Le politiche antipovertà: una questione europea', in S.Fabbrini (ed.), *L'europeizzazione dell'Italia*, Roma-Bari 2003, p. 212.

74   The Italian National Social Plan adopted in April 2001 constituted the basis for the preparation of the NAP. See European Commission, *Joint Report on Social Inclusion*, Bruxelles 2002, p. 129.

75   This is the opinion – shared by the present writer – of T. Padoa Schioppa, *Europa, forza gentile*, Bologna 2001, p. 118.

76   Ibid, p. 105.

77   For instance the Commissione Onofri, previously mentioned at Section 1.3 and the 1997 Giugni Committee set up by the Prime Minister Prodi, for the evaluation of the 1993 Social Pact.

The practice then changed and a large number of experts were recruited at different stages of the law-making process. Furthermore, collective agreements are no longer anticipating widely accepted achievements in the regulation of working conditions. They suffer themselves from the fragmentation of legislative developments and from the different function they are asked to pursue especially with regard to employment policies.

The impression is that the OMC requires a deep transformation of the administration and of the apparatus of bureaucrats. The latter may lead important reforms from inside the administration, while being in close contact with external experts. Expertise is becoming more and more functional to the understanding of supranational policies. This is the reason why a stable group of experts should be established inside relevant branches of the administration, dealing with the many facets of employment policies. It should be combined with external high-level expertise capable of promoting objective field-research.

Labour law is only one component of this strategy, but its influence continues to be extremely important. Because of its constitutional tradition and its deep grounds in the social context, it adds an enormous contribution to the overall identity of the national legal system and to its evolution. Collective bargaining has always contributed to such an evolving pattern of regulation and should not be reduced to a merely ancillary or uncertain role.

Italian judges, as well as those in other Member States, are active components of a 'community of courts' which uses European law as if it were part of the national legal system.[78] This has been achieved through preliminary ruling procedures, activated by Italian courts in some cases of strategic litigation.[79]

Italian labour lawyers have, particularly in the decade taken into consideration in this report, vivaciously interacted with colleagues from other European countries and intervened in European developments. It may suffice to notice that European developments are dealt with in most leading textbooks. Furthermore, a number of texts are specifically devoted to the impact on national labour law of European law and of the ECJ case law.[80]

The auspices are that the evolution of Italian labour law continues along the lines which have been highlighted for the decade 1992-2003, linking together adaptation to new social needs and respect for deeply rooted traditions.

78   This is one of the outcomes of a research on preliminary ruling procedures in which Italy, as well as other European countries, are included. See S. Sciarra (ed), *Labour law in the Courts. National judges and the ECJ*, Oxford 2001, in particular the introductory chapter.

79   See in particular Job Centre, mentioned earlier in Section II.1.

80   M. Roccella, *La Corte di giustizia e il diritto del lavoro*, Torino 1997; R. Foglia, *L'attuazione giurisprudenziale del diritto comunitario del lavoro*, Padova 2002.

THE EVOLUTION OF LABOUR LAW IN LUXEMBOURG

1992-2002

Marie-Ange MOREAU
Professor at the European University Institute (Florence)

Table of contents

Chapter 1:
Introduction: General background to labour relations in Luxembourg

Labour law in Luxembourg is heavily influenced by changes in French and Belgian law, with which it is closely connected. For those involved, these act as a reference in terms of doctrinal and jurisprudential interpretation.[1]

However, the evolution of Luxembourg's labour laws over the last 11 years has been markedly different due to the economic context: up to 2001, Luxembourg experienced strong growth (6% on average), which led to a constant increase in the number of jobs. Although there was a downturn in 2001 and 2002 (1% increase in GDP) growth should return to 2% in 2004.

Labour law is strongly influenced by this economic wealth, which has made emergency legislation to combat job losses (as has occurred in France and Belgium) unnecessary.

This wealth also influences the labour relations system. Until recently, this has been marked by consensus based on economic development and by a preference for employee protection.

Salaries, which are index-linked, remain generous, attracting a skilled cross-border labour force and avoiding social conflict.

As was the case during the post-war growth period in France and other European countries, social dialogue has been aimed more at sharing wealth through salary negotiations than bringing about economic change.

In terms of Luxembourg's labour relations, the law predominates over collective agreements. The latter have to be more favourable than the law.

Changes in labour law come about through legislation. Community law is therefore transposed through the adoption of laws.

Where employment policies are involved, proposals are drawn up within the tripartite consultation plan in place since 1977.

Luxembourg has a tradition of sector-based negotiation with an important role given to the banking and insurance sector, representing 45% of jobs. Collective agreements are usually generally applicable: in other words the agreement is compulsorily extended to the whole sector concerned. They are mandatory and universally applicable.

There is no multi-sector negotiation in Luxembourg and very little company-based negotiation: the latter occasionally takes place where a company is alone in a sector (e.g. Goodyear) or part of a Community-wide group (cf. Auchan). In 1998, the rate of cover for salaried occupations was 41.1%. This rose to 43.1% in 2001 due to renegotiations of collective agreements on the organisation of working time, applying the Act of 12 February 1999. Collective agreements at company level represent 29% of employees covered, while 71% are subject to agreements signed at sector level.[2]

However, the appearance of the branch framework agreement is leading to more company-based agreements, based on 'plans' drawn up by the employer after consultation with employee representatives or joint councils. Although the plan is drawn up by the employer, this prior consultation appears to prevent difficulties in reaching agreement.

In Luxembourg there does not seem to be any movement towards changing the norms in order to increase the amount of company-based negotiation. Nor does this seem likely. The lack of union representatives in companies and the strong tradition of sector-level negotiation are considered to give better protection to employees and to the general interests of employees in the sector.

Since 1999, employers have called strongly for greater flexibility in work organisation. This has been met by a cautious approach on the part of the unions, which have sought to negotiate further working time reductions in exchange for this new flexibility.

---

1   In Luxembourg, labour law issues are dealt with by professionals, who generally set out the norms. There are no labour law reviews. A great deal of the information about trends in Luxembourg labour law comes from conversations with Ministry of Employment advisors, whom the author of the report wishes to thank. An additional source has been the evaluation report on European employment strategy 'An analysis of strategic developments in performance and impact', *Accord International sa*, 28 January 2002. See bibliographical data used, at end of report.

2   Evaluation report on the Act of 12/2/1999, p. 45.

The Act of 12 February 1999 expired at the end of July 2003. Following an evaluation, union and management representatives on the Tripartite Commission decided to extend the Act to 2007 without changing it for the time being.[3]

The positions taken up by Luxembourg's social partners seem to be influenced by French experiences: employers want to avoid the pitfalls of 'RTT' (reduction of working time) and unions want to avoid signing flexibility agreements without sufficient compensation.

Since 1977, Luxembourg has developed a tripartite approach to employment policy. National plans for employment are thus systematically drawn up in a tripartite steering committee. The resulting proposals have brought about numerous changes in labour law in recent years. But while the committee has undoubtedly influenced the development of workplace relations, its role is limited to employment policies and has not fundamentally changed the country's traditional social order.

1.   Basis of labour law

Although the Constitution contains some provisions concerning social law, its influence on labour law is slight. The country's constitutional Court was only created in 1997 so has made only one ruling in the field, relating to the principle of equality. Legislation therefore remains the main source of labour law.

Unlike France, where there has been a considerable increase in legislation, Luxembourg is changing slowly in terms of labour norms. Since the major Act of 1989 on employment contracts, a series of laws have transposed European directives relating to the most urgent issues, leading the Ministry of Employment to treat as a priority those areas covered by Community social law. Legislative changes over the last ten years have therefore been largely influenced by Community requirements.

But Luxembourg is sometimes very reticent: this was particularly evident in its transposition of the 1994 directive on a European Works Council,[4] where the European Court of Justice judged that it had failed to comply with the directive. Transposition times are sometimes long.

The economic downturn since 2002, corporate restructuring plans, and the 'drying-up' of the cross-border market for skilled labour have recently led to proposals for major

reforms. These centre on the 1965 Act governing collective agreements. The proposals aim to re-energise the social dialogue through a reform of representation (see below) and levels of negotiation. Issues relating to working time flexibility are at the heart of conflicts between unions and management.

From 1992-2003, collective bargaining has, however, remained a form of *negotiation for the acquisition of rights,* which has been favourable to employees and supported by the principle of preference, at a sector-based level.

As far as employment contracts are concerned the traditional rule remains, by which contracts should be permanent, and only based on a fixed term in exceptional circumstances.

There have been no 'atypical' agreements, other new sources or involvement of new groups. Changes to contracts to adapt contractual mechanisms to the necessities of unemployment have been insignificant in terms of both quality and quantity.

Within the context of collective work organisation, plans drawn up by the employer (like plans for work organisation and training) are implemented after consultation with employee representatives and/or joint councils. The fact that they are drawn up unilaterally by the employer does not generally pose problems due to the existing consensus.

Although there have been discussions in the banking sector concerning union representativity, due to the place of sector-based unions, overall measures relating to norms are not questioned.

They may be subject to discussion in the future, however, if the government and/or employers decide to question the principle of automatic index-linking of salaries. This is very likely considering recent economic developments, although putting such a sensitive issue up for discussion is also likely to have a profound impact on Luxembourg's labour relations

With regard to **overall changes in professional sources,** it is important to look at the central question of union representativity.

The Act of 12 June 1965 relating to collective employment agreements states that only 'representative' unions have the right to sign collective employment agreements, but does not set out the conditions for this representativity: are we looking at sector-based, national or multi-sector representativity?

---

3   Report published by Accord international, *Analysis of the implementation of provisions relating to work and employment which, by virtue of the Act of 12 February 1999, expire on 31 July 2003* – report II 12/2/03.

4   Council Directive 94/45/EC of 22 September 1994 on the establishment of a European Works Council or a procedure in Community-scale undertakings and Community-scale groups of undertakings for the purposes of informing and consulting employees (OJ L 254 30.09.1994 p. 64).

In practice, the system has worked well for thirty years. Three multi-sector and national unions (OGB-L, LVGB and FEB) have signed agreements. All three are active in the banking sector and pre-eminent at a national level.

Recent difficulties have come partly from a recommendation from the International Labour Office (No.590) and partly from the fact that the FEB has split into a number of sector-based unions, including ALEBA. The International Labour Office recommended the Luxembourg government to bring sectoral but non-national unions into negotiations to defend the collective interests of their members, thus making a distinction between negotiation and the signing of a collective employment agreement. The growth of ALEBA, which has a very strong presence in the banking, insurance and financial sector, but is absent from others, means that the role of sector-based unions will once again be raised.

In 1993, two national-level unions under-represented in the banking and financial sector, signed the collective agreement for banking sector employees, denying ALEBA the right to negotiate the agreement. In 1999, however, ALEBA alone signed the collective agreement for the banking, insurance and share-clearing sectors, but the Employment Minister refused to allow these agreements to be registered. The matter was referred to the administrative Court, which confirmed that ALEBA was representative, accepting its signature for those sectors in which it was strongly representative and stating that it could not sign for those sectors in which it was not established. The administrative Court therefore reversed precedent in relation to the position of the International Labour Office.

A Bill was lodged on 2 November 2002 to re-cast the Act of 1965. It set out the foundations of union representativity, incorporating the rule of concordance between levels of negotiation and representation, and the procedure for negotiating and signing collective agreements.

The aim is to evaluate representativity quantitatively by sector and by professional category. A procedure for acknowledging the status of the union representative at a national or sector-based level may be instituted to ensure that representativity is only questioned where the Employment Minister refuses to an agreement negotiated by a union deemed to be unrepresentative. The Bill therefore aims to introduce a pro-active rather than a reactive procedure. Other changes are also planned. The Bill aims to generalise the use of framework agreements and subordinate agreements, introduced in the Act of 12 February 1999 for matters concerning working time and training for the return of absent employees. It does this by broadening the scope of subordinate agreements to unions which have not signed the framework agreement.

The Bill also plans to alter rules relating to the National Arbitration Office, which intervenes to allow collective agreements and prevent collective conflicts.

In Luxembourg, unions and management are obliged to maintain social peace during arbitration procedures. The Bill seeks to introduce a new form of action during this period: the warning strike.

Lastly, the Bill plans to introduce an interprofessional, multi-sector level allowing European level agreements to be introduced via general collective agreements, and to transfer certain issues currently in the legislative domain to unions and management.

The Bill, drawn up in late 2002, therefore shows that the labour relations system in Luxembourg is changing rapidly and searching for a new equilibrium. By 2003, however, it had not yet been approved.

The Ministry of Employment intends, in the future, both to set out procedures to avoid disputes over contractual policy and to broaden the scope of negotiation, taking account of the weight of each sector and of European requirements.

2. Special features of the labour market in Luxembourg

Over this 11-year period, Luxembourg has experienced continual growth, a very low unemployment rate (between 2 and 3%) and steady growth in jobs. Job creation over this period has been the highest in the EU.

However, since 2002, a certain change of course has been felt, with the first company restructuring plans appearing in 2003.

Nevertheless, job creation has continued, *and Luxembourg continues to have the lowest unemployment rate in Europe.* Although unemployment increased in 2002 to over 3%, it fell again during 2003 and the unemployment rate remains totally at odds with the main employment centres, where it reaches up to 17%.

Long-term unemployment appeared only a few years ago, mainly affecting women and workers aged over 55.

The difference in the level of activity between 1996 (61.9%) and 2000 (64%) shows that the employment rate continues to rise. It is, however, lower than the European average: 59.2% in 1996 and 62.9% in 2000 compared to an EU rate of 63.3%.

Analysis also shows that the differences between the ratios increase when they are broken down by sex and age. Changes in the employment rate according to age and sex show that the employment rate for:

•   15-24 year-olds was 36.6% in 1996, 31.9% in 2000 – EU 40.3%

•   25-54 year-olds was 73.3% in 1996, 78.4% in 2000 – EU 76.6%

•   55-64 year-olds was 22.9% in 1996, 27.4% in 2000 – EU 37.7%

•   men was 74.3% in 1996, 75.1% in 2000 – EU 72.5%

•   women was 43.8% in 1996, 50.3% in 2000 – EU 54%.

In 2001, the employment rate for women rose to 50.9%, then to 51.8% in 2002, showing a progression of 1.16% between 1996 and 2002.[5] The level of activity for women between 25-54 is currently 60%. If the current trend continues, Luxembourg could achieve the level-of-activity objectives set in the guidelines for 2010.

The active population in Luxembourg is therefore predominantly male, and while the female activity rate is growing steadily, it remains below the Community average.

Luxembourg has a strong tradition of women staying at home: until the last few years, the practical effects of European-inspired equality policies were very small. However, the growth in the employment rate for women and its normalisation show that change is slowly taking place.

The second feature of the labour market in Luxembourg is the strong presence of cross-border workers: 27.7% of the labour force in 1996, 33.3% in 2000 and 38% in late 2003. Cross-border workers have outnumbered residents since 2000. Between May 2002 and May 2003, 77% of new jobs were taken by cross-border workers, and only 23% by residents.

The increase in the active population is mainly covered by the use of cross-border workers. Cross-border labour is skilled labour, enabling employers to find highly qualified workers without having to provide training or retraining.

Luxembourg's wealth, high wages and index-linked salaries are factors that attract the cross-border population. The attraction has grown since neighbouring countries (France, Belgium and Germany) have been experiencing economic difficulties.

However, since 2002, Luxembourg has seen a slowdown in the flows of cross-border workers. This has led to a re-consideration of the policy regarding cross-border workers (to enable them to acquire unemployment rights) and local populations, in the area of vocational training.

The third major feature of the labour market is the large banking and financial sector, which represents 45% of economic activity.

5   *National employment plan*, 2003.

Chapter II:
Employee flexibility and labour law

Due to the specific nature of the labour market in Luxembourg, employee flexibility measures have developed very slowly and not very widely. There are no real adaptation measures during employment (sections 1 & 2), except as part of continuous training (section 4), which has developed only haphazardly, and integration measures that are mainly targeted at young people on the labour market (section 5).

1. The lack of a restrictive mechanism to adapt employees to their job

This lack of a specific flexibility mechanism can be seen in the field of individual labour relations and collective relations.

2. The legal framework surrounding the employment contract

Luxembourg has no overall employee flexibility measures for several reasons:

1. Employment has grown over the last eleven years (including 2002-2003, even though the growth rate slowed down).

2. Employers have easily been able to find young, skilled workers on the labour market at an attractive comparative cost, thanks to cross-border labour. Due to changes in technology, the costs of adapting employees have been considered too high. Preference has been given to voluntary redundancies and early retirements so that the quality of the labour force is changed rather than adapted or trained.

3. The sectors most affected by demands for change during 1992-2003 and of most national significance were

metallurgy and the banking and insurance sector. Policies relating to union-management agreements were put in place, removing the need for general rules concerning employee flexibility.

It is therefore perfectly consistent that, as regards the employment contract, the employer does not have a specific obligation to adapt, retrain or redeploy an employee in case of job loss.

While Luxembourg's labour law is very similar to French law in terms of employment contract regulations, development in the area of general contract obligations has not followed.

Due to the synallagmatic nature of the contract, Luxembourg law would have no difficulty, in terms of legal bases and general theory, in 'recognising' an obligation to adapt employees within the employment contract, as the French court of Appeal has done since 1992.

3. Collective bargaining

Collective agreements must contain provisions on the training policy of the company, sector and branch to which the collective agreement applies (article 4-2 of the Act of 1965, as amended). These should, in particular, cover *accumulation of training sessions, work experience, apprenticeship courses and other measures likely to make it easier for a person to integrate into the working environment, particularly in favour of the unemployed, and the development of lifelong training.* In addition, since the Act of 12 February 1999, article 4b states that *companies should give access to continuous training measures to employees who have been absent due to a career break caused particularly by maternity, a training initiative or sabbatical leave, in order to enable them to follow changes in production techniques and procedures.*

The general normative framework therefore encourages unions and management to contractually implement active training policies.

We can see that an emphasis on vocational training has been introduced into the major branch agreements, the banking and insurance sectors and metallurgy.

However, a number of preliminary remarks should be made:

1. The provisions contained in collective agreements are limited and in no way reflect an overall policy for training employees and adapting them to their jobs. There is usually a reference to company training plans, drawn up after consultation between the employer and employee representatives.

2. These contractual provisions were only recently introduced and result from the legislative framework introduced by the Act of 12 February 1999, initiated under the 1998 national employment plan. There is therefore a clear link between this change, which has helped to develop contractual training measures in Luxembourg, and Community strategy relating to employment. The extension in 2003 of the Act of 1999 was also intended to meet the most recent European guideline objectives.

3. However, the introduction into the Act of an obligation to negotiate, and in particular to negotiate vocational training, has been shown to be unsuccessful. There has been a systematic move towards negotiation at company level. Company plans are still the most commonly used method.

4. On the other hand, a study of collective agreement renegotiations since 1999 showed that these largely focused on training. There is therefore a slow and gradual change in vocational training law in Luxembourg.

5. It is therefore perhaps not surprising that provisions relating to continuous training and employee flexibility are only to be found in certain sector-based agreements (bearing in mind that they are generally renegotiated every two or three years).

In collective agreements for the banking sector, which are of obvious importance in Luxembourg, an appendix was introduced from 1999 concerning training and reorientation (1999-2001 agreement, repeated in the 2001-2002 text).

Employees have no general rights to training. Access is instead based on the prior selection of candidates. The employee has no right to be allocated to a new position once the course is completed, nor any right to a financial bonus.

Training is introduced to raise an employee's initial qualification. It is based on 'voluntary participation and consensus' but requires a favourable decision from the employer (internal application possible). This is carried out on the basis of joint investment (50% of courses within working hours) with training costs being borne by branch organisations and the employer financing the total cost where the course is successfully completed. If the employee fails to do so but has attended regularly, he must pay half the training costs, but must pay 100% if he has not attended regularly. The aim of this measure is therefore to instil a sense of commitment to training in the employee. Training is therefore not a guaranteed right for the employee but a possibility based on shared responsibility.

As far as actual obligations to provide training are concerned, these are limited to career breaks and are confined to reproducing the scope imposed by the Act in article 4b. This right to training after a return from leave is, however, very important in preventing the exclusion of young women from the labour market.

In the collective agreement for the insurance sector, the only measure provided for is a training system to help the unemployed integrate into the sector. In addition, insurance companies are required, 'where relevant', to give access to 'catch-up' measures after a career break.

Other collective agreements deal with continuous training but do not grant employees specific rights. For example, in the private healthcare and social welfare sectors, there is reference to training plans drawn up by the employer at company level (also used in other sectors); while in others, the company plan is limited to career breaks (e.g. breweries and lift installers) but is open to integration initiatives for the unemployed.

At present, it is very difficult to assess the practical impact of company training policies.

The case of the steel sector is, however, clear. Dominated by Arbed, one of the country's flagship industrial companies, it suffered a crisis in the 1980s. Major training policies were introduced for employees who had already followed initial courses in developing sectors. However, in the blast furnace sector (definitive closure spread over the reference period), employees were not retrained or redeployed, but instead offered early retirement.

A survey carried out in 1999 by the Federation of Luxembourg Companies (FEDIL), Chamber of Commerce and Ministry of Labour and Employment shows that three-quarters of the firms questioned had employees who had followed a training course. These courses were either internal (47.2%) external (64.8%) or on the job (56.5%).

Although these figures do not allow a qualitative assessment of the effects of the courses, all firms responded that the amount of training on offer should be increased to allow employees to adapt to technological changes. Training needs are thus recognised by employers and at the same time, listed as an objective of the 2003 employment plan, which clearly favours reinforcing training policies and providing young people with new skills. This explains why legislators intervened in 1999 to encourage companies to develop continuous training plans (see below). An Act is being prepared for 2004.

We can therefore see that the movement in Luxembourg for more job flexibility is developing, but remains at an embryonic stage, concentrating more on integrating the unemployed (see below) and improving young people's initial qualifications.

This could change in the years to come if it were to become practically difficult to recruit cross-border workers. It should be emphasised that this is not yet a widespread problem, except in certain sectors, as even in 2003 job creation was still 70% in favour of cross-border workers. Until now, this generally highly-qualified labour resource has allowed employers to avoid the costs of adapting and retraining resident employees whose jobs have been axed.

4. The development of continuous training

Since 1990, faced with the slow take-off of contractual continuous training measures, Luxembourg developed a system of ministerial monitoring of continuous training. This was generally directed at training courses in secondary technical institutions aimed at developing employees' skills. Vocational training courses are organised either by the Department of Education or by professional chambers, communes or approved private associations. These are similar to secondary school training courses and aimed at unemployed people needing to acquire a qualification.

The banking sector is the best organised in providing vocational training adapted to sectoral needs (several levels of training).

These measures, organised by the Act of 4 September 1990, were supplemented in 1999 by the Act of 22 June. This is a tax incentive law, allowing companies to benefit from exemptions on their continuous training expenditure. The number of participants has grown considerably each year and in 2003, and a campaign was organised by all groups involved (Ministry, unions and management) to promote 'vocational training to move forward with the world'.[6]

The government contributes to the cost of investment in training according to the company's preference. This either takes the form of a direct grant or a tax reduction covering 10% of the cost. In the area of approved training courses, the employee may be required to reimburse costs if he terminates his contract, unless there is serious misconduct on the part of the employer. If the training is organised by the employer with no help from government, the employer can include a reimbursement clause in the agreement signed with the employee, that may be graduated and valid for a three-year period.

From the surveys that have been carried out, it seems that employers choose areas of training according to direct needs: information technology, engineering and manufacturing techniques, quality and safety.

Long-term adaptation of qualifications does not seem, for the moment, to be a concern for employers in the manufacturing sector, even though Fedil considers that a number of skills are missing on the labour market in Luxembourg.

More generally, training courses offered to employees in company training plans are usually one-off courses.

The Act of 2000 does not seem to have created sufficient incentives to change the range of training available to employees in Luxembourg. The Ministry of Employment considers the measure to be unsatisfactory and that it needs to be improved through discussion of the failures of the Act of 1999, which included obligations to negotiate vocational training.

However, the tripartite steering committee has not ruled in favour of a legislative change for 2003 on these issues, although unions and management have reaffirmed their commitment to a contractual policy promoting employment. An agreement to introduce individual training leave has shown the new relevance of social dialogue for these issues in the future. A Bill introducing this right seems likely to be put forward. We can see here, on the one hand, the creative effect of contractual policy on the development of labour law, and on the other, the influence of 'good practices' highlighted by the European employment strategy.

In late 2003, bilateral discussions between the government and social partners were launched to boost the social dialogue and improve the use of legislative, statutory and contractual instruments in handling economic changes, especially restructuring operations. After long discussions as to whether a new law was needed, it was decided that it was not necessary to carry out any fundamental reforms.

5. Integration measures and measures concerning young people

The vast majority of provisions concerning young people's entry into the labour market were revised in 1995, then again in 1999.

These provisions are very traditional in nature, as a result of the specific features of the labour market in Luxembourg. They either aim to help young people in achieving basic qualifications (hence a major apprenticeship plan) or in entering the world of work after leaving education (company placements, introductory or integration placements).

Luxembourg also has regulations allowing students to work during the two summer months.

All these contracts have benefited from the Act of 23 March 2001 concerning the protection of workers under 18, and have helped to strengthen requirements for health safety at work. The Act was passed as a result of the 'young people's' directive of 1994. It reinforces the rules to prohibit children from working and protect teenagers authorised to work, in areas such as working time, rest periods and safety (no Sunday working, no night-time working).

In 2000, in order to follow OECD guidelines, Luxembourg decided to draw up a reform bill to improve the coordination of information and guidance services and to improve the performance of the parties involved.

5.1. Apprenticeships

The employment fund (Act of 1978 extended by an Act of 23 December 1995) can allocate apprenticeship grants to companies. Arrangements for this are fixed by grand-ducal regula-

tion (making it easier to adapt to changes in the economic situation). The employment fund can also allocate career guidance allowances to young job seekers starting out in working life under either an employment or apprenticeship contract.

Arrangements for allocating these allowances, both to the employer and the employee, were established by the grand-ducal regulation of 1988. Distinctions are made according to trades and activity sectors in order to respond to the needs of companies. This measure has not been revised during the last eleven years.

Help in promoting apprenticeship is given to employers as part of an apprenticeship contract. A monthly grant is paid (8% of the allowance paid to the apprentice plus payment of employer contributions, with a 12% increase for artisans). The grant is increased for apprenticeship in the professions or in trades where there is a structural labour shortage (list drawn up by the national employment commission). The allowance paid to the apprentice can also be increased, depending on the activity sector. A reform of the system will be drawn up in 2004 to encourage the development of sandwich courses and life-long training.

5.2. The initial company probation and the training scheme

The probationary placement scheme, the mechanism for which was also extended in 1995, allows job seekers under the age of thirty to follow a sandwich course, half theory and half practice. The Act of 12 February 1999 created the integration placement, which is covered by the same legal framework. This form of training is based on a framework agreement between the company and the Government, usually concluded via one of the professional Chambers. The beneficiary continues to receive unemployment benefit, with the company bearing at least 50% of the cost. In addition, it may pay an extra allowance during training. Framework agreements have been signed with the manufacturers federation, the trades' federation and the small businesses federation.

This type of probationary placement is also open to employees not receiving an allowance but agreeing to accept a placement, before the expiry of the period for registering as a job seeker, which opens the way to the right to receive full unemployment benefit. These workers are paid at least 50% of the full unemployment benefit rate by the employer. This is supplemented in certain sectors by a merit allowance. The unemployment fund can also add to this mechanism.

The worker has to accept the placement, or risk losing full unemployment benefit. The minimum period for these agreements is three months and the maximum twelve.

In the event of recruitment, the company is obliged to take on any former probationer who has returned to being unemployed. The company must inform the individual if they match the job profile, and must receive a response within a week.

5.3. The training scheme contract and the temporary work contract

The probationary placement provided for since 1978, extended in 1995 and re-cast as a temporary work contract in the Act of 12 February 1999, aims to provide young job seekers with a practical introduction to working life and to aid the transition from education. These probationary placements and temporary work contracts are intended for workers under the age of thirty. If a worker turns down a placement, contract, training course or skills evaluation offered as part of the temporary work contract, they may be excluded from receiving full unemployment benefits. Companies that want to sign placement contracts should first of all consult employee representatives or the company's joint committee.

The rules for the fixed-term employment contract apply to these probationary placements. The salary is equal to 85% of the minimum for unskilled employees; 25% of this, along with employer contributions, is paid by the employment fund. Placement workers' salaries are not included in the total used for calculating tax. In the case of temporary work contracts, the salary is equal to 80% of the minimum reference level, and 100% if the employee is not kept on following the training.

During the placement, the worker can ask his employer for leave to respond to job offers (maximum eight hours a month), and still receive payment. He may leave his company if he is offered another job, unless the initial employer has offered a permanent contract.

An employer wishing to recruit must, in the three months prior to the end of placement, offer the job to his placement worker if the individual has the appropriate skills. This condition is a helpful integration provision, but can easily be bypassed since it is based on a set of skills requirements drawn up by the employer.

Finally, if youth unemployment continues to grow, employers may in the future be obliged to comply with a 1% probational worker quota.

Although, in principle, probationer contracts should be for a minimum period of three months and a maximum of twelve months, they can be extended for a further six months for jobs in government and local authority service and for professional re-integration associations.

Since 1999, special measures have been in place to provide workers with better allowances (65% of minimum reference salary) in jobs or sectors in which one or other of the sexes is under-represented.

These provisions clearly show that the main concern in Luxembourg is helping young people to integrate by adapting their training and qualifications to the requirements of the labour market. Because of the regular flow of jobs, a second objective is to encourage job seekers to return to work quickly. The law is somewhat authoritarian in that it can lead to removal of unemployment benefits if the worker refuses to accept offers aimed at re-integrating him. Similarly, companies are given a share of responsibility for integrating young people by the provision concerning employment priority.

The measures that have been taken have therefore been appropriate to the labour market and the objective of integration. Since 2002, the Ministry has been working with the permanent employment committee to draw up a bill aimed at providing a proper foundation for measures to help the unemployed, improve ways of coordinating services and increase financial openness. The Bill, as it stood in late 2003, provides for regulations in which the state will pay the cost of integrating the unemployed into the labour market. This Bill is one of the measures being carried out to improve the way in which ADEM operates and encourage the provision of individual support for jobseekers.[7] Luxembourg is therefore not seeking to reform its integration techniques, but to improve the effectiveness of the parties involved in their actions to help the unemployed.

7   See below.

Chapter III:
Employability and job protection

Employment protection in Luxembourg involves checks on contracts offering little job security (section 1) and a range of measures relating to redundancies and restructuring (section 2), which are backed up by specific measures falling under the framework of working time (section 3). The interaction between job requirements and family life (section 4) shows how far Luxembourg has fallen behind in terms of employment for women.

1. The supervision of job security

Luxembourg undoubtedly wants to retain the form of the permanent employment contract as the basic reference, common-law contract. Both the fixed-term contract, regulated since the Act of 24 May 1989, and the temporary employment contract, regulated since the Act of 19 May 1994, fall under legal rules underpinned by the principle that permanent jobs in the company may not be filled by contracts that do not offer security.

The rules surrounding these contracts are also based on strict adherence to an attitude that protects employees, allowing checks on restrictive use of these contracts and on compliance with the principle of equal treatment.

Luxembourg's regulatory regime is very similar to France's. Supreme Court judgements regularly refer to French doctrine. While there is a smaller volume of jurisprudence encouraging permanent employment than in France, it nevertheless follows the same direction of protecting sustainable employment.

Employment contracts that do not offer security are restricted by the conditions when they can be used, and under which they can be drawn up and by penalties for redefining them.

1.1. Supervision of the use of fixed-term and temporary contracts

Filling a permanent-activity post in a non-permanent manner is prohibited (article 5, Act of 24 May 1989). Temporary or fixed-term contracts are therefore limited to particular, non-permanent tasks that must be justified:

1. By the replacement of a temporarily absent employee or an employee whose employment contract is suspended (excluding collective disputes or bad weather stoppages).

2. By the need to use contracts of a seasonal nature, which should not be for a period of more than 12 months (statutory controls on the notion of a season).

3. By the possibility of using customary contracts due to the nature of the jobs and their temporary character (audio-visual, artistic productions, banking sector, training courses and teaching, professional sport, building and public works). It may be surprising to find the banking sector in this list, as it is Luxembuurg's largest employer.

4. By the carrying out of a particular, occasional, one-off task (e.g. audit, translation, installation of a computer system).

5. By the carrying out of urgent works.

6. As part of specific contracts linked to employment policy.

Fixed-term contracts may be concluded from one date to another within the framework of a maximum period of 24 months (except the seasonal contract, which is a maximum 10 months, and contracts linked to employment policy) or without a fixed term where the contract involves a replacement for an absent person named in the contract, a customary or seasonal contract, or for the carrying out of a particular task. In this case, the contract must provide for a minimum period.

Temporary employment contracts are limited to 12 months (except seasonal contracts, maximum 10 months) but may also be concluded without a fixed term (in this case there is a minimum working period). The contract may be renewed twice if a clause has been inserted to this effect within the maximum imposed limit.

Seasonal contracts may contain a renewal clause from one season to the next, but after two renewals they are considered to be permanent. Successive contracts are permitted for the same job if the work is of an intermittent nature, but must have a lawful cause. The employer must, however, wait for a period of one third of the initial period before he can conclude another short-term contract for the same job, except for seasonal contracts, customary contracts and those linked to employment policy.

1.2. Supervision of contracts and their redefinition

The judicial authority is very strict in checking that the contract is concluded in writing and that it contains the necessary components. They therefore refuse any forms of proof other than written ones, and redefine the contract if any one of its compulsory components is not complied with (duration, renewal, truth of the reasons invoked).

As part of the regulation of temporary work, contracts concluded between the temporary worker (subject to ministerial authorisation, whether the head office is in the European Union or not) and the user company are also regulated and controlled in order to guarantee the rights of employees, and especially their right to equal treatment.

The assignment contract also needs to comply with strict formal requirements, so that judges can keep control of cases where companies resort to temporary labour.

Whether the contract is fixed-term or temporary, employees are protected during the contract period by the fact that the contract may not be terminated unless there are serious reasons or misconduct by the other party. The employer may not therefore terminate the contract for a reason linked to the employee's professional inadequacies, other than misconduct.

However, employee protection is limited by the fact that, if the contract is terminated prematurely, the employer pays a maximum compensation of two months' salary.

However, if the contract is irregular in some way, it is redefined as a permanent employment contract, and in this case compensation is limited to a lump sum.

Furthermore, as the Supreme Court states,[8] redefinition is *the only sanction provided by law in the event of a violation of article 5, the aim of the law not being a termination as of right giving rise to compensation, but the right for the employee to maintain working relations after the expiry of the illegal term.*

It should be noted that, contrary to French law, worker representatives in the company are not specifically obliged to control the use of precarious contracts. Of course, they still have the possibility of informing the labour inspectorate, but they do not have any special rights such as the French right of warning created in 2002.

Here again, the favourable state of the labour market, explains why there have only been legal controls to maintain lasting employment, with no support either from employee action (e.g. union action) or a special collective right to fight against job insecurity.

Lastly, it is important to point out that Luxembourg adopted these regulations in 1989 and 1994, i.e. long before the agreements concluded by European unions and management. Luxembourg law complies with agreements that essentially introduce the principle of equal treatment and encourage limited use of fixed-term contracts.

The fact that Community law has been 'timid' as regards the protections it has introduced and has not created a collective right adapted to insecure jobs also helps to explain why Luxembourg has not needed to modify its law as a result of the directives.

1.3. Part-time employment contracts

Part-time employment contracts are governed by the Act of 26 February 1993, and were modified by the Act of 12 February 1999. The part-time employment contract is a voluntary contract, generally chosen by the employee, as the basic rule remains that a standard employment contract should be full-time. Up to now, Luxembourg has limited the flexibility given to employers and continues to control and restrict part-time working.

Regulation of part-time employment contracts is becoming heavier, along with the legal framework governing the contract. Part-time work is defined as any work below the legal period of 40 hours a week, and must set out the distribution of hours worked.

Employees are given guarantees on two points: the creation of part-time posts and changes to working hours.

Concerning the creation of part-time posts, the management of the company is bound to consult the company joint committee or employee representatives. The employer must also inform the company's employees who wish to work part-time. The law guarantees these employees equal treatment compared to full-time workers while those who work more than 16 hours a week are entitled to full unemployment benefit.

Full-time employees may legitimately refuse to work part-time, so this cannot be used by an employer as a reason for dismissal. Part-time employees can also refuse to work full-time.

Concerning changes to working time, jurisprudence has made a distinction (ruling of 22 June 2000 Post c/ Das Dores Paulo) between working hours that are changed during the day itself or on different days of the week. In respect of the spread of working hours over the day, the employer does not need to obtain the employee's agreement. On the other hand, as far as changes in the days worked are concerned, the employer must send a letter by recorded delivery, providing for notice of a substantial modification to the contract (calculated according to length of service). If the employee does not refuse the change and performs his contract under the new terms, the Court considers that the change has been accepted and that the employee can no longer claim his previous status quo back from the employer.

These part-time work regulations show a desire to control and restrict this type of work. This is probably because Luxembourg has never emphasised new ways for women to reconcile family and working life (see below), and has also tried to limit this type of contract and prevent the development of flexibility through part-time work (bearing in mind that occasional work can be organised under fixed-term contracts, see above).

Finally, it should be mentioned that there is no specific legislation on teleworking in Luxembourg.

2. Supervision of employment in cases of redundancy and restructuring

Between 1992-2003, Luxembourg has had to manage a crisis in the metallurgy industry. Due to the dominance of Arbed (the flagship firm in the sector), all the major restructuring issues have been negotiated and settled through a single company.

In other sectors, Community law has been the impetus for legislative changes, due to the obligation to transpose the directive concerning collective redundancies. The law intro-

duces a system with several levels, with the aim of achieving a proper negotiation of restructuring plans and a desire to prevent conflict. But this law has been rarely applied over the last eleven years: restructuring plans appeared in Luxembourg in 2002, when five materialised within a few months.

Here again, the favourable job creation situation in Luxembourg and the skilled labour provided by cross-border workers explain why working practices tend towards the departure of older employees rather than their re-integration and re-adaptation.

There has therefore been very little discussion about employability in Luxembourg. Only in 2002 did the country have to face growing unemployment and the resulting need to transform the skills of the labour force. The only move made was to adapt training courses to needs identified by the companies themselves: no specific support measures were introduced by the public authorities.

It could therefore be argued that Community law compelled Luxembourg to introduce specific legislation on collective redundancies in 2002-2003 to help the country respond to the deteriorating economic situation. In the area of working practices, the law is still influenced by an attitude encouraging the exclusion of older workers and voluntary redundancy, due in particular to the conservative nature of Luxembourg's employers. Only in the area of unemployment have retraining measures appeared.

2.1. Collective redundancies since the Act of 23 July 1993

The Act of 23 July 1993 takes up the provisions of Community law on collective redundancies, including the actual notion of collective redundancy. The 'in good time' negotiation mechanism is based on the desire to reach an agreement on avoiding or reducing the number of redundancies and on the possibilities of lessening the consequences of collective redundancy.

The representatives responsible for this negotiation are the company joint committee or employee representatives and, if there is a collective agreement, the union organisations. If the company does not have any representatives, the procedure is dependent on the introduction of a representative body and thus the organisation of elections. This obligation means that, in the event of economic difficulties or similar reasons, the employer is required to organise and allow the formation of an employee representation body.

Two weeks at the latest after the start of negotiations, an agreement, called the 'restructuring plan', has to be lodged with the employment authorities and passed on to the labour inspectorate. This document has to show:

- Either the content of the agreement and the measures decided under the restructuring plan, setting out placement measures, placement and retraining assistance, possibilities for immediate re-integration into the labour market and financial compensation measures.

- Or an agreement by the parties that it is impossible to draw up a restructuring plan and the reasons for this.

In this case, a report on the negotiations must also be drawn up, including the positions of the parties and the stage of discussions on restructuring measures (placement, retraining assistance, immediate re-integration, financial compensation and all other measures being considered). The parties must then jointly contact the national arbitration office within three days of signing the disagreement report, giving the names of the individuals who will take part in the office's deliberations.

It is an offence to refuse to take part in national arbitration office proceedings. The office has to give a ruling very quickly (within five days) and deliberations must be completed within two weeks.

Any notification of redundancy before a restructuring plan has been put in place (or before the office report putting the restructuring plan in place) is null and void, and this nullity may be recorded by a judge in an emergency procedure requested by the employee. The employee may also decide not to request nullity and ask for the contract to be continued. He may request compensation if he acts within the two-week period and may in all events request damages for unfair termination of the employment contract.

It should be noted that the employer must communicate to worker representatives all information useful to the negotiation. The whole procedure takes place with an obligation to inform the Ministry of Labour and Employment, but the latter has no special powers to intervene. The Employment Minister may, however, take steps to shorten the period in which collective redundancies can take place (usually 75 days), or extend notice periods for employees.

Jurisprudence states that the agreement could also be based on the inability of the parties to draw up a restructuring plan containing measures more favourable than those made compulsory by the employment contract Act (24 May 1989) and the Act of 1966 on paid holidays (CSJ 08/11/2001 Union of Swiss Banks c/ Jengen).

This means that the measures contained in the restructuring plan, as set out in article 7-2, are not compulsory measures that have to be imposed as part of a collective redundancy plan. The rigour of Luxembourg law is based on the obligation on worker representatives and the employer to negotiate, or, in the event of a disagreement, to negotiate at the national arbitration office, but not on the final content of the plan.

Luxembourg law follows the same lines as the Community directive, which has placed the emphasis on consultation with worker representatives 'with a view to an agreement'. Procedures based on negotiation, then on arbitration mediated by an objective authority, provide workers with solid guarantees.

This procedure seems to be well integrated into collective relations in Luxembourg, even though it is little used. It is backed up by working practices that are accepted by union organisations.

2.2. Working practices in the event of restructuring

Up to now, companies have sought to organise restructuring using procedures based on voluntary participation rather than resort to collective redundancy procedures.

A number of examples, especially in the banking sector, show that companies and union organisations prefer to find solutions that have the lowest possible social cost. These are deemed to be those involving early retirement. The metallurgy sector has made considerable use of early retirement as part of the legal mechanism.

But other measures have also appeared in recent years. Dexia (a very large bank), for example, introduced an agreement based on early retirement, changing full-time contracts to part-time contracts and sabbatical leave. These measures are based on voluntary participation.

Sabbatical leave allows employees to be paid throughout their period of leave. The company assumes that, at the end of the leave period (a year, two years) its activity will enable it to re-open the positions (dangerous during a period of decline in growth).

A large number of companies also make use of voluntary redundancies. These measures, as we know, are very costly and are justified in groups that have a strong financial interest in restructuring, in the absence of any financial difficulty. Union organisations are not opposed to these measures: they are favourable to employees as they accept them voluntarily.

Concerns about the labour market have not been sufficiently strong to persuade the public authorities to seek to limit these voluntary exclusions from the labour market. No measures have therefore been taken to force companies to limit early retirements. In the metallurgy sector, for example, the cost of retraining blast furnace employees in other, more competitive sectors has proved to be greater than that for early retirements.

Up to now, employers have preferred to remove older employees (aged over 50) from the labour market rather than contribute towards major retraining schemes: a question of costs, age of employees and the existence on the labour market, thanks to cross-border workers, of a young, skilled (and often cheaper) labour force.

The situation in Luxembourg is out of step with that in neighbouring countries such as France, Belgium and Germany, who have had to cope with crisis situations and even recession. But it seems likely that the downturn in 2002-2003 and the drying-up of cross-border labour will lead companies to restructure using additional measures to early retirement.

Nevertheless, for the time being, there does not seem to be any serious questioning of early retirement as a technique.

In 2002, Luxembourg considered revising its law on collective redundancies to introduce an obligation to negotiate restructuring plans (not to conclude them) and create a fund to finance outplacement. The Ministry of Employment is considering measures to develop retraining as part of employment. However, it was decided in 2003 that no legislative intervention was needed and that the issue of restructuring plan management came within the scope of social dialogue.

2.3. Measures relating to unemployment

The development of a real employment policy in Luxembourg took place under the impetus of European employment strategies. Since 1997, the country has adopted a wider range of measures, including both direct and indirect aids to employment.

2.3.1. Presentation of measures taken to encourage employment

The employment authority (ADEM) has, since 1997, significantly modernised its services to strengthen the preventive approach. The objective has been to optimise placement services (including a new head office, computerisation, circulation of information, exemptions from administrative charges) and new measures have been taken to give the long-term unemployed individual support (individual psychosocial support plan for jobseekers, or PEC). ADEM now draws up a skills profile, then creates an integration or guidance plan backed up by individual support. Up to 2000, the PEC system was mostly used for the 26-54 age band, but since 2001 the measure has been extended to older workers.

Individual support has increased sharply every year and seems to be particularly well suited to women and young people (the proportion of women in the PEC rose from 49.8% in 1999 to 53.2% in 2000, while the percentage of young people grew from 14.8% to 18.5%).

According to figures from 1999 and 2000, around 11% of jobseekers have health and flexibility problems.

Concerning direct aids to employment, apart from the measures mentioned above, work re-integration courses have been set up for the over-30's (one year with theoretical and practical training), along with training programmes introduced by ADEM, often of short duration, motivation workshops and, since 1994, special return-to-work allowances for unemployed persons receiving no benefits.

Indirect aids are also planned: company start-up grants, geographical mobility grants (since 1994), considerable grants for disabled workers (broadened in 1999), and re-employment grants for those made redundant (1982).

Fiscal measures were also introduced during 2001 and 2002 to reduce the tax burden on households, and the minimum wage was reformed to ensure that those receiving it are not penalised by work integration measures. The mechanism is also used to help people on the employment market whose income is below the guaranteed minimum. It is a form of Government aid to compensate for the difference between earned income and the minimum wage. This is the first step towards a negative tax.

Amongst the evaluations carried out by the Ministry of Employment, the most important measures concern young people, through temporary work contracts (see above).

As regards indirect aids, grants to unemployed workers under threat or made redundant (excluding the metallurgy industry) increased by 35% between 1997 and 2000. Grants to the disabled have also increased considerably.

2.3.2. Overall evaluation of changes in employment sectors

It seems clear that employment policy in Luxembourg has been strongly influenced by European guidelines. Particularly since 1999, the government has continually sought to improve employment measures, although these remain sporadic, sparse and targeted (due to the relatively low unemployment rate).

However, it should be noted that aid is mainly directed at integration of young people, and that nothing has been developed to introduce major, long-term retraining programmes for the unemployed.

The reason for this is simple: companies have sought above all to reduce their workforce numbers through retirement and early retirement. The example of metallurgy is highly significant in this regard, as the rights of employees come on stream from the age of 55 and mechanisms are regularly extended to allow employees to leave at that age. A tripartite negotiation is due concerning the situation of workers aged 55 to 68 (28% currently work beyond 55).

The major companies in Luxembourg generally look to find consensual solutions and managed to avoid the need for redundancies up to 2002. Due to their economic wealth, especially in the banking and insurance sectors, employers usually find solutions and finance them themselves, avoiding the need for a government retraining policy.

Between 1992-2003, employers have not sought to place the emphasis on redeployment or retraining; but have rather been more interested in recruiting young employees with new qualifications while financing early retirement. More recently the situation has changed due to the fall in numbers of cross-border workers and the appearance of collective redundancies.

The Ministry of Employment is currently considering options for introducing long-term retraining procedures, developing incentive mechanisms other than tax bonuses and removing obstacles to integrating the unemployed, especially for women. Similarly, there is presently a lack of procedures for relocating employees, not only nationally but also transnationally. Due to the employment guidelines, Luxembourg has taken action to promote 'active ageing':[9] in 2003

it carried out studies with the OECD, but there is currently no proposal for reform to change company behaviour.

3. Working time flexibility authorised by the Act of 12 February 1999

The Act of 12 February 1999 introduced new provisions concerning the organisation of working time. These were, however, more cautious than those proposed at a tripartite employment conference in 1998. The law allows the employer to change the reference period, from a week (40 hours a week) to a longer period of up to 4 weeks, on the condition that the average over the reference period is no more than 40 hours. The collective agreement may lead to an extension of the reference period from 1 month to 12 months.

For the reference period, the employer must draw up a work organisation plan, which must be communicated to employees five days before the start of the period.

The introduction of this type of flexibility was reliant on collective bargaining and was a failure. Very few agreements were reached due to opposition from unions, to the little benefit gained by employees from such flexibility, and to the practical disadvantages arising out of the company's organisation plan.

In fact, the law provides for the plan to be drawn up on the basis of the company's foreseeable activity over the reference period, but that changes may be made in the case of unforeseeable events. 'Unforeseeable events' are defined as *events that could not have been foreseen at the time the working time organisation plan was being drawn up, or following a regular occurrence of the event in previous periods, or following a cautious forecast by the employer of future events that should or could be recognised.*

The uncertainty created by the employer's right to assess what is unforeseeable, despite this definition, has led unions to stall negotiations on greater flexibility. As for the employers, they consider that requirements relating to the organisation plan remove all flexibility.

It is clear that, during 2002 and 2003, this failure has given rise to a great deal of discussion amongst both employers and unions about how to reform the law. Conflicts of interest are obviously considerable on this sensitive issue. Unions

---

9   This is the term used in the national plan. On this issue, as on flexibility, the main effect of the guidelines is to focus attention on reorienting policy, but a measure is only used if necessary in the national context and where it matches the country's political objectives.

and management are closely monitoring developments over the 35-hour week in France and are learning from them.

Against this background, it was decided in late 2003 to extend the Act of 12 February 1999 until 2007, to continue the momentem begun on the renegotiation of agreements. No further flexibility in work organisation or new obligations for employers were introduced, despite requests by the unions.

Despite opposition from the social partners to a possible increase in working time flexibility the existing situation is considered satisfactory by those involved: 'company cultures' are strong enough for 'arrangements' to be worked out for free time. Part of this company culture is the 'informal' settlement of working hours, which does not appear in the agreements but shows that there is a consensus on the flexibility given to employers.[10]

Obviously, this situation has perverse effects: for example, in the construction sector, a large number of people work illegally.

Arrangements, contractual this time, have been made in the banking sector: variable hours were introduced in exchange for greater flexibility. These are popular with employees, but are far from being widespread in Luxembourg, despite the fact that they help to reconcile family and working life.

Labour relations in Luxembourg are therefore rather traditionally organised, but there are nevertheless innovations in working time, such as fixed or variable hours, flexible hours or shift work. Studies carried out to evaluate the Act of 1999[11] show that the introduction of flexibility into working hours was more frequent in women's employment, which is steadily increasing every year.

4. Job protection and family life

Luxembourg has maintained a very ambiguous attitude to the issue of women at work: although women's access to the labour market has accelerated in recent years, it is, from a sociological point of view, still far from favourable.

The percentage of women at work used to be significantly below the Community average, but since 1999, it has tended to rise and now stands at 3% below the European average. Before this, Luxembourg had no policy to encourage women to go out to work or methods to help women reconcile working and family life. Since 1999 however, an action plan has been drawn up to stimulate the involvement of women in the labour market. As we have seen, measures have been taken in favour of women through temporary contracts.

The Act of 12 February 1999 relating to parental leave is very significant as Luxembourg was one of the last countries in Europe not to preserve women's employment after parental leave.

It is a transposal of the Community directive, which, on this issue too, led to a change in the legal situation of parents in Luxembourg.

Parental leave is available for a period of 6 months for full-time workers and 12 months for part-time workers. The employer may only refuse to allow it for a number of specific reasons. These include a shortage of labour, the fact that the company has less than 15 employees and the fact that a senior executive is part of the company's management team (this list reveals much about the social context). The employee retains his job or a similar post and receives a significant allowance over the period (1 500 euros a month for full-time leave).

The parental leave policy has been backed up by a plan to increase the number of crèches in communes since 1998. It is used by women in 93% of cases.

It is difficult to integrate these provisions into the social context as, although the government fully recognises the economic need for a new labour force – in this case, women – there are still a number of cultural and social barriers to be overcome.

In 2001, an initial assessment of the parental leave laws was carried out. Women tend to take this leave after maternity leave, mainly in the 30-34 age group and mainly when they work in the financial sector. Parental leave does not give rise to a significant number of fixed-term replacement jobs for the unemployed (in 700 companies, 278 individuals were recruited, 162 without government support).

Women's employment is still viewed unfavourably, especially in cases of couples with children. As salaries are high, it is often more advantageous to live on one salary and social benefits, rather than be obliged to organise childminding. The woman's salary is still regarded as an extra income of little interest from a financial point of view. Part-time work, which was regulated in 1993, does not offer sufficient financial advantages to reduce social resistance to the concept of women at work.

---

10   This trend is confirmed in the report by Accord international on the evaluation of the Act of 12 February 1999, p. 39.
11   Report by Accord international 2003.

We often come across some very surprising provisions in collective agreements, such as 'household allowances', which aim to encourage women to stay at home.

There are also occasional provisions to improve the legal mechanism for parental leave, or encourage work-life balance by making special working-hour or holiday arrangements.

However, the policy on child-minding is changing. Luxembourg acknowledges that it has been slow to change in this respect. The objective set in 2003 is to provide places in crèches for 50% of working mothers by 2010. But on this issue, government policy remains considerably out of step with the needs of working women.

The Act of 12 February 1999 also provides for a period of leave for family reasons, to look after a child under the age of 15 in the event of an accident or illness. The period of leave may not exceed two days per child per year. An allowance is paid in the same way as for sick leave but it cannot be said that this is a revolutionary measure to reconcile family and working life.

However, the Act of 29 May 2003 reforming the status of civil servants has introduced measures intended to encourage such a reconciliation. The Act has introduced a part-time service (25%, 50%, 75%) which, in principle, is organised on a daily basis but by agreement with the administration manager and depending on the interests of the service, the part-time work may be spread over a part of the week, month or year. Bonuses are also provided to compensate for leave taken to bring up children, and opportunities are organised for returning to work after leave on a part-time basis or without salary.

Although these measures are very new, it is clear that they favour balance between family and working life, and mainly help women to keep their jobs while staying at home to bring up children.

Chapter IV:
Equal opportunities and employment

The position of working women in Luxembourg society obviously influences the way in which the country's labour law develops.

Although policies for male and female workers have had mixed results (section 1), they are changing due to the impact of Community law, which encourages affirmative action (section 2) and imposes the protection of personal data (section 3).

1. An appraisal of policies relating to the legal position of male and female workers

Luxembourg's labour law has changed as a result of its obligations to transpose Community directives. The Act relating to equal treatment for men and women was adopted on 8 December 1981 and revised in 1986. However, equality representatives were introduced into companies from 1998 to encourage action in favour of workplace equality.

The Act has not given rise to many disputes (two rulings by the Supreme Court, dated 28 March 1991 and 13 July 1995 relating to unequal pay).

The Act was modified on 28 June 2001 with regard to proof of discrimination. It takes up the rules provided for in the Community directive.

No bill had been adopted by late 2003 to transpose the directives adopted in application of article 13 of the Treaty on 29 June 2000 and 27 November 2000.

Among the exceptions to the principle of equal treatment is maternity protection. Luxembourg has acquired a new mechanism that aligns itself with Community law (transposition of directive 92/85 of 19 October 1992). An initial law on maternity protection for women was adopted on 7 July 1998, and another on protection for women who are pregnant, have just given birth or are breast-feeding was voted on 1 August 2001. This new law changes the previous system, dating back to 1975, which totally prohibited night work for pregnant or breast-feeding women. From now on, a pregnant woman may be exempted from night work if she expressly asks her employer and if there is a risk to her health or safety, confirmed by a company doctor. The employer must then transfer her to a daytime job.

The law improves the legal position of pregnant women during the probation period, which is suspended until maternity leave. It also protects pupils and students working during school holidays. Maternity leave is still set at 8 weeks before the birth and 8 or 12 weeks afterwards. The job is guaranteed throughout the leave period. Luxembourg labour law stipulates that redundancies during these protection periods are null and void.

Lastly, a law was voted on 6 April 2000 relating to sexual harassment, following the recommendation on the dignity of men and women at work and the code of good practice on sexual harassment. From a legal point of view, harassment is considered as an attack on equal treatment. The law is aimed at all forms of improper or hurtful behaviour of whatever type (verbal or otherwise) which lead to the employee being put at a disadvantage within his job, his training or any other decision relating to the job. The employer, an employee, a customer or a supplier to the company may all be at fault.

The provisions on combating harassment in companies should be considered as part of the collective bargaining process. Employee representatives and equality representatives (instituted in 1998) must formulate proposals for preventing sexual harassment and to help and advise victims. Victims are protected in terms of their job and may be re-integrated. The legislation places the burden of proof on the victim, even after the comments of the Luxembourg Government advisors on the bill. Parliament reversed the burden of proof so that material proof of harassment must be provided by the victim, and it is up to the person accused of the offence to prove that there was no intention on his part.

Currently, issues of violence at work continue to cause concern to those involved. A bill relating to moral harassment was lodged in late 2002; this mostly takes up the provisions of the law on sexual harassment (here, company customers and suppliers are not involved).

Another major concern lies with the deterioration of working conditions and increased stress in companies. Union organisations and factory inspectors are heavily involved in this issue in Luxembourg. A great deal is expected of changes in Europe to the legal approach to workplace stress, as the phenomenon is growing in every EU country.

2. Affirmative action and equality of opportunities

The Act of 12 February 1999 provided for a mechanism relating to affirmative action in the private sector. Practical measures to encourage more women to work or to remove the disadvantages of a professional career are allowed, as long as they obtain authorisation from the Minister, who decides after having obtained the advice of employee representatives or the company joint committee.

Measures may also be adopted to encourage recruitment, new ways of organising working time, special training initiatives, measures relating to changes in job, access to posts of responsibility, or improved reconciliation between working and family life. These may be brought in via either a collective agreement or a company plan. The Minister rules according to the innovative nature of the initiatives and how feasible they are. Special financing has been provided to encourage companies to introduce such initiatives.

The Act of 12 February 1999 also imposed the obligation, within collective agreements, to negotiate an equality plan and continuous training accessible to those wishing to return to work after a career break. Certain major collective agreements (in banking and insurance) actually provide for training courses after maternity or parental leave, but these are very occasional and short-lived. There is no attempt to construct a genuine equality plan or a labour force flexibility plan. The achievements of collective bargaining in Luxembourg have mainly been in acquiring extra days of leave for family reasons.

At present, there does not seem to be an evaluation of how affirmative action initiatives have developed in Luxembourg companies.

It seems fairly clear that equal opportunities are not a priority for social partners and that there is still a great deal of social resistance to the issue, even though ministerial programmes are drawn up to improve the flow of information to representatives in companies concerning the advantages of positive initiatives.

However, action has been taken to promote the presence of women in union life. Equality representatives have been appointed in companies since the Act of 7 July 1998, and union training programmes for equality have been introduced, initially with European funds and, since the end of the relevant programme, with funds from the Ministry for the Promotion of Women.

On the other hand, it is wholly symptomatic that, when summarising achievements in equal opportunities, the Ministry of Employment presents general measures for jobseekers (temporary contract, introductory courses, re-integration courses, see above) and tax measures to lighten the tax burden on single parents before noting that no studies have been carried out on equal opportunities, apart from a study of housewives in 1998. Luxembourg is still approaching the issue from the point of view of the housewife, not of working women, and is even less involved in the integration of women into the labour market. This survey shows that, in the 45-54 age band, 23% do not want to stay at home all their lives; with 64% of those aged 34-44 sharing this view, and 85% of those under 35.

The analysis shows that there is no clear reason, apart from a lack of overall policy on promoting female participation in the labour market, as to why women feel so uncertain when it comes to returning to work.

Measures such as individual social security rights are currently being drawn up. Other measures are being taken, such as training courses specific to setting up a company, or aids to setting up a small firm. Again, these are isolated and the priority still seems to lie in the improvement of parental leave.

Significant funds have been allocated by the ESF in Luxembourg to promote equality between men and women. All kinds of training initiatives are planned, from female participation awareness programmes to decision-making programmes (2003-2004). Research is being carried out into differences in salaries, and training is currently being given on the issues surrounding classification as part of an action plan drawn up by unions and management in 2003.

All these initiatives show that there is a real interest in the issue of women at work in Luxembourg, due to the pressure created by the EES guidelines. But it does not appear that a real policy is emerging to develop and increase women's access to work within the framework of an equal opportunities policy based on the acquisition of new rights. For the authorities, the increase in the number of women at work in Luxembourg is already a success. But this still does not seem enough in comparison with Community equal opportunities objectives.

3. Equality of treatment and principles for protecting employee freedoms

The principle of equal treatment between male and female workers and the arsenal of provisions for fighting discrimination are fully in place in Luxembourg. But it does not appear that the law is being used.

The economic prosperity experienced over the last eleven years also explains why the differences are less painfully felt than in other countries. Where women work, they benefit from index-linked salaries just like other employees. They also work mainly in the banking and insurance sectors, which are covered by collective agreements containing a chapter on equality.

More generally, we can see that litigation (rare) in Luxembourg has not grown significantly in terms of laws introducing basic social rights. There is one ruling on the recourse to the principle of equality of treatment based on the Constitution and one very rare invocation before the ECHR.

In fact, changes to labour law in Luxembourg are mainly brought about by the requirement to transpose Community directives. A further illustration can be found in the adoption, on 2 August 2002,[12] of a law relating to the protection of individuals in matters concerning information of a personal nature. The law concerns persons in general and is transposed from directive 95/46 EC.

In Article 11, the Law provides for specific measures relating to the supervision of the workplace by the employer. The employer may process workers' personal data only if it is necessary. The text states that this must be justified for the following reasons:

- Workers' health and safety

- Protection of company assets

- Checks on the production process concerned with machines

- Temporary checks on production or worker performance where such a measurement is the only way to work out what the worker's exact pay should be

- The processing is part of a move to organise work on a 'flexi-time' basis.

The company joint committee has decision-making powers in the first two cases and in the last. It therefore has a role in checking the processes introduced that may affect the rights of employees. Consent given by the employee to the employer to process his personal data is not an obstacle to the employer implementing proper supervision. The law provides for criminal sanctions. It is also possible to demand that processing contrary to the law should be stopped, subject to a penalty.

The law organises prior information processing within a national Committee: prior notification must be given for all data processing. As fundamental rights and, in particular, private life are likely to be affected, there cannot be a simplified procedure and the national Committee therefore carries out in-depth checks.

The Law (Article 18) contains principles relating to the transfer of data to other countries, requiring the country to provide appropriate protection (definition, Article 18-2).

Luxembourg has certainly acquired a full data protection system, accompanied by systems for checking and supervising data processing through the offices of the national Committee, and an adequate legal right of appeal. Most of the protection covers data relating to employees. The specific chapter on workplace supervision shows, however, that the employer's right to supervise his employees is acknowledged but controlled.

---

12   OJ 13 August 2002.

Chapter V:
Conclusions

An analysis of the evolution of labour law in Luxembourg between 1992 and 2003 shows without a doubt that a shift of emphasis took place in 1999 towards building an employment policy on stronger foundations. Since the Act of 12 February 1999, there has been a clear determination to modernise labour law in Luxembourg, with the impetus given by the tripartite employment committee.

However, the Committee's guidelines do not always have the expected results in practice, as its work has no formal legislative status.

Luxembourg has, in addition, introduced a number of major legislative changes in order to transpose Community directives in the social field. European strategies are also responsible for the development of an employment policy.

Thanks to this change and to the demanding nature of social directives, Luxembourg has acquired new, specific rules for the protection of workers. This is especially true for the protection of young people and women on maternity leave.

With regard to the introduction of transnational worker representation in the context of the European works council, Luxembourg has been very reticent. It was condemned for infringing Community law on 21 October 1999, but is now transposing the legislation. A further directive,[13] relating to the posting of workers in the framework of the provision of services was transposed via the Act of 20 December 2002. It is considered to have been extremely useful in the fight against social dumping, even leading to 'spectacular' results due to measures immediately terminating any work not declared in advance. Jurisprudence has also incorporated Directive 77/187 relating to the transfer of undertakings, and its modification in 2001.

The period has also been characterised by economic growth in Luxembourg, in sharp contrast to neighbouring countries. The very low unemployment rate also explains the lack of a significant body of rules concerning flexibility, redeployment and employability in general. This relative wealth has, however, been less evident since 2002. The country is beginning to see an increase in unemployment and the appearance of restructuring plans. In the future, Luxembourg will have to take into account the fall in growth and the appearance of company failures (after a major timelag with European neighbours) in its labour law rules.

Changes in labour law will also undoubtedly follow the fall in the number of cross-border workers. This will probably require employment policies to be reinforced.

This will lead to changes in the **labour relations system**. The dispute relating to ALEBA's representativity and the bill modifying the Act of 1965, lodged in late 2002, are proof of this. It is necessary to take into account the appearance of various levels of action on the part of union organisations, to establish a precise regulatory framework concerning union representativity, and in particular to set out the domain of sector-based unions. The issue of working out new representativity rules is being dealt with. It would also be useful to create multi-sector negotiation so that the transposition of European directives can be negotiated in Luxembourg.

The area that seems clearly insufficient with regard to employee flexibility and employability is that of vocational training. It would be necessary to introduce the right to adaptation for employees, a right to redeployment, the obligation to introduce real long-term plans in companies, to introduce mechanisms for organising training over the long term and, in particular, for the working life of employees. The only aspect really taken into account is that of integration. The weak vocational training policy has major repercussions for certain employees: over-50's who are excluded, women, and workers in insecure jobs. As Europe is the driving force for change in Luxembourg, we must hope that the chapter relating to vocational training will give rise to progress.

13   Directive 96/71 of 16 December 1996.

In addition, there are plans to re-examine health and safety rules. Since the directives in this domain were transposed, Luxembourg has not yet developed a new policy and issues involving stress are leading the parties involved to take a new look at the rules.

Lastly, the special nature of the labour force should be emphasised: the exclusion of workers over the age of 55 and the fact that so many women stay at home are real problems in Luxembourg. However, despite the impact of Europe, Luxembourg does not seem to want to make any profound changes to its social policies to give women real access to skilled employment and avoid the exclusion of older workers.

Here, the special nature of the labour market in Luxembourg, with its 38% of cross-border workers, the very conservative attitudes of employers, the inertia of society and the wealth of the economy in comparison with neighbouring companies are the main causes.

An analysis of changes in labour law during the period 1992 to 2003 shows, in all cases, that European impetus has been the essential, predominant force for change and modernisation in the labour laws in Luxembourg. This influence is indisputable when it comes to the adoption of European directives.

On the other hand, the influence of the European employment strategy is subtler: Luxembourg is without doubt a 'model pupil' and generally incorporates European demands. This can be clearly seen on the issue of women in work, employee flexibility and, in 2003, the work of employees over 55. The inclusion of the strategy leads to research, studies and incentive programmes, but does not lead to reforms to change the behaviour of the people or companies involved through the acquisition of new rights.

It seems clear that Luxembourg only undertakes labour law reform if national forces demand it. The issue of increased flexibility introduced as part of the re-organisation of working time shows this very clearly by the fact that a law was voted in 1999 and extended in 2003, with no new reforms, despite guideline demands to this effect.

Annexes

1. Brief bibliography

Analysis of legislation and jurisprudence

- Collection of laws and jurisprudence in Luxembourg (listed by key words)
- Official journal of the Grand Duchy of Luxembourg (date of laws quoted in the text), Memorial A – collection of legislation, 1992-2002
- Liaisons sociales Europe 2000-2003, '15 jours dans les pays de l'Union'
- UIMM International, Luxembourg – 1992-2003, monthly review
- Website: www.itm.Government.lu/droit

Labour law manuals

- Dossiers internationaux Francis Lefebvre, Luxembourg, 6th ed.
- Y. Bechet, J. Karp, *Le droit social au Luxembourg, Travail sans frontières*, éd. Kluwer, 2002
- G., *Loi du travail*, 2002
- Marc Feyereisen, *Loi du travail, guide pratique*, published by Promoculture, 2002

Reports

- Accord International sa, *Analyse des développements stratégiques de la performance et de l'impact*, Ministère du Travail et de l'Emploi, 2002
- Accord International, *Analyse de la mise en œuvre des provisions relatives au travail et à l'emploi qui en vertu de la loi du 12 février 1999 expire le 31 juillet 2003*
- Grand Duchy of Luxembourg, *Plan national d'action pour l'inclusion sociale, Rapport national, 2001-2003*
- Grand Duchy of Luxembourg, *Rapport national pour l'emploi 2003*
- Ministère de la promotion féminine, *Femmes et hommes, droits égaux pour filles et garçons*, 2nd ed.
- M. Laroche-Reeff, *Égalité des chances et négociations collectives dans l'Union Européenne – Exemples de conventions collectives de travail au Luxembourg*, Fondation européenne pour l'amélioration des conditions de vie et de travail, Dublin, 1997

Miscellaneous

- G. Auzero, 'La loi du 12 février 1999 au Luxembourg', *Bull. de droit comparé et de la sécurité sociale*, 1999, p. 257
- E. Pichot, *La participation des salariés aux organes des sociétés en Europe*, Les petites Affiches, 16/04/2002

Statistics

- www.europa.eu.int/eurostat
- www.statec.lu
- www.luxembourg.lu

2. List of main Acts quoted

- Act of 12 June 1965 relating to collective agreements – draft modification lodged on 2 November 2002
- Act of 26 February 1993 relating to voluntary part-time work
- Act of 19 May 1994 relating to the regulation of temporary work and the temporary loan of labour
- Act of 17 June 1994 relating to the health and safety of workers
- Act of 11 August 1996 relating to the length of the working week
- Act of 12 February 1999 relating to the implementation of the national employment plan
- Act of 26 May 2000 relating to sexual harassment in working relations
- Act of 28 July 2000 relating to the introduction of a European works council or a procedure into companies operating across the Community
- Act of 23 March 2001 relating to the protection of young people at work
- Act of 28 June 2001 relating to the burden of proof in cases of discrimination based on sex
- Act of 1 August 2001 relating to the protection of pregnant workers
- Act of 2 August 2002 relating to the protection of individuals with regard to the processing of personal information
- Act of 20 December 2002 relating to the posting of workers and checks on the application of labour law

THE EVOLUTION OF LABOUR LAW
IN THE NETHERLANDS
1992-2002

Table of contents

Chapter I:
New ways of regulating

1. Background of developments in the past decade

The Netherlands is often looked upon as a 'model country' for dealing with or solving employment and labour issues. The origins of this Dutch model, often referred to as the 'Polder Model', date back to the end of the Second World War. At that time, the need for national reconstruction was felt so strongly that employers' associations, trade unions and the Government decided to cooperate very closely in order to restore the nation's economy. As a result, a private organisation of the national employers' associations and trade unions, the Foundation of Labour (*Stichting van de Arbeid*), was established. This organisation developed a national decision-making process on wage moderation. Wage levels were kept low in order to restore the national economy and to establish a national social security system with a high level of protection. The cooperation also promoted industrial peace and a low rate of strikes. During the 1960s, this system gradually weakened as workers started to demand higher wages in line with the growth of the economy. Although national consultation, co-ordination and orchestration have remained important, gradually, and particularly over the last decade, the level of wages has increasingly been determined by the social partners on branch and company levels in collective bargaining agreements.

Early evolutions started to take place during the 1960s, when the level of social security costs gradually increased, and in the 1970s when automatic price compensation for inflation was introduced as a general principle in collective bargaining agreements. After the oil crises of the 1970s, these factors created a high unemployment rate at the beginning of the 1980s. In this respect, the Netherlands was no exception compared to other countries.

The employment question was thus placed high on the agenda. An important step in the development of labour rela

tions and labour law in the Netherlands then took place with the 'Wassenaar Agreement'. In 1982, in the village of Wassenaar, near The Hague, the leaders of the most important national trade union (FNV), and the most important employers' association (VNO) reached an historic agreement. They agreed to put an end to the system of automatic compensation of inflation in wages and, alternatively, decided to start by reducing working time in order to fight unemployment. With this agreement, the social partners prevented the Government from interfering in wage negotiations with their own measures. An important aspect of the working time reductions was that they would be implemented with flexibility: rather than introducing a general reduction of working time for everybody, different types of reduction were to be chosen at branch and company levels. The impact of the Wassenaar Agreement on Dutch labour law is still felt today. The drive towards more flexibility has been dealt with through centralised labour-management agreements. This way of dealing with labour issues by unions and employers has served as the basis for what has become known in the 1990s as the Dutch Polder Model.

Whereas the general idea of the Foundation of Labour was to organise central social dialogue in the reconstruction of the country, this Foundation soon came to be recognised as an advising body with regard to social-economic matters. In the 1950s, however, the Social Economic Council (SER or *Sociaal Economische Raad*) was instituted. This body took over the most important and main advising tasks of the Foundation of Labour. Since then, a very strong link has remained between the Foundation and the Council. The secretariat of the Foundation is housed in the SER building. The Foundation of Labour remains the main platform for central social dialogue; the central employers' and workers' organisations agree on broad principles, which are subsequently implemented through – or serve as a basis for – sector social dialogue, or enterprise-level social dialogue.

2. The Polder Model of the 1990s

2.1. The drive towards flexibility

In order to make the labour market more flexible, several different forms of 'flexible work' became popular. Especially in the uncertain economic period of the 1980s, employers increasingly used fixed-term contracts. But the renewal of these contracts was also restricted by statute: after the first renewal of a fixed-term contract, the employment relationship came under the severe dismissal legislation, meaning that it could only be terminated by notice and required prior governmental permission. Consequently, many employers also started to work with other forms of flexible labour relations like the use of workers hired through temporary employment agencies and workers hired on the basis of 'on-call contracts'. The courts accepted these new forms of flexible labour relations, but in case of long-standing relations they often granted the worker the regular protection of employment contracts. The labour unions gradually accepted the need for flexibility in employment contracts and the strong dismissal protection that goes along with it. Deviations from this rule were made possible, within the framework of the Civil Code, by collective bargaining agreements. During the 1990s, many collective bargaining agreements thus accepted that fixed-term contracts could be renewed without the need to give notice when the second or consecutive contract was terminated within the scope of a limited time frame, such as two years after the beginning of the first contract. The use of temporary employment agencies also became more accepted by the unions once they realised that many workers saw this type of employment as a stepping-stone for a permanent job with the contracting enterprise.

In 1995 the Dutch Government published a policy paper in which it discussed the role of government in labour issues within the context of new developments, like globalisation and the rise of the information society. The Dutch Government asked the Foundation of Labour for advice on certain topics of the paper. The Foundation responded to the paper in a 1996 report titled 'Flexibility and Security'.

2.2 Discussion on job security laws

This report on flexibility and security must be understood in the context of the dismissal legislation of the Netherlands. In the Netherlands of the 1980s and the 1990s, the pressure for a radical overhaul of the law on dismissals was high. There was high unemployment in the country and many economists believed that the law on dismissals was one of its main causes. The Dutch law on dismissals was seen as one of the most rigid in Europe, as it required almost all dismissals to be approved beforehand by a governmental body, either at administrative level or before the local district court.

This rather severe system stems from the post-World War conviction that the national economy and the stability of the country were best served by stable employment relationships and low turnover rates. According to the 1946 Extraordinary Decree on Labour Relations (Article 6), apart from some exceptions, every dismissal without the prior consent (i.e. without a governmental permit) of the 'Centre for Work and Income' (CWI, formerly the Director of the Regional Employment Office) is null and void. The employee can therefore claim that, since he was not dismissed and thus remains employed, the provision of work and the payment of salary should be continued. While the CWI can refuse the permit, it may not impose the obligation of severance pay by the employer. Statistics show that the dismissal permit is granted in a high number of cases (almost 80%) in which the employer files a request for the first time. No administrative appeal against the decision of granting or refusing the permit is possible. However, if the employer disagrees with a refusal to grant the dismissal permit, he can renew his request some months later, and, as practice shows, often with greater success.

As an alternative to the system of requiring permission from the CWI to unilaterally terminate an employment contract, an employer may also request the district court to rescind the contract of employment. Either party to an employment contract may request the district court to pronounce the rescission of the contract on the basis of the Civil Code (Article 7:685). The judge will rescind the contract if there are 'serious grounds'. According to the case law of the district courts, a unilateral termination of the contract is also accepted if the employer can demonstrate a change in the employment relationship. This judicial procedure allows wider possibilities for employers to terminate a contract. Because this procedure is neither very time/consuming nor formal, it has become a significant alternative for unilateral termination of employment contracts by employers. Usually the judge will order one party to pay the other compensation according to a 'district court' formula that takes into account the number of years of service, and, the responsibility of either for the termination of the contract as determined by the judge.

These *a priori* forms of control in dismissals are further supplemented by *a posteriori* forms of judicial control, by a wide range of causes and situations in which the law prohibits dismissals and finally by mandatory periods of notice.

If the worker disagrees with the granting of a dismissal permit or with the fact that he is dismissed without severance pay, he can make recourse to the district court on the basis of 'reasonably unfair dismissal' (Article 7:681 of the Civil Code). If this is accepted by the Court, then the employee's reinstatement or the payment of severance compensation can be ordered. The employer can request that compensation be paid in lieu of reinstatement.

In the case of summary dismissal – if one of the parties has shown such misconduct that the other party cannot reasonably be expected to continue the employment relationship – both parties may go to court (Article 7:679-680 of the Civil Code) to obtain the termination of the contract. If the court finds that the summary dismissal is unfounded, the employment relationship will not be considered terminated.

The Dutch dismissal legislation recognises the following situations as unlawful grounds for dismissal: (a) unequal treatment on the basis of religion, conviction, political orientation, race, sex, nationality, sexual orientation or marital status; (b) on the grounds of an employee's marriage, pregnancy or confinement and (c) dismissal during maternity or parental leave. Moreover, the termination of an employment contract by the employer (d) because of trade union membership or because of trade union activities; (e) on the basis of candidacy for elections for or membership in workers' representative bodies or (f) on the grounds of the transfer of the undertaking is not allowed. Furthermore, the Dutch dismissal legislation states that an employer is prohibited from terminating an employment contract during the first two years of an employee's illness (Article 7:670 of the Civil Code).

The entire system of the Dutch dismissal law, and in particular the requirement of governmental permission for dismissals, was widely criticised as opaque, time-consuming and confusing. As the Government considered ways of adapting the system, businesses addressed its shortcomings by bringing about radical changes. This was done by increasing the use of so-called flexible employment contracts – such as on-call contracts, fixed-term contracts, contracts for workers hired through temporary employment agencies, freelance contracts and contracts for quasi self-employed workers. It is estimated that between 7% and 15% of the current Dutch labour market is comprised of these types of workers, although exact numbers vary due to the use of different definitions among statisticians.

2.3. The Dutch package deal on flexicurity

The political debate on the reform of dismissal law jumped from one solution to another; it was only in the mid 1990s that a compromise was found. At that time, the country was governed by a coalition of social-democrats on the left and liberals of the centre and the right (known as the 'purple coalition'). The right-wing forces in the Cabinet and employers insisted on the need to moderate the rise of pay levels. They were prepared to compromise on the issue of dismissals and flexible contracts in exchange for the moderation of pay rises.

The Dutch trade union movement, often considered reformist and pragmatic, was willing to renounce excessive pay claims if the law on dismissals would be maintained. It was also prepared to give up its ideological resistance to flexible work contracts if the law would provide atypical workers with more rights and job security.

In this socio-political climate, a major trade-off could be arranged:

- Employers agreed, in return for a moderation of the pay rise claims by the trade unions, that the law on dismissals would remain essentially unchanged.

- Having obtained guarantees that the law on dismissals would not be changed and that employees would thus remain strongly protected against dismissal, trade unions agreed to give employers more leeway to use flexible employment contracts.

- Having gained this leeway to use flexible employment contracts, especially for fixed-term work, temporary agency work and on-call work, employers agreed to the improved protection of workers on flexible employment contracts.

The social partners endorsed this project in an agreement in 1996 with regard to flexibility and security, summarised in the word 'flexicurity', and which was subsequently implemented by two Acts of Parliament of 14 May 1998: the Act on the Allocation of Workers by Intermediaries and the Act on Flexibility and Security. The former is an independent Statute; the latter contains a modification of several acts and, most importantly, of the Civil Code. The actual content of the new provisions will be discussed below.

The Government changed the legislation almost completely once the Foundation of Labour presented its opinion. This newly found form of cooperation between employers' organisations and national trade unions has become known as the Polder Model. Based on the older tradition of close cooperation at national level, the organisations understood that labour relations had to be changed in order to cope with the high unemployment rates and the new demands of globalised industries. The Polder Model illustrates the ability of employers and unions to cooperate in the interest of both.

3. Trends in industrial relations law and practice

In 2002, the Netherlands' basic **legislative framework** for **collective bargaining** was 75 years old. The relevant laws on industrial relations had changed little over this period and were still not being questioned. However, certain provisions of the legislation – notably on **the extension of collective agreements** to non-signatory employers and on applying agreements to non-union employees – were increasingly being debated in 2002. For example, extension procedures were questioned in the light of the idea among some politicians that the extension of collective agreements should be used more as a political instrument. This implies that collective agreements that do not meet the policy goals of the Cabinet should not be extended and extension is designed to be legally supportive of the conclusion of (sectoral) collective agreements.

For a number of years, **decentralisation pressure** has increased on several sectoral collective agreements. For example, the collective agreement for the banking sector lapsed at the end of 1999 and was replaced by company agreements. More generally, decentralisation was an important subject in 2000, not only in banking and insurance, but also in building, construction and the public utilities. Overall, however, there has been no significant change in the relative importance of sectoral and company agreements. In 1996, sector-wide agreements covered 87% of employees and by 2000 this figure had dropped only slightly to 86%.

In recent years, there has also been an increasing tendency, among both employers' organisations and trade unions, to **cooperate** or even **merge**. FNV Bondgenoten, the Netherlands' largest union, was formed in late 1997 by the merger of four FNV unions in the industry, food, services and transport

sectors. In 1999, occupational unions such as, for example, the union representing nurses, and the union representing railway workers affiliated to create a main union confederation.

Unions have also begun to open their doors to **self-employed individuals** who do not employ any staff. In mid-1999, the largest union in the Netherlands, the FNV-affiliated United Unions (FNV Bondgenoten), created a separate organisation for self-employed people. Other unions have been more hesitant, however, fearing an erosion of the strength of collective agreements.

Unions have also engaged in **broader activities** than mere representation and bargaining. In 1999, several union confederations announced initiatives concerning financial services and education for their members.

Collective agreements increasingly contain provisions on flexible and **performance-related pay**. In February 2002, KPMG Consulting published the findings of their research into variable pay in the Netherlands (results available on www.eiro.eurofound.eu.int). The study found that, since 1997, the number of collective agreements providing for variable pay has increased fourfold; 30% of agreements concluded in 2000 include provisions on the topic. Individual performance-related payment methods are the most common form of variable pay, followed by payments linked to team performance. According to a Labour Inspectorate survey of 125 collective agreements concluded in 2001, flexible pay provisions, mainly in the form of an end-of-year bonus, were found in 78 cases, while more than half of the agreements (65) included a 'motivating' pay policy. The social partners disagree on the effects of performance-related pay, and employers tend to regard them in a more positive light than the unions. In the private sector, 80% of companies were found to use performance-related pay, compared to 40% of public sector organisations. Furthermore, this form of payment covers a larger proportion of the workforce in private sector companies than in public sector organisations. In most cases, the variable component applies to two months' pay, and in 'knowledge-intensive' services it affects as much as three months' pay, while in the governmental and public sector it applies to a maximum of one month.

Chapter II:
From job security to employability

1. The flexicurity deal kept dismissal law unchanged

As mentioned before, the social partners, within the context of the Foundation of Labour, agreed on a package deal with regard to flexibility and security in 1996. It has been pointed out that the Dutch law on dismissal, which was considered very severe due to existence of prior governmental checks, remained basically untouched.

The obligation to obtain prior consent for most dismissals from either a civil servant or the court was retained in Dutch labour law. Only the procedure to obtain prior permission from the CWI has been accelerated slightly for economic dismissal cases, that is, for cases in which dismissal is based on economic grounds and is not contested by the worker(s) concerned.

The statutory periods of notice were also shortened somewhat. For the employer, the minimum statutory period of notice to be taken into account after a period of service of less than five years is one month. If the period exceeds five years but is less then ten years, the period of notice is two months; after more than ten years of service but less then fifteen years the period is three months and for more then fifteen years it is four months (Article 7:672 of the Civil Code). These statutory periods of notice may be shortened by one month to compensate for the waiting period for the request of the CWI-permit, provided that a minimum of one month's notice is retained. There are also special periods of notice for the suspension of payments in case of bankruptcy or judicial leave (Bankruptcy Act). Collective agreements and, to a lesser extent, individual agreements may contain waivers as to the length of the period of notice. The long list of causes and situations in which a dismissal is prohibited was not shortened, but the exceptions in the application of this norm were somewhat enlarged.

The way in which the new statutes deal with the flexible employment contracts, which have become a major instrument to circumvent the burden of the severe Dutch law on dismissals, is of particular interest. The new statutes have enlarged the possibilities of concluding flexible contracts.

1. In the first place, they have done so by relaxing the existing limitations on the repetition of employment contracts of a fixed duration. Previously, a fixed-term contract could not be renewed without becoming a sort of open-ended contract. Since the 'flexibilisation', employers can renew fixed-term contracts twice, provided that the total length of such a chain of contracts does not exceed three years. Only after either the third renewal (i.e. upon the fourth contract) or after three years, the fixed-term contract will automatically become open-ended (Article 7:668a of the Civil Code).

2. Secondly, most of the existing restrictions on the hiring of workers from temporary employment agencies have been abolished. Until 1998, temporary employment agencies had to obtain a governmental license in order to operate. Furthermore, the law contained a maximum term for leasing temporary workers to one and the same job (12 months). Finally, the leasing of temporary workers in the construction business was prohibited. All of these restrictions have now been repealed. However, in the Netherlands the fact that temporary employment agencies and other labour market intermediaries do not require an obligatory governmental permit has been criticised and support has been shown for the re-introduction of the licensing system.

3. The new Act on Flexibility and Security strengthened the rights of workers in flexible situations. There is a further limitation of the trial clauses in contracts of employment. As in the past, such clauses are limited to a maximum of two months. If, however, the length of the contract is less than two years or does not have a stated fixed term, the trial period should not be longer than one month. In addition, such clauses must now be established in advance in writing (Article 7:652 of the Civil Code).

4. Furthermore, a number of legal assumptions have been introduced, such as the determination of whether or not a contract is an employment contract, or the number of hours effectively worked. It is now provided that any person who has performed paid work for another person on a regular basis (over three consecutive months either every week or for at least 20 hours a month) is assumed to have worked under an employment contract (with all its inherent legal protections), unless proof of the contrary (Article 7:610a of the Civil Code) is established. Another provision stipulates that in cases in which no precise working time has been agreed upon or performed, and once the employment contract has lasted for at least three months, the average working time of any month may be calculated according to the average working time during the last three months, except if the employer can prove that the performed working time was irregular (Article 7:610b of the Civil Code).

5. The legal status of workers of temporary employment agencies has been improved. This was largely carried out by way of a collective agreement between the employers' association and the trade unions. The main provision of the temporary employment agency sector agreement is flexibility, provided through with a system of phases that gradually grants more rights to temporary workers depending on their tenure at the agencies.

As the adaptations of the Dutch legislation were the result of a package deal on flexibility and security in 1996, it is often felt that these adaptations have further complicated the Dutch law on dismissals and flexible work. However, the full impact of the measures contained in this legislation will probably take time to filter through. In 2002, research was conducted on the effects of the Act on Flexibility and Security. The report showed that employers generally make greater use of the possibility to enter into several consecutive fixed-term contracts. In addition, vague, unclear labour relationships disappeared as a result of the implementation of the legal presumptions. The labour contracts of flexible workers are more regulated and give more job- and income-security. In 2000, a State Commission under the chairmanship of the late Prof. Max Rood advocated a more radical reform of the Dutch law on dismissals. However, by the fall of 2002 the social partners had failed to reach an agreement over its recommendations. A new overhaul of the Dutch law on dismissals is therefore not likely to take place in the near future.

2. The 'Law Improvement Gatekeeper'

In the past, work incapacity regulations in the Netherlands have caused problems, particularly in budgetary terms. They also created obstacles to the employability and adaptability of the workforce.

New regulations on work incapacity have improved possibilities for the ongoing employment and adaptability of workers. The so-called 'Law Improvement Gatekeeper' (*Wet Verbetering Poortwachter*) is the most recent example of this. Sick workers and their employers have to cooperate to reintroduce workers in the employment process.

Employers in the Netherlands are obliged to fulfil specific statutory duties to safeguard the health and safety of their employees. As the Dutch Government becomes increasingly interested in reducing the number of employees that fall under the so-called '*WAO*' (Disablement Benefits Act), it is important for businesses to ensure they are meeting the appropriate standards in their handling of employee illness. In order to meet the statutory requirements regarding health and safety, the employer is obliged to call on the Certified Health and Safety Service (H&S-Service). This Service assists the employer, amongst other things, in carrying out the appropriate actions during the employee's illness to ensure their quick and smooth return to work.

From 1 April 2002, after registration of illness the H&S-Service must, in a period of six weeks, prepare recommendations that include the possibility for reintegration, especially in case of the severe disablement. Upon receipt of the recommendations, the employer and the employee must jointly compile an 'Action Plan' setting out reintegration agreements, within two weeks. This Action Plan should initially be evaluated every six weeks and adjusted if necessary. The H&S-service is responsible for monitoring the progress from a medical point of view and, if necessary, providing advice on modifications to the Action Plan.

At least eight months after the registration of illness, the employer and the employee should prepare a 'Reintegration Report' based on the Action Plan and the progress reports. This report is necessary for the employee to be able to apply for *WAO* benefits.

If the employer does not comply with their obligations satisfactorily, their obligation to pay the employee's salary can be extended for a maximum of 52 weeks. This extension can take place voluntarily or can be imposed by the Institute for Employee Benefit Schemes. If the employee does not comply with his/her obligations, their salary can be halted or they can risk dismissal. Furthermore, the Institute for Employee Benefit Schemes can impose a reduction on the employee's WAO-benefit.

In summary, from 1 April 2002, any event of employee illness will require a joint constructive strategy from both the employee and the employer.

The new Law Improvement Gatekeeper is to be taken into account during the first year of absence due to illness, and is applicable to every Dutch employer. This will imply a more rigid approach to employee illness in order to decrease the number of disabled workers and to improve their re-integration into employment.

The new Law can be seen as the first step to a new approach on illness and invalidity. A second step has been taken with a law regarding the extension of the obligation to pay the employee's salary for a maximum of 104 weeks, instead of 52 weeks, in case of illness. This law enters into force on 1 January 2004. It means that the Law Improvement Gatekeeper, from that moment onwards, deals with the first two years of illness and also that the employee is only able to apply for a WAO-benefit at the end of the second year of illness, with use of a Reintegration Report. The Government is also preparing a third step towards modernisation which will aim to change the structure of the WAO itself.

3.   Transfer of undertaking

From 1 July 2002, new statutory regulations came into force in the Netherlands to protect employees during a transfer of undertaking, implementing EU Directive (98/50/EC) amending Directive 77/187/EEC on the approximation of the laws of the Member States related to the safeguarding of employees' rights in the event of transfers of undertakings, businesses or parts of businesses.

The relevant definition of a 'transfer' has been adapted in line with the rulings of the European Court of Justice (ECJ). Significant elements of the definition include the 'retention of the identity of the economic unit being transferred' and the 'continuation of activities'. Furthermore, mergers are now explicitly addressed.

The definition of the term 'employee' remains unchanged. The provisions apply only to people with an employment contract as defined by the Dutch Civil Code. Civil servants are therefore excluded. The Government has indicated, however, that with respect to privatisation every attempt will be made to ensure that rights are preserved as far as possible. Further consultation with the Association of Public Sector Employers (*Verbond Sector Werkgevers Overheid*) is taking place regarding this aspect.

Concerning the concept of a transfer, there has been a fair amount of activity regarding the transfer of services, especially cleaning services. This can be seen in the ruling of the ECJ on the *Temco* case on 24 January 2002 (Case C-51/00). The first judgment in the Netherlands related to the transfer of undertakings since the implementation of the new statutory regulations is in many ways similar to this ECJ ruling. On 8 August 2002, the Utrecht Court ruled that, based on the collective agreement for cleaning and window-cleaning businesses, a cleaning company was obliged to retain the services of employees who had been with the company for more than a year (JAR 2002/202).

Soon after implementation of the original Directive in 1982, a question arose on the extent to which employees also enjoyed protection in cases concerning the transfer of an undertaking when a company was faced with suspension of payment or bankruptcy. This question was ultimately answered by the ECJ: in all cases concerning suspension of payment the regulations apply but the Member States are at liberty to reach a decision regarding bankruptcy. At the time, the Netherlands chose not to apply the regulations in cases of a transfer under bankruptcy.

This distinction has been abused under a number of circumstances. A familiar example is the case concerning *Ammerlaan*, where the employer attempted to circumvent labour legislation governing dismissal compensation by having the company declared bankrupt. Although the court ruled that the bankruptcy law had been abused, Dutch law could not compel the employer to re-employ the employees dismissed under the pretext of bankruptcy.

The new statutory regulations have resolved this problem. The Bankruptcy Act (*Faillissementswet*) has been amended in such a way that any measures undertaken by the trustee in bankruptcy (including employee dismissals) can be reversed if it appears that the law relating to bankruptcy has been abused to the disadvantage of the employees.

The most important substantive change introduced by the new regulations is that, in the future, pension schemes will also be transferred to the acquiring employer. Furthermore, the new regulations include provisions stipulating that if the transferor did not offer a pension scheme and the transferee does, the transferee is bound to offer the transferred employees access to the said pension scheme. In this respect, one of the legislator's main aims is to stimulate a further reduction in the number of employees without access to a group pension scheme (approximately 10% of the total number of employees).

The new regulations also differ with respect to employee participation in transfers in the absence of works councils or other forms of staff representation. In such cases, the employer is now obliged to inform and consult the employees. Although these rights are less far-reaching than those enjoyed by works councils, they serve to strengthen the position of employees within smaller companies.

It is not entirely clear what the consequences will be for the transfer if employers fail to fulfil their obligation to inform and consult the employees. It can be assumed, however, that failing to comply with obligations in terms of employee participation will not diminish the validity of the transfer.

A situation such as this arose in February 2002, when employees at *Snap-on* were called to a meeting and informed that two departments would be transferred to another company, along with their staff. No works council or other form of staff representation was in place at the company (which had 147 employees). Shortly after the meeting, the two departments quickly established a staff association. The transfer of the departments was affected at the end of March 2002. The staff association demanded compliance with the provisions of the Works Councils Act (*Wet op de ondernemingsraden, WOR*).

However, the court asserted that the transfer had already taken place and that the employees' interests would no longer be served by their demand (Amsterdam Court, sub-district sector, Amsterdam, 30 August 2002, JAR 2002/265).

Chapter III:
Labour law and adaptability

1. Part-time work

In the Netherlands, most of the part-time workers are women, but some men also prefer to work part-time. Part-time work is generally accepted as 'normal' work, but there are signs that the so-called glass ceiling also exists in the Netherlands. Part-time work is not accepted in every sector, nor is it accepted for the highest positions. For this reason, many women have problems reaching the higher positions.

In principle, the position of part-time workers in the Netherlands is legally no different from that of full-time workers. Since 1996, the Civil Code prescribes the equal treatment of part-time and full-time workers, in proportion to the amount of working hours.

The implementation of **Directive 97/81/EG concerning the Framework agreement on part-time work** (*O.J.* 20 January 1998, L 14) does not seem to pose a problem in the Netherlands.

The Directive has been transposed by means of changes to existing legislation. In the Netherlands, the regulations applicable to part-time work are derived from several sources:

- The Working Time Discrimination Act (*Wet verbod van onderscheid naar arbeidsduur, WOA*).

- The Working Hours Act, which entered into force in 1996, provides more flexibility for employers and employees to come to an agreement regarding working hours, in consultation and within certain limits.

- The Working Hours Adjustment Act (*Wet aanpassing arbeidsduur, WAA*) entered into force on 1 July 2000. The purpose of the *WAA* is to improve the possibilities to combine work and other responsibilities and to make it possible for the employee to harmonise his/her working hours with other tasks.

Dutch legislation does not use the definition 'part-time worker' contained in the Directive. According to the *WOA*,

the system applied must not obstruct the trend towards greater differentiation and flexibility. It is argued that this trend will help blur the distinction between full-time and part-time employment. In most cases, the 'traditional' full-time worker is used as a reference for workers with different working hours. However, given the desire for greater differentiation, workers who assume they are being treated in a less favourable manner on account of their working hours will no longer be compared to a full-time worker. Instead, the reference for comparison will most likely be a colleague who has different working hours.

The principle of non-discrimination is laid down in Article 7:648, paragraph 1, of the Civil Code. This Article was incorporated into the Civil Code via the *WOA*. Article 7: 648, paragraph 1 of the Civil Code stipulates that termination of the employment contract by the employer may be declared invalid if it is contrary to the principle of non-discrimination or if it is due to the fact that the worker has invoked this principle.

The principle of *pro rata temporis* is not contained in the legislation itself, but this does not mean that it is not applied. Dutch legislation does not define access criteria (Clause 4(4) of the Framework Agreement) for part-time workers.

The Netherlands has satisfied the obligation to eliminate most obstacles to part-time work, but this can be said to have been the case prior to the adoption of the Directive. Article 3 of the *WAA* stipulates that the employer cannot terminate an employment relation with a worker because the latter has requested a change in working hours, judicially or extra-judicially. Where a worker requests a change in working hours (Article 2 of the *WAA*), the employer is obliged to comply with this request, unless important interests relating to the enterprise or the service oppose this. The employer is obliged to provide information on full-time and part-time jobs available (this can be based on Article 7:611 of the Civil Code which requires the employer to act as a 'good employer').

Finally, there are no specific rules concerning the provision of information regarding full-time and part-time work by the employer to workers' representative bodies. However, Article 31 of the *WOR* (Law on Works Councils) stipulates that the employer must provide the Works Council with all information the latter considers necessary to accomplish its task, which may include such information.

2. Fixed-term work

It has always been possible in the Netherlands to conclude a (first) fixed-term contract freely, for whatever purpose and whatever period, without legal restrictions. However, up until 1999 the Civil Code stipulated that a second consecutive fixed-term contract could not be ended without prior notification. As explained above, termination would imply the previous permission of the CWI (who checks the validity of the reason for dismissal) and the observance of a notice period. Since these restrictions are no different from that of a contract for an indefinite period, employers felt that this legislation was very restrictive.

There were two ways to avoid these restrictions:

1. The employer could observe a period of at least 31 days between the two contracts. After this period, the second contract was no longer seen as a consecutive contract. In practice, employers would often hire the same worker in the meantime through a temporary employment agency (the so-called 'revolving door construction' – *draaideurconstructie*). However, the *Hoge Raad* (Dutch Supreme Court) decided in the 1991 *Campina*-case that when an employer uses this arrangement for several years, a the fixed-term-contract should be considered as a consecutive fixed-term contract as defined by the Civil Code (*Bootsma a.o./Campina*, Hoge Raad, 22 November 1992, *N.J.* 1992, 707). Another relevant case concerned a worker was hired first through a temporary employment agency and was then employed directly by the hiring company to continue the same work. In this case, it was determined that the time worked for the temporary employment agency was to be included in the calculation of the maximum trial period of two months as foreseen in the Civil Code (*Dingler/Merkelbach*, Hoge Raad, 13 September 1991, *N.J.* 1992, 130).

2. A second way to avoid the restrictive rules has been to make use of the possibility to deviate from the general rule by collective agreement, as provided by the Civil Code. Due to high unemployment rates during the 80's, the unions often accepted exceptions to this rule in collective agreements. In several collective agreements

on branch and company levels it therefore was accepted that the obligation to give notification was only applicable after the worker had worked over a certain period (often two years) for the same employer.

Since the courts, as indicated, restricted the first possibility, the latter option became important. As a result of the aforementioned agreement on flexibility and security of 1996 between the national organisations of employers and trade unions, the Dutch Government introduced a new system of fixed-term contracts in the 1999 Act on Flexibility and Security. This is perhaps the most important change in the new Act.

Under the present rule (Article 7:668a of the Civil Code), it is possible to have three consecutive contracts that may be ended without having to give notice, as long as they fall within a period of three years. The fourth contract, or the contract that makes the total working period exceed 36 months, will automatically become a contract for an indefinite term, which gives the worker the aforementioned protection against dismissal. This change is an important form of deregulation that is expected to make the fixed-term contract more attractive for employers.

Three principles are introduced to avoid abuse of the new articles:

- Contracts that follow each other within a period of three months are considered to be consecutive.

- For consecutive fixed-term contracts between the same employer and the same employee, it is not relevant whether the work done under the different contracts is identical.

- Fixed-term contracts, where the same employee works for two consecutive employers who are considered each other's successors, are also considered consecutive contracts. Thus, the rule is also applicable if the worker worked under some of the consecutive contracts for a temporary employment agency. The fourth contract is decisive: the employer that employs him/her at that time is the employer with a contract for an indefinite term. Of course, in this case the work under the consecutive contracts should be the same.

The above-mentioned regulation is considered to be in line with the recent EC Directive on fixed-term contracts. However, this Directive also requires that the principle of equal treatment of permanent and fixed-term workers be introduced. This required new legislation in the Netherlands. In order to comply with Directive 1999/70/EC, the Dutch Parliament passed the **Law regarding Fixed Term Contracts** of 22 November 2002 (Stb. 2002, 560). This new law inserted two new articles in the Civil Code. Article 7:649 provides that the employer cannot make a distinction between employees, as far as their working conditions are concerned, on the basis of the fixed or permanent status of their employment, unless this distinction can be objectively justified. Article 7:657 obliges the employer to inform the fixed-term worker, clearly and punctually, of any vacant position which offers an employment contract for an indefinite period. However, this provision does not contain the right of the employee to be appointed in the vacant permanent position.

3. On-call work

In traditional on-call contracts, the amount of hours and the time when the work is to be done are not set in advance. It is estimated that around 6% of the workforce work under this type of contract. It is used by 16% of companies, which employ an average of 17% of their personnel on this basis. There is a wide range of contracts – from those with a low number of hours with a high degree of uncertainty of work, to those with a high number of hours (20-30 hours a week) and high levels of certainty of employment.

Often, the legal position of workers working with on-call contracts was often not strong. The Act on Flexibility and Security introduced a few provisions in the Civil Code, to improve their position.

In theory, two forms of on call-contracts were distinguished:

* *Zero hour-contracts:* These contracts do not guarantee that labour will be done or offered. Both sides are entirely free to (give) work once work is available. These are not employment contracts, but only framework agreements that set possible wages and details. Every time a worker responds to a concrete call for work he/she concludes a fixed-term employment contract with the employer.

* *Min/max contracts:* These contracts offer a minimum amount of working hours, for example, between 20 and 30 hours a week. These contracts are employment contracts, even though the working schemes are very flexible and are not set long in advance.

However, because employers that use the so-called `zero hour-contracts' very often make use of the worker, the courts determined that the more intensive the employment relation, the earlier it would be recognised as an employment contract under the Dutch Civil Code. This would entitle the worker to demand wages and access to work. Often, courts declared that since the worker had a regular pattern of work, he/she was entitled to work according to the average of the amount of hours that he/she worked during the preceding period.

This was recognised by the Dutch Supreme Court in the 1994 landmark-case of *Agfa vs. Schoolderman*. Ms. Schoolderman had worked for several years on the so-called 'zero hour-contracts' and was also hired sometimes as a temporary worker through an agency. These contracts were used for persons who were hired by the hour to fill gaps in the workforce. The labour relation developed to the extent that, in practice, Ms. Schoolderman did exactly the same work as the permanent personnel but was paid less and was less sure of her position. The Supreme Court concluded that the originally agreed terms of the contract were not decisive. In addition, significance was to be given to the way the parties executed the employment contract in practice. The Supreme Court also concluded that the generally accepted principle of equal pay for equal work under equal conditions should be taken into consideration, unless objective grounds justified different payment (*Agfa-Gevaert vs. Schoolderman*, Hoge Raad, 8 April 1994, *N.J.* 1994, n°794).

The first rule was not new, but it had never been so formulated. The principle of equal pay for equal work was in fact not intensively discussed in labour law circles before, with the exception of differences between men and women.

As indicated above, the Act on Flexibility and Security first aimed to strengthen the position of the workers with on-call contracts.

As a first measure, two so-called *presumptions of fact* were introduced in the Civil Code. Article 7:610a of the Civil Code determines that, when a worker performs work for the benefit of another person for three consecutive months, weekly or for not less than twenty hours per month, it is presumed that this was done on the basis of an employment contract. Article 7:610b of the Civil Code states that, when an employment contract has lasted for at least three months, the contracted work in any month is presumed to amount to the average working period per month over the three preceding months. This new article may have important effects on cases in which the employer reduces the amount of hours of any worker.

In both cases it is possible for the employer to prove that it was agreed otherwise, for instance in case of temporary overtime and seasonal work. This will, consequently, promote the proper composition of contracts and increased transparency in working schedules for the worker.

The second measure is that it is more difficult for the employer to neglect his/her obligation to pay wages if there is no work under his/her responsibility. In the future, this obligation may only be neglected for the first six months of a contract, unless the applicable collective agreement allows the employer to do so for a longer period (Article 7:628 of the Civil Code).

The third improvement for workers with on-call contracts is the obligation of the employer to pay at least three hours of work for any call. This obligation protects the employee in case of small contracts (less than 15 hours a week and with no certainty of the exact hours of work or with no certainty of the amount of hours at all). The aim is to ensure that workers are not forced to sit near the telephone for a whole day to be called for just one hour of work, or to travel to work just for a very short period.

4. Temporary work

Since 1975, the restrictions on temporary work services have been gradually reduced to the point of almost being abolished. In 1975, the official ban on these services was replaced by a system of licenses. A worker dispatching services needed a government permit to operate, as the Government wanted to closely monitor whether the service was following good practices or not. It demanded that social security premiums be paid by the agencies, that they be properly administrated and that workers earn wages equal to those of ordinary workers in the same company who performed the same job. In some areas (e.g. the construction sector) these services were continuously abolished because of previous bad experiences with uncontrollable 'black work'. In other areas, temporary workers were eventually allowed to be used for a maximum period of three months. Later, this period was prolonged to six months and, in the end, one year was tolerated. However, over the years this type of work became very popular in the Netherlands. Indeed, temporary work became a form of 'employee recruiting'. On the other hand, the legal position of temporary workers remained uncertain. Temporary employment agencies, for example, denied that they concluded employment contracts with their workers. But the growth of this type of work and the desire of temporary employment agencies to gain credibility gradually brought about change. During the 1980s the general trade unions managed to reach a nation-wide collective agreement for temporary workers with the Organisation of Temporary Employment Agencies (ABU), and increasing number of courts considered that, after starting work, a temporary worker was working on the legal basis of an employment contract. Finally, the Attorney General concluded before the Hoge Raad (Supreme Court of the Netherlands) that this was the leading legal opinion (Conclusion Advocate-General T. Koopmans 7 April 1996, Jurisprudentie Arbeidsrecht 1996, 168 – the Hoge Raad did not give a judgment as the case was withdrawn).

At this point, the ABU changed its previous position. In a 1996 Agreement with the unions, it accepted the principle that temporary workers were working on the basis of an employment contract. In exchange, the unions accepted temporary employment agencies as normal employers who, as such, do not require specific government supervision.

By January 1999, this agreement was formalised in the Civil Code with the introduction of Articles 690 and 691 of Book 7 as a result of the Act on Flexibility and Security. Article 7:690 defines the 'secondment contract' as a special type of employment contract. Its flexibility is guaranteed by the exclusion of restrictions on dismissals of prolonged contracts for temporary work during the first 26 weeks, and the possibility to agree on a clause that terminates the contract immediately in case the hiring company ends its assignment during this period. In the case of such a clause, the temporary worker is also allowed to terminate his/her work at any time. It is possible, however, to extend these periods of 26 weeks by collective agreement.

A legal question raised is whether employees who are not members of the contracting union are bound by this derogation of the Civil Code, since the Minister of Labour has not yet extended the Collective Agreement. In practice, not many temporary workers are members of a union. However, most legal experts believe that they are bound by the derogation, mostly for practical reasons. Theoretically, this point is not easy to tackle under the Dutch system of collective agreement legislation.

In the Collective Agreement for Temporary Workers of 1999-2001, an important derogation was made: the legal exceptions were extended from 26 weeks to one full year and even longer. In return, the unions stipulated the temporary worker's right to training and access to a pension scheme when they work longer than 26 weeks for a temporary employment agency. It is expected that the larger temporary employment agencies will hire temporary workers for longer periods in the future.

Since these agencies are generally accepted today, the system of permits was abolished on 1 July 1998, according to the new 'Act on the Allocation of Workers by Intermediates'.

Temporary employment agencies are now free to operate like any other company. Only two principles were sustained in the new Act. The first principle is that temporary workers may not be used to undermine a strike. The second principle is that the wages of a temporary worker should be the same as that of an employee of the company who does the same work. However, the latter rule may be set aside by a collective agreement (either that of the hiring company or that of the temporary employment agency). The temporary employment agencies are in favour of such an independent wage policy, as they argue that they are employers with their own employment policies. Sometimes they hire workers for several years and send them to different companies in consecutive periods. This may be one reason to give the workers a different pay.

5. Telework

On 16 July 2002, the central EU-level social partners formally signed a new EU-level Framework Agreement on telework. However, in 2002 there was no specific legal response in the Netherlands to this agreement.

On 11 September 2003, however, the Foundation of Labour issued a recommendation with regard to telework, explaining how telework is viewed in the Netherlands. In this recommendation, telework is estimated to be used by 4% of Dutch employees as a form of homework and about 2.3% of self-employed workers. Generally, it is estimated that teleworkers account for between 1.5% and 7% of the working population in the Netherlands.

According to the Foundation of Labour, the European Framework Agreement on telework will be implemented through collective agreements or through regulations drafted in the framework of works councils, or through individual employment arrangements.

As far as the legal regulation of telework is concerned, the application of normal labour law provisions is not excluded. For example, the Law on Health and Safety (*Arbo-wet*) is applicable, meaning that the employer must apply his/her health and safety policies to teleworkers. The general principle is that teleworkers (homeworkers) receive the same protection as workers who are employed in the company's premises. Furthermore, the Decree on Health and Safety (*Arbobesluit*) provides that the teleworker's workplace needs to respond to requirements of ergonomy and lighting.

6. Work and care

A recent trend in the Netherlands has been to focus more on internal flexibility than on external flexibility, which implies greater attention to the reconciliation of work and family life.

On 22 November 2001, a new Work and Care Act passed the First Chamber of Parliament and came into force on 1 December 2001. The legislation gathers various existing and new leave provisions and seeks to facilitate the reconciliation of work and family responsibilities.

In addition to the amendment of existing regulations, such as those governing maternity and parental leave, new provisions cover:

- Emergency leave when the employee cannot work because of very exceptional personal circumstances. If taken in conjunction with short-term care leave, the emergency leave terminates after one day.

- Short-term care leave to a maximum of ten days partially-paid leave a year to care for a sick child living at home, a sick partner or a parent.

- Two days of paid paternity leave.

- Four weeks' leave for couples who adopt a child.

Deviation from this regulation that is unfavourable to employees is possible only if it is agreed upon by employers and employees in a Collective Labour Agreement. However, this only concerns the payment of the emergency leave and the right, duration and payment of the short-term care leave and the paternity leave. If there is no Collective Labour Agreement, or if it contains no agreement on this subject, the employer can deviate from the law on the condition that he or she first consults and obtains the (written) approval of the works council or the staff representatives.

The possibilities for saving time or money now for paid leave later at a later stage will be extended. The specific construction of this so-called 'life course arrangement' will be negotiated with the social partners in the first half of 2004; the arrangement will come into force in 2006.

A few years ago, reconciliation of work and family life was at the top of the Dutch agenda, both in terms of collective bargaining – at sectoral and company levels – and government policy. The key issue was flexible working time, to facilitate the reconciliation of work and family life for both working parents.

An agreement was signed within the bipartite Labour Foundation on 28 April 1999 by employees and employers, on a policy document entitled *Moving towards customised conditions of employment.* This agreement aimed to increase the options available to individual employees within collective agreements and had important implications on working time flexibility. Whilst the essential lines of collective agreements will be retained under the Foundation's recommendations, certain conditions of employment can be swapped within a company on a 'multiple-choice' basis. The policy document also lays down a number of conditions for implementing the multiple-choice model. Generally, the introduction of a 'multiple-choice' system offers individual employees the opportunity to put together a package of employment conditions suited to their personal needs, within the framework of conditions set within the collective agreement.

Based on the experiences of companies that have used the multiple-choice model over a longer period of time, the Labour Foundation anticipates the following effects:

* Employees in higher-level function groups will be more inclined to sell their time, and employees in lower-level function groups will be more likely to buy time.

* Single employees will be more likely to sell time while the opposite will be true for those with partners.

* Employees with small children will be more likely to buy time while parents of older children will sooner opt to sell theirs.

The **Working Hours Adjustment Act** came into force in July of 2000. This Act awarded employees the conditional right to increase or reduce their working hours. The Act does not apply to organisations with fewer than ten employees, which are obliged to make their own arrangements regarding the adjustment of working hours.

Deviation from this regulation that is unfavourable to employees is possible, if agreed upon by employers and employees in a collective agreement, but only with regard to an increase in working hours. If there is no collective agreement, or if it contains no agreement on this subject, the employer can deviate from the law on the condition that he or she first consults and obtains the (written) approval of the works council or the staff representatives.

Although the Netherlands has a far greater number of part-time workers than other EU-countries, there is still a discrepancy between the actual working hours of workers and the working hours that are wished for. In 1999, 12% of the men working full-time would have preferred a part-time job, and 14% of professionally active women preferred shorter working hours. On the other hand, 11% of the women stated that they would like to work more hours.[1]

As far as the distribution of part-time work over the different sectors is concerned, figures show that in 2000 part-time jobs were scarce in the building industry, energy and waterworks. In healthcare, three-quarters of the staff have a part-time job and in education nearly half do. Furthermore, the different occupational levels show a different proportion of part-time work. At the academic level, only a quarter of the working men and women have a job for less than 35 hours a week (a part-time job). At the elementary level, 64% work part-time. Moreover, at the elementary level 53% of the jobs require between 1 and 20 hours a week, whereas at the academic level 6.5% of the jobs require the same amount of time. Generally, the proportion of part-timers increases with the proportion of women employees and the degree of autonomy of the employees.[2]

---

1   *Trendrapport Aanbod van arbeid 2000,* The Hague, Organisatie voor Strategisch Arbeidsmarktonderzoek.
2   C. Remery. c.s. (2002), *Zorg als arbeidsmarktgegeven: werkgevers aan zet,* Tilburg, Organisatie voor Strategisch Arbeidsmarktonderzoek.

Chapter IV:
Equal opportunities

In the Netherlands, Article I of the Constitution prohibits discrimination. The 1994 Dutch Equal Treatment Act (AWGB) elaborates on this norm. The AWGB prohibits discrimination in specific fields (employment, education and the provision of goods and services) on a limited number of grounds (religion, belief, political orientation, race, sex, nationality, sexual preference and marital status). The AWGB, which, as mentioned above, covers the most common non-discrimination grounds in the Netherlands for several areas of society, is complemented by the Equal Opportunities Act (*Wet gelijke behandeling mannen en vrouwen, WGB*), which covers discrimination on the ground of sex. This Act contains special chapters on the subject of equal pay and equal treatment in occupational pension schemes.

In addition, several provisions in the Civil Code prohibit discrimination on the ground of sex.

With regard to **sex discrimination**, the Dutch Government has started the preparation of the implementation of Directive 2002/73/EC. This European Directive integrates the existing case law of the European Court of Justice and updates the legislation at a European level.

In the context of **equal treatment on other grounds**, three new bills have been prepared, largely in response to EU Directive 2000/78/EC establishing a general framework for equal treatment in employment and occupation, as well as for the implementation of EU Directive 2000/43 with regard to discrimination on the basis of race and ethnic origin:

- A bill amending the Equal Treatment Act to implement the Racial Equality Directive and the Employment Equality Directive (for the grounds of religion or belief and sexual orientation). Status: accepted by Parliament: 10 February 2004.

- An Act on equal treatment on the ground of age in employment (to implement the Employment Equality Directive for the ground of age). Status: accepted by Parliament: 17 December 2004.

- An Act on equal treatment on the grounds of disability/chronic disease (to implement the Employment Equality Directive for the ground of disability). Status: accepted by Parliament: 3 April 2003.

The new set of provisions that provides for equal treatment of employees with a disability or a chronic illness at work and in employment, provides the opportunity for individual employees to bring cases of potential direct or indirect discrimination before the courts.

- Article 2 of the Act on equal treatment on the ground of disability states that effective accommodation must be provided, unless such would constitute a disproportionate burden to that person. Accommodation is understood to mean both material and immaterial adjustments and measures. They may involve adjusting materials and equipment for work, providing facilities enabling disabled students to take courses, adapted working hours or adapted supervision. Other measures may pertain to the accessibility or design of a building. In other words, accommodation may concern all measures that enable the disabled person to participate in all the fields mentioned in the law. Because it depends on the situation of the person, the bill does not define exactly which accommodation measures should be taken.

- The Act on equal treatment on the ground of disability provides for the possibility of positive action.

The new provisions referring to discrimination based on an employee's **age** seek to do away with unjustified age limitations in employment issues. In the Act on equal treatment on the ground of age in employment, the following exceptions (based on Article 6 of the employment Directive) are foreseen.

- *Employment or labour market policy*: differences in treatment on the ground of age do not constitute discrimination, if they are based on legitimate employment or labour market policy to promote vocational integration of certain age groups (Article 7, section 1, sub a).

- *Dismissal on the ground of age when someone is entitled to a pension under the General Old Age Pensions Act:* employers may dismiss an employee who has reached the age when he or she is entitled to a pension under the General Old Age Pensions Act, or at an older age, when this is based on a law, a collective labour agreement between employer- and employee-organisations or between an individual employer and employee (Article 7, section 1, sub b). However, as the dismissal is allowed rather than obliged, this is not a mandatory retirement age.

- *Objective justification*: the Act prohibits discrimination on the ground of age, unless the distinction made on the ground of age is objectively justified by a legitimate aim and the means of achieving that aim are appropriate and necessary.

Chapter V:
Conclusion

The Netherlands is often looked upon as a model country for solving employment and labour issues. The particular ways of cooperation between employers' associations, trade unions and government are enshrined in the so-called 'Polder Model'.

The most important development in Dutch labour law during the past decade is certainly the Flexibility and Security Act, which entered into force on 1 January 1999. Since the beginning of the 1990s, the pressure for a reform of the Dutch law on dismissal protection was high. The existing system was considered too severe and was held partly responsible for the high unemployment rate. Practically all individual dismissals had to be approved beforehand by a governmental administrative body or a civil court.

Employers pushed to introduce more flexibility in the system. A typical 'Polder Model' compromise emerged in 1996, whereby the trade unions accepted to recognise more flexible forms of work, under the condition that the core concept of the existing dismissal legislation would not be altered and that flexible (atypical) workers would receive high(er) protection.

Typical reforms of the law concerned the relaxing of limitations on the repetition of employment contracts for a fixed duration. A second crucial reform was the abolition of restrictions on the use of temporary work.

The comprehensive Dutch approach to the reconstruction of the law on dismissal and on flexibility was addressed under the word 'flexicurity'. It must be noted, however, that the reforms have not simplified the Dutch labour law. A clear view on the full impact of the measures contained in the legislation involving 'flexicurity' will only appear over the coming years.

In the meantime, earlier discussions on the Polder Model have dissipated since at the end of 2002. At the end of 2003, central social partners and the Dutch Government concluded central agreements on several issues of social economic policy, in order to provide guidelines for the collective agreements at sectoral and company levels. Furthermore, discussions on the system of collective bargaining and collective agreements concentrate on the question of how to use the benefits of that system while developing more flexibility within the framework of collective agreements.

Recent trends in the Netherlands also show an increased focus on internal, rather than external, flexibility, implying a greater attention on the reconciliation of work and family life. On 22 November 2001, a new Work and Care Act was passed, which approaches flexibility from the employee's point of view. The practical effects of the law and its application will be determined over the next few years.

THE EVOLUTION OF LABOUR LAW
IN PORTUGAL

1992-2002

Miguel C. Rodríguez-Piñero Royo
Professor of Labour Law
Carlos III University, Madrid

Table of contents

Table of contents

Chapter I:
Introduction: Labour law and employment relations in Portugal

1. Ten years of legal reform

1.1. The background: Portuguese labour law in the 1990s

The origins of Portuguese labour law stem from the interminable authoritarian period the country underwent, in which the regulation of the main labour market institutions was developed and consolidated. This experience shaped employment legislation in its entirety and a far-reaching reform process was needed with the advent of a democratic regime.

The 1976 Constitution of the Portuguese Republic regulates in detail many aspects of employment rights, influencing the subsequent work of the lawmakers in this area. On account of the historical context in which it was adopted, it is without doubt one of the constitutions which most fully enshrines workers' rights.

During the 1980s, there was considerable pressure to make labour legislation more flexible. This led to a series of reforms in the late 1980s and early 1990s that affected the regulation of fixed-term employment, the recognition of temporary employment agencies, the organisation of working time, rules on dismissals, telework, and so on. On the whole, these measures had one primary goal: as a result of the neoliberal view that rigidity and excessive guarantees stymied firms' competitiveness, they aimed to increase the scope for the flexible management of company workforces. The neoliberal perspective was particularly convincing once Portugal had joined the European Community.

Although the reference period for this report commences in 1992, it is a good idea to go back a little further the years immediately preceding that date saw the introduction of major legislative innovations that dovetailed with those between 1992 and 2002 and formed part of the same reform process. The legal provisions governing fixed-term contracts were reformed in 1989, making them substantially more flexible and simpler. That same year, when the temporary employment agencies that had previously been prohibited made their debut on the labour market, the initial rules governing them were approved in 1989.

Several sweeping employment reforms were carried through in 1991 with the aim of increasing labour flexibility. Firstly, the duration of the trial period in open-ended contracts was lengthened considerably. The reform extended the period from 15 to 60 or 90 days, depending on whether the company had more or less than 20 employees. Indeed, the period could reach up to 180 days for employees in positions of trust, with extensive responsibilities, or performing complex technical tasks, or even 240 days for executives and senior staff.

The dismissal system was also altered in 1991 with the introduction of a new ground related to the worker's impossibility or inability to adapt to changes in his/her job. This reform aimed to make firms more adaptable to technical and organisational change within a regulatory framework that ensured reasonable protection for the worker. That same year, and with the same objective of improving adaptation to technological change and new management processes, a somewhat irregular procedure for suspending the employment contract was introduced. This was known as early retirement, and applied to workers of 55 or over. The early retirement status constitutes suspension of the employment contract by mutual agreement until the worker becomes a pensioner. During the period of early retirement, the worker retains the right to receive a monthly benefit that may not be lower than 25% of the last wage received during the active work period. This measure had a twofold aim: to reduce company payrolls and to facilitate replacement of older workers by younger workers.

In addition, 1991 saw the introduction of a new way of hiring workers, the so-called 'special relationship' employment (*trabalho en comissão de serviço*) to fulfil a promise made in the Economic and Social Agreement of 1990. This new system was used to hire employees that would perform duties implying a special relationship of trust between the employee and the company. Decree-Law 404/91 thus established that staff might be recruited to fill management posts, supervisory posts directly dependent on management, personal secretariat posts relating to these duties and other tasks laid down in the collective labour agreement that are characterised by a special relationship of trust. Previously, these employees had been recruited under ordinary employment contracts to which general labour law was applicable. This new type of contract was crucial to labour flexibility, as it afforded complete freedom to either party to terminate the contract by giving notice.

Law 2/91 reduced the maximum working week from 48 hours (in force in Portugal since 1919) to 44. At the same time, working time became far more flexible and adaptable. However, the maximum overtime was extended by Decree-Law 389/91 from 160 to 200 hours, without including overtime for reasons of *force majeure* or to prevent or repair serious damage to the company. Decree-Law 397/91 concerning far-reaching reform of rules on holidays and leave of absence arrangements also increased flexibility.

Lastly, in conjunction with the above measures, Decree-Law 440/91 on teleworking was introduced. Teleworking had not been previously regulated, apart from a few mentions in Decree-Law No 49 408 of 1969, the Contract of Employment Law (*Lei de Contracto de Trabalho*, LCT). This type of work is economically significant in Portugal and is relatively extensive in certain industries and branches. The reform had a number of goals: to prevent distortions of competition between firms resulting from the lack of control; promote greater flexibility in companies; give the latter access to low-cost labour; and guarantee minimum working conditions for teleworkers, particularly as regards the prevention of risks at work. Similar rules were also introduced for child labour, although these were of course more restrictive.

1.2. Developments in legislation between 1992 and 2002

The reform process that culminated with the various laws of 1991 continued during the last decade of the twentieth century. A vast number of legal provisions were introduced, impacting many of Portugal's institutions of individual and collective labour law. The common objective was to remove restrictions on employers' powers, broadening their scope and making them more coherent. As the effects of the globalising economy and the growing integration of European economies were increasingly felt, particularly with the progression from the internal market to the economic and monetary union, these attempts were stepped up.

In some cases, the reforms resulted from prior social consultation agreements. Many Community directives were also transposed during these years.

Decree-Law No 5/1994 incorporated into Portuguese law Directive 91/533/EEC. This was a major innovation in Portuguese law as there had previously been no rules on how open-ended contracts were to be drawn up. In many cases, the worker was unaware of his/her terms and conditions of employment, particularly in industries such as construction where the cultural and educational level of the labour force was fairly low. The Decree-Law is fairly consistent with the Directive. The Labour Code imposes a comparable obligation on the worker, who is required to inform the employer of personal details relevant to the performance of work.

Law 38/96 brought about new arrangements for dismissals in order to prevent fraud through agreements on terminations of contract. It also aimed to ensure compliance with fixed-term contracts, requiring that the contract include expressly and in concrete terms, the facts and circumstances attached to the reason for the conclusion of a fixed-term contract.

Important legislation on equality and non-discrimination in work and employment was passed in 1997. Law 105/97 was targeted mainly at combating indirect discrimination. The trade unions were afforded the right to take action to prove the existence of discriminatory practices. Decree-Law 307/97, clearly influenced by Community case law on this subject (notably the *Barber* and *Moroni* judgments) and by Directive 96/97/EC, introduced the principle of equal treatment in occupational social security schemes.

Amendments were made to the collective redundancy system in 1999 to implement Directive 98/59/EC, which consolidated the original Directive of 1975 and its reform of 1992. A number of practical effects ensued. Firstly, the undertaking planning to effect collective redundancies is required to include in its notification, *inter alia*, details of the period of time during which the redundancies are to be made and details of the method used for calculating any general compensation afforded to the workers to be made redundant. Secondly, during the consultation process in which the parties attempt to reach an agreement, they may be accompanied by an expert of their choice. Thirdly, any worker affected by a legal collective redundancy may, under express provision of the law and within five working days, request suspension of the redundancy for judicial reasons. Under the previous system, only workers who did not accept redundancy were given this option, which meant that workers accepting financial compensation were unable to appeal against the employer's decision.

Law 103/99 transposed Directive 97/81/EC on part-time employment, fully regulating this type of employment for the first time in Portuguese law. Previously, only the law of 1971 on the duration of work mentioned, but did not regulate, part-time work, merely referring to collective bargaining. Similarly, Law 40/99 incorporated into Portuguese law Directive 94/45/EC on European works councils. Law 9/2000 transposed Directive 96/71/EC of the European Parliament and of the Council on the posting of workers in the framework of the provision of services. This area had not previously been regulated in Portuguese law.

To improve consistency with the Community Directive and honouring the commitments made in the strategic social concertation pact of 1996, a more efficient system was introduced to protect workers' wage claims. A Wage Guarantee Fund was also set up, which was further developed and regulated in 2001. The establishment of this Fund brought major improvements to workers' rights in the event of the insolvency of their employer, as there had previously been no scheme that fulfilled this role adequately. Preferential arrangements for workers' wage claims were also reinforced in 2001.

In 1999 a new Procedural Labour Code was approved replacing the one dating from 1982. This Code includes important changes in procedures for court cases in order to speed them up and make them more effective. In the same year, new arrangements were introduced for infringements of labour law, including updating penalty amounts and classifying non-compliance with the labour law rules. The following year, pursuant to the Strategic Concertation Pact of 1966, the General Labour Inspectorate was reorganised with a view to making it more efficient and increasing its powers.

Returning to the area of non-discrimination, Law 9/2001 was adopted to improve the effectiveness of the means to combat discrimination on grounds of gender, boosting the arrangements for supervision and penalties. Supplementing this reform, Law 10/2001 required the Government to send an annual report to Parliament on progress in equal opportunities for men and women at work, in employment and vocational training.

Law 18/2001 increased the compensation paid to fixed-term workers on termination of their contract and required the employer to notify the trade union representative in the company of the conclusion, extension and termination of fixed-term contracts. Prior to this reform, the employer was only required to notify the workers' legal representatives of the recruitment of workers by means of fixed-term contracts.

The outcome of this entire process was a fragmented, uncoordinated body of labour law that gave rise to many problems in everyday application. We must not forget that Portuguese labour law results from an accumulation of rules and regulations dating from different epochs, mainly the corporatist period and the democratic period. Although most of the rules in force during the decade concerned were introduced subsequent to the Constitution, some of them date from the previous period. Moreover, the post-constitutional period covered quite wide-ranging and varied measures; while the first democratic laws provided strong guarantees, the reforming laws of the early 1990s was aimed primarily at flexibility.

As a result, the body of employment provisions was not only fragmented, but also on occasion incoherent. Consequently, the effectiveness of labour law was impaired, mainly in respect to individual rights, so the stakeholders, workers and employers had serious problems in deciphering the rules in force in order to organise their relations. Labour law specialists attempted to deal with these problems, but it was difficult to achieve any degree of coherence in the system, or even to determine whether a number of provisions were in force. This affected legal certainty and legal safety, both crucial in a State based on the rule of law.

To remedy this situation, a Commission for the Review and Reorganisation of Labour Law was set up. Above all, this was a technical body approved by the Economic and Social Council in order to review, redraft and streamline existing rules, check on applicability, consistency and wording and the situation of current texts, while abiding by the current framework. The Commission never managed to issue proposals. The outcome of its work was two parallel papers, one on the individual employment relationship and the other on collective relationships. These papers reorganised and classified the most important texts on labour law.

However, in the end it was the Government that presented a preliminary draft Labour Code. Unlike that prepared by the Commission, it was vast in scope and contained important innovations. Parliament approved the draft Labour Code in its broad form and its entry into force is planned for November 2003. However, this time schedule may change as it is highly likely that the Portuguese President will question the constitutionality of certain aspects of the Code.

The most important development in Portuguese labour law from 1992 to 2002 is perhaps the fact that, paradoxically, none of the rules and regulations on which it was based will survive. Thus, a completely new set of rules will be applied for the new century.

2. The protagonists of the system

As in all advanced, democratic systems of employment relations, there are three primary traditional players: the State, workers' organisations and employers' organisations.

2.1. The role of the State

Central government takes action in the labour market and in the industrial relations system on four main fronts: as lawmaker, manager, judicial authority and employer.

Responsibility for legislative authority is shared by the Parliament and the Government. A number of special rules are applicable in this context, depending on the field concerned. The regulation of workers' fundamental rights, freedoms and guarantees, such as the right of association, the right to collective bargaining and strike, workers' representation in companies and the stability of employment, falls to the Parliament on the basis of formal law. The same applies to other, similar rights, for example, the limits on working time, pay, daily and weekly rest, holidays, protection against risks at work, protection against involuntary unemployment, and accidents at work and occupational diseases.

The Government also has legislative powers that it exercises by means of decree-laws. The Parliament approves enabling legislation or legislation laying down the general principles of the rules to be introduced and the Government may either adopt a so-called 'authorised decree-law' or a 'development decree-law'. However, both parties are not on the same footing as regards these shared legislative powers. Parliament is afforded a position of privilege with respect to Government, which means, *inter alia*, that MPs can ratify the decree-laws issued by the Government.

Both as a legislative body and in its preeminent role as an executive body, the Portuguese Government fulfils a very important political and administrative role in labour relations. This stems from the traditional relationship between a highly interventionist State and the labour market. This tradition was consolidated during the authoritarian period, when the regime controlled employment relations directly and organised them in corporatist fashion. This intervention was maintained and even increased with the changeover to democracy, given the numerous obligations the Constitution imposed on the State in relation to employment.

State intervention in the labour market and employment relations can be broken down into two major types. On the one hand, there is political intervention at a high level, which could be described as economic and social policy conducted by the Government, which affects the economy as a whole and employment aspects in particular. On the other hand, there is also lower-level intervention, which more political/administrative and sectoral in nature, conducted by the Ministry for Social Security and Employment (*Ministerio da Segurança Social e do Trabalho*).

For the first type of intervention, the Constitution requires that the Government, as the highest level of public authority, promote and implement policies of full employment as well as equality of opportunity at work and vocational development for workers. This is laid down in Article 58 of the Portuguese Constitution. The Government also influences wage policies by setting a minimum wage (which is updated every year), pensions and social pensions, and through the remuneration of its employees, civil servants and workers employed in public undertakings. The increases set by the central government in both the minimum wage and civil servants' salaries have an enormous impact on income policy in general, as they serve as a reference in fixing pay scales in private-sector collective bargaining.

The Ministry for Social Security and Employment is responsible for implementing labour market, social security and employment policies drawn up by the Government. Its numerous duties are extremely varied and it deals with most central government intervention in the employment field. Its most important functions include the management of the labour market, monitoring working conditions, the imposition of administrative penalties in the employment field, the management of collective disputes, registration of various documents and ancillary duties regarding the regulation of working conditions. Where its tasks in **labour market management** are concerned, the top priority in all public action is to fight unemployment by means of a series of measures designed to promote full employment, which is regarded as a strategic objective.

Among the numerous tools used to attain this goal, attention should be drawn to:

- Exemption from social contributions on recruitment of young people or long-term unemployed people (Decree-Law No 89/95)

- Grants for the recruitment of young people and the long-term unemployed (Decree-Law No 34/96)

- Incentives for teleworking by disabled people (Law 31/98)

- The establishment of an observatory for the integration of disabled people (Law 30/98)

- Specific measures to promote employment in certain occupations where gender discrimination is manifest (Decree-Law 111/2000).

Broadly speaking, employment policy in Portugal is based on a number of general principles. These include:

- The integration of employment policies

- Universal access to such policies

- The promotion of social cohesion and the fight against poverty

- The promotion of employability.

The most important of these is the principle of integration, enshrined in Decree-Law 132 of 21 April 1999, which states that employment policies have to be based on a comprehensive, inclusive appraisal of employment. Its importance lies in the fact that it can serve as a basis for the systematic organisation of a series of employment-promotion measures that had previously been implemented in an isolated, one-off fashion.

Within the Ministry for Social Security and Employment, the tasks most directly concerned with the labour market and employment are assigned mainly to two departments, the Directorate-General for Employment and Labour Relations and the Employment and Vocational Training Institute. Among other things, the former is responsible for:

- Strategic planning and technical and regulatory support in the field of employment and vocational training, preparing standards and defining strategies for job creation and worker development

- The collection and processing of information on employment and vocational training

- The preparation of studies

- Participation in the approval of employment and vocational training programmes

- Participation in national and European networks aimed at promoting employment and vocational training.

The Employment and Vocational Training Institute deals with the following:

- Bringing into effect the employment and vocational training policies approved by the Government

- Developing the organisation of the labour market

- Promoting worker placement

- Improving corporate productivity by means of training and retraining

- Supporting job creation initiatives.

The tasks of the Employment and Vocational Training Institute therefore include operating as a public placement agency that both workers and employers can use on a voluntary basis. Discrimination against workers on grounds of nationality is prohibited.

The employment authorities are also responsible for monitoring working conditions and ensuring adherence to legal provisions, rules and regulations and agreements on working conditions, employment, unemployment and social security contributions. These duties are performed by the General Labour Inspectorate, (*Inspecção-Geral do Trabalho*) whose tasks are set out in Decree-Law No 102/2000. This body is similar in setup and operation to others throughout Europe, but has been assigned certain tasks specific to Portugal. These include the approval of undertakings' internal rules and the subsequent monitoring of compliance, as well as the provision of education, training and guidance on the correct application of standards at work.

The Labour Inspectorate is also responsible for imposing penalties, an instrument of persuasion to ensure compliance with standards at work. Accordingly, the Inspectorate may apply the appropriate methods to combat labour law infringements, depending on the case. The labour inspector is required to draw up a record (*auto de noticia*) when, during the performance of duties, he/she personally encounters an infringement of the labour rules liable to penalty. Where the labour inspector did not personally witness the infringement, notification is required (*auto de participação*). In both cases, the inspector takes note in writing of the relevant facts and arguments in order to determine whether there has been an infringement of labour law. There is also a third type of record, the recorded warning (*auto de advertencia*), which is made when the inspector notes a failure to comply with labour law that has not resulted in serious harm to workers, the labour authorities or social security. In this case, penalty procedures are not commenced; measures to be taken to reverse the infringement are communicated to the offender along with a given deadline.

The subsequent stages in penalty proceedings that commence with a recorded offence or notification vary according to the nature of the infringement concerned. Where criminal conduct may be involved, the case goes to the criminal courts. Where failure to comply with labour rules is involved, the case goes to a labour court. Where an infringement is established, the General Labour Inspectorate makes a decision and, on conclusion of the administrative proceedings, action may be taken before a labour court.

The Directorate-General for Employment and Labour Relations also deals with the prevention and settlement of collective disputes. It is responsible for supervising collective bargaining procedures and bringing into effect the conciliation and mediation procedures that arise as a result of collective disputes. Its responsibilities also include participation in the negotiation stage of collective redundancy procedures and monitoring limitations on the working day or suspension of employment contracts for company reasons. In general, the Directorate-General for Employment and Labour Relations is responsible for overseeing and intervening in industrial relations in order to prevent or overcome labour disputes and conflicts of interest.

For a strike to be lawful, notice must be given by the parties entitled to call it (trade unions and workers' meetings, the latter only under certain conditions) to the Ministry for Social Security and Employment. The normal period of notice is five working days, extended to ten working days in cases of strikes that affect sectors or undertakings satisfying imperative social needs. The role of the labour authorities is stronger and more decisive in the event of strikes in essential services and conflicts of interests resulting from the conclusion or revision of a collective agreement.

In the special case of strikes in essential services, the Directorate-General for Employment and Labour Relations is responsible for defining minimum services and for setting up the means to provide them, but only where this matter has not been previously regulated by means of a collective bargaining tool or an agreement between employer or employers' organisation and representatives of the workers on strike. If there is no agreement on minimum services before prior notice is given, the labour authorities are required to promote an agreement between the parties to the dispute. If no agreement can be reached, the corresponding minimum services are established by a joint order of the Minis-

ter for Social Security and Employment and the Minister responsible for the sector of activity affected by the strike. However, these arrangements are only applicable to private-sector strikes. In the event of a strike in services administered directly by the State or by a public undertaking, the minimum services are not laid down by joint order. Instead, arbitration becomes compulsory and the decision is taken by a group of three arbitrators.

In the event of disputes arising as a result of the negotiation or revision of a collective agreement, the parties may agree to arbitration following failure of negotiation and attempts at conciliation and mediation. Where the parties concerned fail to agree to arbitration within two months of the start of the strike, the Minister for Social Security and Employment may impose compulsory arbitration at the request of one of the parties or on the recommendation of the Standing Commission on Social Consultation.

As for registration, the Ministry for Social Security and Employment is required to register trade union organisations, workers' committees and employers' organisations, and to store all related documentation. The register of the articles of association of these organisations serves as a basis for acquiring legal personality. The labour authorities are responsible for publishing the articles of association of these organisations, any amendments thereto and the composition of the management bodies. The aim is to exercise formal control over the establishment of new legal persons, publicise the workers and employers' representative bodies and identify their management bodies. The control over the establishment of these collective bodies is formal and strictly administrative, as it is not for the labour authorities to pass judgment on their lawfulness or the lawfulness of their establishment. That is a matter for the courts alone.

Lastly, let us turn to the ancillary tasks and the establishment of working conditions. This task is related to the nature of collective bargaining in Portuguese law. In Portugal, the collective agreement has limited personal effect and has no effect *erga omnes*. Its provisions apply only to the workers represented by the parties negotiating. Based on this rule, the law provides that where certain presuppositions have been obtained, the original scope of a collective agreement or arbitration decision can be extended. This is arranged via an order by the Minister for Social Security and Employment or a joint order by the Minister together with the Minister responsible for the sector of activity concerned. The agreement will then apply to other undertakings in the same sector, or to workers in the same or similar occupations. Alternatively, the collective agreement or arbitration decision may be extended to workers and employers outside the geographical area of the original agreement as long as the economic and social circumstances are similar or the same.

In cases where the extension of arrangements cannot be used and there are no trade unions or employers' organisations, the Ministers for Social Security and Employment and of the sector of activity concerned may regulate minimum conditions, if justified by social and economic circumstances. This administrative intervention to establish working conditions is quite exceptional and its constitutionality is even under discussion. The tradition of allowing the administrative regulation of working conditions by sectors of activity can be traced to the corporatist period; it survived in the Republic, but no new rules have been drawn up since 1992. Such rules constitute a genuinely exceptional administrative source of labour law. While filling any regulatory gaps in sectors that experience difficulties in collective bargaining, they perform an additional role in the democratic system: combating bad faith in collective bargaining, particularly in cases where one of the parties manifestly uses delaying tactics or impedes the normal development of the bargaining process. This task is not included in the new Labour Code.

2.2. The trade union organisations

The trade union organisations constitute the most powerful mechanism for workers' representation, both in companies and at local, regional and national level. It is also the form of workers' collective organisation to which the Portuguese legal system attaches the greatest importance. There are other channels for representation, such as workers' committees, European works councils and committees on safety and health at work. Workers' meetings also have certain recognised responsibilities and outcomes, such as calling a strike.

The different forms of worker representation in Portugal do not vie with each other. Indeed, they generally operate in conjunction and complement each other.

The personal and geographical scope of the trade unions, as first-stage voluntary organisations, is both varied and distinctive. They are based on occupations (horizontal trade unions) and on sectors of activity (vertical trade unions). Company trade unions also exist. From the geographical standpoint, their coverage may be local, regional or national.

Broadly speaking and as a trend, the trade unions belonging to the General Workers' Union (*União Geral dos Trabalhadores*, UGT), set up mainly after April 1974, make less use of intermediate federation and union structures and favour national trade unions. In contrast, the trade unions belonging to the

General Confederation of Portuguese Workers (*Confederação Geral dos Trabalhadores Portugueses*, CGTP), many of which were established during the corporatist period, are more varied in geographical scope and include local, regional and national unions. Despite attempts to reorganise towards greater vertical integration, the intermediate trade union organisations still carry significant weight.

Not until 1974, with the introduction of the democratic regime, could trade unions be established for public servants. Trade unions for the military and militarised forces are prohibited, while freedom of association is recognised for the judiciary. Police trade unions were prohibited for more than 20 years, but the police was granted the right to establish trade unions from December 2001. In some areas of public service, the trade unions are fragmented and very small unions have been set up.

The Portuguese Constitution and law recognise the right to trade union activity within companies which may have a trade union branch (all the workers in the company affiliated to one and the same trade union). They also recognise the right to trade union delegates (workers elected by the members of each trade union branch), trade union committees (which assemble the delegates of one and the same trade union in the company) and inter-union committees (which assemble the trade union delegates of various trade union committees). The trade union delegate is seen more as a worker of the company who deals with the union than as a representative of the trade union who deals with the workers in the company.

The Portuguese industrial relations system comprises two major trade union confederations, UGT and CGTP. A third group, the General Confederation of Managerial Staff (*Confederação Geral de Quadros*) has little impact on the labour relations system.

CGTP, also known as Intersindical (CGTP-IN), was clandestine or semi-clandestine. It was set up in 1970 by a number of trade unions, whose senior officials were anti-fascist, in order to counter the established authority at that time. They were able to do so because, in its final stages, the corporatist regime no longer required administrative approval of managerial positions in the trade unions. Always predominantly communist, but co-existing happily with progressive socialist and catholic tendencies, CGTP has favoured more aggressive, mass trade unionism. Although it has undergone strategic changes, its position has remained practically unchanged with respect to the different governments.

With great encouragement and support from the then majority parties (the Socialist Party and the Social Democratic Party, then known as the Popular Democratic Party), UGT was set up in 1978 on the basis of an agreement between the socialist and social democratic movements in the context of a break with the CGTP. The socialist tendency clearly continues to dominate and this confederation mainly follows the Christian trade union orientation, although its influence is small. Above all, it practices trade unionism based on bargaining and consensus.

Both confederations belong to the European Trade Union Confederation and participate in the Portuguese delegation to the annual conference of the International Labour Organisation.

Most of the Portuguese trade unions are affiliated to one of the confederations. According to National Statistical Institute data for 2001, which is the most recent in this area, 384 trade unions do not belong to the confederations.

There are no legal criteria on trade union representativeness, nor information on the representativeness of the trade union confederations. All relevant research shows that CGPT is the most representative and the foremost Portuguese confederation from this viewpoint. According to a study published in 1993, 71% of workers affiliated to a trade union belong to CGPT organisations, 23% to the UGT area and 6% to independent trade unions. According to another study dating from 1991, active workers belonging to trade unions (paying membership dues) numbered about one million, with between 550 000 and 600 000 belonging to CGTP, between 300 000 and 350 000 to UGT and between 100 000 and 150 000 to the independent trade unions. The 1995 data provided by the High Authority for Social Communication, for the purposes of allocating broadcasting time to each of the trade union organisations, revealed that CGTP accounted for 737 000 workers belonging to 144 trade unions, UGT accounted for 505 987 workers belonging to 61 trade unions, and 37 independent trade unions accounted for 137 762 workers. There is no reason to believe that the figures have changed substantially since that time.

3. Sources of labour law

Article 12(1) of Decree-Law 49 408 of 1969, generally known as the Contract of Employment Law (LCT), contains the only list available of sources of Portuguese labour law. However, it is scarcely functional as it is so old. It refers to rules no longer existing and does not refer to others that are fully operational nowadays. It is stated that *employment contracts are subject in particular to the legal provisions regulating employment, those issued by the Ministry for Companies and*

Social Security, company rules and rules under collective labour agreements, in that order.

Although it is not mentioned in the LCT, international labour law fully applies in Portugal, which has ratified many ILO conventions. The same applies to European Community law since Portuguese accession to the European Community in 1986. The Community labour law directives have, on the whole, been incorporated into Portuguese law, although occasionally with some delay. The European Social Charter came into force in Portugal in 1991.

3.1. State rules

The internal sources of labour law include the Constitution, laws, decree-laws, regulations and, in the autonomous regions of Madeira and the Azores, regional legislative decrees. Extension directives and labour regulation directives are of a more administrative nature.

The Constitution contains many references to labour and employment. As it is one of the European constitutions that focuses the most attention thereon, it is referred to as a 'labour constitution'. It is fairly extensive and detailed and shapes the development of labour law from state sources and, in general, all acts of the public authorities.

In particular, the Constitution comprises a detailed, ample list of workers' rights. The effectiveness of certain rights, freedoms and guarantees connected with work is afforded special protection in that they have the special status of fundamental rights. This applies to some of the most paradigmatic rights, such as stability in employment, collective bargaining, freedom of association and the right to strike. As these are classified as fundamental rights, they are directly applicable and directly binding on both public and private bodies in accordance with Article 18 of the Portuguese Constitution.

The legal provisions are extremely varied as regards the substance, scope and date of approval. As can be seen throughout this study, rules from the dictatorship co-exist with others from the early years of democracy, including emergency laws from the 1980s and laws promoting flexibility from the 1990s. There is no key law, basic law or framework law regulating the employment contract. The nearest thing to a Workers' Statute or a Labour Code is Decree Law No 49 408 of 1969, known as the Contract of Employment Law. Its title is misleading, however, because the basic rules on employment are dealt with in subsequent specific laws. The normal procedure is that each one-off measure in the labour market and each practical rule are dealt with by means of an *ad hoc* monographic law. In many cases, as labour law rules are not reformed by means of derogations from one rule, both co-exist. The result is an extensive, poorly organised system of labour law that is difficult to manage. This is why it was decided to draw up a Labour Code.

Parliament and the Government are responsible for drafting labour legislation. However, in the field of employment relations and the labour market, these sovereign bodies cannot legislate without giving workers' and employers' organisations the opportunity to give their opinion on draft texts. Up until 1999, only the trade unions had to be afforded this right, but since then the employers' organisations are also involved. The role of both sides of industry is limited to issuing an opinion on the draft; they may attempt to influence the substance of the legislation, but this in no way restricts the powers of the sovereign bodies. Under the Labour Code, the organisations still participate in the legislative process and the Standing Committee on Social Consultation also has the right to take part in the drafting of labour legislation.

In addition to this participation in the legislative process, it is important to note that throughout the period under consideration a good proportion of the labour law adopted resulted from negotiation and social consultation. A case in point is the controversial reform of working time and operational flexibility in 1996. Law 21/96 brought into effect – with some delay – the content of the Economic and Social Pact of 1990.

This was a fruitful period for the production of negotiated legislation, although consensus was not always achieved among all the social players. For example, when the draft Labour Code was put to the social partners some of them put up stiff resistance and others approved it. The consensus reached was translated into a 'tripartite compromise on the proposed Labour Code', in which the Government undertook to include in the text the amendments agreed upon by most of the social partners. These amendments were approved by Parliament and have been included in the Code.

3.2. Social dialogue

Social dialogue is of vital importance in working and political life in Portugal and has held a special place throughout the democratic period. That is why it is reviewed separately. The Constitution refers to social consultation and its role in matters related to economic and social policy.

In 1984, central government set up the Standing Council for Social Consultation (*Conselho Permanente de Concertação Social* (CPCS) with the aim of monitoring labour disputes.

The State needed a special instrument to legitimise its attempts to combat industrial disputes. In line with the prevailing trend in Europe at the time, it tried to do this through forms of social consultation that would legitimise its economic and social policy. The country's most representative trade union, CGTP, refused on principle to take part in this body that it did not trust. This considerably impaired the legitimacy of all social consultation policy at that time.

At the outset, the social consultation covered income policy and the regulation of working conditions. Subsequently, the areas falling within the scope of social dialogue were extended; as more emphasis was placed on dialogue and social consultation, it started to deal with employment, vocational training, the Community Funds, Portugal's position in the European Union and social security.

The 1989 revision of the Constitution introduced the Economic and Social Council (*Conselho Economico e Social*, CES) as a body for consultation in economic and social policies. It inherited the role and position of the former CPCS. Together with the CES, undoubtedly the most important body in the field of social consultation, there is a Standing Committee on Social Consultation (CPCS). This tripartite committee is chaired by the Prime Minister. It has 18 members, six representing the trade unions, six the employers' organisations and six the Government.

Social consultation has resulted in numerous agreements on economic and social matters during the decade under consideration. The most important ones include: the Economic and Social Agreement of 1990, concluded by the Government, one of the trade union confederations and two employers' organisations; the Agreement on Safety, Hygiene and Health at Work concluded in 1991 by all the representative organisations; the Short-term Social Consultation Agreement and the Agreement on Consultation Strategy, both dating from 1996, which had important consequences on labour legislation and gave rise to a number of significant reforms.

Under a socialist government, a milestone in social consultation was reached in 2001 with the signature of four major agreements: the Pact on Employment, Labour Market, Education and Training; the Pact on Working Conditions, Hygiene and Safety at Work and Fight Against Workplace Accidents; the Pact on the Modernisation of Social Protection; and the Pact on the Introduction of Optional Ceilings on Contributions for the Pension System. Only the first two agreements were signed by all of the social partners. At the start of the 21st century, social consultation does not appear to be faring well. By way of example, the drafting of the Labour Code, despite conclusion of a tripartite agreement that amended the Government's original proposal, destroyed the climate of social consensus and resulted in a general strike. Moreover, the current Portuguese Government seems less interested than its predecessor in social consultation.

The agreements concluded under the auspices of the CES have no legal force and are not binding on the signatories. They do not impose obligations on State bodies and the State is not required to put them into effect. Nevertheless, in practice, both public and private bodies usually regard such agreements as references or guidelines to be followed.

In all events, social dialogue has played an important role from 1992 to 2002. It has dealt with some of the most important issues relating to employment and the labour market, providing for the adoption of reforms with wide social support – in a country whose working culture has hardly been inclined towards consensus.

3.3. Collective bargaining

The legislation regulating collective bargaining dates from 1979, when it was approved with the aim of assigning the parties an autonomous, responsible role therein. Nevertheless, its rules are very interventionist and it regulates many aspects of collective bargaining procedures and management in fairly detailed fashion. Decree-law No 519/79 deals with matters such as:

• The capacity of the parties

• The subjects on which negotiations may be held

• The scope and effects of the agreements on individuals and as regards time

• The bargaining process

• The lodging and publication of agreements.

Although the Constitution grants workers who are members of a group or category the right to bargain, these rules only grant trade union organisations the legitimate capacity to conclude collective agreements on their behalf. Thus, workers' committees do not have this right. Trade union confederations and groupings may, in accordance with the conditions laid down by law, enter into collective agreements, but so far this authority has not been used. The trade union confederations are parties to agreements and pacts on social and employment policy within institutionalised

consultation but, as we will see, such pacts are not regarded as collective agreements or formal sources of law.

On the employers' side, agreements may be concluded by individual employers, groups of employers and employers' organisations. Depending on the criteria relating to the identity of the party to the agreement on the employers' side, a distinction is made between the following types of collective agreements:

• Collective agreements concluded by a group of employers or an employers' organisation

• Collective agreements concluded by more than one employer for application in more than one company

• Company agreements entered into by an employer for application in a single company.

The lack of criteria on representativeness in Portuguese labour law has important consequences for collective bargaining. Any trade union or employers' organisation, however small, may negotiate a collective agreement. As a result, employers refuse to negotiate with representative unions in their company or industry and negotiate with others who are scarcely or not at all representative.

As regards the duration of collective agreements, under the Decree-Law of 1979 an agreement remains in force for the time that the parties specify. However, a different rule is in fact applied, in accordance with that same Decree-Law, whereby the agreement remains in force until it is replaced by another one. This general rule applies both to the clauses of the agreement and to its requirements. By law, the minimum period of validity is 12 months from the date of registration for lodging purposes, but no maximum period is laid down. The parties may also opt not to establish a period of validity. With the exception of economic clauses, the parties may not give retroactive effect to clauses in a collective agreement.

In the event of transfer of an undertaking or establishment, the new employer is required to comply with the agreement applying to the previous employer for twelve months following the transfer or until the deadline for termination laid down in the agreement, unless the agreement has been replaced by another one in the meantime. These arrangements were introduced in 1992 by Decree-Law No 209/92.

Where the conditions for replacing collective agreements are concerned, the rule is that the later agreement must be more favourable overall than the previous one. That is, the guarantees provided by the previous agreement may be more limited, but on the whole the later agreement must be more favourable for the workers and this must be express-ly stated in the new agreement. In comparing agreements the criterion of *conglobação* is applied.

The law does not require any particular organisational setup for collective bargaining; the parties concerned choose the bargaining units. The most common units are sector of activity, often covering the whole country or a significant part of it, occupation and company, particularly in large com-panies. In the course of the period under review, sector-level bargaining predominated. A decentralising trend in collec-tive bargaining has never, strictly speaking, emerged in Por-tugal and the traditional industrial relations system has thus always given priority to sectoral bargaining. In some sectors, sectoral collective bargaining and company bargaining have been complementary. This informal bargaining is based on the claims the workers present to the employer.

The coverage rate of collective bargaining, that is, the per-centage of workers covered by a collective agreement or some other instrument for collective regulation, is approxi-mately 60%.

Under Portuguese law, collective agreements apply to their sig-natories and the persons they represent, that is, the employers and workers belonging to the signatory organisations when the bargaining process commences. The consequences for individuals are thus relative or limited, as Portuguese agree-ments do not apply *erga omnes*. This original scope may be extended by means of agreements concluded between the employers' organisations and trade union concerned, or by extension directives, which will be known in the Labour Code as extension regulations. The purpose of this administrative device is to broaden the scope of collective agreements and approximate and standardise occupational status in a specific geographical area or occupation. The scope of an agreement may also be extended as a result of workers and employers subsequently joining the organisations that sign the agreement.

Collective agreements have a necessary, automatic impact on the labour relations they regulate; its effects are similar to those of a law. The only case in which they do not apply is where an individual employment contract includes work-ing conditions that are more favourable for the worker. Oth-erwise, the less favourable contract clause is replaced by the relevant provision of the agreement.

4. Settlement of labour disputes

For resolving individual and collective labour-law disputes, Portugal has a specialised judicial authority, the labour courts.

These labour courts are judicial bodies with special powers; they fall within the system of ordinary courts and are run by professional magistrates. Although the constitution and legis-lation provide for 'social magistrates' (*guises sociais*) who are competent to rule on labour issues, these magistrates, who have to be elected by employers and workers, have never materialised.

The jurisdiction of the Portuguese labour courts is different from that of other countries. It deals with the settlement of disputes that would be handled by ordinary or administrative courts elsewhere. Its jurisdiction can be broken down into three areas: civil issues, contraventions and infringements. Civil proceedings, the area normally covered by labour courts in Europe, include, *inter alia*, issues relating to working condi-tions, the termination of the employment contract, the inter-pretation and cancellation of rules in collective agreements, strikes, freedom of association, accidents at work and occupa-tional diseases. Contraventions include breaches of statutory rules for which fines may be imposed. Infringements include appeals against decisions by the General Labour Inspectorate in proceedings for infringements of labour law. In other Euro-pean judicial systems, the latter areas fall within the scope of the ordinary/administrative courts as they involve administra-tive acts imposing penalties.

Despite the wide jurisdiction of the labour courts, ordi-nary/administrative courts also rule on certain employment questions. These can include legal disputes on fixed-term contracts in the civil service, or appeals against ministerial orders establishing minimum services in the event of strikes in services essential to the community. In short, the admin-istrative courts are competent to decide on appeals against administrative acts that affect the field of work. The criminal courts are naturally competent to deal with cases involving labour law offences covered by the Criminal Code.

The above description refers to the ordinary courts. The Constitutional Court may be called upon to assess the con-stitutionality of the labour rules applied by a court, some-thing which occurs with relative frequency.

As in other European system, the use of independent means for resolving collective disputes, alongside court settlements of labour disputes, is increasingly being promoted. In Portugal, the regulation of these independent means for dispute settlement is directly related to the legal arrangements governing collec-tive agreements.

Individual disputes follow the course of ordinary legal pro-ceedings and are dealt with by the labour courts, as men-tioned earlier. Collective disputes, however, are broken down into two groups under Decree-Law No 519/79: disputes relating to the termination or conclusion of collective agreements and disputes relating to the application of an agreement. This distinction stems from the traditional doctrinal divide between economic disputes or conflicts of interests, and legal disputes.

For the purpose of resolving legal disputes, each collective agreement must establish a joint committee, comprising an equal number of representatives from each side. Agreements adopted unanimously by this committee may be lodged and published as tools for collective regulation and as an extension of the agreement. The operating rules of the joint committee are laid down by the same parties to the agreement. Although agreements usually set up joint committees, they rarely operate in practice and make little contribution to the settlement of disputes resulting from the application of agreements.

Collective legal disputes are settled mainly, if not solely, by the labour courts. The law organising these courts, dating from 1999, assigns them powers to resolve disputes concerning the cancellation and interpretation of tools for the collective regulation of work. However, this does not apply to those resulting from an administrative regulation or an act of extension as the administrative courts are competent for the latter. Under the Portuguese legislation on proceedings, the Supreme Court (*Supremo Tribunal de Justiça*) may rule on the interpretation of a clause in an agreement, or may cancel it. Its decision will have a general, compulsory effect, acting as a mechanism to ensure uniformity in interpretation of the collective agreement.

The laws on proceedings entitle the trade unions and employers' organisations to take action on matters concerning the collective rights and interests they represent. In addition, the Procedural Labour Law Code of 1999 (*Código de Processo de Trabalho*) confers on trade unions the right to appear before the courts representing or acting as a substitute for employees who authorise them to do so. This generally occurs where the individual rights at stake are similar to those of their members.

Conciliation, mediation and arbitration are the specific forms of industrial dispute settlement provided for by law. However, there is nothing to prevent such methods from being used for legal disputes, as Portuguese law states that the parties are free to use any means for settling controversies and may establish their operating rules. The legal system has traditionally fulfilled an essentially voluntary, supplementary role and it comes into play only where the parties do not establish independent arrangements.

As for compulsory arbitration in labour disputes, major changes have occurred during the decade under consideration. These instruments do have some standing as provision was already made for them in the collective bargaining law of 1979. However, it merely provided that arbitration could become compulsory for disputes resulting from the conclusion or revision of collective agreements in public undertakings or publicly funded undertakings. Given the failure of voluntary arbitration, legislation was introduced in 1992 to extend the scope of compulsory arbitration. It could then be used when the instruments for independent settlement (conciliation and mediation) failed and two months from the time the parties decided to put the matter to voluntary arbitration. Where such conditions occur and are fulfilled, at the initiative of one of the parties or on a recommendation from the Economic and Social Council, the Minister responsible for the field concerned may decide, by means of an order, to impose compulsory arbitration.

For the purpose of compulsory arbitration, a list of arbitrators was to be agreed by the social partners belonging to the Economic and Social Council. However, this list has not yet been drawn up, demonstrating that the protagonists of the labour relations system are not very convinced that this is a good system. As many argue, the system cannot operate without agreement first being reached on the arbitrators.

The Labour Code that is about to come into force also includes compulsory arbitration, laying down arrangements very similar to the present ones. A new circumstance for compulsory arbitration has been included, namely strikes in essential services. In the event of a strike affecting services administered directly by the State or public undertakings, where no agreement has been reached on the third day of notice, a group of three arbitrators is assigned the tasks of defining the minimum services and the means to assure them.

The conciliation provided for by law is arranged by the labour authorities at the request of both parties or of only one party. A reform in 1993 endeavoured to boost the role of the labour authorities, entitling them to promote conciliation *ex officio* so that the parties to the dispute would no longer be the only parties entitled to request conciliation. The Labour Code reinforces this aspect in that the parties are required to take steps towards conciliation and mediation under pain of committing a serious infringement of labour law.

During the decade under consideration, the administrative regulation of working conditions was not used to combat bad faith in collective bargaining. This was not because bad faith did not feature in bargaining, but because the State decided not to make use of this facility in disputes arising during negotiations on or review of collective agreements.

Of the various voluntary methods for resolving labour disputes, only conciliation under the auspices of the labour authorities is worthy of mention as it is the only method that has worked.

In 1992, lawmakers wanted to encourage the use of independent procedures for settling disputes involving individuals. The legislation made express provision for collective agreements to include instruments such as conciliation, mediation and arbitration for disputes concerning individual employment contracts. However, this resulted in a mere indicative legal reference with no practical consequences. Even in those sectors where such dispute-settlement instruments were provided for (and a large number of agreements did so), it did not work in practice, with a few exceptions such as professional football. The labour courts continued to deal with disputes relating to employment contracts. Procedural labour law provided for conciliation, the stage at which a fair number of disputes come to an end. However, this is legal conciliation, which has nothing to do with independent machinery for dispute resolution.

This limited success of independent instruments for dispute settlement can be explained by various factors, including shortcomings in the legal framework, an unfavourable cultural environment, the insufficient funds available to the State and easy access to the labour courts.

Chapter II:
From employment security to employability

As mentioned earlier, the Portuguese Constitution contains numerous commitments concerning employment and the labour market, which is regarded as a place where many citizens' rights are exercised. *Inter alia*, Article 58 states that everyone has the right to work. It is the duty of the State to guarantee this by implementing economic and social plans and, in practical terms, by ensuring the implementation of policies on full employment.

1. Protection against dismissal

Employment security is recognised as a fundamental right in Article 53 of the Portuguese Constitution, which expressly prohibits dismissal without just cause or for political or ideological reasons. Nevertheless, this has not prevented this principle from losing ground during the ten years under consideration.

For many years, dismissal was regulated by Decree-Law 372-A/75 which included a relatively limited list of conditions giving just cause for dismissal. For example, the worker's failure to adapt to technological change was not included, nor the employer's need to eliminate jobs on economic, technical, organisational or production grounds.

In light of the rigidity of these rules, which date back to 1975 and could therefore not adequately respond to the requirements of the production system in the 1980s, the Government repeatedly attempted to introduce new rules. These attempts met not only with the trade union's opposition, but also with some reluctance on the part of the Constitutional Court. Approval was eventually gained for Decree-Law 64-A/89, the main legislative text on dismissals throughout the period under consideration, which will remain in force until the Labour Code effectively enters into force.

In 1991 a new form of dismissal was introduced on the ground of the worker's inability to adapt to changes at his/her workplace. Since the introduction of the rules concerned via Decree-Law 400/91, this is has been known as 'dismissal for failure to adapt'.

Law No 38/96 gave workers the option of revoking their consent to termination of the employment contract by mutual agreement of the parties or by unilateral decision of the worker within ten days from the time when the termination was to take effect. The purpose of this measure was to make sure that the worker really wanted to terminate the contract and to protect him/her from pressure exerted by the employer, who conceals the true motive for the dismissal in order to prevent the application of dismissal arrangements.

In a closer analysis of the rules governing dismissal, the first thing to be noted is their imperative nature. Accordingly, Article 2 of the Decree-Law of 1989 specifies that its arrangements cannot be amended by any collective labour regulation tool or collective agreement.

Having reiterated that dismissals without just cause are prohibited, Article 3 of the Decree-Law lists the legal reasons for termination of the employment relationship:

- Expiry of the agreed term of a fixed-term contract

- Mutual agreement between the parties

- Dismissal instigated by the employer for objective or subjective reasons

- Termination of the contract by the worker

- Cancellation by either of the parties during the trial period

- Termination of the jobs for objective reasons of a structural, technological or economic nature related to the undertaking.

Of the various reasons for termination, the most important for our purpose is the one for objective reasons, which are covered in Chapter V of the Decree-Law. This Chapter is comprised of two parts; the first concerns the termination of the employment contract for objective reasons and the second one concerns collective redundancies.

As regards the first type of dismissal, individual redundancy, Article 26(1) of the Decree-Law specifies that this must be justified by economic, technological or structural reasons. The reasons are specified as follows:

- Economic or market grounds, where there is an actual reduction in the enterprise's activity, resulting from a drop in sales or services on account of the practical or legal impossibility of placing such goods or services on the market.

- Technical grounds, where there are changes in the techniques or in the manufacturing or automation processes of production, control or goods transport equipment.

- Structural grounds in the company, when it changes its activity or replaces its main product or when a number of departments definitively close down, resulting in economic and financial imbalance.

However, the presence of one of the above reasons does not justify redundancy by itself. Under Article 27 of the Decree-Law other factors must be present at the same time:

- The reasons invoked cannot be attributed to the fault of the employer

- Practical impossibility of continuing the employment relationship

- There must be no equivalent jobs filled by fixed-term workers

- The appropriate compensation must be made available to the worker.

The Decree-Law deals with other aspects of redundancy, such as the amount of compensation, the criteria for choosing the jobs to be terminated, the procedure for proceeding with termination, and information for the workers' representatives.

Collective redundancy is defined as the simultaneous or successive termination, within a three-month period, of the employment contracts of at least two employees in the case of enterprises with up to 50 employees and at least five employees in enterprises with over 50 employees. Termination may also result from the permanent closure of the enterprise or one or more departments, or the need to reduce the workforce for structural, technological or economic reasons.

This redundancy procedure is fully consistent with Community rules and includes negotiation and consultation, the participation of the public authorities, a period for termination of the contract, etc. The redundant worker is entitled to compensation of one month's pay for each year or part-year of service, subject to a minimum of three months.

Another important ground to be mentioned here is dismissal for failure to adapt, which is not covered by the Decree-Law of 1989 but by a special rule introduced into the legal system by Decree-Law No 400/91. Article 2 describes situations in which the worker fails to adapt to the circumstances and performs his task in a manner that makes it practically impossible to continue the employment relationship. The following objective situations are expressly mentioned:

- Repeated reductions in productivity

- Repeated breakdowns in the facilities connected with the job

- Risks to the health and safety of the worker, his/her colleagues or third parties.

The presence of these circumstances is not sufficient, however. The Decree-Law also requires the simultaneous presence of a series of conditions governing the validity of the dismissal:

- Changes have been made to the job as a result of new manufacturing processes, new technologies or equipment based on more advanced technology. Such changes must have been made no more than six months prior to the decision being taken.

- The worker has received adequate vocational training consistent with the technological change made.

- The worker has been granted an appropriate period of adjustment.

- The company has no other job the worker could fill in the light of his/her occupational skills.

2. Training and work

Under Article 58 of the Portuguese Constitution, the right to work includes an undertaking by the State to promote cultural and technical training and vocational development for workers.

Decree-Law No 401/91 established the vocational training system that was to remain in force for most of the decade, regulating the vocational training to be promoted within the education system and in the labour market, schools and companies. A very wide definition of vocational training was provided: a comprehensive, ongoing process whereby young people and adults, at the start of, or already taking part in working life, prepare themselves for the performance of an occupational activity. Decree-Law 405/91 regulates vocational training in the labour market.

Portugal, like other countries, has various levels of vocational training:

•   Regulated training that forms part of the education system

•   Vocational training for the unemployed, with the aim of improving their employability

•   Continued training to maintain and increase the technical skills of employed persons.

In accordance with Decree-Law No 401/91, responsibility for vocational training falls to a number of bodies: the State, the social players, companies, other entities that provide employment, employers', trade-union and occupational organisations, other public and private bodies, both profit-making and non-profit making, and cooperatives devoted to vocational training. In practice, vocational training may be organised by public, private or cooperative bodies, notably:

1.   Training establishments and centres

2.   Companies and employers' associations

3.   Trade union and occupational organisations

4.   Regional and local authorities

5.   Cultural associations.

Such training is implemented through course-based programmes. The programmes are to be prepared and developed at the initiative of the State through the training bodies that receive financial support from central government and other sources.

Decree-Law 401/91 defines continued training as training that forms part of an individual's working life and is followed throughout the latter with the aim of improving adaptation to technological, organisational and other change, encouraging career advancement, improving quality in employment and contributing to cultural, economic and social development. The bodies responsible for offering such training are the State, the social players, companies and other entities that provide employment, employers', trade-union and occupational organisations, other public and private bodies, both profit-making and non-profit-making, and cooperatives devoted to vocational training. Companies are mainly responsible for funding continued training, although they may receive financial support from the State.

In addition to this legislation, there are also other rules and schemes connected with worker training. For example, Decree-Law No 379/91 introduced long-term unpaid leave (a minimum period of 60 days) for attending training courses. A similar scheme was introduced by Decree-Law 874/76, which also provided for leave to take examinations. That same year, Decree-Law 396/91 was approved, regulating various aspects of work by minors with the aim of preventing school drop-out and promoting vocational training.

Special mention must also be made of schemes for combining training and work, the so-called training contracts. Portuguese labour law essentially recognises two types: apprenticeship contracts and work experience contracts.

From 1992 to 2002, the apprenticeship contract was regulated by Decree-Law 102/84. Apprenticeship is defined as a training process aimed to develop the ability and knowledge required for the performance of a skilled occupation. The main tool for attaining these aims is the apprenticeship contract, defined as an employment contract whereby a qualified company undertakes to assure, in cooperation with other institutions, vocational training for the apprentice, the latter being required to perform tasks inherent to such training. The contract is intended for young people that have completed compulsory schooling, aged between 14 and 24. It must be concluded in writing and includes complicated arrangements for pay, lower than what would be awarded to an ordinary worker in the same job.

The legal arrangements for apprenticeships, which had been introduced in the 1980s and were clearly out of date, were radically reformed in 1996 under the Agreement on Vocational Training Policy of 1991. From that time, these arrangements are understood as forming part of vocational training within the labour market. By boosting the training component in the promotion of employment, this reform helped to extend the levels of employability on the labour market.

The work experience contract was regulated by Decree-Law No 253/84 and has a fairly limited goal: to provide a framework of rules for the organisation of the vocational experiences that correspond to different training courses.

A new system was established in 1997 that provided more protection for student workers. In 2001, support measures were introduced for specific situations of student workers.

3. Integration through work

1996 saw the introduction of a guaranteed minimum income scheme, a measure challenged by some sections of Portuguese society. The measure was aimed at combating poverty and directed mainly at persons excluded from the labour market or employed persons on very low pay. The measure had a twofold goal: to ensure a minimum income and to prepare those receiving the benefit for integration into the labour market. Receipt of this benefit was dependant on participation in an integration programme.

Chapter III:
The right to work and adaptability

Although starting off from a relatively rigid situation, Portuguese labour law nowadays, particularly subsequent to the decade under consideration, is highly flexible and therefore comparable with that of any other European legal system. This is thanks to the reform process that began in the 1980s, although the most significant developments took place between 1992 and 2002. After this series of reforms, flexibility was extended to all aspects of the employment relationship, from its establishment to its termination, including the different aspects of its administration. As we will see, flexibility has been introduced on entry and departure as well as in the internal employment processes and practices. The most obvious outcomes of this flexibility are possible adjustment of working times and content and the introduction of non-standard forms of work.

The Labour Code not yet in force presses ahead with this flexibility, both in terms of the scope and exercise of employers' powers and the increasing prevalence of insecure forms of employment.

1. Internal flexibility

A decisive step towards flexible labour law was taken in 1996 with Law 21/1996. This law comprised two vital measures for facilitating labour management in companies: functional versatility and adaptability of working time.

As regards functional versatility, the reform of 1996 amended Article 22 of Decree-Law No 49 408, the Contract of Employment Law. It contained very traditional rules based on the rationale of worker protection and left little room for employers to adjust their labour force. The worker was required to perform an activity consistent with his/her occupational category. The performance of different activities could be required only under certain fairly strict conditions of *jus variandi*.

Since the reform, Article 22 of the Contract of Employment Law authorises the employer to require the employee to

perform other activities that are functionally related or linked to those corresponding to his/her normal function and for which he/she has the skills and the ability, even where such activities are not included in those laid down for the category. This option is limited, however, as fulfilling the normal task remains the worker's main activity and functional versatility cannot be prejudicial to promotion or lead to any reduction in pay. In addition, functional versatility has to be backed by vocational training and development. In all events, these arrangements are supplementary to those laid down in collective agreements, so long as they are more favourable for the workers and the undertakings.

The Labour Code takes the same approach. Article 147(2) states that the worker's activity under the contract also includes tasks which are functionally related or linked to the activity for which the worker has the appropriate skills and does not involve any downgrading. The Code gives considerable power to employers to change job content unilaterally through a very broad definition of *jus variandi* that enables the employer to increase ordinary executive power, temporarily assigning the worker tasks not included in the activities covered by the contract, provided that such assignment does not result in any substantial change in the worker's position.

Other aspects concerning changes to the content of work and working conditions are still covered by the arrangements under the Contract of Employment Law. Given the time from which it dates, this Contract is based on a very different approach to labour law flexibility.

Where geographical mobility is concerned, Portuguese legislation is relatively restrictive, limiting the employer's powers to change the place of the provision of services agreed in the contract. Under Article 24 of the Contract of Employment Law, the company may transfer the worker to a different workplace only where such a change does not give rise to serious prejudice or if the change results from the complete or partial transfer of the establishment where the work is performed. In that case, the employer is entitled to resign and receive compensation, unless the employer can prove that the transfer is not seriously prejudicial to the worker. If the worker incurs costs as a result of the transfer, they will be charged to the undertaking unless the worker agreed to geographical mobility at the time of recruitment. The Labour Code provides for more flexible arrangements for geographical mobility, eliminating some of the restrictions currently in force.

As for pay, under Article 21 of the Contract of Employment Law the worker's pay may not be reduced with the exception of circumstances expressly laid down by law, administrative provisions on working conditions or collective agreements, or where authorised by the National Labour Institute and with the worker's consent.

The arrangements for altering working time are quite specific and set out in Decree-Law 409/71. Any reduction in the working day may not be harmful to the worker's economic situation, nor result in any change in working conditions that is unfavourable to him/her. Working hours agreed individually with workers may not be altered unilaterally. All changes to the organisation of working time require prior communication and consultation with the legal representatives of the workers in the undertaking. These must be organised at least two weeks in advance and the Labour Inspectorate must be notified. In addition, the working times must be displayed by the undertaking as appropriate.

2. Non-standard forms of employment

Like other systems based on the same legal traditions, which consider the open-ended employment contract a model or prototype and retain strict rules on dismissal, the Portuguese system is attempting to offer a more balanced panoply of non-standard contracts.

Alongside atypical contracts, there are also certain situations where contracts establish special schemes, such as pre-retirement and early retirement, or special arrangements for particular situations such as companies in economic difficulties. These contracts provide for the extensive adjustment of working systems to cope with the different situations of workers and employers.

In addition to the wide range of fixed-term contracts, very long trial periods may now be agreed for open-ended contracts, thus making them fairly flexible.

2.1. Fixed-term contracts

Already in the 1980s, reforms were introduced with a view to greater flexibility in the negotiation of employment contracts. These reforms, in particular Decree-Law 64/89, extended the scope of fixed-term contracts. Two broad groups of reasons justifying fixed-term work were established. The first were related to the employer and the transitional or temporary nature of the activity to be performed. The second were related to the worker and to the need to promote employment in the most problematic sectors of the labour market, such as workers seeking a first job or the long-term unemployed. The need for a just cause for fixed-term work was based on Article 53 of the Portuguese Constitution.

Major reforms in this field were introduced during the period under consideration. Law 38/96 required employers to list in explicit detail the facts and circumstances justifying the conclusion of a fixed-term contract.

Article 11 of the Contract of Employment Law, which is still in force, states that the worker may be recruited on a permanent, seasonal or temporary basis. The various procedures relating to fixed-term contracts are laid down in Decree-Law 64/89.

The fixed-term contract is permitted in limited circumstances:

- Temporary replacement of a worker who is prevented from working, including the replacement of a worker who awaiting the results of a trial on the lawfulness of his/her dismissal

- Temporary or exceptional increase in the company's workload

- Seasonal activities

- Performance of an occasional task or specific service, precisely-defined and not long term

- The launch of an activity of uncertain duration, such as the start of manufacturing in a company or establishment

- Performance, control and supervision of civil building works, public works, industrial assemblies and repairs, including related projects and other complementary control and back-up activities and other similar, fixed-term works, carried out on a contract basis and also administered directly

- Project development, including design, research, control and supervision, not customary in the firm's routine business

- Recruitment of workers that have been long-term unemployed, are seeking a first job or in other situations provided for in the special legislation on employment policy.

Where a fixed-term contract is concluded outside the above limits, the terms of the contract will be considered null and void. A fixed-term contract exceeding the maximum duration laid down by law will also be regarded as an open-ended contract.

The maximum length of the contract will vary from case to case and may be extended where not initially agreed.

There are two types of fixed-term contracts, depending on whether an expiry date is specified. Where an expiry date is specified because of the temporary nature of the work, the duration of the work is known when the contract is concluded. In contracts without a specific expiry date, the employment relationship will last for the period needed to perform the activity concerned. Different rules apply to these contracts, although some provisions are common to both, notably:

- It is compulsory to notify the workers' representatives when workers are recruited under fixed-term contracts

- Fixed-term workers are counted with the rest of the staff for the purposes of determining the social obligations connected with the number of workers in service

- Fixed-term workers are given preference for permanent employment if the company recruits staff from outside

- If preference is not given to the fixed-term worker for permanent employment, the company must pay the worker compensation equivalent to half the basic salary.

In addition to fixed-term contracts where the temporary nature of the need for staff justifies fixed-term recruitment, other fixed-term contracts are concerned with training or justified for employment policy reasons.

During the period under consideration, fixed-term contracts were the main cause of increased instability in employment.

Although in legal terms they are still considered exceptional, in practice they are increasingly used like ordinary contracts and have become a means of evading the strict rules on the termination of open-ended contracts. This trend has been endorsed by a number of important labour market sectors, above all employers, and extended by a number of governments that regard them as a means of combating unemployment.

The Labour Code considerably widens the scope of fixed-term contract terms, increasing employment insecurity in the Portuguese labour market. The duration of fixed-term contracts has been lengthened; although at present fixed-term contracts can be no longer than three years and cannot be renewed more than twice, under the Labour Code they may be renewed three times and the maximum duration will be six years.

2.2. Part-time work

The rules governing the part-time employment contract were also reformed many times from 1992 to 2002. The current rules are set out in Law 103/99, which defines the normal part-time working day as 75% or less than the full-time day in a comparable situation. The Community Directive of 1997 obviously had an impact on this definition, as on many other aspects of the related rules. A principle of proportionality was imposed in respect of remuneration for such workers. The switch from part-time to full-time work and *vice versa* is regulated in detail and must be made voluntarily by the worker. The employer is required to notify part-time workers of full-time vacancies. On the whole, the legal provisions concerning part-time work are fairly detailed, with numerous checks and safeguards for workers.

The approach of Portuguese labour law to part-time employment is similar to that in neighbouring countries. On one hand, it is a very flexible form of atypical work and the rules are designed to balance the interests of workers and employers alike. On the other hand, it is a very important tool for labour market access and job creation and the related rules include measures to enhance these advantages by promoting it and making it attractive for companies. In accordance with the conditions laid down by law, transforming full-time contracts into part-time contracts may give entitlement to reductions in social security contributions and other tax deductions provided that new workers are recruited. Law No 103/99 sets out very detailed rules on support and economic incentives aimed at encouraging the use of part-time work and increasing employment through job-sharing, flexible retirement, etc.

Part-time employment is also used as a way of reconciling working life and family life. Law 4/1984 on the protection of maternity and paternity was reformed in the course of the period in question to adapt it, *inter alia*, to Community rules. The most important reforms resulted from Law 17/95 and Law 142/99 and the implementing rules were set out in Decree-Law 230/2000. Under the current rules, where a worker reduces their working day to take care of a child under 12 years of age, biological or adopted, and the reduction makes the working day part-time (in accordance with the Portuguese labour-law definition of this form of employment), the legislation applicable to calculation of social benefits presumes that the worker has provided services (and paid contributions) full-time during this period. A worker with dependent children under 12 years of age is also entitled to reduced or flexible working hours.

2.3. Telework

Article 1 of Decree-Law 440/91 defines teleworking as working for the purposes of the service performed, without any legal subordination, in the worker's home or where the worker purchases the raw materials and sells them to the seller of the same products as a finished product, provided, in both cases, that a situation of economic dependence exists. Joint work for one and the same employer by up to four workers, without any link of subordination between them, in the home of one of them, is also regarded as telework. In contrast, the law does not apply where the contract concerns the performance of intellectual work.

The teleworker may not be assisted in his/her work, unless the persons concerned are family members. The employer is required to respect the privacy of the worker's home and family leisure and rest times. In contrast, the worker is required to comply with confidentiality rules on techniques and models entrusted to him or her and to adhere to rules on the use and operation of equipment. In the same way, the worker may not use the raw materials and equipment provided by the employer for any purpose other than that intended for the performance of working tasks.

The Labour Code, to be approved in due course, includes special rules on telework.

3. Temporary employment agencies

Portugal belongs to the group of countries that may be regarded as 'intermediate' from the standpoint of legalising tempo-

rary employment agencies. A group of pioneering countries, such as France, the Netherlands and the United Kingdom, introduced such agencies on the labour market before the flexibility and deregulation processes had an impact in the 1960s and 1970s. Other countries, such as Spain, Italy and Sweden, waited until the 1990s to do so in the face of broad resistance to such businesses. Temporary employment agencies were legalised in Portugal in 1989 under Decree-Law 358/89. The legislation concerned is very modern and technically up-to-date. As this law was introduced when the labour law system dealing with flexible forms of employment had not yet reached the decisive, broad acceptance of the 1990s, the rules governing such businesses are relatively rigid and intrusive.

From 1992 to 2002, the legal provisions on temporary employment agencies were amended by Law 39/96 and Law 146/99.

Decree-Law 358/89 defines a temporary employment agency as a natural or legal person whose activities consist in making available temporarily to third parties or users, workers which the latter hires and pays. These agencies may also perform other activities such as selection, vocational guidance and vocational training. They are not required to focus exclusively on temporary work, which is a routine requirement in other EU Member States.

The activities of temporary employment agencies are tightly regulated. To operate as such, a business has to obtain prior approval from the labour authorities subject to the satisfaction of various requirements. These requirements include:

• Suitability

• Technical capacity

• Regular situation vis-à-vis tax and social security authorities

• The lodging of a deposit or security

• Designation as 'temporary employment agency'.

Approved temporary employment agencies are required to register and receive an identifying approval number.

Decree-Law 358/89 limits both the circumstances under which recourse may be had to temporary employment agencies and the maximum duration of assignments. The circumstances in which they may be used include:

• The replacement of a worker who is absent or prevented from working

- Where there are needs resulting from vacant posts and steps are being taken to recruit a worker for that purpose

- Where there is a temporary or exceptional increase in workload of the user undertaking

- For tasks for a precisely-defined length of time

- For seasonal work

- In order to fulfil occasional requirements for labour resulting from fluctuations in the undertaking's workload on certain days or at certain times, provided that the use does not exceed a weekly total equivalent of half the normal working hours in the user undertaking

- Where there are occasional requirements for workers to provide direct family support of a social nature on certain days or at certain times of the day

- Where there are requirements to carry out limited projects of a temporary nature, not including the undertaking's normal activities, such as setting up or reorganising businesses or establishments and industrial assembly and repair.

The maximum duration of assignments varies according to the reason for use of the temporary employment agency. Where a shorter duration is agreed, the agency work contract may be renewed, provided that the relevant reason still exists, up to the limit of the maximum duration allowed. The original contract and the subsequent extensions are regarded as a single contract. Under a temporary agency work contract, a worker may not be assigned a post that was previously filled by another person until expiry of the maximum legal duration. Where the worker continues in the service of the employer for ten days after termination of the temporary agency work contract without having concluded a contract to make it lawful, the worker is considered an employee of the user undertaking under an open-ended contract.

As for the rights of assigned workers, Decree-Law 358/89 recognises the principle of wage comparability, entitling them to receive the minimum pay laid down by law or under the collective agreement applicable to the user undertaking for the category corresponding to the tasks performed. This pay includes a proportional sum for holidays, bonuses and other regular or recurrent allowances. As the employer, the temporary employment agency is required to pay this remuneration. Compensation on termination of contract is also paid in some cases, but only where the employment con-

tract entered into with the temporary employment agency included a clause preventing the worker from employment with the user undertaking.

To supplement the above arrangements, provision has also been made for special rules regulating the responsibility of the temporary employment agency and the user undertaking, keeping the workers' representatives informed, and a detailed system of infringements and penalties.

4. The organisation of working time

During the decade under consideration, most of the rules on working time were set out in an old, basic text, Decree-Law 409 of 27 September 1971. It applied generally to 'work performed under a contract of employment' (Article 1(1)), including within its scope public undertakings and undertakings providing public services, except where their workers were subject to different rules. For example, the Decree-Law expressly stated that its provisions should be adapted for work in ports (Article 1(3)) and in agriculture (Article 2), and do not apply to ship's articles (Article 3) or to domestic service (Article 4). Given the time it dates from, this legislation was relatively rigid; however, it was in line with the 1993 Directive on working time. From 1996 onwards, working time could be adapted extensively. This could not be done previously, mainly because it was not dealt with adequately in collective bargaining. Law 21/96 introduced the maximum working week of 40 hours, which could be calculated as an average over a reference period of up to four months.

The legal provisions on working time were amended by Law 73/98, which transposed Directive 93/104/EC. The maximum working week is 40 hours, with 8 hours per day. Longer reference periods may be laid down, with these limits calculated as an average, if an agreement is reached via collective bargaining. However, there are certain maximum limits in such cases: the working day can only be lengthened by up to 4 hours and the working week may not exceed 60 hours.

However, numerous derogations from these limits are allowed. Under Article 6 of Decree-Law 409/71 they may be exceeded in the following cases: staff carrying out non-profit activities or activities closely connected with the public interest, if it is proven that such activity is completely incompatible with the general limits on the working day; persons whose work is to a large extent intermittent or merely involves being in attendance.

The employer is responsible for establishing the working hours and may amend them unless they were agreed on an individual basis. When establishing the working hours, the employer must adhere to certain specific criteria. They must facilitate the worker's access to technical or vocational training courses and they must take into account the need to protect workers' health and safety and the needs of workers that belong to one and the same family.

Chapter IV:
Equal opportunities at work

In accordance with the Portuguese Constitution, Portuguese labour law lays great emphasis on the different aspects of equality. Article 13(2) of the Constitution states that *no-one shall be privileged or favoured, or discriminated against, or deprived of any right or exempted from any duty, by reason of his/her ancestry, sex, race, language, territory of origin, religion, political or ideological convictions, education, economic situation or social circumstances.* This principle underpins the entire legal system.

In the 1970s, the lawmakers focused in particular on banning discrimination on grounds of sex. Attempts were made to give more substance to the rules in the Constitution and the Committee on Equality at Work and in Employment (CITE) was set up within the Ministry for Social Security and Employment. It was assigned extensive powers to combat gender-based discrimination under Decree-Law No 392 of 20 September 1979. In addition, first steps were taken towards allowing positive discrimination, or in the terms of the abovementioned Decree-Law: *provisions of a fixed-term nature which establish preference on grounds of gender imposed by the need to correct a de facto inequality, and also measures designed to protect maternity as a social value.* Basic concepts were also defined, such as discrimination, remuneration, equal work and work of equal value.

While these and other measures were undoubtedly important, it soon became clear that they were insufficient. However, it is extremely difficult to establish proof in this area and it is not easy to report discrimination, which frequently occurs in a context of dominance.

The above circumstances prompted the lawmakers to attach more importance to the idea of indirect discrimination and the evidence for such discrimination in 1997. They deemed that a 'considerable disproportion' between the percentage of workers of the same sex at the service of an employer and the percentage of workers of that same sex employed in the same branch of activity could constitute evidence of discrimination. What is more, in such cases the burden of proof was reversed and was left to the employer to prove that there were no discriminatory practices, criteria or measures. We can thus confirm compliance with the Council Directives of 1975 and 1976 on equal pay for male and

female workers and equality in access to employment, vocational training and development and working conditions (Directives 75/117/EEC of 10 February 1975 and 76/207/EEC of 9 February 1976, as amended).

Irrespective of legal proceedings taken by the victims of discrimination, the trade unions are entitled to take action to provide proof of any discriminatory practice.

Penalties against discriminatory practices (fines) were increased, reaching between five and ten times the monthly pay of the victim of discrimination. Provision was also made for supplementary penalties, for example, an employer repeating an offence could be legally required to publish the decision on the discriminatory practice in the most widely disseminated newspapers of the country and to display an extract from the decision for 30 days at the workplace.

Directive 96/97/EC, amending Directive 86/378/EC on equal treatment for men and women in supplementary social security schemes, was also incorporated into Portuguese law in 1997.

Portugal's population totals little over 10 million, with more women, who live longer than men. From 1992 to 2001, the female activity rate rose from 41% to 44%. This was a significant increase, bearing in mind that in 1980 it was only 30.6% and is around 57% for men at present. Women also have higher inactivity and unemployment rates than men and account for a greater proportion of part-time work.

In 2001, more effective supervision and harsher penalties were introduced to boost the fight against discriminatory practices. The powers of the General Labour Inspectorate were extended in this respect and more importance was attached to the reports of the Committee on Equality at Work and in Employment. The Government was also required to prepare an annual report for Parliament on progress in equal opportunities for men and women at work, in employment and vocational training.

Portuguese law does not confine itself to combating gender-based discrimination; it also tackles any discrimination that has no rational, objective basis. Generally speaking, no worker or job applicant can be damaged or advantaged by reason of sex, ancestry, age, sexual orientation, genetic heritage, family situation, civil status, reduced capacity for work, chronic illness, political, religious or ideological convictions, trade union membership, nationality or ethnic origin. Portuguese law therefore complies with Directive 2000/43/EC and Directive 2000/78/EC.

The Labour Code also deals with discrimination in employment in a detailed fashion, including protection against sexual harassment.

Chapter V:
Conclusions

Portuguese labour law has undergone a process of change and adjustment for many years, as a result of both the change of regime in the 1970s and the successive economic and employment crises over subsequent years.

During the 1990s, this reform process continued and affected numerous institutions of individual and collective law in Portugal. Legislation was adopted, *inter alia*, on:

- Rights to information on working conditions

- Individual and collective redundancies

- Guarantees for pay claims

- Work by minors

- Work by foreigners

- Temporary posting of workers

- Apprenticeship contracts

- Prevention of risks at work

- Temporary employment agencies

- Working time.

As a result of this process, labour law became fragmented and chaotic, with numerous problems in everyday application. In order to improve the situation, a Commission on Review and Reorganisation of Labour Law was set up. The fruit of its work was a draft Labour Code that received general approval from Parliament and is now at the committee stage.

The numerous changes in Portuguese labour law in the course of the last ten years directly affected the system of labour law sources, as in other European countries. Most of the reforms were one-off, specific measures taken by the lawmakers, introducing legislation on practical aspects of labour law. The general movement towards flexibility did not result in generalised deregulation of the employment relationship. On the contrary,

it was brought about by means of successive legislative measures that increased the number of special rules, making it difficult to determine the legal provisions in force. Also worthy of special mention as regards legislative output during these years is the development of negotiated legislation for many social agreements that were converted into legislation.

Security of employment is guaranteed by Article 53 of the Portuguese Constitution and the individual labour laws reflect this faithfully, entitling the worker unlawfully dismissed to reinstatement. Successive legislative reforms have watered down this principle in various manners, including the facilitation of dismissal on economic and organisational grounds and the extension of the circumstances for temporary hiring by Portuguese companies. The draft Labour Code continues on the same tack.

As regards employability, Portuguese labour law concentrates above all on vocational training, geographical mobility and employment promotion. The latter are organised essentially on the basis of economic assistance with employee recruitment, both through direct payment of funds as well as through exemption from payment of social security contributions.

Various employment procedures have been introduced to facilitate access to employment, the most important including:

- Fixed-term contracts

- Training contracts

- Combined work and training contracts

- Work experience contracts

- Apprenticeship contracts

- Part-time contracts

- Pre-retirement and early retirement

- Contracts in the framework of integration programmes.

After 20 years of legislative reform, Portuguese labour law is highly flexible as regards the different ways of regulating the employment relationship, from its establishment to its termination. Many non-standard forms of employment are permitted, functional versatility and adjustments in working time have been introduced and termination of the employment relationship has been facilitated to a certain extent. These changes have been crucial, particularly if we remember that the starting position was a labour law strongly marked by the corporatist period.

The draft Labour Code continues along the path marked out by these successive reforms, constituting their culmination and consolidation. Its provisions comprise numerous tools for facilitating firms' adaptability to the latest market situation and providing for flexible management of the employment relationship. Accordingly:

- The scope of the work performed by the worker is extended to also include related or functionally related functions. The employer's executive power is also extended as he/she may assign the worker to different posts within the undertaking without this implying any substantial change in working conditions.

- The terms and conditions for workers' geographical mobility are made more flexible.

- Fixed-term employment is facilitated, by extending the duration of fixed-term contracts.

- A wide range of terms and conditions of employment are provided for.

- Special arrangements are introduced for undertakings in crisis.

- The trial period in open-ended contracts is extended.

Annexes:
Reforms to Portuguese labour law during 2003

The most significant development in Portuguese labour law during 2003 was without a doubt the entry into force of the Labour Code, of which the development and meaning were already noted in the Portuguese national report for the period 1992 to 2002. The Code came into force on 1 November 2003, although the effective entry into force of many of the provisions is pending the adoption of implementing legislation, which it is hoped will take place in April 2004. The Portuguese national report will thus be concluded with an analysis of this Labour Code, which defines Portuguese labour law for the start of the 21st century.

1. General aspects of the code

1.1. Structure

The Code is divided into two Books. The first includes a general section, a section on the work contract and a section on collective rights. The second deals with criminal and administrative liabilities. The Code also regulates industrial accidents and occupational diseases, the prevention of workplace risks and vocational training.

1.2. General characteristics

Perhaps the most striking element of the new Code is the attempt to promote adaptability and flexibility in employment relationships. As stated in the Explanatory Memorandum, *the Code recommends that the provision of services by the worker be adapted to the needs of the undertaking.* This is particularly evident in the arrangements for working time, place of work and the definition of the tasks to be performed by the worker. Moreover, elements of a more personal nature, such as the rights of the individual, can also take second place to the needs of the undertaking or the nature of the activity to be carried out.

Furthermore, we can discern a clear shift away from the labour element, making employment relationships subject to civil rather than labour law.

In many areas, the parties are placed on a perfectly equal footing. For example, the regulation on the duty of information, as laid down in Directive 91/533/EEC for employers, is also used as a means to impose other information duties on workers. For the first time, labour law governs the individual rights of the worker and of the employer, as if both parties to the employment relationship were facing the same problems. Civil law concepts such as good faith, abnormal changes to circumstances, *pacta sunt servanda,* etc. are applied to both the employment relationship and collective rights in workplace conflicts and collective bargaining.

1.3. Relationships between the law and collective bargaining: a strategic alteration

Article 4 (1) states that *the regulations of this Code may be superseded by collective bargaining instruments, unless these would have the opposite effect.* This means that, as a rule, the regulations of the Code are voluntary in nature. In other words, they can be superseded by the provisions of an agreement, when the collective ruling is either more favourable or less favourable. The traditional role of collective bargaining, of securing more favourable treatment than that provided for by law, has been replaced.

1.4. Teleworking

An interesting new development relative to both Portuguese labour law and Comparative Law is the express provision made by the Code for teleworking, a new contractual arrangement that is the subject of a complete regulation in Articles 233-244.

2. Individual rights

2.1. The work contract

The concept of the work contract is defined by three well-known elements and has been formulated in such a way that an employee can work for several different employers at the same time, provided that between these there is *a relationship based on equal partnership, ownership or shared group membership* (Article 92). Workers were previously obliged to work for one single employer. One Article is dedicated to the presumption of the existence of a work contract based on a wide-ranging and cumulative set of requirements (Article 12). Essentially, the work contract remains the element that defines the personal scope of the Code, based on the concept of legal subordination.

The system set out in the Code thus applies to workers employed by public legal bodies and who are neither officials nor agents (Article 6 of the Preliminary Law). It should be pointed out that legislation on public employment adopted this year gives priority to the use of the labour market instrument.

The conflict rules on the law applicable to international labour contracts, laid down in the Rome Convention of 1980, which has already been ratified by Portugal, have been expressly transposed in Article 6 of the Code.

Attention should also be given to the following measures geared towards greater adaptability and flexibility of work:

- For 'micro-enterprises' (fewer than 10 workers), special arrangements have been made for disciplinary procedures, the rehiring of unfairly dismissed workers, overtime, fixing of holiday periods, and the termination of contracts following company dissolution

- The scope of *comissão de serviço* ('special relationship' employment arrangements) has been extended

- The concept of work due by the worker has been reformulated

- The probationary period system has been amended

- Incentives have been given for part-time working

- Flexible working time systems are permitted, and the respective reference periods are set

- Night working is defined as that taking place between 22:00 and the 7:00 of the following day, if collective bargaining does not provide otherwise.

2.2. Fixed-term contracts

Portuguese law already includes several instances in which fixed-term work is legal and Article 129 of the Code adds to these instances. It is now possible for a fixed term contract to last as long as six years. Under previous legislation, this period was allowed only in exceptional cases and never by means of successive renewals of a contract. However, this, which was previously exceptional case, now appears to be standard practice (Article 139 (2)). A rather original provision is made whereby the employer's social security contributions (*taxa social única*, single social tax) increases in accordance with the number of workers recruited on fixed-term contracts and in accordance with the duration of their respective contracts (Article 138). This regulation, of which the implementation is subject to special legislation, is intended to make fixed-term contracts more expensive and thus contribute to providing an incentive for open-ended contracts. It must also be stressed that workers' entitlement to vocational training, once they have been recruited for a period longer than six months, is expressly recognised, albeit with numerous restrictions (Article 137).

2.3. Changes to the probationary period

Before the Code came into force, probationary periods lasted 60 or 90 days, depending on whether the company had fewer or more than 20 employees. In addition, the period could last up to 180 days for employees in positions of trust, with extensive responsibilities, or performing complex technical tasks, or even up to 240 days for executives and senior staff. The Code does away with the differences in the duration of probation based on the number of employees in the undertaking. When the probationary period is in excess of 60 days, the employer must give a minimum of seven days notice when terminating the contract (Article 105). This is an important provision, given the long duration of probationary periods that are maintained under the Code.

In case of 'special relationship' employment, the probationary period must be expressly stipulated and cannot exceed 180 days (Article 109).

2.4. Changes to night working

Under the previous law, and in the absence of regulation by collective agreement, night working was defined as work between 20:00 and 7:00. The Code only considers work between 22:00 and 7:00 as night work, unless collective agreements provide otherwise.

2.5. Amendments to the rules governing the transfer of a workplace

Here, a distinction is made between the definitive transfer of the workplace (Article 315) and temporary transfers (Article 316), both of which require prior communication and justification (Article 317). However, the parties are permitted to extend or restrict the possibility of transferring the workplace, meaning that the legal limits in place may not be complied with.

2.6. Changes to the arrangements for functional mobility

The rule that workers must, in principle, perform an activity consistent with their occupational category, laid down in Article 22(1) of the *Ley de Contrato de Trabajo* (Contract of Employment Act), has been replaced by another rule according to which *workers must, in principle, perform tasks consistent with the activity for which they were contracted* (Article 151(1) of the Labour Code). When defining the object of the contract, it needs to be borne in mind that, legally, this includes similar tasks (*funções afins*) and functionally related activities. This was already the case under the previous law, which devoted ample space to functional versatility subject to the limits of the worker's abilities and what he or she could not do. The Code maintains the same requirements but goes further. The employer can, in the interests of the undertaking, oblige the worker to take on tasks that are not included in the activity for which he or she was contracted or in the concept of similar tasks, provided that this does not imply any substantial change to the worker's position (Article 314). The *jus variandi* thus changes from being an exceptional measure to becoming one of the standard powers of management. While previously this was only permitted on the rare occasion of a pressing need in the undertaking, as it went beyond the object of the contract, it is now evolving into a mere contractual vicis-

situde. The Code also permits the parties to extend this power of the employer (Article 314 (2)).

2.7. Working time

There are no major amendments to the regulations regarding working time. The normal maximum working time limits are maintained at eight hours per day and 40 hours per week (Article 163 (1)). Limited flexibility arrangements are permitted, to be established by collective agreements or individual contracts, as are bi-annual or annual reference periods for these flexibility arrangements, in the terms of Directive 93/104/EC.

2.8. Absences

Although the previous system was already somewhat stringent, the fight against absenteeism has become one of the main standards of the new Code. The current regulation does not make any significant changes to the list of justified absences from work (Article 225 (2)). The most significant change lies in the greater power attributed to the employer to check on absences from work, especially sick leave (Article 229).

2.9. Posted workers

Law 90/2000, of 15 June 2000, transposed Directive 96/71/EC of the European Parliament and of the Council of 16 December 1996 concerning the posting of workers in the framework of the provision of services. As is known, the Directive only requires that regulations be laid down on the posting of workers in the host State. The Code not only deals with the situation of posting within Portugal, but also establishes an identical system for the posting of workers to other countries by Portuguese undertakings. The latter aspect constitutes a move away from previously existing arrangements.

2.10. Employment equality

While the structure of this section has changed, no changes have been made to the content of the previous Law. In addition to dealing with equality and non-discrimination on the basis of gender, emphasis is placed on standardising the response to discrimination on any grounds (Articles 22 *et seq.*). For the first time, regulations are laid down on harassment, which is given a broad definition that can be reduced to one of its manifestations, namely sexual harassment (Article 24).

2.11. Changes to the dismissal system

The Code contains important new elements in the area of termination of employment contracts, and special attention can be drawn to the following:

- If the employer is declared legally insolvent, the obligation to comply with the legislation on collective dismissal does not apply to terminations of employment contracts in micro-enterprises (Article 391(3)).

- In cases where dismissal is invalid for reasons of procedure (absence of proceedings, proceedings that are null and void, etc.), there is a possibility of reopening disciplinary proceedings within the period granted to the employer to mount a legal challenge against the ruling on the dismissal (Article 436). This system, unprecedented in previous laws, has given rise to a great deal of controversy in the Portuguese judiciary. The same applies if the contract is terminated on the worker's initiative (Article 445).

- In cases of unfair dismissal, compensation was previously calculated on the basis of one month's salary per year of seniority or part thereof. In the Code, each year of seniority or part thereof corresponds to 15 or 45 days of salary (Article 439 (1)). Within this context the courts can, depending on the level of unfairness or the amount of the salary, fix compensation at a specific level. The system is becoming more confusing and more haphazard.

- For micro-enterprises in general, or where workers employed in administrative or management posts are involved, employers are now permitted to express their opposition to re-hiring the worker, provided that they can demonstrate that this would be prejudicial to the activities of the undertaking (Article 438 (2)). This rule does not apply to dismissals for reasons of politics, ethnicity or religion or where the reasons for opposition to re-hiring were deliberately provoked by the employer (Article 438(4)). Some doubts have been raised concerning the compatibility of this solution with Article 53 of the Constitution, although a (very divided) Constitutional Tribunal found this regulation to be constitutional. If there is opposition to re-hiring, compensation will be calculated by the courts at between 30 and 60 days of salary for each year of seniority or part thereof. This means that, even in cases where dismissal was unjustified or failed to comply with the rules governing dis-

ciplinary procedures, the employer's illicit acts can still prevail if the judge is convinced that that the return of the worker to the undertaking is *highly prejudicial and/or damaging to the continued performance of business activities* (Article (438(2)). The employer will only need to pay a little more.

Regarding non-attendance at work, which is a form of illegal termination of the employment contract by the worker, the period following which abandonment can be presumed has been reduced. Instead of 15 consecutive working days of absence from work, in non-attendance is presumed this code after 15 consecutive working days [*sic*] (Article 450).

2.12. Procedure for drafting employment legislation

In addition to recognising the responsibilities of trade unions employer's associations and workers' commissions, the Labour Code also recognises the contribution of the *Comisión Permanente de Concertación Social* (Standing Commission on Social Concertation) to the drafting of employment legislation.

3. Collective law

One of the Code's structural objectives is to reverse the situation of stagnation in collective bargaining. This is attempted by making multiple allusions to the subjects to be regulated by agreements and restricting the temporal validity of these instruments, as mentioned during parliamentary debates on this subject. All of this is intended to encourage collective bodies to take a more active role in the employment sphere. In order to achieve this, the Code legislators have concentrated on five points:

1. Revitalising collective bargaining

2. Giving new impetus to compulsory arbitration

3. Restricting the use of the regulation of minimum conditions (instruments substituting for the PRT), and reinforcing the requirements for the production of minimum conditions

4. Enshrining the principle that the general protection of workers cannot be reduced by the mere succession of collective agreements

5. Reiterating the principle of civil responsibility with regard to the signatories and affiliates, in case of failure to comply with the agreement.

It is at the very least debatable that the proposed objectives will be achieved using the measures adopted, particularly as concerns the invalidation of agreements in force as provided for in accordance with Article 557(4) of the Labour Code, and the promotion of compulsory arbitration, as provided for in Articles 567 et seq. In fact, one could even view these measures as potentially counter-productive.

As far as the validity of collective agreements is concerned, the law previously stipulated that the agreements would be in force for the period that had been expressly agreed, and added that they would remain in force until the agreement was replaced by another. This general system applied both to the legislative and to the contractual elements. Now, in the system set out in the Code in force, once the period of validity fixed in the agreement has lapsed, Article 557 provides for a supplementary 'grace period'. This period varies, depending mainly on whether the agreement has been denounced, and on whether the collective bodies are bargaining to replace the agreement in force. If the parties do not reach an agreement within this period, or do not call for conciliation or arbitration (which can take up to two and half years), the agreement becomes invalid. Therefore, and in contrast to what happened under previous arrangements, a collective agreement in force can lapse without another taking its place, thus creating a regulatory vacuum. Anyone standing to gain from this regulatory vacuum might be tempted to let the collective agreement lapse in order to then negotiate from scratch, thus freed from the restrictions of the rules on successive agreements.

More generally speaking, the absence of criteria determining representativeness has major consequences in the area of collective bargaining. Any trade union or employers' association, however reduced their scope, may negotiate and sign collective agreements. Under a system of trade union pluralism it is therefore possible, for example, for an employer's organisation to refuse to negotiate with a representative trade union organisation and instead negotiate with one that is hardly representative or not representative at all.

Although compulsory arbitration was already provided for under the previous law, it never worked because the essential list of arbitrators was never compiled. Article 570 of the Code provides for a meticulous and 'infallible' process of constituting lists of arbitrators (lists of arbitrators, presidents and lists of party arbitrators). For the rest, the Code, which

supports compulsory arbitration, makes some changes to the existing system, but essentially the system remains exactly the same. The eligibility requirements, now contained in Article 567, do not change. These lay down the criteria to be respected by the responsible Ministry when defining the compulsory arbitration requested by the parties. However, these criteria are extremely vague and imprecise. This presupposes, as far as strikes in State-administered services or in State-owned undertakings are concerned, that if no agreement on minimum services has been reached on the third day following the notice of strike action, these arrangements will be defined by a college of three arbitrators (599 (4)).

Under the previous system, the conciliation provided for by the law took place in the services of the labour administration, on the request of one or both parties. From 1993 onwards, the law allowed the labour administration to promote conciliation from the outset, meaning that it was no longer on the exclusive initiative of one of the parties. The Labour Code reinforces this by obliging both parties to be present at attempts at conciliation, with failure to do so constituting serious misconduct.

Conversely, the regulations on minimum conditions, laid down in previous laws as a means to counteract bad faith in collective bargaining processes, have disappeared.

Regarding strikes, three significant amendments are made:

1. For strikes in essential community services, the notice of strike action must contain a proposed definition of minimum services and, in general, a proposed definition of the required services in terms of safety and the maintenance of equipment and installations (Article 595(3)).

2. For strikes called in the public employment sector that place essential services in danger, if there is no regulation by a collective instrument or through agreement with workers' representatives, minimum services and the arrangements for these may be defined by a college of arbitrators (Articles 599(4) and (5)).

3. Provision is made for the possibility of collective bargaining reaching an agreement on labour relations in this respect provided that this is made clear in the text of the agreement and that it does not restrict the possibility of calling strikes for other purposes than to amend the content of the agreement.

THE EVOLUTION OF LABOUR LAW IN THE UNITED KINGDOM

1992-2002

Final report 4 June 2003

Professor Alan C. Neal
Employment Law Research Unit
University of Warwick
United Kingdom

Table of contents

Executive summary

This report traces the development of labour law in the United Kingdom during the period 1992-2002 (with an Annex note on further developments during 2003). It draws upon a wide range of material, and includes statistical data derived from both official and non-governmental sources. The framework for presentation reflects agreement in the Group of Experts upon key themes and issues.

CHAPTER I sets the historical background to industrial relations and labour law in the United Kingdom, and highlights dramatic changes which have taken place since the time of the Donovan Report in 1968. The increasing influence of legislation ('hard law') is identified as a consistent trend from the mid-1960s onwards, and a continuing diminution of the role for 'voluntary industrial relations' as the regulatory framework for labour market relationships is noted. This shift of emphasis is observed under both Conservative and Labour governments, and has been continued throughout the post-1997 administrations of Prime Minister Blair.

The make-up of the modern United Kingdom labour market is presented, with particular note being taken of problem issues such as the decline of manufacturing and large-scale manual employment, an apparent 'north-south divide' in terms of economic performance, and the emergence of a 'two-speed labour market'. Data drawn from official sources is used to furnish details of the changing composition of the work force in the decade from 1992.

After describing the labour market and industrial relations actors, there is a consideration of trends in collective bargaining. Drawing upon material from the most recent *Workplace Employee Relations Survey*, it is indicated that (notwithstanding dwindling levels of trade union membership) enterprise bargaining between an employer and one or more trade unions remains the dominant feature of the British scene. Data is provided in relation both to the private and the public sectors.

Consideration of the regulatory techniques adopted in the United Kingdom leads to the conclusion that the historical model of 'collective laissez-faire', based upon 'free collective bargaining', has given way to the technique of normative legislation emanating from parliamentary processes. The role

of collective bargaining has steadily diminished, as has the coverage of collective bargaining – increasingly located at the company level. This is so despite the introduction in 1999 of a mechanism to provide for statutory recognition of trade unions. The introduction through labour law statutes of wide-ranging provisions setting down individual rights of workers (normally enforced through the system of Employment Tribunals) has eclipsed the central role of collective bargaining which had continued prior to that change of policy. It is also observed that the concept of 'social dialogue' and 'social concertation' for the United Kingdom context is extremely difficult to expound with any conviction, albeit that a number of instances of 'co-operative' or 'partnership' activities may be pointed to.

Alongside 'hard law' regulation are also to be found a variety of 'soft law' regulatory techniques, and the positive role and influence of ACAS is noted in this context. However, it is observed that legal *fora* for dispute resolution have acquired a major role for modern United Kingdom industrial relations. Furthermore, recent attempts to introduce variants of 'alternative dispute resolution' (ADR) into the United Kingdom institutional framework have not, so far, proved particularly encouraging.

The coverage of modern statutory employment protections is addressed and significant problems are highlighted in this context. Recent government concern with the existing conceptual and definitional framework is identified, culminating in a formal consultation process being launched on the issue. Nevertheless, some recent trends towards extended protection to particular groups are noted, although there is also evidence of statutory qualification thresholds being utilised as a deliberate device to limit access to labour law rights.

Note is taken of the operation of labour law in the United Kingdom since the introduction of a Human Rights Act 1998, which reinforced the significance of the 1950 European Convention on Human Rights as a reference point for fundamental social rights. Particular mention is made of issues relating to 'privacy', including recent initiatives in relation to freedom of information, data protection, and the right to respect for family and private life.

CHAPTER II considers some of the traditional approaches to 'job security' in the United Kingdom, and looks at how those approaches have been modified in the context of the European employment policy objective of 'employability'. Particular attention is paid to United Kingdom rules relating to dismissal, and note is taken of the increasing modern influence of measures agreed at the level of the European Union in the context of social policy regulation. While noting the influence of international standards (notably, those of the ILO) in this field, and the importance of a post-1972 statutory framework of 'unfair dismissal' to supplement inadequate Common Law protection, a trend is perceived to provide enhanced dismissal protection for particular designated groups within the workforce (especially where those groups are the object of EU level measures). There is also a trend towards setting labour law protections within frameworks designed to address problems of discrimination, equal opportunities, and ensuring 'fundamental rights'.

Amongst the measures designed to promote 'employability', note is taken of policies providing facilities to encourage self-employment, while a significant need is also identified to upgrade United Kingdom workforce skills. The pattern of post-school training opportunities is presented, and a wide range of targeted initiatives taken by post-1997 Labour governments are outlined. 'New Deal' arrangements for young persons and for long-term unemployed adults are presented, and successful outcomes in reducing youth unemployment are highlighted.

Mention is made of the introduction (for the first time) in 1998 of a national minimum wage, as well as the work of the Low Pay Commission, established at the same time. A general impression is reported that positive effects have been forthcoming in the first years of the national minimum wage, including some impact upon the gender pay gap at the bottom of the earnings distribution.

Broader problems of potential social exclusion in the United Kingdom are then addressed by reference to low pay (particularly as regards the impact of the national minimum wage), exclusion related to ethnicity (where a long-standing statutory anti-discrimination framework has been in operation), and exclusion related to disability. In this latter regard, positive experience is reported since the introduction of a Disability Discrimination Act in 1995.

CHAPTER III considers labour law trends in the context of the European employment policy goal of 'adaptability'. It is observed that the responsiveness of United Kingdom labour law to changing patterns of work and issues of adaptability, as technological progress and globalisation have increasingly impacted upon the world of work, has been sluggish. It is suggested that a number of fairly rigid conceptual paradigms (including the issue of 'employee status') remain, while reliance upon strict common law contractual analysis for the contract of employment produces some surprising outcomes. In particular, it is suggested that it has only been with the introduction of measures stimulated by social policy initiatives at the European Union level that any degree of comfort can be detected in United Kingdom labour law's treatment of part-time, fixed-term, temporary, and certain other 'atypical' workers. Indeed, in the United Kingdom context, it is noted that the expression 'atypical' was, even quite recently, commonly used to refer narrowly to work performed by part-time workers, temporary workers, fixed-term workers, and (in so far as they were not already covered by one of the other categories) seasonal workers. It is also noted that the expression 'flexible' lacks any clear definitional basis in United Kingdom labour law, although the term appears to extend rather wider than the earlier expression 'atypical'. One interesting development is noted in the context of European Union social policy initiatives, with the former statutory notion of 'fixed-term contracts' being replaced by a new phenomenon of the 'limited-term contract'. However, difficulties remain in relation to contingent workers, agency workers, and a variety of other work forms.

CHAPTER IV, which touches upon labour law developments in the context of equal opportunities, re-emphasises some of the changing characteristics of the United Kingdom labour market (notably, female activity rates), and draws links to problems in relation to issues of 'employability'. It is pointed out that experience of anti-discrimination and equal opportunities legislation is quite long-standing, with statutory provisions having been in operation in relation to sex and race discrimination for 30 years, while measures in relation to disabled workers have been in force since 1995. In addition, protection has developed in relation to particular groups such as transsexuals. The role of public 'equal opportunities' bodies is emphasised, and the existing arrangements to deal with anti-discrimination and equal opportunities in the labour market are set in the context of implementation for the first two 'Article 13 Directives' adopted in 2000.

In the final CHAPTER V, it is concluded that throughout the decade under consideration, as the shape of the labour force shifted ever further away from the 'traditional' industrial pattern which had formed the backdrop to the report of the Donovan Commission in 1968, the regulatory tools of labour law have struggled to keep up with more diverse work-forms and practices. At the same time, the inability of the traditional actors in an outmoded model of 'free collective bargaining' to define new roles and relationships cleared the stage for the almost unchallenged dominance of the statutory norm as the 'natural' modern regulatory tool.

It is suggested that nothing indicates any kind of return to 'the golden era' of industrial relations, and that the question of whether 'partnership' offers the way forward for trade unionism in the United Kingdom remains open to debate. The impact of the regulatory mechanisms associated with European employment policy is identified as becoming ever more evident, while there appears to be enthusiasm for 'soft law' alternatives to the statutory norm (possibly including benchmarking and other features of the so-called 'open method of co-ordination').

One particular challenge for the United Kingdom collective labour relations actors is identified as being the process of implementation for instruments such as Directive 2002/14/EC on informing and consulting workers. However, it is suggested that the United Kingdom's system of Common Law has shown itself surprisingly flexible in the course of 'receiving' European Union law into the domestic framework and procedures. The prospects are thus not considered to give major cause for concern. This is assisted by the perceived strong desire on the parts of both Conservative and Labour governments to ensure compliance with their European Union obligations, once a directive in the social field has been adopted and falls to be transposed into domestic law. Nevertheless, there has been relatively little success in establishing a wholehearted engagement for the 'social partners', and it is suggested that there is no realistic prospect of the 'social dialogue' route to domestic legislation gaining a significant foothold in the United Kingdom for the foreseeable future.

Although the traditional post-war 'welfare state' model may be scarcely recognisable, and a variety of tensions are evident in United Kingdom society at large, opinions are divided as to whether the current era of rapid change is to be feared, or whether there may have emerged an underlying strength and durability to the foundations of working life in the United Kingdom, such as to offer a more optimistic perspective from which to observe the continuing adaptation which is taking place. In particular, it may be that the apparatus associated with European employment policy may prove to be of bene-fit to a national system in search of new tools and new tech-niques for regulating its variegated labour relationships.

However that may be, it is concluded that labour law in the United Kingdom currently stands ill-equipped to respond effectively to the swiftly-changing phenomena emerging in a labour market which has changed out of all recognition in the course of a quarter of a century. Notably, despite a proven ability to assimilate the value-systems inherent in the regulatory structure and mechanisms of the European Union, it is suggested that the foundations of United King-dom labour law at the beginning of the 21st Century remain constrained by traditional Common Law concepts, such that it struggles to deliver the necessary sensitivity to the indus-trial relations subject-matter with which it is so intimately involved. More problematic still, there appears, to date, to have been little or no sign of the necessary 'freshness of thinking' which would be required to free labour law in the United Kingdom from the shackles of its own history.

Chapter I:
Introduction

1. Labour law in the United Kingdom[1]

An important starting point for any consideration of the industrial relations structures in the United Kingdom and the system of labour law relating to them is the hugely influential report of the *Royal Commission on Trade Unions and Employers' Associations,* (The 'Donovan Report') which was published in 1968.[2] That analysis has imposed an orthodoxy upon later commentators which persists even until today – particularly in relation to legal analyses of labour market and industrial relations trends in the United Kingdom.

However, a variety of developments in the years since 1968 have made it necessary, from time to time, to question some of the 'received fundamental truths' which underpinned the analysis of the Donovan Commission, some thirty-five years ago. In particular, the changing face of the workforce, with ever-increasing numbers of 'flexible' work forms and practices, coupled with a dramatic shift of paradigm from 'autonomous employment relations regulation' in the direction of 'normative intervention' by the legislator, makes it increasingly difficult to embark upon any consideration of trends in the United Kingdom without re-visiting many of the 'traditional' ways of portraying that national system, its institutions, and its practices.[3]

In what follows, a presentation is made of the changing face of the United Kingdom labour market and its associated industrial relationships, followed by consideration of the approaches and techniques adopted by labour law in a Common Law context, faced with the key challenges of 'employability', 'entrepreneurship', 'adaptability' and 'equal opportunities'.[4]

2. Historical background

The historical development of labour law in the United Kingdom up until 1992 is well known.[5] From the early statutes in 1871 and 1875 which provided for the abolition of criminality for trade unions,[6] through the period up until the mid-1960s when trade union freedoms became enshrined in a form of liberty known as the 'Golden Formula immunities',[7] the history of industrial conflict and the regulation of collective labour relations was moulded into its modern form.

In 1963, the beginning of a new era was set under way with the introduction of what proved to be the first in a long line

---

1   This report offers a brief picture of the labour law context for the United Kingdom at the beginning of the year 2003. It draws upon a wide range of material (both directly, and at second-hand – the most significant of which are set out in the selected bibliography contained in Annex I), and includes a selection of statistical data derived from both official and non-governmental sources. Some of the most important material providing data in relation to this report is drawn from regular workplace employment relations surveys ('WERS', formerly 'WIRS'), of which the most recent data was compiled in 1998. Regular reference is made, in particular, to the findings of the 1998 survey ('WERS98'), as well as to work by academic commentators which is based upon those 1998 findings. See M. Cully, S. Woodland, S. O'Reilly & G. Dix, *Britain at Work: As depicted by the 1998 Workplace Employee Relations Survey,* London 1999. Analysis of the data for earlier surveys can be found in W. Daniel & N. Millward, *Workplace Industrial Relations: The DE/PSI/ESRC Survey,* London 1980, N. Millward & M. Stevens, *British Workplace Industrial Relations 1980-1984: The DE/ESRC/PSI/ACAS Surveys,* Aldershot 1986, N. Millward, M. Stevens, D. Smart & W. Hawes, *Workplace Industrial Relations in Transition: The ED/ESRC/PSI/ACAS Surveys,* Aldershot 1992 and N. Millward, A. Bryson & J. Forth, *All Change at Work? – British employment relations 1980-1998, as portrayed by the Workplace Industrial Relations Survey series,* London 2000.

2   Royal Commission on Trade Unions and Employers' Associations (Chairman, Lord Donovan), Cmnd.3623, London 1968.

3   For the extent to which the process of change has been progressing, see inter alia the contributions to R. Crompton, D. Gallie & K. Purcell (eds), *Changing forms of Employment: Organisations, Skills and Gender,* London 1996.

4   See the four underlying 'pillars' for the European Union's employment strategy in the post-Amsterdam Treaty era of the 'Luxembourg Process'. The bases for this process can be gleaned from the contributions in M. Biagi (ed), *Job Creation and Labour Law: From Protection towards Pro-action,* The Hague 2000.

5   The leading text on labour law in the United Kingdom is currently S. Deakin & G. Morris, *Labour Law* (3rd edition), London 2001. For consideration of the socio-political picture at the beginning of the 1990s, see P. Davies & M. Freedland, *Labour Legislation and Public Policy,* Oxford 1993.

6   The Trade Union Act 1871 and the Conspiracy and Protection of Property Act 1875.

7   The expression coined by Wedderburn to describe the formulation originally used by the legislator in the Trade Disputes Act 1906 to express the scope of the statutory protection being provided there. See K.W. Wedderburn, *The Worker and the Law* (2nd edition), 1971, at p. 327.

of individual statutory employment protections – in this case, in the form of the Contracts of Employment Act 1963. Quickly followed by the Redundancy Payments Act 1965, this emerging basis for individual employment protection through statutory labour law was then subjected to a significant shock in 1972, when the revolutionary Industrial Relations Act 1971 came into force amid great political controversy. That new framework launched collective labour relations into a violent and unstable interim phase, which was to last until 1974.

However, in relation to individual labour law, the advent of the regime introduced by the Industrial Relations Act 1971 – and particularly the introduction of a statutory protection against 'unfair dismissal' – was to constitute a watershed. Certainly, by 1974, the presence and hugely influential role of legislation ('hard law') had been confirmed at the expense of traditional 'legal abstentionism'.

When a Labour government returned to power in 1974 under arrangements known as the 'social contract' with the trade union movement, the promises included in that 'contract' involved not only the continuation of the statutory mechanisms for providing individual employment protections (particularly through a new Employment Protection Act 1975), but also a context for the first important debate concerning institutional 'workers participation' (eventually to be explored in the 1977 'Bullock Report').[8]

The relative stability of the re-formulated regime for the regulation of employment relations in law characterised the period of Labour administration between 1974 and 1979. However, yet another 'shock' was then to be suffered, with the advent of a Conservative government in 1979 under the premiership of Mrs Margaret Thatcher. That administration, committed to principles of 'the market', took a radically different view of the employment relationship both at the collective and at the individual levels, and saw the mechanism of statutory regulation as the way in which to implement policies designed to 'redress the balance of power' between labour and capital in the United Kingdom. As has been observed by the authors of the 1998 WERS report:

The election of the Conservative government in 1979 signalled the beginning of a period of policy reform that was to change the face of the British labour market. The overriding concern was to promote the free play of market forces. By restricting the activities of trade unions and weakening some parts of the framework of statutory employment protection, successive Conservative governments aimed to bolster employers' 'right to manage' and increase the degree of flexibility in the labour market, in the expectation that this would increase the competitiveness of British business and promote employment growth. The public sector was transformed by a wave of privatisations, the contracting-out of many services from local and central government and the movement of many functions from core departments to agencies.[9]

That period of reform, as is often emphasised,[10] itself took place as part of a programme of social policy intended to promote 'self-reliance, entrepreneurship and 'acquisitive individualism'.

A succession of statutory provisions between 1979 and 1989 ensured that the role of 'voluntary industrial relations' as the regulatory framework for labour relationships was continuously being pushed to the background, while the role for labour law in its 'hardest' form of statutory provisions was moving inexorably into the ascendancy. This continued through the successor administration under Prime Minister John Major, until a change of government in 1997, and the return for the first time for nearly two decades of a Labour government under the leadership of Prime Minister Tony Blair.

Since the return to office of a Labour government, a variety of initiatives have been undertaken on the trade unions' part, with a view to reawakening a framework for what is often described as 'partnership' in the United Kingdom context.[11] Many claims have already been made for this 'new approach', although it is probably far too early to judge whether, as one leading commentator (writing of developments during 1999) has suggested could be the case, there is solid evidence of:

... a cautious growth of confidence in trade unions, and of a pragmatic increase in the willingness of employers to develop new relationships with them. A common feature of these relationships was

---

8   Report of the Committee of Inquiry on Industrial Democracy (Chairman, Lord Bullock), Cmnd.6706 (London 1977).

9   M. Cully, S. Woodland, A. O'Reilly & G. Dix, *Britain at Work: As depicted by the 1998 Workplace Employee Relations Survey*, London 1999, at 219.

10   See, inter alia, H. Phelps Brown, 'The Counter-Revolution of Our Time', 1990, 29 *Industrial Relations 1*. For a critique of the discourse of United Kingdom governments during this period, set against the discourse of the 'Luxembourg Process' employment policy of the European Union, see Alan C. Neal, 'From "Bad Boy" to European Role Model? The Strange Legacy of United Kingdom Employment Policies Since the Single European Act', in M. Biagi (ed), *Job Creation and labour law: From protection towards Pro-action*, The Hague 2000, 269.

11   See, for some of the earlier examples of this, the 1997 TUC publications *Partners for Progress: Next Steps in the New Unionism* and *Partners for Progress: New Unionism at the Workplace*. As described by Brown, *Six underlying principles of partnership were spelled out. First there should be a shared commitment to the business goals of the organization. Second, there should be a clear recognition that there might be quite legitimate differences of interest and priorities between the partners, differences that needed to be listened to, respected and represented. Third, measures to ensure flexibility of employment must not be at the expense of employees' security, which should be protected by taking such steps as ensuring the transferability of skills and qualifications. Fourth, partnership arrangements must improve opportunities for the personal development of employees. Fifth, they must be based upon open and well informed consultation, involving genuine dialogue. Sixth and finally, effective partnerships should seek to 'add value' by raising the level of employee motivation.* (William Brown, 'Putting Partnership into Practice in Britain', 2000, 38 *British Journal of Industrial Relations 299*, at p. 305. See also J. Knell, 'Partnership at Work', *Employment Relations Research Series No.7*, DTI, London).

the emphasis placed by trade unions on adopting a co-operative rather than confrontational stance. At the national level, the Trades Union Congress (TUC) and Confederation of British Industry (CBI) were involved in employment policy to an extent unknown for twenty years. Social partnership appeared to be taking root.[12]

Nevertheless, this approach is in line with the declaration of the relevant Minister, when introducing the White Paper 'Fairness at Work' in 1998:[13]

The White Paper looks to the future, not the past. There will be no going back to the days of strikes without ballots, mass picketing and the closed shop. We are setting out to foster and support a new culture in the workplace – a culture of partnership. That culture is already evident in many of our most successful and modern companies, but the framework of our existing law all too often undermines or runs clean counter to it.

It should be noted, furthermore, that, at the national policy-making level, relations between the CBI and the TUC have moved on significantly since what became referred to as the era of 'beer and sandwiches' was so widely criticised by employer organisations at times of Labour Party government. In particular, recent consultation activities, in respect of implementation of EU level measures on information and consultation at the level of the workplace,[14] have seen substantial impetus to discussion and the formulation of some degree of 'common positions' – albeit leaving important areas of dispute between 'the two sides of industry'.[15]

3.   The changing face of the British labour market

Setting out some of the key changes leading up to the situation reported by the 1998 WERS, the authors observed that,

The growth in female employment has been one of the most obvious developments, with the proportion of female employees rising from 42% to 47% over the course of our survey series. Women also moved into occupations and positions of authority where their presence had previously been uncommon. At the same time, the extent of labour market participation among young people declined, particularly during the 1990s, as the expansion of further and higher education persuaded many to delay their entry into paid work… These changes have been accompanied by a significant shift towards non-standard forms of employment. Self-employment rose rapidly during the 1980s. Accounting for 7% of all workers in 1980, the proportion stood at 12% in 1998. However, the more significant developments at workplace level concern the increased use of part-time and temporary workers. The proportion of all employees working part-time (defined as 30 hours or less per week) rose from 21% in 1981 to 25% in 1998. The proportion in temporary jobs, which stood at 4% in 1984, had doubled by the time of our fourth survey in 1998.[16]

It is also important to bear in mind that, in the 18 years following the election of Prime Minister Margaret Thatcher in 1979,

*… much of the British economy was being opened up to the forces of international competition. Inflation came down, initially at the expense of higher unemployment. But by 1998, both of these crucial measures of labour market performance were low, compared with their levels in 1980. The economic downturns of the early 1980s and early 1990s hastened incipient shifts in the composition of the economy, notably the decline of manufacturing and large-scale manual employment.[17]

A further feature of the United Kingdom experience – which has been highlighted particularly by the TUC – is the so-called 'north-south divide', and what has been described as a 'two-speed labour market'. Thus, it has been suggested that, for the period December 1998 to December 2001:

… manufacturing jobs were consistently in decline (the current cycle of manufacturing employment decline began in Spring 1998)… The extent of the two-speed labour market over the past three years is self-evident from the data… The service sector continued to forge ahead and generated 1.3 million additional jobs in this period, a proportional increase of 7%. Service sec-

---

12   William Brown, 'Putting Partnership into Practice in Britain', 2000, *38 British Journal of Industrial Relations 299*, at p. 315.

13   The President of the Board of Trade and Secretary of State for Trade and Industry (Mrs. Margaret Beckett), Hansard, 28 May 1998, Col. 1101.

14   In the context, especially, of Directive 2002/14/EC.

15   Thus, a fair measure of agreement between the CBI and the TUC has served to set the agenda for the subsequent consultation process undertaken by the Department of Trade and Industry. This marks an interesting step on from the situation at the time of implementation for the Works Councils provisions in Directive 94/45/EC (extended to the United Kingdom by Directive 97/74/EC), which led to the Transnational Information and Consultation of Employees Regulations 1999 (SI 1999/3323).

16   N. Millward, A. Bryson & J. Forth, 'All Change at Work? British employment relations 1980-1998', as portrayed by the *Workplace Industrial Relations Survey* series, London 2000, at 14.

17   N. Millward, A. Bryson & J. Forth, 'All Change at Work? British employment relations 1980-1998', as portrayed by the *Workplace Industrial Relations Survey* series, London 2000, at 224-5. According to the ILO's Bureau for Workers' Activities (ACTRAV), *Developed countries have lost jobs in manufacturing since 1970. In 1970, manufacturing employed 69.7 million people in the ten major developed economies. In 1992, the last year when data on all ten countries is available, only 63.7 million had their employment in this sector. The biggest decrease was in the United Kingdom, from 8.5 million in 1970 to 4.9 million in 1992. ILO, Labour Market Trends and Globalization's Impact on Them, Geneva.*

tor jobs now account for 79% of all employee jobs compared to 77% three years ago. ... At the same time around 400,000 manufacturing jobs were lost, accounting for a 10% reduction in the sector's employee workforce. The sector now accounts for 14% of all employee jobs compared to 17% three years ago. While other sectors (e.g. construction, energy and agriculture) generated a relatively insignificant number of new jobs at the national level, in some regions the construction industry has been a vital source of employment growth in this period.[18]

4. Current characteristics of the British labour market[19]

According to United Kingdom official statistics for the first quarter of 2003, the working age employment rate was 74.6% in the three months to March 2003, unchanged from the three months to December 2002 but there was a rise of 0.3 percentage points from a year earlier. The employment level was 27.86 million in the three months to March 2003, up 47 000 from the three months to December 2002 and up 283 000 on a year earlier.

The number of men in full-time employment was 13.48 million in the three months to March 2003, down 29 000 from the three months to December 2002. The number of women in full-time employment was 7.21 million in the three months to March 2003, down 5 000 from the three months to December 2002.

The number of people in part-time employment was 7.17 million in the three months to March 2003, up 80 000 from the three months to December 2002. Of this total, 1.52 million were men and 5.65 million were women.

Workforce jobs were up 47 000 over the quarter to 29.56 million in December 2002 and up 44 000 on a year earlier.

Over the year to December, production industry workforce jobs were down 161 000, service sector jobs up 254 000 and other industries down 48 000. Employee jobs were up 25 000 over the quarter to 25.83 million in December 2002.

The unemployment rate was 5.1% in the three months to March 2003, unchanged from both the three months to December 2002, and from a year earlier. The unemployment level was 1.50 million in the three months to March 2003, down 6 000 from the three months to December 2002 but up 11 000 on a year earlier.

The number of unemployed men was 909 000 in the three months to March 2003, up 24 000 from the three months to December 2002. The number of unemployed women was 592 000 in the three months to March 2003, down 29 000 from the three months to December 2002. Unemployment for 18 to 24 year olds was 405 000 in the three months to March 2003, up 21 000 from the three months to December 2002. Unemployment over 12 months was 324 000 in the three months to March 2003, up 16 000 from the three months to December 2002.

5. The actors on the United Kingdom labour law stage

The pattern of involvement for the social actors in the British context focuses upon the 'top organisations' of the TUC and the CBI, together with a variety of sectoral representational organisations on the employers' side, along with chambers of commerce, lined up against the increasingly dwindling number of trade unions to be found in the United Kingdom.

The main umbrella organisation on the employer side is the CBI (the Confederation of British Industry),[20] and within that

---

18   See TUC, *Half the World Away: Making Regional Development Work*, July 2002. The report goes on to note that ... *The national average for employee jobs growth conceals a very mixed labour market performance across the regions. The contrasting fortunes of the jobs market in the two main sectors (services and manufacturing) resulted in a clear regional bias with those regions with the greatest dependency on manufacturing suffering most. While the national proportional increase in total employee jobs in the period stood at 4%, regional variations fall within a range of 0% to 8%... Virtually zero jobs growth was recorded for three regions (the North East, the East Midlands and the West Midlands) while London recorded the best overall jobs performance, at 8%. Also, the three regions recording above average jobs growth (i.e. 5% or more) were located in southern England, showing how the two-speed labour market has exacerbated the north-south divide... The three regions with negligible jobs growth in this period all suffered large declines in manufacturing employment, with the greatest toll being felt on the manufacturing heartlands in the Midlands. Both the Midland regions recorded a decline of 14% in manufacturing employee jobs and nearly 140 000 jobs in total have been lost in the Midlands in the past three years. ... However, the regional labour market data for this period tells a much more complex story than simply that of a two-speed jobs market and unambiguous north-south divide. The interplay between employee job trends in manufacturing, services and 'other sectors' often either reinforced the decline in manufacturing jobs or went some way to compensating for it. For example, the North East recorded the largest proportional decline in jobs in 'other sectors' (-16%) as well as suffering heavy manufacturing losses and only service sector jobs growth prevented negative employment growth. On the other hand, robust growth in jobs in 'other sectors' in the North West went some way to compensating for manufacturing decline, as did an increase in service sector employment growth.* (See pp. 11-13).

19   Taken from Labour Market Statistics (part of National Statistics, published by the United Kingdom government's Office for National Statistics).

20   According to a 1999 survey undertaken for the European Commission (looking at representativeness of the social partners), the density of adhesion to employers' organisations in the United Kingdom revealed a level of 38% for the Confederation of British Industry (CBI). The Annual Report of the Certification Officer for 2001-02, reporting on returns made in respect of the period 2000-2001, reveals a total membership in employers' associations of 272 930, compared with membership of 269 230 in 1999-2000. See pp. 71-73, Appendix 6.

organisation (which is not itself a bargaining body) one of the highest profile organisation members is the Engineering Employers' Federation (EEF). Chambers of commerce have traditionally played a liaising and trade representation role within the United Kingdom pattern, but, as with the CBI itself, have not been involved in collective bargaining.

It is still the case that enterprise bargaining between an employer and one or more trade unions is the dominant feature of the British scene. On the trade union side, the umbrella organisation is the TUC (Trades Union Congress), which acts as a political lobby level and co-ordination vehicle for its affiliate member unions. The traditionally dominant unions representing manual workers in coal, steel, transport and engineering have seen their membership dramatically decline in the last quarter of the century, as heavy manual industry has given way to service activities and light industry.

Both public and private sector workers are represented in trade unions, although there is a marked difference between the density of unionisation in the two sectors, with public sector numbers now being maintained at higher levels than in the private sector.

An indication of union membership and density over the decade up until 2001 can be seen in Table 1. Using survey data from the WIRS/WERS series, *Machin* has observed that:

Aggregate union density shows a remarkable stability in the post-war period (at around 40-45% membership), followed by a sharp rise in the 1970s, but then an even sharper fall from the late 1970s onwards. After 1979 aggregate union density has trended downwards so that, by the end of the 1990s, less than 30% of the workforce were members of trade unions.[21]

Following the WERS98 survey data, he concludes that:

Failure to organise the new establishments that were set up in the private sector in the last twenty years or so is central to falling unionisation. The low rates of recognition and density in new establishments set up in the 1980s and 1990s are seen to be very similar for both decades. The sharpest falls in union recognition are among private manufacturing establishments set up after 1980, with significant falls, albeit from a lower initial level, in private sector services. In the public sector there is no evidence of an establishment-age-based decline in recognition.[22]

Most recent indications of the health of the TUC are provided in that body's own figures for membership (published in July 2002) which suggest a membership of 6 685 000, representing a membership decline of some 37 000 in relation to the previous year.[23]

On the employer side, the position emerging from the WERS98 data is that, so far as concerns the roles of constituting the employers' side of industry-wide or regional negotiating bodies:

… employers' associations diminished in importance during the 1980s, indicating that 'more and more managements seem to be assuming responsibility for their own industrial relations'. Employers' association membership in industry and commerce fell during the 1980s from 22% of workplaces in 1984 to 13% in 1990. The latest results suggest a modest recovery, with 18% of workplaces reporting membership in 1998. The recovery was complete among the largest workplaces with 500 of more employees, among whom membership levels in 1998 returned to the level of 1984.

21   Stephen Machin, 'Union Decline in Britain', 2000, *38 British Journal of Industrial Relations 631*, at 632.
22   Ibid.
23   The two largest unions within the TUC each have something in excess of one million members, and it is noteworthy that, of these two, the second largest is a public sector union (UNISON), which, incidentally, is also the largest affiliate to the Labour Party whose members make up the current United Kingdom government.

Table 1: Trade union membership in Great Britain and United Kingdom; 1991 to 2001, not seasonally adjusted

	Great Britain[a]			United Kingdom[a]		
	Number of members[b] (thousands)	Union density		Number of members[b] (thousands)	Union density	
		All in Employment (%)	Employees (%)		All in Employment (%)	Employees (%)
1991	8 602	33.6	37.5	-	-	-
1992	7 956	32.2	35.8	-	-	-
1993	7 767	31.5	35.1	-	-	-
1994	7 530	30.1	33.6	-	-	-
1995	7 309	28.8	32.1	7 532	29.0	32.3
1996	7 244	28.2	31.2	7 472	28.4	31.5
1997	7 154	27.3	30.2	7 372	27.4	30.4
1998	7 155	26.9	29.6	7 396	27.1	29.9
1999	7 277	27.0	29.5	7 498	27.1	29.6
2000	7 351	27.0	29.4	7 580	27.1	29.5
2001	7 295	26.5	28.8	7 550	26.8	29.1

Source: Labour Force Survey

a   Trade union questions were included in the LFS in Great Britain from 1989 and in Northern Ireland from 1995.

b   Includes all those in employment, excluding members of the armed forces, unpaid family workers, and those on college-based schemes. From 1989-1991 union membership questions were asked in the spring quarter. Since 1992 they have been asked in the autumn quarter. Those who did not report their union status or were not contactable in the autumn quarter have been allocated on a pro-rata basis.

Table 2: Union presence and coverage of collective agreements, United Kingdom; Autumn 1996 to Autumn 2001

				Thousands and per cent
	Number of employees where there are trade union members at the work place (thousands)	Percentage of employees working where trade union members are present	Number of employees whose pay is affected by collective agreements (thousands)	Percentage of employees whose pay is affected by collective agreement
1996	11 358	49.8	8 297	36.4
1997	11 335	48.5	8 247	35.3
1998	11 385	47.6	8 249	34.5
1999[a]	11 735	48.3	8 771	36.1
2000	12 009	48.7	8 924	36.2
2001	11 948	48.0	8 869	35.6

Source: Labour Force Survey

a   Data for 1999 onwards are not directly comparable to earlier years due to changes in the trade union questions in the Labour Force Survey.

Taken from K. Brook, 'Trade Union Membership: An Analysis of Data from the Autumn 2001 LFS', 2002, *Labour Market Trends 343*, at p. 351, Table 6.

The structure of employer-side bargaining also changed, such that:

[m]ulti-employer bargaining, which had greatly diminished in importance in the 1980s, became even more of a rarity in the 1990s. Among workplaces with recognised trade unions, multi-employer negotiations affected the pay of some or all employees in 68% of workplaces in 1980. In 1990 this had fallen to 60%, but in 1998 it was down to 34%. In all three broad sectors of the economy the fall over the whole period 1980 to 1998 was substantial: in public services the drop was from 81 to 47%; in private manufacturing it was from 57 to 25%; and, most dramatically, in private services, from 54 to just 12%.[24]

Post-1996 trends in relation to trade union presence and the coverage of collective agreements appear in Table 2. These show a slight falling back in 2001, after a gentle increase during the previous three-year period.

6. Regulatory techniques

In terms of regulatory techniques to be found in the United Kingdom – the 'home of collective bargaining'[25] – the historical model of 'collective laissez-faire', based upon 'free collective bargaining', has swiftly and dramatically given way, since the end of the 1960s, to the technique of normative legislation emanating from parliamentary processes.

The role of collective bargaining has steadily diminished, as has the coverage of collective bargaining within the United Kingdom labour market. An indication of the present scope of collective bargaining and the influence of that bargaining upon wage levels can be seen in Table 3.[26] Summing up this trend, it has been observed that,

The traditional form of collective bargaining at the multi-employer, industry-wide level has continued its long retreat in favour of single-employer bargaining at some level within the enterprise. The surveys show that the proportion of workplaces (of 25 or more employees) affected by multi-employer bargaining fell from 43% in 1980 to 31% in 1990 and 14% in 1998.[27]

Since the report of the Donovan Commission in 1968, the picture in relation to regulation of employment relations and industrial relations has been radically transformed. The introduction through labour law legislation of wide-ranging provisions setting down individual rights of workers has eclipsed the central role of collective bargaining which had continued prior to that change of policy. Enforcement of these individual rights has generally been provided for through statutory causes of action before the Employment Tribunals, whose range and variety of jurisdictions has expanded dramatically since their creation (in the guise of the 'Industrial Tribunals') in 1964.[28]

A watershed can be seen to have occurred in 1971, when the Industrial Relations Act 1971 was enacted by a Conservative government. Notwithstanding ostensible repeal of that legis-

Table 3: **Employees covered by collective bargaining for pay fixing and principal level of pay bargaining: Great Britain establishments of 25 or more employees, 1960-1998; Public and private sectors (Estimates in italics)**

	1960	**1970**	**1980**	**1984**	**1990**	**1998**
Collective bargaining	*80%*	*80%*	*75%*	*70%*	*54%*	*40%*
of which						
Industry level (multi-employer)	*60%*	*50%*	*43%*	*37%*	*31%*	*14%*
Enterprise level (single-employer)	*20%*	*30%*	*32%*	*33%*	*23%*	*26%*
No collective bargaining	*20%*	*20%*	*25%*	*30%*	*46%*	*60%*

24   M. Cully, S. Woodland, A. O'Reilly & G. Dix, *Britain at Work: As depicted by the 1998 Workplace Employee Relations Survey*, London 1999, at 228.

25   F. Schmidt & A. Neal, 'Collective Bargaining and Collective Agreements', *International Encyclopedia of Comparative Law Tübingen, 1984*, Vol. XV, Ch. 12.

26   Taken from W. Brown, P. Marginson & J. Walsh, 'The Management of Pay as the Influence of Collective Bargaining Diminishes', *ESRC Centre for Business Research*, University of Cambridge, Working Paper No. 213, 2001, and itself drawing upon various sources.

27   W. Brown, S. Deakin, D. Nash & S. Oxenbridge, 'The Employment Contract: From Collective Procedures to Individual Rights', 2000, *38 British Journal of Industrial Relations 611*, at 614.

28   See infra.

lation in 1974 by a Labour government,[29] the prevailing paradigm of legislative frameworks and significant intervention by the legislator was retained.[30] Indeed, the shift in that direction markedly gathered pace during the administrations of Prime Minister Margaret Thatcher between 1979 and 1991, followed by the administrations of Prime Minister John Major between 1991 and 1997. In the years which have followed the change of government to a Labour administration in 1997, the received wisdom is that no deviation has been made from that paradigm of dominant normative legislative techniques holding sway over free collective bargaining.

The concept of 'social dialogue' and 'social concertation' for the United Kingdom context is extremely difficult to expound with any conviction, albeit that a number of instances of 'co-operative' or 'partnership' activities can be pointed to.[31] Since 1999, a statutory scheme providing for recognition of trade unions, in order to permit them the opportunity to bargain with employers who might otherwise be reluctant to accept a collective representative presence at the workplace, has operated under the aegis of the Central Arbitration Committee (CAC).[32] This appears to have delivered some favourable results,[33] and to be providing an additional impetus towards 'social dialogue' of a more constructive kind than arguably was witnessed during the period 1979-1997. Notwithstanding that observation, however, it has to be said that reliance upon such a statutory mechanism for trade

union recognition arguably serves to underline the weakness which has afflicted the trade union movement in the United Kingdom during the past quarter of a century.

In addition to the normative legislative approach (primarily to be found in a series of Acts of Parliament, under the umbrella of which a huge flood of regulatory instruments of a secondary nature have been authorised)[34] one may point to a number of examples of collaboration between employers and representatives of the workforce. This can be seen particularly in the public sector, where the shift away from unionisation and collective bargaining along traditional lines has not been as swift and significant as in much of the private sector.[35]

It is also relevant to note that such industrial action as residually takes place in the United Kingdom tends to be witnessed in the public sector (with high profile instances in relation to the fire services, the National Health Service, and certain parts of transport). That having been said, however, the phenomenon has been detectable in the private sector (for example, in privatised rail operations) and even elsewhere there are clear signs in the private sector to suggest that industrial conflict is by no means dead. Behind the 'hard law' mechanisms of Acts of Parliament and regulations one also finds a variety of so-called 'soft law' techniques, amongst which may be mentioned Codes of Practice,[36] Guidance

---

29   The repeal of the 1971 Act was achieved through Section 1 of the Trade Union and Labour Relations Act 1974, which declared that *The Industrial Relations Act 1971 is hereby repealed*. At the same time, however, the 'non-headline' reality was that large chunks of the frameworks established by the 1971 Act were reintroduced through Schedules to the 1974 statute – the most significant being the (broadly intact) provisions on unfair dismissal contained in Schedule 1 to the Act.

30   For the encapsulation of this process in the notion of 'juridification', see S. Simitis, 'Juridification of Labor Relations', in G. Teubner (ed), *Juridification of Social Spheres,* De Gruyter 1987, pp. 113-161, and, for comment on the Simitis approach in the United Kingdom context, see J. Clark & Lord Wedderburn, 'Juridification – A Universal Trend? The British Experience in Labor Law', in G. Teubner (ed), *Juridification of Social Spheres,* De Gruyter 1987, pp. 163-190.

31   See, for example, the experience discussed in William Brown, 'Putting Partnership into Practice in Britain', 2000, *38 British Journal of Industrial Relations 299*. For discussion of 'social dialogue' at the European Union level through a United Kingdom prism, see Alan C. Neal, 'We love you social dialogue – But who exactly are you?', in Fondazione Giulio Pastore, *La contrattazione collettiva europea: Profili giuridici ed economici,* Milan 2001, 113. Indeed, it is worthwhile noting that annual criticism of the lack of social dialogue in the United Kingdom is to be found in the 'Recommendations' which form part of the process for the European Union's employment policy, without any real account being taken of the historical traditions underlying the operation of industrial relations and other labour market activities in the United Kingdom. In consequence, the ripostes in the annual NAPs prepared on behalf of the United Kingdom government to meet points in respect of this phenomenon appear, on occasion, to indicate the existence of two parallel universes!

32   See Part I, Chapter VA of the Trade Union and Labour Relations (Consolidation) Act 1992, inserted by the Employment Relations act 1999.

33   See the activities of the CAC in 2000-2002, infra Table 4.

34   A list of the principal primary and secondary legislative measures is set out in Annex II.

35   Thus, for example, an interesting apparent shift towards national level bargaining arrangements can be seen in the educational sector during 2000, with an agreement for national level bargaining over pay and conditions.

36   See, for example, the *ACAS Codes on Disciplinary and Grievance Procedures* (No. 1, 2000), on Disclosure of information to trade unions for collective bargaining purposes (Code No. 2, 1998), and on Time off for trade union duties and activities (Code No. 3, 1998). Statutory Codes of Practice are also to be found in relation to health & safety at work, discrimination and equal opportunities, and in relation to data protection. The standing of statutory codes of practice is interesting from the point of view of legislative technique: thus, use of the *ACAS Code No. 1 on Disciplinary and Grievance Procedures,* 2000, is governed by Section 207 of the Trade Union and Labour Relations (Consolidation) Act 1992, which provides that *(1) A failure on the part of any person to observe any provision of a Code of Practice issued under this Chapter shall not of itself render him liable to any proceedings. (2) In any proceedings before an employment tribunal or the Central Arbitration Committee any Code of Practice issued under this Chapter by ACAS shall be admissible in evidence, and any provision of the Code which appears to the tribunal of Committee to be relevant to any question arising in the proceedings shall be taken into account in determining that question.* Section 207(3) makes similar provision for Codes issued under Chapter III of the 1992 Act by the Secretary of State. In other employment-related fields, indeed, such codes of practice are particularly significant – as can be seen in the area of health and safety at work, where the phenomenon of the 'approved code of practice' also carries evidential significance in the context of criminal law enforcement of protections.

emanating either from ministerial sources or from specialist bodies in particular sectors (notably in relation to health and safety at work, which, it should be noted, is an area attracting penal sanctions in the event of non-compliance), as well as a number of 'declarations' on both trade union and employer sides.[37] Nevertheless, the scope of freedom for collective bargaining along the traditional lines of the 1960s kind has without doubt almost vanished as it had been known at the time of the 1971 Industrial Relations Act or the Donovan Commission in 1968.

7. Levels of bargaining in the United Kingdom

The locus of bargaining has been a subject of particular attention throughout the 1980s and into the 1990s. So far as the United Kingdom case is concerned, the picture is described by *Brown et al* in the following terms:[38]

The coverage of collective bargaining, the principal means of governing the employment contract for most of the twentieth century, has been contracting. This is best charted by considering collective bargaining over pay. WERS98 and its predecessors indicate that the proportion of all employees (in workplaces employing 25 or more) covered by collective bargaining over pay fell from 70% in 1984 to 54% in 1990, and to 41% in 1998. The level at which this bargaining occurs has also changed. The traditional form of collective bargaining at the multi-employer, industry-wide level has continued its long retreat in favour of single-employer bargaining at some level within the enterprise. The surveys show that the proportion of workplaces (of 25 or more employees) affected by multi-employer bargaining fell from 43% in 1980 to 31% in 1990 and 14% in 1998.

In a recent study, taking comparative evidence from experience in the European automotive and financial sectors, *Marginson & Sisson* report that,

In the UK, where sector-level bargaining arrangements came to an end in both engineering and banking a decade or more ago,

the issue of balance has been resolved decisively in favour of company-level bargaining arrangements (or in some parts of automotive components and banking and insurance non-union arrangements).[39]

Such work as has been done to test the effect of bargaining levels upon enterprise performance suggests only tenuous links. Thus, taking data from the WERS98, Bryson & Wilkinson maintain that:

Although there has been much debate about the level at which bargaining is conducted in Britain and its influence on wage setting and inflation, bargaining levels had little effect on workplace performance in general. Workplaces with multi-level bargaining enjoyed better climates than other workplaces. This was the only bargaining effect on managerial and employee perceptions of climate. However, this arrangement existed in less than 1% of workplaces. Industry-level bargaining was associated with better financial performance than other levels of bargaining. However, some caution should be exercised in interpreting the finding. Industry-level bargaining has continued to decline in the 1990s, and it may be that those who retain it are those who can 'afford' to do so. There is therefore a question mark about the direction of causation.[40]

8. Dispute resolution and enforcement of labour law rights

With the growth in significance for normative intervention from the legislator since 1971, it comes as no surprise to discover that legal *fora* for dispute resolution have taken on a major role within the United Kingdom industrial relations structures. The 'normal' civil justice institutions for resolving collective labour law disputes have remained the High Court and the appellate levels above (the Court of Appeal and, thereafter, the House of Lords). However, where individual employment rights are involved, the growth in case-load disposed of by the Employment Tribunals (formerly, the Industrial Tribunals) and the extension of the jurisdiction exercised by those bodies has been little short of remarkable.[41]

---

37   For consideration of the impact of such 'soft' approaches, see K. Sisson & P. Marginson, 'Soft Regulation' – Travesty of the real thing or new dimension? (Paper produced for the ESRC's research project on 'Emerging Boundaries of European Collective Bargaining at Sector and Enterprise Levels', within the context of the 'One Europe or Several?' programme, June 2001.

38   W. Brown, S. Deakin, D. Nash & S. Oxenbridge, 'The Employment Contract: From Collective Procedures to Individual Rights', 2000, *38 British Journal of Industrial Relations 611*, at 614.

39   P. Marginson & K. Sisson, 'European dimensions to collective bargaining: new symmetries within an asymmetric process?', 2002, *33 Industrial Relations Journal 332*, at 341.

40   See A. Bryson & D. Wilkinson, 'Collective bargaining and workplace performance: An investigation using the Workplace Employee Relations Survey 1998', *DTI Employment Relations Research Series No.12*, 2001.

41   Thus, during 2001/02, no less than 194,120 cases were lodged with the Employment Tribunals. See *ETS, Annual Report and Accounts 2001-2002* (HC 951), and, for the most recent government investigation into the working of the system, see *Moving Forward: The Report of the Employment Tribunal System Taskforce,* July 2002.

Since the introduction of a statutory procedure for granting recognition to trade unions for bargaining purposes, the Central Arbitration Committee (CAC) has gained substantial influence as the resolution body charged with dealing with disputes under this procedure. The Central Arbitration Committee is a permanent independent body with statutory powers whose main function is to adjudicate on applications relating to the statutory recognition and de-recognition of trade unions for collective bargaining purposes, where such recognition or de-recognition cannot be agreed voluntarily. In addition, the CAC has a statutory role in determining disputes between trade unions and employers over the disclosure of information for collective bargaining purposes, and in disposing of claims and complaints regarding the establishment and operation of European Works Councils in Great Britain. The CAC also provides voluntary arbitration in industrial disputes. CAC activity in the period 2000-2002 can be seen in Table 4.

The Advisory, Conciliation and Arbitration Service (ACAS) – the most important of the bodies active in the field of dispute resolution in relation to industrial relations and labour law matters – undertakes important work in respect of both individual and collective matters. Their activity in relation to collective conciliation can be seen from Table 5. There is also an important statutory duty to conciliate in relation to complaints presented to an Employment Tribunal – giving rise to the bulk of the case-load for ACAS individual conciliation officers (see Table 6).[42] The contribution of ACAS towards dispute resolution at both the collective and the individual levels is widely held to be very positive, and a strong lobby exists which maintains that more should be done to 'shift the balance' back from litigation before the Employment Tribunals towards conciliation, mediation or arbitration.

In this context, however, recent attempts to introduce variants of 'alternative dispute resolution' ('ADR') into the United Kingdom institutional framework have not, so far, proved particularly encouraging.[43] A statutory scheme, using the facilities and expertise of ACAS, was envisaged in terms that:

The central feature of the proposed arbitration scheme is that the process by which cases are dealt with is designed to be largely free of legalism. The arbitrator will rule on his/her own jurisdiction, and on procedural and evidential matters, with appeals against the decision of the arbitrator therefore being limited to alleged serious irregularity. There will be no appeal on a point of law. The intention is to give the arbitration a finality: if this is not achieved then the scheme will come to resemble an Employment Tribunal without its tripartite nature. By obviating the need for legal argument, there is the possibility of reduced costs for the parties. Costs and delays that accompany appeals will also be avoided… As a consequence of the desire to free the scheme from 'legalism' the arbitrator will not have the same powers as an Employment Tribunal chairman to make witness orders or order discovery/production of documents, although he/she will have the right to draw conclusions from the withholding of information. The hearings will be conducted in an inquisitorial rather than an adversarial manner. The parties will be able to state their own cases and comment on the case of the other side and, although there will be no cross-examination, clarification and questioning will be carried out by or through the arbitrator. …The hearings will not be public and the decisions and awards will be confidential.[44]

The underlying concern to avoid 'legalism' and 'formalism' in United Kingdom industrial relations and management practices has long been a matter of comment – although some scepticism has to be expressed as to whether such a longing for 'traditional modes' of conducting these relationships in the 21st Century has long become a forlorn hope.[45]

Some concern has been expressed about the levels of awareness and knowledge on the parts of employers of labour law in the United Kingdom. A recent study, looking at the awareness of individual employment rights on the parts of small firms, has suggested that, overall:

… owner-managers were not confident about their knowledge of individual employment rights. This was most likely to be the result of the absence of an in-house personnel function, and that employment rights were dealt with by these employers on a 'need-to-know' basis.

---

42 According to the statistics presented in the ACAS Annual Report for 2001/02, the case-load was 165 093. However, some caution should be exercised when comparing statistics relating to cases presented to the Employment Tribunals and their disposal by those bodies and by ACAS, since the basis for computing 'multiple complaints' (i.e. A single document presented to an Employment Tribunal which contains more than one jurisdictional complaint) differs as between the two bodies.

43 See, for example, the statutory scheme introduced in relation to unfair dismissal in 2000, by virtue of the ACAS Arbitration Scheme (England and Wales) Order 2001 (brought into effect from 21 May 2001). However, enquiries at the beginning of 2003 indicated that the scheme has only been utilised slightly in excess of 30 times during its first 18 months of operation.

44 See the 'Foreword' to the 1998 Consultation Document, ACAS Arbitration Scheme for the Resolution of Unfair Dismissal Disputes.

45 See the substantial writing on indications of 'growing formalism' in United Kingdom industrial relations, largely dismissed in B. Weekes, M. Mellish, L. Dickins & J. Lloyd, *Industrial Relations and the Limits of Law: The Industrial Effects of the Industrial Relations Act*, 1971, Oxford 1975, as well as in M. Terry, 'The Inevitable Growth of Informality', 1977, *15 British Journal of Industrial Relations* 75. The extent of 'denial' by the labour law community in the United Kingdom for many years after the demise of the Industrial Relations Act 1971 was also remarkable: See, for example, the underlying thrust of the contributions to Lord Wedderburn, R. Lewis & J. Clark, *Labour law and Industrial Relations: Building on Kahn-Freund*, Oxford 1983. This intransigent stance by some of the best-known labour lawyers of the time appears strange, given that Kahn-Freund himself had given a clear signal of a significant re-visiting of his own analytical paradigm in the course of his presentations in O. Kahn-Freund, *Labour Relations: Heritage and Adjustment*, London 1979, written shortly before his death.

Table 4:   Analysis of references to the CAC 2000-2002

Jurisdiction	Brought forward from 31/3/2000	Received between 1/4/2000 – 31/3/2002	References completed or withdrawn	References outstanding 31/3/2002
Voluntary Arbitration (s.212)	-	-	-	-
Disclosure of Information (s.183)	12	17	19	10
Trade Union Recognition (Pt.1)	-	175	123	52
Trade Union Recognition (Pt.2)	-	1	1	0
Trade Union Recognition (Pt.6)	-	2	2	0
Trans-national Information & Consultation	-	1	1	0
TOTALS	12	196	146	62

Table 5:   ACAS collective conciliation (requests and completed cases) 2000-2002

	2001/2002	2000/2001	1999/2000
Requests received	1 371	1 472	1 500
Requests subsequently withdrawn	56	58	81
Requests in which conciliation was completed	1 270	1 226	1 247
Conciliation resulting in a settlement or progress towards a settlement	1 166	1 139	1 152
Conciliation unsuccessful	104	87	95

Table 6:   Employment tribunal applications – Cases received and dealt with by ACAS

Year	Cases received	Settled	Withdrawn	Employment tribunal	Total cases completed
2001/02	165 093	57 660	44 842	34 998	137 500
2000/01	167 186	64 133	41 480	42 967	148 580
1999/00	164 525	57 478	40 312	32 921	130 711

Source: ACAS Annual Report 2001-2002, Table 8.

This lack of confidence, at the level of the sample as a whole, masked minor size and sector variations. Thus, behind the crude relationship between size and knowledge levels there were a number of intervening factors, which would also be influential. One particular example is firms in the Hotels and Catering sector where employers expressed the highest levels of confidence. It is argued that the relative low wages in the sector and the higher proportions of females in the labour force, means that employers have had to come to terms with certain individual employment rights (e.g. NMW [the national minimum wage] and maternity rights) on far more occasions than those

*in other sectors. This further reinforces the theme of employers'
awareness and knowledge on a 'need-to-know' basis. Those firms at
risk from the effects of employment rights because of their particular characteristics will have to become more au fait with the legislation. This implies that there will be variations in employers' knowledge
levels even when size of firm is controlled because of the heteroge-
neous nature of their activities, variations in their labour force composition and events such as an industrial dispute.[46]*

Looking at the awareness and knowledge levels on the parts
of small firms of new, relative to older, established legislation
on individual employment rights, the authors reached the
conclusion that:

*The theme to emerge here was that not only are smaller firms
less likely to be knowledgeable about employment rights, awareness of new legislation takes a longer time to enter the consciousness of the very small employer.[47]*

9. A note on the coverage of statutory labour law rights

It should be noted that the basis for qualification in respect
of the great majority of individual labour law rights in the
United Kingdom is that the protected subject should be an
'employee', as defined in the relevant statutory provisions.[48]
This limiting concept – as in many other legal systems – is
far from clear in terms of identifying precisely who is covered by, and who falls outside, labour law protection, and
involves a variety of assumptions built up over a long history of Common Law case development.[49] Indeed, despite
recent consideration at the level of the House of Lords,[50]
this issue remains highly unsatisfactory for all involved.

The statutory term 'employee' (representing the 'gateway'
to a wide range of individual rights and protections) is used
by way of distinction from what are described in the labour
law statutes as 'workers' – to which category a broader
range of protections is afforded.[51]

A small number of recent provisions have extended protection to particular groups – notably, to 'home workers' and to
'agency workers' – through newly-established statutory definitions.[52] This indication that the United Kingdom legislator
has developed an awareness of some of the problems brought
about by the unsatisfactory state of 'employee status' was also
reinforced by the launch in 1992 of a government-level consultation exercise on precisely that subject.[53] At the same
time, there has been evidence of a more disturbing use of
statutory qualification thresholds as a deliberate device to
limit access to labour law rights – even to the point of raising

---

46 R. Blackburn & M. Hart, *Small firms' awareness and knowledge of individual employment rights, DTI Employment Relations Research Series No.14*, London 2002.

47 The authors go on to observe that, *The theme of size of enterprise as an important determinant in awareness and knowledge levels emerged again and
again in the analysis. Some of the reasons for this are apparent in the results: smaller enterprises were less likely to have to deal with the breadth and depth of
individual employment rights on the statute books merely because they employ fewer people; smaller firms in the sample were likely to have less resources devoted to personnel matters and instead relied on the owner-manager to address issues on a need-to-know basis; and smaller enterprises were less likely to have
experienced employment disputes or have been taken to an Employment Tribunal. The latter was shown to raise awareness and knowledge levels significantly.*

48 Section 230 of the Employment Rights Act 1996 defines an 'employee' as 'an individual who has entered into or works under (or, where the employment has ceased, worked under) a contract of employment' – a definition which itself depends upon the further definition of 'contract of employment' as 'a contract of service or apprenticeship, whether express or implied, and (if it is express) whether oral or in writing'.

49 A number of well-known 'tests' have been developed through the Common Law cases, of which the most important are considered to be the 'control',
the 'integration', the 'in business on one's own account', and the 'mutuality of obligation' tests. None of these is particularly illuminating on its own, and the
exercise of identifying 'who is an employee?' has developed into a composite test with a variety of components being 'placed in the balance'.

50 See Carmichael and Another v. National Power Plc. [2000] I.R.L.R. 43.

51 It may be noted that this 2-category distinction is of relatively recent origin. Indeed, as recently as in the second edition of Wedderburn's The Worker and the Law (1971) one can find the terms 'employee' and 'worker' being used almost interchangeably. A 'worker' is now defined by section
230(3) of the Employment Rights Act 1996 as *an individual who has entered into or works under (or, where the employment has ceased, worked under) –
(a) a contract of employment, or (b) any other contract, whether express or implied and (if it is express) whether oral or in writing, whereby the individual undertakes to do or perform personally any work or services for another party to the contract whose status is not by virtue of the contract that of a client or customer of any profession or business undertaking carried on by the individual.*

52 See s. 34 of the National Minimum Wage Act 1998 and Regulation 36 of the Working Time Regulations 1998, which both contain a definition of 'agency
worker' in terms of an individual who ... (a) is supplied by a person ('the agent') to do work for another ('the principal') under a contract or other arrangements made between the agent and principal; but (b) is not, as respects that work, a worker, because of the absence of a worker's contract between the individual and the agent or the principal; and (c) is not a party to a contract under which he undertakes to do the work for another party to the contract whose status is, buy virtue of the contract, that of a client or customer of any profession or business undertaking carried on by the individual. Meanwhile, s.35 of the
National Minimum Wage Act 1998 contains a provision intended to bring 'home workers' within the scope of the statutory protections, and defines
the protected category of worker as ... (2) ...an individual who contracts with a person, for the purposes of that person's business, for the execution of work
to be done in a place not under the control or management of that person.

53 See DTI, *Discussion Document on Employment Status in Relation to Statutory Employment Rights*, URN 02/1058.

possible conflicts with the approach of the European Court of Justice to this issue at the level of the European Union.[54]

10. A note on fundamental rights and labour law

Regard should also be had for the issue of 'fundamental rights' in the field of labour law as this notion has developed in the United Kingdom. In particular, the enactment of a Human Rights Act 1998, which came into effect in 2000, has raised a debate about the extent to which international human rights instruments – in particular, the European Convention on Human Rights of 1950 – constitute a source of norms for labour law in the United Kingdom. Two points may be made in this context.

First, it has to be appreciated that the Human Rights Act 1998 does not 'incorporate' the European Convention into United Kingdom law. What, instead, is established is the requirement upon every 'public authority' – which, in the present context, includes the Employment Tribunals and the Employment Appeal Tribunal – to conduct its proceedings and to make its decisions in accordance with the provisions in, and the jurisprudence concerning, the Convention.[55]

Second, the 'flood' of employment-related litigation which was forecast to arise in consequence of the coming into force of the Human Rights Act 1998 has not materialised.[56] Consequently, the position in respect of international sources of labour law rights and protections would appear not to have altered markedly from what had gone before – with occasional points of particular importance being raised and considered against the framework of the fundamental rights instrument from which they are said to derive.[57]

However, that having been said, there have been some interesting 'indirect' effects of the concern to operate United Kingdom labour law in strict conformity with the principles and values of the European Convention. One, in particular, concerns the area of 'privacy', with all of the associated issues of freedom of information, data protection, and the need to respect family and private life. Indeed, the appropriate balance to be struck between competing interests in relation to data touching the personal and other circumstances of workers has been the goal of a series of legislative measures introduced into United Kingdom labour law during recent years.[58] A wide range of perspectives underlie these legislative innovations, including concern to protect the employment circumstances of workers who seek to engage in 'whistle blowing' in the public interest.[59]

---

54   See, for example, Regulation 17 of the Part-time Workers (Prevention of Less Favourable Treatment) Regulations 2000, which provides that *These regulations do not apply to any individual in his capacity as the holder of a judicial office if he is remunerated on a daily fee-paid basis* – a category never previously identified as subject to particular treatment in United Kingdom law. This naked move to 'invent' a new class of non-protected member of the working citizenry raises interesting questions in the context both of the loose definitions provided in Clause 3 of the Framework Agreement on Part-Time Work whose transformation into legislative form Directive 97/81/EC purports to deliver, and as regards the traditional formula used by the European Court of Justice to delimit the scope of protected workers under EU Law (identification 'in accordance with national law, collective agreements or practice' in the Member State) – particularly when one bears in mind the concern of the ECJ in Unger C-75/63, that (speaking of the term 'worker' in the context of former Articles 48-51), the relevant Community provisions would be *deprived of all effect and the above-mentioned objectives of the Treaty would be frustrated if the meaning of such a term could be unilaterally fixed and modified by national law.*

55   See section 3, which provides that: *So far as it is possible to do so, primary legislation and subordinate legislation must be read and given effect in a way which is compatible with the Convention rights,* and section 6, which states that: *It is unlawful for a public authority to act in a way which is incompatible with a Convention right.* [Note that the expression 'public authority' includes 'a court or tribunal'].

56   The Employment Tribunals have, since the Human Rights Act came into force, operated a system for recording, and disseminating information about, 'human rights points' raised in the course of proceedings before them. This indicates that, while matters are raised, from time to time, in respect of the 'due process' of the proceedings (by reference to Article 6 of the Convention), very few other areas of Convention coverage are giving rise to regular concern.

57   A process which has been seen in the past in cases such as the 'closed shop' case of Young, James and Webster (1981), the 'telephone tapping' case of Halford (1997), and the religious discrimination case of Tinnelly & Sons Ltd and Others and McElduff and Others (1998). The most recent high-profile labour law case in this context has been Wilson & Others v United Kingdom, [2002] ECHR 568, where the United Kingdom was held to be in violation of Article 11 of the Convention. For presentation of the United Kingdom perspective on the procedures of the ECHR in the light of the revised access rules introduced by Protocol 11 of the European Convention on Human Rights, see House of Commons Research Paper 98/109, Protocol 11 and the New European Court of Human Rights (4 December 1998).

58   See, inter alia, the provisions on disclosure of medical records [contained in the Access to Medical Reports Act 1988]; provisions specifically directed towards data protection [including the framework of the Date Protection Act 1998 and the detailed Data Protection (Processing of Sensitive Personal Data) Order 2000 (SI 2000/417)]; rules relating to third-party access to communications, such as E-mails [under a framework established by the Regulation of Investigatory Powers Act 2000, and including, as part of a long list of related measures, the Telecommunications (Lawful Business Practice) (Interception of Communications) Regulations 2000 (SI 2000/2699)]; and various procedural provisions relating to the making public of sensitive information during the course of Employment Tribunal proceedings (including, importantly, such information produced in the context of sex discrimination and disability discrimination litigation) [the most important of which are to be found in the Employment Tribunals (Constitution and Rules of Procedure) Regulations 2001 (SI 2001/1171)].

59   In relation to which the provisions of the Public Interest Disclosure Act 1998 have been inserted as Part IVA of the Employment Rights Act 1996.

Chapter II:
From job security to employability

1. Introduction

The traditional approach to 'job security' in the United Kingdom – which lasted well into the post-World War II era – was to leave matters to free collective bargaining, and the 'voluntarist' mechanisms whereby strongly organised trade unions could influence workplace management in relation to recruitment, terms of employment, and discipline for workers. Very few examples (outside wartime experience, involving so-called 'emergency powers') can be pointed to where this key approach was departed from – although experience of wage-fixing in 'Wages Council' sectors and, increasingly, in the public sector, provides some evidence of contrasting models.[60] It may be questionable to what extent the reliance upon this framework came at the price of a trade-off between 'collective interests' and the immediate priority interests of individual workers. Certainly, one is entitled to infer that an important consequence was an inconsistent level of 'employment protection' across different parts of the United Kingdom economy.

That 'laissez-faire' tradition came under increasing attention from the legislator at the beginning of the 1960s, and, arguably, came to an abrupt end with the commitments by both major United Kingdom political parties to take a more interventionist approach to the regulation of industrial relations and the labour market in the wake of the report of the Donovan Commission in 1968.[61] With the enactment of an Industrial Relations

Act in 1971, the long-held reluctance to see government-initiated regulatory intervention in the field of labour law was swept aside. Importantly, this not only involved direct intervention into collective labour relations, but also established the roots of what has subsequently developed into a mountainous body of 'individual employment protection' laws.

When a change of political climate came about in 1974, even the ostensible repeal of the Industrial Relations Act 1971 (together with the judicial mechanisms to which it had given birth)[62] did little to reverse this shift of regulatory paradigm. Remarkably, therefore, in the space of little over half a decade, the whole basis for labour law regulation had been remodelled, and the indisputable dominance of the legislative norm by the end of the millennium serves as testimony to the enormity of that shift.

2. Protection against dismissals

Perhaps the most visible legacy of the Industrial Relations Act 1971 has been the United Kingdom's statutory framework of protection against 'unfair dismissal'.[63] This structure, currently generating in excess of 50 000 sets of legal proceedings every year,[64] modelled itself around two of the key components in the then prevailing ILO instruments in the area of termination of employment at the initiative of the employer.[65]

---

60 The general reaction to more 'interventionist' approaches in certain areas was to categorise those sectors of the labour market as essentially those where collective bargaining was too 'weak' to deliver an acceptable level to the 'floor of rights', and thus to require 'supporting measures' imposed by the legislator. See, for example, the analysis of Kahn-Freund in his O. Kahn-Freund, *Labour and the Law,* London 1972.

61 The 1970 general election saw competing programmes for reform. On the part of the Labour Party, the proposals contained in the White Paper In Place of Strife (Cmnd.3888) (London 1969), and a subsequent Industrial Relations Bill 1970, piloted by the then responsible minister, Mrs Barbara Castle, envisaged a very different approach from what had gone before. Meanwhile, the radical change of paradigm sought by the Conservative Party – much of the new proposals being informed by models and practice in the United States of America – became reality after that party's success at the polls in 1970. See, in particular, *Fair Deal at Work* (1968). For analysis and comment on this period, see inter alia O. Kahn-Freund, *Labour and the Law,* London 1972, and the standard text on industrial relations of the time, H. Clegg, *The System of Industrial Relations in Great Britain* (revised edition, Oxford 1972).

62 Notably, the NIRC and the CIR. See B. Weekes, M. Mellish, L. Dickins & J. Lloyd, *Industrial Relations and the Limits of Law: The Industrial Effects of the Industrial Relations Act, 1971,* Oxford 1975.

63 Now contained in Part X of the Employment Rights Act 1996. For data drawn from WERS98 in relation to dismissals and workplace discipline, see K. Knight & P. Latreille, 'Discipline, Dismissals and Complaints to Employment Tribunals', 2000, *38 British Journal of Industrial Relations 533.*

64 According to the statistics presented in the 2002 Annual Report of the Employment Tribunals Service (ETS), the number of unfair dismissal complaints to Employment Tribunals in the year 2001/02 was 51 512. This constituted a substantial proportion of the total 194 120 complaints presented to the Tribunals (of which the next most significant categories of complaint were related to unlawful deduction of wages and breach of contract – 42 205 and 30 791 complaints respectively in 2001/02). See Employment Tribunals Service Annual Report & Accounts 2001-2002 (HC 951), Appendix I.

65 See, in particular, Recommendation 119 on the Termination of Employment at the Initiative of the Employer (1963). However, it may be noted that later ILO Instruments – the 1983 Convention 158 on Termination of Employment at the Initiative of the Employer, together with Recommendation 166 on the Termination of Employment at the Initiative of the Employer – have not been ratified by the United Kingdom. For discussion of the policy context at the end of the 1960s, see G. de N. Clark, 'Remedies for Unjust Dismissal: Proposals for Legislation', PEP Broadsheet 518, 1970.

The modern 'standard' approach taken in respect of individual dismissals therefore consists of two complementary strands.

- First, there is the Common Law protection afforded to workers as parties to a civil law contract as a matter of private bargaining. This is enforced on the basis of standard civil law procedures (in the County Court or the High Court) relating to actions for breach of contract, together with a limited jurisdiction for the specialist first-instance Employment Tribunals to deal with some aspects involving breach of the contract of employment.

- Second, there is the statutory framework now contained in the Employment Rights Act 1996, which requires 'employees'[66] to be made aware of the reason whereby an employer has made a decision to terminate the contract of employment, and requires that, in formulating that decision to terminate, the employer acts 'fairly',[67] both in substantive terms and from a procedural point of view.[68]

Alongside (and complementary to) this 'standard' approach to furnishing labour law protection at the point of termination of the contract of employment have been two significant trends which, in the view of many, have served to segment United Kingdom workers in terms of the levels of protection afforded to them.

- The first trend has been a quickening concern to provide enhanced dismissal protection to particular designated groups within the workforce. An early, and well-established, example of this approach can be seen in relation to protection designed for individual workers in relation to the exercise of the right of freedom of association (normally, as manifested in trade union membership or activity).[69] However, it has increasingly been the case that the United Kingdom legislator has adopted a similar model of enhanced protection where individual protections in relation to dismissal are considered to be required in the context of implementing European Union social policy directives into United Kingdom law.[70]

- The second has been a clear movement (in line with tendencies at the European Union level) towards establishing labour law protections within frameworks designed to address problems of discrimination, equal opportunities, and ensuring 'fundamental rights'.[71] So far as concerns termination of employment in such contexts, dramatically enhanced remedies may be available to qualifying workers who lose their jobs for various discriminatory reasons.[72]

The United Kingdom has long provided for a certain level of employment protection in relation to dismissals for 'economic reasons' (generally referred to as 'redundancy').[73] In addition to these well-established statutory arrangements, additional provi-

---

66   It should be noted that this area of protection, in common with many other matters of labour law protection in the United Kingdom (and, indeed, in common with many other domestic systems of labour law in Europe), is limited only to workers who can establish that they satisfy a statutory definition of 'employee' as a qualifying pre-condition for enjoyment of the right not to be unfairly dismissed. See supra.

67   The core test, contained in Section 98(4) of the 1996 Act requires an Employment Tribunal, having regard to the reason for dismissal established by the employer, to decide the question by reference to a statutory formula, which has been explained and clarified by subsequent case law. Thus, ...the determination of the question whether the dismissal is fair or unfair (having regard to the reason shown by the employer) – (a) depends on whether in the circumstances (including the size and administrative resources of the employer's undertaking) the employer acted reasonably or unreasonably in treating it as a sufficient reason for dismissing the employee; and (b) shall be determined in accordance with equity and the substantial merits of the case.

68   See, for a fuller discussion of this duality and other important aspects of the unfair dismissal regime in action, H. Collins, *Justice in Dismissal*, Oxford 1993.

69   Other examples can be seen in relation to 'public interest disclosure' ('whistle-blowing') cases, and as regards employees seeking to assert their statutory rights. See the respective provisions in the Employments Rights Act 1996, Part IVA (inserted by the Public Interest Disclosure Act 1998) and Section 104.

70   Examples of this can be seen in relation to groups such as 'health and safety representatives' (of which there are several types – depending upon whether they operate in the context of implementing measures deriving from Council Directive 89/391/EEC of 12 June 1989 on the introduction of measures to encourage improvements in the safety and health of workers at work, or whether they act under older provisions which established 'safety committees' in 1997); in respect of works council members within the framework of the arrangements established by Directive 94/45/EC on Council Directive 94/45/EC of 22 September 1994 on the establishment of a European Works Council or a procedure in Community-scale undertakings and Community-scale groups of undertakings for the purposes of informing and consulting employees (as subsequently extended to the United Kingdom); and as regards worker representatives in the context of Council Directive 75/129/EEC of 17 February 1975 on the approximation of the laws of the Member States relating to collective redundancies (as subsequently amended) and Council Directive 77/187/EEC of 14 February 1977 on the approximation of the laws of the Member States relating to the safeguarding of employees' rights in the event of transfers of undertakings, businesses or parts of businesses (also as subsequently amended).

71   For a comment on the 'fundamental rights' aspect of United Kingdom labour law, see supra. In relation to the more general issue of protecting 'fundamental social rights', see the contributions to Alan C. Neal, *Fundamental Social Rights at Work in the European Community*, Aldershot 1997, reflecting studies undertaken by the European Association of Labour Court Judges for DG/V (Social Affairs) of the European Commission.

72   Including unlimited financial awards following removal of earlier statutory 'ceilings'.

73   See the provisions introduced by the Redundancy Payments Act 1965, now contained in Part XI of the Employment Rights Act 1996.

sions concerning collective dismissals derive from the relevant 1975 European Union directive,[74] while prior consultation and notification duties provide an interface with certain aspects of the 'collective' labour law regime for the United Kingdom.[75]

3. Measures to promote 'employability'

While the rhetoric underlying 'employability' initiatives is generally located in documentation associated with arrangements under the Employment Chapter of the Treaty of Amsterdam,[76] it is worth a reminder that the United Kingdom had already undertaken large-scale and highly controversial labour market reform during the two decades preceding the launch of the Luxembourg Process.[77] In consequence, a substantial amount of 'pain' had already been endured by those in the United Kingdom labour market – including particularly high levels of unemployment, as traditional heavy industries shed substantial numbers of workers – well before the initiation of NAPs and Guidelines at the European level.

One particular emphasis in the United Kingdom has been upon providing facilities to encourage self-employment – a category of the workforce which increased slightly in 2002, following three years of slight decline from a level in 1998 of 3 290 000 (see Table 7).[78] Thus, as *Metcalf* describes it, for the last two decades of the 20th century:

... the state has provided assistance to unemployed people wishing to enter self-employment. The approach has varied over time and location, with, variously, advice, training, grants, loans and income support being available for unemployed people. At the same time, unemployed people have been able to access assistance through mainstream government business support agencies. However, this approach has not been free from criticism.[79]

Table 7: Employment status of the UK workforce (thousands)

	1998	1999	2000	2001	2002
Employees	23 657	24 119	24 622	24 889	25 060
Self-employed	3 290	3 232	3 178	3 193	3 249
Unpaid family workers	102	102	110	98	96
Government-supported training and employment programmes	178	159	144	151	105
Employment of whom:	**27 227**	**27 611**	**28 053**	**28 332**	**28 511**
Full-time workers	20 473	20 761	21 083	21 293	21 400
Part-time workers	6 755	6 850	6 970	7 038	7 111
Workers with a second job	1 190	1 282	1 191	1 185	1 151
Temporary workers	1 745	1 712	1 727	1 728	1 588

Source: Labour Force Survey, Office for National Statistics (Taken from UK 2003, Table 11.3, p. 124).

74 Directive 75/129/EEC, as amended by Directive 92/56/EEC and Directive 98/59/EC.

75 The (sometimes rather artificial) desire to keep separate 'individual' and 'collective' issues can be seen clearly from 1974 onwards. Indeed, a particularly good example of this attempt to maintain the division can be seen in relation to the rules on dismissal occurring during industrial action – see sections 237-239 of the Trade Union and Labour Relations (Consolidation) Act 1992. However, whether the concerns to 'keep out the judges' which were commonly articulated thirty years ago still have the same relevance in a new Millennium may be open to question.

76 Title VIII, Articles 125-130 (formerly Articles 109n – 109s). See, for an example of some of the 'incidental' consequences of this innovation, the comments of M. Rodríguez-Piñero Bravo-Ferrer & M. Rodríguez-Piñero Royo, 'The Role of Labour Law and Industrial Relations in Job Creation Policies', in M. Biagi (ed), *Job Creation and Labour Law: From Protection towards Pro-action*, The Hague 2000, 11.

77 See Alan C. Neal, 'From 'Bad Boy' to European Role Model? – The Strange Legacy of United Kingdom Employment Policies since the Single European Act', in M. Biagi (ed), *Job Creation and Labour Law: From Protection towards Pro-action*, The Hague 2000, 269.

78 Further on this, see inter alia K. Kellard & S. Middleton, *Helping Unemployed People into Self-employment*, DfEE Research Report RR46, Sheffield 1998, and H. Metcalf, *Self-employment for the Unemployed: the Role of Public Policy*, DfEE Research Report No. 47, Sheffield 1998.

79 See H. Metcalf & R. Benson, 'From Unemployment to Self-Employment: Developing an Effective Structure of Micro-Finance Support', *PSI Discussion Paper No. 170*, October 2000. In particular, it is suggested that: *Research has indicated that low initial financing may contribute to business failure and that unemployed people face barriers to accessing commercial loans... And lack of access to bank finance may be a barrier to entry to self-employment... Yet government financial assistance, other than in the form of financial advice to improve access to commercial loans, has been limited, with grants and loans restricted both in size and availability.*

4. Upgrading workforce skills: towards a higher 'quality' workforce

At the root of many of the developments within the United Kingdom context were initiatives to address the skills levels of the workforce, and significant political policies were developed by both Conservative and Labour administrations during the last decade of the 20th century. One feature which deserves particular mention in the United Kingdom context was the removal of formal trade union involvement in what had hitherto been broadly 'tripartite' mechanisms for developing national training policy and the means for its implementation.[80] This diminution of direct trade union participation and influence at the national policy-making level was in line with other moves consequent upon various actions taken (especially) by the first two administrations of Prime Minister Margaret Thatcher between 1979 and 1987.[81]

A brief indication of the nature of the post-school training picture in the United Kingdom is provided by *Kim & Kurz*, drawing upon work published in 1995 and 1998:[82]

Post-compulsory education is commonly represented as a tripartite system with an academic, broad vocational, or an occupational pathway... The majority of pupils remain at school for two post-compulsory years and embark on a one year course to achieve the Scottish Certificate of Education (Higher Grade, in general 'Higher') or A levels in England and Wales. The SCE at the Higher Level and A levels are standard qualifications for entering a university. The full time vocational courses at further education (FE) colleges or schools (called the 'broad vocational pathway') provide both A level and vocational training courses in England. In Scotland, FE colleges offer a range of vocational courses for the General Scottish Vocational Qualification (GSVQ). The third post-compulsory pathway is the work-based route to occupational qualifications generally offered through an apprenticeship or with on-the-job training. Both are supported by government funding. Another alternative for young people is to enter a training place supported by government funding, but without the status of being employed. This option is commonly referred to as Youth Training (YT) in England/Wales and Skill-seekers in Scotland. Youth Training is aimed to provide 16-18 year olds with integrated programmes of work experience and vocational training, catering in particular for the rising number of unemployed young people.[83]

In terms of training provision, the main active measures are currently 'Work-based Training for Young People' (now incorporating 'Youth Training' and 'Modern Apprenticeships') and 'Work-based Training for Adults' (previously known as 'Training for Work').[84]

The 'New Deal for Young People' is the largest active labour market policy introduced by the post-1997 United Kingdom Labour government. Participation is effectively compulsory for 18-24 year-olds with six months or more of unemployment. Following an initial 'Gateway' programme (intensive counselling and guidance), participants face a range of options, including a subsidised job, environmental or voluntary work, or full-time education or training (without loss of benefit).

The 'New Deal for Long-term Unemployed Adults (25+)' is a measure introduced in June 1998, which is considerably smaller than the New Deal for Young People.[85] It shares, however, some of the latter's design features, the main difference being that eligibility is confined to those with two years of unemployment (subject to exceptions for certain groups, including people with English language needs).[86]

5. Young people

One area of continuing concern for the United Kingdom has been the problem of youth unemployment, which was highlighted throughout the transition period of labour law reform under successive Conservative governments in the

---

80 The outcome reflected something of 'an own goal' on the part of the trade union movement, which had publicly snubbed the then government's initiatives in this field.

81 See, for example, changes made to the basis for appointing 'lay members' to sit on the Employment Tribunals – formerly the effective fiefdom of the CBI and the TUC.

82 See W.D. Halls, 'United Kingdom', in T. Neville Postlethwaite (ed.), *International Encyclopedia of National Systems of Education,* Hamburg 1995, 1025-1033, and D. Raffe, A. Biggart, J. Fairgrieve, C. Howieson, J. Rodger & S. Burinston, *OECD Thematic Review: The Transition From Initial Education to Working Life,* OECD, Paris 1998.

83 A. Kim & K. Kurz, 'Precarious Employment, Education and Gender: A Comparison of Germany and the United Kingdom' (Paper prepared for the RC 28 meeting 'Social Stratification and Mobility: Integrating Theory and Research', Oxford, 10-13 April, 2002).

84 For updated material on this, see N. Meager, 'National Labour Market Policies, Trends: United Kingdom' *European Employment Observatory,* EU Commission, regular updates. Detailed presentation of many of the initiatives are to be seen in the United Kingdom's 'National Action Plans' developed under the reporting cycle of the European Union's employment policy.

85 See DfEE, New Deal for Young People and long-term unemployed people aged 25+: Statistics, *DfEE Statistical First Release,* 2/99, London, 5 January 1999.

86 Although these schemes are not specifically targeted at ethnic minorities, it is worth noting that the eligibility requirement (six months of registered unemployment) for adult training is relaxed for people for whom English is a second language and who need assistance with their spoken English to enter employment – most such people will be from ethnic minorities (including recent immigrants). In addition, there is an incentive system for Training and Enterprise Councils (TECs, which deliver the mainstream labour market measures) known as Performance Related Funding (PRF), whereby TECs which meet specific performance targets in a year (including targets to increase ethnic minority participation in training and reduce the gap in subsequent job outcomes) receive a funding bonus from central government. See Meager (supra).

last quarter of the 20th century. An indication of the activity levels of young persons as part of the age distribution of the workforce in the United Kingdom labour force can be found in Table 8.[87] On the basis of the most recent consolidated statistics, it is considered that:[88]

The economic activity of 16-19 year olds is closely linked to their participation in full-time education (FTE). Of those not in FTE in spring 2002, 85% were economically active, of whom 18% were ILO unemployed. For those in FTE, 44% were economically active. There has been an increase in youth ILO unemployment, with 406,000 people aged 18 to 24 unemployed in spring 2002, 5% higher than a year earlier. However, the number who had been out of work for more than a year fell by 19%, suggesting that long-term unemployment among younger people continues to fall.

It is worth noting that some research has been undertaken into whether unemployment early in an individual's career influences later employment prospects. However, the results are by no means clear-cut:

We find small positive effects on later unemployment of early-career unemployment for the unskilled, and small negative effects for the more skilled. One implication of this is that the unemployment experiences of cohorts coming of age in poor labour market conditions are more unequal within the cohort than those of luckier cohorts.[89]

6. The national minimum wage

In 1998 the recently elected Labour government enacted the National Minimum Wage Act, introducing, for the first time in the United Kingdom, a pay threshold sanctioned by inspection and legal sanctions. In connection with that innovation, the Government created the Low Pay Commission, whose role was to recommend the coverage and initial level of the minimum wage. Following the adoption of unanimous recommendations, the national minimum wage was introduced at a lower rate for under-25s, and at a lower general rate (£3.60 per hour) than the trades unions and many anti-poverty organisations had been advocating.

Table 8:   United Kingdom – Employment by age

	All aged 16 over	16-59/64	16-17	18-24	25-34	35-49	50-64 (M) 50-59 (W)	65+ (M) 60+ (W)
In Employment								
All Persons								
Jan-Mar 2001	27 428	26 620	658	3 249	6 674	10 160	5 880	808
Jan-Mar 2002	27 576	26 696	662	3 325	6 484	10 259	5 967	880
Jan-Mar 2003	27 859	26 939	670	3 353	6 320	10 442	6 154	920
Male								
Jan-Mar 2001	14 844	14 582	329	1 702	3 618	5 426	3 506	262
Jan-Mar 2002	14 560	14 560	322	1 747	3 499	5 456	3 536	285
Jan-Mar 2003	14 997	14 670	323	1 756	3 399	5 550	3 641	327
Female								
Jan-Mar 2001	12 585	12 039	329	1 547	3 055	4 734	2 374	546
Jan-Mar 2002	12 730	12 136	340	1 578	2 985	4 803	2 432	595
Jan-Mar 2003	12 269	12 269	347	1 597	2 921	4 892	2 513	592

---

87   See Office for National Statistics, Labour Force Survey (pre-release data set – to 1st quarter 2003).

88   Drawn from *National Statistics, UK 2003*: 'The Official Yearbook of the United Kingdom of Great Britain and Northern Ireland', HMSO, London 2002, see p. 124.

89   S. Burgess, C. Propper, H. Rees & A. Shearer, The Class of '81: The effects of early-career unemployment on subsequent unemployment experiences (University of Bristol, October 1999). The authors go on to observe that *An interpretation of these results has to focus on two things. First, the relative importance of different sources of information in the labour market is important. The issue is whether an individual's underlying ability sooner or later outweighs the adverse signal of a poor employment record. Alternatively, it may be that employers generally judge applicants' employment records in a sophisticated way and condition on general labour market conditions at the time. Second, the impact of the macro-environment on an individual's decision when to leave school matters. Evidence for Britain on this matter is mixed, with no consensus view on the effect of unemployment rates on school-leaving rates.*

National minimum wage rates at the time of writing were £4.20 per hour for those aged 22 and over (the adult rate) and £3.60 per hour for those aged 18-21 (the 'Development Rate'). There is provision for the Development Rate also to apply to workers aged 22 and over who are receiving accredited training during the first six months in a new job with a new employer. The Government has accepted the recommendation of the Low Pay Commission that these rates should be increased to £4.50 and £3.80 respectively in October 2003. It has also accepted the recommendation that, subject to confirmation in early 2004, there should be further increases to £4.85 and £4.10 in October 2004.

Notwithstanding that there appears to be evidence that some employers are evading the recommendations by changing employees' hours of work and other aspects of their contract,[90] the general impression is that positive effects have been forthcoming in the first years of the national minimum wage. In particular, according to the most recent report of the Low Pay Commission:

The minimum wage has had a significant impact on the gender pay gap at the bottom of the earnings distribution.[91]

7. The problem of social exclusion

The notion and terminology of 'social exclusion' have made their way into the United Kingdom context from policy documents developed at the level of the European Union.[92] Given the disparate make-up of the United Kingdom workforce and labour market, it will suffice here to indicate a small selection of factors (low pay related, ethnic related, and disability related) giving rise to potential for social exclusion.

7.1. Low pay related

As previously indicated, the problem of poverty and low pay has been approached, in part, through the introduction of a national minimum wage since 1998.

7.2. Ethnicity related

By 1997, among the UK population aged 16+ there were some 2.4 million adults in ethnic minority groups in 1997, amounting to 5.4% of the overall adult population and 6.4% of people of working age.[93] The difference in these percentages was reflective of the fact that the ethnic minority population has a younger than average age structure. Ethnic minorities are regionally concentrated, with around 70% resident in four urban areas (Greater London, the West Midlands, Greater Manchester and West Yorkshire), whereas less than a quarter of whites are resident in these areas.[94]

The make-up of the population by ethnic origin at the start of the period under consideration in this report (1991) is shown in Table 9 for Great Britain.

7.3. Disability related

Since the enactment of the Disability Discrimination Act 1995, significantly more data has been emerging in relation to the situation of disabled people in the British workforce. Some of that data confirms what has long been suspected – for example, according to the Low Pay Commission, disabled workers (those with a work-limiting disability) are generally more likely to be low-paid than non-disabled workers.[95]

The extent to which active measures are now required of employers in the United Kingdom in order to combat discrimination in relation to disabled workers can be recognised from the observations of the President of the EAT in the case of *Kenrick v Heinz*:[96]

---

90 See Katherine Duffy, United Kingdom National Report to the EAPN Conference on National & European Policies to Combat Poverty and Social Exclusion, Helsinki, 8-9 November 1999.

91 See Fourth Report of the *Low Pay Commission*, 'The National Minimum Wage: Building on Success', March 2003, para. 3.

92 See Katherine Duffy, United Kingdom National Report to the EAPN Conference on National & European Policies to Combat Poverty and Social Exclusion, Helsinki, 8-9 November 1999.

93 F. Sly, T. Thair & A. Risdon, 'Labour Market Participation of Ethnic Groups', 1998, *Labour Market Trends* (December).

94 For a broader picture, see inter alia Office for National Statistics, Social Focus on Ethnic Minorities (HMSO, London 1996), and T. Madood, R. Berthoud, J. Lakey, J. Nazroo, P. Smith, S. Virdee & S. Beishon, Ethnic Minorities in Britain: Diversity and Disadvantage, Policy Studies Institute, London 1997.

95 See Fourth Report of the *Low Pay Commission*, 'The National Minimum Wage: Building on Success', March 2003, para.2.17. The observation is based upon Labour Force Survey data, which uses a very broad definition of disability (broader, for example, than that used to monitor the effects of the Disability Discrimination Act 1995). It should also be noted that, according to Smith & Twomey, since 1998, there has been a significant increase in the proportion of employees reporting a disability. See A. Smith & B. Twomey, 'Labour Market Experiences of People with Disabilities. National Statistics Feature', 2002, *110 Labour Market Trends* 415.

96 Commented upon in Alan C. Neal, 'Disability Discrimination at Work', in A. Numhauser-Henning (ed), *Legal Perspectives on Equal Treatment and Non-Discrimination*, The Hague 2001, 351. The author goes on to observe that *What is clear, however, is that a complex of legislative goals – to penalise those who discriminate, to shift attitudes, to raise awareness of disability as an issue in employment relations, and to promote the integration of disabled persons into the active workforce – calls for new and imaginative regulatory techniques. Such a need is, one might suggest, finding a tangible response, and we are now witnessing (both at national and, particularly, at European level) the emergence of novel instruments and mechanisms seeking to deliver this ambitious combination of goals.* (at p. 358).

Table 9:   Population by ethnic origin: Great Britain

Ethnic group	Population (in 1 000s)	% of total population	% of ethnic minority populations
Black Caribbean	500	0.9	16.6
Black African	212	0.4	7.0
Other Black	178	0.3	5.9
Indian	840	1.5	27.9
Pakistani	477	0.9	15.8
Bangladeshi	163	0.3	5.4
Chinese	157	0.3	5.2
Other Asian	198	0.4	6.6
Other ethnic minorities	290	0.5	9.6
White	51 874	94.5	-
Total	54 889	100.0	100.0

...we would not wish to leave the case without some expression of sympathy for Heinz's position. Heinz has not, on the facts of this case, been a 'bad' employer in any moral sense. It responded to Mr Kenrick's long and indefinite absence with real patience; it frequently consulted Mr Kenrick, it listened to him and his Union Representative. It repeatedly made Dr MacIntyre's services available to him. Whether or not the Employment Tribunal, on remission of unfair dismissal, ultimately finds the decision fair or unfair, (which will be entirely a matter for them) Heinz's decision to dismiss could not, in our view, be described as harsh. For all that, it has been held to be guilty of disability discrimination, a finding which may attract some opprobrium to the perpetrator and which Heinz has accordingly very properly sought to resist. It has failed in that task not because it is a bad employer – there is no reason to think it is – but because, at a stage when the difficult disability discrimination legislation was in its infancy, it failed to give such full consideration as is now necessary to the possibility of disability and to discrimination by reason of it. That legislation was, well after the time at which Heinz was grappling with the unfolding facts in 1997, described in Clark v. Novacold ... by Counsel as revolutionary and described by the Court of Appeal itself as being unusually complex. It is hard to be very critical of an employer faced in early 1997 not only with such legislation but also with so nebulous a disability as CFS. The legislation has also been described, rightly in our view, as passed in order to change the attitudes and behaviour of employers – British Sugar plc v. Kirker [1998] IRLR 624 EAT; it may fairly be said that Heinz's principal shortcoming in 1997 was in not changing fast enough.

Chapter III:
Labour law and adaptability

The responsiveness of United Kingdom labour law to changing patterns of work and issues of adaptability, as technological progress and globalisation have increasingly impacted upon the world of work, has been sluggish. A number of fairly rigid conceptual paradigms remain, amongst which the issue of 'employee status' has consequences across almost the whole field, while reliance upon strict Common Law contractual analysis for the contract of employment can give rise to some surprising outcomes.[97]

Despite a lively debate for some considerable time over the emergence of 'atypical work forms',[98] little formal response was forthcoming from the legal regulatory forum, and it has only been with the introduction of measures stimulated by social policy initiatives at the European Union level that any degree of comfort can be detected in the law's treatment of part-time, fixed-term, temporary, and certain other 'atypical' workers.

One of the best-known categorisations of 'the flexible workforce' is that which makes use of the notion of 'core/peripheral' workers, developed by Atkinson *et al* at the IES in Sussex. Using this form of classification, the authors of the 1998 WERS observe that:

The ability of managers to adjust the size of their workforces in line with requirements and demand – usually referred to as 'numerical flexibility' – appears to be quite widespread. It has also

increased over the past five years .... In each of the four categories, the number of workplaces reporting greater use of contracting out and 'non-standard' workers far outweighs the number where it has gone down. ... Another form of flexibility is 'functional' flexibility, which refers to the ability to move workers from one task to another. We asked managers to tell us what proportion of employees in the occupation with the most employees at the workplace were formally trained to be able to do jobs other than their own. In more than half of all workplaces this form of flexibility is either non-existent or negligible, but in around a quarter of workplaces, most employees in the largest occupational group are trained to be adaptable. There are negative associations between the use of 'non-standard' workers – particularly, the use of temporary agency workers – and the proportion of employees who are trained to be functionally flexible.[99]

Even here, however, the need to introduce measures designed to implement the recent group of directives which have resulted from the social dialogue at the European level has not obviously brought about a re-visiting of some of the fundamental premises contained within United Kingdom labour law[100] – although a few examples of more creative approaches can be seen in recent statutory definitions accorded to 'home-workers' and 'agency workers'.[101]

It is, of course, widely held that the use of 'flexible' work forms presents a dramatic challenge for labour law regula-

---

97 See, for example, the variety of problems which have come to the fore in relation to 'illegal contracts', 'undue influence or duress', and the doctrine of 'frustration' (supervening impossibility).

98 See the contributions by J. Atkinson, 'Manning for Uncertainty: Some emerging UK Work Patterns', University of Sussex Institute of Manpower Studies, Brighton 1984, and J. Atkinson, 'Manpower strategies for flexible organisatons', 1984, *Personnel Management 28*. The terminology of 'the flexible firm' has passed into common usage, although the model has given rise to criticism: see, for example, A. Pollert, 'The flexible firm – fixation or fact?', 1988, 2 *Work, Employment and Society 281*, and, for a robust rejection of the Pollert view, C. Hakim, 'Workforce Restructuring in Europe in the 1980s', 1989, 5 *The International Journal of Comparative Labour Law and Industrial Relations 167*. The general debate is addressed in Alan C. Neal, 'Atypical Workforms and European Labour Law', 1992, *45 Recht der Arbeit 115*.

99 WERS98, First Findings, p. 9.

100 Notably, Council Directive 97/81/EC of 15 December 1997 concerning the Framework Agreement on part-time work concluded by UNICE, CEEP and the ETUC (as subsequently extended to the United Kingdom), Council Directive 1999/70/EC of 28 June 1999 concerning the framework agreement on fixed-term work concluded by ETUC, UNICE and CEEP, as well as in relation to the earlier Council Directive 91/383/EEC of 25 June 1991 supplementing the measures to encourage improvements in the safety and health at work of workers with a fixed-duration employment relationship or a temporary employment relationship. For a comment on the United Kingdom's approach to defining the scope of labour law protections through use of the statutory terms 'employee' and 'worker', see supra.

101 See the definition of 'home worker' which was first introduced by the s.35 of the National Minimum Wage Act 1998, and the definition of 'agency worker', contained in s.34 of the National Minimum Wage Act 1998 and Regulation 36 of the Working Time Regulations 1998. These definitions serve to modify the 'default' application of definitions for 'workers' and 'employees', which underlie employment protections in the form of such mechanisms as 'unfair dismissal'. See supra.

tion and the ability to ensure fundamental social rights at the workplace.[102] What one is referring to in using the expression 'flexible', however, calls for comment, as does the implication of using the term 'atypical' in respect of workers. In the United Kingdom context, the expression 'atypical' was, even quite recently, commonly used to refer narrowly to work performed by part-time workers, temporary workers, fixed-term workers, and (in so far as they were not already covered by one of the other categories) seasonal workers[103] – although the rather obvious point has been made that it is difficult to speak of 'atypical' in a context where the categories embraced by that label would seem to make up a majority of employment in the national economy. Use of the expression 'flexible' also lacks any empirical basis in the United Kingdom context, although it seems that the expression goes rather wider than the earlier expression 'atypical'. In specific terms, as has previously been mentioned,[104] there is some assistance in the statutory provisions as regards the definition of 'home worker' and 'agency worker'. One interesting recent example of United Kingdom statutory terminological amendment (which owes its origins directly to EU initiatives) can be pointed to in relation to 'fixed-term contracts' – where the expression 'limited-term contract' has been substituted throughout the relevant legislative provisions.[105]

A recent concern has arisen in relation to so-called 'contingent workers',[106] while the relatively widespread use of 'agency workers' in the United Kingdom has attracted the same kind of adverse comment which has led to (so far unsuccessful) efforts at the level of the European Union to introduce regulation of 'temporary work agencies' through a Directive based upon the 'social dialogue' provisions of the Treaty.

Care also needs to be taken in relation to pay levels as these relate to various forms of 'flexible' work-forms. By way of example, the Low Pay Commission comments, in relation to one particular group:

Low pay is common among home workers. Analysis of this group using LFS data is limited due to small sample sizes, and focuses on home workers who do not work with a computer or telephone essential to their job. The data suggest that manual home workers are over-represented among gainers from the October 2001 uprating [of the national minimum wage].[107]

---

102 As the ILO has put it, when commenting on the particular problem of how to categorise the 'self-employed':... *Like unemployment, flexible forms of work pose a challenge to social security arrangements. Flexible forms of work lack continuity. Spans of work and unemployment alternate, as do weekly working hours. Defining the periods during which flexi-workers are entitled to various benefits (e.g. To unemployment benefits) is becoming more difficult as the forms or work continue to multiply and definitions of various forms of work become blurred. Home workers resemble the self-employed, the self-employed resemble on-call workers, employees resemble entrepreneurs, etc.,* ILO Bureau for Workers' Activities (ACTRIV), *Labour Market Trends and Globalization's Impact on Them,* ILO, Geneva.

103 For treatment of this, with criticism of that contemporary limited perspective, see Alan C. Neal, 'Atypical Workforms and European Labour Law', 1992, *Recht der Arbeit 115* – especially at footnotes 5 and 6.

104 See supra.

105 See, for example, in section 95(1)(b) of the Employment Rights Act 1996, as substituted by the Fixed-term Employees (Prevention of Less Favourable Treatment) Regulations 2002 (SI 2002/2034).

106 The ILO's Bureau for Workers' Activity, drawing from the practice of the United States, uses the term as follows: *Contingent workers are those who do not have an implicit or explicit contract for ongoing employment, and who do not expect their jobs to last. Wage and salaried workers are included, even if they already held the job for more than a year and expect to hold the job for at least an additional year. Self-employed persons and independent contractors are included, if they expect their employment to last for an additional year or less, and if they had been self-employed or independent contractors for one year or less.*

107 Fourth Report of the *Low Pay Commission*, 'The National Minimum Wage: Building on Success', March 2003, para.2.18.

Chapter IV:
Promoting equal opportunities

An indication of some of the fields in which equal opportunities promotion has been addressed in the United Kingdom context emerges from earlier presentation of some of the characteristics of the labour market and problems in relation to issues of 'employability'. From a regulatory perspective, the experience of anti-discrimination and equal opportunities legislation is quite long-standing, with particular provisions having been in operation in relation to sex discrimination and race discrimination for some thirty years,[108] while statutory provision in relation to disabled workers has been in force since 1995.[109] Alongside these areas, there has also been development of protection in relation to transsexuals.[110]

The handling of discrimination issues through litigation before the Employment Tribunals gives rise to a fairly substantial case-load for both ACAS and the Tribunals themselves. Outcomes from conciliation undertaken in relation to discrimination complaints concerning equal pay, sex, race, and disability, are set out in Table 10. It should also be noted that this is an area where particularly widespread use has been made of 'complementary non-legislative and/or quasi-legislative measures', often in the form of 'Codes of Practice'. So, too, has the opportunity been taken to establish specialist public bodies charged with duties *inter alia* to promote good practice – whether this be in relation to sex (through

Table 10: Discrimination, etc. Cases received and dealt with by ACAS

Year/ Jurisdiction	Cases received	Settled	Withdrawn	Employment Tribunal	Total cases completed
Equal Pay Act					
2001/2002	2 614	619	969	264	1 852
2000/2001	4 933	614	834	190	1 638
1999/2000	2 786	819	451	165	1 435
Sex Discrimination Act					
2001/2002	7 525	2 993	2 191	1 161	6 345
2000/2001	9 082	3 021	1 900	1 206	6 127
1999/2000	7 038	2 937	1 782	1 185	5 904
Race Relations Act					
2001/2002	3 825	1 455	1 253	989	3 697
2000/2001	4 153	1 322	1 303	1 041	3 666
1999/2000	3 922	1 231	1 054	915	3 200
Disability Discrimination Act					
2001/2002	5 057	1 957	1 317	791	4 065
2000/2001	4 422	1 647	1 102	679	3 428
1999/2000	3 583	1 410	934	572	2 916

108   Currently contained in the Sex Discrimination Acts 1975 and 1986, and the Race Relations Act 1976.
109   As introduced by the Disability Discrimination Act 1995.
110   See the Sex Discrimination (Gender Reassignment) Regulations 1999 (SI 1999 No.1102).

the Equal Opportunities Commission, EOC), to race (through the Commission on Racial Equality, CRE), or disability (through the Disability Rights Commission, DRC) – as well as to assist alleged victims of such discrimination in bringing their complaints before a court or tribunal.[111]

The need to implement the first two 'Article 13 Directives' adopted in 2000 have caused the United Kingdom legislator to undertake a thoroughgoing assessment of the extent to which existing statutory protections designed to combat discrimination in working life need adjustment and/or extension.[112] It may be noted that, already, the United Kingdom position had been modified in the light of developments at the level of the European Union – notably, with the enactment of the Sex Discrimination Act 1986 (following the judgment of the ECJ in the *Marshall* case),[113] with provisions on gender re-assignment (in the wake of a later case brought before the ECJ),[114] with changes in relation to the burden of proof (in accordance with the 'burden of proof Directive'),[115] and in relation to a variety of pay-related issues following upon the copious case law of the Luxembourg Court under Article 141 (formerly Article 119).[116]

---

111 Proposals are currently being brought forward to merge the various public bodies into a single equal opportunities body – coinciding with the substantial overhaul of the legal provisions in the context of transposing the provisions of the two 'Equality Directives' of 2000 into United Kingdom domestic law.

112 Council Directive 2000/43/EC of 29 June 2000 implementing the principle of equal treatment between persons irrespective of racial or ethnic origin, which is to be implemented by 19 July 2003 (see Article 16), and Council Directive 2000/78/EC of 27 November 2000 establishing a general framework for equal treatment in employment and occupation, which (subject to derogations in respect of age and disability discrimination – see Article 18) is to be implemented by 2 December 2003 (see Article 17).

113 C-152/84: M.H. Marshall v Southampton and South West Hampshire Area Health Authority (Teaching) [1986] E.C.R. 0723.

114 C-13/94: P v S and Cornwall County Council [1996] E.C.R. I-2143.

115 Council Directive 97/80/EC of 15 December 1997 on the burden of proof in cases of discrimination based on sex, implemented in the shape of Section 63A of the Sex Discrimination Act 1975.

116 Particularly in relation to the line of cases following C-262/88: Douglas Harvey Barber v Guardian Royal Exchange Assurance Group [1990] E.C.R. I-1889.

Chapter V:
Overview and comment

The period 1992-2003 has witnessed a continuation of the rapid change which had already been impacting upon the United Kingdom labour market for a decade and a half under Conservative administrations since 1979. As the shape of the labour force shifted ever further away from the 'traditional' industrial pattern which had formed the backdrop to the report of the Donovan Commission in 1968, the regulatory tools of labour law were struggling to keep up with more diverse work-forms and practices. At the same time, the inability of the traditional actors in an outmoded model of 'free collective bargaining' to define new roles and relationships had cleared the stage for the almost unchallenged dominance of the statutory norm as the 'natural' regulatory tool.[117]

The weakness of the trade union movement has been of particular significance in this process. If ever the decline of 'the old ways' needed confirmation, it was encapsulated in the blunt observation that:

In 1979 membership stood at 12.9 million, and collective bargaining coverage extended over 70% of the workforce. By 1998 membership stood at 7.8 million, while coverage had declined to 36%.[118]

What support there might be for trade unions does nothing to suggest any kind of return to 'the golden era' of membership.[119] Nor do the small number of voices sounding any more optimistic notes yet carry with them the ring of conviction. Certainly, in spite of much heralding (as well as regular consideration of experience elsewhere in the European Union),[120] the question of whether 'partnership' offers the way forward for trade unionism in the United Kingdom remains open to debate.[121] Furthermore, the recognition that there is 'no way back' has also been dawning upon commentators of all shades of persuasion – particularly as the true impact of the regulatory mechanisms associated with EU employment policy has become more evident. It is not only lawyers and socio-legal commentators who are concerned to stress the significance of 'soft law' alternatives to the statutory norm.[122] Thus,

Rather than legal enactment and collective bargaining being the main engines of the 'Europeanisation' of industrial relations, benchmarking and 'soft' forms of regulation are increasingly to the fore.[123]

---

117 Something which has not, of course, been confined to experience in the United Kingdom. See Alan C. Neal, 'Industrial Relations in Europe: Assessing the Regulatory Challenge for Labour Law', in M. Biagi (ed), *Towards a European Model of Industrial Relations? Building on the First Report of the European Commission*, The Hague 2001, 109, especially at pp. 113-115.

118 D. Metcalf, 'British Unions: Dissolution or Resurgence Revisited?', *Discussion Paper 493, Centre for Economic Performance, LSE*, London 2001.

119 For some comment of related issues, see A. Charlwood, 'Why Do Non-Union Employees Want to Unionise? Evidence from Britain', 2002, *40 British Journal of Industrial Relations 463*.

120 See, for example, discussions such as that contained in P. Marginson & K. Sisson, 'European dimensions to collective bargaining: new symmetries within an asymmetric process?', 2002, *33 Industrial Relations Journal 332*, or K. Sisson, K. Arrowsmith & P. Marginson, 'All Benchmarkers Now? Benchmarking and the "Europeanisation" of Industrial Relations', 2003, *34 Industrial Relations Journal 15*. For a more critical approach, see R. Hyman, 'The Europeanisation – Or the Erosion – of Industrial Relations?', 2001, *32 Industrial Relations Journal 280*.

121 See the comments of E. Heery, 'Partnership versus Organising: Alternative Futures for British Trade Unionism', 2002, *33 Industrial Relations Journal 20*, as well as the contributions from William Brown, 'Putting Partnership into Practice in Britain', 2000, *38 British Journal of Industrial Relations 299*, and J. Knell, 'Partnership at Work', *Employment Relations Research Series No.7, DTI, London*. Supra note 9.

122 See, on this phenomenon, J. Kenner, 'EC Labour Law: The Softly, Softly Approach', 1995, *11 The International Journal of Comparative Labour Law and Industrial Relations 307*, and his later 'The EC Employment Title and the "Third Way": Making Soft Law Work?', 1999, *15 The International Journal of Comparative Labour Law and Industrial Relations 33*. More recently, see K. Sisson & P. Marginson, 'Soft Regulation' – Travesty of the real thing or new dimension? (Paper produced for the ESRC's research project on 'Emerging Boundaries of European Collective Bargaining at Sector and Enterprise Levels', within the context of the 'One Europe or Several?' programme, June 2001.

123 K. Sisson, K. Arrowsmith & P. Marginson, 'All Benchmarkers Now? Benchmarking and the "Europeanisation" of Industrial Relations', 2003, *34 Industrial Relations Journal 15*.

Nor can one ignore the continuing question marks which hang over a United Kingdom outside the group of EU Member States which have committed themselves to economic and monetary union (EMU).[124]

Perhaps, though, the real test for British collective labour relations actors will be in the course of implementation for instruments such as the 2002 'Consultation Directive'.[125] Here, the mix of post-Thatcherite labour market and 'old Europe' normative intervention will have to be worked out on the battlefield of 'the home of collective bargaining'.

In terms of the 'tools' for regulation, the United Kingdom's system of Common Law has shown itself surprisingly flexible in the course of 'receiving' European Union law into the domestic framework and procedures. On a formal level, there have not been the same kinds of 'constitutional integrity' problems in relation to the doctrine of the 'supremacy' of Community Law, such as have been faced in France, Germany or Italy. Nor has the House of Lords been reticent to ensure that the 'intention of the legislator' can be read as giving full effect to directives in the social field.[126]

So, too, there is a (perhaps surprising) strong desire on the part of the United Kingdom government – in common with its Conservative predecessors – to ensure compliance with their European Union obligations, once a directive in the social field has been adopted and falls to be transposed into domestic law. As a result, the legislative process undertakes thorough evaluation of the practical implications of various drafting possibilities – rather than relying purely upon a linguistic transposition 'onto the statute book'. That process of transposition has not, however, so far succeeded in establishing a wholehearted engagement for the 'social partners' – nor is there a real prospect of the 'social dialogue' route to domestic legislation gaining a real foothold in the foreseeable future for the United Kingdom.[127] The notion of *erga omnes*, so beloved of continental jurists, finds no resonance in the courts of the United Kingdom, while the traditional view of the collective bargain constituting a 'gentlemen's agreement' continues to distort any comparative discussion of the role of the collective agreement as a regulatory instrument.[128]

The more one reflects upon the particular United Kingdom situation, however, the more sharply one is struck by the legacy of 'the Thatcher years' – certainly, in respect of the extent to which so many fundamental socio-economic institutions were torn down and replaced. In social terms, there can be little dispute that the experience of exposing the United Kingdom economy of the 1980s to the full rigours of 'market forces' was 'nasty, brutish and short', as an open welcome was extended to those preaching the gospel from the shores of Lake Ontario. Nevertheless, the underlying stability of the national economy, together with a 'sea change' in attitudes towards industrial relations and their conduct, have combined to provide relatively satisfactory levels of inflation, employment and unemployment, and 'an increasing standard of living' – much as aspired to by the rhetoric of the Treaties establishing and framing the European Union.

The 'welfare state' of the immediate post-Second World War era may no longer be recognisable in much of the detail, and the scale of privatisations during the 1980s and early 1990s have altered the perception of 'public services' in key ways.

124   See P. Whyman, 'British Trade Unions and Economic and Monetary Union', 2002, *41 Industrial Relations 467*. Attention in this context is drawn to the requirement placed upon the European Investment Bank by Article 2 of its Statute, in the framework of Article 105 of the Treaty to the effect that: *The primary objective of the ESCB shall be to maintain price stability. Without prejudice to the objective of price stability, the ESCB shall support the general economic policies in the Community with a view to contributing to the achievement of the objectives of the Community as laid down in Article 2. The ESCB shall act in accordance with the principle of an open market economy with free competition, favouring an efficient allocation of resources, and in compliance with the principles set out in Article 4.* A key discussion, as outlined in Alan C. Neal, 'From 'Bad Boy' to European Role Model? The Strange Legacy of United Kingdom Employment Policies Since the Single European Act', in M. Biagi (ed), *Job Creation and Labour Law: From protection towards Pro-action,* The Hague 2000, 269, at pp. 280-281, has been over the extent to which the European Central Bank should or should not take considerations other than 'price stability' into account in its deliberations on monetary policy. See, for example, the view of the former Commissioner for Social Affairs, Padraig Flynn, speaking at the Hubert Detremmerie Seminar in Brussels, on 11 March 1999, under the title 'Social Europe after the Euro': *For me, the issue is relatively straightforward. Of course, the ECB must take employment considerations into account. Can you imagine the Chairman of the Federal Reserve, telling the US Congress that the FED would ignore the impact of its decisions on employment? ... Secondly, the Treaty is clear. Article 105 of the Treaty sets two basic principles for guiding monetary policy for EMU as a whole. The primary objective is price stability. Its second objective, without prejudice to the first, is to support general economic policies to contribute to achieving the core objectives of the Community, as set out in Article 2 of the Treaty: those of growth and employment.* A number of issues touching upon the potential impact of EMU on industrial relations systems are considered in M. Biagi, 'The European Monetary Union and Industrial Relations', 2000, *16 The International Journal of Comparative Labour Law and Industrial Relations 39*. More wide-ranging are the contributions to T. Kauppinen (ed), 'The Impact of EMU on Industrial Relations in European Union', *Finnish Labour Relations Association,* Helsinki 1998.

125   Directive 2002/14/EC of the European Parliament and of the Council of 11 March 2002 establishing a general framework for informing and consulting employees in the European Community. See the comments in Alan C. Neal, 'Information and Consultation for Employees – Still Seeking the Philosopher's Stone?' in M. Biagi (ed), *Quality of Work and Employee Involvement in Europe,* The Hague 2002, 83.

126   As was vividly demonstrated in the labour law case of *Litster v Forth Dry Dock and Engineering Co Ltd* [1989] ICR 341.

127   For some of the problems associated with notions of 'social dialogue' and the 'social partners', see Alan C. Neal, 'We love you social dialogue – But who exactly are you?', in Fondazione Giulio Pastore, *La contrattazione collettiva europea: Profili giuridici ed economici,* Milan 2001, 113.

128   See Alan C. Neal, 'The Collective Agreement as a Public Law Instrument', in F.K. Banakas (ed), *United Kingdom Law in the 1980s,* London 1988.

So, too, are the social scars of the changes wrought during nearly two decades of Conservative administrations clearly visible in terms of wealth distribution and the current extent of poverty in the United Kingdom. 'Equal opportunities' may not have been developed as fast or as broadly as might have been aspired to, and the emergence of a 'multi-cultural' society with continuing high levels of immigration creates tensions for the social fabric of United Kingdom society at the dawn of the 21st century.

For many, the weakness of traditional collective organisations, the uncertainties of post-EMU enlargement Europe, and the challenges of a fast-changing labour market in a rapidly regenerating society, present a fearful threat to the future of 'a social dimension' to temper the 'market excesses' of recent years in the United Kingdom. For others, however, the recognition that dramatic change has already taken place, and a sense that there may have emerged an underlying strength and durability to the foundations of working life in the UK, offer a more optimistic perspective from which to observe the continuing adaptation which is taking place.

For the policy-makers, the challenge now is to integrate the best features of 'the European social model' with the benefits which have followed from the last quarter of a century of turmoil, change, and adaptation for 'the home of collective bargaining'. To that end, the objectives embedded in the 'pillars' of the European employment strategy, coupled with the developing tools of 'the open method of co-ordination, legislation, the social dialogue, the Structural Funds, the support programmes, the integrated policy approach, analysis and research',[129] may prove to be of benefit to a national system in search of new tools, new techniques, and – one might almost go so far as to add – new horizons.

As this commentator has suggested elsewhere:[130]

Whether it will prove possible for the European Union to achieve its economic objectives within the discipline of economic and monetary union, and, at the same time, satisfy the social (and, consequently, political) needs of its citizens, only time will tell. Certainly, if 'the partnership approach', with strong overtones of corporatism embedded in the 'social dialogue' upon which so much hinges, is to prove capable of delivering both necessary change and broad socio-political stability, it will have responded to a challenge much greater than anything previously asked of the continent of Europe. ...In the meantime, more anxious observers await some evidence that dramatic change – which has undeniably been achieved within the United Kingdom economy and labour market over the course of the last two decades – can effectively be secured throughout the European Union without paying the social price which, at the same time, gave rise to such a 'divided Britain' by the last decade of the 20th century.[131]

Labour law in the United Kingdom currently stands ill-equipped to respond effectively to the swiftly-changing phenomena emerging in a labour market which has changed out of all recognition in the course of a quarter of a century. Unrecognised as a 'discipline' in its own right,[132] and without the institution of a true specialist 'Labour Court',[133] it struggles to deliver the necessary sensitivity to the industrial relations subject matter with which it is so intimately involved. Notwithstanding a proven ability to assimilate the value systems inherent in the regulatory structure and mechanisms of the European Union, the foundations of labour law at the beginning of the 21st century remain constrained by traditional Common Law concepts – 'the employee', 'equality of bargaining power', the undesirability of restrictive covenants on grounds of 'public policy', inappropriately applied doctrines relating to 'duress' and to 'illegal contracts', and a whole host of other issues.

Perhaps it is already something of a miracle that labour law in the United Kingdom has managed to respond as substantially as it has to date. Whatever its shortcomings so far, however, one thing remains almost certain: the miracle will have to carry on, because there has, to date, been little or no sign of the necessary 'freshness of thinking' which would be required to free labour law from the shackles of its own history.

---

129   See the *Social Policy Agenda*, Annexed to the Presidency Conclusions, Nice European Council Meeting, 7, 8 and 9 December 2000, para.28.

130   Alan C. Neal, 'From 'Bad Boy' to European Role Model? The Strange Legacy of United Kingdom Employment Policies Since the Single European Act', in M. Biagi (ed.), *Job Creation and Labour Law: From protection towards Pro-action*, The Hague 2000, 269, at 279.

131   For an indication of the increase in United Kingdom income inequality between 1979 and 1989, see T. Stark, *Income and Wealth in the 1980s*, Fabian Society, 2nd ed. London 1990. Nearly fifteen years on from the last administration headed by Prime Minister Thatcher, concern is heightened by looking at the Labour government which has been in power in the United Kingdom since 1997, whose policies in these key fields have continued much of the foundation work set in train by predecessor Conservative administrations, notwithstanding a high-profile discourse of 'Europeanism' and 'social rights'. See, for example, some of the statements in the 1998 White Paper entitled Fairness at Work (Cm 3968). *There will be no going back. The days of strikes without ballots, mass picketing, closed shops and secondary action are over. Even after the changes we propose, Britain will have the most lightly regulated labour market of any leading economy in the world.* (Foreword, by the Prime Minister).

132   See the observations in Alan C. Neal, 'Comparative Labour law and Industrial Relations: 'Major Discipline? – Who Cares?', in C. Engels & M. Weiss (eds.), *Labour Law and Industrial Relations at the Turn of the Century: Liber Amicorum for Roger Blanpain*, The Hague 1998, 55.

133   The Employment Tribunals (at first instance) and the Employment Appeals Tribunal (at the first appellate level) are both subject to the 'normal' civil justice framework dominated by the Court of Appeal (Civil Division) and the House of Lords. Indeed, even in relation to the standing and functions of the Employment Tribunals, the resistance to designating 'specialist status' has recently been affirmed by the report of Sir Andrew Leggatt, *Tribunals for Users: One System, One Service*, 2001, notwithstanding the acknowledgement that the Employment Tribunals 'are effectively labour courts in all but name' (at para. 5.7).

Annexes

1. Selected bibliography

Atkinson 1984(a)	J. Atkinson, *Manning for Uncertainty: Some emerging UK Work Patterns,* University of Sussex Institute of Manpower Studies, Brighton 1984
Atkinson 1984(b)	J. Atkinson, 'Manpower strategies for flexible organisations', 1984, *Personnel Management* 28
Biagi 2000	M. Biagi (ed), *Job Creation and Labour Law: From Protection towards Pro-action,* The Hague 2000
Biagi 2002	M. Biagi (ed), *Quality of Work and Employee Involvement in Europe,* The Hague 2002
Blackburn & Hart 2002	R. Blackburn & M. Hart, 'Small firms' awareness and knowledge of individual employment rights', *DTI Employment Relations Research Series No.14,* London 2002
Brook 2002	K. Brook, 'Trade Union Membership: An Analysis of Data from the Autumn 2001 LFS', 2002, *Labour Market Trends* 343
Brown 2000	William Brown, 'Putting Partnership into Practice in Britain', 2000, 38 *British Journal of Industrial Relations* 299
Brown *et al* 2000	W. Brown, S. Deakin, D. Nash & S. Oxenbridge, 'The Employment Contract: From Collective Procedures to Individual Rights', 2000, 38 *British Journal of Industrial Relations* 611
Brown *et al* 2001	W. Brown, P. Marginson & J. Walsh, *The Management of Pay as the Influence of Collective Bargaining Diminishes* (ESRC Centre for Business Research, University of Cambridge, Working Paper No. 213, 2001)
Bryson & Wilkinson 2001	A. Bryson & D. Wilkinson, Collective bargaining and workplace performance: An investigation using the Workplace Employee Relations Survey 1998, *DTI Employment Relations Research Series No.12,* 2001
Burgess *et al* 1999	S. Burgess, C. Propper, H. Rees & A. Shearer, *The Class of '81: The effects of early-career unemployment on subsequent unemployment experiences,* University of Bristol, October 1999
Chorlwood 2002	A. Charlwood, 'Why Do Non-Union Employees Want to Unionise? Evidence from Britain', 2002, 40 *British Journal of Industrial Relations* 463
Clark & Wedderburn 1987	J. Clark & Lord Wedderburn, 'Juridification – A Universal Trend? The British Experience in Labor Law', in G. Teubner (ed), *Juridification of Social Spheres,* De Gruyter 1987, 163
Cully *et al* 1999	M. Cully, S. Woodland, S.O' Reilly & G. Dix, *Britain at Work: As depicted by the 1998 Workplace Employee Relations Survey,* London 1999
Davies & Freedland 1993	P. Davies & M. Freedland, *Labour Legislation and Public Policy,* Clarendon Press 1993
De N. Clark 1968	G. de N. Clark, 'Remedies for Unjust Dismissal: Proposals for Legislation', PEP Broadsheet 518, 1970
Deakin & Morris 2001	S. Deakin & G. Morris, *Labour Law,* 3rd edition, London 2001
DfEE 1999	DfEE, 'New Deal for Young People and long-term unemployed people aged 25+: Statistics', *DfEE Statistical First Release, 2/99,* London , 5 January 1999
DTI 2002	DTI, *Discussion Document on Employment Status in Relation to Statutory Employment Rights* (URN 02/1058)
Duffy 1999	K. Duffy, *United Kingdom National Report to the EAPN Conference on National & European Policies to Combat Poverty and Social Exclusion* (Helsinki, 8-9 November 1999)

Hakim 1989	C.Hakim, 'Workforce Restructuring in Europe in the 1980s', 1989, 5 *The International Journal of Comparative Labour Law and Industrial Relations* 167
Halls 1995	W.D. Halls, 'United Kingdom', in T.Neville Postlethwaite (ed.), *International Encyclopedia of National Systems of Education,* Hamburg 1995, 1025-1033
Heery 2002	E. Heery, 'Partnership versus Organising: Alternative Futures for British Trade Unionism', 2002, 33 *Industrial Relations Journal* 20
HMSO 1968	*Report of the Royal Commission on Trade Unions and Employers' Associations 1965-1968* (Chairman, Lord Donovan), Cmnd.3623 (HMSO, London 1968)
HMSO 1977	*Report of the Committee of Inquiry on Industrial Democracy* (Chairman, Lord Bullock), Cmnd.6706 (London 1977).
HMSO 1996	Office for National Statistics, *Social Focus on Ethnic Minorities* (HMSO, London 1996)
HMSO 1998(a)	*Fairness at Work* (Cm 3968)
HMSO 1998(b)	Consultation Document, *ACAS Arbitration Scheme for the Resolution of Unfair Dismissal Disputes* (London 1998)
HMSO 2001	*Tribunals for Users: One System, One Service* (London 2001)
HMSO 2002(a)	*Annual Report of the Certification Officer for 2001-02* (London 2002)
HMSO 2002(b)	ETS, *Annual Report and Accounts 2001-2002* (HC 951)
HMSO 2002(c)	*Moving Forward: The Report of the Employment Tribunal System Taskforce* (HMSO, London 2002)
HMSO 2002(d)	ACAS Annual Report for 2001/02 (London 2002)
HMSO 2002 (e)	*Employment Tribunals Service Annual Report & Accounts 2001-2002* (HC 951)
HMSO 2003	Fourth Report of the Low Pay Commission, *The National Minimum Wage: Building on Success* (HMSO, London 2003)
HMSO (continuing)	Office for National Statistics, *Labour Market Statistics* (HMSO, London, regular updates)
HMSO (continuing)	Office for National Statistics, *Labour Force Survey* (regular quarterly updates)
Hyman 2001	R. Hyman, 'The Europeanisation – Or the Erosion – of Industrial Relations?', 2001, 32 *Industrial Relations Journal* 280
ILO	*Labour Market Trends and Globalization's Impact on Them*, ILO, Geneva
ILO	ILO Bureau for Workers' Activities (ACTRIV), *Labour Market Trends and Globalization's Impact on Them,* ILO, Geneva
Kellard & Middleton 1998	K. Kellard & S. Middleton, 'Helping Unemployed People into Self-employment', *DfEE Research Report RR46*, Sheffield 1998
Kenner 1995	J. Kenner, 'EC Labour Law: The Softly, Softly Approach', 1995, 11 *The International Journal of Comparative Labour Law and Industrial Relations* 307
Kenner 1999	J. Kenner, 'The EC Employment Title and the 'Third Way': Making Soft Law Work?, 1999, 15 *The International Journal of Comparative Labour Law and Industrial Relations* 33
Kim & Kurz 2002	A. Kim & K. Kurz, 'Precarious Employment, Education and Gender: A Comparison of Germany and the United Kingdom', Paper prepared for the RC 28 meeting 'Social Stratification and Mobility: Integrating Theory and Research', Oxford, 10-13 April, 2002
Knell	J. Knell, 'Partnership at Work', *Employment Relations Research Series No.7*, DTI, London
Knight & Latreille 2000	K. Knight & P. Latreille, 'Discipline, Dismissals and Complaints to Employment Tribunals', 2000 38 *British Journal of Industrial Relations* 533
Machin 2000	S. Machin, 'Union Decline in Britain', 2000, 38 *British Journal of Industrial Relations* 631
Madood et al 1997	T. Madood, R. Berthoud, J. Lakey, J. Nazroo, P. Smith, S. Virdee & S. Beishon, *Ethnic Minorities in Britain: Diversity and Disadvantage*, Policy Studies Institute, London 1997
Marginson & Sisson 2002	P. Marginson & K. Sisson, 'European dimensions to collective bargaining: new symmetries within an asymmetric process?', 2002, 33 *Industrial Relations Journal* 332

Meager	N. Meager, 'National Labour Market Policies, Trends: United Kingdom', *European Employment Observatory*, EU Commission, regular updates
Metcalf 1998	H. Metcalf, 'Self-employment for the Unemployed: the Role of Public Policy', *DfEE Research Report No.47*, Sheffield 1998
Metcalf 2001	D. Metcalf, *British Unions: Dissolution or Resurgence Revisited?*, Discussion Paper 493, Centre for Economic Performance, LSE, London 2001
Metcalf & Benson 2000	H. Metcalf & R. Benson, 'From Unemployment to Self-Employment: Developing an Effective Structure of Micro-Finance Support', *PSI Discussion Paper No.170*, October 2000
Millward *et al* 2000	N. Millward, A. Bryson & J. Forth, *All Change at Work? – British employment relations 1980-1998, as portrayed by the Workplace Industrial Relations Survey series,* London 2000
Neal 1992	Alan C. Neal, 'Atypical Workforms and European Labour Law', 1992, 45 *Recht der Arbeit* 115
Neal 1997	Alan C. Neal, *Fundamental Social Rights at Work in the European Community,* Aldershot 1997
Neal 1998	Alan C. Neal, 'Comparative Labour law and Industrial Relations: 'Major Discipline?' – Who Cares?', in C.Engels & M.Weiss (eds), *Labour Law and Industrial Relations at the Turn of the Century: Liber Amicorum for Roger Blanpain,* The Hague 1998, 55
Neal 2000	Alan C. Neal, 'From 'Bad Boy' to European Role Model? The Strange Legacy of United Kingdom Employment Policies Since the Single European Act, in M.Biagi (ed), *Job Creation and Labour Law: From protection towards Pro-action,* The Hague 2000, 269
Phelps-Brown 1990	H. Phelps Brown, 'The Counter-Revolution of Our Time', 1990, 29 *Industrial Relations* 1
Pollert 1988	A. Pollert, 'The flexible firm – fixation or fact?', 1988, 2 *Work, Employment and Society* 281
Raffe *et al* 1998	D. Raffe, A. Biggart, J. Fairgrieve, C. Howieson, J. Rodger & S. Burinston, *OECD Thematic Review: The Transition From Initial Education to Working Life,* OECD, Paris 1998
Schmidt & Neal 1984	F. Schmidt & A. Neal, 'Collective Bargaining and Collective Agreements', *International Encyclopedia of Comparative Law,* Tübingen 1984, Vol. XV, Ch. 12
Simitis 1987	S. Simitis, 'Juridification of Labor Relations', in G. Teubner (ed), *Juridification of Social Spheres,* De Gruyter 1987, 113
Sisson & Marginson 2001	K. Sisson & P. Marginson, *'Soft Regulation' – Travesty of the real thing or new dimension?,* Paper produced for the ESRC's research project on 'Emerging Boundaries of European Collective Bargaining at Sector and Enterprise Levels', within the context of the 'One Europe or Several?' programme, June 2001
Sisson *et al* 2003	K. Sisson, K. Arrowsmith & P. Marginson, 'All Benchmarkers Now? Benchmarking and the 'Europeanisation' of Industrial Relations', 2003, 34 *Industrial Relations Journal* 15
Sly *et al* 1998	F. Sly, T. Thair & A. Risdon, 'Labour Market Participation of Ethnic Groups', 1998, *Labour Market Trends* (December)
Smith & Twomey 2002	A. Smith & B. Twomey, 'Labour Market Experiences of People with Disabilities. National Statistics Feature', 2002, 110 *Labour Market Trends* 415
Stark 1990	T. Stark, *Income and Wealth in the 1980s,* Fabian Society, 2nd ed. London 1990
TUC 1977(a)	TUC, *Partners for Progress: Next Steps in the New Unionism,* London 1977
TUC 1977(b)	TUC, *Partners for Progress: New Unionism at the Workplace,* London 1977
TUC 2002	TUC, *Half the World Away: Making Regional Development Work,* London 2002
Weekes *et al* 1975	B. Weekes, M. Mellish, L. Dickins & J. Lloyd, *Industrial Relations and the Limits of Law: The Industrial Effects of the Industrial Relations Act, 1971,* Oxford 1975
Whyman 2002	P. Whyman, 'British Trade Unions and Economic and Monetary Union', 2002, 41 *Industrial Relations* 467

2. Principal United Kingdom legislative measures

2.1. Primary legislation

- Equal Pay Act 1970
- Employment Agencies Act 1973
- Health and Safety at Work Act 1974
- Rehabilitation of Offenders Act 1974
- Sex Discrimination Act 1975
- Race Relations Act 1976
- Sex Discrimination Act 1986
- Employment Act 1988
- Access to Medical Reports Act 1988
- Employment Act 1989
- Trade Union and Labour Relations (Consolidation) Act 1992
- Disability Discrimination Act 1995
- Employment Tribunals Act 1996
- Employment Rights Act 1996
- Employment Rights (Dispute Resolution) Act 1998
- Public Interest Disclosure Act 1998
- Data Protection Act 1998
- National Minimum Wage Act 1998
- Human Rights Act 1998
- Disability Rights Commission Act 1999
- Employment Relations Act 1999
- Regulation of Investigatory Powers Act 2000
- Employment Act 2002

2.2. Secondary legislation

- The Safety Representatives and Safety Committees Regulations 1977
- The Transfer of Undertakings (Protection of Employment) Regulations 1981
- The Employment Tribunals (Extension of Jurisdiction) (England & Wales) Order 1994
- The Health and Safety (Consultation with Employees) Regulations 1996
- The Working Time Regulations 1998
- The National Minimum Wage Regulations 1999
- The Management of Health and Safety at Work Regulations 1999

- The Transnational Information and Consultation of Employees Regulations 1999
- The Data Protection (Processing of Sensitive Personal Data) Order 2000
- The Trade Union Recognition (Method of Collective Bargaining) Order 2000
- The Employment Tribunals Act 1996 (Application of Conciliation Provisions) Order 2000
- The Part-time Workers (Prevention of Less Favourable Treatment) Regulations 2000
- The Telecommunications (Lawful Business Practice) (Interception of Communications) Regulations 2000
- The Employment Tribunals (Constitution and Rules of Procedure) Regulations 2001
- The ACAS Arbitration Scheme (England and Wales) Order 2001
- The Right to Time off for Study or Training Regulations 2001
- The Fixed-Term Employees (Prevention of Less Favourable Treatment) Regulations 2002
- The Paternity and Adoption Leave Regulations 2002
- The Flexible Working (Eligibility, Complaints and Remedies) Regulations 2002

3. A note on further United Kingdom developments in 2003

This Annex, indicating further developments in the United Kingdom during 2003, follows the pattern of the main report covering 1992-2002.

The initiatives designed to strengthen a form of 'partnership' in the United Kingdom between the two sides of industry continued during 2003, with, in particular, consultation taking place over the form for implementing Directive 2002/14/EC on information and consultation. Notwithstanding this, however, the United Kingdom was, once again, subjected to a criticism as regards the low level of development of 'social dialogue', and received a recommendation (as part of the European Union's employment strategy process) that this matter should be improved.[134]

Labour market trends continued positively. According to United Kingdom official statistics,[135] the working age employment rate was 74.8% in the three months to January 2004, a rise of 0.2 per-

---

134   See Council Recommendation of 22 July 2003 on the implementation of Member States' employment policies (2003/579/EC), OJ L197/22 of 5.8.2003, at L197/30. This states that the United Kingdom should ... *4. further develop social partnership at all levels to help improve productivity and quality in work, in particular by addressing low levels of basic skills and skills gaps amongst the workforce*. It may be noted that the United Kingdom's National Action Plan 2003 has undergone an impressive editorial process, whereby a variety of events have been accorded the description 'social dialogue' – although the appropriateness of this label may be open to some scepticism.

135   Provided by United Kingdom National Statistics (quarterly).

centage points from a year earlier. The employment level was 28.27 million in the same period, up 262 000 on a year earlier.

The number of men in full-time employment was 13.67 million, and the number of women in full-time employment was 7.25 million – both up from the previous year. The number of people in part-time employment was 7.36 million in the three months to January 2004, of which 1.58 million were men and 5.78 million were women.

Workforce jobs over the quarter to December 2003 increased 29.89 million, while production industries workforce jobs fell by 90 000. Service sector jobs were up by 273,000 and other industries were also up by 139 000. The number of employee jobs stood at 25.89 million – a rise of 67 000 over the quarter.

The unemployment rate was 4.8% in the three months to January 2004 (a drop of 0.2% from the previous year), with an unemployment level of 1.44 million – down 34 000 on a year earlier. The number of unemployed men was 862 000 in the three months to January 2004, while the number of unemployed women was 574 000 – both showing a continuing downward trend. Unemployment for 18 to 24 year olds was 383 000 in the same period, while the level of unemployment over 12 months stood at 312 000.

Trade union membership showed little change over the previous year, with membership density standing at 26.6% of all in employment (29% of employees), while collective bargaining coverage extended to 8.7 million (35.6%).[136]

The strong emphasis upon normative statutory regulation continued, although there was a slight reduction in the volume of measures introduced during 2003. Almost all of the new provisions were contained in Statutory Instruments (secondary legislation).

The Central Arbitration Committee (CAC) continued its activity in relation to trade union recognition, with a downturn in the number of applications made under that jurisdic-

tion, while the number of applications in relation to information remained tiny.[137]

Meanwhile, applications to the Employment Tribunals saw a slight dip from the previous year, with a total across all jurisdictions of 172 322 applications for 2002/03.[138]

A complete overhaul of the rules of procedure for the Employment Tribunals and the Employment Appeal Tribunal is being undertaken, with a view to coming into effect in October 2004. Meanwhile, ministerial responsibility for these two judicial dispute resolution bodies is to move from the Department of Trade and Industry to the Department for Constitutional Affairs – envisaged to take place at the end of 2005.

ACAS saw 1 353 requests for collective conciliation during 2002/03 (broadly in line with the previous year's situation), along with 80 requests for trade dispute arbitration (a marked increase on the previous two years). In the context of bringing the provisions of the Employment Act 2002 into force (with new requirements for employers and employees to observe statutory dispute resolution procedures), a revised draft of the *ACAS Code of Practice on Disciplinary and Grievance Procedures* is being completed. One particularly interesting observation made by ACAS in its *Annual Report and Accounts 2002-2003* relates to the statutory arbitration scheme intended to offer 'ADR' in place of litigation before the Employment Tribunals, finally acknowledging that, *The statutory arbitration scheme which ACAS administers did not meet the target for growth we set this year. After two years of operation, we must conclude that it does not appear to appeal to employers and applicants as a practical alternative to employment tribunal hearings in unfair dismissal cases.*[139]

The impact of this ongoing 'sea' of legislation continued regularly to be a subject of complaint on the parts of the CBI and employer organisations.[140] However, a study commissioned by the Department of Trade and Industry and published in September 2003 finds that the effects of employment legislation on small firms can be small.[141] Although the effect on firms may be severe

---

136 The most recent figures are taken from the Labour Force Survey for the Autumn quarter of 2002 (not seasonally adjusted).

137 Central Arbitration Committee Annual Report 2002/03 (HMSO, London 2003). The report confirms that *At 31 March 2003, the CAC had received 255 applications for recognition under Part I of Schedule A1 to the 1992 Act. There were therefore 80 applications in the year 1 April 2002 to 31 March 2003 and, in addition, there were a further two applications under Part II of the Schedule and one application under Part III. The Disclosure of Information provisions provided us with seven cases but no applications were made under the legislative provisions relating to the establishment of European Works Councils.*

138 See ETS Annual Report and Accounts 2002-2003 (HMSO, London 2003). Only complaints relating to working time saw any significant rise, although there was a slight increase in the number complaining of disability discrimination. All other jurisdictions saw some diminution compared with the previous year.

139 *ACAS Annual Report and Accounts 2002/03,* HMSO, London 2003, p. 34.

140 The Confederation of British Industry's annual employment trends survey, published in September 2003, argues that the prospect of further employment regulation, especially from the EU, threatens to undermine the UK's flexible labour market.

141 See P. Edwards, M. Ram & J. Black, The impact of employment legislation on small firms: a case study analysis, *DTI, Employment Research Series No. 20*, London 2003.

by reason of limited administrative resources or economic vulnerability, benefits such as improved disciplinary procedures or a better work-life balance are also indicated.

However, it is in respect of the framework for equal opportunities and anti-discrimination that some of the most dramatic developments have occurred. In particular, the implementation into United Kingdom labour law of Directives 2000/43/EC and 2000/78/EC has seen significant reformulation of the pattern for dealing with unlawful discrimination in the workplace. Thus, the Employment Equality (Sexual Orientation) Regulations 2003 and the Employment Equality (Religion or Belief) Regulations 2003 have extended the scope of protection to cover sexual orientation and religion with effect from December 2003.[142] Alongside these provisions, important amendments have been made to the existing United Kingdom framework of protection against sex, race and disability discrimination at work. At the same time, a scheme to unify the specialist non-judicial bodies dealing with discrimination[143] under one umbrella is being put into place.

The national minimum wage was uprated, as recommended by the independent Low Pay Commission, so that the adult rate increased in October 2003 to £4.50 per hour, with the rate for 18-21 year olds rising to £3.80.

In relation to issues concerning the employability of workers in the United Kingdom labour market, the government unveiled, in July 2003, its new skills strategy white paper aimed at addressing England's long-standing skills and productivity weaknesses.[144]

In respect of questions touching labour law and adaptability, an important discussion document (launched in 2002) on 'employment status' as the basis for benefiting from labour law protections completed its consultation phase,[145] and a response is awaited from the government as to whether any shift away from the traditional categorisation of 'employee/worker' in British labour law might be under consideration. However, there is little indication that any radical change might be in contemplation.[146]

In April 2003, new legislation came into force giving parents of children aged under six or of disabled children aged under 18 a statutory right to request flexible working and to have their request seriously considered by their employer.[147] These new provisions are based on recommendations made by the Work and Parents Taskforce, and reflect policy designed to facilitate dialogue between working parents and their employers about working patterns to meet both childcare responsibilities and the business needs of employers.

More generally, a review (initiated in July 2002) of the impact of the Employment Relations Act 1999 was published in February 2003, indicating that a series of detailed amendments were called for in order to improve the operation of the trade union recognition procedure contained in the statute. This has led, at the end of the year, to the introduction of an Employment Relations Bill, which is intended to become law during 2004. The new legislation will amend the statutory recognition procedure, as well as making changes to the law on ballots for industrial action. Provisions are also included to enable the government to make regulations on employee information and consultation. In relation to individual rights, the Bill also amends the law on the right to be accompanied at disciplinary or grievance hearings.

---

142   See also the Employment Equality (Religion or Belief) (Amendment) Regulations 2003 and the Employment Equality (Sexual Orientation) (Amendment) Regulations 2003.

143   Currently, the Equal Opportunities Commission (EOC), the Commission for Racial Equality (CRE) and the Disability Rights Commission (DRC).

144   See the White Paper, 21ˢᵗ century skills: realising our potential, published on 8 July 2003.

145   See URN 02/1058, Discussion Document on Employment Status in Relation to Statutory Employment Rights, DTI, London, July 2002.

146   Certainly, most of the particularly sensitive issues raised by the Perulli report on 'para-subordination' have not been addressed in this context. See Adalberto Perulli, Economically dependent/quasi-subordinate (parasubordinate) employment: legal, social and economic aspects (Brussels 2003). Meanwhile the debate stimulated by the Supiot report on Transformation of labour and future of labour law in Europe (Brussels 1998) has found little voice outside academic circles. See, for example, the published results of the colloquium held by the Centre for Economic Performance, London School of Economics and Political Science, Labour Law and Social Insurance in the New Economy: A Debate on the Supiot Report, London 2001.

147   Employment Act 2002, together with the accompanying Flexible Working (Procedural Requirements) Regulations 2002 and the Flexible Working (Eligibility, Complaints and Remedies) Regulations 2002.

European Commission

The evolution of labour law (1992-2003) – Volume 2: National reports

Luxembourg: Office for Official Publications of the European Communities

2005 – 526 pp. – 21 x 29.7 cm

ISBN 92-894-9894-3